# CLASSICS IN POLITICAL PHILOSOPHY

## SECOND EDITION

# CLASSICS IN POLITICAL PHILOSOPHY

## SECOND EDITION

### JENE M. PORTER

**EDITOR**

Prentice Hall Canada Inc., Scarborough, Ontario

**Canadian Cataloguing in Publication Data**

Main entry under title:

Classics in political philosophy (second edition)

Includes index.

ISBN 0-13-546913-9

1. Political science–Philosophy. 2. Political science–History. I. Porter, J.M. (Jene M.), 1937–

JA81.C53 1989 320'.01 C88-094849-3

Prentice-Hall, Inc., Englewood Cliffs, New Jersey
Prentice-Hall International (UK) Limited, London
Prentice-Hall of Australia, Pty. Limited, Sydney
Prentice-Hall Hispanoamericana, S.A., Mexico City
Prentice-Hall of India Private Limited, New Delhi
Prentice-Hall of Japan, Inc., Tokyo
Simon & Schuster Asia Private Limited, Singapore
Editora Prentice-Hall do Brasil, Ltda., Rio de Janeiro

ISBN 0-13-546913-9

Acquisitions Editor: Allan Gray
Developmental Editor: Maurice Esses
Production Editor: Kelly Dickson
Copy Editor: Lana Kong
Production Coordinator: Jane Schell
Permissions: Marijke Leupen
Cover Design: Petra Phillips
Interior Design: Petra Phillips
Cover Image: The Granger Collection
Page Layout: Arlene Edgar, Graphic Design and Formatting

2 3 4 5    RRD    00 99

Printed and bound in the United States

We welcome readers' comments, which can be sent by e-mail to
**phabinfo_pubcanada@prenhall.com**

TO SUSAN

Hang up philosophy!
Unless philosophy can make you a Juliet.

SHAKESPEARE

Those who seek the direct road to truth should not bother
with any object of which they cannot have a certainty equal
to the demonstrations of arithmetic and geometry.

DESCARTES

The slenderest knowledge that may be obtained of the
highest things is more desirable than the most certain
knowledge obtained of lesser things.

ST. THOMAS AQUINAS

# TABLE OF CONTENTS

# PREFACE TO THE
# FIRST EDITION

## (1989)

This textbook was born from desperation. It has become increasingly hard to justify requiring students, particularly at the introductory level, to purchase a series of expensive paperbacks covering each major political philosopher. Yet no professor would happily rely solely on a secondary text. A reader was necessary. The search for a suitable textbook of readings, though, quickly led to a sense of despair. There are readers providing snippets from Plato to Mussolini. There are those devoted to one theme, such as the development of democracy or the concept of rights. There are many that simply begin with Hobbes. What was needed was a text that contains the major political thinkers: Plato, Aristotle, St. Augustine, Aquinas, Machiavelli, Hobbes, Locke, Rousseau, Hegel, Mill, and Marx. The usual problem with a book of readings is that it is difficult to have a consensus on the selection, but by listing only the indisputable classics and by having lengthy selections this problem is solved.

Modern translations and editions have been used throughout this book. In the cases where the work is a recognized masterpiece, such as Plato's *The Republic* or Rousseau's *On the Social Contract,* brief summaries of omitted sections have been provided so that the student can see better the entire structure of the work. Some writings have been included which are not tightly constructed literary wholes but nevertheless are held to be "classics," owing to their influence and insights. Knowledge of Aristotle's *The Politics,* the most disjointed and tedious of ancient texts for students, is considered indispensable simply because of its extraordinary influence and encyclopedic scope. Similarly, neither St. Augustine nor Aquinas wrote a masterpiece on political philosophy, but the impact of Christian theology on political philosophy is not disputed; thus both thinkers must be included. Finally, there are some thinkers whose political philosophy cannot be perceived in one work but in a combination of publications. Marx is the best example of such a thinker. In all cases, literary masterpieces or not, the selections offered in this book are large enough for the student to see the whole of a thinker's vision.

Editing requires excising. I have tried to err on the side of having more than enough material for each thinker, and certainly more than found in other readers. In order to make certain that this would be an adequate text, I went to most of the standard secondary textbooks and noted the themes discussed for each major thinker. Then I included all the passages necessary to parallel the coverage in the secondary material.

Editorial comments and footnotes included are those found in the editions of the texts used. My own additional notes are indicated by the initials J.M.P.

I would be remiss if I failed to thank my colleagues for their suggestions as to what material to include and to excise. All of them, I suspect, would wish to be arrayed only on the side of those who suggested inclusions: Stewart Farnell, Hans J. Michelmann, Richard A. Nordahl, Jeffrey S. Steeves, and Donald C. Story. I will bravely accept the responsibility for the excisions.

Finally, in spite of the untiring efforts of my two young daughters, Julia and Jeannette, the time was found to complete the manuscript. They were unknowingly right, however, in assuming that the time spent with them was of more lasting significance. I am grateful to my wife, Susan, for her editing and for her support.

J. M. PORTER
UNIVERSITY OF SASKATCHEWAN

# PREFACE TO THE
# SECOND EDITION
## (1997)

The policy of including a large selection from each classic work in political philosophy has been again followed in this second edition, based upon the premise that large selections enable the reader to see each of these great works as a whole. In the case of a thinker who does not have a single classic work in political philosophy, such as Karl Marx or St. Augustine, the selections chosen are designed to present the full range of that person's philosophy.

There have been many revisions throughout for the second edition. The major changes include the additions of *The Apology* to the Plato section and the *Nicomachean Ethics* to the Aristotle section, a significant expansion of the selections by Karl Marx, and a completely new section devoted to the works of Frederick Nietzsche. Better or newer versions of certain philosophic works have changed from the first edition. Finally, the bibliography for each thinker has been updated and expanded.

I am particularly grateful for the many colleagues who made suggestions for these revisions. This reader has been much improved, thanks to these colleagues and their students. Professor Don Carmichael (University of Alberta), Professor Frederick Vaughn (University of Guelph), Professor Richard Noble (University of Winnipeg), and Professor Lee McDonald (Pomona College) will be able to detect their contributions. I am indebted to them and to the following additional reviewers for Prentice-Hall: Margaret Moore (University of Waterloo) and Paul Vogt (University of Winnipeg).

J. M. PORTER
UNIVERSITY OF SASKATCHEWAN

# PLATO

*Plato (427–347 B.C.) was the most famous student of Socrates (470–399 B.C.). Although Plato was born into a leading aristocratic family of Athens, the trial and death of Socrates and the general political and moral decay of the city-state convinced him to pursue philosophy rather than the expected political career. Socrates never wrote a word, but his lasting influence is in no small degree a result of Plato's Dialogues. In them one again can hear Socrates, the powerfully built stonemason, questioning his fellow citizens about justice and truth. Following Socrates' execution, Plato prudently withdrew from Athens. By 387 B.C. he had returned and founded the Academy, a school which endured for over 900 years. Plato died at the age of 81.*

*Beginning with a series of biographical dialogues defending Socrates and the philosophic life, Plato wrote some 25 Dialogues. Throughout these works he uses the name of Socrates, never his own. A discussion of politics can be found in most of his writings, but three of them—*The Republic, The Laws, *and* The Statesman—*are the primary sources of Plato's political philosophy. The most celebrated is* The Republic. *It remains without question one of the greatest works in political philosophy.* The Apology *serves both as an introduction to the sort of man Socrates was and an introduction to the life of philosophy.*

— J.M.P.

PLATO

# THE APOLOGY¹ OF SOCRATES

## ⇢ SCENE: A LAW COURT AT ATHENS ⇠

### 1. During the Trial

[St. I, p. 17.] **SOCRATES.** I do not know, gentlemen, how you feel after listening to my accusers. As for myself, I almost forgot my own identity, so convincingly did they talk; yet there is hardly a word of truth in what they have said. I was particularly amazed, however, by one of the many lies they told—when they urged you to take care not to be deceived by me, because I was a cunning speaker. I thought it the most shameless part of their conduct that they were not ashamed at the prospect of my forthwith showing them up as liars by the evidence of fact, when I prove myself to be not in the least of "cunning speaker"—unless of course they apply those words to one who speaks the truth, in which case I agree that I am an orator, though not in their style.

As I say, they have said little or nothing that is true. But you shall hear from me nothing but the truth; not, mark me, gentlemen, speeches finely decked with words and phrases, as theirs are, nor carefully arranged, but you will hear things uttered impromptu in such words as may occur to me. I trust that what I say is just, and let none of you expect anything else; for it would indeed be unfitting for a man of my age to come before you like a youngster composing a set speech. Gentlemen, I adjure you not to be surprised and upset if you hear me defend myself in the language I have been accustomed to use at the bankers' tables in the Agora, where many of you have listened to me, and elsewhere. The fact is that this is the first time I have appeared in court, although I am now seventy years old; I am therefore a complete stranger to the manner of speech here. If I were really a foreigner you would of course excuse me if I spoke in the dialect and that manner [18] to which I had been brought up. Very well then, I think it fair to ask you in the present circumstances to disregard the style of my speech—which, though it might be better, might also be worse—and simply consider carefully whether or not my words are just; for to do that is the peculiar excellence of a judge, while an orator's excellence is to speak the truth....

¹ [The word *apology* comes from the Greek *apologia,* which means "defence." —J.M.P.]

Now let us go to the root of the matter and ask this question: What is the charge that has made me the object of false prejudice and upon which Meletus relied when he brought this suit against me? What did those who aroused the prejudice say to arouse it? I must, as it were, read their affidavit as if they were plaintiffs: "Socrates is a criminal busybody, seeking to understand what abides in heaven and beneath the earth, making the weaker argument the stronger and teaching others to do likewise." That is the kind of thing they said; indeed you yourselves have witnessed as much in Aristophanes' play[2]—Socrates carried about proclaiming that he was treading on air, and talking a great deal of other nonsense, about which I know absolutely nothing at all. I say this, gentlemen, not to disparage those who may be learned in such matters— heaven forbid I should ever be called upon to defend myself against Meletus on so grave a charge—but because I have no part in such things. My witnesses are the majority of you now here. Many of you have listened to me talking; I ask them to decide among themselves and openly declare whether anyone has ever heard me so much as refer to such matters. If they will do so you will discover that these and similar allegations are mere vulgar gossip.

No indeed, not one of these accusations is true. Nor is the suggestion that I make money by undertaking to teach others....

Now someone may take me up and ask: "But what *is* the matter with you, Socrates? Why the prejudice against you? All this rumour and criticism is not the result merely of your achievements being greater than those of the average man. Tell us what the trouble is then, and save us from coming to a rash decision in this case." Well, that seems to me a fair question, and I will try to explain what it is that has given rise to my reputation and stirred the prejudice against me. Pay attention, therefore. Maybe some of you will think I am joking; be assured, however, that I shall tell you the absolute truth.

The fact is, gentlemen, that I have acquired this reputation simply and solely on account of a certain brand of wisdom. What kind of wisdom is this? Perhaps just *human* wisdom, in respect of which it is possible that I am wise. Those other people,[3] of whom I was speaking a little while ago, may be wise with some *superhuman* wisdom; I really don't know what to say, for I have no part in it, and anyone who says I have is lying with a view to rousing prejudice against me.

---

2 [The Clouds.]

3 [Gorgias, Prodicus and others, all famous sophists.]

Now gentlemen, no noisy interruptions, please, even though I seem to be boasting; the words I utter are not mine. I am going to refer you to a speaker of great authority. As witness of my wisdom—if such it can be called—I shall present to you the God of Delphi. You know Chaerephon, I believe; [21] he was a close friend of mine since boyhood days, and as a member of your democratic party he shared your recent exile and return.[4] You know too the kind of man Chaerephon was, how impetuous in everything he undertook. Well, he once went to Delphi and made so bold as to ask the oracle this question—quiet now, please, gentlemen! He asked whether there was anyone wiser than Socrates; and the Pythia[5] replied that there was no one wiser. Chaerephon himself is dead, but his brother here will bear you witness to the truth of that event.

Now see why I tell you the story: it will help to explain the prejudice against me. When I learned of the oracle I thought to myself: "What on earth does the god mean; what riddle is he propounding? I know well that I am not wise in the slightest degree, so what does he mean by declaring me the wisest of all men? He certainly cannot be lying, for to do so would be contrary to his very nature." For a long time I was at a loss as to his meaning; then with great reluctance I proceeded to investigate the matter somewhat as follows.

I approached one of those who had a reputation for wisdom, thinking that there if anywhere I should prove the oracle wrong and be able to tell the god: "This man is wiser than I, but you said I was the wisest." I need not tell you the man's name, gentlemen, but he was a politician. At all events this is what happened. As I talked with him I found that he was not really wise, although many others (and not least himself) considered him to be so. I then tried to convince him that he was not wise, despite his own opinion. As a result I became hateful to him and to many of those present; and as I went away I thought to myself: "I *am* wiser than this man; neither of us really knows anything worth knowing, but *he* thinks he knows something when in fact he does not, whereas *I*, knowing nothing at all, make no pretence of doing so." From him I went to another of those who were reported to be even wiser than he, received the same impression as before, and made myself unpopular both with him and with many of his friends.

---

[4] [This refers to the restoration of democracy at Athens in 404 B.C., when the exiles, led by Thrasybulus, returned and overthrew the oligarchical government of the Thirty.]

[5] [The priestess of Apollo at Delphi, who spoke the oracles.]

After that I went from one to another, unhappy and apprehensive because I could see that I was hated, but believing it my duty to put the god's business before everything else. Consequently my investigation of the oracle's meaning led me perforce into the company of all who were reputed to know anything. And by the Dog, gentlemen—[22] for I must speak the truth—this, I do declare, was my experience: those with the greatest reputation seemed to me to be almost the most deficient, while those of less renown seemed endowed with a higher degree of good sense. I must tell you then about my wandering as I performed what I may call my Herculean Labours in an endeavour to prove the oracle irrefutable. From the politicians I went to the authors of tragedy, dithyramb and the rest, thinking to receive from them incontrovertible evidence that I was less learned than they. So I took up those of their works that seemed to have been most carefully constructed, and I tried to discover what they meant, hoping at the same time to learn something from them. Now I am ashamed, gentlemen, to tell you the truth, but still it must be told. For there was hardly a man present, one might say, who would not talk better than they about the works they themselves have composed. So in the case of the poets also I quickly perceived that what they wrote was the fruit not of wisdom, but of nature and inspiration. The experience of the poets, in fact, is obviously very much akin to that of the prophets and givers of oracles, who make many fine utterances but do not understand a word of what they say. At the same time I became aware that their skill as poets has led them to the false belief that they are the wisest of men in all other respects as well. I left them, therefore, convinced that I was superior to them in the same way as I excelled the representatives of public life.

Finally I went to the craftsmen, conscious of knowing practically nothing, but confident of discovering that they know many fine things. Nor was I disappointed; they did know what I did not, and to that extent they were wiser than I. And yet, gentlemen, they appeared to me to have the same failing as the poets: each of them was expert at his trade, and for that reason he believed himself very wise in all other matters of consequence. Indeed this folly of theirs obscured their wisdom as craftsmen, and I asked myself on behalf of the oracle whether I should prefer to be as I am, neither wise with their wisdom nor foolish with their folly, or to be in both respects as they are. I replied through myself to the oracle that it was better for me to be as I am.

Now, gentlemen, as a result of this investigation [23] I am become the object of much bitter and determined hostility; there is a lot of prejudice against me and

I am called a sophist. For whenever I convict someone else of ignorance those listening to me think I am learned in the matters under discussion. But the fact is, gentlemen, that real wisdom belongs most probably to the god, and that his oracle means this: "Human wisdom is of little or no value." It is clear that he is not referring to me in particular, but merely uses my name by way of example, as if to say: "The wisest of you mortals is the one who, like Socrates, recognizes himself as truly of no account in respect of wisdom."

I have therefore till this very day been going about seeking and questioning at the god's behest anyone, whether citizen or foreigner, who I think is wise; and whenever such a man does not appear to me to be so, I lend support to my opinion by *demonstrating* that he is not wise. And because I am thus busily engaged I have no time for any public business worth mentioning or for my own affairs; indeed my service to the god has reduced me to penury.

Furthermore young men of leisure, members of the wealthiest class, volunteer to follow me about; they enjoy hearing people cross-examined, often imitate me and finally undertake to question others. When they get to that stage, I imagine they find a whole host of people who think they know something but in fact know little or nothing; with the result that their victims are angry with me instead of with themselves, declaring that "Socrates is a most abominable person and is corrupting youth." If anyone asks them "by doing or teaching what?" they do not know and have nothing to say; but in order not to reveal their perplexity they have recourse to phrases that are handy for use against all philosophers, talking about "things in the air and things beneath the earth," "not believing in the gods" and "making the weaker argument the stronger." For they would not, I fancy, care to admit the hard fact that they are being shown up as pretending to know but knowing nothing. And so, jealous of their reputation, determined, and speaking with one persuasive voice about me, they have long been filling your ears with vehement slander. Three angry men of their number have attached me: Meletus on behalf of the poets, Anytus on behalf of the craftsmen [24] and Lycon on behalf of the orators.[6] Accordingly, as I said at the beginning of my speech, I should be surprised if I were able to eradicate this prejudice from your minds in so short a time when it has grown so great. There you have the truth, gentlemen; I speak without the slightest concealment or prevarication. And yet I am

---

[6] [These are presumably the "politicians" mentioned above.]

fairly sure I am making myself hated by doing just that; which is also evidence that I speak the truth—that the prejudice against me and its causes are such as I have described. Whether you investigate this matter now or later on, you will find that I am right.

So much then for my defence against the charges long since brought against me. Next I will try to refute Meletus—the good and patriotic Meletus, as he styles himself—and those who seconded him. Once again therefore let us turn to *their* affidavit, as if they were a different set of accusers. It is more or less as follows: it states that Socrates does wrong by corrupting the youth and not believing in the gods recognized by the State, but in other new spiritual beings.

That is the accusation. let us examine it point by point. Meletus says I do wrong by corrupting the youth. But I, gentlemen, say that he does wrong inasmuch as he jests in earnest, light-heartedly involving people in a lawsuit, pretending to be zealous and concerned about things in which he was never interested at all. That this is a fact I will try to make plain to you also.

Here, Meletus, tell me: don't you consider it of great importance that the youth should be as good as possible?

MELETUS. I do....

SOCR. ...Be so kind as to tell us whether it is better to live among good citizens or bad. Answer, man! I am not asking you a difficult question. Do not the bad exert some evil influence upon those who are their constant companions, and the good some beneficial influence?

MEL. Certainly.

SOCR. Is there anyone then who prefers to be injured by his associates rather than benefited? Answer, my dear sir; the law bids you answer. Is there anyone who prefers to be injured?

MEL. Of course not.

SOCR. Come then, do you drag me here on a charge of corrupting the youth and ruining them voluntarily or involuntarily?

MEL. Voluntarily, I say.

SOCR. What then, Meletus? Are you at your age so much wiser than I at my age that whereas you have recognized that bad men always do some harm to those nearest them, and the good some good, I have reached such a depth of ignorance that I do not even know that if I make any one of my associates bad I am in danger of suffering some harm from him, and therefore perpetuate this great evil voluntarily as you say? I don't believe it, Meletus, nor do I think anyone else on earth does. [26] Either I *do not* corrupt the youth or, if I *do*, I do so involuntarily—which makes you a liar in either event. Suppose I corrupt them involuntarily: the law is that instead of being haled before a court for involuntary errors one should be taken for private admonition and instruction. That is what you should have done with me; for if I am told about it, I shall obviously cease from what I am doing involuntarily. But you avoided associating with an instructing me; rather than do that you bring me here, whither the law summons those who need punishment, not instruction.

Well then, gentlemen, it is clear, as I said, that Meletus never cared a jot for these things. Nevertheless, Meletus, tell us by what means you hold me to be corrupting the youth. According to the terms of your indictment it is by teaching them to believe not in the gods recognized by the State, but in other new spiritual beings. Do you say that it is by teaching this that I corrupt them?

**MEL.** That is definitely what I say.

**SOCR.** Then, Meletus, for the sake of those very gods now in question, be still more explicit for the benefit both of myself and of these gentlemen. I want to know whether your point is (*a*) that I teach that there *are* gods (and am therefore not guilty of atheism), but (*b*) that those gods are not the ones in whom the State believes—that you have indicted me for believing in gods other than those recognized by the State. Or do you maintain (*c*) that I don't believe in gods at all, and that I teach this unbelief to other people?

**MEL.** That is what I maintain—that you don't believe in gods at all.

**SOCR.** Meletus, you astonish me. Why do you say this? Do I not believe that the sun and moon are gods, as the rest of mankind believes?

**MEL.** By Zeus, no! He says, gentlemen, that the sun is a stone and the moon earth.

**SOCR.** Do you realize you are insulting these gentlemen, my dear Meletus? Do you so despise them and think them so illiterate as not to know that the works of Anaxagoras are full of such utterances?[7] Learn them from me, indeed! Why, it

---

[7] [Anaxagoras of Clazomenae (*c.* 500–428 B.C.), a philosopher of the Ionian school, settled at Athens *c.* 463 B.C. Socrates was at one time interested in his physical theories, but was quickly disillusioned. Anaxagoras' statement that the sun was a red-hot stone and the moon earth led to an accusation of impiety, and he was obliged to leave Athens.]

is sometimes possible to buy them in the Orchestra for a drachma[8] (and dear at that); anyone who did so would laugh at Socrates if he claimed them as his own, especially as they are so absurd. But for heaven's sake, do you really think I believe that there is no such thing as a god?

**MEL.** That, by Zeus, is just what you do believe.

**SOCR.** You are untruthful, Meletus, even, it appears to me, in your own eyes. Gentlemen, it is my opinion that this fellow is overweening and lacks self-control; that presumption, intemperance and rashness have caused him to bring this indictment. [27] He is like a man who uses a riddle to make a test: "Will Socrates the wise," he says, "recognize that I am playing the fool and contradicting myself, or will I manage to deceive him and others who hear me?" For he manifestly contradicts himself in the indictment, as if to say "Socrates is guilty of not believing in gods, but does believe in gods." Now surely that is playing the fool.

Help me then, gentlemen, to discover why he appears to take this view. Meletus, you must give us answers to our questions. And as for you, gentlemen, I beg of you once again not to interrupt if I argue my case in the way I have always done.

Now, Meletus, is there a man on earth who believes that there are human affairs but no human beings? If so, let him answer straightforwardly, gentlemen. Is there anyone who does not believe there is such a things as a horse, but does believe in equestrianism? Is there anyone who does not believe there is such a thing as a flautist, but does believe that there is such a thing as the art of playing the flute? Of course not, my dear sir; I tell you and the whole court no, regardless of whether or not you are willing to reply. But do at least give me an answer to *this* question: Is there anyone who believes in the existence of spiritual beings but does not believe in spirits?

**MEL.** There is not.

**SOCR.** Thank you for a grudging answer squeezed from you by the court. Well, you say that I believe in spiritual beings, new or old, and teach that belief; so according to your statement I do believe in spiritual beings at any rate, and you swore to that in your indictment. But if I believe in spiritual beings

---

[8] [From this it appears that the orchestra of the theatre, at times other than the annual dramatic festivals, was frequented by booksellers.]

it is absolutely inevitable that I believe also in spirits. Isn't that so? It is; I infer your agreement from the fact that you don't answer. But do we not take spirits to be gods or the offspring of gods? Yes or no?

**MEL.** Certainly.

**SOCR.** Then if, as you admit, I believe in spirits, and spirits are a kind of gods, here we have that silly riddle which I say you employ when you declare that I do not believe in gods, and yet do believe in gods, since I believe in spirits. Likewise, assuming spirits to be bastard children of gods, by nymphs or some other class of females if you like, what man would believe that there are children of gods but no gods? It would be just as absurd as believing that there are offspring of horses and asses, namely mules, but no horses or asses. Yes, Meletus, you must certainly have brought this indictment either by way of testing our intelligence or because you were at a loss for any real crime with which to charge me. There is, however, no device whereby you can convince any man with a grain of sense that it is possible for one and the same individual to believe in spiritual or divine entities and not to believe in spirits or gods.

[28] And so, gentlemen, I do not think much argument is required, beyond what I have already said, to prove myself not guilty of the charges brought against me by Meletus in his indictment. Be assured that I was speaking the truth earlier on when I said that many people had conceived an intense hatred of me. If I am eventually condemned, it will be due not to Meletus or Anytus, but to this widespread prejudice and dislike. Many a good man has been condemned because of prejudice, and I think many another will be thus condemned; I am not likely to be the last of them....

Gentlemen, the fact indeed is that wherever a man is stationed, either by his commanding officer, or by his own free choice in the belief that it is best for him to occupy that position, there he must, I think, stay, fearing neither death nor anything else more than disgrace. Take my own case. At Potidaea, at Amphipolis and at Delium[9] I remained like everyone else at the post assigned to me by the officers whom you had appointed, and ran the risk of death. It would therefore have been a most shameful act on my part if, being fully convinced that the god had given me a station with orders to spend my life as a philosopher, examining myself and others, I had deserted my post through fear of

---

9 [Three military operations of the Peloponnesian War.]

death or anything else whatsoever. [29] Yes, if I disobeyed the oracle, feared death and believed myself wise, which I am not, it would have been a heinous crime, for which I might justly be summoned before a court of law. To fear death, gentlemen, is nothing else than to think one is wise when one is not. It is thinking one knows what one does not; for no one call tell whether death be not the very greatest of all human blessing, and yet it is feared as though it were the greatest of evils. Now to think one knows what one does not is surely the most culpable form of ignorance. In taking this view, gentlemen, it may be that I am different from the majority of men; if I were to declare myself wiser in any respect it would be upon the grounds that I do not know much about the Underworld, and therefore do not claim to know. I do know, however, that it is shamefully wicked to do wrong by disobeying one who is better than I, be he god or man. So I shall never shirk or fear anything which I am unable with certainty to describe either as good or as evil, but only such things as I know are bad. Anytus has urged that either (*a*) I ought not to have been brought to trial at all, or (*b*) now that I *have* been brought to trial I must inevitably suffer death, because my acquittal would mean the ruin of your son through practising what I teach. Well, you may not be convinced by what he says, and may let me go free. You may say me: "This time, Socrates, we will not do what Anytus asks. We will let you go, but upon the sole condition that you no longer spend your time in this sort of inquiry or in philosophical studies; if you are caught doing so again you shall die." If you should propose to free me on that condition, I should reply as follows: "Gentlemen, I respect and love you, but I shall obey the god rather than you; so long as I live and am able to continue I shall never abandon philosophy or cease from exhorting you and pointing out the truth to any one of you whom I happen to meet. 'Most excellent sir,' I shall say in my usual way, 'you are a citizen of Athens, the greatest of states and the most celebrated for wisdom and power; are you not ashamed then to concern yourself with the acquisition of enormous wealth, or with reputation and honour, and yet to care nothing for wisdom, truth and the perfecting of your soul?' " If any such man disputes the point and says he does care, I shall not let him go, nor shall I move on. No, I shall question and examine and cross-examine him; and if I find he does not possess virtue, but claims to do so, I shall rebuke him [30] for regarding what is most important as of least account and caring more for what is of less worth. This I shall do to whomsoever I meet, young and old, alien and citizen, but above all to you citizens inasmuch as you are more closely related to me. Be assured that this charge is laid upon me by the god. Nay, I believe that no greater good was ever accomplished in Athens than my service of the god. For I go about doing nothing else than urging you, young and old, not to care for your persons or property more than (or even as much as) for the perfecting of your souls; and I tell you that virtue is not derived from wealth, but that virtue itself is the source of wealth and all other goods, both for the individual and for the State. If by saying these things I corrupt the youth, these things must be injurious; but if anyone maintains that I say something different, his statement is untrue. Therefore I tell you, gentlemen, do what Anytus advocates or not, condemn or acquit me, in the certain knowledge that I shall not alter my conduct, even though I am to die a thousand deaths.

No uproar now, gentlemen; continue to refrain from interrupting me and listen to what I have to say, for I believe you will profit by the hearing. I am going to tell you certain things at which you might perhaps cry out; but don't do so, please. If you put to death a man such as I claim to be, you will do more harm to yourselves than to me. It is impossible for Meletus or Anytus to injure me, for I believe it is not in the order of things that a better man should be injured by a worse. He might, of course, kill me, banish me or deprive me of citizen rights; and he may think that by doing so he would do me serious harm, but I do not. I think he does himself far more harm by doing what he is doing now—seeking to kill a man unjustly. And so, gentlemen, I must needs defend myself on this occasion not for my own sake, as might be imagined, but for yours, lest in condemning me you sin against the god by your treatment of the gift he gave you. For if you put me to death you will not easily find another who, to use a rather undignified simile, attaches himself to the State like a gadfly to a horse, which, though a large and noble beast, is sluggish on account of its size and needs to be aroused by stinging. I think the god has fastened me upon the State in some such capacity, and I go about rousing, [31] urging and reproaching each one of you, constantly alighting on you everywhere the whole day long. Such another is not likely to come your way, gentlemen; so if you will take my advice you will spare me. Annoyed perhaps, like someone awakened from a snooze, you may hit out, as Anytus has done, and easily destroy me; then you would pass the remainder of your life in slumber, unless the god, in his concern for you, should send someone else to apply the goad. Here is one consideration from which you might recognize me as being what I claim to be—a sort of heaven-sent gift. For many years now I have neglected all my private concerns and have been ready to lay aside my own affairs, and have constantly busied myself in your interest, coming to each of you like a father or an elder brother and imploring you to care for virtue. Now that is not characteristic of mere man. If I derived any profit from this by way of emolument for my exhortations, there would be some sense in it. But you can see for yourselves that in point of fact my accusers, though charging me with everything else in this shameless way, have not been able to attain such a peak of shamelessness as to produce a single witness to testify that I have ever exacted or requested payment from anyone. I think my very poverty is sufficient evidence that I speak the truth.

It may appear strange that I go about prying into other people's affairs to give this advice in private, but do not openly venture into your Assembly and advise the State. Well, the reason for this, as you have often heard me declare in many places, is that I am visited by something divine and spiritual, something which Meletus ridiculed in his indictment. I have had this experience from childhood upwards; it is a sort of voice that comes to me, and when it comes it never urges me forward, but always holds me back from doing what I have a mind to do. This it is which prevents my taking any part in public life. And I think this opposition is a very good thing; for you may be quite sure, gentlemen, that if I had undertaken a political career I should have been put to death long ago and should have benefited neither you nor myself. Now don't be angry with me for telling the truth; the fact is that no man will escape disaster who bravely opposes you or any other citizen body and saves his country from a host of wrongs that violate her laws. [32] If a man intends to stand up for the right, and hopes to preserve his life for even a little while, he must remain a private citizen and take no part in public life.

I will offer you cogent proof of that in the shape not of mere words, but of actions—which you hold in greater esteem. Listen then to an account of something within my own experience; it will convince you that I would never agree to do anything wrong through fear of death, even though such refusal cost me my life. The story I am going to tell you is ordinary and commonplace, but true. Only once, gentlemen, did I hold political office, and then I was a member of the Boule.[10] It happened that my tribe was the presiding committee when you sought to pass collective rather than individual judgment upon ten

---

[10] [In 406 B.C.]

officers who had failed to pick up the victims of a naval action[11]—an illegal proceeding, as all of you later recognized. At that time I was the sole member of the committee who opposed a course of action that ran counter to the laws. Well, the orators were ready to arrest and impeach me, and you clamoured for them to do so; but I thought it my duty to run any risk with law and justice on my side rather than fall in with your unlawful purpose through fear of imprisonment or death. That was before the abolition of democracy. After the establishment of oligarchy[12] the Thirty ordered me and four others to put in an appearance at the Council Chamber, bringing with us Leon of Salamis for execution. They gave many such orders to others besides ourselves, hoping thereby to implicate as many as possible in their crimes. On that occasion too my deeds proclaimed no less eloquently than my words that I didn't care a damn for death—if you'll excuse the colloquialism—but was at infinite pains to do nothing unjust or unholy. For that Government, powerful as it was, could not scare me into committing an injustice. When we left the City Hall my four companions went to Salamis and arrested Leon, but I went off home; and I might well have been put to death for it, if the Government had not been overthrown. Of these facts you have many witnesses....

Well, gentlemen, this is about all I have to say in my defence. Maybe one of your number has stood his trial on a less serious charge than this; and when he remembers how he begged and implored the judges with a flood of tears, and sought to arouse their compassion by bringing forward his children with a host of friends and relations, he will perhaps feel some antagonism towards me because I will do no such thing, notwithstanding the mortal danger that confronts me. Someone with these thoughts in mind, I say, may be harshly disposed towards me and may cast his vote in anger. Now I don't really suppose there is one of you who feels like that; but if there should be, I think I should be speaking fairly in saying to him: "My good sir, I too have relations, for I am, as

---

[11] [The Athenian Boule, or city council, consisted of five hundred members chosen annually by lot, fifty from each tribe. Each group of fifty served for a fixed period as *prutancis*, i.e. a presiding or superintending committee of the whole council. In 406 B.C. the Athenian admiral Conon defeated a Spartan fleet off the islands of Arginusae. Towards the end of the battle a storm arose, and the Athenian commanders ran for shelter without attempting to rescue the crews of twelve sinking ships. Those of them who returned home were tried for dereliction of duty and put to death.]

[12] [The tyrannical oligarchy of the Thirty ruled for almost a year in Athens in 404-3 B.C. before democracy was restored.— J.M.P.]

Homer puts it, 'not born of an oak or a rock,' but of human beings." Indeed yes, I have relations; indeed, gentlemen, I have three sons, one nearly grown up and two still mere boys. Nevertheless I shall bring none of them here in support of my plea for acquittal. Any why not? Not because I am defiant, gentlemen, or lack respect for you. Whether or not I face death boldly is another matter; but for the sake of my good name and yours and that of the whole State, I think it would be wrong of me at my age to herd my family into court. Besides, there is my reputation, deserved or not; the general view is that [35] Socrates is in some way superior to the ordinary run of men. Imagine how disgraceful it would be if those of you who are considered to excel in wisdom or courage, or indeed any other virtue whatsoever, were to act in such a way. Do you know, I have often seen quite distinguished men behave in the most extraordinary fashion when on trial, as if they thought that acquittal meant immortality and looked upon death as an appalling fate. In my view such persons are a disgrace to Athens; a foreigner might come to the conclusion that those of our citizens who are renowned for virtue, and whom they themselves honour with official rank and other marks of esteem, are in fact no better than women. No, gentlemen, we who have any reputation at all ought not to indulge in such behaviour, and you must not tolerate our doing so; you must make it clear that you will be far more ready to condemn a man who stages these pathetic scenes in your presence, and makes Athens ridiculous, than one who holds his peace.

Apart, however, from reputation, gentlemen, I think it wrong to grovel before a judge or to seek acquittal by begging; one should rather inform and convince him. A judge does not sit to dispense favours, but to administer justice; indeed his is bound by oath *not* to oblige defendants at his own sweet will, but to give judgment according to the laws. We must not, therefore, habituate you to breaking your oaths, nor must you make a practice of behaving so; divine law forbids either of us to do that. I ask you therefore, gentlemen, not to expect from me here conduct which I regard as neither honourable not just nor pious, especially when impiety is the very charge brought against me by this fellow Meletus. For it is clear that if I compelled you to violate your oath by means of persuasion and supplication, I would be teaching you to disbelieve in the existence of gods, and my very defence would declare my own unbelief in them. But this is far from being the case; I do believe in them, gentlemen, more than any of my accusers, and I leave you and the god to decide my case as may be best for me and for you.

## 2. *After the Verdict of Guilty*

I am not grieved, gentlemen, [36] at this vote of condemnation you have cast against me, and that for many reasons—among them the fact that it came as no surprise to me. I am much more amazed by the apportionment of votes; I expected that the majority against me would be larger than this. It seems in fact that a mere thirty votes on the other side would have meant my acquittal.[13] I think then that so far as Meletus is concerned I have actually been acquitted; and *more* than acquitted, for it is clear that if Anytus and Lycon had not come forward to accuse me he would have been fined a thousand drachmas for failing to secure a fifth part of the votes.

So the man proposes the penalty of death, does he? Well, gentlemen, what shall I propose as the alternative?[14] Surely that which I deserve. Well no, what do I deserve to suffer or be fined? My offence is that I have not kept silent upon the lessons I have learned from life; I have scorned what most men cherish—money-making and the adminstration of their property, military command and mob-leadership, and all the various political offices, cabals and backstairs intrigue. Thinking myself really too honourable a man to meddle in such affairs without disaster, I have refrained from those activities wherein I should have been of no use to you or to myself, and have spent my time conferring upon each of my fellow citizens individually what I regard as the greatest of all blessings. I have tried to persuade each of you to care for himself, for his own moral and intellectual improvement, rather than for any of his belongings; for the State itself rather than for its possessions; and so on. What then is due to such a man as I? Some benefit, gentlemen, if I am to be rewarded strictly in accordance with my deserts; and that benefit should be such as befits me. Now what is fitting for a poor man who is your benefactor, and who needs leisure to exhort you? There is nothing, gentlemen, more suitable than that such a man be provided with free meals in the City Hall? That would be far more appropriate in my case than it is when one

---

[13] [Cases involving religion were tried before the heliastic court, consisting of six thousand citizens chosen by lot, six hundred from each of the ten tribes. This court, however, was almost always divided into smaller, even-numbered groups ranging from two hundred to a thousand. One additional member was added to avoid a tie. Socrates was tried by a court of 501.]

[14] [Since Athenian law prescribed no penalty for the crime alleged against Socrates, the rule was that, as soon as a verdict of guilty had been returned, the accused should suggest an alternative penalty to the one demanded by the prosecution. The court had to choose between the two, and were not allowed to compromise.]

of you has won a two- or four-horse chariot race at the Olympic games. For while the charioteer makes you *seem* happy I make you *really* happy; besides, he doesn't want for food, whereas I am needy. So if I must propose a penalty in accordance with my deserts, [37] I propose maintenance in the City Hall....

Someone may ask me: "Socrates, can't you leave us and live quietly without talking?" Now to convince some of you that I cannot do so is the hardest of all tasks. If I say (*a*) that such conduct would be disobedience to the god, and that consequently it is impossible for me to remain silent, you will think I am jesting and will not believe me; [38] and you will believe me still less if I say (*b*) that to discourse every day upon virtue, and other topics about which you hear me talking and examining both myself and others, is the greatest benefit to mankind, and that life without debate is not worth living. Herein, gentlemen, I speak the truth, but it is not easy to convince you. Moreover, I am not used to regarding myself as worthy of an evil fate. If I had money I would have proposed the heaviest fine I could pay, for that would have done me no harm. But in point of fact I have none—unless you are willing to propose a fine that I could pay. I might perhaps pay you a mina of silver; so I propose that penalty....

No, gentlemen, Plato here and Crito, Critobulus and Apollodorus tell me to propose as fine of thirty minas, and offer to go surety. So I propose a fine of that amount, guaranteed by these men who have ample resources.

### 3. *After Sentence of Death*

Gentlemen, you have stolen a short march on time; and your reward, conferred by those who seek to besmirch the name of Athens, will be the evil reputation of having slain Socrates, a sage. Yes, those who mean to reproach you will call me a wise man, even though I am not. Now if you had waited a little while, what you desired would have been fulfilled without your intervention; for you see my age, how far advanced in life and how close to death I am. I say this not to all of you, but to those who voted for my death. And here is something else I say to them. You may think, gentlemen, that I have been convicted through a lack of such arguments as would have moved you to acquit me, had I considered it right to stop at nothing, in word or deed to secure acquittal. By no means....

No, gentlemen, it is not difficult to escape death, it is much harder to escape wickedness, an enemy more fleet of foot than death. Here I am now, aged and slow, caught by the slower runner, and you, my accusers, clever and quick though you be, by the faster—wickedness. Now I shall depart, convicted by you and sentenced to death, while they go convicted by truth of villainous injustice. I abide by my doom, and they by theirs. Perhaps these things were inevitable; I do not consider them ill done....

Here is another point of view from which there is sound reason to believe that my condemnation is a good. The state of death is one of two things; either it is virtual nothingness, so that the dead man has no consciousness of anything, or it is, as people say, a change, ie. a migration of the soul from here to another place. If it is unconsciousness, like a sleep in which the sleeper does not even dream, death would be a wonderful gain. Suppose a man had to pick out that night in which he slept a dreamless sleep, and were to compare it with the other nights and days of his life; and then suppose he had to say, after due consideration, how many days and nights had passed more pleasantly than that night: I believe that the great King of Persia himself, let alone an ordinary individual, would conclude that they were few in comparison. If such is the nature of death, then, I count it a gain; for in that case all time seems to be no longer than one night. If, on the other hand, death is a sort of removal hence to some other home, and if we are rightly given to understand that all the dead are there, what greater blessing, my judges, could there be? Can the change of home be undesirable if one reaches [41] the Underworld, after leaving behind these self-styled judges, and finds the true judges who are said to administer justice there—Minos, Rhadamanthus, Aeacus, Triptolemus and all those other demigods who were just men in their lives? Again, what would not any of you give to enjoy the company of Orpheus, Musaeus, Hesiod and Homer? I am prepared to die many deaths if these things are true; for I myself should find the life there wonderful, when I met Palamedes, Telamonian Ajax and other men of old who lost their lives through an unjust judgment, and compared my experience with theirs. That, I think, would not be unpleasant. But the greatest pleasure of all would be to spend my time as I have done here, studying and cross-questioning the inhabitants, to discover who among them is wise and who imagines he is though he is not. What price, my judges, would not any of you pay to examine him[15] who led the great army against Troy, or Odysseus, or Sisyphus, or innumerable others, men and women, whom I might name? To associate and converse with them and examine them would be

---

15 [Agamemnon.]

immeasurable bliss. At all events, folk there do not put men to death for doing so; for, if what we are told is true, everyone there is everlastingly immortal, besides being happier in other respects than we are here.

Yes, my judges, you too must entertain high hopes of death and must bear in mind this one truth, that no evil can befall a good man either in life or after death, and that the gods are not forgetful of his woes. Nor indeed has my present fate overtaken me by chance: I see clearly that it was better for me to die now and be delivered from trouble. That is why the sign made no effort to deter me, and I bear no grudge against those who accused or condemned me. It was not, however, with my welfare in mind that they did so, but because they thought to injure me; and to that extent they are blameworthy. Never mind, I make this request of them: When my sons reach manhood, gentlemen, punish them by troubling them as I have troubled you; if they seem to put money or anything else before virtue, or think themselves of consequence when they are not, rebuke them as I have rebuked you, because they care not for what they ought and believe themselves great men whereas in fact they are worthless. If you do this, [42] both I and my sons shall have received just treatment at your hands.

Well, now it is time to part. I go to die, and you to live; but which of us goes to the better lot is known to none but God.

# THE REPUBLIC

## ❧ BOOK I ❧

### *Cephalus: Justice as Truthfulness and Repayment*

327  I went down to the Piraeus yesterday with Glaucon, the son of Ariston. I intended to say a prayer to the goddess, and I also wanted to see how they would manage the festival, since this was its first celebration. I thought our own procession

b  was a fine one and that which the Thracians had sent was no less outstanding. After we had said our prayer and witnessed the procession we started back toward the city. Polemarchus saw us from a distance as we were setting off for home and he told his slave to run and bid us wait for him. So the slave caught hold of my cloak from behind: Polemarchus, he said, bids you wait for him. I turned round and asked where Polemarchus was. There he is, coming up behind you, he said, please wait for him. And Glaucon said: All right, we'll wait.

c  Just then Polemarchus caught up with us. Adeimantus, the brother of Glaucon,[1] was with him, and so were Niceratus, the son of Nicias, and some others, presumably on their way from the procession.

Then Polemarchus said: Socrates, it looks to me as if you had started on your way back to the city.

Quite right, said I.

Do you see how many we are? he said.

Of course I do.

---

*The Republic*, by Plato, translated by G.M.A. Grube. Indianapolis: Hackett Publishing Company (1974). Reprinted by permission of the publisher.

**N.B.** The topic headings inserted in the text have been added by J.M.P.

[1] [Glaucon and Adeimantus are the brothers of Plato, who is not present. They carry the main burden of the conversation with Socrates from the beginning of the second book to the end of the work. The scene is the house of old Cephalus, father of Polemarchus, Lysias, and Euthydemus. Lysias is a well-known writer of speeches of the late fifth century, and a number of them are extant. He later became the model of the simple style. He takes no part. We have a dialogue named after Euthydemus. Thrasymachus was a Sophist of the younger generation, known for his powerful emotional appeals. He is the main objector in the first book, but after that says very little. We have a short dialogue, the *Cleitophon*, which criticizes Socrates for his lack of positive teaching. The first book, like many early or "Socratic" dialogues, discusses several definitions of "justice" but comes to no conclusion. The whole discussion is probably supposed to have taken place about 411 B.C.]

Well, he said, you must either be stronger than we are, or you must stay here.

Is there not another alternative, said I, namely that we may persuade you to let us go?

Could you, said he, persuade men who do not listen?

Not possibly, said Glaucon.

Well, you can take it that we are certainly not going to listen.

Adeimantus intervened: Do you really not know that there is to be a torch race on horseback this evening in honour of the goddess? 328

On horseback? said I, that is a novelty. Are they going to race on horseback and hand the torches on in relays, or how do you mean?

That's it, said Polemarchus, and there will be an all night festival besides, which will be worth seeing, and which we intend to watch after dinner. We shall be joined by many of our young men here and talk with them. So please do stay. b

And Glaucon said: It seems that we'll have to stay.

If you think so, said I, then we must.

So we went to the home of Polemarchus, and there we found Lysias and Euthydemus, the brothers of Polemarchus, also Thrasymachus of Chalcedon, Charmantides of Paiania, and Cleitophon the son of Aristonymus. Polemarchus' father Cephalus was also in the house. I thought he looked quite old, as I had not c seen him for some time. He was sitting on a seat with a cushion, a wreath on his head, for he had been offering a sacrifice in the courtyard. There was a circle of seats there, and we sat down by him.

As soon as he saw me Cephalus welcomed me and said: Socrates, you don't often come down to the Piraeus to see us. You should. If it were still easy for me to walk to the city you would not need to come here, we would come to you, d but now you should come more often. You should realize that, to the extent that my physical pleasures get feebler, my desire for conversation, and the pleasure I take in it, increase. So be sure to come more often and talk to these youngsters, as you would to good friends and relations.

I replied: Indeed, Cephalus, I do enjoy conversing with men of advanced e years. As from those who have travelled along a road which we too will probably have to follow, we should enquire from them what kind of a road it is, whether rough and difficult or smooth and easy, and I should gladly learn from you what you think about this, as you have reached the point in life which the poets call "the threshold of old age," whether it is a difficult part of life, or how your experience would describe it to us.

329     Yes by Zeus, Socrates, he said, I will tell you what I think of old age. A number of us who are more or less the same age often get together in accordance with the old adage. When we meet, the majority of us bemoan their age: they miss the pleasures which were theirs in youth; they recall the pleasures of sex, drink, and feasts, and some other things that go with them, and they are angry as if they

b    were deprived of important things, as if they then lived the good life and now were not living at all. Some others deplore the humiliations which old age suffers in the household, and because of this they repeat again and again that old age is the cause of many evils. However, Socrates, I do not think that they blame the real cause. For if old age were the cause, then I should have suffered in the same way, and so would all others who have reached my age. As it is, I have met other old

c    men who do not feel like that, and indeed I was present at one time when someone asked the poet Sophocles: "How are you in regard to sex, Sophocles? Can you still make love to a woman?" "Hush man," the poet replied, "I am very glad to have escaped from this, like a slave who has escaped from a mad and cruel master." I thought then that he was right, and I still think so, for a great peace and freedom from these things come with old age: after the tension of one's desires re-

d    laxes and ceases, then Sophocles' words certainly apply, it is an escape from many mad masters. As regards both sex and relations in the household there is one cause, Socrates, not old age but the manner of one's life: if it is moderate and contented, then old age too is but moderately burdensome; if it is not, then both old age and youth are hard to bear.

I wondered at his saying this and I wanted him to say more, so I urged him

e    on by saying: Cephalus, when you say this, I don't think most people would agree with you; they think you endure old age easily not because of your manner of life but because you are wealthy, for the wealthy, they say, have many things to encourage them.

What you say is true, he said. They would not agree. And there is something in what they say, but not as much as they think. What Themistocles said is quite

330   right: when a man from Seriphus was insulting him by saying that his high reputation was due to his city and not to himself, he replied that, had he been a Seriphian, he would not be famous, but neither would the other had he been an Athenian. The same can be applied to those who are not rich and find old age hard to bear—namely that a good man would not very easily bear old age in poverty, nor would a bad man, even if wealthy, be at peace with himself.

Did you inherit most of your wealth, Cephalus, I asked, or did you acquire it?

How much did I acquire, Socrates? As a moneymaker I stand between my    b
grandfather and my father. My grandfather and namesake inherited about the
same amount of wealth which I possess but multiplied it many times. My father,
Lysanias, however, diminished that amount to even less than I have now. As for me,
I am satisfied to leave to my sons here no less but a little more than I inherited.

The reason I asked, said I, is that you did not seem to me to be overfond of    c
money, and this is generally the case with those who have not made it themselves. Those who have acquired it by their own efforts are twice as fond of it as
other men. Just as poets love their own poems and fathers love their children, so
those who have made their money are attached to it as something they have made
themselves, besides using it as other men do. This makes them poor company, for
they are unwilling to give their approval to anything but money.

What you say is true, he said.

It surely is, said I. Now tell me this much more: What is the greatest benefit    d
you have received from the enjoyment of wealth?

I would probably not convince many people in saying this, Socrates, he said,
but you must realize that when a man approaches the time when he thinks he will
die, he becomes fearful and concerned about things which he did not fear before. It is then that the stories we are told about the underworld, which he ridiculed    e
before—that the man who has sinned here will pay the penalty there—torture his
mind lest they be true. Whether because of the weakness of old age, or because he
is now closer to what happens there and has a clearer view, the man himself is
filled with suspicion and fear, and he now takes account and examines whether he
has wronged anyone. If he finds many sins in his own life, he awakes from sleep
in terror, as children do, and he lives with the expectation of evil. However, the    331
man who knows he has not sinned has a sweet and good hope as his constant
companion, a nurse to his old age, as Pindar too puts it. The poet has expressed
this charmingly, Socrates, that whoever lives a just and pious life

> Sweet is the hope that nurtures his heart,
> companion and nurse to his old age,
> a hope which governs the rapidly changing thoughts of mortals.

This is wonderfully well said. It is in this connection that I would say that
wealth has its greatest value, not for everyone but for a good and well-balanced    b

man. Not to have lied to or deceived anyone even unwillingly, not to depart yonder in fear, owing either sacrifices to a god or money to a man: to this wealth makes a great contribution. It has many other uses, but benefit for benefit I would say that its greatest usefulness lies in this for an intelligent man, Socrates.

c     Beautifully spoken, Cephalus, said I, but are we to say that justice or right is simply to speak the truth and to pay back any debt one may have contracted? Or are these same actions sometimes right and sometimes wrong? I mean this sort of thing, for example: everyone would surely agree that if a friend has deposited weapons with you when he was sane, and he asks for them when he is out of his mind, you should not return them. The man who returns them is not doing right, nor is one who is willing to tell the whole truth to a man in such a state.

d     What you say is correct, he answered.

This then is not a definition of right or justice, namely to tell the truth and pay one's debts.

It certainly is, said Polemarchus interrupting, if we are to put any trust in Simonides.

And now, said Cephalus, I leave the argument to you, for I must go back and look after the sacrifice.

Do I then inherit your role? asked Polemarchus.

You certainly do, said Cephalus laughing, and as he said it he went off to sacrifice....

[*Polemarchus enters the discussion by suggesting another definition: justice is that which benefits one's friends and harms one's enemies. Socrates confounds Polemarchus by pointing out that justice is not a list of duties nor is it a type of skill or craft used for friends and against enemies. —J.M.P.*]

### Thrasymachus: Justice as Advantage of the Stronger

336b     While we were speaking Thrasymachus often started to interrupt, but he was restrained by those who were sitting by him, for they wanted to hear the argument to the end. But when we paused after these last words of mine he could no longer keep quiet. He gathered himself together like a wild beast about to spring, and he came at us as if to tear us to pieces.

c     Polemarchus and I were afraid and flustered as he roared into the middle of our company: What nonsense have you two been talking, Socrates? Why do you play the fool in thus giving way to each other? If you really want to know what justice is, don't only ask questions and then score off anyone who answers, and refute him.

You know very well that it is much easier to ask questions than to answer them. Give    d
an answer yourself and tell us what you say justice is. And don't tell me that it is the needful, or the advantageous, or the beneficial, or the gainful, or the useful, but tell me
clearly and precisely what you mean, for I will not accept it if you utter such rubbish.

His words startled me, and glancing at him I was afraid. I think if I had not
looked at him before he looked at me, I should have been speechless. As it was I had
glanced at him first when our discussion began to exasperate him, so I was able to    e
answer him and I said, trembling: do not be hard on us, Thrasymachus, if we
have erred in our investigation, he and I; be sure that we err unwillingly. You surely
do not believe that if we were searching for gold we would be unwilling to give way
to each other and thus destroy our chance of finding it, but that when searching
for justice, a thing more precious than much gold, we mindlessly give way to one
another, and that we are not thoroughly in earnest about finding it. You must believe that, my friend, for I think we could not do it. So it is much more seemly that    337
you clever people should pity us than that you should be angry with us.

When he heard that he gave a loud and bitter laugh and said: By Heracles, that
is just Socrates' usual irony. I knew this, and I warned these men here before that
you would not be willing to answer any questions but would pretend ignorance, and
that you would do anything rather than give an answer, if anyone questioned you.

You are clever, Thrasymachus, I said, for you knew very well that if you asked anyone how much is twelve, and as you asked him you warned him: "Do not, my man,    b
say that twelve is twice six, or three times four, or six times two, or four times three,
for I will not accept such nonsense," it would be quite clear to you that no one can
answer a question asked in those terms. And if he said to you: "What do you mean,
Thrasymachus? Am I not to give any of the answers you mention, not even, you
strange man, if it happens to be one of those things, but am I to say something
which is not the truth, or what do you mean?" What answer would you give him?

Well, he said, do you maintain that the two cases are alike?

They may well be, said I. Even if they are not, but the person you ask thinks
they are, do you think him less likely to answer what he believes to be true,
whether we forbid him or not?

And you will surely do the same, he said. Will you give one of the forbidden
answers?

I shouldn't wonder, said I, if after investigation that was my opinion. What, he
said, if I show you a different answer about justice from all these and a better    d
one? What penalty do you think you should pay then?

What else, said I, but what is proper for an ignorant man to pay? It is fitting for him to learn from one who knows. And that is what I believe I would deserve.

You amuse me, he said. You must not only learn but pay the fee.

Yes, when I have the money, I said.

We have the money, said Glaucon. If it is a matter of money, speak, Thrasymachus, for we shall all contribute for Socrates.

e

Quite so, said he, so that Socrates can carry on as usual: he gives no answer himself, and then, when someone else does give one, he takes up the argument and refutes it.

My dear man, I said, how could one answer, when in the first place he does not know and does not profess to know, and then, if he has an opinion, an eminent

338

man forbids him to say what he believes? It is much more seemly for you to answer, since you say you know and have something to say. Please do so. Do me that favour, and do not begrudge your teaching to Glaucon and the others.

While I was saying this, Glaucon and the others begged him to speak. It was obvious that Thrasymachus was eager to do so and earn their admiration, and that he thought he had a beautiful answer, but he pretended that he wanted to win

b

his point that I should be the one to answer. However, he agreed in the end, and then said: There you have Socrates' wisdom; he himself is not willing to teach but he goes around learning from others, and then he is not even grateful.

When you say that I learn from others you are right, Thrasymachus, said I, but when you say that I am not grateful, that is not true, I show what gratitude I can, but I can only give praise. I have no money, but how enthusiastically I praise when someone seems to me to speak well is something you will realize quite soon after you have given your answer, for I think you will speak well.

c

Listen then, said he. I say that the just is nothing else than the advantage of the stronger. Well, why don't you praise me? But you will not want to.

I must first understand your meaning, said I, for I do not know it yet. You say that the advantage of the stronger is just. What do you mean, Thrasymachus? Surely you do not mean such a thing as this: Poulydamas, the pancratist athlete, is stronger than we are; it is to his advantage to eat beef to build up his physical

d

strength. Do you mean that this food is also advantageous and just for us who are weaker than he is?

You disgust me, Socrates, he said. Your trick is always to take up the argument at the point where you can damage it most.

Not at all, my dear sir, I said, but tell us more clearly what you mean.

Do you not know, he said, that some cities are ruled by a despot, others by the people, and others again by the aristocracy? —Of course.

And this element has the power and rules in every city? —Certainly.

Yes, and each government makes laws to its own advantage: democracy makes democratic laws, a despotism makes despotic laws, and so with the others, and when they have made these laws they declare this to be just for their subjects, that is, their own advantage, and they punish him who transgresses the laws as lawless and unjust. This then, my good man, is what I say justice is, the same in all cities, the advantage of the established government, and correct reasoning will conclude that the just is the same everywhere, the advantage of the stronger.

Now I see what you mean, I said. Whether it is true or not I will try to find out. But you too, Thrasymachus, have given us an answer that the just is the advantageous whereas you forbade that answer to me. True, you have added the words "of the stronger."

Perhaps, he said, you consider that an insignificant addition!

It is not clear yet whether or not it is significant. Obviously, we must investigate whether what you say is true. I agree that the just is some kind of advantage, but you add that it is the advantage of the stronger. I do not know. We must look into this. —Go on looking, he said.

We will do so, said I. Tell me, do you also say that obedience to the rulers is just? —I do.

And are the rulers in all cities infallible, or are they liable to error? —No doubt they are liable to error.

When they undertake to make laws, therefore, they make some correctly and make others incorrectly? —I think so.

"Correctly" means that they make laws to their own advantage, and "incorrectly" not to their own advantage. Or how would you put it? —As you do.

And whatever laws they make must be obeyed by their subjects, and this is just? —Of course.

Then, according to your argument, it is just to do not only what is to the advantage of the stronger, but also the opposite, what is not to their advantage.

What is that you are saying? he asked.

The same as you, I think, but let us examine it more fully. Have we not agreed that, in giving orders to their subjects, the rulers are sometimes in error as to

e
339
b
c
d

what is best for themselves, yet it is just for their subjects to do whatever their rulers order. Is that much agreed? —I think so.

e

Think then also, said I, that you have agreed that it is just to do what is to the disadvantage of the rulers and the stronger whenever they unintentionally give orders which are bad for themselves, and you say it is just for the others to obey their given orders. Does it not of necessity follow, my wise Thrasymachus, that it is just to do the opposite of what you said? The weaker are then ordered to do what is to the disadvantage of the stronger.

340

Yes by Zeus, Socrates, said Polemarchus, that is quite clear.

Yes, if you bear witness for him, interrupted Cleitophon.

What need of a witness? said Polemarchus. Thrasymachus himself agrees that the rulers sometimes give orders that are bad for themselves, and that it is just to obey them.

Thrasymachus maintained that it is just to obey the orders of the rulers, Polemarchus.

He also said that the just was the advantage of the stronger, Cleitophon.

b

Having established those two points he went on to agree that the stronger sometimes ordered the weaker, their subjects, to do what was disadvantageous to themselves. From these agreed premises it follows that what is of advantage to the stronger is no more just than what is not.

But, Cleitophon replied, he said that the advantage of the stronger is what the stronger believes to be of advantage to him. This the weaker must do, and that is what he defined the just to be.

That is not how he stated it, said Polemarchus.

c

It makes no difference, Polemarchus, I said. If Thrasymachus now wants to put it that way, let us accept it. Tell me, Thrasymachus, was this what you intended to say justice is, namely that which appears to the stronger to be to his advantage, whether it is so or not? Shall we say that this is what you mean?

Not in the least, said he. Do you think that I would call stronger a man who is in error at the time he errs?

I did think you meant that, said I, when you said that the rulers were not infallible but were liable to error.

d

You are being captious, Socrates, he said. Do you call a man a physician when he is in error in the treatment of patients, at the moment of, and in regard to this very error? Or would you call a man an accountant when he makes a miscalculation at the moment of, and with regard to this miscalculation? I think that we express ourselves in words which, taken literally, do say that the physician is in error, or the accountant, or the grammarian. But each of these, in so far as he is what we call him, never errs, so that, if you use language with precision —and you want to be precise—no practitioner of a craft ever errs. It is when the knowledge of his craft leaves him that he errs, and at that time he is not a practitioner of it. No craftsman, wise man, or ruler is in error at the time that he is a ruler in the precise sense. However, everyone will say that the physician or the ruler is in error. Take it then that this is now my answer to you. To speak with precision, the ruler, in so far as he is a ruler, unerringly decrees what is best for himself and this the subject must do. The just then is, as I said from the first, to do what is advantageous to the stronger.

Very well, Thrasymachus, said I. You think I am captious?

You certainly are, he said.

And you think that it was deliberate trickery on my part to ask you the questions I did ask?

I know it very well, he said, but it will not do you any good, for I would be well aware of your trickery; nor would you have the ability to force my agreement in open debate.

I would not even try, my good sir, I said, but in order to avoid a repetition of this, do define clearly whether it is the ruler in the ordinary or the precise sense whose advantage is to be pursued as that of the stronger.

I mean, he said, the ruler in the most exact sense. Now practise your trickery and your captiousness on this if you can, for I will not let any statement of yours pass, and you certainly won't be able to.

Do you think, I said, that I am crazy enough to try to shave a lion or trick Thrasymachus?

You certainly tried just now, he said, though you are no good at it.

Enough of this sort of thing, I said. But tell me: is the physician in the strict sense, whom you mentioned just now, a moneymaker or one who treats the sick? Tell me about the real physician. —He is one who treats the sick, said he.

What about the ship's captain? Is he, to speak correctly, a ruler of sailors or a sailor? —A ruler of sailors.

We should not, I think, take into account the fact that he sails in a ship, and we should not call him a sailor, for it is not on account of his sailing that he is called

e

341

b

c

d

a ship's captain, but because of his craft and his authority over sailors. —True.

And there is something which is advantageous to each of these, that is: patients and sailors? —Certainly.

And is not the purpose of a craft's existence to seek and secure the advantageous in each case? —That's right.

Now is there any other advantage to each craft, except that it be as perfect as possible? —What is the meaning of that question?

e

It is this, said I. If you asked me whether our body is sufficient unto itself, or has a further need I should answer: "It certainly has needs, and for this purpose the craft of medicine exists and has now been discovered, because the body is defective, not self-sufficient. So to provide it with things advantageous to it the craft of medicine has been developed." Do you think I am correct in saying this or not? —Correct.

342

Well then, is the craft of medicine itself defective, or is there any other craft which needs some further excellence—as the eyes are in need of sight, the ears of hearing, and, because of this need, they require some other craft to investigate and provide for this? —is there in the craft itself some defect, so that each craft requires

b

another craft which will investigate what is beneficial to it, and then the investigating craft needs another such still, and so ad infinitum? Or does a craft investigate what is beneficial to it, or does it need neither itself nor any other to investigate what is required because of imperfections? There is in fact no defect or error of any kind in any craft, nor is it proper to any craft to seek what is to the advantage of anything but the object of its concern; it is itself pure and without fault, being itself correct, as long as it is wholly itself in the precise sense. Consider this with that preciseness of language which you mentioned. Is it so or otherwise? —It appears to be so.

c

The craft of medicine, I said, does not seek its own advantage but that of the body. —Yes.

Nor does horse-breeding seek its own advantage but that of horses. Nor does any other craft seek its own advantage—it has no further need—but that of its object. —That seems to be the case.

And surely, Thrasymachus, the crafts govern and have power over their object.

He agreed, but with great reluctance at this point.

No science of any kind seeks or orders its own advantage, but that of the

d

weaker which is subject to it and governed by it.

He tried to fight this conclusion, but he agreed to this too in the end. And after he had, I said: Surely no physician either, in so far as he is a physician, seeks or orders what is advantageous to himself, but to his patient? For we agreed that the physician in the strict sense of the word is a ruler over bodies and not a moneymaker. Was this not agreed?

He said yes.

So the ship's captain in the strict sense is a ruler over sailors, and not a sailor? —That has been agreed.

Does it not follow that the ship's captain and ruler will not seek and order what is advantageous to himself, but to the sailor, his subject.

He agreed, but barely.

So then, Thrasymachus, I said, no other ruler in any kind of government, in so far as he is a ruler, seeks what is to his own advantage or orders it, but that which is to the advantage of his subject who is the concern of his craft; it is this he keeps in view; all his words and actions are directed to this end.

When we reached this point in our argument and it was clear to all that the definition of justice had turned into its opposite, Thrasymachus, instead of answering, said: Tell me, Socrates, do you have a nanny?

What's this? said I. Had you not better answer than ask such questions?

Because, he said, she is letting you go around with a snotty nose and does not wipe it when she needs to, if she leaves you without any knowledge of sheep or shepherds.

What is the particular point of that remark? I asked.

You think, he said, that shepherds and cowherds seek the good of their sheep or cattle, whereas their sole purpose in fattening them and looking after them is their own good and that of their master. Moreover, you believe that rulers in the cities, true rulers that is, have a different attitude towards their subjects than one has towards sheep, and that they think of anything else, night and day, than their own advantage. You are so far from understanding the nature of justice and the just, of injustice and the unjust, that you do not realize that the just is really another's good, the advantage of the stronger and the ruler, but for the inferior who obeys it is a personal injury. Injustice on the other hand exercises its power over those who are truly naive and just, and those over whom it rules do what is of advantage to the other, the stronger, and, by obeying him, they make him happy, but themselves not in the least.

You must look at it in this way, my naive Socrates: the just is everywhere at a disadvantage compared with the unjust. First, in their contracts with one another: wherever two such men are associated you will never find, when the partnership ends, the just man to have more than the unjust, but less. Then, in their relation to the city: when taxes are to be paid, from the same income the just man pays more, the other less; but, when benefits are to be received, the one gets nothing while the other profits much; whenever each of them holds a public office, the just man, even if he is not penalized in other ways, finds that his private affairs deteriorate through neglect while he gets nothing from the public purse because he is just; moreover, he is disliked by his household and his acquaintances whenever he refuses them an unjust favour. The opposite is true of the unjust man in every respect. I repeat what I said before: the man of great power gets the better deal. Consider him if you want to decide how much more it benefits him privately to be unjust rather than just. You will see this most easily if you turn your thoughts to the most complete form of injustice which brings the greatest happiness to the wrongdoer, while it makes those whom he wronged, and who are not willing to do wrong, most wretched. This most complete form is despotism; it does not appropriate other people's property little by little, whether secretly or by force, whether public or private, whether sacred objects or temple property, but appropriates it all at once.

When a wrongdoer is discovered in petty cases, he is punished and faces great opprobrium, for the perpetrators of these petty crimes are called temple robbers, kidnappers, housebreakers, robbers, and thieves, but when a man, besides appropriating the possessions of the citizens, manages to enslave the owners as well, then, instead of those ugly names he is called happy and blessed, not only by his fellow citizens but by all others who learn that he has run through the whole gamut of injustice. Those who give injustice a bad name do so because they are afraid, not of practising but of suffering injustice.

And so, Socrates, injustice, if it is on a large enough scale, is a stronger, freer, and more powerful thing than justice and, as I said from the first, the just is what is advantageous to the stronger, while the unjust is to one's own advantage and benefit.

Having said this and poured this mass of close-packed words into our ears as a bathman might a flood of water, Thrasymachus intended to leave, but those present did not let him, and made him stay for a discussion of his views. I too begged him to stay and I said: My dear Thrasymachus, after throwing such a

speech at us, you want to leave before adequately instructing us or finding out    e
whether you are right or not? Or do you think it a small thing to decide on a
whole way of living, which, if each of us adopted it, would make him live the
most profitable life?

Do I think differently? said Thrasymachus.

You seem to, said I, or else you care nothing for us nor worry whether we'll
live better or worse, in ignorance of what you say you know. Do, my good sir,    345
show some keenness to teach us. It will not be without value to you to be the
benefactor of so many of us. For my own part, I tell you that I do not believe that
injustice is more profitable than justice, not even if one gives it full scope and does
not put obstacles in its way. No, my friend. Let us assume the existence of an unjust man with every opportunity to do wrong, either because his misdeeds remain
secret or because he has the power to battle things through; nevertheless he
does not persuade me that injustice is more profitable than justice. Perhaps    b
some other of us feels the same, and not only I. Come now, my good sir, really
persuade us that we are wrong to esteem justice more highly than injustice in
planning our life.

And how, said he, shall I persuade you, if you are not convinced by what I
said just now? What more can I do? Am I to take my argument and pour it into
your mind?

Zeus forbid! Don't you do that, but first stick to what you have said and, if you
change your position, do so openly and do not deceive us. You see now,    c
Thrasymachus—let us examine again what went before—that, while you first
defined the true physician, you did not think it necessary later to observe the
precise definition of the true shepherd, but you think that he fattens sheep, in so
far as he is a shepherd, not with what is best for the sheep in mind, but like a
guest about to be entertained at a feast, with a banquet in view, or again a sale, like
a moneymaker, not a shepherd. The shepherd's craft is concerned only to provide
what is best for the object of its care; as for the craft itself, it is sufficiently provided
with all it needs to be at its best, as long as it does not fall short of being the craft
of the shepherd. That is why I thought it necessary for us to agree just now that
every kind of rule, as far as it truly rules, does not seek what is best for anything
else than the subject of this rule and care, and this is true both of public and pri-    e
vate kinds of rule. Do you think that those who rule over cities, the true rulers,
rule willingly? —I don't think it, by Zeus, I know it, he said.

Well but, Thrasymachus, said I, do you not realize that in other kinds of rule no one is willing to rule, but they ask for pay, thinking that their rule will benefit not themselves but their subjects. Tell me, does not every craft differ from every other in that it has a different function? Please do not give an answer contrary to what you believe, so that we can come to some conclusion.

Yes, that is what makes it different, he said.

And each craft benefits us in its own particular way, different from the others. For example, medicine gives us health, navigation safety while sailing, and so with the others. —Quite so.

And the craft of earning pay gives us wages, for that is its function. Or would you call medicine the same craft as navigation? Or, if you wish to define with precision as you proposed, if the ship's captain becomes healthy because sailing benefits his health, would you for that reason call his craft medicine? —Not at all, he said.

Nor would you call wage-earning medicine if someone is healthy while earning wages? —Certainly not.

Nor would you call medicine wage-earning if someone earns pay while healing? —No.

So we agree that each craft brings its own benefit? —Be it so.

Whatever benefit all craftsmen receive in common must then result clearly from some craft which they pursue in common, and so are benefited by it. —It seems so.

We say then that if the practitioners of these crafts are benefited by earning a wage, this results from their practising the wage earning craft.

He reluctantly agreed.

So this benefit to each, the receiving of pay, does not result from the practice of their own craft, but if we are to examine this precisely, medicine provides health while the craft of earning provides pay; house building provides a house, and the craft of earning which accompanies it provides a wage, and so with the other crafts; each fulfills its own function and benefits that with which it is concerned. If pay is not added, is there any benefit which the practitioner gets from his craft? —Apparently not.

Does he even provide a benefit when he works for nothing? —Yes, I think he does.

Is this not clear now, Thrasymachus, that no craft or rule provides its own advantage, but, as we have been saying for some time, it procures and orders what is of advantage to its subject; it aims at his advantage, that of the weaker, not of the stronger. That is why, my dear Thrasymachus, I said just now that no one willingly wants to rule, to handle and straighten out the affairs of others. They ask for pay because the man who intends to practise his craft well never does what is best for himself, nor, when he gives such orders, does he give them in accordance with his craft, but he pursues the advantage of his subject. For that reason, then, it seems one must provide remuneration if they are to be willing to rule, whether money or honour, or a penalty if he does not rule.

What do you mean, Socrates? said Glaucon. I understand the two kinds of remuneration, but I do not understand what kind of penalty you mean, which you mention under the heading of remuneration.

Then you do not understand the remuneration of the best men, I said, which makes them willing to rule. Do you not know that the love of honour and money are made a reproach, and rightly so? —I know that.

b

Therefore good men will not be willing to rule for the sake of either money or honour. They do not want to be called hirelings if they openly receive payment for ruling, nor, if they provide themselves with it secretly, to be called thieves. Nor will they do it for honour's sake, for they have no love for it. So, if they are to be willing to rule, some compulsion or punishment must be brought to bear on them. That is perhaps why to seek office willingly, before one must, is thought shameful. Now the greatest punishment is to be ruled by a worse man than oneself if one is not willing to rule. I think it is the fear of this which makes men of good character rule whenever they do. They approach office not as something good or something to be enjoyed, but as something necessary because they cannot entrust it to men better than, or even equal to, themselves. In a city of good men, if there were such, they would probably vie with each other in order not to rule, not, as now, in order to be rulers. There it would be quite clear that the nature of the true ruler is not to seek his own advantage but that of his subjects, and everyone, knowing this, would prefer to receive benefits rather than take the trouble to benefit others. In this matter I do not at all agree with Thrasymachus that the just is the advantage of the stronger....

c

d

e

[*In the final portion of Book I Socrates debates Thrasymachus' claim that injustice is "more powerful and stronger than justice" and that the practice of justice is at best a "high-minded foolishness." Socrates argues that justice is an excellence of the soul and to live well the soul must use this excellence. Justice benefits the soul. However, Socrates concludes Book I by stating he "knows nothing" because he does not know precisely what justice itself is. —J.M.P.*]

# → BOOK II ←

## *The Question Restated*

357 When I had said this I thought I had done with the discussion, but evidently this was only a prelude. Glaucon on this occasion too showed that boldness which is characteristic of him, and refused to accept Thrasymachus' abandon-

b ing the argument. He said: Do you, Socrates, want to appear to have persuaded us, or do you want truly to convince us that it is better in every way to be just than unjust?

I would certainly wish to convince you truly, I said, if I could.

Well, he said, you are certainly not attaining your wish. Tell me, do you think there is a kind of good which we welcome not because we desire its consequences but for its own sake: joy, for example, and all the harmless pleasures which have no further consequences beyond the joy which one finds in them?

Certainly, said I, I think there is such a good.

c Further, there is the good which we welcome for its own sake and also for its consequences, knowledge, for example, and sight and health. Such things we somehow welcome on both counts.

Yes, said I.

Are you also aware of a third kind, he asked, such as physical training, being treated when ill, the practice of medicine, and other ways of making money? We

d should say that these are wearisome but beneficial to us; we should not want them for their own sake, but because of the rewards and other benefits which result from them.

There is certainly such a third kind, I said, but why do you ask?

Under which of these headings do you put justice? he asked.

358 I would myself put it in the finest class, I said, that which is to be welcomed both for itself and for its consequences by any man who is to be blessed with happiness.

That is not the opinion of the many, he said; they would put it in the wearisome class, to be pursued for the rewards and popularity which come from a good reputation, but to be avoided in itself as being difficult.

I know that is the general opinion, I said. Justice has now for some time been objected to by Thrasymachus on this score while injustice was extolled, but it seems I am a slow learner.

Come then, he said, listen to me also to see whether you are still of the same    b
opinion, for I think that Thrasymachus gave up before he had to, charmed by you
as by a snake charmer. I am not yet satisfied by the demonstration on either side. I
am eager to hear the nature of each, of justice and injustice, and what effect its presence has upon the soul. I want to leave out of account the rewards and consequences    c
of each. So, if you agree, I will do the following: I will renew the
argument of Thrasymachus; I will first state what people consider the nature and
origin of justice; secondly, that all who practise it do so unwillingly as being something
necessary but not good; thirdly, that they have good reason to do so, for, according
to what people say, the life of the unjust man is much better than that of the just.

It is not that I think so, Socrates, but I am perplexed and my ears are deafened
listening to Thrasymachus and innumerable other speakers; I have never heard from    d
anyone the sort of defence of justice that I want to hear, proving that it is better
than injustice. I want to hear it praised for itself, and I think I am most likely to
hear this from you. Therefore I am going to speak at length in praise of the unjust life and in doing so I will show you the way I want to hear you denouncing
injustice and praising justice. See whether you want to hear what I suggest.

I want it more than anything else, I said. Indeed, what subject would a man
of sense talk and hear about more often with enjoyment?

Splendid, he said, then listen while I deal with the first subject I mentioned:    e
the nature and origin of justice.

They say that to do wrong is naturally good, to be wronged is bad, but the suffering of injury so far exceeds in badness the good of inflicting it that when men
have done wrong to each other and suffered it, and have had a taste of both,
those who are unable to avoid the latter and practise the former decide that it is
profitable to come to an agreement with each other neither to inflict injury nor    359
to suffer it. As a result they begin to make laws and covenants, and the law's command they call lawful and just. This, they say, is the origin and essence of justice; it stands between the best and the worst, the best being to do wrong without
paying the penalty and the worst to be wronged without the power of revenge. The
just then is a mean between two extremes; it is welcomed and honoured because    b
of men's lack of the power to do wrong. The man who has that power, the real man,
would not make a compact with anyone not to inflict injury or suffer it. For him
that would be madness. This then, Socrates, is, according to their argument, the
nature and origin of justice.

Even those who practise justice do so against their will because they lack the
power to do wrong. This we could realize very clearly if we imagined ourselves
granting to both the just and the unjust the freedom to do whatever they liked.
We could then follow both of them and observe where their desires led them,
and we would catch the just man redhanded travelling the same road as the unjust. The reason is the desire for undue gain which every organism by nature
pursues as a good, but the law forcibly sidetracks him to honour equality. The freedom I just mentioned would most easily occur if these men had the power which
they say the ancestor of the Lydian Gyges possessed. The story is that he was a shepherd in the service of the ruler of Lydia. There was a violent rainstorm and an earthquake which broke open the ground and created a chasm at the place where he was
tending sheep. Seeing this and marvelling, he went down into it. He saw, besides
many other wonders of which we are told, a hollow bronze horse. There were
window-like openings in it; he climbed through them and caught sight of a corpse
which seemed of more than human stature, wearing nothing but a ring of gold on
its finger. This ring the shepherd put on and came out. He arrived at the usual
monthly meeting which reported to the king on the state of the flocks, wearing
the ring. As he was sitting among the others he happened to twist the hoop of the
ring towards himself, to the inside of his hand, and as he did this he became invisible to those sitting near him and they went on talking as if he had gone. He
marvelled at this and, fingering the ring, he turned the hoop outward again and
became visible. Perceiving this he tested whether the ring had this power and so
it happened: if he turned the hoop inwards he became invisible, but was visible
when he turned it outwards. When he realized this, he at once arranged to become
one of the messengers to the king. He went, committed adultery with the king's
wife, attacked the king with her help, killed him, and took over the kingdom.

Now if there were two such rings, one worn by the just man, the other by the
unjust, no one, as these people think, would be so incorruptible that he would
stay on the path of justice or bring himself to keep away from other people's
property and not touch it, when he could with impunity take whatever he
wanted from the market, go into houses and have sexual relations with anyone
he wanted, kill anyone, free all those he wished from prison, and do the other
things which would make him like a god among men. His actions would be in
no way different from those of the other and they would both follow the same
path. This, some would say, is a great proof that no one is just willingly but
under compulsion, so that justice is not one's private good, since wherever either

thought he could do wrong with impunity he would do so. Every man believes    d
that injustice is much more profitable to himself than justice, and any expo-
nent of this argument will say that he is right. The man who did not wish to do
wrong with that opportunity, and did not touch other people's property, would
be thought by those who knew it to be very foolish and miserable. They would
praise him in public, thus deceiving one another, for fear of being wronged. So
much for my second topic.

As for the choice between the lives we are discussing, we shall be able to make    e
a correct judgment about it only if we put the most just man and the most unjust
man face to face; otherwise we cannot do so. By face to face I mean this: let us grant
to the unjust the fullest degree of injustice and to the just the fullest justice, each
being perfect in his own pursuit. First, the unjust man will act as clever craftsmen
do —a top navigator for example or physician distinguishes what his craft can do    361
and what it cannot; the former he will undertake, the latter he will pass by, and
when he slips he can put things right. So the unjust man's correct attempts at
wrongdoing must remain secret; the one who is caught must be considered a
poor performer, for the extreme of injustice is to have a reputation for justice,    b
and our perfectly unjust man must be granted perfection in injustice. We must not
take this from him, but we must allow that, while committing the greatest crimes,
he has provided himself with the greatest reputation for justice; if he makes a
slip he must be able to put it right; he must be a sufficiently persuasive speaker if
some wrongdoing of his is made public; he must be able to use force, where force
is needed, with the help of his courage, his strength, and the friends and wealth
with which he has provided himself.

Having described such a man, let us now in our argument put beside him
the just man, simple as he is and noble, who, as Aeschylus put it, does not wish
to appear just but to be so. We must take away his reputation, for a reputation for    c
justice would bring him honour and rewards, and it would then not be clear
whether he is what he is for justice's sake or for the sake of rewards and honour.
We must strip him of everything except justice and make him the complete opposite of the other. Though he does no wrong, he must have the greatest reputation
for wrongdoing so that he may be tested for justice by not weakening under ill repute and its consequences. Let him go his incorruptible way until death with a rep-    d
utation for injustice throughout his life, just though he is, so that our two men may
reach the extremes, one of justice, the other of injustice, and let them be judged
as to which of the two is the happier.

Whew! My dear Glaucon, I said, what a mighty scouring you have given those two characters, as if they were statues in a competition.

I do the best I can, he replied. The two being such as I have described, there should be no difficulty in following the argument through as to what kind of life awaits each of them, but it must be said. And if what I say sounds rather boorish, Socrates, realize that it is not I who speak, but those who praise injustice as preferable to justice. They will say that the just man in these circumstances will be whipped, stretched on the rack, imprisoned, have his eyes burnt out, and, after suffering every kind of evil, he will be impaled and realize that one should not want to be just but to appear so. Indeed, Aeschylus' words are far more correctly applied to the unjust than to the just, for we shall be told that the unjust man pursues a course which is based on truth and not on appearances; he does not want to appear but to be unjust:

> He harvests in his heart a deep furrow
> from which good counsels grow.

He rules his city because of his reputation for justice, he marries into any family he wants to, he gives his children in marriage to anyone he wishes, he has contractual and other associations with anyone he may desire, and, beside all these advantages, he benefits in the pursuit of gain because he does not scruple to practise injustice. In any contest, public or private, he is the winner, getting the better of his enemies and accumulating wealth; he benefits his friends and does harm to his enemies. To the gods he offers grand sacrifices and gifts which will satisfy them, he can serve the gods much better than the just man, and also such men as he wants to, with the result that he is likely to be dearer to the gods. This is what they say, Socrates, that both from gods and men the unjust man secures a better life than the just.

After Glaucon had thus spoken I again had it in mind to say something in reply, but his brother Adeimantus intervened: You surely do not think that enough has been said from this point of view, Socrates?

Why not? said I.

The most important thing, that should have been said, has not been said, he replied.

Well then, I said, let brother stand by brother. If Glaucon has omitted something, you come to his help. Yet what he has said is sufficient to throw me and to make me incapable of coming to the help of justice.

Nonsense, he said. Hear what more I have to say, for we should also go fully   e
into the arguments opposite to those he mentioned, those which praise justice and
censure injustice, so that what I take to be Glaucon's intention may be clearer.
When fathers speak to their sons, they say one must be just—and so do all who
care for them, but they do not praise justice itself, only the high reputations it leads
to, in order that the son, thought to be just, shall enjoy those public offices, mar-   363
riages, and the rest which Glaucon mentioned, as they belong to the just man
because of his high repute; they lay even greater emphasis on the results of reputation. They add popularity granted by the gods, and mention abundant blessings
which, they say, the gods grant to the pious. So too the noble Hesiod and Homer
declare, the one that for the just the gods make "the oak trees bear acorns at the   b
top and bees in the middle and their fleecy sheep are heavy with their burden of
wool" and many other blessings of like nature. The other says similar things:

> (like the fame) of a goodly king who, in his piety, upholds justice;
> for him the black earth bears wheat and barley and the trees are
> heavy with fruit; his sheep bear lambs continually and the sea pro-   c
> vides its fish.

Musaeus and his son grant from the gods more robust pleasures to the just.
Their words lead the just to the underworld, and, seating them at table, provide
them with a banquet of the saints, crown them with wreaths, and make them
spend all their time drinking, as if they thought that the finest reward of virtue was   d
perpetual drunkenness. Others stretch the rewards of virtue from the gods even further, for they say that the children and the children's children and the posterity
of the pious man who keeps his oaths will survive into the future. Thus, and in other
such ways, do they praise justice. The impious and unjust they bury in mud in the
underworld, they force them to carry water in a sieve, they bring them into disrepute
while still living, and they attribute to them all the punishments which Glaucon   e
enumerated in the case of the just with a reputation for injustice, but they have nothing else to say. This then is the way people praise and blame justice and injustice.

Besides this, Socrates, look at another kind of argument which is spoken in private, and also by the poets, concerning justice and injustice. All go on repeating
with one voice that justice and moderation are beautiful, but certainly difficult and   364
burdensome, while incontinence and injustice are sweet and easy, and shameful
only by repute and by law. They add that unjust deeds are for the most part more
profitable than just ones. They freely declare, both in private and in public, that

b  the wicked who have wealth and other forms of power are happy. They honour them but pay neither honour nor attention to the weak and the poor, though they agree that these are better men than the others.

What men say about the gods and virtue is the most amazing of all, namely that the gods too inflict misfortunes and a miserable life upon many good men, and the opposite fate to their opposites. Begging priests and prophets frequent the doors of the rich and persuade them that they possess a god-given power to remedy by sacrifices and incantations at pleasant festivals any crime that the rich

c  man or one of his ancestors may have committed. Moreover, if one wishes to harass some enemy, then at little expense he will be able to harm the just and the unjust alike, for by means of spells and enchantments they can persuade the gods to serve them. They bring the poets as witnesses to all this, some harping on the easiness of vice, that

d  Vice is easy to choose in abundance, the path is smooth and it dwells  
very near, but sweat is placed by the gods on the way to virtue,

and a path which is long, rough, and steep; others quote Homer as a witness that the gods can be influenced by men, for he too said:

e  the gods themselves can be swayed by prayer, for suppliant men  
can turn them from their purpose by sacrifices and gentle prayers,  
by libations and burnt offerings whenever anyone has transgressed  
and sinned.

They offer in proof a mass of writings by Musaeus and Orpheus, offspring, as they say, of Selene and the Muses. In accordance with these they perform their ritual and persuade not only individuals but whole cities that, both for the living and

365  for the dead, there are absolutions and purifications for sin by means of sacrifices and pleasurable, playful rituals. These they call initiations which free from punishment yonder, where a dreadful fate awaits the uninitiated.

When all such sayings about the attitudes of men and gods toward virtue and vice are so often repeated, what effect, my dear Socrates, do we think they have upon the minds of our youth? One who is naturally talented and able, like a bee flitting from flower to flower gathering honey, to flit over these sayings and to

b  gather from them an impression of what kind of man he should be and of how best to travel along the road of life, would surely repeat to himself the saying of Pindar: should I by justice or by crooked deceit scale this high wall and thus live my life fenced off from other men? The advantages said to be mine if I am just are of no use, I am told, unless I also appear so; while the troubles and penalties are obvious. The unjust man, on the other hand, who has secured for himself a reputation for justice, lives, they tell me, the life of a god. Therefore, since appearance, as the wise men tell me, forcibly overwhelms truth and controls happiness, this is altogether the way I should live. I should build around me a facade that gives the illusion of justice to those who approach me and keep behind this the greedy and crafty fox of the wise Archilochus.

"But surely," someone objects, "it is not easy for vice to remain hidden always." We shall reply that nothing is easy which is of great import. Nevertheless, this is the way we must go if we are to be happy, and follow along the lines of all we have been told. To protect our secret we shall form sworn conspiratorial societies and political clubs. Besides, there are teachers of persuasion who make one clever in dealing with assemblies and with the courts. This will enable us to use persuasion here and force there, so that we can secure our own advantage without penalty.

"But one cannot force the gods nor have secrets from them." Well, if either they do not exist or do not concern themselves with human affairs, why should we worry about secrecy? If they do exist and do concern themselves, we have heard about them and know them from no other source than our laws and our genealogising poets, and these are the very men who tell us that the gods can be persuaded and influenced by gentle prayers and by offerings. We should believe both or neither. If we believe them, we should do wrong and then offer sacrifices from the proceeds. If we are just, we shall not be punished by the gods but we shall lose the profits of injustice. If we are unjust we shall get the benefit of sins and transgressions, and afterwards persuade the gods by prayer and escape without punishment. "But in Hades we will pay the penalty for the crimes committed here, either ourselves or our children's children." "My friend, the young man will reply as he does his reckoning, mystery rites have great potency, and so have the gods of absolution, as the greatest cities tell us, and the children of the gods who have become poets and prophets tell us that this is so."

For what reason then should we still choose justice rather than the greatest injustice? If we practise the latter with specious decorum we shall do well at the hands of gods and of men; we shall live and die as we intend, for so both the many and the eminent tell us. From all that has been said, Socrates, what possibility is there that any man of power, be it the power of mind or of wealth, of body or of birth, will be willing to honour justice and not laugh aloud when he hears it praised? And surely any man who can show that what we have said is untrue and has full knowledge that justice is best, will be full of forgiveness, and not of anger, for the unjust. He knows that only a man of godlike character whom injustice disgusts, or one who has superior knowledge, avoids injustice, and that no other man is willingly just, but through cowardice or old age or some other weakness objects to injustice, because he cannot practise it. That this is so is obvious, for the first of these men to acquire power is the first to do wrong as much as he is able.

The only reason for all this talk, Socrates, which led to Glaucon's speech and mine, is to say to you: Socrates, you strange man, not one of all of you who profess to praise justice, beginning with the heroes of old, whose words are left to us, to the present day—not one has ever blamed injustice or praised justice in any other way than by mentioning the reputations, honours, and rewards which follow justice. No one has ever adequately described, either in poetry or in private conversation, what the very presence of justice or injustice in his soul does to a man even if it remains hidden from gods and men; one is the greatest evil the soul can contain, while the other, justice, is the greatest good. If you had treated the subject in this way and had persuaded us from youth, we should then not be watching one another to see we do no wrong, but every man would be his own best guardian and he would be afraid lest, by doing wrong, he live with the greatest evil.

Thrasymachus or anyone else might say what we have said, and perhaps more in discussing justice and injustice. I believe they would be vulgarly distorting the effect of each. To be quite frank with you, it is because I am eager to hear the opposite from you that I speak with all the emphasis I can muster. So do not merely give us a theoretical proof that justice is better than injustice, but tell us how each, in and by itself, affects a man, the one for good, the other for evil. Follow Glaucon's advice and do not take reputations into account, for if you do not deprive them of true reputation and attach false reputations to them, we shall say that you are not praising justice but the reputation for it, or blaming injustice but the appearance of it, that you are encouraging one to be unjust in secret, and that you agree with Thrasymachus that the just is another's good, the advantage of the stronger, while the unjust is one's own advantage and profit, though not the advantage of the weaker.

Since you have agreed that justice is one of the greatest goods, those which are worthy of attainment for their consequences, but much more for their own sake —sight, hearing, knowledge, health, and all other goods which are creative by what they are and not by what they seem—do praise justice in this regard: in what way does its very possession benefit a man and injustice harm him? Leave rewards and reputations for others to praise.

For others would satisfy me if they praised justice and blamed injustice in this way, extolling the rewards of the one and denigrating those of the other, but from you, unless you tell me to, I will not accept it, because you have spent your whole life investigating this and nothing else. Do not, therefore, give us a merely theoretical proof that justice is better than injustice, but tell us what effect each has in and by itself, the one for good, the other for evil, whether or not it be hidden from gods and men.

### Origins of the State

I had always admired the character of Glaucon and Thrasymachus, and on this occasion I was quite delighted with them as I listened and I said: You are the sons of a great man, and Glaucon's lover began his elegy well when he wrote, celebrating the repute you gained at the battle of Megara:

> Sons of Ariston, godlike offspring of a famous man.

That seems well deserved, my friends; you must be divinely inspired if you are not convinced that injustice is better than justice, and yet can speak on its behalf as you have done. And I do believe that you are really convinced by your own words. I base this belief on my knowledge of the way you live, for, if I had only your words to go by, I would not trust you. The more I trust you, however, the more I am at a loss what to do. I do not see how I can be of help; I feel myself incapable. I see a proof of this in the fact that I thought what I said to Thrasymachus showed that justice is better than injustice, but you refuse to accept this as adequate. On the other hand I do not see how I can refuse my help, for I fear it is even impious to be present when justice is being charged and to fail to come to her help as long as there is breath in one's body and one is still able to speak. So the best course is to give her any assistance I can.

Glaucon and the others begged me to give any help I could, not to abandon the argument but to track down the nature of justice and injustice, and where the truth lay as regards the benefits of both. So I said what I had in mind: This investigation we are undertaking is not easy, I think, but requires keen eyesight. As we are not very clever, I said, I think we should adopt a method like this: if men who did not have keen eyesight were told to read small letters from a distance, and

45

then someone noticed that these same letters were to be found somewhere else on a larger scale and on a larger object, it would, I think, be considered a piece of luck that they could read these first and then examine the smaller letters to see if they were the same.

That is certainly true, said Adeimantus, but what relevance do you see in it to our present search for justice?

e

I will tell you, I said. There is, we say, the justice of one man, and also the justice of a whole city? —Certainly.

And a city is larger than one man? —It is.

Perhaps there is more justice in the larger unit, and it may be easier to grasp. So, if you are willing, let us first investigate what justice is in the cities, and afterwards let us look for it in the individual, observing the similarities to the larger in the smaller. —Your proposal seems sound.

369

Well then, I said, if we observed the birth of a city in theory, we would also see its justice and injustice beginning to exist. —Probably.

And as the process went on, we may hope that the object of our search would be easier to discover. —Much easier.

b

Do you think we should attempt to carry this through? It is no small task, I think. Think it over.

We have, said Adeimantus. Carry on.

I think a city comes to be, I said, because not one of us is self-sufficient, but needs many things. Do you think a city is founded on any other principles? —On no other.

c

As they need many things, people make use of one another for various purposes. They gather many associates and helpers to live in one place, and to this settlement we give the name of city. Is that not so? —It is.

And they share with one another, both giving and taking, in so far as they do, because they think this better for themselves? —Quite so.

Come then, I said, let us create a city from the beginning in our discussion. And it is our needs, it seems, that will create it. —Of course.

d

Surely our first and greatest need is to provide food to sustain life. —It certainly is.

Our second need is for shelter, our third for clothes and such things. —Quite so.

Consider then, said I, how the city will adequately provide for all this. One man obviously must be a farmer, another a builder, and another a weaver. Or should we add a cobbler and some other craftsman to look after our physical needs? —All right.

So the essential minimum for the city is four or five men. —Apparently.

A further point: must each of them perform his own work as common for them all, for example the one farmer provide food for them all, and spend four times as much time and labour to provide food which is shared by the others, or will he not care for this but provide for himself a quarter of such food in a quarter of the time and spend the other three quarters, one in building a house, one in the production of clothes, and one to make shoes, and not trouble to associate with the others but for and by himself mind his own business?

Perhaps, Socrates, Adeimantus replied, the way you suggested first would be easier than the other.

By Zeus, said I, there is nothing surprising in this, for even as you were speaking I was thinking that, in the first place, each one of us is born somewhat different from the others, one more apt for one task, one for another. Don't you think so? —I do.

Further, does a man do better if he practises many crafts, or if, being one man, he restricts himself to one craft. —When he restricts himself to one.

This at any rate is clear, I think, that if one misses the proper time to do something, the opportunity to do it has gone. —Clear enough.

For I do not think that the thing to be done awaits the leisure of the doer, but the doer must of necessity adjust himself to the requirements of his task, and not consider this of secondary importance. —He must.

Both production and quality are improved in each case, and easier, if each man does one thing which is congenial to him, does it at the right time, and is free of other pursuits. —Most certainly.

We shall then need more than four citizens, Adeimantus, to provide the things we have mentioned. It is likely that the farmer will not make his own plough if it is to be a good one, nor his mattock, nor other agricultural implements. Neither will the builder, for he too needs many things; and the same is true of the weaver and the cobbler, is it not? —True.

Carpenters, metal workers, and many such craftsmen will share our little city and make it bigger. —Quite so.

Yet it will not be a very big settlement if we add cowherds, shepherds, and other herdsmen in order that our farmers have oxen to do their ploughing, and the builders will join the farmers in the use of them as beasts of burden to transport their materials, while the weavers and cobblers will use their wool and hides.

Neither will it be a small city, said he, if it has to hold all these things.

And further, it is almost impossible to establish the city in the kind of place that will need no imports. —Impossible.

So we shall still need other people to bring what is needed from other cities. —We shall.

371 Now if one who serves in this way goes to the other city without a cargo of the things needed by those from whom he is to bring what his own people need, he will come away empty-handed, will he not? —I think so.

Therefore our citizens must not only produce enough for themselves at home, but also the things these others require, of the right quality and in the right quantity. —They must.

So we need more farmers and other craftsmen in our city. —We do.

Then again we need more people to service imports and exports. These are merchants, are they not? —Yes.

So we shall need merchants too. —Quite so.

And if the trade is by sea, we shall need a number of others who know how to
b sail the seas. —A good many, certainly.

A further point: how are they going to share the things that each group produces within the city itself? This association with each other was the very purpose for which we established the city.

Clearly, he said, they must do this by buying and selling.

It follows that we must have a market place and a currency for this exchange. —Certainly.

c If the farmer brings some of his produce to market, or any other craftsman, and he does not arrive at the same time as those who want to exchange things with him, will he be sitting idly in the market place, away from his own work?

Not at all, he said. There will be people who realize this and engage in this service. In well-organized cities this will be pretty well those of feeble physique who are not
d fit for other work. They must stay around the market, buying for money from those who have something to sell, and then again selling at a price to those who want to buy.

To fill this need there will be retailers in our city. Do we not call retailers those who establish themselves in the market place for this service of buying and selling, while those who travel between cities are called merchants? —Quite so.

e There are some others to serve, as I think, who are not worth admitting into our society for their intelligence, but they have sufficient physical strength for heavy labour. These sell the use of their strength; their reward for this is a wage and they are, I think, called wage-earners. Is that not so? —Certainly.

So the wage-earners complete our city. —I think so.

Well, Adeimantus, has our city now grown to its full size? —Perhaps.

Where then would justice and injustice be in it? With which of the parts we have examined has it come to be?

I do not notice them, Socrates, he said, unless it is in the relations of these very people to one another.

372

You may be right, I said, but we must look into it and not grow weary….

[*Glaucon protests that their city is primitive and is at best a city of pigs. Socrates then adds some luxuries, and this leads to the creation of new roles and even the need to expand the state by war. Warriors or guardians have become necessary, and in order to ensure that they develop the proper qualities Socrates begins a discussion of their education. He advocates the censorship of impious and immoral literature.* —J.M.P.]

## ⤇ BOOK III ⤆

### *Selection of Rulers*

[*Socrates continues his criticism of the poets and dramatists for the impious and immoral features of their works, and he criticizes some styles and harmonies found in music. Training for the body is also prescribed.* —J.M.P.]

…Very well, I said. Shall we choose as our next topic of discussion which of these same men shall rule, and which be ruled? —Why not?

412b

Now it is obvious that the rulers must be older men and that the younger must be ruled. —Obviously.

And that the rulers must be the best of them? —That too.

The best farmers are those who have to the highest degree the qualities required for farming? —Yes.

Now as the rulers must be the best among the guardians, they must have to the highest degree the qualities required to guard the city? —Yes.

And for this they must be intelligent, able, and also care for the city? —That is so.

d

Now one cares most for that which one loves. —Necessarily.

And one loves something most when one believes that what is good for it is good for oneself, and that when it is doing well the same is true of oneself, and so with the opposite. —Quite so, he said.

We must therefore select from among our guardians those who, as we test them, hold throughout their lives to the belief that it is right to pursue eagerly what e    they believe to be to the advantage of the city, and who are in no way willing to do what is not. —Yes, for they are good men.

I think we must observe them at all ages to see whether they are guardians of this principle, and make sure that they cannot be tempted or forced to discard or forget the belief that they must do what is best for the city. —What, he said, do you mean by discarding?

I will tell you, I said. I think the discarding of a belief is either voluntary or 413    involuntary; voluntary when the belief is false, and as a result of learning one changes one's mind, involuntary when the belief is true. —I understand the voluntary discarding, but not the involuntary.

Really? Do you not think that men are unwilling to be deprived of good things, but willingly deprived of bad things? Is not untruth and missing the truth a bad thing, while to be truthful is good? And is not to have a true opinion to be truthful? —You are right, he said, and people are unwilling to be deprived of a true opinion.

b    But they can be so deprived by theft, or compulsion, or under a spell? —I do not understand even now.

I fear I must be talking like a tragic poet! I apply the word "theft" to those who change their mind or those who forget, not realizing that time or argument has robbed them of their belief. Do you understand now? —Yes.

By compulsion I mean those whom pain or suffering causes to change their mind. —That too I understand and you are right.

c    Those under a spell I think you would agree are those who change their mind because they are bewitched by pleasure or fear. —It seems to me, he said, that anything which deceives bewitches.

As I said just now, we must find out who are the best guardians of their belief that they must always do whatever they think to be in the best interest of the city. We must keep them under observation from childhood and set them tasks which would most easily lead one to forget this belief, or to be deceived. We d    must select the one who keeps on remembering and is not easily deceived, the other we will reject. Do you agree? —Yes.

We must also subject them to labours, sufferings, and contests in which to observe this. —Right.

Then, I said, for the third kind we must observe how they face bewitchment. Like those who lead colts into noise and tumult to see if they are fearful, so we must e    expose our young to fears and pleasures to test them, much more thoroughly than one tests gold in fire, and see whether a guardian is hard to bewitch and behaves well in all circumstances as a good guardian of himself and of the cultural education he has received, always showing himself a gracious and harmonious personality, the best man for himself and for the city. The one who is thus tested as a child, as a youth, and as an adult, and comes out of it untainted, is to be made a ruler as well as a guardian. He is to be honoured both in life and after death and receive the most esteemed rewards in the form of tombs and memorials. The one who does not prove himself in this way is to be rejected. It seems to me, Glaucon, I said, that rulers and guardians must be selected and established in some such way as this, to speak in a general way and not in exact detail. —I also think it must be done in some such way.

These are the men whom it is most correct to call proper guardians, so that the enemies without shall not have the power, and their friends within shall not have the desire, to harm the city. Those young men whom we have called guardians hitherto we shall call auxiliaries to help the rulers in their decisions. —I agree.

What device could we find to make our rulers, or at any rate the rest of the city, believe us if we told them a noble fiction, one of those necessary untruths of which we have spoken? —What kind of fiction?

Nothing new, I said, but a Phoenician story which the poets say has happened in many places and made people believe them; it has not happened among us, though it might, and it will take a great deal of persuasion to have it believed.

You seem hesitant to tell your story, he said.

When you hear it you will realize that I have every reason to hesitate.

Speak without fear.

This is the story—yet I don't know that I am bold enough to tell it or what words I shall use. I shall first try to persuade the rulers and the soldiers, and then the rest of the city, that the upbringing and the education we gave them, and the experience that went with them, were a dream as it were, that in fact they were then being fashioned and nurtured inside the earth, themselves and their weapons and their apparel. Then, when they were quite finished, the earth, being their mother, brought them out into the world. So even now they must take counsel for, and defend, the land in which they live as their mother and nurse, if someone attacks it, and they must think of their fellow-citizens as their earth-born brothers.

It is not for nothing that you were shy, he said, of telling your story.

Yes, I said, I had very good reason. Nevertheless, hear the rest of the tale. "All of you in the city are brothers," we shall tell them as we tell our story, "but the god who fashioned you mixed some gold in the nature of those capable of ruling because they are to be honoured most. In those who are auxiliaries he has put silver, and iron

b   and bronze in those who are farmers and other workers. You will for the most part produce children like yourselves but, as you are all related, a silver child will occasionally be born from a golden parent, and vice versa, and all the others from each other. So the first and most important command of the god to the rulers is that there is nothing they must guard better or watch more carefully than the mixture in the souls of the next generation. If their own offspring should be found to have

c   iron or bronze in his nature, they must not pity him in any way, but give him the esteem appropriate to his nature; they must drive him out to join the workers and farmers. Then again, if an offspring of these is found to have gold or silver in his nature they will honour him and bring him up to join the rulers or guardians, for there is an oracle that the city will be ruined if ever it has an iron or bronze guardian." Can you suggest any device which will make our citizens believe this story?

d       I cannot see any way, he said, to make them believe it themselves, but the sons and later generations might, both theirs and those of other men.

Even that, I said, would help to make them care more for their city and each other, for I do understand what you mean. But let us leave this matter to later tradition. Let us now arm our earthborn and lead them forth with their rulers in charge. And as they march let them look for the best place in the city to have

e   their camp, a site from which they could most easily control those within, if anyone is unwilling to obey the laws, and ward off any outside enemy who came like a wolf upon the flock. When they had established their camp and made the right sacrifices, let them see to their sleeping quarters, or what do you suggest? —I agree.

These must protect them adequately both in winter and summer.

Of course, he said, you mean their dwellings.

Yes, I said, dwellings for soldiers, not for money-makers.

416       What would you say is the difference? he asked.

I will try to tell you, I said. The most terrible and shameful thing for a shepherd is to train his dogs, who should help the flocks, in such a way that, through lack of discipline or hunger or bad habit, those very dogs maltreat the animals and behave like wolves rather than dogs. —Quite true.

b       We must therefore take every precaution to see that our auxiliaries, since they are the stronger, do not behave like that toward the citizens, and become cruel masters instead of kindly allies. —We must watch this.

And a really good education would endow them with the greatest caution in this regard? —But surely they have had that.

And I said: Perhaps we should not assert this dogmatically, my dear Glaucon. What we can assert is what we were saying just now, that they must have the correct education, whatever that is, in order to attain the greatest degree of gentleness toward each other and toward those whom they are protecting. —Right.

Besides this education, an intelligent man might say that they must have the amount of housing and of other property which would not prevent them from being the best guardians and would not encourage them to maltreat the other citizens. —That would be true.

Consider then, said I, whether they should live in some such way as this if they are to be the kind of men we described: First, not one of them must possess any private property beyond what is essential. Further, none of them should have a house or a storeroom which anyone who wishes is not permitted to enter. Whatever moderate and courageous warrior-athletes require will be provided by taxation upon the other citizens as a salary for their guardianship, no more and no less than they need over the year. They will have common messes and live together as soldiers in a camp. We shall tell them that the gold and silver they always have in their nature as a gift from the gods makes the possession of human gold unnecessary, indeed that it is impious for them to defile this divine possession by any admixture of the human kind of gold, because many an impious deed is committed in connection with the currency of the majority, and their own must remain pure. For them alone among the city's population it is unlawful to touch or handle gold or silver; they must not be under the same roof with it, or wear any, or drink from gold or silver goblets; in this way they may preserve themselves and the city. If they themselves acquire private land and houses and currency, they will be household managers and farmers instead of guardians, hostile masters of the other citizens instead of their allies; they will spend their whole life hating and being hated, plotting and being plotted against; they will be much more afraid of internal than of external enemies, and they will rush themselves and their city very close to ruin. For all these reasons, I said, let us say that the guardians must be provided with housing and other matters in this way, and these are the laws we shall establish.

Certainly, said Glaucon.

## ⇥ BOOK IV ⇤

### *The Guardians and Happiness*

419    Adeimantus took up the argument and said: What defence, Socrates, would you offer against the charge that you are not making your guardians very happy, and that through their own fault? The city is really in their power, yet they derive no good from this. Others own land, build grand and beautiful houses, acquire furnishings appropriate to them, make their own private sacrifices to the gods, entertain, also, as you mentioned just now, have gold and silver and all the possessions which are thought to belong to people who will be happy. One might well say that your guardians are simply settled in the city like paid mercenaries, with nothing

420    to do but to watch over it.

Yes, said I. Moreover, they work for their keep and get no extra wages as the others do, so that if they want to leave the city privately they cannot do so; they have nothing to give their mistresses, nothing to spend in whatever other way they wish, as men do who are considered happy. You have omitted these and other such things from the charge. —Let these accusations be added, he said.

b        Now you ask what defence we shall offer? —Yes.

I think we shall discover what to say if we follow the same path as before, I said. We shall say that it would not be at all surprising if these men too were very happy. In any case, in establishing our city, we are not aiming to make any one group outstandingly happy, but to make the whole city so, as far as possible. We thought that in such a city we would most easily find justice, find injustice in a

c        badly governed one, and then decide what we have been looking for all the time. Now we think we are fashioning the happy city not by separating a few people in it and making them happy, but by making the whole city so. We shall look at the opposite kind of city presently. If someone came to us while we were painting a statue and objected because we did not apply the finest colours to the finest parts of the body, for the eyes are the most beautiful part, and they are not made

d        purple but black, we should appear to offer a reasonable defence if we said: "My good sir, do not think that we must make the eyes so beautiful that they no longer appear to be eyes at all, and so with the other parts, but look to see whether by dealing with each part appropriately we are making the whole statue beautiful." And so now, do not force us to give our guardians the kind of happiness which would make them anything but guardians.

We know how to clothe our farmers too in purple robes, surround them with gold and tell them to work the land at their pleasure, and how to settle our potters on couches by the fire, feasting and passing the wine, put their wheel by them and tell them to make pots as much as they want; we know how to make all the others also happy in the same way, so that the whole city is happy. Do not exhort us to do this, however. If we do, the farmer will not be a farmer, nor the potter a potter; nor would anyone else fulfill any of the functions which make up the state. For the others this is less important: if shoemakers become inferior and corrupt, and claim to be what they are not, the state is not in peril, but, if the guardians of our laws and city only appear to be guardians and are not, you surely see that they destroy the city utterly, as they alone have the opportunity to govern it well and to make it happy.

If then we are making true guardians who are least likely to work wickedness upon the city, whereas our accuser makes some farmers into banqueters, happy as at some festival but not in a city, he would be talking about something else than a city. We should examine then, with this in mind, whether our aim in establishing our guardians should be to give them the greatest happiness, or whether we should in this matter look to the whole city and see how its greatest happiness can be secured. We must compel and persuade the auxiliaries and the guardians to be excellent performers of their own task, and so with all the others. As the whole city grows and is well governed, we must leave it to nature to provide each group with its share of happiness....

[*Socrates warns that the unity and vigour of the city can be destroyed by wealth and poverty. The city should be kept small and self-sufficient. The unity of the city, he also argues, depends upon rigorously preserving the educational and religious systems from innovations. He places a prohibition, explained later in Book IV, on the guardian class: "the acquiring of wives and children which must all accord with the old proverb, that the possessions of friends must be held in common."*—J.M.P.]

## Virtues in the State

Well, son of Ariston, I said, your city might now be said to be established. The next step is for you to look inside it with what light you can procure, if we can somehow see where justice resides in it, and where injustice, what the difference is between them, and which of the two the man who intends to be happy should possess, whether gods and men recognize it or not.

Nonsense, said Glaucon. You promised to look for them yourself because you said
it was impious for you not to come to the rescue of justice in every way you could.

True, I said, as you remind me; I must do so, but you must help. —We will,
he said.

I hope to find it, I said, in this way. I think our city, if it is rightly founded, is
completely good. —Necessarily so, he said.

Clearly then it is wise, brave, moderate, and just. —Clearly.

Therefore whichever of these we find in the city, the rest will be what we have
not found? —You mean?

As with any four things, if we were looking for any one of them in anything,
if we first recognize it, that would be enough, but if we recognize the other three
first, then by that very fact we recognize what we are looking for. For clearly it can
be no other than what is left. —Correct, he said.

So with these, since there are four, we must look for them in the same way.
—Obviously.

Now the first of them which I believe to be clear is wisdom; and there seems
to be something strange about it. —What is that? he said.

I think that the city which we have described is wise in fact because it has
sound judgment, is it not so? —Yes.

Now this very thing, sound judgment, is clearly some kind of knowledge, for
it is through knowledge, not ignorance, that people judge soundly. —Clearly.

There are many kinds of knowledge in the city. —Of course.

Would we call the city wise and sound in judgment because of the knowledge of its carpenters? —Never through that, he said; we would then call it sound
in carpentry.

Nor through the knowledge by which it judges which wooden furniture is
best would we call the city wise. —No indeed.

Nor because of its knowledge of brazen things or of any similar things?
—Not through any of them.

Nor through the knowledge of how to raise a harvest from the earth, but then
we should call it agricultural. —I think so.

Well then, I said, is there some knowledge in the city we have just founded and
among some of the citizens, which does not deliberate about any particular matter but about the city as a whole, how best to maintain good relations both
internally and with other cities? —There is.

What is this knowledge, I asked, and in whom does it reside?

It is the knowledge of guardianship, he said, and it resides in those rulers whom just now we named the complete guardians.

Then what does this knowledge entitle us to call the city?

Really wise, he said, and of good judgment.

Do you think, I asked, that the metal-workers or these true guardians are the more numerous in our city? —The metal-workers, he said, by far.

Of all those who are called by a certain name because they have some knowledge, the guardians would be the least numerous? —They are by far the fewest.

Then a whole city which is established according to nature would be wise because of the smallest group or part of itself, the commanding or ruling group. This group seems to be the smallest by nature and to it belongs a share in that knowledge which, alone of them all, must be called wisdom. —What you say is very true, he said.

We have now found, I don't know how, this to be itself one of the four, and also where in the city it resides. —Our way of finding it, he said, seems good enough to me.

It is surely not very difficult to see courage itself, through which the city is to be called brave, and where in the city it is to be found. —How?

Who, I said, when calling the city cowardly or brave, would look anywhere else but to that part of it which makes war and campaigns on its behalf? —No one, he said, would look anywhere else.

I do not think, I said, that whether the other citizens were cowardly or brave would cause the city to be called one or the other. —It would not.

The city then is brave because of a part of itself which has the capacity always to preserve its belief about things to be feared, that they are those things and those kinds of things which the lawgiver declared to be such in the course of their education. Or don't you call that courage? —I do not, he said, quite understand what you mean. Please repeat it.

I mean, said I, that courage is a kind of preservation. —What kind?

The preservation of the belief which has been inculcated by the law through one's education as to what things and what kinds of things are to be feared, and by always I meant to preserve this belief and not to lose it when one is in pain, beset by pleasures and desires, and by fears, I will, if you like, make clear what I think this resembles by a simile. —I should like you to do so.

e

429

b

c

d

You know, I said, that dyers who want to dye wool purple, first of all pick out from many colours the natural white, and then prepare this in a number of ways so that it will absorb the colour as well as possible, and only then dye it. In what is dyed in this way the colour is fast; no washing with or without soap can take it away. You also know what becomes of material which has not been dyed in this way, whether someone dyes it other colours or does not prepare the wool beforehand. —I know, he said, that it looks washed out and ridiculous.

Understand then, I said, as far as we could, we were doing something similar when we were selecting our soldiers and were educating them in the arts and physical culture. What we were in fact contriving was that, in obeying us, they should absorb the laws most beautifully like a dye, so that, as they had the right nature and the proper education, their belief as to what they should fear and so on should become fast and that the detergents which are extremely effective should not wash it out: pleasure, which is much more potent than any powder or soda or soap, and pain, and fear and appetite. Now this capacity to preserve through everything the right and lawful belief as to what is to be feared and what is not, this is what I call and define as courage, unless you say otherwise.

I have, he said, nothing to say, for I assume that the right opinion about these same things which is not the result of education, such as you find in animals and slaves, you do not consider to be inculcated by law, and you do not call it courage but something else.

Very true, I said. —Then I accept your description of courage.

Accept also, I said, that it is civic courage, and your acceptance will be sound. We shall discuss this subject more fully some other time, if you want to, but it is not the object of our investigation; justice is, and for that purpose I think this is sufficient. —You are quite right, he said.

There are now two qualities left for us to find in the city: moderation and that at which our whole investigation is aimed, justice. —Quite so.

How could we find justice, so that we need not bother with moderation any further?

I do not know, he said, and I should not want it to appear first, if that means that we do not investigate moderation. If you want to please me, look for moderation before the other.

I am certainly willing, I said; it would be wrong not to be. —Look then.

We must do so, I said. Looked at from here, it is more like a consonance or harmony than the others we have considered hitherto. —How?

Moderation is a certain orderliness, I said, and mastery over certain pleasures and appetites, as people somehow indicate by using the phrase self-control and other expressions which give a clue to its nature. Is that not so? —Most certainly.

Yet the expression self-control is laughable, for the controller of self and the self that is weaker and controlled is the same person, and so with all those expressions. It is the same person that is referred to. —Of course.

431

But, I said, the expression seems to want to indicate that in the soul of the man himself there is a better and a worse part; whenever what is by nature the better part is in control of the worse, this is expressed by saying that the man is self-controlled or master of himself, and this is a term of praise. When, on the other hand, the smaller and better part, because of poor upbringing or bad company, is overpowered by the larger and worse, this is made a reproach and called being defeated by oneself, and a man in that situation is called uncontrolled. —Properly so.

b

Look now, I said, at our new city and you will find one of those alternatives in it. You will say that it is rightly called self-controlled, since that in which the better rules the worse should be called moderate and self-controlled. —I am looking at it, and what you say is true.

Further, one would mostly find many and various appetites and pleasures of all kinds as well as pains in children and women and household slaves, and in the many and the inferior among those called free men. —Quite so.

c

But those that are simple and measured and directed by reasoning with intelligence and right belief you will meet with in but few people who are the best by nature and the best educated. —True.

You will see this also in your city; there the desires of the inferior many are controlled by the desires and the knowledge of the fewer and better? —I do indeed.

d

If any city is to be called in control of its pleasures and desires and of itself, this city is. —Most certainly.

And will it not be called moderate in all these respects? —Definitely.

Further, if the same opinion exists in any city among the rulers and also the ruled as to who should rule, it will be found in this city, do you not think? —Definitely.

e

And when that is the case, in which of the two kinds of citizens will you say that moderation exists, among the rulers or the ruled? —Among both, I suppose.

You see now how right we were to foresee that moderation resembles a kind of harmony? —How so?

Because, unlike courage and wisdom, each of which resided in one part of the city and made it, the one brave, the other wise, moderation spreads throughout the whole, among the weakest and the strongest and those who are in between, be it in regard to knowledge or, if you wish, in physical strength or in numbers or in wealth or in anything else, and it makes them all sing the same tune. This unanimity would rightly be called moderation; agreement, that is, between the naturally worse and the naturally better as to which of the two must rule, both in the city and in each individual. —I quite agree.

Very well, I said. We have now found three of the four in the city, as far as our present discussion takes us. What would the remaining kind be which still makes the city share in virtue? Or is it clear that this is justice? —Quite clear.

So now we must concentrate our attention like hunters surrounding a coppice, lest justice escape us and vanish without our seeing it, for obviously it is somewhere around here. Look eagerly, now, in case you see it before I do, and tell me.

I wish I could, he said, but you will make a more sensible use of me if you take me to be a follower who can see things when you point them out.

Follow then, I said, and join me in a prayer. —I will do that, but you lead.

Indeed, I said, the place seems impenetrable and full of shadows; it is certainly dark and hard to hunt in. However, go on we must. —We must indeed.

As I looked I exclaimed: Aha! Glaucon, it looks as if there was a track, and I don't think our prey will altogether escape us. —Good news.

Surely, I said, we are being stupid. —In what way?

My good friend, it seems to have been rolling about right in front of our feet for some time, in fact from the beginning, and we did not see it. This was quite ridiculous of us. As people sometimes look for the very thing they are holding in their hands, so we paid no attention to it, but were looking away in the distance, which accounts for our not seeing it. —What do you mean?

I mean, I said, that we have been mentioning it, and hearing it mentioned, for a long time without understanding ourselves that we were, in a way, speaking of it. —This is a long prelude for someone who is impatient to hear.

Well, I said, listen whether I am talking sense. I think that justice is the very thing, or some form of the thing which, when we were beginning to found our city, we said had to be established throughout. We stated, and often repeated, if you remember, that everyone must pursue one occupation of those in the city, that for which his nature best fitted him. —Yes, we kept saying that.

Further, we have heard many people say, and have often said ourselves, that justice is to perform one's own task and not to meddle with that of others. —We have said that.

This then, my friend, I said, when it happens, is in some way justice, to do one's own job. And do you know what I take to be a proof of this? —No, tell me.

I think what is left over of those things we have been investigating, after moderation and courage and wisdom have been found, was that which made it possible for those three qualities to appear in the city and to continue as long as it was present. We also said that what remained after we found the other three was justice. —It had to be.

And surely, I said, if we had to decide which of the four will make the city good by its presence, it would be hard to judge whether it is a common belief among the rulers and the ruled, or the preservation among the soldiers of a law-inspired belief as to the nature of what is, and what is not, to be feared, or the knowledge and guardianship of the rulers, or whether it is, above all, the presence of this fourth in child and woman, slave and free, artisan, ruler and subject, namely that each man, a unity in himself, performed his own task and was not meddling with that of others. —How could this not be hard to judge?

It seems then that the capacity for each in the city to perform his own task rivals wisdom, moderation, and courage as a source of excellence for the city. —It certainly does.

You would then describe justice as a rival to them for excellence in the city? —Most certainly.

Look at it this way and see whether you agree: you will order your rulers to act as judges in the courts of the city? —Surely.

And will their exclusive aim in delivering judgment not be that no citizen should have what belongs to another or be deprived of what is his own? —That would be their aim.

That being just? —Yes.

In some way then possession of one's own and the performance of one's own task could be agreed to be justice. —That is so.

Consider then whether you agree with me in this: if a carpenter attempts to do the work of a cobbler, or a cobbler that of a carpenter, and they exchange

b

c

d

e

434

their tools and the esteem that goes with the job, or the same man tries to do both, and all the other exchanges are made, do you think that this does any great harm to the city? —No.

b    But I think that when one who is by nature a worker or some other kind of moneymaker is puffed up by wealth, or by the mob, or by his own strength, or some other such thing, and attempts to enter the warrior class, or one of the soldiers tries to enter the group of counsellors and guardians, though he is unworthy of it, and these exchange their tools and the public esteem, or when the same man tries to perform all these jobs together, then I think you will agree that these exchanges and this meddling bring the city to ruin. —They certainly do.

The meddling and exchange between the three established orders does very

c    great harm to the city and would most correctly be called wickedness. —Very definitely.

And you would call the greatest wickedness worked against one's own city injustice? —Of course.

That then is injustice. And let us repeat that the doing of one's own job by the moneymaking, auxiliary, and guardian groups, when each group is performing its

d    own task in the city, is the opposite, it is justice and makes the city just. —I agree with you that this is so.

### Three Parts of the Soul

Do not let us, I said, take this as quite final yet. If we find that this quality, when existing in each individual man, is agreed there too to be justice, then we can assent to this —for what can we say? —but if not, we must look for something else. For the present, let us complete that examination which we thought we should make, that if we tried to observe justice in something larger which contains

e    it, this would make it easier to observe it in the individual. We thought that this larger thing was a city, and so we established the best city we could, knowing well that justice would be present in the good city. It has now appeared to us there, so let us now transfer it to the individual and, if it corresponds, all will be well. But if it is seen to be something different in the individual, then we must go

435    back to the city and examine this new notion of justice. By thus comparing and testing the two, we might make justice light up like fire from the rubbing of fire-sticks, and when it has become clear, we shall fix it firmly in our own minds. —You are following the path we set, and we must do so.

Well now, when you apply the same name to a thing whether it is big or small, are these two instances of it like or unlike with regard to that to which the same name applies? —They are alike in that, he said.

So the just man and the just city will be no different but alike as regards the very form of justice. —Yes, they will be.

Now the city was thought to be just when the three kinds of men within it each performed their own task, and it was moderate and brave and wise because of some other qualities and attitudes of the same groups. —True.

And we shall therefore deem it right, my friend, that the individual have the same parts in his own soul, and through the same qualities in those parts will correctly be given the same names. —That must be so.

Once again, my good man, I said, we have come upon an easy inquiry whether the soul has these three parts or not!

It does not look easy to us, he said. Perhaps the old saying is true, that all fine things are difficult.

So it seems, said I. I want you to know, Glaucon, that in my opinion we shall certainly not attain any precise answer by following our present methods. There is another longer and fuller way which leads to such an answer. However, this way is perhaps good enough to accord with our previous statements and inquiries.

Is it not satisfactory? he asked. It is enough for me at the present time.

And indeed, I said, it will quite satisfy me. —Do not weary, he said, but continue.

Well then, I said, we are surely compelled to agree that each of us has within himself the same parts and characteristics as the city? Where else would they come from? It would be ridiculous for anyone to think that spiritedness has not come to be in the city from individuals who are held to possess it, like the inhabitants of Thrace and Scythia and others who live to the north of us, or that the same is not true of the love of learning which one would attribute most to our part of the world, or the love of money which one might say is conspicuously displayed by the Phoenicians and the Egyptians. —Certainly, he said.

This then is the case, I said, and it is not hard to understand. —No indeed.

But this is: whether we do everything with the same part of our soul, or one thing with one of the three parts, and another with another. Do we learn with one part of ourselves, get angry with another, and with some third part desire the pleasures of food and procreation and other things closely akin to them, or, when

b

c

d

e

436

b

we set out after something, do we act with the whole of our soul in each case? This will be hard to determine satisfactorily. —I think so too.

Let us try to determine in this way whether these parts are the same or different. —How?

It is clear that one thing cannot act in opposite ways or be in opposite states at the same time and in the same part of itself in relation to the same other thing; so if we find this happening we shall know that we are not dealing with one thing but with several. —Be it so.

Examine then what I am about to say. —Say on.

Is it possible for the same thing to stand still and to move at the same time in the same part of itself? —In no way.

Let us go into this more precisely to avoid disagreements later on. If someone were to say that a man is standing still but moving his hands and his head, and that therefore he is moving and standing still at the same time, I think we would not deem that the proper way to put it, but that one part of him is standing still and another part is moving. Is not that the way to express it? —It is.

Then if our interlocutor carried the objection further, and was smart enough to say that whole spinning tops stand still and move at the same time for, while remaining in the same spot, they turn round their axis, and so with anything else moving in a circular motion while staying in the same place, we would not agree because the parts of them in respect to which they stand still and move are not the same. We should say that these objects have an axis and a circumference; in their axis they stand still, for they do not wobble in any way, and their circumference moves in a circle; then, when the axis inclines left or right, frontward or backward, while the top goes round, it is not still at all. —And we would be right.

No such statements shall disturb us or make us believe that anything while remaining itself, can ever be affected, or be, or act, in opposite ways at the same time, in the same part of itself in relation to the same other object. —They will not make me believe it at any rate.

Nevertheless, I said, in order to avoid having to go through all these objections one by one and taking a long time proving them untrue, let us assume that it is so and carry on. We agree that if the matter should ever be shown to be otherwise, all the consequences we have drawn from it will also be invalidated. —We must do so.

Would you not, I said, consider all the following as pairs of opposites: assent and dissent, to want to have something and to deny oneself, to take something to oneself and to cast it off? Whether they are actions or passive states makes no difference in this respect. —They are opposites.

Further, I said, thirst and hunger and the appetites as a whole, then again inclination and willingness, would you not include all these among the class of things we were mentioning? Would you not say that the soul of one who desires something longs for the object of his desire, or wants to take to itself what he wants to have, or again, in so far as he wants to be provided with something, the soul nods assent to itself as if someone were questioning it, because it yearns for it to be? —Yes.

Then we would include among what is altogether the opposite of these: being unwilling, lacking desire, since these lead to driving away or casting off from the soul. —Of course.

That being so, we will say that there is a class of things named appetites and that the most obvious of these are hunger and thirst? —We agree.

One of these is for drink, the other for food? —Yes.

Now in so far as it is mere thirst, is it a desire in the soul for something more than what we mentioned? For example, is thirst a thirst for a hot drink or a cold drink, a long or a short one, or, in a word, is it for a drink of a certain kind? Or is it that if you feel hot as well as thirsty, this adds a desire for cold or, if you feel cold, for hot. If the desire is great because of the presence of quantity it will make it a desire for much, and if it is little, for a little one, but thirst itself is never for anything different from its natural objects, drink unqualified, and so too with hunger, for food.

That's it, he said, each desire itself is only for its natural object in each case, and additional circumstances add the qualifications, that is, for such and such an object.

Do not let us be disturbed, I said, because we are unprepared for it, by someone saying that no one just wants a drink but a good drink, or any food but good food. All men want good things. So that if thirst is a desire, it will be a desire for good, be it a drink or anything else for which it is a desire, and so with the other desires. —Perhaps the man who says this has a point, he said.

But surely, I said, in the case of all things that are related to another, when the first is qualified by a predicate, the second is too, but each in itself is unqualified and directed to an unqualified object. —I do not understand.

You do not understand that the greater is such as to be greater than something? —Quite so.

It is greater than the smaller? —Yes.

c And that which is much greater is related to something much smaller? —Yes.

And that which is sometimes greater is related to that which is sometimes smaller. —Certainly.

So is the more numerous to the less numerous, the double to the half, and so with all things of the kind, the heavier to the lighter, the swifter to the slower, also the hot to the cold, and all similar things. Is that not so? —Quite.

Then what about knowledge? Does the same apply? Knowledge itself is directed
d to the thing which is learned, or whatever one should say that knowledge is related to, and, when knowledge is qualified, it is of a qualified object. I mean this: when knowledge is of building a house it is called building-knowledge? —Yes indeed.

And is this not qualified as no other knowledge is? —Yes.

So when it becomes knowledge of a certain object, it becomes a certain kind of knowledge, and this is true of all crafts and sciences? —That is so.

This is what I was wanting to say, I said, if you understand now. In a relation between two things, when the first is unqualified by a predicate, so is the second, and when the first is qualified by a predicate, the second is too. I do not mean
e that the predicate need be the same for them both—for example, knowledge of health or disease is not healthy or diseased, or the knowledge of good and evil does not itself become good or evil—but that when knowledge is no longer of its simple object but a qualification is added to the object, it follows that the knowledge itself is qualified. It is then no longer simply called knowledge but is qualified, as in this case it becomes medical knowledge. —I understand and I think that it is so.

439 As for thirst, I said, would you not include it as something which in itself is related to something else? Thirst is related to ...
—I know, to drink.

Therefore when a predicate is added to the drink, one is also added to the thirst, but in itself thirst is not for a long drink or a short one, a good drink or a bad one, in a word not for a qualified drink, but thirst in itself is by nature for a drink without any qualification. —Quite true.

b The soul of the thirsty, in so far as he is thirsty, does not want anything else, only to drink; this is what it longs for and sets out to get. —Obviously.

Therefore if anything pulls it back when it is thirsty, there must be a different part in the soul from the part that is thirsty and, like an animal, leads him to drink: for we say that the same thing cannot act in contrary ways with the same part of itself toward the same object at the same time. —It cannot.

Just as I think it wrong to say that a man's hands at the same time push the bow away and draw it toward him. One ought to say that one hand pushes it away and the other draws it toward him. —Most certainly one should.

Shall we say that there are times when thirsty people are not willing to drink? —Certainly it happens often and to many people.

What then, I said, should one say about this? Is there not in their soul that which bids them drink, and also that which prevents them, that the latter is different and overrules the other part? —I think so, he said.

And the preventing part comes into play as a result of reasoning, whereas the impulses that lead and drag him are due to emotive states and diseases? —Apparently.

It is therefore not unreasonable for us to say that these are two distinct parts, to call that with which it reasons the rational part of the soul, and that with which it lusts and feels hungry and thirsty and gets excited with other desires the irrational and appetitive part, the companion of repletions and pleasures. —That is a natural way for us to think.

Let these two then be described as two parts existing in the soul. Now is the spirited part by which we get angry a third part, or is it of the same nature as either of the other two? —Perhaps it is like the appetitive part.

I have, I said, heard a story which I believe, that Leontius, the son of Aglaion, as he came up from the Piraeus on the outside of the northern wall, saw the executioner with some corpses lying near him. Leontius felt a strong desire to look at them, but at the same time he was disgusted and turned away. For a time he struggled with himself and covered his face, but then, overcome by his desire, pushing his eyes wide open and rushing toward the corpses: "Look for yourselves," he said, "you evil things, get your fill of the beautiful sight!" —I've heard that story myself.

It certainly proves, I said, that anger sometimes wars against the appetites as one thing against another. —It does.

Besides, I said, we often see this elsewhere, when his appetites are forcing a man to act contrary to reason, and he rails at himself and is angry with that within himself which is compelling him to do so; of the two civic factions at odds, as it were, the spirited part becomes the ally of reason. I do not think that you can say that when reason has decided that it must not be opposed, you have ever perceived the spirited part associating itself with the appetites, either in yourself or in anyone else. —No by Zeus I have not.

67

c What happens, I said, when anyone thinks he is doing wrong? Is it not true that the nobler a man is, the less he can resent it if he suffers hunger or cold or anything of that kind at the hands of one whom he believes to be inflicting this on him justly, and as I say, does not his spirited part refuse to be aroused? —True.

d What if a man believes himself wronged? I asked. Is the spirit within him not boiling and angry, fighting for what he believes to be just? Will he not endure hunger and cold and such things and carry on till he wins out? and not cease from noble actions until he either wins out or dies, or, like a dog by his shepherd, is called to heel by the reason within himself and quieted down?

The spirit certainly behaves as you say, he said. Moreover, in our city, we made the auxiliaries, like dogs, obey the rulers, the shepherds of the city.

You understand very well, I said, what I want to convey. In addition, reflect on this further point. —What point?

e The position of the spirited part seems the opposite of what we thought a short time ago. Then we thought of it as something appetitive, but now we say it is far from being that; in the civil war of the soul it aligns itself far more with the reasonable part. —Very much so.

441 Is it different from that also, or is it some part of reason, so that there are two parts of the soul instead of three, the reasonable and the appetitive? Or, as we had three separate parts holding our city together, the money-making, the auxiliary and the deliberative, so in the soul the spirited is a third part, by nature the helper of reason, if it has not been corrupted by a bad upbringing? —It must be a third part.

Yes, I said, if it now appears to be different from the reasonable part, as earlier from the appetitive part.

It is not difficult, he said, to show that it is different. One can see this in chil-dren; they are full of spirit from birth, whereas a few of them seem to me never b to acquire a share of reason, while the majority do not do so until late.

By Zeus, I said, that is very well put. One can see this also in animals. Besides, our earlier quotation from Homer bears witness to it, where he says:

Striking his chest, he addressed his heart,

c for clearly Homer represents the part which reasons about the better and the worse course, and which strikes his chest, as different from that which is angry with-out reasoning. —You are definitely right.

## *The Virtues in the Individual*

We have now made our difficult way through a sea of argument to reach this point, and we have fairly agreed that the same kinds of parts, and the same number of parts, exist in the soul of each individual as in our city. —That is so.

It necessarily follows that the individual is wise in the same way, and in the same part of himself, as the city. —Quite so.

And the part which makes the individual brave is the same as that which    d
makes the city brave, and in the same manner, and everything which makes for virtue is the same in both? —That necessarily follows.

Moreover, Glaucon, I think we shall say that a man is just in the same way as the city is just. —That too is inevitable.

We have surely not forgotten that the city was just because each of the three classes in it was fulfilling its own task. —I do not think, he said, that we have forgotten that.

We must remember then that each one of us within whom each part is fulfilling its own task will himself be just and do his own work. —We must certainly    e
remember this.

Therefore it is fitting that the reasonable part should rule, it being wise and exercising foresight on behalf of the whole soul, and for the spirited part to obey it
and be its ally. —Quite so.

Is it not then, as we were saying, a mixture of artistic and physical culture which makes the two parts harmonious, stretching and nurturing the reasonable    442
part with fine speech and learning, relaxing and soothing the spirited part, and making it gentle by means of harmony and rhythm. —Very definitely, he said.

These two parts, then, thus nurtured and having truly learned their own role and being educated in it, will exercise authority over the appetitive part which is the largest part in any man's soul and is insatiable for possessions. They will watch over it to see that it is not filled with the so-called pleasures of the body, and by becoming enlarged and strong thereby no longer does its own job but attempts to    b
enslave and to rule over those over whom it is not fitted to rule, and so upsets every-
body's whole life. —Quite so, he said.

These two parts will also most effectively stand on guard on behalf of the whole soul and the body, the one by planning, the other by fighting, following its leader, and by its courage fulfilling his decisions. —That is so.

c It is this part which causes us to call an individual brave, when his spirit preserves in the midst of pain and pleasure his belief in the declarations of reason as to what he should fear and what he should not. —Right.

And we shall call him wise because of that small part of himself which ruled in him and made those declarations, which possesses the knowledge of what is beneficial to each part, and of what is to the common advantage of all three. —Quite so.

d Further, shall we not call him moderate because of the friendly and harmonious relations between these same parts, when the rulers and the ruled hold a common belief that reason should rule, and they do not rebel against it? —Moderation, he said, is surely just that, both in the individual and the city.

And he will be just in the way we have often described. —Necessarily.

Now, I said, has our notion of justice become at all indistinct? Does it appear to be something different from what it was seen to be in the city? —I do not think so.

e If any part of our soul still disputes this, we could altogether confirm it by bringing up common arguments. —What are they?

For example, concerning the city and the man similar to it by nature and training, if we had to come to an agreement whether we think that this man has embezzled a deposit of gold and silver, who, do you think, would consider him to

443 have done this rather than men of a different type? —No one would.

And he would have nothing to do with temple robberies, thefts, or betrayals, either of friends in his private life, or, in public life, of cities? —Nothing.

Further, he would be in no way untrustworthy in keeping an oath or any other agreement. —How could he be?

Adultery too, disrespect for parents, neglect of the gods would suit his character less than any other man's. —Much less.

b And the reason for all this is that every part within him fulfills its own function, be that ruling or being ruled? —Certainly that, and nothing else.

Are you still looking for justice to be anything else than this power which produces such men and such cities as we have described? —By Zeus, he said, not I.

c We have then completely realized the dream we had when we suspected that, by the grace of god, we came upon a principle and mould of justice right at the beginning of the founding of our city. —Very definitely.

Indeed, Glaucon —and this is why it is useful —it was a sort of image of justice, namely that it was right for one who is by nature a cobbler to cobble and to do nothing else, and for the carpenter to carpenter, and so with the others. —Apparently.

And justice was in truth, it appears, something like this. It does not lie in a man's external actions, but in the way he acts within himself, really concerned with himself and his inner parts. He does not allow each part of himself to perform the work of another, or the sections of his soul to meddle with one another. He orders what are in the true sense of the word his own affairs well; he is master of himself, puts things in order, is his own friend, harmonizes the three parts like the limiting notes of a musical scale, the high, the low, and the middle, and any others there may be between. He binds them all together, and himself from a plurality becomes a unity. Being thus moderate and harmonious, he now performs any action, be it about the acquisition of wealth, the care of his body, some public actions, or private contract. In all these fields he thinks the just and beautiful action, which he names as such, to be that which preserves this inner harmony and indeed helps to achieve it, wisdom to be the knowledge which oversees this action, an unjust action to be that which always destroys it, and ignorance the belief which oversees that. —Socrates you are altogether right.

Very well, I said, we would then not be thought to be lying if we claim that we have found the just man, the just city, and the justice that is in them. —No by Zeus, we would not.

Shall we say so then? —Yes, let us.

Let that stand then, I said. After this we must, I think, look for injustice. —Obviously.

Surely it must be a kind of civil war between the three parts, a meddling and a doing of other people's task, a rebellion of one part against the whole soul in order to rule it, though this is not fitting, as the rebelling part is by nature fitted to serve, while the other part is by nature not fit to serve, for it is of the ruling kind. We shall say, I think, that such things, the turmoil and the straying, are injustice and license and cowardice and ignorance and, in a word, every kind of wickedness. —That is what they are.

If justice and injustice are now sufficiently clear to us, then so are unjust actions and wrongdoing on the one hand, just actions on the other, and all such things. —How so?

Because they are no different from healthy and diseased actions; what those are in the body, these are in the soul. —In what way?

Healthy actions produce health, diseased ones, disease. —Yes.

Therefore just actions produce justice in a man, and unjust actions, injustice? —Inevitably.

To produce health in the body is to establish the parts of the body as ruler and ruled according to nature, while disease is that they rule and are ruled contrary to nature. —That is so.

Therefore to produce justice is to establish the parts of the soul as ruler and ruled according to nature, while injustice means they rule and are ruled contrary to nature. —Most certainly.

e    Excellence then seems to be a kind of health and beauty and well-being of the soul, while vice is disease and ugliness and weakness. —That is so.

Then do not fine pursuits lead one to acquire virtue, ugly ones to acquire vice? —Of necessity.

445    It is left for us to enquire, it seems, if it is more profitable to act justly, to engage in fine pursuits and be just, whether one is known to be so or not, or to do wrong and be unjust, provided one does not pay the penalty and is not improved by punishment.

But Socrates, he said, this enquiry strikes me as becoming ridiculous now that justice and injustice have been shown to be such as we described. It is generally thought that life is not worth living when the body's nature is ruined, even if every kind of food and drink, every kind of wealth and power are available; yet we are to enquire whether

b    life will be worth living when our soul, the very thing by which we live, is confused and ruined, if only one can do whatever one wishes, except that one cannot do what will free one from vice and injustice and make one acquire justice and virtue.

Ridiculous indeed, I said, but as we have reached the point from which we can see the state of these things most clearly, we must not give up….

## ⇥ BOOK V ⇤

### *Philosophers as Kings*

[*Challenged to explain what he meant by holding wives and children in common, Socrates first discusses the position of women in the guardian class.*]

451b    …We must now, said I, go back to what should have been said earlier in sequence.
c    However, this may well be the right way: after we have completed the parts that men must play, we turn to those of women, especially as you call on me to do so.

For men of such a nature and education as we have described there is, in my opinion, no other right way to deal with wives and children than following the road upon which we started them. We attempted, in our argument, to establish the men as guardians of the flock. —Yes.

Let us then give them for the birth and upbringing of children a system        d
appropriate to that function and see whether it suits us or not. —How?

Like this: do we think that the wives of our guardian watchdogs should join
in whatever guardian duties the men fulfill, join them in the hunt, and do everything else in common, or should we keep the women at home as unable to do so
because they must bear and rear their young, and leave to the men the labour
and the whole care of the flock?

All things, he said, should be done in common, except that the women are        e
physically weaker and the men stronger.

And is it possible, I asked, to make use of living creatures for the same purposes
unless you give them the same upbringing and education? —It is not possible.

So if we use the women for the same tasks as the men, they must be taught the
same things. —Yes.                                                              452

Now we gave the men artistic and physical culture. —Yes.

So we must give both also to the women, as well as training in war, and use
them for the same tasks. —That seems to follow from what you say.

Perhaps, I said, many of the things we are saying, being contrary to custom,
would stir up ridicule, if carried out in practice in the way we are telling them.
—They certainly would, he said.

What, I asked, is the most ridiculous feature you see in this? Or is it obviously that women should exercise naked in the palaestra along with the men,        b
not only the young women but the older women too, as the old men do in the
gymnasia when their bodies are wrinkled and not pleasant to look at and yet
they are fond of physical exercise? —Yes, by Zeus, he said, it would appear ridiculous as things stand now.

Surely, I said, now that we have started on this argument, we must not be
afraid of all the jokes of the kind that the wits will make about such a change in
physical and artistic culture, and not least about the women carrying arms and        c
riding horses. —You are right, he said.

As we have begun this discussion we must go on to the tougher part of the law
and beg these people not to practise their own trade of comedy at our expense but
to be serious and to remember that it is not very long since the Greeks thought
it ugly and ridiculous, as the majority of barbarians still do, for men to be seen
naked. When first the Cretans and then the Lacedaemonians started their phys-        d
ical training, the wits of those days could have ridiculed it all, or do you not
think so? —I do.

But I think that after it was found in practice to be better to strip than to cover up all those parts, then the spectacle ceased to be looked on as ridiculous because reasonable argument had shown that it was best. This showed that it is foolish to think anything ridiculous except what is bad, or to try to raise a laugh

e    at any other spectacle than that of ignorance and evil as being ridiculous, as it is foolish to be in earnest about any other standard of beauty than that of the good. —Most certainly....

454d    Therefore, I said, if the male and the female are seen to be different as regards a particular craft or other pursuit we shall say this must be assigned to one or the other. But if they seem to differ in this particular only, that the female bears children while the male begets them, we shall say that there has been no kind of

e    proof that a woman is different from a man as regards the duties we are talking about, and we shall still believe that our guardians and their wives should follow the same pursuits. —And rightly so.

Next we shall bid anyone who holds the contrary view to instruct us in this:

455    with regard to what craft or pursuit concerned with the establishment of the city is the nature of man and woman not the same but different? —That is right.

Someone else might very well say what you said a short time ago, that it is not easy to give an immediate reply, but that it would not be at all difficult after considering the question. —He might say that.

Do you then want us to beg the one who raises these objections to follow us

b    to see whether we can show him that no pursuit connected with the management of the city belongs in particular to a woman? —Certainly.

Come now, we shall say to him, give us an answer: did you mean that one person had a natural ability for a certain pursuit, while another had not, when the first learned it easily, the latter with difficulty? The one, after a brief period of instruction, was able to find things out for himself from what he had learned, while the other, after much instruction, could not even remember what he had learned; the

c    former's body adequately served his mind, while the other's physical reactions opposed his. Are there any other ways in which you distinguished the naturally gifted in each case from those who were not? —No one will say anything else.

Do you know of any occupation practised by mankind in which the male sex is not superior to the female in all these respects? Or shall we pursue the argument at length by mentioning weaving, baking cakes, cooking vegetables, tasks in

d    which the female sex certainly seems to distinguish itself, and in which it is most laughable of all for women to be inferior to men?

What you say is true, he said, namely that one sex is much superior to the other in almost everything, yet many women are better than many men in many things, but on the whole it is as you say.

There is therefore no pursuit connected with city management which belongs to woman because she is a woman, or to a man because he is a man, but various natures are scattered in the same way among both kinds of persons. Woman by nature shares all pursuits, and so does man, but in all of them woman is a physically weaker creature than man. —Certainly.

e

Shall we then assign them all to men, and none to a woman? —How can we?

One woman, we shall say, is a physician, another is not, one is by nature artistic, another is not. —Quite so.

One may be athletic or warlike, while another is not warlike and has no love of athletics. —I think so.

456

Further, may not one woman love wisdom, another hate it, or one may be high-spirited, another be without spirit? —That too.

So one woman may have a guardian nature, the other not. Was it not a nature with these qualities which we selected among men for our male guardians too? —We did.

Therefore the nature of man and woman is the same as regards guarding the city, except in so far as she is physically weaker, and the man's nature stronger. —So it seems.

Such women must then be chosen along with such men to live with them and share their guardianship, since they are qualified and akin to them by nature. —Certainly.

b

Must we not assign the same pursuits to the same natures? —The same....

You then, as their lawgiver, just as you chose the men, will in the same manner choose the women and provide as far as possible those of the same nature. Since they have their dwellings and meals together and none of them possess anything of the kind as private property, they will be together and mix together both in the gymnasia and in the rest of their education, and they will, I think, be driven by inborn necessity to have intercourse with one another. Or do you not think that what I say will of necessity happen?

458c

d

The necessity is not of a mathematical but of an erotic kind, he said, and this is probably stronger in persuading and compelling the mass of the people.

Yes indeed, I said. The next point is, Glaucon, that promiscuity is impious in a city of fortunate people, nor will the rulers allow it. —It is not right.

e

After this we must obviously make marriage as sacred as possible, and sacred marriages will be those which are the most beneficial. —Most certainly.

459 How then will they be most beneficial? Tell me, Glaucon: I see that at home you have hunting dogs and quite a number of pedigree birds. Did you then, by Zeus, pay any attention to their unions and breeding? —In what way? he asked.

In the first place, though they are all of good stock, are there not some who are and prove themselves to be best? —There are.

Do you breed equally from them all, or are you anxious to breed most from the best? —From the best.

b Further, do you breed from the youngest, or from the oldest, or from those in their prime? —From those in their prime.

And do you think that if they were not bred in this way, your stock of birds and dogs would deteriorate considerably? —I do.

Do you think things are any different in the case of horses and the other animals? —That would indeed be absurd.

Good gracious, my friend, I said, how great is our need for extremely able c rulers if the same is true for the human race. —It is, but what about it?

Because they will need to use a good many drugs. For people who do not need drugs but are willing to follow a diet even an inferior physician will be sufficient, but when drugs are needed, we know that a bolder physician is required. —True, but what do you have in mind?

This, I said: our rulers will probably have to make considerable use of lies d and deceit for the good of their subjects. We said that all such things are useful as a kind of drug. —And rightly so.

This "rightly" will occur frequently in matters of marriage and the bearing of children. —How so?

It follows from our previous agreement that the best men must have intercourse with the best women as frequently as possible, and the opposite is true of e the very inferior men and women; the offspring of the former must be reared, but not the offspring of the latter, if our herd is to be of the highest possible quality. Only the rulers should know of these arrangements, if our herd of guardians is to avoid all dissension as far as possible. —Quite right.

Therefore certain festivals will be established by law at which we shall bring the 460 brides and grooms together; there will also be sacrifices, and our poets must compose hymns to celebrate the marriages. The number of marriages we shall leave to the rulers to decide, in such a way as to keep the number of males as stable as possible, taking into account war, disease, and similar factors so that our city shall, as far as possible, become neither too big nor too small. —Right.

There will have to be some clever lots introduced, so that at each marriage celebration the inferior man we mentioned will blame chance but not the rulers. —Quite so.

The young men who have distinguished themselves in war or in other ways must be given awards consisting of other prizes and also more abundant permission to sleep with women, so that we may have a good excuse to have as many children as possible begotten by them. —Right. b

As the children are born, officials appointed for the purpose—be they men or women or both, since our offices are open to both women and men—will take them. —Yes.

The children of good parents they will take to a rearing pen in the care of nurses living apart in a certain section of the city; the children of inferior parents, or any child of the others born defective, they will hide, as is fitting, in a secret and unknown place.[2] —Yes, he said, if the breed of the guardians is to remain pure. c

The nurses will also see to it that the mothers are brought to the rearing pen when their breasts have milk, but take every precaution that no mother shall know her own child; they will provide wet nurses if the number of mothers is insufficient; they will take care that the mothers suckle the children for only a reasonable time; the care of sleepless children and all other troublesome duties will belong to the wet nurses and other attendants. d

You are making it very easy, he said, for the wives of the guardians to have children.

And that is fitting, I said....

However, I think that when women and men have passed the age of having children, we shall leave them free to have intercourse with anyone they wish, with these exceptions: for a man, his daughter or mother, or the daughter's daughters, or his mother's female progenitors; for a woman, a son or father, their male issue or progenitors. Having received these instructions they should be very careful 461b

c

---

[2] [There can be no doubt that Plato is here recommending infanticide by exposure for these babies, a practice which was quite common even in classical times (cp. 459d–e and 461b–c). Presumably the point of exposure rather than direct infanticide was that the responsibility was felt to be thrown upon the gods, for the child might be saved, as Oedipus was.]

not to bring a single child into the light, but if one should be conceived, and forces its way to the light, they must deal with it knowing that no nurture is available for it.

d  This too, he said, is sensibly spoken, but how shall they know their fathers and daughters and those other relationships you mentioned?

They have no means of knowing, I said, but all the children who are born in the tenth and seventh month after a man became a bridegroom he will call sons if they are male, daughters if they are female, and they will call him father, and so too he will call their offspring his grandchildren who in turn will call the first group their grandfathers and grandmothers. Those born during the time when their fathers and mothers were having children they will call their brothers and sisters, so that, as I said, these groups will have no sexual relations with each other. But

e  the law will allow brothers and sisters to live together if the lot so falls and the Pythian approves. —Quite right.

This then is the holding in common of wives and children for the guardians of your city. We must now confirm in our argument that it conforms with the rest of our constitution and is by far the best. Or how are we to proceed? —In that way, by Zeus.

471c  …But I think, Socrates, that if one lets you talk on these subjects, you will never remember the subject you postponed before you said all this, namely, that it is possible for this city to exist and how it can be brought about. I agree that, if it existed, all the things we have mentioned would be good for the city in which they

d  occurred, including this you are leaving out: they would be excellent fighters against an enemy because they would be least likely to desert each other, since they know each other as, and call each other by the name of, brothers, fathers, sons. Moreover, if their women joined their campaigns, whether in the same ranks or drawn up behind as reserves, either to frighten the enemy or as reinforcements, should they ever be needed, I know that this would make them quite unbeatable. I also see that a number of good things would ensue for them at home

e  which have not been mentioned. Take it that I agree that all these things would happen as well as innumerable others, if this kind of government were to exist. Say no more on this subject but let us now try to convince ourselves of this, namely that it is possible and how it is possible. Let the rest go.

472  This is a sudden attack you have made upon my arguments, I said, and you show no leniency towards my loitering. You may not realize that I have barely

escaped from the first two waves of objections as you bring the third upon me, the biggest and most difficult to deal with.[3] When you hear and see it you will surely be more lenient towards my natural hesitation and my fear to state, and attempt thoroughly to examine, such a paradox.

The more you speak like this, he said, the less we shall let you off from telling us how this city is possible. So speak and do not waste time. b

Well then, I said, we must first remember that we have come to this point while we were searching for the natures of justice and injustice. —We must, but what of it?

Nothing, but if we find out what justice is, shall we require that the just man be in no way different from that justice itself, and be like justice in every respect, c or shall we be satisfied if he comes as close to it as possible, and share in it far more than others? —That will satisfy us.

It was then to have a model, I said, that we were seeking the nature of justice itself, and of the completely just man, if he should exist, and what kind of man he would be if he did, and so with injustice and the most unjust man. Our purpose was, with these models before us, to see how they turned out as regards happiness and its opposite. Thus we would be forced to come to an agreement about ourselves, that he who was as like them as possible would also have a life most like theirs. It was not our purpose to prove that these could exist. —What you say is true. d

Do you think a man is any less a good painter if, having painted a model of what the most beautiful man would be, and having rendered all the details satisfactorily in this picture, he could not prove that such a man can come into being? —By Zeus, I do not.

Well then, do we not also say that we were making a model of a good city in e our argument? —Certainly.

Do you think our discussion less worthwhile if we cannot prove that it is possible to found a city such as we described? —Not at all.

And indeed, I said, that is the truth. But if we must, to please you, exert ourselves to pursue this topic, namely to show how and in what respect this might best be possible, then you in turn should agree that the same thing applies to this demonstration. —What thing?

---

[3] [The first wave of objection was that women could equally be guardians, and the second was that the guardian class would have wives and children in common. —J.M.P.]

473    Is it possible to realize anything in practice as it can be formulated in words or is it natural for practice to have a lesser grip on truth than theory, even if some people do not think so? Will you first agree to this or not? —I agree.

Then do not compel me to show that the things we have described in theory can exist precisely in practice. If we are able to discover how the administration b    of a city can come closest to our theories, shall we say that we have found that those things are possible which you told us to prove so? Or will you not be satisfied with that measure of success? For I would be satisfied. —So would I.

Next, it seems, we should try to find out and to show what is now badly done in the cities which prevents them from being governed in this way, and what is the smallest change which would enable a city to reach our type of government— c    one change if possible, or, if not one, then two, or at any rate as few changes and as insignificant in their effects as possible. —By all means.

There is one change to which I think we could point which would accomplish this. It is certainly neither small nor easy, but it is possible.—What is it?

I have now come, I said, to what we likened to the greatest wave. However, it shall be said even if, like a wave of laughter, it will simply drown me in ridicule and contempt. —Say on.

And I said: Cities will have no respite from evil, my dear Glaucon, nor will the d    human race, I think, unless philosophers rule as kings in the cities, or those whom we now call kings and rulers genuinely and adequately study philosophy; until, that is, political power and philosophy coalesce, and the various natures of those who now pursue the one to the exclusion of the other are forcibly debarred from doing e    so. Otherwise the city we have been describing will never grow into a possibility or see the light of day. It is because I saw how very paradoxical this statement would be that I have for some time hesitated to make it. It is hard to realize that there can be no happiness, public or private, in any other city.

Socrates, he said, you have uttered such a speech and statement that after speaking it you must expect a great many not undistinguished people to cast off 474    their cloak at once and, thus stripped for action, to snatch any available weapon, make a determined rush at you and do astonishing things to you. Unless you can hold them off by argument and escape, you will really pay the penalty of general derision.

Well, I said, it is you who brought this on me.

And I was quite right, he said. However, I will not betray you but defend you by any means I can, by good will, by urging you on, and perhaps I could give you more appropriate answers than another. Try, with this assistance, to show the unbelievers that things are as you state them.

b

I must try, I said, with the considerable support that you offer....

[*Socrates argues that knowledge "is directed to what is, while ignorance is of necessity directed to what is not." Opinion is intermediate. A philosopher, as one example, knows Beauty itself but a man of opinion can perceive only beautiful things. A philosopher can see, Socrates says, what "remains eternally the same in all respects." The beautiful things seen by the man of opinion are always in flux and changing. The objects of the philosopher's knowledge are "what is," the unchanging, eternal Form of Beauty itself. —J.M.P.*]

## ⤙ BOOK VI ⤚

### Four Stages of Cognition: The Line Allegory

[*The philosopher is now defined as the lover of Forms, and in this book Socrates returns more than once to the qualities required to become one. He puts the love of truth first and from this he derives a number of moral qualities, including the traditional virtues. He also emphasizes that some of these qualities, such as quickness and stability, are almost contradictory and rarely found together. Adeimantus accepts this but points out that, although Socrates compels his hearers to agree with him step by step, the majority will still believe that the best philosophers are useless, and most of them are wicked, and Socrates startles his audience by his ironic reply that the majority is right. He explains the uselessness by the parable of the ship of state in which the crew in their blindness believe that the art of navigation consists of getting hold of the helm and regard the true navigator as a useless stargazer.*

*As for the wickedness, he points out that the rare philosophic nature is led into temptations which corrupt it by its very virtues and by the tremendous power of public opinion. Compared with that, the Sophists, who merely study the moods of the beast and take that to be knowledge, do little harm. Then, when philosophic natures have been tempted away from philosophy, unworthy and quarrelsome little souls invade it and bring it into disrepute.*

*Philosophers must be capable of the highest studies, and the highest study is that of the Good. Asked to describe the Good, he says he cannot, but will describe "the offspring of the Good which is most like it," and we get the simile of the Sun which fulfills in the physical world much the same functions as the Good does in the intelligible. This is worked out in some detail, and is immediately followed by another image, that of the Line, which illustrates the Platonic dream of the upward journey from mere sense awareness to perfect and complete knowledge, and which is also an ascending scale of reality.*]

509 ...Understand then, I said, that, as we say, there are those two, one reigning over the intelligible kind and realm, the other over the visible (not to say heaven, that I may not appear to play the sophist about the name). So you have two kinds, the visible and the intelligible. —Right.

It is like a line divided into two unequal parts, and then divide each section in the same ratio, that is, the section of the visible and that of the intelligible.[4] You will then have sections related to each other in proportion to their clarity and obscurity. The first section of the visible consists of images—and by images
510 I mean shadows in the first instance, then the reflections in water and all those

---

[4] [It is clear that Plato visualizes a vertical line (511d and throughout) with B as the highest point in the scale of reality and A as the lowest form of existence. The main division is at C. AC is the visible, CB is the intelligible world, AD is the world of images (and perhaps, though Plato does not say so, works of art), mathematical realities are contained in CE, the Platonic Forms in EB, with the Good presumably at B.

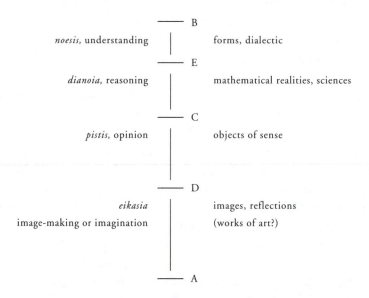

The names of the four mental processes —*noesis, dianoia, pistis,* and *eikasia*—are more or less arbitrary, and Plato does not use them regularly in these precise senses in the rest of *The Republic.*]

on close-packed, smooth, and bright materials, and all that sort of thing, if you understand me. —I understand.

In the other section of the visible, place the models of the images, the living creatures around us, all plants, and the whole class of manufactured things. —I so place them.

Would you be willing to say that, as regards truth and untruth, the division is made in this proportion: as the opinable is to the knowable so the image is to the model it is made like? —Certainly.

Consider now how the section of the intelligible is to be divided. —How?   b

In such a way that in one section the soul, using as images what before were models, is compelled to investigate from hypotheses, proceeding from these not to a first principle but to a conclusion. In the second section which leads to a first principle that is not hypothetical, the soul proceeds from a hypothesis without using the images of the first section, by means of the Forms themselves and proceeding through these. —I do not, he said, quite understand what you mean.

Let us try again, I said, for you will understand more easily because of what has   c
been said. I think you know that students of geometry, calculation, and the like assume the existence of the odds and the even, of figures, of three kinds of angles, and of kindred things in each of their studies, as if they were known to them. These they make their hypotheses and do not deem it necessary to give any account of them either to themselves or to others as if they were clear to all; these are their starting   d
points, and going through the remaining steps they reach an agreed conclusion on what they started out to investigate. —Quite so, I understand that.

You know also that they use visible figures and talk about them, but they are not thinking about them but about the models of which these are likenesses; they are making their points about the square itself, the diameter itself, not about   e
the diameter which they draw, and similarly with the others. These figures which they fashion and draw, of which shadows and reflections in the water are images, they now in turn use as images, in seeking to understand those others in themselves, which one cannot see except in thought. —That is true.   511

This is what I called the intelligible class, and said that the soul is forced to use hypotheses in its search for it, not travelling up to a first principle, since it cannot reach beyond its hypotheses, but it uses as images those very things which at a lower level were models and which, in comparison with their images, were thought to   b
be clear and honoured as such. —I understand, he said, that you mean what happens in geometry and kindred sciences.

83

Understand also that by the other section of the intelligible I mean that which reason itself grasps by the power of dialectic. It does not consider its hypotheses as first principles, but as hypotheses in the true sense of stepping stones and starting points, in order to reach that which is beyond hypothesis, the first principle of all that exists. Having reached this and keeping hold of what follows from it, it does come down to a conclusion without making use of anything visible at all, but proceeding by means of Forms and through Forms to its conclusions which are Forms.

I understand, he said, but not completely, for you seem to be speaking of a mighty task—that you wish to distinguish the intelligible reality contemplated by the science of dialectic as clearer than that viewed by the so-called sciences, for which their hypotheses are first principles. The students of these so-called sciences are, it is true, compelled to study them by thought and not by sense perception, yet because they do not go back to a first principle but proceed from hypotheses, you do not think that they have any clear understanding of their subjects, although these can be so understood if approached from a first principle. You seem to me to call the attitude of mind of geometers and such reasoning but not understanding, reasoning being midway between opinion and understanding.

You have grasped this very satisfactorily, I said. There are four such processes in the soul, corresponding to the four sections of our line: understanding for the highest, reasoning for the second; give the name of opinion to the third, and imagination to the last. Place these in the due terms of a proportion and consider that each has as much clarity as the content of its particular section shares in truth. —I understand, and I agree and arrange them as you say.

## ✦ BOOK VII ✦

### *The Allegory of the Cave*

Next, I said, compare the effect of education and the lack of it upon our human nature to a situation like this: imagine men to be living in an underground cave-like dwelling place, which has a way up to the light along its whole width, but the entrance is a long way up. The men have been there from childhood, with their neck and legs in fetters, so that they remain in the same place and can only see ahead of them, as their bonds prevent them turning their heads. Light is provided by a fire burning some way behind and above them. Between the fire and the prisoners, some way behind them and on a higher ground, there is a path across the cave and along this a low wall has been built, like the screen at a puppet show in front of the performers who show their puppets above it. —I see it.

See then also men carrying along that wall, so that they overlap it, all kinds of artifacts, statues of men, reproductions of other animals in stone or wood fashioned in all sorts of ways, and, as is likely, some of the carriers are talking while others are silent. —This is a strange picture, and strange prisoners.

They are like us, I said. Do you think, in the first place, that such men could see anything of themselves and each other except the shadows which the fire casts upon the wall of the cave in front of them? —How could they, if they have to keep their heads still throughout life?

And is not the same true of the objects carried along the wall? —Quite.

If they could converse with one another, do you not think that they would consider these shadows to be the real thing? —Necessarily.

What if their prison had an echo which reached them from in front of them? Whenever one of the carriers passing behind the wall spoke, would they not think that it was the shadow passing in front of them which was talking? Do you agree? —By Zeus I do.

Altogether then, I said, such men would believe the truth to be nothing else than the shadows of the artifacts? —They must believe that.

Consider then what deliverance from their bonds and the curing of their ignorance would be if something like this naturally happened to them. Whenever one of them was freed, had to stand up suddenly, turn his head, walk, and look up toward the light, doing all that would give him pain, the flash of the fire would make it impossible for him to see the objects of which he had earlier seen the shadows. What do you think he would say if he was told that what he saw then was foolishness, that he was now somewhat closer to reality and turned to things that existed more fully, that he saw more correctly? If one then pointed to each of the objects passing by, asked him what each was, and forced him to answer, do you not think he would be at a loss and believe that the things which he saw earlier were truer than the things now pointed out to him? —Much truer.

If one then compelled him to look at the fire itself, his eyes would hurt, he would turn round and flee toward those things which he could see, and think that they were in fact clearer than those now shown to him. —Quite so.

And if one were to drag him thence by force up the rough and steep path, and did not let him go before he was dragged into the sunlight, would he not

c

515

b

c

d

e

516 be in physical pain and angry as he was dragged along? When he came into the light, with the sunlight filling his eyes, he would not be able to see a single one of the things which are now said to be true. —Not at once, certainly.

I think he would need time to get adjusted before he could see things in the world above; at first he would see shadows most easily, then reflections of men and other things in water, then the things themselves. After this he would see objects in the

b sky and the sky itself more easily at night, the light of the stars and the moon more easily than the sun and the light of the sun during the day. —Of course.

Then, at last, he would be able to see the sun, not images of it in water or in some alien place, but the sun itself in its own place, and be able to contemplate it. —That must be so.

After this he would reflect that it is the sun which provides the seasons and the

c years, which governs everything in the visible world, and is also in some way the cause of those other things which he used to see. —Clearly that would be the next stage.

What then? As he reminds himself of his first dwelling place, of the wisdom there and of his fellow prisoners, would he not reckon himself happy for the change, and pity them? —Surely.

And if the men below had praise and honours from each other, and prizes for the man who saw most clearly the shadows that passed before them, and who could best remember which usually came earlier and which later, and which came

d together and thus could most ably prophesy the future, do you think one man would desire those rewards and envy those who were honoured and held power among the prisoners, or would he feel, as Homer put it, that he certainly wished to be "serf to another man without possessions upon the earth" and go through

e any suffering, rather than share their opinions and live as they do? —Quite so, he said, I think he would rather suffer anything.

Reflect on this too, I said. If this man went down into the cave again and sat down in the same seat, would his eyes not be filled with darkness, coming suddenly out of the sunlight? —They certainly would.

And if he had to contend again with those who had remained prisoners in rec-

517 ognizing those shadows while his sight was affected and his eyes had not settled down—and the time for his adjustment would not be short—would he not be ridiculed? Would it now be said that he had returned from his upward journey with his eyesight spoiled, and that it was not worthwhile even to attempt to travel upward? As for the man who tried to free them and lead them upward,

if they could somehow lay their hands on him and kill him, they would do so. —They certainly would.

This whole image, my dear Glaucon, I said, must be related to what we said before. The realm of the visible should be compared to the prison dwelling, and the fire inside it to the power of the sun. If you interpret the upward journey and the contemplation of things above as the upward journey of the soul to the intelligible realm, you will grasp what I surmise since you were keen to hear it. Whether it is true or not only the god knows, but this is how I see it, namely that in the intelligible world the Form of the Good is the last to be seen, and with difficulty; when seen it must be reckoned to be for all the cause of all that is right and beautiful, to have produced in the visible world both light and the fount of light, while in the intelligible world it is itself that which produces and controls truth and intelligence, and he who is to act intelligently in public or in private must see it. —I share your thought as far as I am able.

Come then, share with me this thought also: do not be surprised that those who have reached this point are unwilling to occupy themselves with human affairs, and that their souls are always pressing upward to spend their time there, for this is natural if things are as our parable indicates. —That is very likely.

Further, I said, do you think it at all surprising that anyone coming to the evils of human life from the contemplation of the divine behaves awkwardly and appears very ridiculous while his eyes are still dazzled and before he is sufficiently adjusted to the darkness around him, if he is compelled to contend in court or some other place about the shadows of justice or the objects of which they are shadows, and to carry through the contest about these in the way these things are understood by those who have never seen Justice itself? —That is not surprising at all.

Anyone with intelligence, I said, would remember that the eyes may be confused in two ways and from two causes, coming from light into darkness as well as from darkness into light. Realizing that the same applies to the soul, whenever he sees a soul disturbed and unable to see something, he will not laugh mindlessly but will consider whether it has come from a brighter life and is dimmed because unadjusted, or has come from greater ignorance into greater light and is filled with a brighter dazzlement. The former he would declare happy in its life and experience, the latter he would pity, and if he should wish to laugh at it, his laughter would be less ridiculous than if he laughed at a soul that has come from the light above. —What you say is very reasonable.

We must then, I said, if these things are true, think something like this about them, namely that education is not what some declare it to be; they say that

c    knowledge is not present in the soul and that they put it in, like putting sight into blind eyes. —They surely say that.

Our present argument shows, I said, that the capacity to learn and the organ with which to do so are present in every person's soul. It is as if it were not possible to turn the eye from darkness to light without turning the whole body; so one must turn one's whole soul from the world of becoming until it can endure to con-

d    template reality, and the brightest of realities, which we say is the Good. —Yes.

Education then is the art of doing this very thing, this turning around, the knowledge of how the soul can most easily and most effectively be turned around; it is not the art of putting the capacity of sight into the soul; the soul possesses that already but it is not turned the right way or looking where it should. This is what education has to deal with. —That seems likely.

Now the other so-called virtues of the soul seem to be very close to those of the

e    body—they really do not exist before and are added later by habit and practice— but the virtue of intelligence belongs above all to something more divine, it seems, which never loses its capacity but, according to which way it is turned, becomes useful and beneficial or useless and harmful. Have you ever noticed in men who are said to be wicked but clever, how sharply their little soul looks into things to which it turns its attention? Its capacity for sight is not inferior, but it is compelled to serve evil ends, so that the more sharply it looks the more evils it works. —Quite so.

Yet if a soul of this kind had been hammered at from childhood and those excrescences had been knocked off it which belong to the world of becoming

b    and have been fastened upon it by feasting, gluttony, and similar pleasures, and which like leaden weights draw the soul to look downward—if, being rid of these, it turned to look at things that are true, then the same soul of the same man would see these just as sharply as it now sees the things towards which it is directed. —That seems likely.

Further, is it not likely, I said, indeed it follows inevitably from what was said before, that the uneducated who have no experience of truth would never govern

c    a city satisfactorily, nor would those who are allowed to spend their whole life in the process of educating themselves; the former would fail because they do not have a single goal at which all their actions, public and private, must aim; the latter because they would refuse to act, thinking that they have settled, while still alive, in the faraway islands of the blessed. —True.

It is then our task as founders, I said, to compel the best natures to reach the study which we have previously said to be the most important, to see the Good and to follow that upward journey. When they have accomplished their journey and seen it sufficiently, we must not allow them to do what they are allowed to do today. —What is that?

To stay there, I said, and to refuse to go down again to the prisoners in the cave, there to share both their labours and their honours, whether these be of little or of greater worth.

Are we then, he said, to do them an injustice by making them live a worse life when they could live a better one?

You are again forgetting, my friend, I said, that it is not the law's concern to make some one group in the city outstandingly happy but to contrive to spread happiness throughout the city, by bringing the citizens into harmony with each other by persuasion or compulsion, and to make them share with each other the benefits which each group can confer upon the community. The law has not made men of this kind in the city in order to allow each to turn in any direction they wish but to make use of them to bind the city together. —You are right, I had forgotten.

Consider then, Glaucon, I said, that we shall not be doing an injustice to those who have become philosophers in our city, and that what we shall say to them, when we compel them to care for and to guard the others, is just. For we shall say: "Those who become philosophers in other cities are justified in not sharing the city's labours, for they have grown into philosophy of their own accord, against the will of the government in each of those cities, and it is right that what grows of its own accord, as it owes no debt to anyone for its upbringing, should not be keen to pay it to anyone. But we have made you in our city kings and leaders of the swarm, as it were, both to your own advantage and to that of the rest of the city; you are better and more completely educated than those others, and you are better able to share in both kinds of life. Therefore you must each in turn go down to live with other men and grow accustomed to seeing in the dark. When you are used to it you will see infinitely better than the dwellers below; you will know what each kind of image is and of what it is an image, because you have seen the truth of things beautiful and just and good, and so, for you as for us, the city will be governed as a waking reality and not as in a dream, as the majority of cities are now governed by men who are fighting shadows and striving against each other in order to rule as if this were a great good." For this is the truth: a city in which the prospective rulers are least keen to rule must

d

e

520

b

c

d

of necessity be governed best and be most free from civil strife, whereas a city with the opposite kind of rulers is governed in the opposite way. —Quite so.

Do you think that those we have nurtured will disobey us and refuse to share the labours of the city, each group in turn, though they may spend the greater part of their time dwelling with each other in a pure atmosphere?

e      They cannot, he said, for we shall be giving just orders to just men, but each of them will certainly go to rule as to something that must be done, the opposite attitude from that of the present rulers in every city.

521      That is how it is, my friend, I said. If you can find a way of life which is better than governing for the prospective governors, then a well-governed city can exist for you. Only in that city will the truly rich rule, not rich in gold but in the wealth which the happy man must have, a life with goodness and intelligence. If beggars hungry for private goods go into public life, thinking that they must snatch their good from it, the well-governed city cannot exist, for then office is fought for, and such a war at home inside the city destroys them and the city as well. —Very true.

b      Can you name, I said, any other life than that of true philosophy which disdains political office? —No, by Zeus.

And surely it is those who are no lovers of governing who must govern. Otherwise, rival lovers of it will fight them. —Of course.

What other men will you compel to become guardians of the city rather than those who have the best knowledge of the principles that make for the best government of a city and who also know honours of a different kind, and a better life than the political? —No one else....

*[Socrates then turns to the higher education of the philosopher-ruler. Education, he remarks, does not consist in putting knowledge into the soul, but in turning the eyes of the soul towards the right objects, and the young must be taught in play, for no free man learns anything worthwhile under compulsion.*

*What studies will do this? Socrates finds the answer in the mathematical studies, arithmetic, geometry, stereometry, astronomy (the study of the laws of motion), and harmonics (the study of the laws of sound). He then draws up a time-table and it is interesting to find him insisting that after five years of dialectic, at the age of thirty-five, his philosophers must return into the cave, i.e. take part in practical politics, for fifteen years in order to acquire the experience which is necessary for a ruler. Even after fifty, when their education is completed, the philosophers must take turns in ruling the city, even though they know a better life. We should also note that they must not be allowed to start a course on dialectic too young, or they will merely use it as a debating skill to confuse other people. The exclusion from the city of everyone over ten years of age seems a drastic way of establishing a new constitution, but it certainly emphasizes Plato's point that education, to be effective, must start early. Socrates also reminds his hearers that all he has said applies to women too.]*

# ⇥ BOOK VIII ⇤

## *The Decline of the State*

Very well. These things then, Glaucon, are agreed. If a city is to be well governed, wives, children, and all education must be in common, and so too their occupations in peace and war must be common to both sexes; their kings must be those who are best in the practice of philosophy and the waging of war. —That is agreed.

We have further agreed that as soon as the rulers are established they will lead the soldiers and settle them in such dwellings as we have mentioned, in which there is no private property but which are common to all. Besides the houses, we have also agreed, if you remember, what kind of possessions they will have.

I remember, he said, that we thought that no one should acquire any of the things that other people now do, but that, as athletes of war and guardians, they should receive their yearly keep from the other citizens as wages of their guardianship, their duty being to look after themselves and the rest of the city.

That is correct, I said. But come, since we have completed this discussion, let us recall the point at which we digressed to reach our present position, so that we may continue along the same path.

That offers no difficulty, he said, for then, much the same as now, you were talking as if you had completed the discussion of the city; you said that you would class as good the city which you had described, and that the good man was he who resembled it, although it seems that you still had a finer city and man about which to tell us. You then mentioned the other cities which were of the wrong kind, if this one was right. You said, as I remember, that there were four kinds of other cities which would be worth discussing, observing their errors, as well as the men corresponding to them. Our aim was to observe them all, to agree which was the best man and which the worst, and then to examine whether

543

b

c

d
544

the best man was the happiest and the worst most wretched, or whether mat-
b    ters stood otherwise. I was asking you to say which were these four kinds of
cities when Polemarchus and Adeimantus interrupted, and so you took up the
argument again and have now arrived at this point. —Your recollection, I said,
is quite correct.

Well then, like a wrestler, give me the same hold again and, as I ask the same
question, do you try to give the answer which you were about to give then. —If
indeed I can, said I.

Indeed, he said, I am myself eager to hear what four cities you meant.

c    You will hear these without difficulty, for they are those which have names.
There is that which is praised by most people, the Cretan or Laconian. The second kind, which is also second in the praise it receives, is called oligarchy and it
is full of many evils. Then there is a different one which comes into existence
next, namely democracy. Then the noble dictatorship which stands out from all
d    these is the fourth and last diseased city. Or can you name another kind which is
in a clearly different class? For hereditary dynasties and bought kingships and
some such other forms of rule are somewhere between these named kinds and
one can find as many of them among the barbarians as among the Greeks.
—One hears of many strange kinds, he said.

You realize, I said, that there are of necessity as many ways of life for men as
there are types of cities? Or do you think that governments are born "from oak or
e    rock" and not from the characters of the men who live in the cities, which characters tip the scales and drag other things after them?

I do not believe, he said, that they have any other origin.

Then if the cities are of five kinds, the dispositions of the individuals' souls must
be five also. —Quite so.

We have already described the man who is like aristocracy, whom we cor-
545    rectly state to be the good and just man. —We have.

After this we must describe the worse types: the lover of victory and honour
who corresponds to the Laconian city, then the oligarchic man, the democratic,
and the dictatorial, in order to observe the most unjust man and contrast him with
the most just. Thus we will complete our investigation of the relation between pure
justice and pure injustice with regard to the happiness and wretchedness of the men
who possess these qualities. We shall then be persuaded either by Thrasymachus
b    to practise injustice, or, in the light of our present argument, to pursue justice.
—This we must certainly do.

92

Shall we then, just as we began by seeking moral qualities in the cities, as being clearer, before we did so in individuals, also now examine the city which loves honour—I have no other name for it, or should we call it a timocracy or timarchy —and then examine that kind of individual, then oligarchy and the oligarchic man, then again after examining democracy we shall observe the democratic man; then fourthly we shall come to the city under a dictator and observe it, and then look into the dictatorial soul? Thus we shall try to become well-qualified judges of the problem which we set ourselves. —It would be reasonable for our investigation and decision to proceed in this way, he said.…

c

[*The harmonies of the universe can be mathematically expressed, and Plato explains the fall from aristocracy to timocracy by playfully indicating how rulers can miscalculate the proper time for mating. Rulers eventually come to power who have inadequate virtue.* —J.M.P.]

## *Timocracy*

I think, he said, that this is how the change started.

547

This government then, I said, stands between aristocracy and oligarchy? —Certainly.

This is how it will change. And, having changed, how will it be managed? Clearly, it will be like the earlier government in some respects, and like oligarchy in others, being between the two, and it will also have some features of its own. —That is so.

b

It will honour the rulers; the fighting section of the state will take no part in agriculture, manual labour, or other ways of making money; it will eat communally and devote itself to physical exercise and training for war; in all these ways it will be like the earlier city? —Yes.

On the other hand it will be afraid to appoint wise men to office, because such men are no longer simple and earnest, but of mixed nature; it then turns to spirited and simpler-minded men who are born for war rather than for peace; the tricks and devices of war are now held in high esteem, and the city spends all its time in making war. Most of these features will be all its own. —Yes.

c

548

Such men, I said, will be greedy for money, as men are in oligarchies; they will prize gold and silver without restraint but in secret; they will have private treasuries and storing places where they can keep it hidden; their houses will enclose them, like private nests where they can spend a great deal of money on women and anyone else they may wish. —Very true.

b

They will also be mean with money, since they prize it and do not acquire it openly, but they will be ready to spend other people's money because of their passion for it. They will enjoy their pleasures in secret, escaping from the law as sons from their father. They have not been educated by persuasion but by force, because they have neglected the true Muse, that of discussion and philosophy, and have honoured physical training more highly than the arts.

The city you mention, he said, is altogether a mixture of good and bad.

Yes, I said, it is indeed a mixture. There is only one thing which appears in it most clearly under the rule of the spirited part, namely the love of victory and of honours. —Very definitely.

This then, I said, is the kind of government it would be and how it would arise, to sketch the shape of it without working it out in detail, for even from a sketch we shall discern the most just and the most unjust man, and it would be an intolerably long task to describe every kind of city and every kind of character without omitting any detail. —Correct.

Who is now the man who corresponds to this city? How does he come to be and what kind of a man is he?

I think, said Adeimantus, that he would be very like Glaucon here as far as the love of victory goes.

Perhaps in that respect, I said, but in the following respects he would be very different. —In what respects? he said.

He must be rather obstinate and somewhat uncultured, though he likes the arts; he must like to hear things, but is in no way a speaker; he would be harsh to his slaves, but not because he looks down on them as a man of good education does; toward free men, however, he would be gentle and quite obedient to those in power, being himself a lover of power and honours. He does not believe that the capacity to express oneself, or anything of that kind, should lead to power, but rather deeds in war and concerning war, as he is a lover of physical training and the hunt. —Yes, he said, that is the character of that city.

Such a man, I said, would despise money while young, but welcome it more and more as he grows older, for he has his share of the money-loving nature. He is not pure in his attitude to virtue because he lacks the best of guardians. —What is that?

Reasonable discourse, I said, with an admixture of the arts, for this dwells in a man as the sole preserver of his virtue throughout his life. —Well said.

This then is the timocratic youth, and he resembles this kind of city. —Quite so.

And he comes to be, I said, in some such manner as this. He is the son of a good father who lives in a city which is not well governed. The father avoids honours and office and lawsuits and all that kind of business; he is even willing to be put at a disadvantage in order to avoid trouble.

How, he said, does the timocrat come to be?

He becomes such in the first instance, I said, when he hears his mother being angry because her husband is not one of the rulers and she is less esteemed among other women on that account. Then she sees that he is not very concerned about money, that he does not fight back when he is insulted in private or in the courts or in public, and that he bears all this with indifference. She also sees him always concentrating his mind upon his own thoughts, neither greatly honouring nor slighting her. Angered by all this, she tells her son that his father is unmanly and too easygoing, and all the things which women repeat over and over again about such men. —Yes, said Adeimantus, they do say many things which are characteristic of them.

You know too, I said, that these men's servants sometimes say similar things to the sons covertly, those servants who are thought to be well disposed. When they see the father failing to prosecute someone who owes him money or wrongs him in some other way, they advise the son that when he grows up he must take vengeance on all those people and be more of a man than his father. The boy hears and sees the same kind of thing when he goes out, that those who restrict themselves to their own affairs are called foolish in the city and held in low esteem, while those who meddle with the affairs of others are honoured and praised. The young man hears and sees all this, but on the other hand he also listens to what his father says, observes what he does from close at hand, and compares his actions with those of the others. So he is pulled both ways; his father nourishes the reasonable part of his soul and makes it grow, the others foster the spirited and the appetitive parts. As he is not a bad man by nature but keeps bad company, pulled both ways he has settled in the middle and has surrendered the rule over himself to the middle part, the victory-loving and spirited part, and becomes a proud and ambitious man.

I certainly think, he said, that you have given a full account of the birth of this type.

We have then, I said, the second type of city and the second type of man. —We have.

d

e

550

b

c

## *Oligarchy*

After this then, to quote Aeschylus, let us talk of "another man placed over against another city," or rather, according to our plan, talk of the city first. —Quite so.

The one to come after this city is, as I think, oligarchy.

And what kind of constitution would you call oligarchy? he asked.

d   The constitution based on income, I said, in which the rich rule, while the poor have no share of power. —I understand.

So now we must first tell how the timarchy changes into an oligarchy? —Yes.

Surely, I said, the manner of this change is clear even to the blind. —How?

That private treasury, I said, which each man has, becomes filled with gold and destroys the constitution. First they find ways of spending it on themselves, they twist the laws for this purpose, and they themselves disobey it along with their wives. —Likely enough.

e   Then as one man sees another doing this and envies him, they make the masses like themselves in this. —That is probable.

Then as they proceed further into money-making, the more they honour this the less they honour virtue. Or does not virtue stand in such opposition to wealth that if each were in the scale of a balance, they would ever incline in opposite directions? —Certainly.

551   When wealth and the wealthy are honoured in a city, virtue and the virtuous are prized less. —Clearly.

What is honoured is always practised, and what is slighted is neglected. —That is so.

In the end the lovers of victory and honours become money-lovers and money-makers; they praise and admire the wealthy man and appoint him to office while they disregard the poor man. —Quite so.

b   Then they pass a law which is the characteristic of oligarchy by establishing a wealth qualification, higher where the government is more oligarchic, of a lesser amount where it is less so, having previously declared that those whose possessions do not reach the stated amount are not qualified for office. They either enforce this by force of arms, or else they have terrorized people before they established this kind of government. Is that not so? —It is.

This, in general terms, is how this kind of government is established.

c   Yes, he said, but how does it work? And what are the flaws which we said it had?

First of all, I said, is the very nature of the characteristic we mentioned. For look, would anyone appoint the pilots of a ship this way, by their wealth, and not entrust the ship to a poor man even if he was a better pilot?

People who did that, he said, would make a poor voyage.

Is that not also true of the rule of anything else? —I think so.

Except a city? I said, or does it also apply to a city?

More than to anything else, he said, in so far as this is the most difficult and the most important kind of rule.

This then is one considerable flaw of oligarchy? —So it appears.

Further, is the following flaw less than this? —What?

The fact that it is of necessity not one city but two, one of the poor and the other of the rich, living in the same place and always plotting against each other. —This, by Zeus, is just as big a flaw.

And this is not a fine feature either, that they are probably unable to fight a war, because they would be compelled either to arm the people and use them, and be more afraid of them than of the enemy, or, if they did not do so, they would indeed be oligarchs, being so few, in the actual fighting. At the same time they would be unwilling to pay taxes, being lovers of money. —Not a fine feature.

Moreover, there is also what we strongly disapproved of before, that the same men in such a state would fulfill many functions, being farmers and money-makers and warriors all at the same time. Or do you think this right? —Not right at all.

But look whether of all the evils this is not the greatest, which is first found in this city. —What evil?

That a man may sell all his possessions and another may buy them, and, having sold them, he lives in the city without being any part of the community, neither a money-maker nor a craftsman, neither cavalry man nor hoplite, but one they call a pauper without means. —Yes, and this is the first city to allow this.

Yet this is not forbidden in an oligarchy. If it were, some would not be excessively rich and others utter paupers. —Correct.

However, consider this: when this man was rich and spending his money, was he of any greater use to the city in the ways we have just mentioned? He appeared to be one of the rulers, but in fact was neither ruler nor subject in the city, but merely someone who was spending money that was ready to hand. —That is so, he said. He appeared to be part of the community, but he was nothing but a spender.

Should we say then, I said, that, as a drone exists in a cell and is an affliction to the hive, so this man is a drone in the house and an affliction to the city? —Quite so, Socrates.

The god, Adeimantus, has fashioned all the winged drones without stings, but of these two-footed drones some are stingless, while others have dangerous stings. The stingless ones continue as beggars into old age, but it is from among d    those endowed with stings that all those we call criminals come. —Very true.

Clearly then, in any city where you see beggars there are thieves hidden in the place, and footpads and temple robbers, and the doers of all such evil deeds. —Clearly.

And do you not notice the presence of beggars in oligarchies? —Almost everyone, he said, except the rulers.

e    Shall we not believe then that there are many criminals with stings in these cities, whom those in office deliberately keep in check by force? —We think so.

And shall we not say that it is the lack of education and a poor upbringing, as well as the condition of the city, that are the cause of the drones' presence? —We shall.

This then, or something like this, is the oligarchic city; it contains these many evils, and perhaps even more. —I think so....

[*The change from timocratic to oligarchic man parallels the change in the society. When the timocratic father comes to ruin, the son, seeing the decline of the father, changes his own way of life and pursues wealth rather than honour. —J.M.P.*]


## *Democracy*

555    After this we must consider democracy, how it originated and how it functions once it has come into existence, in order that we should know the manner of life of the democratic man and put him beside the city for judgment. —We would be proceeding consistently in doing so.

Well, I said, the city changes from an oligarchy to a democracy in some such way as this, because of its insatiable desire to attain what it has set before itself as the good, namely the need to become as rich as possible. —How so?

c    I think that, in as much as those who rule in the city do so because they have accumulated great possessions, they are not willing to prevent by law the intemperate among the young from spending and wasting their substance. Their intention is to buy them up and lend them money so that they themselves will become even richer and more honoured.

Now this is quite clear: it is impossible to honour wealth in a city and at the same time for the citizens to acquire sufficient moderation; one or the other is inevitably neglected. —Quite clear.

Because of this neglect, and because they do not restrain the intemperate, men of good birth are often reduced to poverty in oligarchies. —Quite so.

So there they are in the city, with their stings and their weapons; some of them are in debt; some are disfranchised, some are both; they hate those who have acquired their property and plot against them as well as against others, and they long for revolution. —That is so.

The money-makers on the other hand keep their eyes on the ground and do not appear to see them, but they injure anyone of the others who yields to them by providing him with money and exacting as interest many times the principal sum, and so they create a considerable number of drones and beggars in the city. —Certainly a good many.

And as this evil flares up in the city they do not wish to quench it either in the way we mentioned, by preventing people doing whatever they please with their own, or by another law which might solve the problem. —What law?

One which is a second best but which compels people to pay attention to virtue, if it prescribes that the majority of private contracts be entered into at one's own risk; they would then be less shameless in their pursuit of money in the city and fewer of those evils we were mentioning just now would develop. —Far fewer.

But as it is now, I said, for all these reasons this is the condition to which the rulers reduce their subjects in the city. As for themselves and their children, do they not make the young fond of luxury, incapable of effort either physical or mental, soft in the face of pleasure and pain, and lazy besides? —Surely.

They neglect everything except making money, and care no more for virtue than the poor do. —Indeed they do not.

When rulers and subjects in this condition meet each other on a journey or on some other common pursuit, at festivals or on an embassy or on a campaign, on shipboard or in the army, and observe each other facing danger, on those occasions the poor are not despised by the rich. Often a poor man, spare and sun-tanned, stands in battle next to a rich man who is pale for lack of sun with much superfluous flesh, and sees him panting and at a loss. Do you not think that he would consider that it is through the cowardice of the poor that people like that are rich, and one poor man would say to the other as they met privately: "These men are at our mercy; they are no good." —I know very well that they do this.

d

e

556

b

c

d

e

Then, as a sick body needs only a slight shock from outside to fall into illness and sometimes even without this it is in a state of civil strife, so a city which is in the same plight needs but a small excuse and, as one side brings in allies from an oligarchic city or the other from a democracy, the city is ill and

fights itself, and sometimes a revolution occurs even without outside help. —Most certainly.

I think democracy comes when the poor are victorious, kill some of the other side, expel others, and to the rest they give an equal share of political power and offices, and generally the offices are filled by lot in this city.

Yes, he said, that is how democracy is established, be it by force of arms or because those on the other side are frightened into exile.

How do they live then? I asked. Of what kind is this city? For clearly a man of this kind will turn out to be a democratic man. —Clearly.

First of all they are free, and the city becomes full of liberty and freedom of speech, and in it one can do anything one pleases. —So they say.

Where this opportunity exists, everyone will arrange his own life in any manner that pleases him. —Obviously.

And in this city above all others there would, I think, be all sorts of people. —Of course.

This is probably the most beautiful of all constitutions. Like a cloak embroidered with every kind of ornament, so this city, embroidered with every kind of character, would seem the most beautiful, and perhaps many would judge it to be so, like children and women gazing at embroideries of many colours. —They certainly would.

It is also, my good friend, I said, a convenient place to look for a constitution. —How do you mean?

It contains all kinds of constitutions because of its permissiveness, and the man who wants to establish a city, as we were doing, should probably go to a democracy, as if it were an emporium of constitutions, pick out whatever type

pleases him and establish that. —Perhaps he would not be at a loss for models.

In this city, I said, there is no compulsion to rule, even if you are capable of it, or again to be ruled if you do not want to be, or to be at war when the others are, or at peace unless you desire peace. If some law forbids you to hold office or to go

to law, you nevertheless do both if it occurs to you to do so. Is that not a divine and pleasant life for the time being? —Perhaps, he said, for the time being.

And is the placidity of some of their condemned criminals not civilized? Or have you not seen in this city men who have been condemned to death or exile stay in the city in spite of this? The criminal strolls around like a hero's ghost, without anyone seeing him or giving him a thought. —Yes, I have seen many such.

The tolerance in such a city! It certainly does not show any petty concern for trifles. Indeed it despises those things we solemnly spoke of when we were founding our city, as that, unless a man had an exceedingly fine nature, he would never become a good man unless from early childhood he played fine games and followed fine pursuits. How magnificently this city tramples all this underfoot and does not give a thought to what a man was doing before he enters public life. It honours him if only he says that he wishes the crowd well. —An altogether noble city!

These are the qualities of democracy, and others like these, and it would seem to be a pleasant constitution without any rulers and with much variety, distributing a kind of equality to the equal and the unequal alike. —We certainly know what you mean....

[*The democratic man develops when the young man's soul is no longer controlled by the necessary desires found in the thrifty oligarchic father. As unnecessary and useless desires predominate, reason and knowledge are dispelled, and the soul becomes rudderless. In such a person, Socrates notes, "insolence becomes good breeding, anarchy freedom, extravagance munificence, and shamelessness courage."*—J.M.P.]

After this, I think, such a man spends his money, effort, and time no less upon unnecessary than upon necessary pleasures. If he is lucky and does not overstep the boundary of frenzy, then, as he grows older and the great tumult has spent itself, he welcomes back some of the exiles and does not surrender himself completely to the newcomers, he puts pleasures on an equal footing and so spends his life, always surrendering the government of himself to one, as if chosen by lot, until he is satisfied and then to another, not disdaining any but fulfilling them all equally. —Quite so.

He does not welcome true reasoning or allow it into the guardhouse; if someone tells him that some pleasures belong to good and beautiful desires, but others belong to evil ones, that one should prize and pursue the former while the latter must be restrained and mastered, he denies all this and declares that all pleasures are equal and must be equally prized. —A man in that condition would certainly do so.

b

c

561

b

c

And he lives on, yielding day by day to the desire at hand. At one time he drinks heavily to the accompaniment of the flute, at another he drinks only water and is wasting away; at one time he goes in for physical exercise, then again he does nothing and cares for nothing; at times he pretends to spend his time on philosophy; often he takes part in public affairs; he then leaps up from his seat and says and does whatever comes into his mind; if he happens to admire military men, he is carried in that direction, if moneyed men, he turns to making money; there is no plan or discipline in his life but he calls it pleasant, free, and blessed, and he follows it throughout his time. —You have certainly described the life of a man who believes in legal equality.

I also think, I said, that he is a fine man of great variety full of all sorts of characters, just like that city. Many men and many women might envy his life, for it contains the greatest number of governments and ways of living. Shall we then place this man beside democracy as being correctly called the democratic man? —Let him so be placed.

### *Tyranny*

The finest government and the finest kind of man remain for us to discuss, dictatorship and the dictatorial man. —They certainly do remain.

Come, my dear friend, what is dictatorship like? That it evolves from democracy is pretty clear. —Obviously.

Does it not evolve from democracy in much the same way as democracy does from oligarchy? —How?

What they put before them as the good, which was the basis of oligarchy, was wealth, was it not? —Yes.

Then their insatiable desire for wealth, and their neglect of other things for money-making was what destroyed it, was it not? —True.

Now insatiability for what democracy defines as the good also destroys it. —And what do you say it defines as such?

Liberty, I said. This is what you would hear in a democracy is its finest possession and that this is the reason why it is the only city worth living in for a man who is by nature free. —That too is very often said.

Well, this is just what I was going to say, that insatiability regarding this, and neglect of other things because of it, is the thing which changes this government too, and puts it in a condition in which it needs dictatorship. —How so?

I think that whenever a democracy athirst for liberty has bad cup-bearers to preside over it and drinks too deeply of the pure wine of liberty, then the rulers, unless they are very accommodating and give plenty of liberty, are punished by the city and accused of being foul oligarchs. —Yes, that is so.

It abuses those who obey the rulers as willing slaves and of no account, but it praises and honours, both in public and in private, rulers who behave like subjects and subjects who behave like rulers. Must not such a city reach the extreme of liberty? —Of course.

Liberty makes its way into private households and in the end it breeds anarchy even among the animals....

The same disease, I said, which developed in oligarchy develops here also, more widespread and virulent because of the permissiveness, and it enslaves democracy. In fact, excessive action in one direction usually sets up a reaction in the opposite direction. This happens in weather, in plants, in bodies, and not least in politics. So excessive liberty, whether in the individual or the state, is likely to change to excessive servitude and nothing else. —Likely enough.

So, I said, dictatorship is likely to evolve from democracy, the most severe and cruel servitude from pure liberty. —That is reasonable.

I do not think that was your question, however, but you asked what was the disease which developed in oligarchy and also in democracy and enslaved it. —That is true.

I mentioned that class of idle and extravagant men, some of whom were very brave leaders while others were their more cowardly followers. This class we compared to drones, the former endowed with stings, the latter stingless. —Quite correct.

Now these two groups cause disturbances in any city they inhabit, as phlegm and bile do in the body. The good physician therefore, and the lawgiver of a city, must, no less than the good beekeeper, take precautions ahead of time, in the first instance to prevent their presence, and if they should be present, to cut them out of the hive as quickly as possible, cells and all. —Yes, by Zeus, he must certainly do that.

Shall we take up the question in this way, so that we may see our way more clearly to decide what we want? —Which way?

Let us divide a democracy into three parts in our argument as it is in reality. One part is this class of idlers, and it grows here no less than in oligarchy because of the permissiveness. —That is so.

And it is much more bitter here than there. —How so?

There it is bitter because it is disdained but, as it is kept out of office, it is lacking in experience and does not become strong. In a democracy, however, this class is the presiding element, with few exceptions. The most bitter speak and act, while the rest of them settle, buzzing around the speakers' platform, and will not tolerate the opposition of another speaker so that everything is managed by them in this city, with a few exceptions. —That is certainly so.

Then there is also the following group which can be distinguished in the crowd. —Which is that?

When everybody is trying to make money, those who are the most steady by nature generally become the wealthiest. —Probably so.

They would provide the most and the most easily available honey for the drones. —Yes, for how can one take honey from those who have very little?

So I think that these rich are called the drones' pasture. —Pretty well.

The people would be a third part, those who work with their own hands. They take no part in politics and have but few possessions. This is the most numerous and the most powerful element in a democracy whenever they are assembled.

It is, he said, but they are not willing to gather often, unless they get a share of the honey.

They always do take a share, I said, as much as their leaders can give them as they take it from the prosperous and distribute it to the people, though they keep the greater share of it to themselves. —Yes, he said, that is how the people get their share.

And those from whom it is taken are compelled to defend themselves by speaking and acting before the people in so far as they can. —Of course.

They are accused by the other side of plotting against the people and of being oligarchs, even when they have no desire for revolution. —Quite so.

So in the end, when they see the people trying to harm them, not of its own free will but through ignorance and being deceived by their accusers, then indeed they truly do become oligarchs, not willingly but that drone stings them with this evil too. —Definitely.

Then there are impeachments and judgments and trials on both sides. —Quite.

Now the people are always in the habit of elevating one man as their champion above all others, and they nurture him and make him great. —That is the custom.

It is clear that this championship of the people is the one and only root from which dictatorship and the dictator can grow....

Shall we now, I said, describe the happiness of the man, and of the city in which such a mortal arises? —Certainly, let us describe it.

Will he not, during the first days, and indeed for some time, smile in welcome at anyone he meets. He says he is no dictator and makes many promises both in private and in public. He has freed people from debt and redistributed the land to the people and to his own entourage, and he pretends to be gracious and gentle to all. —He must do that.

But I think that when he has dealt with his outside enemies by making peace with some and destroying others, and all is quiet on the external fronts, the first thing he always does is to stir up a war, so that the people shall feel the need of a leader. —That is likely.

Also in order that by paying war taxes they become poor and are compelled to concern themselves with their daily needs and thus are less likely to plot against him. —Obviously.

Besides, if he suspects some of having thoughts of freedom and of not favouring his rule, he would have an excuse to destroy them by giving them up to the enemy. For all these reasons a dictator must always stir up war. —He must.

And because he does this, he is the more readily hated by the citizens? —Of course.

Then some of those who have helped to establish the dictatorship and hold positions of power speak freely to him and to each other; that is, the bravest of them reproach him for what is happening. —That is likely.

The dictator must eliminate them all if he is intending to rule, until he leaves no one who is of any account among his friends or his enemies. —Clearly.

He must therefore keep a sharp lookout for anyone who is brave, proud, wise, or rich; so happy is he that he must be the enemy of them all, whether he wants to be or not, and plot against them until he has purged the city. —A fine purge!

Yes, I said, the opposite of that which the physicians apply to the body. They eliminate the worst and leave the best, he does the opposite. —He is compelled to do this, it seems, if he is to rule.

A happy kind of necessity! said I, which binds him and orders him to live with a crowd of inferior people and to be hated by them, or not live at all. —That is how he must live.

And the more his actions make the citizens hate him, the more numerous and loyal a bodyguard he needs. —Of course.

Who will these loyal people be, and where will he get them from?

They will come flocking of their own accord, he said, if he pays them.

Drones by the dog! I think you mean foreign drones, I said, from all kinds of places. —You are right.

But whom will he get from the city? For he would not want to... —Do what?

Deprive citizens of their slaves by freeing them and enlisting them in his bodyguard.

He certainly will, he said, since they will also be the most loyal to him.

What a blessed sort of person you make the dictator out to be, I said, if those are the kind of friends and loyal followers he has, after doing away with his earlier ones. —Anyway, that is the kind he has.

These friends admire him, I said, and the new citizens associate with him while the good citizens hate him and avoid him. —How could they not do so?

It is not for nothing that tragedy as a whole is thought to be wise, and Euripides is outstanding in it. —How so?

Because he said, and this shows a subtle mind, that "dictators are wise who keep company with the wise"; and he clearly meant that the wise are the company they keep. Also, he said, he eulogizes dictatorship as something godlike, and both he and the other poets say many things like that.

Surely, I said, being wise, the tragic poets will forgive us and those whose government is close to ours, if we do not admit them into our city because they praise dictatorship.

I think, he said, that the more subtle among them will.

I believe, I said, that they go round the other cities, collect crowds, hire men with beautiful, resounding, and persuasive voices, and draw the cities to dictatorship and democracy. —They do indeed.

Besides this they receive pay and honours, especially from the dictators, as is natural, then from the democracies, but the higher they go on the ascending scale of governments, the more their honours fail, as if unable to keep up with them for lack of breath. —That is certainly true.

But, I said, we have digressed here. Let us say again from what source the dictator's army, that beautiful, numerous, and varied body which never remains the same, draws its sustenance.

Clearly, he said, if there are sacred treasures in the city, he will spend them, as well as the property of his victims, for as long as these last, thus necessitating smaller taxes from the people.

What when these give out?

Obviously, he said, he and his fellow revellers and companions and mistresses will have to be fed from his father's estate.

I understand, I said. You mean that the people, who fathered the dictatorship, will have to feed him and his companions. —They will certainly be compelled to do so.

How do you mean? said I. If the people get angry and say that it is not right for a young son to be kept by his father, but on the contrary for the father to be kept by the son, and that they did not father the dictatorship and put him in power, in order that, when he had grown great, they should be enslaved to their own slaves and feed him and his slaves and the other rabble; but they hoped that his championship would free them from the rich, the so-called best people in the city. They now order him and his companions to leave the city, like a father driving a son with his mob of fellow revellers from the house.

Then by Zeus, he said, the people will learn what kind of creature they fathered, welcomed, and caused to grow, and that they are the weaker trying to drive out the stronger.

How do you mean? I said. Will he dare to use violence against his father, and to strike him if he does not obey?

Yes, he said, after he has taken away his arms.

You are saying that the dictator is a parricide, I said, and a cruel nurse to old age. This is now an acknowledged tyranny and, as the saying goes, the people, in trying to avoid the smoke of servitude to free men, have fallen into the fire of having slaves as their masters, and, in the place of that vast and pure liberty, they have put upon themselves the harshest and most bitter slavery to slaves. That indeed is what happened.

Well then, I said, shall we not be justified in saying that we have adequately described how dictatorship evolves from democracy, and what its nature is when it has so evolved? —Quite adequately.

## ⇥ BOOK IX ⇤

### *Justice Benefits*

[ *The ninth book is devoted to a description of the dictatorial or tyrannical man. He is the completely unjust man whom Glaucon had challenged Socrates to put beside the just man in order to judge adequately which of the two was the happier. This judgment is given in this book.*

*It begins with a distinction between the necessary and unnecessary desires. The latter are the lawless desires which exist in almost every man and usually betray themselves only in sleep, but they rule in the soul of the dictatorial man who knows nothing of friendship and conceives all relationships between men as that between master and slave. Full of fears, surrounded by enemies, both city and individual are wretched indeed.*

*Of special interest is the discussion of pleasure. We learn that each part of the soul has its own proper pleasures which it can enjoy when the soul as a whole is governed by reason. When appetites rule, then in the resulting chaos no part can enjoy even its own legitimate pleasures.*

*There are three lives, the philosophic, the ambitious, and the appetitive, and each man believes his own life to be the most pleasant. The philosopher, however, is the best judge because he has some experience of the others' pleasures, whereas they have no experience of his. Moreover the means of judgment—intelligence and reasoned discourse—are peculiarly his.*

*Pleasure is not the mere absence of pain, but the pleasures of the ordinary man are always mixed with pain, unlike those of the philosopher which are more true, more real, and more lasting. By a somewhat acrobatic calculation Socrates finds that the dictatorship is 729 times more miserable than the kings of his ideal city.]*

588b   …Very well, I said. As we have come to this point in our discussion, let us take up again what was said at first, which has led us to this. It was said at some point that injustice was to the benefit of the completely unjust man who had a reputation for justice, was it not? —It certainly was.

Since we have fully agreed, I said, upon the effect of each, that is, of just and unjust behaviour, let us now talk to the man who maintains this point of view. —How?

Let us in our argument fashion an image of the soul, so that he may understand

c   the kind of thing he was saying. —What kind of image?

One of the kind that are told in ancient legends about creatures like the Chimera, Scylla, Cerberus, and many others in whose natures many different kinds had grown into one. —We are told of such creatures.

Fashion me then one kind of multiform beast with many heads, a ring of heads of both tame and wild animals, who is able to change these and grow them all out of himself.

d   A work for a clever modeller, he said. However, as words are more malleable than wax and such things, take it as fashioned.

Then one other form, that of a lion, and another of a man, but the first form of all is much the largest, and the second second. —That is easy and it is done.

Gather the three into one, so that they somehow grow together. —All right.

Model around them on the outside the appearance of being one, a man, so that anyone who cannot see what is inside but only the outside cover will think it is one creature, a man. —Done.

e

Let us now tell the one who maintains that injustice benefits this man, and that justice brings him no advantage, that his words simply mean that it benefits the man to feed the multiform beast well and make it strong, as well as the lion and all that pertains to him, but to starve and weaken the man within so that he is dragged along whithersoever one of the other two leads. He does not accustom one part to the other or make them friendly, but he leaves them alone to bite and fight and kill each other. —This is most certainly what one who praises injustice means.

589

On the other hand, one who maintains that justice is to our advantage would say that all our words and deeds would tend to make the man within the man the strongest. He would look after the many-headed beast as a farmer looks after his animals, fostering and domesticating the gentle heads and preventing the wild ones from growing. With the lion's nature as his ally, he will care for all of them and rear them by making them all friendly with each other and with himself. —This is most definitely the meaning of him who praises justice.

b

What is said of justice is true in every way, and what is said on the other side is false, whether one examines it from the point of view of pleasure, of good repute, or of advantage; whereas he who condemns justice has nothing sound to say, and he does not know what he is condemning. —I don't think he does at all.

c

Let us then gently persuade him—he is not willingly wrong—by asking him: "My good sir, should we not say that beautiful and ugly traditions have originated as follows: the beautiful are those which subordinate the beastlike parts of our nature to the human, or perhaps we should say to the divine, while the ugly enslave the gentler side to the wilder?" Will he agree or what? —He will agree if he takes my advice.

d

Can it benefit anyone, I said, to acquire gold unjustly if when he takes the gold he enslaves the best part of himself to the most vicious part? Or, if by taking the gold he should make a slave of his son or daughter in the house of wild and evil men, it would certainly not benefit him to acquire even a great deal of gold on those terms.

e

If then he enslaves the most divine part of himself to the most ungodly and disgusting part and feels no pity for it, is he not wretched and is he not accepting a bribe of gold for a more terrible death than Eriphyle when she accepted the necklace for her husband's life? —Much more, said Glaucon. I will answer for him.

Then do you think that licentiousness has long been condemned because in a licentious man that terrible, that big, that multiform beast is let loose more than it should be? —Clearly.

Obstinacy and irritability are condemned whenever the lion and snake-like part is increased and stretched disproportionately? —Surely.

Are luxury and softness condemned because the slackening and looseness of this same part produce cowardice? —Of course.

And do not flattery and meanness come when this same spirited part is subordinated to the turbulent beast which accustoms it from youth to being abused for the sake of money and the beast's insatiability, and to become an ape instead of a lion? —Certainly.

Why do you think the mechanical work of one's own hands is subject to reproach? Shall we say that it is so only when the best part of one's soul is naturally weak and cannot rule the animals within but pampers them and can learn nothing except ways to flatter them. —That is likely.

Therefore, in order that such a man be ruled by a principle similar to that which rules the best man, we say he must be enslaved to the best man, who has a divine ruler within himself. It is not to harm the slave that we believe he must be ruled, as Thrasymachus thought subjects should be, but because it is better for everyone to be ruled by divine intelligence. It is best that he should have this within himself, but if he has not, then it must be imposed from outside, so that, as far as possible, we should all be alike and friendly and governed by the same principle. —Quite right.

This, I said, is clearly the aim of the law which is the ally of everyone in the city, and of our rule over children. We should not allow them to be free until we establish a government within them, as we did in the city, fostering the best in them with what is best in ourselves and securing within the child a similar guardian and ruler, and then let him go free. —The law does make that clear.

How then and by what argument can we maintain, Glaucon, that injustice, licentiousness, and shameful actions are profitable, since they make a man more wicked, though he may acquire more riches or some other form of power? —We cannot.

Or that to do wrong without being discovered and not to pay the penalty is profitable? Does not one who remains undiscovered become even more vicious, whereas within the man who is discovered and punished the beast is calmed down and tamed; his whole soul, settling into its best nature, as it acquires moderation and justice together with wisdom, attains a more honoured condition than a strong, beautiful, and healthy body, in so far as the soul is to be honoured more than the body. —Most certainly.

The man of sense then will direct all his efforts to this end; firstly, he will prize such studies as make his soul like this, and he will disregard the others. —Obviously.

Then, I said, he will see to his bodily condition and nurture it in such a way that he does not entrust it to the irrational pleasure of the beast, turn himself that way, and live on that level. It is not even health he aims at, nor does he consider it most important that he should be strong, healthy, or beautiful, unless he acquires moderation as a result, but he will cultivate harmony in his body for the sake of consonance in his soul. —That is altogether true, if he is truly to be a cultured man.

To the same end, there will be order and measure in his acquisition of wealth. He will not be panicked by the numbers of the crowd into accepting their idea of blessedness and increase his wealth without limit, and so have unlimited ills. —I do not think he will do so.

Looking to the government within, I said, he will guard against disturbances being caused there by too much wealth or too little, and he will direct, as far as he can, both the acquiring and spending of his possessions. —Very definitely.

He will have the same end in view as regards honours. He will share in, and willingly taste, those which he believes will make him a better man, but he will avoid both public and private honours which he believes will destroy the existing condition of his soul.

He will not then, he said, if that is his concern, be willing to go into politics.

Yes, by the dog, he will, I said, at least in his own kind of city, but not in his fatherland perhaps, unless divine good luck should be his.

I understand, he said, you mean in the city which we were founding and described, our city of words, for I do not believe it exists anywhere on earth.

Perhaps, I said, it is a model laid up in heaven, for him who wishes to look upon, and as he looks, set up the government of his soul. It makes no difference whether it exists anywhere or will exist. He would take part in the public affairs of that city only, not of any other. —That is probable, he said.

111

## ⇢ BOOK X ⇠

### The Myth of Er

[*The main argument of The Republic has now been completed, and justice has definitely been proved to bring happiness. The tenth book is a kind of addendum: the first half of it discusses poetry again in the light of the metaphysics and the psychology of the intervening books; then follows an argument professing to prove the immortality of the soul and finally, the myth of Er.*

*Socrates begins by confirming the ban on "imitative poetry" and by showing "imitations" to be at three removes from the truth, that is, from the Forms. It only imitates particulars, and indeed only their appearance. He illustrates this by the art of painting, but, he tells us, it is just as true of tragedy. The poet has no knowledge. The user of an instrument has knowledge, the maker of it has right opinion as he follows the user's instructions, the imitator has neither. Moreover, poetry appeals to the emotional part of the soul. We are emotionally affected in the theatre by the uncontrolled emotions of the characters; we identify with them and this is likely to cause us to lose control in our own lives. This applies to comedy as well as tragedy.*

*The argument for immortality is that anything which is not destroyed by its own peculiar evil cannot be destroyed at all and it is absurd to suggest that dying people become more unjust. The argument is not convincing, but it is hardly fair to condemn Plato for not finding a convincing proof of what no one has ever proved.*]

614 …So these are, I said, the prizes and rewards and gifts which gods and men give to the just man while he lives, in addition to those which justice itself provides for him. —They are fine and lasting awards.

They are as nothing in number and magnitude compared with those that await each of the two after death. These should be heard, in order that both

b should receive in full what the argument owes them. —Tell us, he said, for there are few things I would more gladly hear.

It is not a tale of Alcinous I shall tell you, but that of a brave man, Er, the son of Armenias, a Pamphylian by race who once died in war. When the dead were picked up ten days later, putrefaction had already set in but his corpse was quite fresh. He was picked up and taken home and preparations were made for his funeral. On the twelfth day, as he was already laid out on the funeral pyre, he revived.

c When he had revived he told what he had seen yonder. He said that after his soul had left him it travelled with many others until they came to a marvellous place, where there were two openings side by side into the earth, and opposite them two others upward into heaven, and between them sat judges. These, when they had given judgment, ordered the just to go upward through the heavens by the opening on the right, and they attached signs of the judgment on them in front. The unjust they ordered to travel downward by the opening on the left with signs of all their deeds on their back. When Er himself came forward they told him that he was to be a messenger to mankind of what happened there, and that he was to listen and to observe everything in the place. He said he saw souls leaving by either opening into the heavens and into the earth after their judgment. As for the other two openings, from one souls emerged from the earth covered with dust and dirt, by the other souls came down from heaven clean. And all the time those who arrived appeared to have been on a long journey; they gladly went and camped in the meadow, like a festival crowd. Those who knew each other exchanged greetings and enquiries. If they had come up from the earth they asked what happened in the other place, and if they came from heaven what had happened to the others. They recounted it to each other, those from the earth wailing and weeping as they recalled all they had suffered and seen on their journey below the earth—it lasted a thousand years—while those who came down from heaven told how well they had fared and the incredibly beautiful sights they had seen. There was much to tell, Glaucon, and it took a long time, but the main point was this: for all the wrongs they had done to any person they paid a tenfold penalty one after the other, that is, once in every century of their journey, as human life is reckoned of that length, so that they should pay a tenfold price for every injustice. If, for example, some of them had caused many deaths by betraying a city or an army and had thrown many people into slavery, or had been accomplices in other misdeeds, they had to suffer ten times the pain they had caused to each individual. Then again, if they had done good deeds and had become just and pious, they would receive a reward on the same scale. He said some other things about the stillborn and those who had lived but a short time, but these are not worth mentioning. He also spoke of even greater penalties or rewards for piety and impiety toward the gods and parents, and for the murder of kindred.

For he said he was present when a man was asked where the great Ardiaius was. This Ardiaius was said to have been dictator in a city of Pamphylia a thousand years before, had killed his father and his elder brother, and committed many other impious deeds. Er said he heard the answer: "He has not come, and never will, for this was one of the dreadful sights we saw: when we came near the opening on our way out after all our sufferings, we suddenly saw him and others; most of them were dictators but there were some private people who had been great sinners. They thought they were now going to get out but the opening did not admit them; it roared whenever one of those incurably wicked men, or someone who had not paid a sufficient penalty, tried to come out, and then, he said, some savage men, all fiery to look at, who were standing by and recognised the road, took hold of them and led them away. They bound the feet, hands, and head of Adriaius and others, threw them down and beat them, took them out of our path and by the side of the road, tortured them on thorny bushes, and indicated to those who were continually passing by why this was done, and that they would be led away and dropped into Tartarus." Of their many fears, he said that this was the greatest, lest the roar should be heard as each of them came up, and each was immensely relieved if silence greeted him. Such were the penalties and retributions and the rewards corresponding to them.

When those in the meadow had each been there seven days, on the eighth they had to get up and go on a journey, and on the fourth day of that journey they came to a place where they could look down from above upon a light stretching straight through the whole of heaven and earth like a column, very like a rainbow but brighter and more pure. They went on and arrived there after another day and from there in the middle of the light they saw the extremities of the bonds stretched from heaven, for the light holds together its whole revolution in the same way as the cables underpinning a trireme. From the extremities hangs the spindle of Necessity, by means of which all the orbits revolve; its staff and book are made of adamant, whereas in the whorl adamant is mixed with other materials. The nature of the whorl was as follows:

Its shape was like that of an ordinary whorl, but we must understand Er's account of the parts which composed it. It was as if in one big whorl which had been thoroughly scooped out, another smaller one had been closely fitted like boxes fitting into one another, so there was a third and a fourth and four more, eight whorls altogether inside one another, their rims showing in a circle and a continuous surface of one whorl round the shaft which has driven right through the middle of the eighth circle.

The first and outside whorl had the widest circular rim, that of the sixth was second in width, the fourth was third, the eighth was fourth, the seventh was fifth, the fifth was sixth, the third was seventh, and the second was eighth. The circle of the largest was spangled; the circle of the seventh was the brightest; that of the eighth took its colour from the brightest; the seventh, the second, and the fifth were about equal in brightness, more yellow than the others; the third was the whitest in colour; the fourth was rather red; and the sixth was second in whiteness. The whole spindle turned at the same speed, but as the whole turned the inner circles were carried round at a slower pace in a motion contrary to that of the whole. Of these the eighth was the swiftest; then second were seventh, sixth, and fifth at an equal pace; third in speed as it appeared to them as it turned was the fourth; fourth was the third; and the second was fifth. The spindle turned on the knees of Necessity. On each of the circles stood a Siren who was carried along with it and uttered one note, and the eight notes made up a concordance. Three others were sitting around at equal distances: the daughters of Necessity, the Fates, dressed in white with garlands on their heads; Lachesis and Clotho and Atropos; and they sang to the music of the Sirens—Lachesis sang of the past, Clotho of the present, and Atropos of the future. Clotho with her right hand touched the outer part of the spindle and helped it turn, and then left off for a time; Atropos did the same to the inner circles with her left hand; Lachesis would help both motions in turn, one with one hand and one with the other.

When the souls arrived, they had to go to Lachesis right away, and an interpreter of the divine first arranged them in order, then took from Lachesis a number of lots and samples of lives, ascended a high platform and spoke: "This is the message of Lachesis, the maiden daughter of Necessity. Souls of a day, this is the beginning of another mortal round which will bring death. Your guardian spirit will not be assigned to you, you will choose him. Let him who has the first lot be the first to choose a life which will of necessity be his. Virtue knows no master, each will possess it in greater or lesser degree according as he honours or disdains it. The responsibility is his who makes the choice, the god has not." When he had said this he threw the lots to them all and each one picked up that which fell at his feet, except Er who was not allowed to do so. As each man picked it up his place in the order of choice was made clear to him. Next after this the samples of lives were placed on the ground before them, far more numerous than the souls present. They were of all kinds, for the lives of animals were there as well as all kinds of human lives. There were dictatorships, some that lasted throughout life, others that lasted half way through and ended in poverty, exile, and beggary. There were lives of men famous for their physical powers, for beauty and strength and athletic success, others famed for high birth and the virtues of ancestors, also the lives of men of no fame at all for these things, and the same with lives of women. The state

617

b

c

d

e

618

b

of the soul was not included, for this unavoidably depended upon the kind of life one chose. The other qualities were mixed with wealth and poverty, with health and disease, and some too were moderate in these respects.

c
d

It is here, my dear Glaucon, that man faces every danger, and because of this we should be most concerned that each of us neglect other studies in order to seek for and learn the knowledge which will enable him to discover who will enable him to distinguish the good life from the bad, and always to make the best possible choice everywhere. He should think over all that has now been said about the nature of the virtuous life, separately and together, and know what good or evil physical beauty can accomplish mixed with wealth and poverty and with what state of the soul.

e

619

b

He should know the effects of high or low birth, of private life and public office, of physical strength or weakness, of ease and difficulty in learning, of all such things as affect the soul by nature or as acquired characteristics, and what they achieve when mixed with one another, so that with all this in mind he should be able to make a thoughtful choice, while considering the nature of the soul, between the better life and the worse. He will call the worse that which leads the soul to being more unjust, the better that which leads it to being more just; for we have seen that this is the best choice for a man, both in life and after. Everything else he will ignore. One should hold on to this belief with adamantine determination as one goes down to the underworld, so that there too one should not be dazzled by wealth and similar evils and should not stumble into a dictator's life and actions of that kind, and perform many incurable evils and suffer even worse oneself, but know how always to choose the mean in such lives, avoid excesses both ways, and live as far as possible such a life forever. That is where a man will find the greatest happiness.

c

Then our messenger from the other world reported that the interpreter spoke as follows: "Even for the one who comes last a life which is not bad but satisfactory is available if he chooses intelligently and lives consistently. Let not the first be careless in his choice nor the last be discouraged." When the interpreter had thus spoken, Er said, the one who came up first chose the mightiest dictatorship. In his folly and greed he chose without a careful look and did not notice that he was fated to devour his own children and other evils, but when he examined his chosen life at leisure, he beat his breast and bemoaned his choice, nor did he abide by the warning of the interpreter for he did not blame himself for these evils, but fortune and the gods, and everyone but himself. He was one of those who had come down from heaven; he had lived his previous life in a well-ordered city, and had been virtuous by habit without philosophy. One might say that among those who were caught that way the souls who had come down from heaven were not in a minority because they had no experience of evil. The majority of those who had come up from the earth, having suffered themselves and seen others suffer, were in no rush to make their choice. There was thus an interchange of evils and blessings for the majority of souls, and also because of the chance of the lot.

d

Therefore if someone, whenever he comes to live here on earth, pursues philosophy soundly, and the lot of the choice does not place him among the last, he is likely to be happy here, according to the message received from the other world, and his journey from here to there and back again will not be along the rough path below the earth, but along the smooth and heavenly.

e

Er said that it was a spectacle worth seeing how the souls each chose their lives. It was pitiful, ridiculous, and surprising. For the most part their choice depended upon the character of their previous life. He said that he saw the soul which had once been that of Orpheus choosing the life of a swan in his hatred of women; because of his death at their hands he did not want to be born of a woman. He saw the soul of Thamyris choosing the life of a nightingale, and on the other hand a swan changing to choose the life of a man, and so with other musical birds. The twentieth soul chose the life of a lion. This was the soul of Ajax, son of Telamon, avoiding human life because he remembered the judgment about the armour. The soul which came after him was that of Agamemnon. His sufferings too made him hate the human race and he changed to the life of an eagle. The lot had assigned a place about the middle to the soul of Atalanta; as she saw great honours being paid to an athlete she could not pass it by and chose it. After her he saw the soul of Epeius the son of Panopeus entering the life of a craftswoman. Far on among the last the soul of the ridiculous Thersites entered the life of a monkey. By chance the soul of Odysseus had been allotted the very last place to make its choice. Remembering its former ills and taking a rest from ambition it went around for a long time looking for the quiet life of a private individual and had difficulty finding it as it lay neglected by everybody. He gladly chose it and said he would have made the same choice if he had been first. As for the others, animals chose men's lives and each other's, the unjust ones choosing the life of wild beasts, the just ones choosing the tame lives, and all sorts of mixtures occurred.

620

b

c

d

After all the souls had chosen their lives, they went forward to Lachesis in the same order in which they had chosen, and she sent with each the genius he had chosen as guardian of his life and to fulfill his choice. This genius first led the soul to Clotho, under her hand, and the rotation of the spindle confirming the fate which the lot and his choice had given him. After contacting her he led the soul to the spinning of Atropos, making what had been spun irreversible. Thence they went under the throne of Necessity without turning around and after passing through there, when all had gone through, they all went to the plain of forgetfulness in burning, choking, terrible heat, for it was empty of trees and of the plants that grow from the earth. There they camped, as it was now evening, by the stream of Oblivion whose water no vessel can hold.

All had to drink a measure of this water, but those who were not preserved by wisdom drank more, and as each drank they forgot everything. After they had slept and it was the middle of the night, there was a clap of thunder and an earthquake, and suddenly they were carried upward to birth in different directions, rushing like stars. Er himself was forbidden to drink of the water. He did not know how and in what way he arrived back in his body, but looking up suddenly he saw himself lying on the pyre at dawn.

And so, Glaucon, the story was preserved and not lost. It could save us if we believe it, and we shall safely cross the stream of Forgetfulness and not be defiled in our soul. If we are persuaded by me to believe that the soul is immortal and that it can endure all evils and all blessings, we shall always hold on to the upward journey and we shall in every way practise justice with wisdom, in order that we may be at peace with ourselves and with the gods while we remain here on earth, and in order that afterwards we may receive the rewards of justice like the victors at the games who collect their pay, and may fare well both here and on the thousand-year journey we have described.

# ARISTOTLE

*Aristotle (384-322 B.C.) was born not in Athens but in Stagira, a town near Macedonia. His father was a physician at the court of Macedonia. At the age of 17 Aristotle went to Plato's Academy and studied there for 20 years. After Plato's death, Aristotle left Athens for ten years. During this time he tutored for a short period Alexander, the young heir to the Macedonian Kingdom. Eventually, Aristotle returned to Athens and established his own school, the Lyceum. When Alexander the Great died in 323 B.C. there were strong anti-Macedonian sentiments in Athens, and Aristotle left for Chalcis where he died.*

*The scope of Aristotle's work has not been surpassed. He wrote separate treatises on physics, biology, logic, psychology, metaphysics and philosophy, political philosophy and ethics, and aesthetics and literary criticism. The power and scope of Aristotle's work was so admired in the Middle Ages that he was called simply "The Philosopher."*

*The* Nicomachean Ethics *and* The Politics *together form Aristotle's greatest work. Whereas Plato's* The Republic *is a tightly constructed work of art, Aristotle's writings take the form of a series of lectures and an encyclopedic reference work for students.*

— J.M.P.

# NICOMACHEAN ETHICS

## ＋ BOOK ONE ＋

## The Goal of Human Life

### *1. Every human action aims at some end, goal, or good.*

1094a  Every craft and every investigation, and likewise every action and decision, seems to aim at some good; hence the good has been well described as that at which everything aims.

However, there is an apparent difference among the ends aimed at. For the end is sometimes an activity, sometimes a product beyond the activity; and when there is an end beyond the action, the product is by nature better than the activity.

Since there are many actions, crafts and sciences, the ends turn out to be many as well; for health is the end of medicine, a boat of boatbuilding, victory of generalship, and wealth of household management.

But whenever any of these sciences are subordinate to some one capacity—as e.g. bridlemaking and every other science producing equipment for horses are subordinate to horsemanship, while this and every action in warfare are in turn subordinate to generalship, and in the same way other sciences are subordinate to further ones— in each of these the end of the ruling science is more choiceworthy than all the ends subordinate to it, since it is the end for which those ends are also pursued. And here it does not matter whether the ends of the actions are the activities themselves, or some product beyond them, as in the sciences we have mentioned.

### *2. The science that studies the good for man is political science.*

Suppose, then, that (a) there is some end of the things we pursue in our actions which we wish for because of itself, and because of which we wish for the other things; and (b) we do not choose everything because of something else, since (c) if we do, it will go on without limit, making desire empty and futile; then clearly (d) this end will be the good, i.e. the best good.

---

*Nicomachean Ethics*, by Aristotle, translated by Terence Irwin. Indianapolis: Hackett Publishing Company (1985). Reprinted by permission.

**N.B.** The book and chapter titles are by J.M.P.

Then surely knowledge of this good is also of great importance for the conduct of our lives, and if, like archers, we have a target to aim at, we are more likely to hit the right mark. If so, we should try to grasp, in outline at any rate, what the good is, and which science or capacity is concerned with it.

It seems to concern the most controlling science, the one that, more than any other, is the ruling science. And political science apparently has this character.

(1) For it is the one that prescribes which of the sciences ought to be studied in cities, and which ones each class in the city should learn, and how far.

1094b

(2) Again, we see that even the most honoured capacities, e.g. generalship, household management and rhetoric, are subordinate to it.

(3) Further, it uses the other sciences concerned with action, and moreover legislates what must be done and what avoided.

Hence its end will include the ends of the other sciences, and so will be the human good.

[This is properly called political science;] for though admittedly the good is the same for a city as for an individual, still the good of the city is apparently a greater and more complete good to acquire and preserve. For while it is satisfactory to acquire and preserve the good even for an individual, it is finer and more divine to acquire and preserve it for a people and for cities. And so, since our investigation aims at these [goods, for an individual and for a city], it is a sort of political science.

### 3. *The study of politics cannot be an exact science.*

Our discussion will be adequate if its degree of clarity fits the subject-matter; for we should not seek the same degree of exactness in all sorts of arguments alike, any more than in the products of different crafts.

Moreover, what is fine and what is just, the topics of inquiry in political science, differ and vary so much that they seem to rest on convention only, not on nature. Goods, however, also vary in the same sort of way, since they cause harm to many people; for it has happened that some people have been destroyed because of their wealth, others because of their bravery.

Since these, then, are the sorts of things we argue from and about, it will be satisfactory if we can indicate the truth roughly and in outline; since [that is to say] we argue from and about what holds good usually [but not universally], it will be satisfactory if we can draw conclusions of the same sort.

Each of our claims, then, ought to be accepted in the same way [as claiming to hold good usually], since the educated person seeks exactness in each area to the extent that the nature of the subject allows; for apparently it is just as mistaken to demand demonstrations from a rhetorician as to accept [merely] persuasive arguments from a mathematician.

1095a    Further, each person judges well what he knows, and is a good judge about that; hence the good judge in a particular area is the person educated in that area, and the unconditionally good judge is the person educated in every area.

This is why a youth is not a suitable student of political science; for he lacks experience of the actions in life which political science argues from and about.

Moreover, since he tends to be guided by his feelings, his study will be futile and useless; for its end is action, not knowledge. And here it does not matter whether he is young in years or immature in character, since the deficiency does not depend on age, but results from being guided in his life and in each of his pursuits by his feelings; for an immature person, like an incontinent person, gets no benefit from his knowledge.

If, however, we are guided by reason in forming our desires and in acting, then this knowledge will be of great benefit.

These are the preliminary points about the student, about the way our claims are to be accepted, and about what we intend to do....

## 7. The good for man is happiness.

1097a    But let us return once again to the good we are looking for, and consider just what it could be, since it is apparently one thing in one action or craft, and another thing in another; for it is one thing in medicine, another in generalship, and so on for the rest.

What, then, is the good in each of these cases? Surely it is that for the sake of which the other things are done; and in medicine this is health, in generalship victory, in housebuilding a house, in another case something else, but in every action and decision it is the end, since it is for the sake of the end that everyone does the other things.

And so, if there is some end of everything that is pursued in action, this will be the good pursued in action; and if there are more ends than one, these will be the goods pursued in action.

Our argument has progressed, then, to the same conclusion [as before, that the highest end is the good]; but we must try to clarify this still more.

Though apparently there are many ends, we choose some of them, e.g. wealth, flutes and, in general, instruments, because of something else; hence it is clear that not all ends are complete. But the best good is apparently something complete. Hence, if only one end is complete, this will be what we are looking for; and if more than one are complete, the most complete of these will be what we are looking for.

An end pursued in itself, we say, is more complete than an end pursued because of something else; and an end that is never choiceworthy because of something else is more complete than ends that are choiceworthy both in themselves and because of this end; and hence an end that is always [choiceworthy, and also] choiceworthy in itself, never because of something else, is unconditionally complete.

Now happiness more than anything else seems unconditionally complete, since we always [choose it, and also] choose it because of itself, never because of something else.

Honour, pleasure, understanding and every virtue we certainly choose because of themselves, since we would choose each of them even if it had no further result, but we also choose them for the sake of happiness, supposing that through them we shall be happy. Happiness, by contrast, no one ever chooses for their sake, or for the sake of anything else at all.

The same conclusion [that happiness is complete] also appears to follow from self-sufficiency, since the complete good seems to be self-sufficient.

Now what we count as self-sufficient is not what suffices for a solitary person by himself, living an isolated life, but what suffices also for parents, children, wife and in general for friends and fellow-citizens, since a human being is a naturally political [animal]. Here, however, we must impose some limit; for if we extend the good to parents' parents and children's children and to friends of friends, we shall go on without limit; but we must examine this another time.

Anyhow, we regard something as self-sufficient when all by itself it makes a life choiceworthy and lacking nothing; and that is what we think happiness does.

Moreover, we think happiness is most choiceworthy of all goods, since it is not counted as one good among many. If it were counted as one among many, then, clearly, we think that the addition of the smallest of goods would make it more choiceworthy; for [the smallest good] that is added becomes an extra quantity of goods [so creating a good larger than the original good], and the larger of two goods is always more choiceworthy. [But we do not think any addition can make happiness more choiceworthy; hence it is most choiceworthy.]

Happiness, then, is apparently something complete and self-sufficient, since it is the end of the things pursued in action.

But presumably the remark that the best good is happiness is apparently something [generally] agreed, and what we miss is a clearer statement of what the best good is.

Well, perhaps we shall find the best good if we first find the function of a human being. For just as the good, i.e. [doing] well, for a flautist, a sculptor, and every craftsman, and, in general, for whatever has a function and [characteristic] action, seems to depend on its function, the same seems to be true for a human being, if a human being has some function.

Then do the carpenter and the leatherworker have their functions and actions, while a human being has none, and is by nature idle, without any function? Or, just as eye, hand, foot and, in general, every [bodily] part apparently has its functions, may we likewise ascribe to a human being some function besides all of theirs?

What, then, could this be? For living is apparently shared with plants, but what we are looking for is the special function of a human being; hence we should set aside the life of nutrition and growth. The life next in order is some sort of life of sense-perception; but this too is apparently shared, with horse, ox and every animal. The remaining possibility, then, is some sort of life of action of the [part of the soul] that has reason.

1098a

Now this [part has two parts, which have reason in different ways], one as obeying the reason [in the other part], the other as itself having reason and thinking. [We intend both.] Moreover, life is also spoken of in two ways [as capacity and as activity], and we must take [a human being's special function to be] life as activity, since this seems to be called life to a fuller extent.

(a) We have found, then, that the human function is the soul's activity that expresses reason [as itself having reason] or requires reason [as obeying reason]. (b) Now the function of F, e.g. of a harpist, is the same in kind, so we say, as the function of an excellent F, e.g. an excellent harpist. (c) The same is true unconditionally in every case, when we add to the function the superior achievement that expresses the virtue; for a harpist's function, e.g. is to play the harp, and a good harpist's is to do it well. (d) Now we take the human function to be a certain kind of life, and take this life to be the soul's activity and actions that express reason. (e) [Hence by (c) and (d)] the excellent man's function is to do this finely and well. (f) Each function is completed well when its completion expresses the proper virtue. (g) Therefore [by (d), (e) and (f)] the human good turns out to be the soul's activity that expresses virtue.

124

And if there are more virtues than one, the good will express the best and most complete virtue. Moreover, it will be in a complete life. For one swallow does not make a spring, nor does one day; nor, similarly, does one day or a short time make us blessed and happy.

This, then, is a sketch of the good; for, presumably, the outline must come first, to be filled in later. If the sketch is good, then anyone, it seems, can advance and articulate it, and in such cases time is a good discoverer or [at least] a good co-worker. That is also how the crafts have improved, since anyone can add what is lacking [in the outline].

However, we must also remember our previous remarks, so that we do not look for the same degree of exactness in all areas, but the degree that fits the subject-matter in each area and is proper to the investigation. For the carpenter's and the geometer's inquiries about the right angle are different also; the carpenter's is confined to the right angle's usefulness for his work, whereas the geometer's concerns what, or what sort of thing, the right angle is, since he studies the truth. We must do the same, then, in other areas too, [seeking the proper degree of exactness], so that digressions do not overwhelm our main task.

Nor should we make the same demand for an explanation in all cases. Rather, in some cases it is enough to prove that something is true without explaining why it is true. This is so, e.g. with origins, where the fact that something is true is the first principle, i.e. the origin.                                                          1098b

Some origins are studied by means of induction, some by means of perception, some by means of some sort of habituation, and others by other means. In each case we should try to find them out by means suited to their nature, and work hard to define them well. For they have a great influence on what follows; for the origin seems to be more than half the whole, and makes evident the answer to many of our questions.

## ✦ BOOK FIVE ✦

### Justice and Injustice

### *1. What is meant by justice and injustice in persons or actions?*

The questions we must examine about justice and injustice are these: What sorts         1129a
of actions are they concerned with? What sort of mean is justice? What are the extremes between which justice is intermediate? Let us examine them by the same type of investigation that we used in the topics discussed before....

Let us, then, find the number of ways an unjust person is spoken of. Both the lawless person and the greedy and unfair person seem to be unjust; and so, clearly, both the lawful and the fair person will be just. Hence what is just will be both what is lawful and what is fair, and what is unjust will be both what is lawless and what is unfair.

Since the unjust person is greedy, he will be concerned with goods—not with all goods, but only with those involved in good and bad fortune, goods which are, [considered] unconditionally, always good, but for this or that person not always good. Though human beings pray for these and pursue them, they are wrong; the right thing is to pray that what is good unconditionally will also be good for us, but to choose [only] what is good for us.

Now the unjust person [who chooses these goods] does not choose more in every case; in the case of what is bad unconditionally he actually chooses less. But since what is less bad also seems to be good in a way, and greed aims at more of what is good, he seems to be greedy. In fact he is unfair; for unfairness includes [all these actions], and is a common feature [of his choice of the greater good and of the lesser evil].

Since, as we saw, the lawless person is unjustified and the lawful person is just, it clearly follows that whatever is lawful is in some way just; for the provisions of legislative science are lawful, and we say that each of them is just. Now in every matter they deal with the laws aim either at the common benefit of all, or at the benefit of those in control, whose control rests on virtue or on some other such basis. And so in one way what we call just is whatever produces and maintains happiness and its parts for a political community.

Now the law instructs us to do the actions of a brave person—not to leave the battle-line, e.g., or to flee, or to throw away our weapons; of a temperate person—not to commit adultery or wanton aggression; of a mild person—not to strike or revile another; and similarly requires actions that express the other virtues, and prohibits those that express the vices. The correctly established law does this correctly, and the less carefully framed one does this worse.

This type of justice, then, is complete virtue, not complete virtue unconditionally, but complete virtue in relation to another. And this is why justice often seems to be supreme among the virtues, and "neither the evening star nor the morning star is so marvellous," and the proverb says "And in justice all virtue is summed up."

Moreover, justice is complete virtue to the highest degree because it is the complete exercise of complete virtue. And it is the complete exercise because the person who has justice is able to exercise virtue in relation to another, not only in what concerns himself; for many are able to exercise virtue in their own concerns but unable in what relates to another.

And hence Bias seems to have been correct in saying that ruling will reveal the man, since a ruler is automatically related to another, and in a community. And for the same reason justice is the only virtue that seems to be another person's good, because it is related to another; for it does what benefits another, either the ruler or the fellow-member of the community.

1130a

The worst person, therefore, is the one who exercises his vice towards himself and his friends as well [as towards others]. And the best person is not the one who exercises virtue [only] towards himself, but the one who [also] exercises it in relation to another, since this is a difficult task.

This type of justice, then, is the whole, not a part, of virtue, and the injustice contrary to it is the whole, not a part, of vice.

At the same time our discussion makes clear the difference between virtue and this type of justice. For virtue is the same as justice, but what it is to be virtue is not the same as what it is to be justice. Rather, in so far as virtue is related to another, it is justice, and in so far as it is a certain sort of state unconditionally it is virtue.

## 2. What is special (particular) justice and injustice? Particular justice is either distributive or rectifying.

But we are looking for the type of justice, since we say there is one, that consists in a part of virtue, and correspondingly for the type of injustice that is a part [of vice].

Here is evidence that there is this type of justice and injustice:

First, if someone's activities express the other vices—if, e.g., cowardice made him throw away his shield, or irritability made him revile someone, or ungenerosity made him fail to help someone with money—what he does is unjust, but not greedy. But when one acts from greed, in many cases his action expresses none of these vices—certainly not all of them; but it still expresses some type of wickedness, since we blame him, and [in particular] it expresses injustice. Hence there is another type of injustice that is a part of the whole, and a way for a thing to be unjust that is a part of the whole that is contrary to law.

Moreover, if A commits adultery for profit and makes a profit, while B commits adultery because of his appetite, and spends money on it to his own loss, B seems intemperate rather than greedy, while A seems unjust, not intemperate. Clearly, then, this is because A acts to make a profit.

Further, we can refer every other unjust action to some vice—to intemperance if he committed adultery, to cowardice if he deserted his comrade in the battle-line, to anger if he struck someone. But if he made an [unjust] profit, we can refer it to no other vice except injustice.

Hence evidently (a) there is another type of injustice, special injustice, besides the whole of injustice; and (b) it is synonymous with the whole, since the definition is in the same genus. For (b) both have their area of competence in relation to another. But (a) special injustice is concerned with honour or wealth or safety, or whatever single name will include all these, and aims at the pleasure that results from making a profit; but the concern of injustice as a whole is whatever concerns the excellent person.

1130b

Clearly, then, there is more than one type of justice, and there is another type besides [the type that is] the whole of virtue; but we must still grasp what it is, and what sort of thing it is.

What is unjust is divided into what is lawless and what is unfair, and what is just into what is lawful and what is fair. The [general] injustice previously described, then, is concerned with what is lawless. But what is unfair is not the same as what is lawless, but related to it as part to whole, since whatever is unfair is lawless, but not everything lawless is unfair. Hence also the type of injustice and the way for a thing to be unjust [that expresses unfairness] are not the same as the type [that expresses lawlessness], but differ as parts from wholes. For this injustice [as unfairness] is a part of the whole of injustice, and similarly justice [as fairness] is a part of the whole of justice.

Hence we must describe special[1] [as well as general] justice and injustice, and equally this way for a thing to be just or unjust.

Let us, then, set to one side the type of justice and injustice that corresponds to the whole of virtue, justice being the exercise of the whole of virtue, and injustice of the whole of vice, in relation to another.

---

[1] [A better translation for "special" would be *particular*. —J.M.P.]

And it is evident how we must distinguish the way for a thing to be just or unjust that expresses this type of justice and injustice; for the majority of lawful actions, we might say, are the actions resulting from virtue as a whole. For the law instructs us to express each virtue, and forbids us to express each vice, in how we live. Moreover, the actions producing the whole of virtue are the lawful actions that the laws prescribe for education promoting the common good.

We must wait till later, however, to determine whether the education that makes an individual an unconditionally good man is a task for political science or for another science; for, presumably, being a good man is not the same as being every sort of good citizen.

Special justice, however, and the corresponding way for something to be just [must be divided].

One species is found in the distribution of honours or wealth or anything else that can be divided among members of a community who share in a political system; for here it is possible for one member to have a share equal or unequal to another's.

Another species concerns rectification in transactions. This species has two parts, since one sort of transaction is voluntary, and one involuntary. Voluntary transactions include selling, buying, lending, pledging, renting, depositing, hiring out—these are called voluntary because the origin of these transactions is voluntary. Some involuntary ones are secret, e.g. theft, adultery, poisoning, pimping, slave-deception, murder by treachery, false witness; others are forcible, e.g. assault, imprisonment, murder, plunder, mutilation, slander, insult.

1131a

### 3. *Distributive justice is proportionate.*

Since the unjust person is unfair, and what is unjust is unfair, there is clearly an intermediate between the unfair [extremes], and this is what is fair; for in any action where too much and too little are possible, the fair [amount] is also possible. And so if what is unjust is unfair, what is just is fair (*ison*), as seems true to everyone even without argument.

And since what is equal (*ison*) [and fair] is intermediate, what is just is some sort of intermediate. And since what is equal involves at least two things [equal to each other], it follows that what is just must be intermediate and equal, and related to some people. In so far as it is intermediate, it must be between too much and too little; in so far as it is equal, it involves two things; and in so far as it is just, it is just for some people. Hence what is just requires four things at least; the people for whom it is just are two, and the [equal] things that are involved are two.

Equality for the people involved will be the same as for the things involved, since [in a just arrangement] the relation between the people will be the same as the relation between the things involved. For if the people involved are not equal, they will not [justly] receive equal shares; indeed, whenever equals receive unequal shares, or unequals equal shares, in a distribution, that is the source of quarrels and accusations.

This is also clear from considering what fits a person's worth. For everyone agrees that what is just in distributions must fit some sort of worth, but what they call worth is not the same; supporters of democracy say it is free citizenship, some supporters of oligarchy say it is wealth, others good birth, while supporters of aristocracy say it is virtue.

Hence what is just [since it requires equal shares for equal people] is in some way proportionate....

## 6. *What is political justice? How is it different from family justice?*

1134a

We have previously described, then, the relation of reciprocity to what is just. We must now notice that we are looking not only for what is just unconditionally but also for what is just in a political association. This is found among associates in a life aiming at self-sufficiency, who are free and either proportionately or numerically equal.

Hence those who lack these features have nothing politically just in their relations, though they have something just in so far as it is similar [to what is politically just].

For what is just is found among those who have law in their relations. Where there is law, there is injustice, since the judicial process is judgment that distinguishes what is just from what is unjust. Where there is injustice there is also doing injustice, though where there is doing injustice there need not also be injustice. And doing injustice is awarding to oneself too many of the things that, [considered] unconditionally, are good, and too few of the things that, [considered] unconditionally, are bad.

1134b

This is why we allow only reason, not a human being, to be ruler; for a human being awards himself too many goods and becomes a tyrant, but a ruler is a guardian of what is just and hence of what is equal [and so must not award himself too many goods].

If a ruler is just, he seems to profit nothing by it. For since he does not award himself more of what, [considered] unconditionally, is good if it is not proportionate to him, he seems to labour for another's benefit; that is why justice is said, as we also remarked before, to be another person's good. Hence some payment [for ruling] should be given; this is honour and privilege, and the people who are unsatisfied by these are the ones who become tyrants.

What is just for a master and a father is similar to this, not the same. For there is no unconditional injustice in relation to what is one's own; one's own possession, or one's child until it is old enough and separated, is as though it were a part of oneself, and no one decides to harm himself. Hence there is no injustice in relation to them, and so nothing politically unjust or just either. For we found that what is politically just must conform to law, and apply to those who are naturally suited for law, hence to those who have equality in ruling and being ruled. [Approximation to this equality] explains why relations with a wife more than with children or possessions allow something to count as just—for that is what is just in households; still, this too is different from what is politically just.

## 7. Political justice may be derived from natural law, or from civil law and convention.

One part of what is politically just is natural, and the other part legal. What is natural is what has the same validity everywhere alike, independent of its seeming so or not. What is legal is what originally makes no difference [whether it is done] one way or another, but makes a difference whenever people have laid down the rule—e.g. that a mina is the price of a ransom, or that a goat rather than two sheep should be sacrificed; and also laws passed for particular cases, e.g. that sacrifices should be offered to Brasidas,[2] and enactments by decree.

Now it seems to some people that everything just is merely legal, since what is natural is unchangeable and equally valid everywhere—fire, e.g, burns both here and in Persia—while they see that what is just changes [from city to city].

This is not so, though in a way it is so. With us, though presumably not at all with the gods, there is such a thing as what is natural, but still all is changeable; despite the change there is such a thing as what is natural and what is not.

---

2 [Brasidas was a Spartan general who after his death received sacrifices in Amphipolis as a liberator; his cult is introduced as an example of a strictly local observance initiated by decree.]

What sort of thing that [is changeable and hence] admits of being otherwise is natural, and what sort is not natural, but legal and conventional, if both natural and legal are changeable? It is clear in other cases also, and the same distinction [between the natural and the unchangeable] will apply; for the right hand, e.g., is naturally superior, even though it is possible for everyone to become ambidextrous.

1135a    The sorts of things that are just by convention and expediency are like measures. For measures for wine and for corn are not of equal size everywhere, but in wholesale markets they are bigger, and in retail smaller. Similarly, the things that are just by human [enactment] and not by nature differ from place to place, since political systems also differ; still, only one system is by nature the best everywhere....

## ⇒ BOOK EIGHT ⇐

### Kinds of Friendships and Politics

*1. Friendship is necessary for a full life and is superior to political justice.*

1155a    After that the next topic to discuss is friendship; for it is a virtue, or involves virtue, and besides is most necessary for our life.

For no one would choose to live without friends even if he had all the other goods. For in fact rich people and holders of powerful positions, even more than other people, seem to need friends. For how would one benefit from such prosperity if one had no opportunity for beneficence, which is most often displayed, and most highly praised, in relation to friends? And how would one guard and protect prosperity without friends, when it is all the more precarious the greater it is? In poverty also, and in the other misfortunes, people think friends are the only refuge.

Moreover, the young need it to keep them from error. The old need it to care for them and support the actions that fail because of weakness. And those in their prime need it, to do fine actions; for "when two go together ...," they are more capable of understanding and acting.

Further, a parent would seem to have a natural friendship for a child, and a child for a parent, not only among human beings but also among birds and most kinds of animals. Members of the same race, and human beings most of all, have a natural friendship for each other; that is why we praise friends of humanity. And in our travels we can see how every human being is akin and beloved to a human being.

Moreover, friendship would seem to hold cities together, and legislators would seem to be more concerned about it than about justice. For concord would seem to be similar to friendship and they aim at concord above all, while they try above all to expel civil conflict, which is enmity.

Further, if people are friends, they have no need of justice, but if they are just they need friendship in addition; and the justice that is most just seems to belong to friendship....

### 3. There are three kinds of friendship: utility, pleasure, and good.

... Hence friendship has three species, corresponding to the three objects of love. For each object of love has a corresponding type of mutual loving, combined with awareness of it, and those who love each other wish goods to each other in so far as they love each other.

1156a

Those who love each other for utility love the other not in himself, but in so far as they gain some good for themselves from him. The same is true of those who love for pleasure; for they like a witty person not because of his character, but because he is pleasant to themselves.

And so those who love for utility or pleasure are fond of a friend because of what is good or pleasant for themselves, not in so far as the beloved is who he is, but in so far as he is useful or pleasant.

Hence these friendships as well [as the friends] are coincidental, since the beloved is loved not in so far as he is who he is, but in so far as he provides some good or pleasure.

And so these sorts of friendships are easily dissolved, when the friends do not remain similar [to what they were]; for if someone is no longer pleasant or useful, the other stops loving him.

What is useful does not remain the same, but is different at different times. Hence, when the cause of their being friends is removed, the friendship is dissolved too, on the assumption that the friendship aims at these [useful results]. This sort of friendship seems to arise especially among older people, since at that age they pursue what is advantageous, not what is pleasant, and also among those in their prime or youth who pursue what is expedient.

Nor do such people live together very much. For sometimes they do not even find each other pleasant. Hence they have no further need to meet in this way if they are not advantageous [to each other]; for each finds the other pleasant [only] to the extent that he expects some good from him. The friendship of hosts and guests is taken to be of this type too.

The cause of friendship between young people seems to be pleasure. For their lives are guided by their feelings, and they pursue above all what is pleasant for themselves and what is near at hand. But as they grow up [what they find] pleasant changes too. Hence they are quick to become friends, and quick to stop; for their friendship shifts with [what they find] pleasant, and the change in such pleasure is quick. Young people are prone to erotic passion, since this mostly follows feelings, and is caused by pleasure; that is why they love and quickly stop, often changing in a single day.

1156b

These people wish to spend their days together and to live together; for this is how they gain [the good things] corresponding to their friendship.

But complete friendship is the friendship of good people similar in virtue; for they wish goods in the same way to each other in so far as they are good, and they are good in themselves. [Hence they wish goods to each other for each other's own sake.] Now those who wish goods to their friend for the friend's own sake are friends most of all; for they have this attitude because of the friend himself, not coincidentally. Hence these people's friendship lasts as long as they are good; and virtue is enduring.

Each of them is both good unconditionally and good for his friend, since good people are both unconditionally good and advantageous for each other. They are pleasant in the same ways too, since good people are pleasant both unconditionally and for each other. [They are pleasant for each other] because each person finds his own actions and actions of that kind pleasant, and the actions of good people are the same or similar.

It is reasonable that this sort of friendship is enduring, since it embraces in itself all the features that friends must have. For the cause of every friendship is good or pleasure, either unconditional or for the lover; and every friendship reflects some similarity. And all the features we have mentioned are found in this friendship because of [the nature of] the friends themselves. For they are similar in this way [i.e. in being good]. Moreover, their friendship also has the other things—what is unconditionally good and what is unconditionally pleasant; and these are lovable most of all. Hence loving and friendship are found most of all and at their best in these friends.

These kinds of friendships are likely to be rare, since such people are few. Moreover, they need time to grow accustomed to each other; for, as the proverb says, they cannot know each other before they have shared the traditional [peck of] salt, and they cannot accept each other or be friends until each appears lovable to the other and gains the other's confidence. Those who are quick to treat each other in friendly ways wish to be friends, but are not friends, unless they are also lovable, and know this. For though the wish for friendship comes quickly, friendship does not.

This sort of friendship, then, is complete both in time and in the other ways. In every way each friend gets the same things and similar things from each, and this is what must be true of friends. Friendship for pleasure bears some resemblance to this complete sort, since good people are also pleasant to each other. And friendship for utility also resembles it, since good people are also useful to each other....

1157a

### 9. *The relationship between friendship and the community.*

As we said at the beginning, friendship and justice would seem to have the same area of concern and to be found in the same people. For in every community there seems to be some sort of justice, and some type of friendship also. At any rate, fellow-voyagers and fellow-soldiers are called friends, and so are members of other communities. And the extent of their community is the extent of their friendship, since it is also the extent of the justice found there. The proverb "What friends have is common" is correct, since friendship involves community. But while brothers and companions have everything in common, what people have in common in other types of community is limited, more in some communities and less in others, since some friendships are also closer than others, some less close....

1159b

### 10. *Types of political systems and friendships.*

There are three species of political system (*politeia*), and an equal number of deviations, which are a sort of corruption of them. The first political system is kingship; the second aristocracy; and since the third rests on property (*timēma*) it appears proper to call it a timocratic system, though most people usually call it a polity (*politeia*). The best of these is kingship and the worst timocracy.

1160a

The deviation from kingship is tyranny. For, though both are monarchies, they show the widest difference, since the tyrant considers his own advantage, but the king considers the advantage of his subjects. For someone is a king only if he is self-sufficient and superior in all goods; and since such a person needs nothing more, he will consider the subjects' benefit, not his own. For a king who is not like this would be only some sort of titular king. Tyranny is contrary to this; for the tyrant pursues his own good....

1160b

## *11.* *Friendship and justice in political systems.*

Friendship appears in each of the political systems, to the extent that justice appears also. A king's friendship to his subjects involves superior beneficence. For he benefits his subjects, since he is good and attends to them to ensure that they do well, as a shepherd attends to his sheep; hence Homer also called Agamemnon shepherd of the peoples.

Paternal friendship resembles this, but differs in conferring a greater benefit, since the father is the cause of his children's being, which seems to be the greatest benefit, and of their nurture and education. These benefits are also ascribed to ancestors; and by nature father is ruler over sons, ancestors over descendants, and king over subjects.

All these are friendships of superiority; that is why parents are also honoured. And what is just in these friendships is not the same in each case, but corresponds to worth; for so does the friendship.

The friendship of man to woman is the same as in an aristocracy. For it reflects virtue, in assigning more good to the better, and assigning what is fitting to each. The same is true for what is just here.

The friendship of brothers is similar to that of companions, since they are equal and of an age, and such people usually have the same feelings and characters. Friendship in a timocracy is similar to this. For there the citizens are meant to be equal and decent, and so rule in turn and on equal terms. The same is true, then, of their friendship.

In the deviations, however, justice is found only to a slight degree; and hence the same is true of friendship. There is least of it in the worst deviation; for in a tyranny there is little or no friendship.

For where ruler and ruled have nothing in common, they have no friendship, since they have no justice either. This is true for a craftsman in relation to his tool, and for the soul in relation to the body. For in all these cases the user benefits what he uses, but there is neither friendship nor justice towards soulless things.

Nor is there any towards a horse or cow, or towards a slave, in so far as he is a slave. For master and slave have nothing in common, since a slave is a tool with a soul, while a tool is a slave without a soul. In so far as he is a slave, then, there is no friendship with him.

But there is friendship with him in so far as he is a human being. For every human being seems to have some relations of justice with everyone who is capable of community in law and agreement. Hence there is also friendship, to the extent that a slave is a human being.

Hence there are friendships and justice to only a slight degree in tyrannies also, but to a much larger degree in democracies; for there people are equal, and so have much in common.

# THE POLITICS

## BOOK 1

## The City and the Household

### Chapter 1

### The City and the Man

1252a   (1) Since we see that every city is some sort of partnership, and that every partnership is constituted for the sake of some good (for everyone does everything for the sake of what is held to be good), it is clear that all partnerships aim at some good, and that the partnership that is most authoritative of all and embraces all the others does so particularly, and aims at the most authoritative good of all. This is what is called the city or the political partnership.

  (2) Those who suppose that the same person is expert in political [rule], kingly [rule], managing the household and being a master [of slaves] do not argue rightly. For they consider that each of these differs in the multitude or fewness [of those ruled] and not in kind—for example, [the ruler] of a few is a master, of more a household manager, and of still more an expert in political or kingly [rule]—the assumption being that there is no difference between a large household and a small city; and as for the experts in political and kingly [rule], they consider an expert in kingly [rule] one who has charge himself, and in political [rule] one who, on the basis of the precepts of this sort of science, rules and is ruled in turn. But these things are not true. (3) This will be clear to those investigating in accordance with our normal sort of inquiry. For just as it is necessary elsewhere to divide a compound into its uncompounded elements (for these are the smallest parts of the whole), so too by investigating what the city is composed of we shall gain a better view concerning these [kinds of rulers] as well, both as to how they differ from one another and as to whether there is some expertise characteristic of an art that can be acquired in connection with each of those mentioned.

---

**N.B.** The titles of each book and chapter are adapted from Carnes Lord.

*Chapter 2*

(1) Now in these matters as elsewhere it is by looking at how things develop naturally from the beginning that one may best study them. (2) First, then, there must of necessity be a conjunction of persons who cannot exist without one another: on the other hand, male and female, for the sake of reproduction (which occurs not from intentional choice but—as is also the case with the other animals and plants—from a natural striving to leave behind another that is like oneself); on the other, the naturally ruling and ruled, on account of preservation. For that which can foresee with the mind is the naturally ruling and naturally mastering element, while that which can do these things with the body is the naturally ruled and slave; hence the same thing is advantageous for the master and slave. (3) Now the female is distinguished by nature from the slave. For nature makes nothing in an economizing spirit, as smiths make the Delphic knife, but one thing with a view to one thing; and each instrument would perform most finely if it served one task rather than many. (4) The barbarians, though, have the same arrangement for female and slave. The reason for this is that they have no naturally ruling element; with them, the partnership [of man and woman] is that of female slave and male slave. This is why the poets say "it is fitting for Greeks to rule barbarians" —the assumption being that barbarian and slave are by nature the same thing.

1252b

(5) From these two partnerships, then, the household first arose, and Hesiod's verse is rightly spoken: "first a house, and woman, and ox for ploughing"—for poor persons have an ox instead of a servant. The household is the partnership constituted by nature for [the needs of] daily life; Charondas calls its members "peers of the mess," Epimenides of Crete "peers of the manger." The first partnership arising from [the union of] several households and for the sake of nondaily needs is the village. (6) By nature the village seems to be above all an extension of the household. Its members some call "milk-peers"; they are "the children and the children's children." This is why cities were at first under kings, and nations are even now. For those who joined together were already under kings: every household was under the eldest as king, and so also were the extensions [of the household constituting the village] as a result of kinship. (7) This is what Homer meant when he says that "each acts as law to his children and wives"; for [men] were scattered and used to dwell in this manner in ancient times. And it is for this reason that all assert that the gods are under a king—because they themselves are under kings now, or were in ancient times. For human beings assimilate not only the looks of the gods to themselves, but their ways of life as well.

(8) The partnership arising from [the union of] several villages that is complete is the city. It reaches a level of full self-sufficiency, so to speak; and while coming into being for the sake of living, it exists for the sake of living well. Every city, therefore, exists by nature, if such also are the first partnerships. For the city is their end, and nature is an end: what each thing is—for example, a human being, a horse, or a household—when its coming into being is complete is, we assert, the nature of that thing. (9) Again, that for the sake of which [a thing exists], or the end, is what is best; and self-sufficiency is an end and what is best.

From these things it is evident, then, that the city belongs among the things that exist by nature, and that man is by nature a political animal. He who is without a city through nature rather than chance is either a mean sort or superior to man; he is "without clan, without law, without hearth," like the person reproved by Homer; (10) for the one who is such by nature has by this fact a desire for war, as if he were an isolated piece in a game of chess. That man is much more a political animal than any kind of bee or any herd animal is clear. For, as we assert, nature does nothing in vain; and man alone among the animals has speech. (11) The voice indeed indicates the painful or pleasant, and hence is present in other animals as well; for their nature has come this far, that they have a perception of the painful and pleasant and indicate these things to each other. But speech serves to reveal the advantageous and the harmful, and hence also the just and the unjust. (12) For it is peculiar to man as compared to the other animals that he alone has a perception of good and bad and just and unjust and other things [of this sort]; and partnership in these things is what makes a household and a city.

The city is thus prior by nature to the household and to each of us. (13) For the whole must of necessity be prior to the part; for if the whole [body] is destroyed there will not be a foot or a hand, unless in the sense that the term is similar (as when one speaks of a hand made of stone), but the thing itself will be defective. Everything is defined by its task and its power, and if it is no longer the same in these respects it should not be spoken of in the same way, but only as something similarly termed. (14) That the city is both by nature and prior to each individual, then, is clear. For if the individual when separated [from it] is not self-sufficient, he will be in a condition similar to that of the other parts in relation to the whole. One who is incapable of participating or who is in need of nothing through being self-sufficient is no part of a city, and so is either a beast or a god.

1253a

(15) Accordingly, there is in everyone by nature an impulse toward this sort of partnership. And yet the one who first constituted [a city] is responsible for the greatest of goods. For just as man is the best of the animals when completed, when separated from law and adjudication he is the worst of all. (16) For injustice is harshest when it is furnished with arms; and man is born naturally possessing arms for [the use of] prudence and virtue which are nevertheless very susceptible to being used for their opposites. This is why, without virtue, he is the most unholy and the most savage [of the animals], and the worst with regard to sex and food. [The virtue of] justice is a thing belonging to the city. For adjudication is an arrangement of the political partnership, and adjudication is judgment as to what is just.

## Chapter 3

### The Household

(1) Since it is evident out of what parts the city is constituted, it is necessary first to speak of household management; for every city is composed of households. The parts of household management correspond to the parts out of which the household itself is constituted. Now the complete household is made up of slaves and free persons. Since everything is to be sought for first in its smallest elements, and the first and smallest parts of the household are master, slave, husband, wife, father, and children, three things must be investigated to determine what each is and what sort of thing it ought to be. (2) These are expertise in mastery, in marital [rule] (there is no term for the union of man and woman), and thirdly in parental [rule] (this too has not been assigned a term of its own). (3) So much, then, for the three we spoke of. There is a certain part of it, however, which some hold to be [identical with] household management, and others its greatest part; how the matter really stands has to be studied. I am speaking of what is called business expertise.

Let us speak first about master and slave, so that we may see at the same time what relates to necessary needs and whether we can not acquire something in the way of knowledge about these things that is better than current conceptions. (4) For some hold that mastery is a kind of science, and that managing the household, mastery, and expertise in political and kingly [rule] are the same, as we said at the beginning. Others hold that exercising mastery is against nature, for [as they believe] it is by law that one person is slave and another free, there being no difference by nature, and hence it is not just, since it rests on force.

1253b

## Chapter 4

### Slavery

(1) Now possessions are a part of the household, and expertise in acquiring possessions a part of household management (for without the necessary things it is impossible either to live or to live well); and just as the specialized arts must of necessity have their proper instruments if their work is to be performed, so too must the expert household manager. (2) Now of instruments some are inanimate and other animate—the pilot's rudder, for example, is an inanimate one, but his lookout an animate one; for the subordinate is a kind of instrument for the arts. A possession too, then, is an instrument for life, and one's possessions are the multitude of such instruments; and the slave is a possession of the animate sort. Every subordinate, moreover, is an instrument that wields many instruments, (3) for if each of the instruments were able to perform its work on command or by anticipation, as they assert those of Daedalus did, or the tripods of Hephaestus (which the poet says "of their own accord came to the gods' gathering"), "so that shuttles would weave themselves and picks play the lyre," master craftsmen would no longer have a need for subordinates, or masters for slaves. (4) Now the instruments mentioned are productive instruments, but a possession is an instrument of action. For from the shuttle comes something apart from the use of it, while from clothing or a bed the use alone. Further, since production and action differ in kind and both require instruments, these must of necessity reflect the same difference. (5) Life is action, not production; the slave is therefore a subordinate in matter concerning action.

1254a

A possession is spoken of in the same way as a part. A part is not only part of something else, but belongs wholly to something else; similarly with a possession. Accordingly, while the master is only master of the slave and does not belong to him, the slave is not only slave to the master but belongs wholly to him.

(6) What the nature of the slave is and what his capacity, then, is clear from these things. For one who does not belong to himself by nature but is another's, though a human being, is by nature a slave; a human being is another's who, though a human being, is a possession; and a possession is an instrument of action and separable [from its owner].

*Chapter 5*

(1) Whether anyone is of this sort by nature or not, and whether it is better and just for anyone to be a slave or not, but rather all slavery is against nature, must be investigated next. It is not difficult either to discern [the answer] by reasoning or to learn it from what actually happens. (2) Ruling and being ruled belong not only among things necessary but also among things advantageous. And immediately from birth certain things diverge, some toward being ruled, others toward ruling. There are many kinds both of ruling and ruled [things], and the better rule is always that over ruled [things] that are better, for example over a human being rather than a beast; (3) for the work performed by the better is better, and wherever something rules and something is ruled there is a certain work belonging to these together. For whatever is constituted out of a number of things—whether continuous or discrete—and becomes a single common thing always displays a ruling and a ruled element; (4) this is something that animate things derive from all of nature, for even in things that do not share in life there is a sort of rule, for example in a harmony. But these matters perhaps belong to a more external sort of investigation. But an animal is the first thing constituted out of soul and body, of which the one is the ruling element by nature, the other the ruled. (5) It is in things whose condition is according to nature that one ought particularly to investigate what is by nature, not in things that are defective. Thus the human being to be studied is one whose state is best both in body and in soul—in him this is clear; for in the case of the depraved, or those in a depraved condition, the body is often held to rule the soul on account of their being in a condition that is bad and unnatural.

1254b

(6) It is then in an animal, as we were saying, that one can first discern both the sort of rule characteristic of a master and political rule. For the soul rules the body with the rule characteristic of a master, while intellect rules appetite with political and kingly rule; and this makes it evident that it is according to nature and advantageous for the body to be ruled by the soul, and the passionate part [of the soul] by intellect and the part having reason, while it is harmful to both if the relation is equal or reversed. (7) The same holds with respect to man and the other animals: tame animals have a better nature than wild ones, and it is better for all of them to be ruled by man, since in this way their preservation is ensured. Further, the relation of male to female is by nature a relation of superior to inferior and ruler to ruled. The same must of necessity hold in the case of human beings generally.

(8) Accordingly, those who are as different [from other men] as the soul from the body or man from beast—and they are in this state if their work is the use of the body, and if this is the best that can come from them—are slaves by nature. For them it is better to be ruled in accordance with this sort of rule, if such is the case for the other things mentioned. (9) For he is a slave by nature who is capable of belonging to another—which is also why he belongs to another—and who participates in reason onto to the extent of perceiving it, but does not have it. (The other animals, not perceiving reason, obey their passions.) Moreover, the need for them differs only slightly: bodily assistance in the necessary things is forthcoming from both, from slaves and from tame animals alike.

(10) Nature indeed wishes to make the bodies of free persons and slaves different as well [as their souls]—those of the latter strong with a view to necessary needs, those of the former straight and useless for such tasks, but useful with a view to a political way of life (which is itself divided between the needs of war and those of peace); yet the opposite often results, some having the bodies of free persons while others have the souls. It is evident, at any rate, that if they were to be born as different only in body as the images of gods, everyone would assert that those not so favored merited being their slaves. (11) But if this is true in the case of the body, it is much more justifiable to make this distinction in the case of the soul; yet it is not as easy to see the beauty of the soul as it is that of the body. That some persons are free and others slaves by nature, therefore, and that for these slavery is both advantageous and just, is evident.

## Chapter 13

1259b

(1) It is evident, then, that household management gives more serious attention to human beings than to inanimate possessions, to the virtue of these than that of possessions (which we call wealth), and to the virtue of free persons rather than that of slaves. (2) First, then, one might raise a question concerning slaves: whether there is a certain virtue belonging to a slave besides the virtues of an instrument and a servant and more honorable than these, such as moderation and courage and justice and the other dispositions of this sort, or whether there is none besides the bodily services. (3) Questions arise either way, for if there is [such a virtue], how will they differ from free persons? But if there is not, though they are human beings and participate in reason, it is odd. Nearly the same question arises concerning a woman and a child, whether there are virtues belonging

to these as well—whether the woman should be moderate and courageous and just, and whether a child is [capable of being] licentious and moderate or not. (4) And in general, then, this must be investigated concerning the ruled by nature and the ruler, whether virtue is the same or different. For if both should share in gentlemanliness, why should the one rule and the other be ruled once and for all? For it is not possible for them to differ by greater and less, since being ruled and ruling differ in kind, not by greater and less; (5) but that one should [have such virtue] and the other not would be surprising. For unless the ruler is moderate and just, how will he rule finely? And unless the ruled is, how will he be ruled finely? For if he is licentious and cowardly he will perform none of his duties. It is evident, then, that both must of necessity share in virtue, but that there are differences in their virtue, as there are in [that of] those who are by nature ruled. (6) Consideration of the soul guides us straightway [to this conclusion]. For in this there is by nature a ruling and a ruled element, and we assert there is a different virtue of each—that is, of the element having reason and of the irrational element. It is clear, then, that the same thing holds in the other cases as well. Thus by nature most things are ruling and ruled. (7) For the free person rules the slave, the male the female, and the man the child in different ways. The parts of the soul are present in all, but they are present in a different way. The slave is wholly lacking the deliberative element; the female has it but it lacks authority; the child has it but it is incomplete. (8) It is to be supposed that the same necessarily holds concerning the virtues of character: all must share in them, but not in the same way, but to each in relation to his own work. Hence the ruler must have complete virtue of character (for a work belongs in an absolute sense to the master craftsman, and reason is a master craftsman); while each of the others must have as much as falls to him. (9) It is thus evident that there is a virtue of character that belongs to all these mentioned, and that the moderation of a woman and a man is not the same, nor their courage or justice, as Socrates supposed, but that there is a ruling and a serving courage, and similarly with the other virtues. (10) This is further clear if we investigate the matter in more detail. For those who say in a general way that virtue is a good condition of the soul or acting correctly or something of this sort deceive themselves. Those who enumerate the virtues, like Gorgias, do much better than those who define it in this way. (11) One should thus consider that matters stand with everyone as the poet said of woman: "to a woman silence is an ornament," though this is not the case for a man. Since the child is incomplete,

1260a

it is clear that its virtue too is not its own as relating to itself, but as relating to its end and the person leading it. (12) The same is true of that of the slave in relation to a master. We laid it down that the slave is useful with respect to the necessary things, so that he clearly needs only a small amount of virtue—as much as will prevent him from falling short in his work through licentiousness or cowardice. One might raise the question whether, if what has just been said is true, artisans too will need virtue, since they often fall short in their work through licentiousness. (13) Or is the case very different? For the slave is a partner in [the master's] life, while the other is more remote, and shares in virtue only so far as he also shares in slavery. For the vulgar artisan is under a special sort of slavery, and while the slave belongs among those [persons or things that are] by nature, no shoemaker does, nor any of the other artisans. (14) It is evident, therefore, that the master should be responsible for [instilling] this sort of virtue in the slave; he is not merely someone possessing an expertise in mastery which instructs the slave in his work. Those who deny reason to slaves and assert that commands only should be used with them do not argue rightly: admonition is to be used with slaves more than with children. (15) But concerning these matters let our discussion stand thus. Concerning husband and wife and children and father and the sort of virtue that is connected with each of these, and what is and what is not fine in their relations with one another and how one should pursue what is well and avoid the bad, these things must necessarily be addressed in the [discourses] connected with the regimes. For since the household as a whole is a part of the city, and these things of the household, and one should look at the virtue of the part in relation to the virtue of the whole, both children and women must necessarily be educated looking to the regime, at least if it makes any difference with a view to the city's being excellent that both its children and its women are excellent. (16) But it necessarily makes a difference: women are a part amounting to a half of the free persons, and from the children come those who are partners in the regime. So since there has been discussion of these matters, and we must speak elsewhere of those remaining, let us leave off the present discourses as having reached an end and make another beginning to the argument. Let us investigate in the first instance the views that have been put forward about the best regime.

*[The rest of Book 1 consists of a detailed description of the various modes of acquiring property (natural, unnatural and intermediate) and a short discussion of types of authority (marital and parental) found in the household. —J.M.P.]*

1260b

## → BOOK 2 ←

## Views Concerning the Best Regime

### *Chapter 1*

### *The Regime of Plato's* Republic

(1) Since it is our intention to study the sort of political partnership that is superior to all for those capable of living as far as possible in the manner one would pray for, we should also investigate other regimes, both those in use in some of the cities that are said to be well managed and any other spoken about by certain persons that are held to be in a fine condition, in order that both what is correct in their condition and what is useful may be seen—and further, that to seek something apart from them may not be held wholly to belong to those who wish to act the sophist, but that we may be held to enter into this inquiry because those regimes now available are in fact not in a fine condition. (2) We must make a beginning that is the natural beginning for this investigation. It is necessary that all the cities be partners either in everything, or in nothing, or in some things but not in others. Now it is evident that to be partners in nothing is impossible; for the regime is a certain sort of partnership, and it is necessary in the first instance to be partners in a location: a single city occupies a single location, and the citizens are partners in the single city. (3) But, of the things in which there can be participation, is it better for the city that is going to be finely administered to participate in all of them, or is it better to participate in some but not in others? For it is possible for the citizens to be partners with one another in respect to children and women and property, as in the *Republic* of Plato; for there Socrates asserts that children and women and property should be common. Which is better, then, the condition that exists now or one based on the law that is described in the *Republic?*

1260a

1261a

### *Chapter 2*

### *Community of Wives and Children*

(1) Having women common to all involves many difficulties; but a particular difficulty is that the reason Socrates gives as to why there should be legislation of this sort evidently does not result from his arguments. Further, with respect to the end

which he asserts the city should have, it is, as has just been said, impossible; but how one should distinguish [a sense in which it is possible] is not discussed. (2) I mean, that it is best for the city to be as far as possible entirely one; for this is the presupposition Socrates adopts. And yet it is evident that as it becomes increasingly one it will no longer be a city. For the city is in its nature a sort of multitude, and as it becomes more a unity it will be a household instead of a city, and a human being instead of a household; for we would surely say that the household is more a unity than the city, and the individual than the household. So even if one were able to do this, one ought not do it, as it would destroy the city. (3) Now the city is made up not only of a number of human beings, but also of human beings differing in kind: a city does not arise from persons who are similar. A city is different from an alliance. The latter is useful by its quantity, even if [its parts are] the same in kind (since an alliance exists by nature for mutual assistance), as when a greater weight is added to the scale. In this sort of way, too, a city differs from a nation, when the multitude is not separated in villages but rather is like the Arcadians. Those from whom a unity should arise differ in kind. (4) It is thus reciprocal equality which preserves cities, as was said earlier in the [discourses on] ethics. This is necessarily the case even among persons who are free and equal, for all cannot rule at the same time, but each rules for a year or according to some other arrangement or period of time. (5) In this way, then, it results that all rule, just as if shoemakers and carpenters were to exchange places rather than the same persons always being shoemakers and carpenters. (6) But since that condition is better also with respect to the political partnership, it is clear that it is better if the same always rule, where this is possible; but in cases where it is not possible because all are equal in their nature, and where it is at the same time just for all to have a share in ruling (regardless of whether ruling is something good or something mean), there is at least an imitation of this. (7) For some rule and some are ruled in turn, as if becoming other persons. And, in the same way, among the rulers different persons hold different offices. It is evident from these things, then, that the city is not naturally one in this sense as some argue, and what was said to be the greatest good for cities actually destroys them; yet the good of each thing is surely what preserves it. (8) It is evident in another way as well that to seek to unify the city excessively is not good. For a household is more self-sufficient than one person, and a city than a household; and a city tends to come into being at the point when the partnership formed by a multitude is self-sufficient. If, therefore, the more self-sufficient is more choiceworthy, what is less a unity is more choiceworthy than what is more a unity.

1261b

148

*Chapter 3*

*Criticism of the Means*

(1) But even if it is best for the partnership to be as far as possible a unity, even this does not appear to be proved by the argument [that it will follow] if all say "mine" and "not mine" at the same time; for Socrates supposes this is an indication of the city being completely one. (2) For "all" has a double sense. If it means "each individually," perhaps this would be closer to what Socrates wants to do, for each will then speak of the same boy as his own son and the same woman as his own wife, and similarly with regard to property and indeed to everything that comes his way. But those who have wives and children in common will not speak of them in this way, but as "all" [collectively] and not individually; (3) and similarly with respect to property, as "all" [collectively] but not individually. It is evident, then, that a certain fallacy is involved in the phrase "all say"—indeed, the double sense of "all," "both," "odd," and "even" produces contentious syllogisms in arguments as well. Therefore that "all say the same thing" is in one way fine, though impossible, while in another way it is not even productive of concord.

(4) Furthermore, the formula is harmful in another way. What belongs in common to the most people is accorded the least care: they take thought for their own things above all, and less about things common, or only so much as falls to each individually. For, apart from other things, they slight them on the grounds that someone else is taking thought for them—just as in household service many attendants sometimes do a worse job than fewer. (5) Each of the citizens comes to have a thousand sons, though not as an individual, but each is in similar fashion the son of any of them; hence all will slight them in similar fashion.

Further, each says "mine" of a citizen who is acting well or ill only in this sense, that he is one of a certain number, each really says "mine or his," meaning by this every individual of the thousand or however many the city has. And even then he is in doubt, for it is unclear who has happened to have offspring, or whether any have survived. (6) Yet which is superior—for each of two thousand (or ten thousand) individuals to say "mine" and address the same thing, or rather the way they say "mine" in cities now? (7) For now the same person is addressed as a son by one, by another as a brother, by another as a cousin, or according to some other sort of kinship, whether of blood or of relation and connection by marriage—in the first instance of himself, then of his own; and further, another describes him as clansman or tribesman. It is better, indeed, to have a cousin of one's own than a son in the sense indicated.

1262a

(8) Actually, though, it is impossible to avoid having some suspect who their brothers and sons or fathers and mothers really are; for they will of necessity find proofs of this in the similarities that occur between children and their parents. (9) Indeed, some of those who have composed accounts of travels assert that this in fact happens; for they say that some inhabitants of upper Libya have women in common, yet the children they bear are distinguishable according to their similarities. There are some women [and some females] of other animals such as horses and cattle that are particularly inclined by nature to produce offspring similar to the parents, like the mare at Pharsalus called the Just.

## Chapter 4

### Other Difficulties

(1) Further, it is not easy for those establishing this sort of partnership to avoid such difficulties as outrages or involuntary homicides, for example, or voluntary homicides, assaults, or verbal abuse. None of these things is holy when it involves fathers, mothers, or those not distant in kinship, as distinct from outsiders; yet they must necessarily occur more frequently among those who are ignorant [of their relatives] than among those who are familiar [with them], and when they do occur, only those who are familiar [with their relatives] can perform the lawful expiations, while the others cannot. (2) It is also odd that while sons are made common, only sexual intercourse between lovers is eliminated, but love is not forbidden, or other practices which are improper particularly for a father in relation to his son or a brother in relation to his brother, as indeed is love by itself. (3) It is also odd that sexual intercourse is eliminated for no other reason than that the pleasure involved is too strong, it being supposed that it makes no difference whether this occurs between a father and a son or between brothers.

(4) It would seem to be more useful for the farmers to have women and children in common than for the guardians. For there will be less affection where children and women are common; but the ruled should be of this sort if they are to obey their rulers and not engage in subversion. (5) In general, there must necessarily result from a law of this sort the very opposite of what correctly enacted laws ought properly to cause, and of what caused Socrates to suppose that the matter of children and women should be arranged in this way. (6) For we suppose affection to be the greatest of good things for cities, for in this way they would least of all engage in factional conflict; and Socrates praises above all the city's being one,

1262b

which is held to be, and which he asserts to be, the work of affection—just as in the discourses on love we know that Aristophanes speaks of lovers who from an excess of affection "desire to grow together," the two of them becoming one. (7) Now here it must necessarily happen that both, or one of them, disappear [in the union]; in the city, however, affection necessarily becomes diluted through this sort of partnership, and the fact that a father least of all says "mine" of his son, or the son of his father. (8) Just as adding much water to a small amount of wine makes the mixture imperceptible, so too does this result with respect to the kinship with one another based on these terms, it being least of all necessary in a regime of this sort for a father to take thought for his sons as sons, or a son for his father as a father, or brothers for one another [as brothers]. (9) For there are two things above all which make human beings cherish and feel affection, what is one's own and what is dear; and neither of these can be available to those who govern themselves in this way.

There is also considerable uncertainty concerning the manner in which children are to be transferred from the farmers and artisans to the guardians as well as from the latter to the former; at any rate, those who transfer and assign them necessarily know who has been assigned to whom. (10) Further, what was mentioned before must necessarily result above all in these cases—that is, outrages, love affairs, homicides; for those who have been assigned to the other [class of] citizens will no longer address the guardians as brothers, children, fathers, or mothers, nor will those among the guardians so address the other [class of] citizens, so that they avoid doing any of these things on account of their kinship. Concerning the partnership in children and women, then, let our discussion stand thus.

## Chapter 5

### Community of Possessions

(1) Next after this it remains to investigate the manner in which possessions should be instituted for those who are going to govern themselves under the best regime—whether possessions should be common or not. (2) This may be investigated even apart from the legislation concerning children and women. I mean, as regards what is connected with possessions, even if the former are held separately, which is the way all do it now, [one may investigate in particular whether] it is better for both possessions and uses to be common[, or whether one should be held in common and the other separately]. For example, farmland

1263a

151

could be held separately while the crops are brought into a common [store] and consumed [in common], as some [barbarian] nations do; or the opposite could happen, land being held and farmed in common and the crops divided for private use (some barbarians are said to have this mode of partnership as well); or both farmland and crops could be common. (3) Now if the farmers were [of a] different [class than the citizens] the mode would be different and easier, but if they undertake the exertion for themselves, the arrangements concerning possessions would give rise to many resentments. For if they turn out to be unequal rather than equal in the work and in the gratifications deriving from it, accusations against those who can gratify themselves or take much while exerting themselves little must necessarily arise on the part of those who take less and exert themselves more. (4) In general, to live together and be partners in any human matter is difficult, and particularly things of this sort. This is clear in the partnerships of fellow travelers, most of whom are always quarreling as a result of friction with one another over everyday and small matters. Again, friction particularly arises with the servants we use most frequently for regular tasks. (5) Having possessions in common involves, then, these and other similar difficulties, and the mode that prevails now— if provided with the adornment of character and an arrangement of correct laws—would be more than a little better. For it would have what is good in both—by both I mean what comes from having possessions in common and what from having them privately. For they should be common in some sense, yet private generally speaking. (6) Dividing the care [of possessions] will cause them not to raise these accusations against one another, and will actually result in improvement, as each applies himself to his own; and it will be through virtue that "the things of friends are common," as the proverb has it, with a view to use. Even now this mode can be found in outline in some cities, so it is not impossible; in finely administered cities especially some of these things already exist, while others could be brought into being. (7) [In these cities] everyone has his own possessions, but he makes some of them useful to his friends, and some he uses as common things. In Lacedaemon, for example, they use each other's slaves, as well as their horses and dogs, as practically their own, and anything they need by way of provisions from the fields [when they travel] in their territory. (8) It is evident, then, that it is better for possessions to be private, but to make them common to use. That [the citizens] become such [as to use them in common]— this is a task peculiar to the legislator.

Further, it makes an immense difference with respect to pleasure to consider a thing one's own. It is surely not to no purpose that everyone has affection for himself; this is something natural. (9) Selfishness is justly blamed; but this is not having affection for oneself [simply], but rather having more affection than one should—just as in the case of the greedy person; for practically everyone has affection for things of this sort. Moreover, it is a very pleasant thing to help or do favors for friends, guests, or club mates; and this requires that possessions be private. (10) Those who make the city too much of a unity not only forfeit these things; in addition, they manifestly eliminate the tasks of two of the virtues, moderation concerning women (it being a fine deed to abstain through moderation from a woman who belongs to another) and liberality concerning possessions. For it will not be possible to show oneself as liberal or to perform any liberal action, since the task of liberality lies in the use of possessions.

1263b

(11) This sort of legislation has an attractive face and might be held humane; he who hears of it accepts it gladly, thinking it will produce a marvellous affection in all for each other, especially when it is charged that the ills that now exist in regimes come about through property not being common—I am speaking of lawsuits against one another concerning contracts, trials involving perjury, and flattery of the rich. (12) Yet none of these things comes about because of the lack of partnership [in property], but through depravity. For it is precisely those who possess things in common and are partners whom we see most at odds, not those who hold their property separately; but those at odds as a result of their partnerships are few to observe in comparison with those who own possessions privately. (13) Further, it is only just to speak not only of the number of ills they will be deprived of by being partners, but also the number of goods. Indeed, it is a way of life that appears to be altogether impossible.

The cause of Socrates' going astray one should consider to be the incorrectness of the presupposition. (14) Both the household and the city should be one in a sense, but not in every sense. On the one hand, as the city proceeds [in this direction], it will at some point cease to be a city; on the other hand, while remaining a city, it will be a worse city the closer it comes to not being a city—just as if one were to reduce a consonance to unison, or a meter to a single foot. (15) Rather, as was said before, [the city,] being a multitude, must be made one and common through education. It is odd that one who plans to introduce education and who holds that it is through this that the city will be excellent

153

should suppose it can be corrected by things of that sort, and not by habits, philosophy, and laws, just as the legislator in Lacedaemon and Crete made common what is connected with possessions by means of common messes....

1264a

[*Following his criticism of* The Republic, *Aristotle examines Plato's* Laws. *He then provides a short critique of two other great thinkers, Phaleas of Chalcedon and Hippodamus of Miletus. Last, he analyzes three well-governed regimes (Sparta, Crete, and Carthage), and discusses nine famous law-givers who combined theory and practice.*—J.M.P.]

## ⤞ BOOK 3 ⤝

### The City and the Regime

#### *Chapter 1*

#### *Citizenship*

1275a

...We are seeking the citizen in an unqualified sense, one who has no defect of this sort requiring correction, since questions may be raised and resolved concerning such things in the case of those who have been deprived of [civic] prerogatives or exiled as well. (6) The citizen in an unqualified sense is defined by no other thing so much as by sharing in decision and office. Now some offices are divided on the basis of time, so that in some cases the same person is not permitted to hold them twice, or only after some definite period of time has passed; but other offices are indefinite, such as that of juror or assemblyman. (7) Perhaps someone might say that the latter are not rulers and do not share in office on account of these things; yet it would be ridiculous to deprive those with greatest authority of [the title of] office. But it should make no difference: the argument is over a term, for what is common to juror and assemblyman lacks a name that could apply to both. For the sake of definition, then, let it be "indefinite office." (8) We set it down, then, that citizens are those who share in this way.

The [notion of] citizen that fits best with all those who are called citizens is, therefore, something of this sort. But it should not be overlooked that of [types of] things where the constituent elements differ in kind—one of them being primary, one secondary, another derivative—the common element either is not present at all insofar as they are such, or only slightly. (9) We see that regimes differ

154

from one another in kind, and that some are prior and some posterior; for those
that are errant and deviant must necessarily be posterior to those that are with-out error. (In what sense we are speaking of deviant regimes will be evident
later.) Hence the citizen must necessarily differ in the case of each sort of regime.
(10) Accordingly, the citizen that was spoken of is a citizen above all in a democ-racy; he may, but will not necessarily, be a citizen in the others. In some [regimes]
there is no people, nor is an assembly recognized in law, but [only a consultative
meeting of specially] summoned persons, and cases are adjudicated by groups [of
officials]. In Lacedaemon, for example, different overseers try different cases in-volving agreements, the senators those involving murder, and another office
perhaps others; (11) and it is the same in the case of Carthage, where certain
offices try all cases. But the definition of the citizen admits of correction. In the
other regimes, it is not the indefinite ruler who is assemblyman or juror, but
one whose office is definite. For of these either all or some are assigned to de-liberate and adjudicate, either concerning all matters or concerning some.

(12) Who the citizen is, then, is evident from these things. Whoever is enti-tled to participate in an office involving deliberation or decision is, we can now
say, a citizen in this city; and the city is the multitude of such persons that is ad-equate with a view to a self-sufficient life, to speak simply.

## Chapter 3

### The Identity of the City

... (7) For if the city is a type of partnership, and if it is a partnership of citizens
in a regime, if the regime becomes and remains different in kind, it might be
held that the city as well is necessarily not the same. At any rate, just as we assert
that a chorus which is at one time comic and at another tragic is different even
though the human beings in it are often the same, (8) it is similar with any other
partnership and any compound, when the compound takes a different form—for
example, we would say that the mode is different even when the notes are the
same, if it is at one time Dorian and at another Phrygian. (9) If this is indeed
the case, it is evident that it is looking to the regime above all that the city must
be said to be the same; the term one calls it can be different or the same no mat-ter whether the same human beings inhabit it or altogether different ones. As to
whether it is just to fulfill or not to fulfill [agreements] when the city undergoes
revolution into another regime, that is another argument.

1275b

1276b

## Chapter 4

### The Good Man and the Good Citizen

(1) Connected with what has been said is the investigation of whether the virtue of the good man and the excellent citizen is to be regarded as the same or as not the same. If we are indeed to examine this, however, the virtue of the citizen must first be grasped in some sort of outline. Now just as a sailor is one of a number of partners, so, we assert, is the citizen. (2) Although sailors are dissimilar in their capacities (one is a rower, another is a pilot, another a lookout, and others have similar sorts of titles), it is clear that the most precise account of their virtue will be that peculiar to each sort individually, but that a common account will in a similar way fit all. For the preservation of the ship in its voyage is the work of all of them, and each of the sailors strives for this. (3) Similarly, although citizens are dissimilar, preservation of the partnership is their task, and the regime is [this] partnership; hence the virtue of the citizen must necessarily be with a view to the regime. If, then, there are indeed several forms of regime, it is clear that it is not possible for the virtue of the excellent citizen to be single, or complete virtue. (4) That it is possible for a citizen to be excellent yet not possess the virtue in accordance with which he is an excellent man, therefore, is evident....

## Chapter 6

### The Typology of Regimes

1278b   (1) Since these things have been discussed, what comes after them must be investigated—whether we are to regard them as being one regime or many, and if many, which and how many there are and what the differences are between them. The regime is an arrangement of a city with respect to its offices, particularly the one that has authority over all [matters]. For what has authority in the city is everywhere the governing body, and the governing body *is* the regime. (2) I mean, for example, that in democratic regimes the people have authority, while by contrast it is the few in oligarchies. The regime too, we say, is different in these cases; and we shall speak in the same way concerning the others as well.

First, then, we must lay down by way of presupposition what it is for the sake of which the city is established, and how many kinds of rule are connected with man and the partnership in life. (3) It was said in our initial discourses, where household management and mastery were discussed, that man is by nature a political animal. Hence [men] strive to live together even when they have no need of assistance from one another, though it is also the case that the common advantage brings them together, to the extent that it falls to each to live finely. It is this above all, then, which is the end for all both in common and separately; but they also join together, and maintain the political partnership, for the sake of living itself. For there is perhaps something fine in living just by itself, provided there is no great excess of hardships. It is clear that most men will endure much harsh treatment in their longing for life, the assumption being that there is a kind of joy inherent in it and a natural sweetness.

As for the modes of rule that are spoken of, it is easy to distinguish them, and we discuss them frequently in the external discourses. Mastery, in spite of the same thing being in truth advantageous both to the slave by nature and to the master by nature, is still rule with a view to the advantage of the master primarily, and with a view to that of the slave accidentally (for mastery cannot be preserved if the slave is destroyed). Rule over children and wife and the household as a whole, which we call household management, is either for the sake of the ruled or for the sake of something common to both—in itself it is for the sake of the ruled, as we see in the case of the other arts such as medicine and gymnastic, but accidentally it may be for [the sake of the rulers] themselves. For nothing prevents the trainer from being on occasion one of those engaging in gymnastic, just as the pilot is always one of the sailors: the trainer or pilot looks out for the good of the ruled, and when he becomes one of them himself, he shares accidentally in the benefit; for the one is a sailor, and the other becomes one of those engaging in gymnastic, though still a trainer. Hence with respect to political offices too, when [the regime] is established in accordance with equality and similarity among the citizens, they claim to merit ruling in turn. Previously, as accords with nature, they claimed to merit doing public service by turns and having someone look to their good, just as when ruling previously they looked to his advantage. Now, however, because of the benefits to be derived from common [funds] and from office, they wish to rule continuously, as if they were sick persons who were always made healthy by ruling; at any rate, these would perhaps pursue office in a similar fashion.

It is evident, then, that those regimes which look to the common advantage are correct regimes according to what is unqualifiedly just, while those which look only to the advantage of the rulers are errant, and are all deviations from the correct regimes; for they involve mastery, but the city is a partnership of free persons.

1279a

## Chapter 7

### *Rule by the One, Few, or Many*

(1) These things having been discussed, the next thing is to investigate regimes—how many in number and which sorts there are, and first of all the correct ones; for the deviations will be evident once these have been discussed. (2) Since "regime" and "governing body" signify the same thing, since the governing body is the authoritative element in cities, and since it is necessary that the authoritative element be either one or a few or the many, when the one or the few or the many rule with a view to the common advantage, these regimes are necessarily correct, while those with a view to the private advantage of the one or the few or the multitude are deviations. For either it must be denied that persons sharing [in the regime] are citizens, or they must participate in its advantages. (3) Now of monarchies, that [form] which looks toward the common advantage we are accustomed to call kingship; [rule] of the few (but of more than one person) we are accustomed to call aristocracy—either because the best persons are ruling, or because they are ruling with a view to what is best for the city and for those who participate in it; and when the multitude governs with a view to the common advantage, it is called by the term common to all regimes, polity. (4) This happens reasonably. It is possible for one or a few to be outstanding in virtue, but where more are concerned it is difficult for them to be proficient with a view to virtue as a whole, but [some level of proficiency is possible] particularly regarding military virtue, as this arises in a multitude; hence in this regime the warrior element is the most authoritative, and it is those possessing [heavy] arms who share in it. (5) Deviations from those mentioned are tyranny from kingship, oligarchy from aristocracy, democracy from polity. Tyranny is monarchy with a view to the advantage of the monarch, oligarchy [rule] with a view to the advantage of the well off, democracy [rule] with a view to the advantage of those who are poor; none of them is with a view to the common gain.

1279b

## Chapter 8

### *Rule Based on Social Class*

(1) It is necessary to speak at somewhat greater length of what each of these regimes is. For certain questions are involved, and it belongs to one philosophizing in connection with each sort of inquiry and not merely looking toward

action not to overlook or omit anything, but to make clear the truth concerning each thing. (2) Tyranny, as was said, is monarchic rule of a master over the political partnership; oligarchy is when those with property have authority in the regime; and democracy is the opposite, when those who have authority do not possess a [significant] amount of property but are poor. (3) The first question has to do with the definition. If a well-off majority has authority, and similarly in the other case, if it somewhere happened that the poor were a minority with respect to the well off but were superior and had authority in the regime, although when a small number has authority it is called oligarchy, this definition of the regimes would not be held to be a fine one. (4) But even if one were to combine fewness with being well off and number with being poor and described the regimes accordingly (oligarchy being that in which those who are well off and few in number have the offices, and democracy that in which those who are poor and many in number have them), another question is involved. (5) What shall we say of the regimes that were just mentioned—those in which the majority is well off and the poor are few and each has authority in the regime—if there is no other regime beside those we spoke of? (6) The argument seems to make clear, therefore, that it is accidental that few or many have authority in oligarchies on the one hand and democracies on the other, and that this is because the well off are everywhere few and the poor many. Hence it also turns out that the causes of the differences are not what was mentioned. (7) What makes democracy and oligarchy differ is poverty and wealth: wherever some rule on account of wealth, whether a minority or a majority, this is necessarily an oligarchy, and wherever those who are poor, a democracy. (8) But it turns out, as we said, that the former are few and the latter many; for few are well off, but all share in freedom—which are the causes of both [groups] disputing over the regime.

1280a

## Chapter 9

### Oligarchy and Democracy

(1) It is necessary first to grasp what they speak of as the defining principles of oligarchy and democracy and what just is [from] both oligarchic and democratic [points of view]. For all fasten on a certain sort of justice, but proceed only to a certain point, and do not speak of the whole of justice in its authoritative sense. For example, justice is held to be equality, and it is, but for equals and not for all; (2) and inequality is held to be just and is indeed, but for unequals and not for all;

but they disregard this element of persons and judge badly. The cause of this is that the judgment concerns themselves, and most people are bad judges concerning their own things. (3) And so since justice is for certain persons, and is divided in the same manner with respect to objects and for persons, as was said previously in the [discourses on] ethics, they agree on the equality of the object, but dispute about it for persons. They do this particularly because of what was just spoken of, that they judge badly with respect to what concerns themselves, but also because both, by speaking to a point of a kind of justice, consider themselves to be speaking of justice simply. (4) For the ones, if they are unequal in a certain thing, such as goods, suppose they are unequal generally, while the others suppose that if they are equal in a certain thing, such as freedom, they are equal generally. (5) But of the most authoritative [consideration] they say nothing. For if it were for the sake of possessions that they participated and joined together, they would share in the city just to the extent that they shared in possessions, so that the argument of the oligarchs might be held a strong one; for [they would say] it is not just for one who has contributed one mina to share equally in a hundred minas with the one giving all the rest, whether [he derives] from those who were there originally or the later arrivals. (6) But if [the city exists] not only for the sake of living but rather primarily for the sake of living well (for otherwise there could be a city of slaves or of animals—as things are, there is not, since they do not share in happiness or in living in accordance with intentional choice) and if it does not exist for the sake of an alliance to prevent their suffering injustice from anyone, nor for purposes of exchange and of use of one another—for otherwise the Tyrrhenians and Carthaginians, and all who have agreements with one another, would be as citizens of one city—(7) at any rate, there are compacts between them concerning imports, agreements to abstain from injustice, and treaties of alliance. But no offices common to all have been established to deal with these things, but different ones in each [city]; nor do those [in one city] take thought that the others should be of a certain quality, or that none of those coming under the compacts should be unjust or depraved in any way, but only that they should not act unjustly toward one another. (8) Whoever takes thought for good management, however, gives careful attention to political virtue and vice. It is thus evident that virtue must be a care for every city, or at least every one to which the term applies truly and not merely in a manner of speaking. For otherwise the partnership becomes an alliance which differs from others—from [alliances of] remote allies—only by location. And law becomes a compact and, as the sophist

1280b

Lycophron says, a guarantor among one another of the just things, but not the sort of thing to make the citizens good and just. (9) But that the matter stands thus is evident. For even if one were to bring the locations together into one, so that the city of the Megarians were fastened to that of the Corinthians by walls, it would still not be a single city. (10) Nor would it be if they practiced intermarriage with one another, although this is one of the aspects of the partnership that is peculiar to cities. Nor, similarly, if certain persons dwelled in separate places, yet were not so distant as to have nothing in common, but had laws not to commit injustice toward one another in their transactions—for example, if one were a carpenter, one a farmer, one a shoemaker, one something else of this sort, and the multitude of them were ten thousand, yet they had nothing in common except things of this sort, exchange and alliance; not even in this way would there be a city. (11) What, then, is the reason for this? It is surely not on account of a lack of proximity of the partnership. For even if they joined together while participating in this way, but each nevertheless treated his own household as a city and each other as if there were a defensive alliance merely for assistance against those committing injustice, it would not by this fact be held a city by those studying the matter precisely—if, that is, they participated in a similar way when joined together as they had when separated. (12) It is evident, therefore, that the city is not a partnership in a location and for the sake of not committing injustice against each other and of transacting business. These things must necessarily be present if there is to be a city, but not even when all of them are present is it yet a city, but [the city is] the partnership in living well both of households and families for the sake of a complete and self-sufficient life. (13) This will not be possible, however, unless they inhabit one and the same location and make use of intermarriage. It was on this account that marriage connections arose in cities, as well as clans, festivals, and the pastimes of living together. This sort of thing is the work of affection; for affection is the intentional choice of living together. Living well, then, is the end of the city, and these things are for the sake of this end. (14) A city is the partnership of families and villages in a complete and self-sufficient life. This, we assert, is living happily and finely. The political partnership must be regarded, therefore, as being for the sake of noble actions, not for the sake of living together. (15) Hence those who contribute most to a partnership of this sort have a greater part in the city than those who are equal or greater in freedom and family but unequal in political virtue, or those who outdo them in wealth but are outdone in virtue.

1281a

That all who dispute about regimes speak of some part of justice, then, is evident from what has been said.

[*Book 3 concludes with an assessment of the conflicting claims made on behalf of oligarchies and democracies, and with a depiction of five forms of kingship found in the ancient world.*—J.M.P.]

# ⇥ BOOK 4 ⇤

## Types of Regimes:
## What Preserves and Destroys Them

### *Chapter 1*

### *Scope of the Study of Regimes*

1288b    (1) In all arts and sciences which have not arisen on a partial basis but are complete with respect to some one type of thing, it belongs to a single one to study what is fitting in the case of each type of thing. In the case of training for the body, for example, it belongs to it to study what sort is advantageous for what sort of body; which is best (for the best is necessarily fitting for the body that is naturally the finest and is most finely equipped); which is best—a single one for all—for most bodies (for this too is a task of gymnastic expertise); (2) and further, if someone should desire neither the disposition nor the knowledge befitting those connected with competitions, it belongs no less to the sports trainer and the gymnastic expert to provide this capacity as well. We see a similar thing occurring in the case of medicine, shipbuilding, [the making of] clothing, and every other art.

(3) So it is clear that, with regard to the regime, it belongs to the same science to study what the best regime is, and what quality it should have to be what one would pray for above all, with external things providing no impediment; which regime is fitting for which [cities]—for it is perhaps impossible for many to obtain the best, so neither the one that is superior simply nor the one that is the best that circumstances allow should be overlooked by the good legislator and the political [ruler] in the true sense; (4) further, thirdly, the regime based on a presupposition—for any given regime should be studied [with a view to determining] both how it might arise initially and in what manner it might be preserved

for the longest time once in existence (I am speaking of the case where a city happens neither to be governed by the best regime—and is not equipped even with the things necessary for it—nor to be governed by the regime that is [the best] possible among existing ones, but one that is poorer); (5) and besides all these things, the regime that is most fitting for all cities should be recognized. Thus most of those who have expressed views concerning the regime, even if what they say is fine in other respects, are in error when it comes to what is useful. (6) For one should study not only the best regime but also the regime that is [the best] possible, and similarly also the regime that is easier and more attainable for all. As it is, however, some seek only the one that is at the peak and requires much equipment, while others, though speaking of an attainable sort of regime, disregard those that exist and instead praise the Spartans or some other [single one]. (7) But one ought to introduce an arrangement of such a sort that they will easily be persuaded and be able to participate in it [by the fact that it arises directly] out of those that exist, since to reform a regime is no less a task than to institute one from the beginning, just as unlearning something is no less a task than learning it from the beginning. Hence in addition to what has been said the political expert should be able to assist existing regimes as well, as was also said earlier. (8) But this is impossible if he does not know how many kinds of regime there are. As it is, some suppose there is one sort of democracy and one sort of oligarchy; but this is not true. So the varieties of the regimes—how many there are and in how many ways they are combined—should not be overlooked. (9) And it is with this same prudence that one should try to see both what laws are best and what are fitting for each of the regimes. For laws should be enacted—and all are in fact enacted—with a view to the regimes, and not regimes with a view to the laws. (10) For a regime is an arrangement in cities connected with the offices, [establishing] the manner in which they have been distributed, what the authoritative element of the regime is, and what the end of the partnership is in each case; and there are distinct laws among the things that are indicative of the regime—those in accordance with which the rulers must rule and guard against those transgressing them. (11) So it is clear that it is necessary to have a grasp of the varieties of each regime and their number with a view to the enactment of laws as well. For it is impossible for the same laws to be advantageous for all oligarchies or for all democracies, at least if there are several kinds of them and not merely a single sort of democracy or of oligarchy.

1289a

## Chapter 2

### Types of Regimes

(1) Since in our first inquiry concerning regimes we distinguished three correct regimes—kingship, aristocracy, and polity—and three deviations from these—tyranny from kingship, oligarchy from aristocracy, and democracy from polity, and since aristocracy and kingship have been spoken of—for to study the best regime is the same as to speak about [the regimes designated by] these terms as well, as each of them wishes to be established on the basis of virtue that is furnished with equipment; and further, since the difference between aristocracy and kingship and when [a regime] should be considered kingship were discussed earlier, what remains is to treat polity—that which is called by the name common [to all regimes]—and the other regimes—oligarchy and democracy, and tyranny....

## Chapter 4

### Democracy

1290a

(1) One should not regard democracy, as some are accustomed to do now, as existing simply wherever the multitude has authority, since in oligarchies and indeed everywhere the major part has authority, nor oligarchy as existing wherever the few have authority over the regime. (2) For if [the male inhabitants of a city] were one thousand three hundred in all, and a thousand of these were wealthy and gave no share in ruling to the three hundred poor, though these were free persons and similar in other respects, no one would assert that they are under a democracy. (3) Similarly, if the poor were few, but superior to a majority of well-off persons, no one would describe this sort of thing as an oligarchy, if the others had no part in the prerogatives although they were wealthy. It must rather be said, therefore,

1290b

that [rule of] the people exists when [all] free persons have authority, and oligarchy when the wealthy have it; (4) but it turns out that the former are many and the latter few, for many are free but few wealthy. Otherwise, there would be an oligarchy where they distributed offices on the basis of size, as some assert happens in Ethiopia, or on the basis of good looks; for the number of both good-looking and tall persons is few. (5) Yet neither is it adequate to define these regimes by these things alone. But since there are a number of parts both in the case of [rule of] the people and of oligarchy, it must be grasped further that [rule of] the people does not exist even where a few free persons rule over a majority who are not free, as at Apollonia on the Ionian Sea, for example, or Thera (in each of these cities those who were outstanding in good birth on account of descent from the first settlers of the colony—a few among many—held the prerogatives); nor is there [rule of] the people where the wealthy [rule] through being preeminent in number, as was formerly the case at Colophon (there the majority possessed large properties prior to the war against the Lydians). (6) Democracy exists when the free and poor, being a majority, have authority to rule; oligarchy, when the wealthy and better born have authority and are few....

(20) That there are several sorts of regimes, then, and what the reasons are for this, was stated earlier; we may now say that there are also several kinds of democracy and of oligarchy. This is evident from what has been said as well. (21) For there are several kinds both of the people and of the so-called notables. In the case of the people, for example, there are the farmers, the element engaged in the arts, the marketing element whose pursuits are buying and selling, and the element connected with the sea; of the latter, there is the military element, the element engaged in business, the ferrying element, and the fishing element. (In many places one of these elements amounts to a considerable mass—for example, the fishermen in Tarentum and Byzantium, the warship crews at Athens, the trading element in Aegina and Chios, and the ferrying element in Tenedos.) In addition, there is the menial element and that having little property, so as to be incapable of being at leisure; and further, the free element that is not descended from citizen parents on both sides, and whatever other similar kind of multitude there may be. (22) In the case of the notables, [there are kinds distinguished by] wealth, good birth, virtue, education, and whatever is spoken of as based on the same sort of difference as these.

The first sort of democracy, then, is that which is particularly said to be based on equality. The law in this sort of democracy asserts that there is equality when the poor are no more preeminent than the well off, and neither have authority, but they are both [treated as] similar. (23) For if freedom indeed exists particularly in a democracy, as some conceive to be the case, as well as equality, this would particularly happen where all participate in the regime as far as possible in similar fashion. But since the people are a majority, and what is resolved by the majority is authoritative, this will necessarily be a democracy. (24) This is one kind of democracy; another is the kind where offices are

1291b

filled on the basis of assessments, but these are low, and it is open to anyone possessing [the amount] to share, while anyone losing it does not share. Another kind of democracy is where all citizens of unquestioned descent share, but law rules. (25) Another kind of democracy is where all have a part in the offices provided only they are citizens, but law rules. Another kind of democracy is the same in other respects, but the multitude has authority and not the law. This comes about when decrees rather than law are authoritative, and this happens on account of the popular leaders. (26) For in cities under a democracy that is based on law a popular leader does not arise, but the best of citizens preside; but where the laws are without authority, there popular leaders arise. For the people become a monarch, from many combining into one—for the many have authority not as individuals but all together. (27) What Homer means when he says "many-headed rule is not good" is not clear—whether it is this sort of rule, or the sort when there are a number of rulers acting as individuals. At any rate, such a people, being a sort of monarch, seek to rule monarchically on account of their not being ruled by law, and become like a master: flatterers and held in honor, and this sort of [rule of] the people bears comparison with tyranny among the forms of monarchy. (28) Hence their character is the same as well: both are like masters with respect to the better persons; the decrees of the one are like the edicts of the other; and the popular leader and the flatterers are the same or comparable. These are particularly influential in each case, flatterers with tyrants and popular leaders with peoples of this sort. (29) These are responsible for decrees having authority rather than the laws because they bring everything before the people. For they become great through the people's having authority in all matters, and through having authority themselves over the opinion of the people, since the multitude is persuaded by them. (30) Moreover, some bring accusations against [certain persons holding] offices and assert that the people should judge; the invitation is gladly accepted, and all the offices are thus overthrown. One may hold it a reasonable criticism to argue that a democracy of this sort is not a regime. For where the laws do not rule there is no regime. (31) The law should rule in all matters, while the offices and the regime should judge in particular cases. So if democracy is one of the sorts of regime, it is evident that such a system, in which everything is administered through decrees, is not even democracy in the authoritative sense, since no decree can be general. This may stand, then, as our discussion of the kinds of democracy.

## Chapter 5

## *Oligarchy*

(1) Of the kinds of oligarchy, one is where the offices are filled on the basis of assessments of such a size that the poor do not share, though they are a majority, while it is open to anyone possessing [the amount] to share in the regime. Another is when the offices are filled on the basis of large assessments, and they themselves elect in filling vacancies (if they do this out of all of these it is held to be more aristocratic, but if from certain special ones, oligarchic). (2) Another form of oligarchy is when father succeeds son. A fourth is when what was just spoken of occurs, and not law but the officials rule. This is the counterpart among oligarchies to tyranny among monarchies, and to the sort of democracy we spoke of law among democracies; they call such an oligarchy a "dynasty."

(3) There are, then, this many kinds of oligarchy and democracy. But it should not be overlooked that it has happened in many places that, although the regime insofar as it is based on the laws is not a popular one, it is governed in popular fashion as a result of the character and upbringing [of the citizens]. Similarly, it has happened elsewhere that the regime insofar as it is based on the laws tends toward the popular, but through the [citizens'] upbringing and habits tends to be oligarchically run. (4) This happens particularly after revolution in regimes. For the transition is not immediate: they are content at first to aggrandize themselves at the expense of the others only in small ways, so that the laws that existed before remain, although those who have effected revolution in the regime are dominant.

1292b

## Chapter 8

## *Origins of the Polity*

(1) It remains for us to speak of what is termed polity as well as of tyranny. We have arranged it thus, although polity is not a deviation, nor are those sorts of aristocracies just spoken of, because in truth all fall short of the most correct regime, and because [usually] enumerated with them are those which are themselves deviations from them, as we said in our initial [discourses]. (2) It is reasonable to make mention of tyranny last since of all of them this is least a regime, while our inquiry concerns the regime. The reason it has been arranged in this manner, then, has been spoken of; now we must set out [our view of] polity. Its power should be more evident now that we have discussed what pertains to oligarchy and democracy.

1293b

(3) Simply speaking, polity is a mixture of oligarchy and democracy. It is customary, however, to call polities those [sorts of polities] which tend toward democracy, and those tending more toward oligarchy, aristocracies, on account of the fact that education and good birth particularly accompany those who are better off. (4) Further, those who are well off are held to possess already the things for the sake of which the unjust commit injustice; this is why they are referred to as gentlemen and notables. Since aristocracy tries to assign preeminence to the best of the citizens, it is asserted that oligarchies too are made up particularly of gentlemen. (5) Also, it is held to be impossible for a city to be well managed if it is run not aristocratically but by the base, and similarly, for one that is not well managed to be aristocratically run. For good management does not exist where the laws have been well enacted yet are not obeyed. (6) Hence one should conceive it to be one sort of good management when the laws are obeyed as enacted, and another sort when the laws being upheld have been finely enacted (for it is possible that even badly enacted ones will be obeyed). This may be done in two ways: [they may obey] either the laws that are the best of those possible for them, or those that are the best simply.

1294a

(7) Aristocracy is held to be most particularly the distribution of prerogatives on the basis of virtue; for the defining principle of aristocracy is virtue, as that of oligarchy is wealth, and of [rule of] the people freedom. (The [principle of] what the major part resolves is present in all: in an oligarchy, an aristocracy, or in [regimes ruled by] peoples, what is resolved by the greater part of those sharing in the regime is authoritative.) (8) Now in most cities the kind of regime [that is commonly called aristocracy is not correctly so] called. For the mixture aims only at the well off and the poor, at wealth and freedom, since in most places the well off are held to occupy the place of gentlemen. (9) Since there are three things disputing over equality in the regime, freedom, wealth, and virtue (for the fourth—what they call good birth—accompanies the latter two, good birth being old wealth and virtue together), it is evident that a mixture of the two—of the well off and the poor—is to be spoken of as polity, while a mixture of the three should (apart from the genuine and first form) be spoken of most particularly as aristocracy. (10) That there are other kinds of regimes apart from monarchy, democracy, and oligarchy, then, has been stated, and it is evident which sorts these are, in what ways aristocracies differ among themselves and polities from aristocracy, and that they are not far from one another.

## Chapter 11

### Polity

(1) What regime is best and what way of life is best for most cities and most human beings, judging with a view neither to virtue of the sort that is beyond private persons, nor to education, in respect to those things requiring [special advantages provided by] nature and an equipment dependent on chance, nor to the regime that one would pray for, but a way of life which it is possible for most to participate in, and a regime in which most cities can share? (2) For those that are called aristocracies—the ones we were just speaking of—either fall outside [the range] of most cities, or border on so-called polity; hence we may speak of both as one.

Judgment in all these matters rests on the same elements. (3) If it was correctly said in the [discourses on] ethics that the happy life is one in accordance with virtue and unimpeded, and that virtue is a mean, then the middling sort of life is best—the mean that is capable of being attained by each sort of individual. These same defining principles must also define virtue and vice in the case of a city or a regime; for the regime is the way of life of a city. (4) Now in all cities there are three parts of the city, the very well off, the very poor, and third, those in the middle between these. Since, however, it is agreed that what is moderate and middling is best, it is evident that in the case of the goods of fortune as well a middling possession is the best of all. (5) For it is readiest to obey reason, while for one who is overly handsome, overly strong, overly well born, or overly wealthy—or the reverse of these things, overly indigent, overly weak, or very lacking in honor—it is difficult to follow reason. The former sort tend to become arrogant and base on a grand scale, the latter malicious and base in petty ways; and acts of injustice are committed either through arrogance or through malice. Moreover, these are least inclined either to avoid ruling or to wish to rule, both of which things are injurious to cities. (6) In addition, those who are preeminent in the goods of fortune—strength, wealth, friends, and the other things of this sort—neither wish to be ruled nor know how to be. This is something that marks them from the time they are children at home, for the effect of living in luxury is that they do not become habituated to being ruled even at school; but those who are excessively needy with respect to these things are too humble. (7) So the ones do not know how to rule but only how to be ruled, and then only in the fashion of rule of a master, and the others do not know how to be ruled by any sort of rule, but only to rule in the fashion of rule of a master. What comes into being, then, is a city not of free persons but of slaves and masters, the ones consumed by envy, the others by contempt. Nothing is further removed from affection and from a political partnership; for partnership involves the element of affection—enemies do not wish to have even a journey in common. (8) The city wishes, at any rate, to be made up of equal and similar persons to the extent possible, and this is most particularly the case with the middling elements. So this city must necessarily be governed in the best fashion if it is made up of the elements out of which we assert the city is by nature constituted. Also, of citizens in cities these most particularly preserve themselves. (9) For neither do they desire the things of others, as the poor do, nor others their [property], as the poor desire that of the wealthy; and as a result of not being plotted against or plotting against others they pass their time free from danger. On this account, the prayer of Phocylides was a fine one: "Many things are best for the middling; I would be of the middling sort in the city."

(10) It is clear, therefore, that the political partnership that depends on the middling sort is best as well, and that those cities are capable of being well governed in which the middling element is numerous—most particularly if it is superior to both [of the other] parts, but if not, superior to either of them; for when added to one it will tip the scale and prevent the opposing excesses from arising. (11) Thus it is the greatest good fortune for those who are engaged in politics to have a middling and sufficient property, because where some possess

1296a

very many things and others nothing, either [rule of] the people in its extreme form must come into being, or unmixed oligarchy, or—as a result of both of these excesses—tyranny. For tyranny arises from the most headstrong sort of democracy and from oligarchy, but much less often from the middling sorts [of regime] and those close to them. (12) We will speak of the reason for this later in the [discourses] on revolutions in regimes. But that the middling sort is best is evident. It alone is without factional conflict, for where the middling element is numerous, factional conflicts and splits over [the nature of] the regimes occur least of all. (13) And large cities are freer of factional conflict for the same reason—that the middling element is numerous. In small cities it is easier for all to be separated into two [factions] and have no one left in the middle, and nearly everyone is either poor or well off. (14) And democracies are more stable than oligarchies and more durable on account of those of the middling sort, who are more numerous and have a greater share in the prerogatives in democracies than in oligarchies. When the poor predominate numerically in the absence of these, they fare badly and are quickly ruined. (15) It should be considered an indication of this that the best legislators are from the middling citizens. Solon was one of these, as is clear from his poems, and Lycurgus (for he was not king), Charondas, and most of the others....

## Chapter 12

### Which Regimes Suit Which Cities

(1) What regime is advantageous for which [cities], and what sort for which sort [of persons], is to be treated next after what has been spoken of. Now the same thing must first be grasped about all of them generally: the part of the city that wants the regime to continue must be superior to the part not wanting this. Every city is made up of both quality and quantity. By quality I mean freedom, wealth, education, and good birth; by quantity, the preeminence belonging to the multitude. (2) It is possible that, while quality belongs to one part of the city among all those of which a city is constituted, and quantity to another part (for example, the ignoble may be more in number than those of good family, or the poor than the wealthy), [the larger part] is nevertheless not preeminent in quantity to the same extent that it falls short in quality. Hence these [two factors] must be judged in relation to one another. (3) Where the multitude of the poor is preeminent, therefore, with respect to the proportion mentioned, there a democracy is what accords with nature—and each kind of democracy according to the preeminence belonging to each sort of people. If, for example, the multitude of farmers predominates, it will be the first sort of democracy; if that of vulgar persons and wage earners, the last sort, and similarly for the others between these. But where the element of the well off and the notables predominates in quality to a greater extent than it falls short in quantity, there it is oligarchy that accords with nature, and in a similar manner each of its kinds according to the preeminence belonging to the oligarchic multitude.

(4) The legislator should always add those of the middling sort [to the dominant class] in the regime. If he enacts oligarchic laws, he ought to aim at the middling sort; if democratic ones, he ought to attach these to them. Where the multitude of middling persons predominates either over both the extremities together or over one alone, there a lasting polity is capable of existing. (5) For there is no reason to fear that the wealthy and the poor will come to an agreement against them: neither will want to be the slaves of the other, and if they seek a

1296b

1297a

regime in which they will have more in common, they will find none other than this. They would not put up with ruling in turn on account of their distrust toward one another. The most trustworthy person everywhere is the arbitrator; but the middling person is a sort of arbitrator. (6) The better the mixture in the polity, the more lasting it will be. Many of those who want to set up aristocratic regimes as well [as polities] thoroughly err not only by the fact that they distribute more to the well off, but also by deceiving the people. For in time from things falsely good there must result a true evil, and the aggrandizements of the wealthy are more ruinous to the polity than those of the people.

*[In the remaining chapters of Book 4, Aristotle elaborates on the institutional devices used by oligarchies and democracies in maintaining power. This leads to a discussion of a variety of legislative, executive, and judicial institutions and functions. —J.M.P.]*

## ⇥ BOOK 5 ⇤

### What Preserves and Destroys Regimes

### *Chapter 1*

### *Conflict and Revolution in General*

1301a    (1) Nearly everything else that we intended to speak of has been treated. What things bring about revolutions in regimes and how many and of what sort they are; what are the sources of destruction for each sort of regime and into which sort of regime a regime is most particularly transformed; further, what are the sources of preservation both [for regimes] in common and for each sort of regime separately; and further, by what things each sort of regime might most particularly be preserved—these matters must be investigated in conformity with what has been spoken of.

(2) It is necessary first to take as a beginning point the fact that many sorts of regimes have arisen because, while all agree regarding justice and proportionate equality, they err about this, as was also said earlier. (3) [Rule of] the people arose as a result of those who are equal in any respect supposing they are equal simply, for because all alike are free persons, they consider themselves to be equal simply; and oligarchy arose as a result of those who are unequal in some one respect conceiving

themselves to be wholly unequal, for as they are unequal in regard to property they conceive themselves to be unequal simply. (4) Then the former claim to merit a share in all things equally on the grounds that they are equal, while the latter seek to aggrandize themselves on the grounds that they are unequal, since "greater" is something unequal. (5) All [regimes of this kind] have, then, a certain sort of justice, but in an unqualified sense they are in error. And it is for this reason that, when either [group] does not share in the regime on the basis of the conception it happens to have, they engage in factional conflict. (6) Those who are outstanding in virtue would engage in factional conflict most justifiably, yet they do it the least of all; for it is most reasonable for these only to be unequal in an unqualified sense. (7) There are also certain persons who are preeminent on the basis of family and claim not to merit equal things on account of this inequality: they are held to be well-born persons, to whom belong the virtue and wealth of their ancestors.

These, then, are in a manner of speaking the beginning points and springs of factional conflicts. (8) Hence revolutions also occur in two ways. Sometimes [factional conflict] is with a view to the regime, so that it will be transformed from the established one into another sort, for example from democracy into oligarchy or from oligarchy into democracy, or from these into a polity or aristocracy, or from the latter into the former; sometimes it is not with a view to the established regime, and they intend that the system remain the same, but want to have it in their own hands, as in the case of oligarchy or monarchy. (9) Further, [there may be factional conflict] concerning more and less—for example, where there is an oligarchy, to make it more oligarchically run or less, or where there is a democracy, to make it more democratically run or less, and similarly in the case of the remaining regimes, either to tighten or to loosen them. (10) Further, [there may be factional conflict] with a view to changing a part of the regime—for example, to establish or abolish a certain office. Some assert that Lysander tried to eliminate the kingship at Sparta, and King Pausanias the board of overseers; in Epidamnus too the regime was altered partially—a council replaced the tribal officials, (11) but it is still compulsory [only] for those of the governing body [who hold] offices to come to the hall when there is voting for an office, and the single [supreme] official was also an oligarchic feature of that regime. Factional conflict is everywhere the result of inequality, at any rate where there is no proportion among those who are unequal (a permanent kingship is unequal if it exists among equal persons); in general it is equality they seek when they engage in factional conflict.

(12) Equality is twofold: one sort is numerical, the other is according to merit. By numerical I mean being the same and equal in number or size; by according to merit, [being equal] in respect to a ratio. For example, three exceeds two and two one by an equal amount numerically, whereas four exceeds two and two one by an equal amount with respect to a ratio, both being halves. (13) Now while there is agreement that justice in an unqualified sense is according to merit, there are differences, as was said before: some consider themselves to be equal generally if they are equal in some respect, while others claim to merit all things unequally if they are unequal in some respect.

(14) Hence two sorts of regimes particularly arise—[rule of] the people and oligarchy. Good birth and virtue exist among few persons, these things among more: nowhere are there a hundred well-born and good persons, but in many places the well off are many. Yet to have everywhere an arrangement that is based simply on one or the other of these sorts of equality is a poor thing. This is evident from the result: none of these sorts of regimes is lasting. (15) The reason for this is that, once the first and initial error is committed, it is impossible not to encounter some ill in the end. Hence numerical equality should be used in some cases, and in others equality according to merit. Nevertheless, democracy is more stable and freer from factional conflict than oligarchy. (16) In oligarchies two sorts of factional conflict arise, one against each other, the other against the people; in democracies, though, there is only that against the oligarchy, there being none that arises among the people against itself that is worth mentioning. Moreover, the regime made up of the middling elements is closer to [rule of] the people than to [rule of] the few, and this is the most stable of regimes of this sort.

1302a

## Chapter 8

### Preserving Regimes

1307b

(1) We have to speak next about the preservation of regimes, both in common and separately for each sort. Now in the first place it is clear that if we have an understanding of the things that destroy them, we will also have an understanding of the things that preserve them; for opposites are productive of opposite things, and destruction is the opposite of preservation. (2) In well-blended regimes, then, one should watch out to ensure there are no transgressions of the laws, and above all be on guard against small ones. Transgression of the laws slips in unnoticed, just as small expenditures consume a person's property when frequently repeated.

(3) The expenditure goes unnoticed because it does not happen all at once: the mind is led to reason fallaciously by this, as in the sophistical argument "if each is small, so are all." This is so in one sense, but in another sense not. The whole and all things are not something small, but are composed of small things.

(4) One must be on guard in the first instance, then, against this sort of beginning [of destruction]. Next, one should not trust to those things that have been devised against the multitude, for they are thoroughly refuted by the facts. (As to which sort of devices in regimes we mean, this was spoken of earlier.)

1308a

(5) Further one should see that not only some aristocracies but even some oligarchies last, not because the regimes are stable, but because those occupying the offices treat well those outside the regime as well as those in the governing body—those who do not have a share, by not acting unjustly toward them and by bringing into the regime those among them who have the mark of leaders, not acting unjustly toward the ambitious by depriving them of prerogatives or toward the many with regard to profit; and themselves and those who do have a share, by treating one another in a popular spirit. (6) For the quality that those of the popular sort seek for the multitude is not only just but advantageous for persons who are similar. Hence where there are a number of persons in the governing body, many legislative measures of a popular sort are advantageous, such as having offices be for six months, so that all those who are similar may have a share in them. For similar persons are already a people, as it were, and hence popular leaders often arise among them, as was said earlier. (7) Oligarchies and aristocracies will then be less apt to decline into dynasties, for it is not easy for rulers to act as criminally in a short time as over a longer one. Indeed, it is on this account that tyrannies arise in oligarchies and democracies. For those who aim at tyranny in either regime are either the greatest persons—the popular leaders in the one, the powerful in the other—or those who hold the greatest offices, when they rule for a long time.

(8) Regimes are preserved not only through the things that destroy them being far away, but sometimes also through their being nearby; for when [men] are afraid, they get a better grip on the regime. Thus those who take thought for the regime should promote fears—so that they will defend and not overturn the regime, keeping watch on it like a nocturnal guard—and make the far away near.

(9) Further, one should try to guard against the rivalries and factional conflicts of the notables, both through laws and [by guarding against] those who are outside the rivalry getting caught up in it themselves—for to recognize an ill as it arises in the beginning belongs not to an ordinary person but rather to a man expert in politics.

(10) With regard to the revolution from oligarchy and polity that occurs on account of assessments, when this happens while the assessments remain the same but money becomes abundant, it is advantageous to investigate what the amount of the common assessment is compared with that of the past (in cities which assess every year, on the basis of that period; in larger ones, every third or fifth year), and if the amount is many times greater or less than before at the time when the assessment rates for the regime were established, to have a law that tightened or relaxes the assessments—if [the total current amount] exceeds [the old amount], tightening [the assessments] in proportion to the increase, if it falls short, relaxing the rate of assessment and making it less. (11) If this is not done in oligarchies and polities, the result in the one case is that in the latter and oligarchy arises and in the former a dynasty, while in the other case a democracy arises from polity, and from oligarchy a polity or [rule of the] people.

1308b

(12) It is a thing common to [rule of the] people and oligarchy and to monarchy and every regime not to allow any person to grow overly [great] contrary to proportion, but to attempt to give small prerogatives over a long period of time rather than great ones quickly (for they become corrupted—it does not belong to every man to bear good fortune), or failing this, at least not to give them all at the same time and then take them back all at the same time, but rather gradually. Above all, one should try to shape matters by means of the laws so that there arises no one especially preeminent by the power of his friends or riches, or failing this, that such persons have sojourns abroad.

(13) Since [men] also attempt subversion on account of their private lives, one should create an office to oversee those who live in a manner that is disadvantageous relative to the regime—in a democracy, relative to democracy, in an oligarchy, relative to oligarchy, and similarly for each of the other regimes. For the same reasons the prospering of a part of the city should be guarded against. (14) A remedy for this is always to place actions and offices in the hands of the opposing parts (I speak of the respectable as opposed to the multitude, and the poor as opposed to the well off), and to try either to mix together the multitude of the poor and that of the well off, or to increase the middling element, for this dispels the factional conflicts that result from inequality.

(15) But a very great thing in every regime is to have the laws and management of the rest arranged in such a way that it is impossible to profit from the

offices. This is something that must be looked after particularly in oligarchies. (16) The many do not chafe as much at being kept away from ruling—they are even glad if someone leaves them the leisure for their private affairs—as they do when they suppose that their rulers are stealing common [funds]; then it pains them both not to share in the prerogatives and not to share in the profits. (17) Indeed, the only way it is possible for democracy and aristocracy to exist together is if someone instituted this. For it would then be possible for both the notables and the multitude to have what they want. Having it open to all to rule is characteristic of democracy; having the notables in the offices is characteristic of aristocracy. (18) But this is what will happen when it is impossible to profit from the offices. The poor will not want to rule on account of not profiting, but rather will want to attend to their private affairs; the well off will be able to rule because they will need nothing from the common [funds]. The result for the poor is that they will become well off through spending their time at work; for the well off, that they will not be ruled by ordinary persons. (19) To prevent the stealing of common [funds], then, let the transfer of funds occur in the presence of all the citizens, and let records of this be deposited with each clan, company, and tribe. But to ensure profitless rule, there should be legislation assigning honors to those of good reputation.

1309a

(20) In democracies, the well off should be spared, not only by not having their possessions redivided, but not even their incomes, which in some regimes happens unnoticed; it is better to prevent them from taking on expensive but useless public services, such as leading choruses, officiating at torch races, and other similar things, even if they are willing. In oligarchy, on the other hand, much care should be taken of the poor, and offices from which gains accrue distributed to them, and if one of the well off behaves arrogantly toward them, the penalty should be greater than if toward one of their own. Also, inheritances should be passed on not by bequest but on the basis of family, and the same person should not receive more than one inheritance. In this way, properties would be more on a level, and more of the poor could establish themselves among the well off. (21) And it is advantageous both in a democracy and in an oligarchy to assign equality or precedence to those who participate least in the regime—in [rule of] the people, to the well off, in oligarchy, to the poor—in all respects other than the authoritative offices of the regime; these should be kept in the hands only or mainly of those from the regime.

## Chapter 11

### Preserving Kingships and Tyrannies

1313a

(1) It is clear that they are preserved, on the other hand, by opposite things simply speaking, and in the case of kingships in particular, by drawing them toward greater moderateness. For the fewer the things over which [kings] have authority, the greater the period of time their rule as a whole will necessarily last: they themselves are less like masters and more equal in their characters, and are less envied by those they rule. (2) It is on this account that the kingship of the Molossians has lasted for a long time, and also that of the Lacedaemonians, both because the office was divided from the beginning into two parts and because Theopompus moderated it, among other things by establishing in addition the office of the overseers. By taking away from its power, he increased the duration of the kingship, and so in a certain manner made it not less but greater. (3) This is just what he is supposed to have answered his wife when she asked him whether he was not ashamed to hand over to his sons a kingship that was lesser than the one he had received from his father, and he said: "Not at all—I am handing over one that will be longer lasting."

(4) Tyrannies are preserved in two modes that are quite opposite to one another. One is the mode that has been handed down, according to which most tyrants administer their rule. Most of these [tyrannical methods] are said to have been established by Periander of Corinth; many such things may also be seen in the rule of the Persians. (5) These include both what was spoken of some time ago as relating to the preservation (so far as this is possible) of tyrannies—lopping off the preeminent and eliminating those with high thoughts—and also not permitting

1313b

common messes, clubs, education, or anything else of this sort, but guarding against anything that customarily gives rise to two things, high thoughts and trust. Leisured discussions are not allowed, or other meetings connected with leisure, but everything is done to make all as ignorant of one another as possible, since knowledge tends to create trust of one another. (6) Also, residents [of the city] are made to be always in evidence and pass their time about the doors [of the tyrant's palace]; in this way their activities would escape notice least of all, and they would become habituated to having small thoughts through always acting like slaves. And there are other such features of tyranny, in Persia and among the barbarians, which have the same power. (7) Also, to attempt to let nothing that is done or said by any of those he rules escape his notice, but to have spies, like the women called "inducers" at Syracuse, and the "eavesdroppers" Hiero sent out whenever there was some meeting or gathering (for men speak less freely when they fear such persons, and if they do speak freely they are less likely to escape notice). (8) Also [a feature of tyranny is] to slander them to one another, and set friends at odds with friends, the people with the notables, and the wealthy with themselves. It is also a feature of tyranny to make the ruled poor, so that they cannot sustain their own defense, and are so occupied with their daily [needs] that they lack the leisure to conspire. (9) Examples of this are the pyramids in Egypt, the monuments of the Cypselids, the construction of the temple of Olympian Zeus by the Pisistratids, and the work done by Polycrates on the [temples] at Samos. All of these things have the same effect—lack of leisure and poverty on the part of the ruled. (10) There is also the matter of taxes, as in Syracuse, where in the time of Dionysius it happened that they were taxed for their entire property over a period of five years. The tyrant is also a warmonger, so that they will always be kept lacking in leisure and in need of a leader. Kingship is preserved by friends [of the king], but it is characteristic of the tyrant to distrust his friends, on the assumption that all wish [to overthrow him], but these are particularly capable of it.

(11) Everything that happens in connection with democracy of the extreme sort is characteristic of tyranny—dominance of women in the household, so that they may report on their husbands, and laxness toward slaves for the same reasons. Slaves and women do not conspire against tyrants, and as they prosper [under such circumstances] they necessarily have a benevolent view both of tyrannies and of democracies (for, indeed, the people wish to be a monarch). (12) Hence also the flatterer is held in honor by both—the popular leader by peoples, as the popular leader is a flatterer of the people, and by tyrants, persons approaching them in obsequious fashion, which is the work of flattery. On this account tyranny is friendly to the base, for they delight in being flattered, and no one would do this who had free thoughts: respectable persons may be friends, but they will certainly not flatter. (13) And the base are useful for base things: "nail [is driven out] by nail," as the proverb has it. It is also a feature of tyranny not to delight in anyone who is dignified or free; for the tyrant alone claims to merit being such, and one who asserts a rival dignity and a spirit of freedom takes away the preeminence and the element of mastery of tyranny; hence these are hated as persons

1314a

undermining [the tyrant's] rule. (14) It is also characteristic of the tyrant to have foreigners rather than persons from the city as companions for dining and entertainment, the assumption being that the former are enemies, while the latter do not act as rivals.

Such things are, then, characteristic of tyrants and help preserve their rule—though in no respect do they fall short in depravity. All of these things are encompassed, so to speak, under three heads. (15) For tyranny aims at three things: one, that the ruled have only modest thought (for a small-souled person will not conspire against anyone); second, that they distrust one another (for a tyranny will not be overthrown before some persons are able to trust each other—hence they make war on the respectable as being harmful to their rule not merely because they claim not to merit being ruled in the fashion of a master, but also because they are trustworthy, both among themselves and with respect to others, and will not denounce one another or others); (16) and third, an incapacity for activity, for no one will undertake something on behalf of those who are incapable, so that not even a tyranny will be overthrown where the capacity is lacking. The defining principles to which the wishes of tyrants may be reduced are, then, these three. For one might reduce all things characteristic of tyranny to these presuppositions—that they not trust one another, that they not be capable, that they have modest thought.

(17) The one mode of preservation for tyrannies, then, is of this sort; the other involves a sort of superintendence that is practically the opposite of what has been spoken of. (18) One may grasp this in connection with the destruction of kingships. For just as one mode of destruction for kingship is to make the rule more tyrannical, so it is a source of preservation for tyranny to make it more kingly, provided one thing only is safeguarded—his power, so that he may rule not only willing persons, but also those who are unwilling; for if this is thrown away, so is the tyranny. (19) This must remain as a presupposition, then, but in whatever else he does or is held to do he should give a fine performance of the part of the kingly [ruler]. In the first place, he should be held to take thought for the common [funds], not only by not making expenditures on gifts which enrage the multitude (when they take from persons working and exerting themselves in penury, and give lavishly to prostitutes, foreigners, and artisans), but also by rendering an account of what has been taken in and what expended, as some tyrants have in fact done in the past. One administering matters in this way might be held a manager [of the city] rather than a tyrant....

1314b

*[Book 5 is primarily devoted to outlining the general causes of revolution and change, and the particular causes of revolution and change in each type of constitution: democracy, oligarchy, aristocracy, kingships, and tyrannies. Book 6 develops at greater length the means for constructing democracies and oligarchies. —J.M.P.]*

## ✦ BOOK 7 ✦

## Education and the Best Regime

### *Chapter 1*

### *The Highest Good*

(1) Concerning the best regime, one who is going to undertake the investigation appropriate to it must necessarily discuss first what the most choiceworthy way of life is. As long as this is unclear, the best regime must necessarily be unclear as well; for it is appropriate for those who govern themselves best on the basis of what is available to them to act in the best manner, provided nothing occurs contrary to reasonable expectation. (2) Hence there should first be agreement on which is the most choiceworthy way of life for all, so to speak, and after this, whether the same or a different way of life is choiceworthy [for men] in common and separately [as individuals]. Considering as adequate, then, much of what is said in the external discourses concerning the best way of life, we must use that here as well.

(3) For in truth no one would dispute that, there being a distinction among three groups [of good things], those that are external, those of the body, and those of the soul, all these things ought to be available to the blessed. (4) No one would assert that a person is blessed who has no part of courage, moderation, [the virtue of] justice, or prudence, but is afraid of the flies buzzing around him, abstains from none of the extremes when he desires to eat or drink, destroys his dearest friends for a trifle, and similarly regarding the things connected with the mind, is as senseless and as thoroughly deceived [by a false perception of things] as a child or a madman. (5) Yet while all would admit what has been said, they differ in regard to how much [of each type of good is desirable] and their [relative degree of] preeminence. For [men] consider any amount of virtue to be adequate, but wealth, goods, power, reputation, and all such things they seek to excess without limit. (6) We shall say to them that it is easy to convince oneself concerning these matters through the facts as well [as through argument], when one sees

1323a

that men do not acquire and safeguard the virtues by means of external things, but the latter by means of the former, and that living happily—whether human beings find it in enjoyment or in virtue or in both—is available to those who have to excess the adornments of character and mind but behave moderately in respect to the external acquisition of good things, rather than to those who possess more of the latter than what is useful but are deficient in the former. Yet this can also be readily seen by those investigating on the basis of argument.

(7) External things, like any instrument, have a limit: everything useful belongs among those things an excess of which must necessarily be either harmful or not beneficial to those who have them. In the case of each of the good things connected with the soul, however, the more it is in excess, the more useful it must necessarily be—if indeed one should attribute to these things not only nobility but utility as well. (8) In general, it is clear, we shall assert, that the best state of each thing in relation to other things corresponds with respect to its preeminence to the distance between the things of which we assert that these are states. So if the soul is more honorable than both possessions and the body both simply and for us, the best state of each must necessarily stand in the same relation as these things [among themselves]. (9) Further, it is for the sake of the soul that these things are naturally choiceworthy and that all sensible persons should choose them, and not the soul for the sake of them.

(10) That the same amount of happiness falls to each person as of virtue and prudence and action in accordance with these, therefore, may stand as agreed by us. We may use the god as testimony to this: he is happy and blessed, yet not through any of the external good things but rather through himself and by being of a certain quality in his nature. And it is on this account that good fortune necessarily differs from happiness. Of the good things that are external to the soul the cause is chance and fortune; but no one is just or sound by fortune or through fortune.

(11) Next, and requiring the same arguments, is [the assertion] that the best city is happy and acts nobly. It is impossible to act nobly without acting [to achieve] noble things; but there is no noble deed either of a man or of a city that is separate from virtue and prudence. (12) The courage, justice, and prudence of a city have the same power and form as those things human beings share in individually who are called just, prudent, and sound.

(13) These things, so far as they go, may stand as a preface to our discourse. For it is not possible either not to touch on them or to exhaust all of the arguments

pertaining to them (these things are a task for [an inquiry belonging to] another sort of leisure). For the present let us presuppose this much, that the best way of life both separately for each individual and in common for cities is that accompanied by virtue—virtue that is equipped to such an extent as to [allow them to] share in the actions that accord with virtue. (14) With regard to those who dispute [such an argument], we must pass over them for the purposes of the present inquiry, but shall make a thorough investigation later, if anyone happens not to be persuaded by what has been said.

1324a

## Chapter 2

### The Best Way of Life

(1) Whether happiness must be asserted to be the same both for a single individual human being and for a city or not the same, however, remains to be spoken of. But this too is evident: all would agree it is the same. (2) For those who ascribe living well to wealth in the case of a single person also call the city as a whole blessed if it is wealthy; those who honor the tyrannical way of life above all would also assert that the city is happiest which rules the greatest number of persons; and if anyone accepts that the individual [is happy] on account of virtue, he will also assert that the more excellent city is the one that is happier.

(3) But the following two things are in need of investigation: one, which is the most choiceworthy way of life, that which involves engaging jointly in politics and participating in a city, or rather than characteristic of the foreigner and divorced from the political partnership; and further, which regime and which state of the city are to be regarded as best (regardless of whether participating in a city is choiceworthy for all or only for the most and not for certain persons).

(4) Since this [question]—but not [that concerning] what is choiceworthy for the individual—is a task for political thought and study, and since at present we have intentionally chosen [to limit ourselves to] this sort of investigation, the former is incidental to, the latter a task for, this inquiry.

(5) Now that the best regime must necessarily be that arrangement under which anyone might act in the best manner and live blessedly is evident. Yet there is a dispute among those who agree that the most choiceworthy way of life is that accompanied by virtue as to whether the political and active way of life is choiceworthy, or rather that which is divorced from all external things—that involving some sort of study, for example—which some assert is the only philosophic way of life.

(6) For it is evident that these two ways of life are the ones intentionally chosen by those human beings who are most ambitious with a view to virtue, both in former times and at the present; the two I mean are the political and the philosophic. It makes no small difference on which side the truth lies, for a sensible person, at any rate, must necessarily organize matters with a view to the better aim both in the case of human beings individually and for the regime in common. (7) There are some who consider rule over one's neighbors, if undertaken after the fashion of a master, to be accompanied by injustice of the greatest sort, and if in political fashion, not to involve injustice but to be an impediment to one's own well-being. Others hold opinions that are virtually the opposite of these. [They believe] that the active and political way of life is the only one for a man, and that in the case of each sort of virtue there is no more room for action on the part of private individuals than on the part of those who are active with respect to common matters and engage in politics. (8) This is the conception some of them have; but others assert that the mode of regime involving mastery and tyranny is the only happy one. Indeed, among some [peoples] this is the defining principle of the regime and the laws—that they exercise mastery over their neighbors. (9) Hence while most of the usages existing among most [peoples] are, so to speak, a mere jumble, nevertheless if the laws anywhere look to one thing, it is domination that all of them aim at. In Sparta and Crete, for example, it is with a view to wars that education and the greatest part of the laws are organized. (10) Further, among all nations that are capable of aggrandizing themselves, power of this sort is honored—for example, among the Scythians, the Persians, the Thracians, and the Celts. Among some of them there are also certain laws stimulating [men] to this sort of virtue; for example at Carthage, so it is asserted, they receive armlets to adorn themselves for each campaign they go on. (11) There was once a law in Macedonia as well that any man who had killed an enemy had to wear a tether for a belt; among the Scythians one who had not killed an enemy was not permitted to drink from the cup passed around at a banquet; among the Iberians, a warlike nation, they fix in the ground a tomb as many spits as the number of enemies [the deceased] has destroyed; (12) and there are many other things of this sort among other [peoples], some of them prescribed by laws, others by customs.

Yet it may perhaps seem overly odd to those wishing to investigate [the matter] that this should be the task of the expert in politics, to be able to discern how to rule and exercise mastery over those nearby, whether they wish it or not. (13) How could this be characteristic of the political expert or the legislator when it is not even lawful? It is not lawful to rule [a city in this fashion] justly, let alone unjustly; and it is possible to dominate unjustly. Yet not even in the other sciences do we see this: it is not the task of the doctor or the pilot to either persuade or [failing that] compel persons [to submit to their rule]—patients in the case of the one, voyagers in the case of the other. (14) But the many seem to suppose that expertise in mastery is [the same as] political expertise, and they are not ashamed to train [to do] in relation to others what they deny is just or advantageous for themselves. For among themselves they seek just rule, but they care nothing about justice toward others. (15) It would be odd if there did not exist by nature that which exercises mastery and that which does not exercise mastery, so that if matters stand in this manner, one should not try to exercise mastery over all things but only over those that are to be mastered, just as one should not hunt human beings for a feast or sacrifice, but rather that which is to be hunted for this (that which is to be hunted is any wild animal that is edible). (16) But even by itself a single city could be happy—one that is finely governed (if indeed it is possible for a city to be settled by itself somewhere using excellent laws)—and the organization of its regime will not be with a view to war and the domination of enemies; for [under this assumption] nothing of this sort would exist.

1325a

(17) It is clear, therefore, that all of the concerns that are with a view to war are to be regarded as noble, but not as the highest end of all, but rather as being for the sake of that. It belongs to the excellent legislator to see how a city, a family of human beings, and every other sort of partnership will share in the good life and in the happiness that is possible for them. (18) There will be different arrangements, however, with regard to certain usages [in accordance with differing circumstances]; and where neighboring [peoples] are present, it belongs to legislative expertise to see what sorts of training are to be undertaken with a view to what sorts [of neighboring peoples] or how the things suitable for each sort are to be practiced. But this [question]—toward what end the best regime should be directed—may be appropriately investigated later.

## Chapter 3

### *The Life of Action*

(1) In regard to those who agree that the most choiceworthy way of life is the one accompanied by virtue but differ about the practice of it, we must say to both—on the one side they reject [the holding of] political offices, since they consider the way of life of the free person to be different from that of the political [ruler]

and the most choiceworthy of all; on the other, they consider the latter the best, [arguing that] it is impossible for one who acts in nothing to act well, and that acting well and happiness are the same thing—that they both argue correctly in some respects and incorrectly in others. (2) The one side is correct in saying that the way of life of the free person is better than that involving mastery. This is true: there is nothing dignified about using a slave as a slave; giving commands concerning necessary things has no share in the noble things. But to consider every sort of rule as mastery is not correct. There is no less distance between rule over free persons and rule over slaves than between what is by nature free and what is by nature slavish. But these things were discussed adequately in the initial discourses.

(3) To praise inactivity more than activity is also not true. Happiness is a sort of action, and the actions of just and moderate persons involve an end for many noble things. Now when such matters are discussed in this way, one might perhaps conceive that having authority over all [persons] is best, for in this way one would have authority over the greatest number of the noblest of actions. (4) So [on this understanding] one who is capable of doing so should not leave those nearby to rule themselves but should deprive them of it, and a father should take no account of his children nor children of their father nor a friend for his friend not take any thought for this: the best is what is most choiceworthy, and acting well is best. Perhaps they argue true in this if the most choiceworthy of existing things will be available to those who plunder and use force. (5) But perhaps it is impossible that it be available, and this presupposition of theirs is false. For actions can no longer be noble for one who does not differ as much [from those he rules] as husband differs from wife, father from children, or master from slaves. So the transgressor could never make up later for the deviation from virtue he has already committed. Among similar persons nobility and justice are found in [ruling and being ruled] in turn, for this is something equal and similar: (6) [to assign] what is not equal to equal persons and what is not similar to similar persons is contrary to nature, and nothing contrary to nature is noble. Hence when another person is superior on the basis of virtue and of the power that acts [to achieve] the best things, it is noble to follow this person and just to obey him. (7) (Not only virtue should be present but also power, on the basis of which he will be active.) But if these things are argued rightly and happiness is to be regarded as [the same as] acting well, the best way of life both in common for every city and for the individual would be the active one.

1325b

(8) Yet the active way of life is not necessarily to be regarded as being in relation to others, as some suppose, nor those thoughts alone as being active which arise from activity for the sake of what results, but rather much more those that are complete in themselves, and the sorts of study and ways of thinking that are for their own sake. Acting well is the end, so it too is a certain action; and even in the case of external actions we speak of those who by means of their thoughts are master craftsmen as acting in the authoritative sense. (9) Indeed, not even cities that are situated by themselves and intentionally choose to live in this way are necessarily inactive. For this [activity] can come about on the basis of [a city's] parts: there are many sorts of partnership that belong to the parts of the city in relation to one another. (10) This is available in a similar way to any individual human being as well. For otherwise the god and the entire universe could hardly be in a fine condition, since they have no external actions beyond those that are proper to themselves. That the same way of life must necessarily be the best both for each human being individually and for cities and human beings in common, then, is evident.

## Chapter 13

### Education and Leisure

(1) We must [now] speak of the regime itself, and of which and what sort of things the city that is going to be blessed and finely governed should be constituted from. (2) There are two things that [living] well consists in for all: one of these is in correct positing of the aim and end of actions; the other, discovering the actions that bear on the end. These things can be consonant with one another or dissonant, for sometimes the aim is finely posited but in acting they miss achieving it, and sometimes they achieve everything with a view to the end, but the end they posited was bad. And sometimes they miss both. In connection with medicine, for example, [doctors] sometimes neither judge rightly what the quality of a healthy body should be nor achieve what is productive in relation to the object they set for themselves. But in all arts and sciences both of these should be kept in hand, the end and the actions directed to the end.

(3) Now that everyone strives for living well and for happiness is evident. It is open to some to achieve these things, but to others not, on account of some sort of fortune or nature; for living nobly requires a certain equipment too—less of it for those in a better state, more for those in a worse one. (4) Some, on the other

1331b

1332a

187

hand, seek happiness incorrectly from the outset although it is open to them to achieve it. Since our object is to see the best regime, and this is one in accordance with which a city would be best governed, and it would be best governed in accordance with one that would make it possible for the city to be happy most of all, it is clear that one should not overlook what happiness is.

(5) We assert—and we have defined it thus in the [discourses on] ethics, if there is anything of benefit in those discourses—that happiness is the actualization and complete practice of virtue, and this not on the basis of a presupposition but unqualifiedly. (6) By "not on the basis of a presupposition" I mean necessary things, by "unqualifiedly," nobly. In the case of just actions, for example, just retributions and punishments derive from virtue, but they are necessary, and have the element of nobility only in a necessary way (for it would be more choiceworthy if no man or city required anything of the sort); but actions directed to honors and to what makes one well off are very noble in an unqualified sense. (7) For the one is the choice of an evil, but actions of this [latter] sort are the opposite; they are providers and generators of good things. An excellent man would deal in noble fashion with poverty, disease, and other sorts of bad fortune, but blessedness is in their opposites. Indeed, it was defined thus in the ethical discourses—that the excellent person is one of a sort for whom on account of his virtue the things that are good unqualifiedly are good; (8) and it is clear that his uses of these [good things] must necessarily also be excellent and noble in an unqualified sense. Hence human beings consider the causes of happiness to be those good things that are external—as if the lyre rather than the art were to be held the cause of brilliant and beautiful lyre playing.

Necessarily, therefore, some of the things mentioned must be present, while others must be supplied by the legislator. (9) Hence we pray for the city to be constituted on the basis of what one would pray for in those matters over which fortune has authority (we regard it as having authority [over the external things we regard as being desirable for the best city to have present]); but the city's being excellent is no longer the work of fortune, but of knowledge and intentional choice. But a city is excellent, at any rate, by its citizens'—those sharing in the regime—being excellent; and in our case all the citizens share in the regime. (10) This, then, must be investigated—how a man becomes excellent. Now even if it is possible for all to be excellent but not each of the citizens individually, the latter is more choiceworthy; for all [being excellent] follows from [all] individually [being excellent].

Now [men] become good and excellent through three things. (11) These three are nature, habit, and reason. For one must first develop naturally as a human being and not some one of the other animals, and so also be of a certain quality in body and soul. But there is no benefit in certain [qualities] developing naturally, since habits make them alter: certain [qualities] are through their nature ambiguous, through habits [tending] in the direction of worse or better. (12) The other animals live by nature above all, but in some slight respects by habit as well, while man lives also by reason (for he alone has reason); so these things should be consonant with the other. For [men] act in many ways contrary to their habituation and their nature through reason, if they are persuaded that some other condition is better. (13) Now as to the sort of nature those should have who are going to be readily taken in hand by the legislator, we discussed this earlier. What remains at this point is the work of education. For [men] learn some things by being habituated, others by listening.

1332b

## Chapter 14

### Education and Citizenship

(1) Since every political partnership is constituted of rulers and ruled, this must then be investigated—if the rulers and the ruled should be different or the same throughout life; for it is clear that education too will have to follow in accordance with this distinction. (2) Now if the ones were as different from the others as we believe gods and heroes differ from human beings—much exceeding them in the first place in body, and then in soul, so that the preeminence of the rulers is indisputable and evident to the ruled—it is clear that it would always be better for the same persons to rule and the same to be ruled once and for all. (3) But since this is not easy to assume, there being none so different from the ruled as Scylax says the kings in India are, it is evident that for many reasons it is necessary for all in similar fashion to participate in ruling and being ruled in turn. For equality is the same thing [as justice] for persons who are similar, and it is difficult for a regime to last if its constitution is contrary to justice. (4) For the ruled [citizens] will have with them all those [serfs] in the countryside who want to subvert it, and it is impossible that those in the governing body will be numerous enough to be superior to all of these. Nevertheless, that the rulers should differ from the ruled is indisputable. How this will be the case and how they will share [in ruling and being ruled], then, should be investigated by the legislator.

(5) This was spoken of earlier. Nature has provided the distinction by making that which is the same by type have a younger and an older element, of which it is proper for the former to be ruled and the latter to rule. No one chafes at being ruled on the basis of age or considers himself superior, particularly when he is going to recover his contribution when he attains the age to come. (6) In one sense, therefore, it must be asserted that the same persons rule and are ruled, but in another sense different persons. So education too must necessarily be the same in a sense, and in another sense different. For, so it is asserted, one who is going to rule finely should first have been ruled. Now rule, as was said in our first discourses, is on the one hand for the sake of the ruler, and on the other for the sake of the ruled. Of these [sorts of rule] we assert the former to be characteristic of a master, and the latter to belong to free persons. (7) Now certain commands differ not by the works [involved] but by the [end] for the sake of which [they are carried out]. Hence it is noble for the free among the young to serve in many of the tasks that are held to be characteristic of servants; for, with a view to what is noble and what not noble, actions do not differ so much in themselves as in their end and that for the sake of which [they are performed].

(8) Since we assert that the virtue of citizen and ruler is the same as that of the good man, and the same person must be ruled first and ruler later, the legislator would have to make it his affair to determine how men can become good and through what pursuits, and what the end of the best life is.

(9) The soul is divided into two parts, of which the one has reason itself, while the other does not have it in itself, but is capable of obeying reason. To these belong, we assert, the virtues in accordance with which a man is spoken of as in some sense good. As to which of these the end is more to be found in, what must be said is not unclear to those who distinguish in the way we assert should be done. (10) The worse is always for the sake of the better—this is evident in a similar way both in what accords with art and in what accords with nature; and the element having reason is better. This is divided in two in the manner we are accustomed to distinguish: there is reason of the active sort on the one hand and reason of the studying sort on the other. (11) It is clear, therefore, that this part [of the soul] must also be divided in the same fashion. And we shall say that actions stand in a comparable relationship: those belonging to that [part] which is better by nature are more choiceworthy for those who are capable of achieving either all of them or [those belonging to] the two [lower parts]. For what is most choiceworthy for each individual is the highest it is possible for him to achieve.

1333a

(12) Life as a whole is divided, too, into occupation and leisure and war and peace, and of matters involving action some are directed toward necessary and useful things, others toward noble things. (13) Concerning these things there must of necessity be the same choice as in the case of the parts of the soul and their actions: war must be for the sake of peace, occupation for the sake of leisure, necessary and useful things for the sake of noble things. The political [ruler] must legislate, therefore, looking to all [these] things in the case both of the parts of the soul and of their actions, but particularly to the things that are better and [have more the character of] ends. (14) And [he must do so] in the same manner in connection with the ways of life and the divisions among activities; for one should be capable of being occupied and going to war, but should rather remain at peace and be at leisure, and one should act [to achieve] necessary and useful things, but noble things more so. So it is with a view to these aims that they must be educated when still children as well as during the other ages that require education.

[*In order to construct the best state, Aristotle discusses in Book 7 the effect of several key factors: size and character of population, type of territory, social system, proximity to the sea, city planning, and even climate. Book 8, apparently unfinished, is an inquiry about a system of public education and a proper curriculum.* —J.M.P.]

# ST. AUGUSTINE

~

*Augustine (354-430 A.D.) was born in a North African province of the
Roman Empire, in what today is Algeria. He converted to Christianity in his
twenties and became a major expositor and defender of Christianity.
St. Augustine did not write systematic works in general and certainly none
on political philosophy. Although his immense writings were primarily responses
to urgent theological controversies of his day, he became the most influential
Christian thinker until Thomas Aquinas.*

*The City of God was written between 413 and 427. It was begun
after Alaric and the Goths conquered Rome in 410, and was initially designed
to defend Christianity against charges of undermining the Empire through
the displacement of the Roman gods and rendering the Empire soft through
Christian ethics. In addition to being an important theological work, The City
of God is of major significance to Western civilization because it is the first
serious attempt to explain political existence and to develop a political
philosophy through Christian theology.*

— J.M.P.

## THE CITY OF GOD

### Fallen Nature and the Two Cities

[a]God, desiring not only that the human race might be able by their similarity of
nature to associate with one another, but also that they might be bound together
in harmony and peace by the ties of relationship, was pleased to derive all men from

From *The Political Writings of St. Augustine,* edited by Henry Paolucci. (Translation by M. Dods, J.J. Smith,
and Cr. Wilson, 1872.) Gateway Editions (1985). Reprinted by permission of Regnery Gateway, Inc.

[a]  *City of God,* XIV, 1.

one individual. And He created men with such a nature that the members of the race should not have died, had not the first two (of whom one was created out of nothing, and the other out of him) merited this with their disobedience; for by them so great a sin was committed, that by it the human nature was altered for the worse, and was transmitted also to their posterity.

[b]That the whole human race has been condemned in its first origin, this life itself, if life it is to be called, bears witness by the host of cruel ills with which it is filled. Is not this proved by the profound and dreadful ignorance which produces all the errors that enfold the children of Adam, and from which no man can be delivered without toil, pain, and fear? Is it not proved by his love of so many vain and hurtful things, which produces gnawing cares, disquiet, griefs, fears, wild joys, quarrels, law-suits, wars, treasons, angers, hatreds, deceit, flattery, fraud, theft, robbery, perfidy, pride, ambition, envy, murders, parricides, cruelty, ferocity, wickedness, luxury, insolence, impudence, shamelessness, fornications, adulteries, incests, and the numberless uncleannesses and unnatural acts of both sexes, which it is shameful so much as to mention; sacrileges, heresies, blasphemies, perjuries, oppression of the innocent, calumnies, plots, falsehoods, false witnessings, unrighteous judgments, violent deeds, plunderings, and innumerable other crimes that do not easily come to mind, but that never absent themselves from the actuality of human existence? These are indeed the crimes of wicked men, yet they spring from that root of error and misplaced love which is born with every son of Adam. For who is there that has not observed with what profound ignorance, manifesting itself even in infancy, and with what superfluity of foolish desires, beginning to appear in boyhood, man comes into this life, so that, were he left to live as he pleased, and to do whatever he pleased, he would plunge into all, or certainly into many of those crimes and iniquities which I mentioned, and could not mention?

But because God does not wholly desert those whom He condemns, nor shuts up in His anger His tender mercies, the human race is restrained by law and education, which keep guard against the ignorance that besets us, and oppose the assaults of vice, but are themselves full of labour and sorrow. For what mean those multifarious threats which are used to restrain the folly of children? What mean pedagogues, masters, the birch, the strap, the cane, the schooling which Scripture

---

[b]  *Ibid.*, XXII, 22.

says must be given a child, "beating him on the sides lest he wax stubborn"[1] and it be hardly possible or not possible at all to subdue him? Why all these punishments, save to overcome ignorance and bridle evil desires—these evils with which we come into the world? For why is it that we remember with difficulty, and without difficulty forget? learn with difficulty, and without difficulty remain ignorant? are diligent with difficulty, and without difficulty are indolent? Does not this show that vitiated nature inclines and tends to by its own weight, and what succour it needs if it is to be delivered? Inactivity, sloth, laziness, negligence, are vices which shun labour, since labour, though useful, is itself a punishment.

But, besides the punishments of childhood, without which there would be no learning of what the parents wish—and the parents rarely wish anything useful to be taught—who can describe, who can conceive the number and severity of the punishments which afflict the human race—pains which are not only the accompaniment of the wickedness of godless men, but are a part of the human condition and the common misery—what fear and what grief are caused by bereavement and mourning, by losses and condemnations, by fraud and falsehood, by false suspicions, and all the crimes and wicked deeds of other men? For at their hands we suffer robbery, captivity, chains, imprisonment, exile, torture, mutilation, loss of sight, the violation of chastity to satisfy the lust of the oppressor, and many other dreadful evils. What numberless casualties threaten our bodies from without—extremes of heat and cold, storms, floods, inundations, lightning, thunder, hail, earthquakes, houses falling; or from the stumbling, or shying, or vice of horses; from countless poisons in fruits, water, air, animals; from the painful or even deadly bites of wild animals; from the madness which a mad dog communicates, so that even the animal which of all others is most gentle and friendly to its own master, becomes an object of intenser fear than a lion or dragon, and the man whom it has by chance infected with this pestilential contagion becomes so rabid, that his parents, wife, children, dread him more than any wild beast! What disasters are suffered by those who travel by land or sea! What man can go out of his own house without being exposed on all hands to unforeseen accidents? Returning home sound in limb, he slips on his own door-step, breaks his leg, and never recovers. What can seem safer than a man sitting in his chair? Eli the priest fell from his, and broke his neck. How many accidents do farmers, or rather all men,

---

[1] Ecclus. xxx. 12.

fear that the crops may suffer from the weather, or the soil, or the ravages of destructive animals? Commonly they feel safe when the crops are gathered and housed. Yet, to my certain knowledge, sudden floods have driven the labourers away, and swept the barns clean of the finest harvest. Is innocence a sufficient protection against the various assaults of demons? That no man might think so, even baptized infants, who are certainly unsurpassed in innocence, are sometimes so tormented, that God, who permits it, teaches us hereby to bewail the calamities of this life, and to desire the felicity of the life to come. As to bodily diseases, they are so numerous that they cannot all be contained even in medical books. And in very many, or almost all of them, the cures and remedies are themselves tortures, so that men are delivered from a pain that destroys by a cure that pains. Has not the madness of thirst driven men to drink human urine, and even their own? Has not hunger driven men to eat human flesh, and that the flesh not of bodies found dead, but of bodies slain for the purpose? Have not the fierce pangs of famine driven mothers to eat their own children, incredibly savage as it seems? In fine, sleep itself, which is justly called repose, how little of repose there sometimes is in it when disturbed with dreams and visions; and with what terror is the wretched mind overwhelmed by the appearances of things which are so presented, and which, as it were, so stand out before the senses, that we cannot distinguish them from realities! How wretchedly do false appearances distract men in certain diseases! With what astonishing variety of appearances are even healthy men sometimes deceived by evil spirits, who produce these delusions for the sake of perplexing the senses of their victims, if they cannot succeed in seducing them to their side!

From this hell upon earth, [c] the deserved penalty of sin would have hurled all headlong even into the second death, of which there is no end, had not the undeserved grace of God saved some therefrom. And thus it has come to pass, that though there are very many and great nations all over the earth, whose rites and customs, speech, arms, and dress, are distinguished by marked differences, yet there are no more than two kinds of human society, which we may justly call two cities, according to the language of our Scriptures. The one consists of those who wish to live after the flesh, the other of those who wish to live after the spirit.

First, we must see what it is to live after the flesh, and what to live after the spirit. For any one who either does not recollect, or does not sufficiently weigh,

---

[c] *City of God*, XIV, 1–2.

the language of sacred Scripture, may, on first hearing what we have said, suppose that the Epicurean philosophers live after the flesh, because they place man's highest good in bodily pleasure; and that those others do so who have been of opinion that in some form or other bodily good is man's supreme good; and that the mass of men do so who, without dogmatizing or philosophizing on the subject, are so prone to lust that they cannot delight in any pleasure save such as they receive from bodily sensations: and he may suppose that the Stoics, who place the supreme good of men in the soul, live after the spirit; for what is man's soul, if not spirit? But in the sense of the divine Scripture both are proved to live after the flesh. For by flesh it means not only the body of a terrestrial and mortal animal, as when it says, "All flesh is not the same flesh, but there is one kind of flesh of men, another flesh of beasts, another of fishes, another of birds,"[2] but it uses this word in many other significations.... If we are to ascertain what it is to live after the flesh (which is certainly evil, though the nature of flesh is not itself evil), we must carefully examine that passage of the epistle which the Apostle Paul wrote to the Galatians, in which he says, "Now the works of the flesh are manifest, which are these: adultery, fornication, uncleanness, lasciviousness, idolatry, witchcraft, hatred, variance, emulations, wrath, strife, seditions, heresies, envyings, murders, drunkenness, revellings, and such like: of the which I tell you before, as I have also told you in time past, that they which do such things shall not inherit the Kingdom of God."[3] This whole passage of the apostolic epistle being considered, so far as it bears on the matter in hand, will be sufficient to answer the question, what it is to live after the flesh.

[d]In enunciating this proposition of ours, then, that because some live according to the flesh and others according to the spirit there have arisen two diverse and conflicting cities, we might equally well have said, "because some live according to man, others according to God." For Paul says very plainly to the Corinthians, "For whereas there is among you envying and strife, are ye not carnal, and walk according to man?"[4] So that to walk according to man and to be carnal are the same; for by *flesh,* that is, by a part of man, man is meant.

---

[2]  I. Cor. xv. 39.

[3]  Gal. v. 19–21.

[d]  *City of God,* XIV, 4.

[4]  I. Cor. iii. 3.

ᵉBut the character of the human will is of moment; ... for the man who lives according to God, and not according to man, ought to be a lover of good, and therefore a hater of evil. And since no one is evil by nature, but whosoever is evil is evil by vice, he who lives according to God ought to cherish toward evil men a perfect hatred, so that he shall neither hate the man because of his vice, nor love the vice because of the man. For the vice being cursed, all that ought to be loved, and nothing that ought to be hated, will remain.

He who resolves to love God, and to love his neighbour as himself, not according to man but according to God, is on account of this love said to be of a good will; and this is in Scripture more commonly called charity, but it is also, even in the same books, called love.... The right will is, therefore, well-directed love, and the wrong will is ill-directed love. Love yearning to have what is loved, is desire; and having and enjoying it, is joy; fleeing what is opposed to it, is fear; and feeling what is opposed to it, when it has befallen it, is sadness. Now these motions are evil if the love is *evil;* good if the love is good.

ᶠTwo cities have been formed, therefore, by two loves: the earthly by love of self, even to contempt of God; the heavenly by love of God, even to contempt of self. The former glories in itself, the latter in the Lord. For the one seeks glory from men; but the greatest glory of the other is God, the witness of conscience. The one lifts up its head in its own glory; the other says to its God, "Thou art my glory, and the lifter up of mine head."[5] In the one, the princes and the nations it subdues are ruled by the love of ruling; in the other, the princes and the subjects serve one another in love, the latter obeying, while the former take thought for all. The one delights in its own strength, represented in the persons of its rulers; the other says to its God, "I will love Thee, O Lord, my strength."[6] And therefore the wise men of the one city, living according to man, have sought for profit to their own bodies or souls, or both, and those who have known God "glorified Him not as God, neither were thankful, but became vain in their imaginations, and their foolish hearts were darkened; professing themselves to be wise"—that is, glorying in their own wisdom, and being possessed by pride—"they became fools, and

---

ᵉ  *City of God,* XIV, 6–7.

ᶠ  *City of God,* XIV, 28.

5  Ps. iii. 3.

6  Ps. xviii. 1.

changed the glory of the incorruptible God into an image made like to corruptible man, and to birds, and four-footed beasts, and creeping things." For they were either leaders or followers of the people in adoring images, "and worshipped and served the creature more than the Creator, who is blessed for ever."[7] But in the other city there is no human wisdom, but only godliness, which offers due worship to the true God, and looks for its reward in the society of the saints, of holy angels as well as holy men, "that God may be all in all."[8] [g]And when these two cities severally achieve what they wish, they live in peace, each after its kind.

[h]Now peace is a good so great, that even in this earthly and mortal life there is no word we hear with such pleasure, nothing we more strongly desire, or enjoy more thoroughly when it comes. So that if we dwell for a little longer on this subject, we shall not, in my opinion, be wearisome to our readers who will bear with us both for the sake of understanding what is the end of this city of which we speak, and for the sake of the sweetness of peace which is dear to all.

Everyone who has observed the conduct of men's affairs and common human nature will agree with me in this: that just as there is no man who does not long for joy, so there is no man who does not long for peace. Even those who want war, want it really only for victory's sake: that is, they want to attain a glorious peace by fighting. For what is victory if not the subjugation of those who resist us? And when this is done, peace follows.

It is therefore with the desire for peace that wars are waged, even by those who take pleasure in exercising their warlike nature in command and battle. And hence it is obvious that peace is the end sought for by war. For every man seeks peace by waging war, but no man seeks war by making peace. For even they who intentionally interrupt the peace in which they are living have no hatred of peace, but only wish it changed into a peace that suits them better. They do not, therefore, wish to have no peace, but only one more to their mind. And in the case of sedition, when men have separated themselves from the community, they yet do not effect what they wish, unless they maintain some kind of peace with their fellow-conspirators. And therefore even robbers take care to maintain peace with

---

[7] Rom. i. 21–25.

[8] I. Cor. xv. 28.

[g] *City of God*, XIV, 1.

[h] *Ibid.*, XIX, 11–12.

their comrades, that they may with greater effect and greater safety invade the peace of other men. And if an individual happens to be of such unrivalled strength, and to be so jealous of partnership, that he trusts himself with no comrades, but makes his own plots, and commits depredations and murders on his own account, yet he maintains some shadow of peace with such persons as he is unable to kill, and from whom he wishes to conceal his deeds. In his own home, too, he makes it his aim to be at peace with his wife and children, and any other members of his household; for unquestionably their prompt obedience to his every look is a source of pleasure to him. And if this be not rendered, he is angry, he chides and punishes; and even by this storm he secures the calm peace of his own home, as occasion demands. For he sees that peace cannot be maintained unless all the members of the same domestic circle be subject to one head, such as he himself is in his own house. And therefore if a city or nation offered to submit itself to him, to serve him in the same style as he had made his household serve him, he would no longer lurk in a brigand's hiding-places, but lift his head in open day as a king, though the same covetousness and wickedness should remain in him. And thus all men desire to have peace with their own circle whom they wish to govern as suits themselves. For even those whom they make war against they wish to make their own, and impose on them the laws of their own peace.

But let us suppose a man such as poetry and mythology speak of—a man so insociable and savage as to be called rather a semi-man than a man. Although, then, his kingdom was the solitude of a dreary cave, and he himself was so singularly bad-hearted that he was named Cacus, which is the Greek word for *bad;* though he had no wife to soothe him with endearing talk, no children to play with, no sons to do his bidding, no friend to enliven him with intercourse, not even his father Vulcan (though in one respect he was happier than his father, not having begotten a monster like himself); although he gave to no man, but took as he wished whatever he could, from whomsoever he could, when he could; yet in that solitary den, the floor of which, as Virgil[9] says, was always reeking with recent slaughter, there was nothing else than peace sought, a peace in which no one should molest him, or disquiet him with any assault or alarm. With his own body he desired to be at peace; and he was satisfied only in proportion as he had this peace. For he ruled his members, and they obeyed him; and for the sake of pacifying his mortal nature, which rebelled when it needed anything, and of allaying the sedition of

---

[9] *Aeneid,* viii, 195.

hunger which threatened to banish the soul from the body, he made forays, slew, and devoured, but used the ferocity and savageness he displayed in these actions only for the preservation of his own life's peace. So that, had he been willing to make with other men the same peace which he made with himself in his own cave, he would neither have been called bad, nor a monster, nor a semi-man. Or if the appearance of his body and his vomiting smoky fires frightened men from having any dealings with him, perhaps his fierce ways arose not from a desire to do mischief, but from the necessity of finding a living. But he may have had no existence, or, at least, he was not such as the poets fancifully describe him, for they had to exalt Hercules, and did so at the expense of Cacus. It is better, then, to believe that such a man or semi-man never existed, and that this, in common with many other fancies of the poets, is mere fiction. For the most savage animals (and he is said to have been almost a wild beast) encompass their own species with a ring of protecting peace. They cohabit, beget, produce, suckle, and bring up their young, though very many of them are not gregarious, but solitary—not like sheep, deer, pigeons, starlings, bees, but such as lions, foxes, eagles, bats. For what tigress does not gently purr over her cub, and lay aside her ferocity to fondle them? What kite, solitary as he is when circling over his prey, does not seek a mate, build a nest, hatch the eggs, bring up the young birds, and maintain with the mother of his family as peaceful a domestic alliance as he can? How much more powerfully do the laws of man's nature move him to hold fellowship and maintain peace with all men so far as in him lies, since even wicked men wage war to maintain the peace of their own circle, and wish that, if possible, all men belonged to them, that all men and things might serve but one head, and might, either through love or fear, yield themselves to peace with him!

[i]But the dominion of bad men harms themselves far more than their subjects, for they destroy their own souls in their greater license to exercise their lusts; while those who are put under them in service are not hurt except by their own iniquities. For to the just all the evils imposed on them by unjust rulers are not the punishment of crime, but the test of virtue. Therefore the good man, although he is a slave, is free; but the bad man, even if he reigns, is a slave, and that not of one man, but what is far more grievous, of as many masters as he has vices; of which vices where the divine Scripture treats, it says: "Of whatsoever a man is overcome, to that he is in bondage."[10]

---

[i] *City of God*, IV, 3.

[10] 2 Pet. ii. 19.

ʲThis earthly city, which shall not be everlasting (for it will no longer be a city when it has been committed to perpetual pains) has all its good in this world, and rejoices in it with such joy as such things can afford. ᵏIt is spread throughout the world in the most diverse places, and, though united by a common nature, is for the most part divided against itself, and the strongest oppress the others, because all follow after their own interests and lusts, while what is longed for either suffices for none, or not for all, because it is not the true good. ˡEach part of it that arms against another desires to be the world's master, whereas it is itself in bondage to vice. If, when it has conquered, it is inflated with pride, its victory is self-destroying; but if it turns its thoughts upon the common casualties of our mortal condition, and is rather anxious concerning the disasters that may befall it than elated with the successes already achieved, this victory, though of a higher kind, is still only short-lived; for it cannot abidingly rule over those whom it has subjugated by conquest. Yet one cannot say that the things this earthly city desires are not good, since it itself is, of its kind, better than all other human beings. For it desires earthly peace for the sake of enjoying earthly goods, and it makes war in order to attain this peace; since, if it has conquered, and there remains no one to resist it, it enjoys a peace which it had not while there were opposing parties to contest it for the enjoyment of those things which were too little to satisfy both.

ᵐAnd the vanquished readily succumb to the victors, preferring any sort of peace and safety to freedom itself; so that they who choose to die rather than be slaves have been greatly wondered at. For nature seems to cry out with one voice through all peoples of the world, that it is better to serve the conqueror than be destroyed by war. Thus it happens (but not without God's providence) that some are endowed with kingdoms and others made subject to kings.

## True Justice: Not Of This World

ᵃJustinus, who wrote Greek or rather foreign history in Latin, and briefly, like Trogus Pompeius whom he followed, begins his work thus: "In the beginning of the affairs of peoples and nations the government was in the hands of kings,

---

ʲ  *City of God,* XIV, 4.

ᵏ  *Ibid.,* XVIII, 2.

ˡ  *Ibid.,* XV, 4.

ᵐ  *Ibid.,* XVIII, 2.

ᵃ  *City of God,* IV, 6.

who were raised to the height of this majesty not by courting the people, but by the knowledge good men had of their moderation. The people were held bound by no laws; the decisions of the princes were instead of laws. It was the custom to guard rather than to extend the boundaries of the empire; and kingdoms were kept within the bounds of each ruler's native land. Ninus king of the Assyrians first of all, through new lust of empire, changed the old and, as it were, ancestral custom of nations. He first made war on his neighbours, and wholly subdued as far as to the frontiers of Libya the nations as yet untrained to resist." And a little after he says: "Ninus established by constant possession the greatness of the authority he had gained. Having mastered his nearest neighbours, he went on to others, strengthened by the accession of forces, and by making each fresh victory the instrument of that which followed, subdued the nations of the whole East." Now, with whatever fidelity to fact either he or Trogus may in general have written—for that they sometimes told lies is shown by other more trustworthy writers—yet it is agreed among other authors, that the kingdom of the Assyrians was extended far and wide by King Ninus. And it lasted so long, that the Roman empire has not yet attained the same age; for, as those write who have treated of chronological history, this kingdom endured for twelve hundred and forty years from the first year in which Ninus began to reign, until it was transferred to the Medes. But to make war on your neighbours, and thence to proceed to others, and through mere lust of dominion to crush and subdue people who do you no harm, what else is this to be called than great robbery?

[b]Indeed, without justice, what are kingdoms but great robberies? For what are robberies themselves, but little kingdoms? The band itself is made up of men; it is ruled by the authority of a prince, it is knit together by the pact of the confederacy; the booty is divided by the law agreed on. If, by the admittance of abandoned men, this evil increases to such a degree that it holds places, fixes abodes, takes possession of cities, and subdues peoples, it assumes the more plainly the name of a kingdom, because the reality is now manifestly conferred on it, not by the removal of covetousness, but by the addition of impunity. Indeed, that was an apt and true reply which was given to Alexander the Great by a pirate who had been seized. For when that king had asked the man what he meant by keeping hostile possession of the sea, he answered with bold pride, "What thou

---

[b]  *City of God*, IV, 4.

meanest by seizing the whole earth; but because I do it with a petty ship, I am called a robber, whilst thou who dost it with a great fleet art styled emperor."[1]

ᶜYet, at the end of the second book of Cicero's *De Republica,* Scipio says: "As, among the different sounds which proceed from lyres, flutes, and the human voice, there must be maintained a certain harmony which a cultivated ear cannot endure to hear disturbed or jarring, but which may be elicited in full and absolute concord by the modulation even of voices very unlike one another; so where reason is allowed to modulate the diverse elements of the state, there is obtained a perfect concord from the upper, lower, and middle classes as from various sounds; and what musicians call harmony in singing, is concord in matters of state, which is the strictest bond and best security of any republic, and which by no ingenuity can be retained where justice has become extinct." Then, when he had expatiated somewhat more fully, and had more copiously illustrated the benefits of its presence and the ruinous effects of its absence upon a state, Pilus, one of the company present at the discussion, struck in and demanded that the question should be more thoroughly sifted, and that the subject of justice should be freely discussed for the sake of ascertaining what truth there was in the maxim which was then becoming daily more current, that "the republic cannot be governed without injustice." Scipio expressed his willingness to have this maxim discussed and sifted, and gave it as his opinion that it was baseless, and that no progress could be made in discussing the republic unless it was established, not only that this maxim, that "the republic cannot be governed without injustice," was false, but also that the truth is, that it cannot be governed without the most absolute justice. And the discussion of this question, being deferred till the next day, is carried on in the third book with great animation. For Pilus himself undertook to defend the position that the republic cannot be governed without injustice, at the same time being at special pains to clear himself of any real participation in that opinion. He advocated with great keenness the cause of injustice against justice, and endeavoured by plausible reasons and examples to demonstrate that the former is beneficial, the latter useless, to the republic.

---

[1] Nonius Marcell. borrows this anecdote from Cicero, *De Repub.* iii.

[Nonius Marcellus was a fourth-century A.D. grammarian and lexicographer who collected and preserved extracts from ancient writers. — J.M.P.]

ᶜ *City of God,* II, 21.

Then, at the request of the company, Laelius attempted to defend justice, and strained every nerve to prove that nothing is so hurtful to a state as injustice; and that without justice a republic can neither be governed, nor even continue to exist.

When this question has been handled to the satisfaction of the company, Scipio reverts to the original thread of discourse, and repeats with commendation his own brief definition of a republic, that it is the weal of the people. "The people" he defines as being not every assemblage or mob, but an assemblage associated by a common acknowledgement of law, and by a community of interests. Then he shows the use of definition in debate; and from these definitions of his own he gathers that a republic, or "weal of the people," then exists only when it is well and justly governed, whether by a monarch, or an aristocracy, or by the whole people. But when the monarch is unjust, or as the Greeks say, a tyrant; or the aristocrats are unjust, and form a faction; or the people themselves are unjust, and become, as Scipio for want of a better name calls them, themselves the tyrant, then the republic is not only blemished (as had been proved the day before), but by legitimate deduction from those definitions, it altogether ceases to be. For it could not be the people's weal when a tyrant factiously lorded it over the state; neither would the people be any longer a people if it were unjust, since it would no longer answer the definition of a people—"an assemblage associated by a common acknowledgement of law, and by a community of interests."

Cicero himself, speaking not in the person of Scipio or any one else, but uttering his own sentiments, uses the following language in the beginning of the fifth book, after quoting a line from the poet Ennius, in which he said, "Rome's severe morality and her citizens are her safeguard." "This verse," says Cicero, "seems to me to have all the sententious truthfulness of an oracle. For neither would the citizens have availed without the morality of the community, nor would the morality of the commons without outstanding men have availed either to establish or so long to maintain in vigour so grand a republic with so wide and just an empire. Accordingly, before our day, the hereditary usages formed our foremost men, and they on their part retained the usages and institutions of their fathers. But our age, receiving the republic as a *chef d'œuvre* of another age which has already begun to grow old, has not merely neglected to restore the colours of the original, but has not even been at the pains to preserve so much as the general outline and most outstanding features. For what survives of that primitive morality which the poet called Rome's safeguard? It is so obsolete and forgotten, that, far from practising it, one does not even know it. And of the citizens what shall I say? Morality has perished through poverty of great men; a poverty for which we must not only assign a reason, but for the guilt of which we must answer as criminals charged with a capital crime. For it is through our vices, and not by any mishap, that we retain only the name of a republic, and have long since lost the reality."

This is the confession of Cicero, long indeed after the death of Africanus, whom he introduced as an interlocutor in his work *De Republica*.... But Rome's admirers have need to inquire whether, even in the days of primitive men and morals, true justice flourished in it; or was it not perhaps even then, to use the casual expression of Cicero, rather a coloured painting than the living reality? If God will, I mean in its own place to show that—according to the definitions in which Cicero himself, using Scipio as his mouthpiece, briefly propounded what a republic is, and what a people is, and according to many testimonies, both of his own lips and of those who took part in that same debate—Rome never was a republic, because true justice had never a place in it.

[d]Away with deceitful masks, with deluding whitewashes; look at the naked deeds; weigh them naked, judge them naked! [e]Sallust says that "equity and virtue prevailed among the Romans not more by force of laws than of nature."[2] ...

---

[d] *City of God*, III, 14.

[e] *Ibid.*, II, 17–18.

[2] Sallust, *Cat. Con.* ix.

[Gaius Sallustius Crispus was a first-century B.C. Roman historian and politician. After the death of Julius Caesar he wrote several works about the decline of the Roman Republic, including the *Conspiracy of Cataline,* from which this quotation is taken. —J.M.P.]

# ST. THOMAS AQUINAS

⟳

*St. Thomas Aquinas (1224-1274) was born near Aquino, Italy, into a noble Italian family. Against the wishes of his family he entered a Dominican order and spent his life primarily as a university scholar and teacher in Paris, Cologne, Rome, and Naples. With the revival of Greek philosophy and, particularly, of Aristotelianism, the Church faced the task of determining the proper relationship between theology and Greek philosophy. St. Thomas devoted himself to this task of reconciling faith and reason into a synthesis. He died at the age of 50, but his writings were judged by the Church to be so successful that in 1879 they were declared the official teaching of the Church.*

*St. Thomas wrote commentaries on the chief works of Aristotle, including* The Politics. *Of his own works, there are two that are essential for understanding his Christian political philosophy:* On Kingship, *written in 1266-1267 for the King of Cyprus; and sections of the* Summa Theologica, *written between 1267-1274 and never finished. In both works one can see St. Thomas synthesizing the writings of "the Philosopher" (Aristotle) and the tenets of Christian theology.*

— J.M.P.

## ON KINGSHIP

### To the King of Cyprus

[1] As I was turning over in my mind what I might present to Your Majesty as a gift at once worthy of Your Royal Highness and befitting my profession and office, it seemed to me a highly appropriate offering that, for a king, I should write

*On Kingship, to the King of Cyprus,* by St. Thomas Aquinas, translated by Gerald B. Phelan, revised by I. Th. Eschmann, OP. Reprinted by permission of the publishers. © 1949, 1982 The Pontifical Institute of Mediaeval Studies, Toronto.

a book on kingship, in which, so far as my ability permits, I should carefully expound, according to the authority of Holy Writ and the teachings of the philosophers as well as the practice of worthy princes, both the origin of kingly government and the things which pertain to the office of a king, relying for the beginning, progress and accomplishment of this work, on the help of Him, Who is King of Kings, Lord of Lords, through Whom kings rule, God the Mighty Lord, King great above all gods.

## Chapter I

### What is Meant by the Word "King"

[2] The first step in our undertaking must be to set forth what is to be understood by the term *king*.

[3] In all things which are ordered towards an end wherein this or that course may be adopted, some directive principle is needed through which the due end may be reached by the most direct route. A ship, for example, which moves in different directions according to the impulse of the changing winds, would never reach its destination were it not brought to port by the skill of the pilot. Now, man has an end to which his whole life and all his actions are ordered; for man is an intelligent agent, and it is clearly the part of an intelligent agent to act in view of an end. Men also adopt different methods in proceeding towards their proposed end, as the diversity of men's pursuits and actions clearly indicates. Consequently man needs some directive principle to guide him towards his end.

[4] To be sure, the light of reason is placed by nature in every man, to guide him in his acts towards his end. Wherefore, if man were intended to live alone, as many animals do, he would require no other guide to his end. Each man would be a king unto himself, under God, the highest King, inasmuch as he would direct himself in his acts by the light of reason given him from on high. Yet it is natural for man, more than for any other animal, to be a social and political animal, to live in a group.

[5] This is clearly a necessity of man's nature. For all other animals, nature has prepared food, hair as a covering, teeth, horns, claws as means of defence or at least speed in flight, while man alone was made without any natural provisions for these things. Instead of all these, man was endowed with reason, by the use of which he could procure all these things for himself by the work of his

hands. Now, one man alone is not able to procure them all for himself, for one man could not sufficiently provide for life, unassisted. It is therefore natural that man should live in the society of many.

[6] Moreover, all other animals are able to discern, by inborn skill, what is useful and what is injurious, even as the sheep naturally regards the wolf as his enemy. Some animals also recognize by natural skill certain medicinal herbs and other things necessary for their life. Man, on the contrary, has a natural knowledge of the things which are essential for his life only in a general fashion, inasmuch as he is able to attain knowledge of the particular things necessary for human life by reasoning from natural principles. But it is not possible for one man to arrive at a knowledge of all these things by his own individual reason. It is therefore necessary for man to live in a multitude so that each one may assist his fellows, and different men may be occupied in seeking, by their reason, to make different discoveries—one, for example, in medicine, one in this and another in that.

[7] This point is further and most plainly evidenced by the fact that the use of speech is a prerogative proper to man. By this means, one man is able fully to express his conceptions to others. Other animals, it is true, express their feelings to one another in a general way, as a dog may express anger by barking and other animals give vent to other feelings in various fashions. But man communicates with his kind more completely than any other animal known to be gregarious, such as the crane, the ant or the bee. —With this in mind, Solomon says: "It is better that there be two than one; for they have the advantage of their company."

[8] If, then, it is natural for man to live in the society of many, it is necessary that there exist among men some means by which the group may be governed. For where there are many men together and each one is looking after his own interest, the multitude would be broken up and scattered unless there were also an agency to take care of what appertains to the common weal. In like manner, the body of a man or any other animal would disintegrate unless there were a general ruling force within the body which watches over the common good of all members. —With this in mind, Solomon says: "Where there is no governor, the people shall fall."

[9] Indeed it is reasonable that this should happen, for what is proper and what is common are not identical. Things differ by what is proper to each: they are united by what they have in common. But diversity of effects is due to diversity of causes. Consequently, there must exist something which impels towards the common good of the many, over and above that which impels towards

the particular good of each individual. Wherefore also in all things that are ordained towards one end, one thing is found to rule the rest. Thus in the corporeal universe, by the first body, *i.e.* the celestial body, the other bodies are regulated according to the order of Divine providence; and all bodies are ruled by a rational creature. So, too, in the individual man, the soul rules the body; and among the parts of the soul, the irascible and the concupiscible parts are ruled by reason. Likewise, among the members of a body, one, such as the heart or the head, is the principal and moves all the others. Therefore in every multitude there must be some governing power.

[10] Now it happens in certain things which are ordained towards an end that one may proceed in a right way and also in a wrong way. So, too, in the government of a multitude there is a distinction between right and wrong. A thing is rightly directed when it is led towards a befitting end; wrongly when it is led towards an unbefitting end. Now the end which befits a multitude of free men is different from that which befits a multitude of slaves, for the free man is one who exists for his own sake, while the slave, as such, exists for the sake of another. If, therefore, a multitude of free men is ordered by the ruler towards the common good of the multitude, that rulership will be right and just, as is suitable to free men. If, on the other hand, a rulership aims, not at the common good of the multitude, but at the private good of the ruler, it will be an unjust and perverted rulership. The Lord, therefore, threatens such rulers, saying by the mouth of Ezechiel: "Woe to the shepherds that feed themselves (seeking, that is, their own interest): should not the flocks be fed by the shepherd?" Shepherds indeed should seek the good of their flocks, and every ruler, the good of the multitude subject to him.

[11] If an unjust government is carried on by one man alone, who seeks his own benefit from his rule and not the good of the multitude subject to him, such a ruler is called a *tyrant*—a word derived from "*strength*"—because he oppresses by might instead of ruling by justice. Thus among the ancients all powerful men were called tyrants. If an unjust government is carried on, not by one but by several, and if they be few, it is called an *oligarchy*, that is, the rule of a few. This occurs when a few, who differ from the tyrant only by the fact that they are more than one, oppress the people by means of their wealth. If, finally, the bad government is carried on by the multitude, it is called a *democracy, i.e.* control by the populace, which comes about when the plebeian people by force of numbers oppress the rich. In this way the whole people will be as one tyrant.

[12] In like manner we must divide just governments. If the government is administered by many, it is given the name common to all forms of government, *viz. polity*, as for instance when a group of warriors exercise dominion over a city or province. If it is administered by a few men of virtue, this kind of government is called an *aristocracy, i.e.* noble governance, or governance by noble men, who for this reason are called the *Optimates*. And if a just government is in the hands of one man alone, he is properly called a *king*. Wherefore the Lord says by the mouth of Ezechiel: "My servant, David, shall be king over them and all of them shall have one shepherd."

[13] From this it is clearly shown that the idea of king implies that he be one man who is chief and that he be a shepherd seeking the common good of the multitude and not his own....

# SUMMA THEOLOGICA

## → PART II ←
### (First Part)
### Significance of the State

*The Value of the State*
(Question 21, Article 4)

Man is not ordained to the body politic, according to all that he is and has; and
so it does not follow that every action of his acquires merit or demerit in relation
to the body politic. But all that man is, and can, and has, must be referred to
God: and therefore every action of man, whether good or bad, acquires merit or
demerit in the sight of God, as far as the action itself is concerned.

*Political, Divine and Natural Orders*
(Question 72, Article 4)

Now there should be a threefold order in man:—one in relation to the rule of
reason, in so far as all our actions and passions should be commensurate with
the rule of reason:—another order is in relation to the rule of the Divine law,
whereby man should be directed in all things: and if man were by nature a solitary animal, this twofold order would suffice. —But since man is naturally a civic
and social animal, as is proved in *Politics*, I. 2, hence a third order is necessary,
whereby man is directed in relation to other men among whom he has to dwell.

## Treatise on Law

*The Essence of Law*
(Question 90, Article 1)

Law is a rule and measure of acts, whereby man is induced to act or is restrained
from acting: for *lex* (law) is derived from *ligare* (to bind), because it binds one

*Summa Theologica,* by St. Thomas Aquinas, translated by Fathers of the English Dominican
Province. Originally published in English 1911. Revised edition published 1920, London.
Copyright © 1948 by Benziger Brothers, Inc. Reprinted by permission of Glencoe Publishing
Company, a division of Macmillan, Inc. All rights reserved.

to act. Now the rule and measure of human acts is the reason, which is the first principle of human acts, as is evident from what has been stated elsewhere; since it belongs to the reason to direct to the end, which is the first principle in all matters of action, according to the Philosopher....

Reason has its power of moving from the will, as stated above: for it is due to the fact that one wills the end, that the reason issues its commands as regards things ordained to the end. But in order that the volition of what is commanded may have the nature of law, it needs to be in accord with some rule of reason. And in this sense is to be understood the saying that the will of the sovereign has the force of law; otherwise the sovereign's will would savour of lawlessness rather than of law.

### Law and the Common Good

#### (Question 90, Article 2)

Now the first principle in practical matters, which are the object of the practical reason, is the last end: and the last end of human life is bliss or happiness, as stated above. Consequently the law must needs regard principally the relationship to happiness. Moreover, since every part is ordained to the whole, as imperfect to perfect; and since one man is a part of the perfect community, the law must needs regard properly the relationship to universal happiness. Wherefore the Philosopher, in the above definition of legal matters mentions both happiness and the body politic: for he says (*Ethics,* V. 1) that we call those legal matters *just, which are adapted to produce and preserve happiness and its parts for the body politic:* since the state is a perfect community, as he says in *Politics,* I. 1.

### Promulgation of Law

#### (Question 90, Article 3)

A law, properly speaking, regards first and foremost the order to the common good. Now to order anything to the common good, belongs either to the whole people, or to someone who is the vicegerent of the whole people. And therefore the making of a law belongs either to the whole people or to a public personage who has care of the whole people: since in all other matters the directing of anything to the end concerns him to whom the end belongs....

A private person cannot lead another to virtue efficaciously: for he can only advise, and if his advice be not taken, it has no coercive power, such as the law should have, in order to prove an efficacious inducement to virtue, as the

Philosopher says (*Ethics,* X. 9). But this coercive power is vested in the whole people or in some public personage, to whom it belongs to inflict penalties....

As one man is a part of the household, so a household is a part of the state: and the state is a perfect community, according to *Politics,* I. 1. And therefore, as the good of one man is not the last end, but is ordained to the common good; so too the good of one household is ordained to the good of a single state, which is a perfect community. Consequently he that governs a family, can indeed make certain commands or ordinances, but not such as to have properly the force of law.

### Definition of Law
### (Question 90, Article 4)

Thus from the four preceding articles, the definition of law may be gathered; and it is nothing else than an ordinance of reason for the common good, made by him who has care of the community, and promulgated.

## The Various Kinds of Law

### Eternal Law
### (Question 91, Article 1)

As stated above, a law is nothing else but a dictate of practical reason emanating from the ruler who governs a perfect community. Now it is evident, granted that the world is ruled by Divine providence, as was stated in the First Part (Question 22, Arts. 1, 2), that the whole community of the universe is governed by Divine Reason. Wherefore the very Idea of the government of things in God the Ruler of the universe, has the nature of a law. And since the Divine Reason's conception of things is not subject to time but is eternal, according to Prov. viii. 23, therefore it is that this kind of law must be called eternal.

### Natural Law
### (Question 91, Article 2)

Wherefore, since all things subject to Divine providence are ruled and measured by the eternal law, as was stated above; it is evident that all things partake somewhat of the eternal law, in so far as, namely, from its being imprinted on them, they derive their respective inclinations to their proper acts and ends. Now among all others, the rational creature is subject to Divine providence in the most excellent way, in so far as it partakes of a share of providence, by being provident both for itself and for others. Wherefore it has a share of the Eternal Reason, whereby it has a natural inclination to its proper act and end: and this participation of the eternal law in the rational creature is called the natural law. Hence the Psalmist after saying (Ps. iv. 6): *Offer up the sacrifice of justice,* as though someone asked what the works of justice are, adds: *Many say, Who showeth us good things?* in answer to which question he says: *The light of Thy countenance, O Lord, is signed upon us:* thus implying that the light of natural reason, whereby we discern what is good and what is evil, which is the function of the natural law, is nothing else than an imprint on us of the Divine light. It is therefore evident that the natural law is nothing else than the rational creature's participation of the eternal law.

## Human Law

### (Question 91, Article 3)

Accordingly we conclude that just as, in the speculative reason, from naturally known indemonstrable principles, we draw the conclusions of the various sciences, the knowledge of which is not imparted to us by nature, but acquired by the efforts of reason, so too it is from the precepts of the natural law, as from general and indemonstrable principles, that the human reason needs to proceed to the more particular determination of certain matters. These particular determinations, devised by human reason, are called human laws, provided the other essential conditions of law be observed, as stated above (Question 90, Arts. 2, 3, 4). Wherefore Cicero says in his *Rhetoric (De Invent. Rhet.* ii) that *justice has its source in nature; thence certain things came into custom by reason of their utility; afterwards these things which emanated from nature and were approved by custom, were sanctioned by fear and reverence for the law.*

## Divine Law

### (Question 91, Article 4)

Besides the natural and the human law it was necessary for the directing of human conduct to have a Divine law. And this for four reasons. First, because it is by law that man is directed how to perform his proper acts in view of his last end. And indeed if man were ordained to no other end than that which is proportionate to his natural faculty, there would be no need for man to have any further direction on the part of his reason, besides the natural law and human law which is derived from it. But since man is ordained to an end of eternal happiness which is inproportionate to man's natural faculty, as stated above (Question 5, Art. 5), therefore it was necessary that, besides the natural and the human law, man should be directed to his end by a law given by God.

Secondly, because, on account of the uncertainty of human judgment, especially on contingent and particular matters, different people form different judgments on human acts; whence also different and contrary laws result. In order, therefore, that man may know without any doubt what he ought to do and what he ought to avoid, it was necessary for man to be directed in his proper acts by a law given by God, for it is certain that such a law cannot err.

Thirdly, because man can make laws in those matters of which he is competent to judge. But man is not competent to judge of interior movements, that are hidden, but only of exterior acts which appear: and yet for the perfection of virtue it is necessary for man to conduct himself aright in both kinds of acts. Consequently human law could not sufficiently curb and direct interior acts; and it was necessary for this purpose that a Divine law should supervene.

Fourthly, because, as Augustine says (*De Lib. Arb.* i. 5, 6), human law cannot punish or forbid all evil deeds: since while aiming at doing away with all evils, it would do away with many good things, and would hinder the advance of the common good, which is necessary for human intercourse. In order, therefore, that no evil might remain unforbidden and unpunished, it was necessary for the Divine law to supervene, whereby all sins are forbidden.

# Just War

## (Question 40, Article 1)

In order for a war to be just, three things are necessary. First, the authority of the sovereign by whose command the war is to be waged. For it is not the business of a private individual to declare war, because he can seek for redress of his rights from the tribunal of his superior. Moreover it is not the business of a private individual to summon together the people, which has to be done in wartime. And as the care of the common weal is committed to those who are in authority, it is their business to watch over the common weal of the city, kingdom or province subject to them. And just as it is lawful for them to have recourse to the sword in defending that common weal against internal disturbances, when they punish evil-doers, according to the words of the Apostle (Rom. xiii. 4): *He holdeth not the sword in vain: for he is God's minister, an avenger to execute wrath upon him that doth evil;* so too, it is their business to have recourse to the sword of war in defending the common weal against external enemies. Hence it is said to those who are in authority (Ps. lxxxi. 4): *Rescue the poor: and deliver the needy out of the hand of the sinner;* and for this reason Augustine says (*Contra Faust.* xxii. 75): *The natural order conducive to peace among mortals demands that the power to declare and counsel war should be in the hands of those who hold the supreme authority.*

Secondly, a just cause is required, namely that those who are attacked, should be attacked because they deserve it on account of some fault. Wherefore Augustine says (*QQ. in Hept.*, qu. x., *super Jos.*): *A just war is wont to be described as one that avenges wrongs, when a nation or state has to be punished, for refusing to make amends for the wrongs inflicted by its subjects, or to restore what it has seized unjustly.*

Thirdly, it is necessary that the belligerents should have a rightful intention, so that they intend the advancement of good, or the avoidance of evil. Hence Augustine says *(De Verb. Dom.[1]): True religion looks upon as peaceful those wars that are waged not for motives of aggrandisement, or cruelty, but with the object of securing peace, of punishing evil-doers, and of uplifting the good.* For it may happen that the war is declared by the legitimate authority, and for a just cause, and yet be rendered unlawful through a wicked intention. Hence Augustine says (*Contra Faust.* xxii. 74): *The passion for inflicting harm, the cruel thirst for vengeance, an unpacific and relentless spirit, the fever of revolt, the lust of power, and suchlike things, all these are rightly condemned in war.*

## Resisting Tyrannical Government

### (Question 42, Article 2)

A tyrannical government is not just, because it is directed, not to the common good, but to the private good of the ruler, as the Philosopher states (*Politics,* III. 5; *Ethics,* VIII. 10). Consequently there is no sedition in disturbing a government of this kind, unless indeed the tyrant's rule be disturbed so inordinately, that his subjects suffer greater harm from the consequent disturbance than from the tyrant's government. Indeed it is the tyrant rather that is guilty of sedition, since he encourages

---

[1]  [The words quoted are to be found, not in St. Augustine's works, but Can. *Apud.* Caus. xxiii., qu. I.]

discord and sedition among his subjects, that he may lord over them more securely; for this is tyranny, being conducive to the private good of the ruler, and to the injury of the multitude.

## Right To Property

### (Question 66, Article 1)

External things can be considered in two ways. First, as regards their nature, and this is not subject to the power of man, but only to the power of God Whose mere will all things obey. Secondly, as regards their use, and in this way, man has a natural dominion over external things, because, by his reason and will, he is able to use them for his own profit, as they were made on his account: for the imperfect is always for the sake of the perfect, as stated above. It is by this argument that the Philosopher proves (*Politics,* I. 3) that the possession of external things is natural to man. Moreover, this natural dominion of man over other creatures, which is competent to man in respect of his reason wherein God's image resides, is shown forth in man's creation (Gen. i. 26) by the words: *Let us make man to Our image and likeness: and let him have dominion over the fishes of the sea,* etc.

## Property Useful to Human Life

### (Question 66, Article 2)

Two things are competent to man in respect of exterior things. One is the power to procure and dispense them, and in this regard it is lawful for man to possess property. Moreover this is necessary to human life for three reasons. First because every man is more careful to procure what is for himself alone than that which is common to many or to all: since each one would shirk the labour and leave to another that which concerns the community, as happens where there is a great number of servants. Secondly, because human affairs are conducted in more orderly fashion if each man is charged with taking care of some particular thing himself, whereas there would be confusion if everyone had to look after any one thing indeterminately. Thirdly, because a more peaceful state is ensured to man if each one is contented with his own. Hence it is to be observed that quarrels arise more frequently where there is no division of the things possessed.

The second thing that is competent to man with regard to external things is their use. In this respect man ought to possess external things, not as his own, but as common, so that, to wit, he is ready to communicate them to others in their need. Hence the Apostle says (I Tim. vi. 17, 18): *Charge the rich of this world ... to give easily, to communicate to others,* etc.

Community of goods is ascribed to the natural law, not that the natural law dictates that all things should be possessed in common, and that nothing should be possessed as one's own: but because the division of possessions is not according to the natural law, but rather arose from human agreement which belongs to positive law, as stated above. Hence the ownership of possessions is not contrary to the natural law, but an addition thereto devised by human reason.

## Need and Charity

### (Question 66, Article 8)

Things which are of human right cannot derogate from natural rights or Divine right. Now according to the natural order established by Divine providence, inferior things are ordained for the purpose of succouring man's needs by their means. Wherefore the division and appropriation of things which are based on human law, do not preclude the fact that man's needs have to be remedied by means of these very things. Hence whatever certain people have in superabundance is due, by natural law, to the purpose of succouring the poor. For this reason Ambrose says, and his words are embodied in the Decretals: *It is the hungry man's bread that you withhold, the naked man's cloak that you store away, the money that you bury in the earth is the price of the poor man's ransom and freedom.*

Since, however, there are many who are in need, while it is impossible for all to be succoured by means of the same thing, each one is entrusted with the stewardship of his own things, so that out of them he may come to the aid of those who are in need. Nevertheless, if the need be so manifest and urgent, that it is evident that the present need must be remedied by whatever means be at hand (for instance when a person is in some imminent danger, and there is no other possible remedy), then it is lawful for a man to succour his own need by means of another's property, by taking it either openly or secretly: nor is this properly speaking theft or robbery.

# Usury

## *Profit*

### (Question 77, Article 4)

A tradesman is one whose business consists in the exchange of things. According to the Philosopher (*Politics,* I. 3), exchange of things is twofold; one, natural as it were, and necessary, whereby one commodity is exchanged for another, or money taken in exchange for a commodity, in order to satisfy the needs of life. Suchlike trading, properly speaking, does not belong to tradesmen, but rather to house-keepers or civil servants who have to provide the household or the state with the necessaries of life. The other kind of exchange is either that of money for money, or of any commodity for money, not on account of the necessities of life, but for profit, and this kind of exchange, properly speaking, regards tradesmen, according to the Philosopher (*Politics,* I. 3). The former kind of exchange is commendable because it supplies a natural need: but the latter is justly deserving of blame, because, considered in itself, it satisfies the greed for gain, which knows no limit and tends to infinity. Hence trading, considered in itself, has a certain debasement attaching thereto, in so far as, by its very nature, it does not imply a virtuous or necessary end. Nevertheless gain which is the end of trading, though not implying, by its nature, anything virtuous or necessary, does not, in itself, connote anything sinful or contrary to virtue: wherefore nothing prevents gain from being directed to some necessary or even virtuous end, and thus trading becomes lawful. Thus, for instance, a man may intend the moderate gain which he seeks to acquire by trading for the upkeep of his household, or for the assistance of the needy: or again, a man may take to trade for some public advantage, for instance, lest his country lack the necessaries of life, and seek gain, not as an end, but as payment for his labour.

## *The Injustice of Usury*

### (Question 78, Article 1)

To take usury for money lent is unjust in itself, because this is to sell what does not exist, and this evidently leads to inequality which is contrary to justice.

In order to make this evident, we must observe that there are certain things the use of which consists in their consumption: thus we consume wine when we use it for drink, and we consume wheat when we use it for food. Wherefore in such-like things the use of the thing must not be reckoned apart from the thing itself, and whoever is granted the use of the thing, is granted the thing itself; and for this reason, to lend things of this kind is to transfer the ownership. Accordingly if a man wanted to sell wine separately from the use of the wine, he would be selling the same thing twice, or he would be selling what does not exist, wherefore he would evidently commit a sin of injustice. In like manner he commits an injustice who lends wine or wheat, and asks for double payment, *viz.* one, the return of the thing in equal measure, the other, the price of the use, which is called usury.

On the other hand there are things the use of which does not consist in their consumption: thus to use a house is to dwell in it, not to destroy it. Wherefore in such things both may be granted: for instance, one man may hand over to another the ownership of his house while reserving to himself the use of it for a time, or vice versa, he may grant the use of the house, while retaining the ownership. For this reason a man may lawfully make a charge for the use of his house, and, besides this, revendicate the house from the person to whom he has granted its use, as happens in renting and letting a house.

Now money, according to the Philosopher (*Ethics*, V. 5; *Politics*, I. 3) was invented chiefly for the purpose of exchange: and consequently the proper and principal use of money is its consumption or alienation whereby it is sunk in exchange. Hence it is by its very nature unlawful to take payment for the use of money lent, which payment is known as usury: and just as a man is bound to restore other ill-gotten goods, so is he bound to restore the money which he has taken in usury....

Human laws leave certain things unpunished, on account of the condition of those who are imperfect, and who would be deprived of many advantages, if all sins were strictly forbidden and punishments appointed for them. Wherefore human law has permitted usury, not that it looks upon usury as harmonizing with justice, but lest the advantage of many should be hindered. Hence it is that in civil law it is stated that *those things according to natural reason and civil law which are consumed by being used, do not admit of usufruct*, and that *the senate did not (nor could it) appoint a usufruct to such things, but established a quasi-usufruct*, namely by permitting usury. Moreover the Philosopher, led by natural reason, says (*Politics*, I. 3) that *to make money by usury is exceedingly unnatural.*

# NICCOLÒ MACHIAVELLI

*Machiavelli (1469–1527) was a citizen of the city-state of Florence. He served the Florentine Republic for 14 years as a secretary to the city council and as a diplomatic envoy. The Republic was overthrown by the Medici family in 1512, and Machiavelli was dismissed and tortured. He remained in political exile until 1526, when the Medici finally gave him a minor government post. The Medici themselves were overthrown shortly afterwards, and Machiavelli was again dismissed, but this time for being pro-Medici.*

*During his long period of exile Machiavelli wrote several literary works, including* The Golden Ass, *a poem;* Mandragola, *a comic play; and* Felfagor, *a short novel. His fame rests on the political realism, or, some would argue, the sinister advice, found in his political-historical works:* The Art of War, The History of Florence, Discourses on the First Ten Books of Titus Livius, *and* The Prince. *Relatively unknown during his lifetime, his reputation has resulted mainly from the* Discourses *and* The Prince. The Prince, *his most famous work, was published five years after his death. In 1557 Pope Paul IV placed the book on the* Index Expurgatorious, *the Catholic church's list of banned works.*

— J.M.P.

# THE PRINCE

## ⤤ DEDICATORY LETTER ⤦

### Niccolò Machiavelli to His Magnificence Lorenzo de' Medici[1]

Those who wish to be viewed with favour by a ruler usually approach him with things from among their possessions that are very dear to them, or with things that they expect will please him. Hence, it often happens that they are presented with horses, weapons, a cloth of gold, precious stones and similar ornaments, which are worthy of their exalted position. Wishing myself to offer Your Magnificence some token of my devotion to you, I have not found among my belongings anything that I hold more dear or valuable than my knowledge of the conduct of great men, learned through long experience of modern affairs and continual study of ancient history: I have reflected on and examined these matters with great care, and have summarised them in a small volume, which I proffer to Your Magnificence.

And although I consider this work unworthy to be presented to Your Magnificence, I trust very much that your humanity will lead you to accept it, since it is not in my power to offer you a greater gift than one which in a very short time will enable you to understand all that I have learned in so many years, and with much difficulty and danger. I have not embellished this work by filling it with rounded periods, with high-sounding words or fine phrases, or with any of the other beguiling artifices of apparent beauty which most writers employ to describe and embellish their subject-matter; for my wish is that, if it is to be honoured at all, only its originality and the importance of the subject should make it acceptable.

I hope it will not be considered presumptuous for a man of very low and humble condition to dare to discuss princely government, and to lay down rules about it. For those who draw maps place themselves on low ground, in order to

---

[1] [Not Lorenzo the Magnificent, but the son of Piero de' Medici, and nephew of Pope Leo X.]

understand the character of the mountains and other high points, and climb higher in order to understand the character of the plains. Likewise, one needs to be a ruler to understand properly the character of the people, and to be a man of the people to understand properly the character of rulers.

May Your Magnificence, then, accept this little gift in the spirit in which I am sending it; if it is read and pondered diligently, my deep wish will be revealed, namely, that you should achieve that greatness which propitious circumstances and your fine qualities promise. And if Your Magnificence, from the heights of your exalted position, should sometimes deign to glance down towards these lowly places, you will see how much I am unjustly oppressed by great and cruel misfortune.

## Chapter V

### How one should govern cities or principalities that, before being conquered, used to live under their own laws

When states that are annexed have been accustomed to living under their own laws and in freedom, as has been said, there are three ways of holding them: the first, to destroy their political institutions; the second, to go to live there yourself; the third, to let them continue to live under their own laws, exacting tribute and setting up an oligarchical government that will keep the state friendly towards you. Since the government has been set up by that ruler, it knows that it will be dependent upon his goodwill and power, and will be very concerned to maintain the status quo. If one wants to preserve a city that is accustomed to being independent and having free institutions, it is more easily held by using its citizens to govern it than in any other way.

The Spartans and the Romans provide good examples. The Spartans held Athens and Thebes by establishing oligarchies there; yet they eventually lost control over them. In order to hold Capua, Carthage and Numantia, the Romans destroyed them and consequently never lost them. They tried to hold Greece in a similar manner to the Spartans, by granting it freedom and letting it live under its own laws. This was unsuccessful, so they were then forced to destroy many cities in that country, in order to maintain their hold over it. In fact, destroying cities is the only certain way of holding them. Anyone who becomes master of a city accustomed to a free way of life, and does not destroy it, may expect to be destroyed by it himself, because when it rebels, it will always be able to appeal to the spirit of freedom and its ancient institutions, which are never forgotten, despite the passage of time and any benefits bestowed by the new ruler. Whatever he does, whatever provisions he makes, if he does not foment internal divisions or scatter the inhabitants, they will never forget their lost liberties and their ancient institutions, and will immediately attempt to recover them whenever they have an opportunity, as Pisa did after enduring a century of subjection to the Florentines.

However, when cities or countries are accustomed to living under a prince, and the ruling family is wiped out, the inhabitants are used to obeying but lack their older ruler; they are unable to agree on making one of themselves ruler, and they do not know how to embrace a free way of life. Consequently, they are slow to resort to arms, and a ruler can more easily win them over, and be sure that they will not harm him.

But in republics there is greater vitality, more hatred, and a stronger desire for revenge; they do not forget, indeed cannot forget, their lost liberties. Therefore, the surest way is to destroy them or else go to live there.

## Chapter VI

### New principalities acquired by one's own arms and ability

Nobody should be surprised if, in discussing completely new principalities, both as regards the ruler and the type of government, I shall cite remarkable men as examples. For men almost always follow in the footsteps of others, imitation being a leading principle of human behaviour. Since it is not always possible to follow in the footsteps of others, or to equal the ability of those whom you imitate, a shrewd man will always follow the methods of remarkable men, and imitate those who have been outstanding, so that, even if he does not succeed in matching their ability, at least he will get within sniffing distance of it. He should act as skilful archers do, when their target seems too distant: knowing well the power of their bow, they aim at a much higher point, not to hit it with the arrow, but by aiming there to be able to strike their target.

I maintain, then, that in a completely new principality, where there is a new ruler, the difficulty he will have in maintaining it will depend on how much ability he possesses. And because for a private citizen to become ruler presupposes that he is either able or lucky, it might seem that one or other of these would, to some degree, mitigate many of the difficulties. Nevertheless, rulers maintain themselves better if they owe little to luck. It is also very helpful when the ruler is compelled to go and live in his principality, because he does not possess other states.

However, to come to those who have become rulers through their own ability and not through luck or favour, I consider that the most outstanding were Moses, Cyrus, Romulus, Theseus and others of that stamp. And although one should not discuss Moses, because he was merely an executor of what had been ordained by God, yet he should be admired even if only for that favour which made him worthy to speak with God. But let us consider Cyrus and others who have acquired or founded kingdoms. They will all be found remarkable, and if their actions and methods are considered, they will not appear very different from those of Moses, who had such a great master.

If their deeds and careers are examined, it will be seen that they owed nothing to luck except the opportunity to shape the material into the form that seemed best to them. If they had lacked the opportunity, the strength of their spirit would have been sapped; if they had lacked ability, the opportunity would have been wasted.

It was necessary, then, for Moses to find the people of Israel in Egypt, enslaved and oppressed by the Egyptians, so that they would be disposed to follow him, in order to escape from their servitude. It was necessary that Romulus, who was exposed at birth in Alba, did not find there full scope for his abilities, so that he should have wanted to become King of Rome and, indeed, its founder. It was necessary that Cyrus should have found the Persians discontented under the rule of the Medes, and that the Medes should have been soft and weak because of the long peace. And Theseus could not have fully revealed his abilities had he not found the Athenians dispersed. These opportunities, then, permitted these men to be successful, and their surpassing abilities enabled them to recognise and grasp these opportunities; the outcome was that their own countries were ennobled and flourished greatly.

Those who, like them, become rulers through their own abilities, experience difficulty in attaining power, but once that is achieved, they keep it easily. The difficulties encountered in attaining power arise partly from the new institutions and laws they are forced to introduce in order to establish their power and make it secure. And it should be realised that taking the initiative in introducing a new form of government is very difficult and dangerous, and unlikely to succeed. The reason is that all those who profit from the old order will be opposed to the innovator, whereas all those who might benefit from the new order are, at best, tepid supporters of him. This lukewarmness arises partly from fear of their adversaries, who have the laws on their side, partly from the sceptical temper of men, who do not really believe in new things unless they have been seen to work well. The result is that whenever those who are opposed to change have the chance to attack the innovator, they do it with much vigour, whereas his supporters act only half-heartedly; so that the innovator and his supporters find themselves in great danger.

In order to examine this matter thoroughly, we need to consider whether these innovators can act on their own or whether they depend upon others; that is, whether they need to persuade others if they are to succeed, or whether they are capable of establishing themselves by force. In the former case, they always fare badly and accomplish nothing. But if they do not depend upon others and have sufficient forces to take the initiative, they rarely find themselves in difficulties. Consequently, all armed prophets succeed whereas unarmed ones fail. This happens because, apart from the factors already mentioned, the people are fickle; it is easy to persuade them about something, but difficult to keep them persuaded. Hence, when they no longer believe in you and your schemes, you must be able to force them to believe.

If Moses, Cyrus, Theseus and Romulus had been unarmed, the new order which each of them established would not have been obeyed for very long. This is what happened in our own times to Fra' Girolamo Savonarola, who perished together with his new order as soon as the masses began to lose faith in him; and he lacked the means of keeping the support of those who had believed in him, as well as of making those who had never had any faith in him believe.

Such innovators, then, have to confront many difficulties; all the dangers come after they have begun their enterprises, and need to be overcome through their own ability. But once they have succeeded, and begin to be greatly respected (after they have extinguished those envious of their success), they remain powerful, secure, honoured and successful.

I should like to add a less important example than the eminent ones already discussed. But it certainly is worthy of mention in this context, so let it suffice for all the others like it: I refer to Hiero of Syracuse. From being a private citizen, he became ruler of Syracuse. He enjoyed a fine opportunity but, apart from that, his success owed nothing to luck. For when the Syracusans were in desperate straits, they chose him as their general; afterwards he was deservedly made their ruler. And even in private life he showed so much ability that it was written of him *"quod nihil illi deerat ad regnandum praeter regnum."*[2] He disbanded the old army and raised a new one; he abandoned the old alliances and formed new ones; and as soon as he possessed his own troops and had reliable allies he could build any edifice he wanted upon this foundation. Thus, it was very difficult for him to attain power, but not to keep it.

## Chapter VII

### New principalities acquired through the power of others and their favour

Private citizens who become rulers only through favour or luck achieve that rank with little trouble, but experience great difficulty in retaining it. In arriving at that position there are no problems, because they fly there; all the difficulties arise afterwards. This is the situation if a state or territory is granted to someone either for money or by favour of the giver, as happened to many in Greece, in the cities of Ionia and the Hellespont, where Darius set up rulers so that they would hold them to increase his security and enhance his glory. Other cases are those private citizens who became emperors, attaining the imperial throne by bribing the soldiers. Such men are entirely dependent on the goodwill and prosperity of those who gave them their positions, and these are two things that are exceedingly variable and uncertain. Such men lack the knowledge and capacity to maintain their power. They lack the knowledge because, unless he has great intelligence and ability, it is not to be expected that a man who has always lacked direct experience of public life should know how to rule. They lack the capacity because they do not have devoted and loyal forces at their disposal. Moreover, like all other natural things that are born and grow rapidly, states that grow quickly cannot sufficiently develop their roots, trunks and branches, and will be destroyed by the first chill winds of adversity. This happens unless those who have so quickly become rulers have the ability to profit by what luck or favour has placed in their laps, and know how to make provision very speedily to preserve their power, developing afterwards the foundations that others have laid before they become rulers.

To illustrate these two methods of becoming ruler, namely, through ability or through favour or luck, I want to cite two recent examples: Francesco Sforza and Cesare Borgia. Francesco, through using appropriate methods and exploiting

---

[2] [Justinus, XXIII, 4: "that the only thing he lacked to be a ruler was a kingdom."]

his great ability, from being a private citizen became Duke of Milan; and he maintained with very little trouble the position that he attained only with count-less difficulties. On the other hand, Cesare Borgia, popularly called the Duke Valentino, attained his position through the favour and help of his father, and lost it when these disappeared, despite having used every means and having done all those things that a far-seeing and able man should do, in order to put down his roots in territories that he had acquired thanks to the power and favour of others. For, as I have said, a man who does not lay his foundations at first may be able to do it later, if he possesses great ability, although this creates difficulties for the builder and the edifice itself may well prove unstable.

If the whole career of the Duke is considered, then, it will be seen that he succeeded in laying very strong foundations for his future power. I do not consider it superfluous to discuss it, for I do not know what better precepts to offer to a new ruler than to cite his actions as a pattern; and although his efforts were in the end unsuccessful, he should not be blamed, because it resulted from extraordinarily bad luck....

## Chapter VIII

### Those who become rulers through wicked means

But because there still remain two ways in which one can become a ruler, which cannot be attributed entirely either to favour or luck or to ability, I do not want to neglect them, even though one of them could be discussed at greater length when dealing with republics. These two ways are seizing power through utterly wicked means, and a private citizen becoming ruler of his country through the favour of his fellow-citizens. Considering the first way now, I shall cite two examples, one ancient and the other modern, without considering explicitly the merits of this way of gaining power, for I think they should be enough for anyone who needs to imitate them.

Agathocles the Sicilian, who became King of Syracuse, was not only an or-dinary citizen, but of the lowest and most abject origins. He was the son of a pot-ter, and he always led a very dissolute life. Nevertheless, his evil deeds were combined with such energy of mind and body that, after having entered the militia, he rose through the ranks to become praetor of Syracuse. Holding that position, he resolved to become ruler, and to hold violently and without being beholden to others the power that had been conferred on him. In order to achieve this purpose, he conspired with Hamilcar the Carthaginian, who was campaigning in Sicily. One morning he called together the people and the senate of Syracuse, as if some matter concerning the republic had to be decided. Then, at a prearranged signal, his soldiers killed all the senators and the richest men of the city. After this massacre, he seized control of the city, and thereafter held it without any civil strife.

Although he was twice defeated by the Carthaginians, and eventually besieged by them, he not only showed himself capable of defending his besieged city but, leaving part of his army to resist the siege, he attacked Africa with the rest. Very soon he was able to relieve Syracuse from the siege, and went on to reduce Carthage to the direst straits. Consequently, the Carthaginians were forced to make an agreement with him, according to which they were to remain in Africa and leave Sicily to Agathocles.

If Agathocles's conduct and career are reviewed, then, it will be seen that luck or favour played little or no part in his success, since (as has been said above) it was not through anyone's favour, but through overcoming countless difficulties and dangers, that he rose up through the ranks of the militia, and gained power, which he afterwards maintained by undertaking many courageous and dangerous courses of action.

Yet it cannot be called virtue[3] to kill one's fellow-citizens, to betray one's friends, to be treacherous, merciless and irreligious; power may be gained by acting in such ways, but not glory. If one bears in mind the ability displayed by Agathocles in confronting and surviving dangers, and his indomitable spirit in enduring and overcoming adversity, there is no reason for judging him inferior to even the ablest general. Nevertheless, his appallingly cruel and inhumane conduct, and countless wicked deeds, preclude his being numbered among the finest men. One cannot, then, attribute either to luck or favour or to ability[4] what he achieved without either.

In our own times, when Alexander VI was pope, Oliverotto of Fermo, whose father died when he was very young, was brought up by Giovanni Fogliani, his maternal uncle, and when still a youth was sent to train as a soldier under Paulo

---

[3] [*virtú*: this word is used in several senses in M.'s account of Agathocles; usually it denotes "energy," "drive," "ability" or "courage," but here it has overtones, at least, of "moral virtue."]

[4] [*virtú*: M. did not mean that Agathocles lacked *virtú* (in the senses of "ability," "energy" or "courage"), but that it was through wicked means (*scelleratezze*) that he became ruler.]

Vitelli, with a view to his achieving high rank when he had become proficient in things military. After Paulo's execution, he trained under Vitellozzo, Paulo's brother; and since he was clever, and strong in body and spirit, in a very short time he became a leader of Vitellozzo's troops. But because he considered it demeaning to serve under another, he resolved to seize power in Fermo, with Vitellozzo's assistance, and with the help of some citizens of Fermo, to whom the servitude of their native city was preferable to its free institutions.[5] Accordingly, he wrote to Giovanni Fogliani, saying that since he had been away from home for many years, he wanted to come to see him and his own city, and to inspect in some measure his own patrimony. Since achieving honour had been the only goal of all his efforts, so that his fellow-citizens would realise that he had not spent his time in vain, he wanted to return in a way that did him honour, and accompanied by a hundred cavalrymen drawn from his friends and followers. And he beseeched Giovanni to arrange for him to be received with due honour by the citizens of Fermo; this would not only honour himself, but also Giovanni, who had educated him.

Giovanni did not fail to treat his nephew with the utmost courtesy, and after the citizens (thanks to Giovanni) had received him with every honour, he was lodged in Giovanni's house, where, after he had spent some days secretly arranging everything that was necessary for carrying out his intended crime, Oliverotto held a formal banquet, to which he invited Giovanni Fogliani and all the leading citizens of Fermo. After the banquet, and all the entertainments customary on such occasions, Oliverotto artfully raised some serious matters, speaking of the great power of Pope Alexander and his son Cesare, and of their various enterprises. When Giovanni and the others began to reply to what Oliverotto had said, he suddenly arose, saying that such matters should be discussed in a more private place. And he went into another room followed by Giovanni and all the others. No sooner were they all seated than his soldiers emerged from hiding-places, and killed Giovanni and all the others.

After this massacre, Oliverotto mounted his horse and rode through the city, taking possession of it, and besieged the chief magistrates in their palace. They were so afraid that they felt constrained to obey him, and they formed a new

---

5   [*la libertà:* Fermo was a free commune or republic. M. should not be understood to have meant that they really "preferred" (*era piú cara*) Fermo's servitude as such (i.e., its subjection to a princely ruler like Oliverotto); rather (as Sasso suggests) they were doubtless prominent citizens who hoped to have greater weight under a ruler whom they had helped to attain power.]

government, of which he made himself the head. And when he had killed all the malcontents who could have harmed him, he consolidated his power by means of new civil and military institutions, so that in the space of the year that he held power he was not only secure in the city of Fermo, but made all the neighbouring powers fear him. And ousting him would have been as difficult as ousting Agathocles, if he had not let himself be tricked by Cesare Borgia, when the Orsini leaders and Vitellozzo Vitelli were captured ... at Senigallia. He too was captured there, a year after his parricide, and together with Vitellozzo, his former mentor in prowess and villainy, strangled.

It may well be wondered how it could happen that Agathocles, and others like him, after committing countless treacherous and cruel deeds, could live securely in their own countries for a long time, defend themselves against external enemies and never be plotted against by their citizens. For many others have not been able to maintain their power by acting cruelly even in peaceful times let alone in times of war, which are always uncertain.

I believe that this depends upon whether cruel deeds are committed well or badly. They may be called well committed (if one may use the word "well" of that which is evil) when they are all committed at once, because they are necessary for establishing one's power, and are not afterwards persisted in, but changed for measures as beneficial as possible to one's subjects. Badly committed are those that at first are few in number, but increase with time rather than diminish. Those who follow the first method can in some measure remedy their standing both with God and with men, as Agathocles did. Those who follow the second cannot possibly maintain their power.

Hence, it should be noted that a conqueror, after seizing power, must decide about all the injuries he needs to commit, and do all of them at once, so as not to have to inflict punishments every day. Thus he will be able, by his restraint, to reassure men and win them over by benefiting them. Anyone who does not act in this way, either because he is timid or because he lacks judgement, will always be forced to stand with sword in hand. He will never be able to rely upon his subjects, for they can never feel safe with him, because of the injuries that continue to be inflicted. For injuries should be done all together so that, because they are tasted less, they will cause less resentment; benefits should be given out one by one, so that they will be savoured more. And above all a ruler must live with his subjects in such a way that no unexpected events, whether favourable or unfavourable, will make him change course. For when difficult times put you under pressure you will not have enough time to take harsh measures, and any benefits that you confer will not help you, because they will be considered to be done unwillingly, and so you will receive no credit for them.

## Chapter IX

### The civil principality

I turn now to the other case, when a private citizen becomes ruler of his own country through the favour of his fellow-citizens, not through villainy or intolerable violence of other kinds: this may be called a civil principality (and to attain it, it is not necessary to have only ability or only good luck, but rather a lucky astuteness). I say that one rises to this position either through being favoured by the people or through being favoured by the nobles; for these two classes are found in every city. And this situation arises because the people do not want to be dominated or oppressed by the nobles, and the nobles want to dominate and oppress the people. And from these two different dispositions there are three possible outcomes in cities: a principality, a republic or anarchy.

This kind of principality is brought about either by the people or by the nobles, according to whether one or the other has the opportunity to act. As for the nobles, when they are unable to resist popular pressure, they begin to favour and advance one of themselves, and make him ruler so that, under his protection, they will be able to satisfy their appetites. On the other hand, the people, when they realise that they cannot resist the nobles, favour and advance one of themselves, and make him ruler, so that through his authority he will be able to protect them.

A man who becomes ruler through the help of the nobles will find it harder to maintain his power than one who becomes ruler through the help of the people, because he is surrounded by many men who consider that they are his equals, and therefore he cannot give them orders or deal with them as he would wish. On the other hand, a man who becomes ruler through popular support finds himself standing alone, having around him nobody or very few not disposed to obey him.

Moreover, the nobles cannot be satisfied if a ruler acts honourably, without injuring others. But the people can be thus satisfied, because their aims are more honourable than those of the nobles: for the latter want only to oppress and the former only to avoid being oppressed. Furthermore, a ruler can never protect himself from a hostile people, because there are too many of them; but he can protect himself from the nobles, because there are few of them. The worst that can befall a ruler from a hostile people is being deserted by them; but he has to fear not only being abandoned by hostile nobles, but also that they will move against him. Since they are more far-seeing and cunning, they are able to act in time to save themselves, and seek to ingratiate themselves with the one whom they expect to prevail. Again, a ruler is always obliged to co-exist with the same people, whereas he is not obliged to have the same nobles, since he is well able to make and unmake them at any time, advancing them or reducing their power, as he wishes.

To clarify this matter, let me say that two main considerations need to be borne in mind with regard to the nobles. Either they conduct themselves in a way that links your success with theirs, or they do not. You should honour and esteem those of the former who are not rapacious. As for those who do not commit themselves to you, two different kinds of reason for their conduct must be distinguished. If they act in this way because of pusillanimity or natural lack of spirit, you should make use of them, especially those who are shrewd, because in good times they will bring you honour, and in troubled times you will have nothing to fear from them. But if they do not commit themselves to you calculatingly and because of ambition, it is a sign that they are thinking more of their own interests than of yours. And a ruler must watch these nobles very carefully, and fear them as much as if they were declared enemies, because if he finds himself in trouble they will always do their best to bring him down.

A man who becomes ruler through popular favour, then, must keep the people well disposed towards him. This will be easy, since they want only not to be oppressed. But a man who becomes ruler against the wishes of the people, and through the favour of the nobles, must above all else try to win over the people, which will be easy if you protect them. And if men are well treated by those from whom they expected ill-treatment, they become more attached to their benefactor; the people will at once become better disposed towards him than if he had attained power through their favour. A ruler can win over the people in many ways; but because these vary so much according to the circumstances one cannot give any definite rules, and I shall therefore leave this matter on one side. I shall affirm only that it is necessary for a ruler to have the people well disposed towards him; otherwise, in difficult times he will find himself in desperate straits.

Nabis, ruler of the Spartans, withstood a siege by all the other Greek powers and by a triumphant Roman army, defending both his country and his own power against them. When danger threatened, he needed only to act against a few;[6] but if the people had been hostile to him, this would not have been enough. And doubt should not be cast on my opinion by quoting the trite proverb, "He who builds upon the people, builds upon mud." This is true if it is a private citizen who builds his power upon them, and believes that the people will come to his rescue if he is oppressed by his enemies or by the rulers. In such circumstances one may often be disappointed, as the Gracchi were in Rome and messer Giorgio Scali in Florence. But if it is a ruler who builds his power upon the people, and if he knows how to command and if he is courageous, does not despair in difficult times, and maintains the morale of his people by his spiritedness and the measures that he takes, he will never find himself let down by them, and he will realise he had laid sound foundations for his power....

## Chapter XI

### Ecclesiastical principalities

It remains now only to discuss ecclesiastical principalities, in which all the difficulties occur before they are acquired, for they are gained either through ability or through favour or luck, and maintained without the help of either. This in turn is because they are sustained by ancient religious institutions, which have been sufficiently strong to maintain their rulers in office however they live or act. Only they have states and do not defend them, and subjects whom they do not trouble to govern; and although their states are undefended, they are not deprived of them. And their subjects, although not properly governed, do not worry about it; they cannot get rid of these rulers, nor even think about doing so. Only these principalities, then, are secure and successful.

However, since they are controlled by a higher power, which the human mind cannot comprehend, I shall refrain from discussing them; since they are raised up and maintained by God, only a presumptuous and rash man would examine them. Nevertheless, someone might ask me how it has happened that the temporal power of the Church has become so great, although before Alexander's[7]

---

[6] [Few "of his subjects" is implied. Nabis favoured the people at the expense of the nobles, and Livy (XXXIV, 27) relates that he imprisoned and then killed about eighty prominent young men.]

[7] [Alexander VI.]

236

pontificate the leading Italian powers[8] (and not only those called "powers," but every baron and lord, however unimportant) held this temporal power in little account, whereas now a King of France stands in awe of it, for it has been able to drive him out of Italy, and to ruin the Venetians. Accordingly it does not seem out of place to recall it, although it is well known.

Before King Charles of France invaded Italy,[9] this country was dominated by the popes, the Venetians, the King of Naples, the Duke of Milan and the Florentines. Each of these powers had two main preoccupations: first, that a foreign power should not invade Italy; secondly, that none of the other Italian powers should acquire more territory and power. Those who caused most concern were the popes and the Venetians. To limit the power of Venice, the others had to form an alliance, as happened in the defence of Ferrara. And the Roman barons were used to limit papal power. As these were divided into two factions, the Orsini and the Colonna, they were always quarrelling among themselves, but carrying their arms under the very eyes of the popes, they kept the Papacy weak and ineffectual. And although there sometimes arose a spirited pope, such as Sixtus, yet he could not overcome this problem, either because of the particular circumstances or because of lack of skill. The shortness of pontificates was the reason, for it was very difficult to destroy one of the factions during the period of ten years that most popes reigned. And if it happened that one pope almost succeeded in destroying the Colonna faction, the next pope would be hostile to the Orsini, which had the effect of reviving the Colonna faction, and yet he did not have enough time to destroy the Orsini faction. The result was that the temporal power of the Papacy was held in little regard in Italy.

Then Alexander VI came to the papal throne; more than any previous pope, he showed how much a pope could achieve through money and military means. Using the Duke Valentino,[10] and exploiting the opportunities provided by the French invasion, he did all those things which I have discussed above, when considering the career of the Duke. And although Alexander's aim was to aggrandise the Duke, not the Church, nevertheless the outcome was to increase the power of the Church

---

[8] [i.e., Milan, Venice, Florence and Naples.]

[9] [Charles VIII; in 1494.]

[10] [Cesare Borgia.]

which, after his death, and the downfall of the Duke, became the beneficiary of his labours. Then came Pope Julius, who found the Church already powerful, possessing all the Romagna, the Roman barons reduced to impotence, and their factions destroyed by the strong measures of Alexander. Moreover, Julius had opportunities for accumulating money which Alexander before him had never had Julius not only maintained what he had inherited, but added to it. He planned to capture Bologna, to destroy the power of Venice, and to expel the French from Italy. All these enterprises were successful, and it was very much to his credit that he did everything in order to increase the power of the Church, and not any individual. He kept the Orsini and Colonna factions in the same impotent condition in which he found them; and although they had some leaders capable of causing trouble, two factors militated against it. The first was the great power of the Church, which overawed them; the second was that there were no cardinals to lead either faction, the cause of the rivalries between them. These factions will always cause trouble whenever they have cardinals as leaders, because it is they who foster these factions, inside Rome and outside, and those barons are compelled to support their own factions. Thus, the ambition of prelates is at the root of the quarrels and tumults among the barons.

His Holiness Pope Leo, then, has found the Papacy very powerful; and it is to be hoped that, just as his predecessors made it great by the use of force, he will make it very great and respected through his natural goodness and countless other virtues.

## Chapter XII

### The different types of army, and mercenary troops

I have discussed in detail all the different types of principality that I mentioned at the beginning, and have given some consideration to the reasons for their prosperity and decline; and I have examined the ways in which many men have sought to acquire them and to hold them. I now turn to consider in a general way the means that can be used in attacking and defending them. I said earlier how necessary it is for a ruler to have firm foundations for his power; otherwise, he will always come to grief. The main foundations of all states (whether they are new, old or mixed) are good laws and good armies. Since it is impossible to have good laws if good arms are lacking, and if there are good arms there must also be good laws,[11] I shall leave laws aside and concentrate on arms.

---

[11] [If "laws" are understood in the usual sense, this would be false (for a country may possess a fine army and yet have laws that are censurable or a defective legal system). But if *buone legge* is understood in the sense of "good order," M.'s position seems stronger.]

I say, then, that the arms with which a ruler defends his state are his own, or they are mercenaries, or auxiliaries, or a mixture of all three. Mercenaries and auxiliaries are useless and dangerous; and anyone who relies upon mercenaries to defend his territories will never have a stable or secure rule. For they are dis-united, ambitious, undisciplined and treacherous; they are powerful when among those who are not hostile, but weak and cowardly when confronted by deter-mined enemies; they have no fear of God, and do not maintain commitments with men. One's ruin is only postponed until the time comes when they are required to fight. In peaceful times you will be despoiled by them, in war by your ene-mies. The reason for all this is that they have no affection for you or any other rea-son to induce them to fight for you, except a trifling wage, which is not sufficient to make them want to risk their lives for you. They are very glad to be in your ser-vice as long as you do not wage war, but in time of war they either flee or desert. I should not need to spend very much time in arguing this case, since the present ruin of Italy has been caused by nothing else than the reliance over so many years on mercenary armies. Some of these mercenary armies were not ineffective, and they appeared powerful when fighting other mercenary armies, but when the foreign invasions began, their real character was soon revealed. Thus, King Charles of France was permitted to conquer Italy with a piece of chalk;[12] and he who said that our sins were responsible[13] spoke the truth. However, they were not the sins that he meant, but those that I have specified; and because they were the sins of rulers, they too have been punished for them.

I want to show more effectively the defects of these troops. Mercenary generals are either very capable men, or they are not. If they are, you cannot trust them, because they will always be aspiring to achieve a great position for themselves, either by attacking you, their employer, or by attacking others contrary to your wishes. If they are mediocre, you will be ruined as a matter of course.

And if it is objected that anyone who has forces at his disposal (whether mer-cenaries or not) will act in this way, I would reply by first drawing a distinction: arms are used either by a ruler or by a republic. If the former, the ruler should per-sonally lead his armies, acting as the general. If the latter, the republic must send its own citizens as generals; and if someone is sent who turns out not to be very

---

[12] [Commynes (*Mémoires*, VII, 14) attributes this witticism to Pope Alexander VI: they met with so little resistance that the had only to mark houses where their soldiers were to be billeted.]

[13] [Savonarola, in a sermon preached before Charles VIII on 1 Nov. 1494, spoke of such sins as fornication, usury and cruelty as being responsible for the present "tribulations."]

capable, he must be replaced; and if the general sent is capable, there should be legal controls that ensure that he does not exceed his authority. Experience has shown that only rulers and republics that possess their own armies are very successful, whereas mercenary armies never achieve anything, and cause only harm. And it is more difficult for a citizen to seize power in a republic that possesses its own troops than in one that relies upon foreign troops.

For many centuries both Rome and Sparta were armed and independent. Today the Swiss are very well armed and completely independent. An example of the worth of ancient mercenaries is provided by the Carthaginians: they were attacked by their own mercenary troops after the first war against the Romans, despite the fact that the generals were Carthaginians. Similarly, after the death of Epaminondas, the Thebans made Philip of Macedon general of their armies; and after he was victorious, he deprived them of their independence. After the death of Duke Filippo, the Milanese engaged Francesco Sforza to lead their armies against the Venetians. But when Sforza had defeated the Venetians at Caravaggio, he joined forces with them and attacked the Milanese, who had been his employers. Sforza's own father, who was employed as a general by Queen Giovanna of Naples, suddenly left her unprotected; and, in order not to lose her Kingdom, she was forced to seek help from the King of Aragon.

And although the Venetians and the Florentines augmented their dominions in the past by using mercenaries, and their generals did not seize power but defended them, my opinion is that in this matter the Florentines were very lucky; for some of the able generals who could have become a threat to them did not win victories, some met with opposition, and others went elsewhere to achieve their ambitions.

The general who did not conquer was John Hawkwood; his loyalty could not be put to the test, just because he did not win victories; but everyone will acknowledge that if he had been victorious, the Florentines would have been at his mercy. The Sforza always had the Bracceschi troops to contend with, and each faction checked the other: Francesco went to Lombardy to satisfy his ambitions, and Braccio moved against the Church and the Kingdom of Naples.

But let us turn to more recent events. The Florentines made Paulo Vitelli their general; he was a very able man, who from modest beginnings had acquired a very high reputation. Nobody can deny that if he had captured Pisa, the Florentines would have been forced to retain his services because, if he had then become general of one of the armies of their enemies, the Florentines would have found themselves in desperate straits; and if they had retained him, he would have been in a commanding position.

If the conquests of the Venetians are reviewed, it is evident that they were secure and glorious when they fought their own wars (which was before they undertook campaigns in Italy), in which their nobles and the people in arms fought very skillfully and courageously. But when they began to fight on the mainland, they forsook this very effective policy, and followed the Italian custom.[14] When they first began to expand their land empire, they had little reason to be afraid of their mercenary generals, because not very much territory had yet been annexed and because the reputation of Venice was very high. But as they expanded further, under Carmagnola, their blunder became evident. They knew that he was very able (since they had defeated the Duke of Milan under his command) but, on the other hand, they realised that he was pursuing the war half-heartedly. They decided that they would not be able to win again by using his services (because he did not want to win), and yet they could not dismiss him without losing the territory that had been annexed. Hence, to protect themselves, they were forced to kill him. Afterwards they had as generals Bartolomeo da Bergamo, Roberto da San Severino, the Count of Pitigliano and others. With regard to these generals, what they had to fear was losing, not the dangers arising from their being victorious, as indeed happened later at Vailà where, in a single battle, they lost what they had gained with so much effort over eight hundred years. For using mercenaries results only in slow, tardy and unimportant gains but sudden and astonishing losses.

Since these examples have brought me to Italy, which for many years has been controlled by mercenary armies, I want to examine them at greater length so that, when their rise and development have been surveyed, it will be easier to find a solution.

You must realise, then, how in recent times the Empire began to lose much ground in Italy, the temporal power of the Papacy was greatly increased, and Italy came to be divided into many states. For in many of the large cities there were revolts against the nobles who (previously supported by the Emperor) had ruled oppressively, and the Church encouraged these revolts in order to increase its temporal power; and in many other cities rulers had emerged from the ranks of

---

[14] [i.e., of using mercenaries.]

the citizens. Hence, because Italy had largely come under the control of the Church and of some republics, and because these priests and citizen-rulers had little experience of military matters, they all began to use outsiders to fight their battles.

Alberigo da Cunio, a Romagnol, was the first to make these mercenary troops important. From this source other mercenary forces came to the fore, including those of Braccio and Sforza, who in their day were the arbiters of Italy. After them came all the others who controlled mercenary armies up to our own times. And the result of their prowess has been that Italy has been overrun by Charles, plundered by Louis, ravaged by Ferdinand and treated with contempt by the Swiss. What happened, first, was that to enhance their own reputations, they neglected the infantry. They did this because, since they were men who did not possess states of their own and lived by being mercenaries, small numbers of foot-soldiers did not enhance their position, and they were incapable of maintaining large numbers of them. Therefore, they resorted to having enough cavalry to maintain themselves and achieve a position of some importance. And things came to such a pass that an army of twenty thousand soldiers would contain scarcely two thousand foot-soldiers. Moreover, they employed all possible means to lessen the hardships and dangers, both to themselves and their troops, by inflicting few casualties in battle; instead, they took prisoners and did not demand ransoms. They did not attack fortified cities at night; mercenaries who defended cities were very reluctant to attack the besiegers; they did not fortify their camps with stockades or ditches; and they did not undertake sieges during winter. All these practices were permitted by the prevailing military code, and were adopted, as I have said, to avoid hardship and danger. The outcome of their activities is that Italy has become enslaved and despised.

## Chapter XIII

### Auxiliaries, mixed troops and native troops

Auxiliaries, which are the other kind of troops that are useless, are troops that are sent to you to aid and defend you when you call on a powerful ruler for help. They were used recently by Pope Julius who, when he had seen the bad showing of his own mercenary troops in the campaign of Ferrara, resorted to auxiliaries, arranging with King Ferdinand of Spain that that ruler would help him with his own troops. In themselves, these auxiliaries can be capable and effective but they are almost always harmful to those who use them; for if they lose you will be ruined, and if they win you will be at their mercy.

Although ancient history provides many examples, I do want to discuss this recent case of Pope Julius II. His decision can only be judged rash: to put himself completely into the hands of a foreign ruler, in order to gain possession of Ferrara! But his good luck meant that he did not reap the fruits of his bad policy, for when the auxiliaries he was using were defeated at Ravenna, and the Swiss arrived and chased out the victors (contrary to what he and others had any reason to expect), he did not find himself at the mercy either of his enemies (who had fled) or of these auxiliaries, because the victory had been achieved by others, not by them. Again, the Florentines, because they were completely unarmed, brought ten thousand French troops to besiege Pisa: and this policy involved them in more danger than at any other time in their troubled history. Similarly, the Emperor of Constantinople brought ten thousand Turkish troops in order to fight his fellow-Greeks; but when that war was finished they did not want to go away, which marked the beginning of the servitude of Greece to the infidels.

Therefore, anyone who wants to be unable to conquer should use such troops, because they are much more dangerous than mercenaries: for with them ruin is complete. They form a united force, and are used to obeying others. But when mercenaries conquer, more time and greater opportunities are required before they will be in a position to do you harm. They do not form a united body, since they have been engaged and paid by you. And an outsider whom you appoint as their leader cannot at once assume such authority over them that harm to you will result. In short, with mercenaries, their cowardice or reluctance to fight is more dangerous; with auxiliaries their skill and courage.

Wise rulers, then, always avoid using these troops, and form armies composed of their own men; and they prefer to lose using their own troops rather than to conquer through using foreign troops, for they do not consider a victory that is gained by using foreign forces to be genuine.

I never hesitate to cite Cesare Borgia and his actions. This Duke invaded the Romagna using auxiliaries (all his troops being French), and with them he captured Imola and Forli. But since he distrusted them, he then used mercenaries, which he thought less dangerous, employing the Orsini and Vitelli troops. When he later found them to be of doubtful value and loyalty, and therefore dangerous, he disbanded them and formed an army composed of his own men. And the difference between these kinds of army is very obvious if one compares the reputation of the Duke when he used only French troops or when he used the Orsini and Vitelli troops, and when he possessed his own soldiers, and was self-sufficient militarily. Then it became much greater, and he was never more esteemed than when everyone saw that he was the complete master of his own forces....

## Chapter XIV

### How a ruler should act concerning military matters

A ruler, then, should have no other objective and no other concern, nor occupy himself with anything else except war and its methods and practices, for this pertains only to those who rule. And it is of such efficacy that it not only maintains hereditary rulers in power but very often enables men of private status to become rulers. On the other hand, it is evident that if rulers concern themselves more with the refinements of life than with military matters, they lose power. The main reason why they lose it is their neglect of the art of war; and being proficient in this art is what enables one to gain power.

Because Francesco Sforza was armed, from being a private citizen he became Duke of Milan; since his descendants did not trouble themselves with military matters, from being dukes they became private citizens. For being unarmed (apart from other bad consequences) results in your being despised, which is one of those disgraceful things against which a ruler must always guard, as will be explained later. There is an enormous difference between an armed and an unarmed man; and it cannot be expected that a man who is armed will obey willingly a man who is unarmed, or that an unarmed man can be safe among armed servants. Since the latter will be contemptuous and the former suspicious and afraid, they will not be able to work well together. Therefore, apart from the other disadvantages already mentioned, a ruler who does not understand military matters cannot be highly regarded by his soldiers, and he cannot trust them.

A ruler should therefore always be concerned with military matters, and in peacetime he should be even more taken up with them than in war. There are two ways of doing this: one is by going on exercises; the other is by study.

With regard to exercises, besides keeping his troops well disciplined and trained, he should very frequently engage in hunting, thus hardening his body and, at the same time, becoming familiar with the terrain: how mountains rise, how valleys open out and plains spread out, as well as with the characteristics of rivers and swamps; he should concern himself very much with all these matters.

This practical knowledge is valuable in two ways. First, one learns well the terrain of one's own country, and understands better its natural defences; secondly, through knowing and exercising in the countryside, one easily grasps the characteristics of any new terrain that must be explored. For the hills, valleys, plains, rivers and swamps that are found in Tuscany, for instance, are in many respects similar to those found in other regions. Thus, knowing well the terrain of one region readily permits one to become familiar with that of other regions. A ruler who lacks such expertise lacks the elements of generalship. For it enables one to track down the enemy, to encamp one's army properly, to lead an army towards the enemy, to prepare for battle, to besiege fortresses or fortified towns, in ways that conduce to victory.

One of the reasons why historians have praised Philopoemen, the leader of the Achaean League, is that in peacetime he was always thinking about military matters; and when he was in the countryside with companions, he often stopped and asked questions: "If the enemy happened to be up on that hill, and we were here with our army, who would be better placed? How should we attack them, while still preserving proper military formation? How should we be able to retreat? If they retreated, how should we pursue them?" As they travelled he used to put to them all the situations in which an army might be placed. He used to listen to their opinions, then give his own, supporting them with reasons. Because of these continual discussions, when he was leading his armies he was able to overcome any difficulties.

As for mental exercise, a ruler should read historical works, especially for the light they shed on the actions of eminent men: to find out how they waged war, to discover the reasons for their victories and defeats, in order to avoid reverses and achieve conquests; and above all, to imitate some eminent man, who himself set out to imitate some predecessor of his who was considered worthy of praise and glory, always taking his deeds and actions as a model for himself, as it is said that Alexander the Great imitated Achilles, Caesar imitated Alexander, and Scipio imitated Cyrus. And anyone who reads the life of Cyrus, written by Xenophon, will realise, when he considers Scipio's life and career, how greatly Scipio's imitation of Cyrus helped him to attain glory, and how much Scipio's sexual restraint, affability, humanity and generosity derived from his imitating the qualities of Cyrus, as recorded in this work by Xenophon. A wise ruler should act in such ways, and never remain idle in quiet times, but assiduously strengthen his position through such activities in order that in adversity he will benefit from them. Thus, when his situation worsens, he will be well equipped to overcome dangers and to flourish.

## Chapter XV

### The things for which men, and especially rulers, are praised or blamed

It remains now to consider in what ways a ruler should act with regard to his subjects and allies. And since I am well aware that many people have written about this subject I fear that I may be thought presumptuous, for what I have to say differs from the precepts offered by others, especially on this matter. But because I want to write what will be useful to anyone who understands, it seems to me better to concentrate on what really happens rather than on theories or speculations. For many have imagined republics and principalities that have never been seen or known to exist. However, how men live is so different from how they should live that a ruler who does not do what is generally done, but persists in doing what ought to be done, will undermine his power rather than maintain it. If a ruler who wants always to act honourably is surrounded by many unscrupulous men his downfall is inevitable. Therefore, a ruler who wishes to maintain his power must be prepared to act immorally when this becomes necessary.

I shall set aside fantasies about rulers, then, and consider what happens in fact. I say that whenever men are discussed, and especially rulers (because they occupy more exalted positions), they are praised or blamed for possessing some of the following qualities. Thus, one man is considered generous, another miserly (I use this Tuscan term because *avaro* in our tongue also signifies someone who is rapacious, whereas we call *misero* someone who is very reluctant to use his own possessions); one is considered a free giver, another rapacious; one cruel, another merciful; one treacherous, another loyal; one effeminate and weak, another indomitable and spirited; one affable, another haughty; one lascivious, another moderate; one upright, another cunning; one inflexible, another easy-going; one serious, another frivolous; one devout, another unbelieving, and so on.

I know that everyone will acknowledge that it would be most praiseworthy for a ruler to have all the above-mentioned qualities that are held to be good. But because it is not possible to have all of them, and because circumstances do not permit living a completely virtuous life, one must be sufficiently prudent to know how to avoid becoming notorious for those vices that would destroy one's power and seek to avoid those vices that are not politically dangerous; but if one cannot bring oneself to do this, they can be indulged in with fewer misgivings. Yet one should not be troubled about becoming notorious for those vices without which it is difficult to preserve one's power, because if one considers everything carefully, doing some things that seem virtuous may result in one's ruin, whereas doing other things that seem vicious may strengthen one's position and cause one to flourish.

## Chapter XVI

### Generosity and meanness

To begin, then, with the first of the above-mentioned qualities, I maintain that it would be desirable to be considered generous; nevertheless, if generosity is practised in such a way that you will be considered generous, it will harm you. If it is practised virtuously, and as it should be, it will not be known about, and you will not avoid acquiring a bad reputation for the opposite vice. Therefore, if one wants to keep up a reputation for being generous, one must spend lavishly and ostentatiously. The inevitable outcome of acting in such ways is that the ruler will consume all his resources in sumptuous display; and if he wants to continue to be thought generous, he will eventually be compelled to become rapacious, to tax the people very heavily, and raise money by all possible means. Thus, he will begin to be hated by his subjects and, because he is impoverished, he will be held in little regard. Since this generosity of his has harmed many people and benefited few, he will feel the effects of any discontent, and the first real threat to his power will involve him in grave difficulties. When he realises this, and changes his ways, he will very soon acquire a bad reputation for being miserly.

Therefore, since a ruler cannot both practise this virtue of generosity and be known to do so without harming himself, he would do well not to worry about being called miserly. For eventually he will come to be considered more generous, when it is realised that, because of his parsimony, his revenues are sufficient to defend himself against any enemies that attack him, and to undertake campaigns without imposing special taxes on the people. Thus he will be acting generously towards the vast majority, whose property he does not touch, and will be acting meanly towards the few to whom he gives nothing.

Those rulers who have achieved great things in our own times have all been considered mean; all the others have failed. Although Pope Julius cultivated a reputation for generosity in order to become pope,[15] he did not seek to maintain it afterwards, because he wanted to be able to wage war. The present King of France[16] has fought many wars without imposing any special taxes on his subjects, because his parsimonious habits have always enabled him to meet the extra expenses. If the present King of Spain[17] had a reputation for generosity, he would not have successfully undertaken so many campaigns.

Therefore, a ruler should worry little about being thought miserly: he will not have to rob his subjects; he will be able to defend himself; he will avoid being poor and despised and will not be forced to become rapacious. For meanness is one of those vices that enable him to rule. It may be objected that Caesar obtained power through his open-handedness, and that many others have risen to very high office because they were open-handed and were considered to be so. I would reply that either you are already an established ruler or you are trying to become a ruler. In the first case, open-handedness is harmful; in the second, it is certainly necessary to be thought open-handed. Caesar was one of those who sought power in Rome; but if after gaining power he had survived,[18] and had not moderated his expenditure, he would have undermined his power. And if it should be objected that many rulers who have been considered very generous have had remarkable military successes, I would reply: a ruler spends either what belongs to him or his subjects, or what belongs to others. In the former case, he should be parsimonious; in the latter, he should be as open-handed as possible. A ruler who accompanies his army, supporting it by looting, sacking and extortions, disposes of what belongs to others; he must be open-handed, for if he is not, his soldiers will desert. You can be much more generous with what does not belong to you or to your subjects, as Cyrus, Caesar and Alexander were. This is because giving away what belongs to others in no way damages your reputation; rather, it enhances it. It is only giving away what belongs to yourself that harms you.

There is nothing that is so self-consuming as generosity: the more you practise it, the less you will be able to continue to practise it. You will either become poor and despised or your efforts to avoid poverty will make you rapacious and

---

[15] [i.e., by bribes.]

[16] [Louis XII.]

[17] [Ferdinand the Catholic.]

[18] [i.e., if he had not been assassinated.]

hated. A ruler must above all guard against being despised and hated; and being generous will lead to both. Therefore, it is shrewder to cultivate a reputation for meanness, which will lead to notoriety but not to hatred. This is better than being forced, through wanting to be considered generous, to incur a reputation for rapacity, which will lead to notoriety and to hatred as well.

## Chapter XVII

### Cruelty and mercifulness; and whether it is better to be loved or feared

Turning to the other previously mentioned qualities, I maintain that every ruler should want to be thought merciful, not cruel; nevertheless, one should take care not to be merciful in an inappropriate way. Cesare Borgia was considered cruel, yet his harsh measures restored order to the Romagna, unifying it and rendering it peaceful and loyal. If his conduct is properly considered, he will be judged to have been much more merciful than the Florentine people, who let Pistoia be torn apart, in order to avoid acquiring a reputation for cruelty. Therefore, if a ruler can keep his subjects united and loyal, he should not worry about incurring a reputation for cruelty; for by punishing a very few he will really be more merciful than those who over-indulgently permit disorders to develop, with resultant killings and plunderings. For the latter usually harm a whole community, whereas the executions ordered by a ruler harm only specific individuals. And a new ruler, in particular, cannot avoid being considered harsh, since new states are full of dangers. Virgil makes Dido say:

> Res dura, et regni novitas me talia cogunt
> moliri, et late fines custode tueri.[19]

Nevertheless, he should be slow to believe accusations and to act against individuals, and should not be afraid of his own shadow. He should act with due prudence and humanity so that being over-confident will not make him incautious, and being too suspicious will not render him insupportable.

A controversy has arisen about this: whether it is better to be loved than feared, or vice versa. My view is that it is desirable to be both loved and feared; but it is difficult to achieve both and, if one of them has to be lacking, it is much safer to be feared than loved.

---

[19] [Virgil, *Aeneid*, 563-4: "Harsh necessity and the newness of my kingdom force me to do such things, and to guard all the frontiers."]

For this may be said of men generally: they are ungrateful, fickle, feigners and dissemblers, avoiders of danger, eager for gain. While you benefit them they are all devoted to you: they would shed their blood for you; they offer their possessions, their lives, and their sons, as I said before, when the need to do so is far off. But when you are hard pressed, they turn away. A ruler who has relied completely on their promises, and has neglected to prepare other defences, will be ruined, because friendships that are acquired with money, and not through greatness and nobility of character, are paid for but not secured, and prove unreliable just when they are needed.

Men are less hesitant about offending or harming a ruler who makes himself loved than one who inspires fear. For love is sustained by a bond of gratitude which, because men are excessively self-interested, is broken whenever they see a chance to benefit themselves. But fear is sustained by a dread of punishment that is always effective. Nevertheless, a ruler must make himself feared in such a way that, even if he does not become loved, he does not become hated. For it is perfectly possible to be feared without incurring hatred. And this can always be achieved if he refrains from laying hands on the property of his citizens and subjects, and on their womenfolk. If it is necessary to execute anyone, this should be done only if there is a proper justification and obvious reason. But, above all, he must not touch the property of others, because men forget sooner the killing of a father than the loss of their patrimony. Moreover, there will always be pretexts for seizing property; and someone who begins to live rapaciously will always find pretexts for taking the property of others. On the other hand, reasons or pretexts for taking life are rarer and more fleeting.

However, when a ruler is with his army, and commands a large force, he must not worry about being considered harsh, because armies are never kept united and prepared for military action unless their leader is thought to be harsh. Among the remarkable things recounted about Hannibal is that, although he had a very large army, composed of men from many countries, and fighting in foreign lands, there never arose any dissension, either among themselves or against their leader, whether things were going well or badly. This could be accounted for only by his inhuman cruelty which, together with his many good qualities, made him always respected and greatly feared by his troops. And if he had not been so cruel, his other qualities would not have been sufficient to achieve that effect. Thoughtless writers admire this achievement of his, yet condemn the main reason for it.

That his other qualities would not have sufficed is proved by what happened to Scipio, considered a most remarkable man not only in his own times but in all others, whose armies rebelled against him in Spain. The only reason for this was that he was over-indulgent, and permitted his soldiers more freedom than was consistent with maintaining proper military discipline. Fabius Maximus rebuked him for this in the senate, and called him a corrupter of the Roman army. And when Locri was ravaged by one of Scipio's legates, the inhabitants were not avenged by him, and the legate was not punished for his arrogance, all because Scipio was too easy-going. Indeed, a speaker in the senate who wished to excuse him said that there were many men who were better at not committing misdeeds themselves than punishing the misdeeds of others. This character of his would eventually have tarnished his fame and glory, if he had continued his military command unchecked; but since he was controlled by the senate, this harmful quality was not only concealed but contributed to his glory.

Returning to the matter of being feared and loved, then, I conclude that whether men bear affection depends on themselves, but whether they are afraid will depend on what the ruler does. A wise ruler should rely on what is under his own control, not on what is under the control of others; he should contrive only to avoid incurring hatred, as I have said.

## Chapter XVIII

### How rulers should keep their promises

Everyone knows how praiseworthy it is for a ruler to keep his promises, and live uprightly and not by trickery. Nevertheless, experience shows that in our times the rulers who have done great things are those who have set little store by keeping their word, being skilful rather in cunningly confusing men; they have got the better of those who have relied on being trustworthy.

You should know, then, that there are two ways of contending: one by using laws, the other, force. The first is appropriate for men, the second for animals; but because the former is often ineffective, one must have recourse to the latter. Therefore, a ruler must know well how to imitate beasts as well as employing properly human means. This policy was taught to rulers allegorically by ancient writers: they tell how Achilles and many other ancient rulers were entrusted to Chiron the centaur, to be raised carefully by him. Having a mentor who was half-beast and half-man signifies that a ruler needs to use both natures, and that one without the other is not effective.

Since a ruler, then, must know how to act like a beast, he should imitate both the fox and the lion, for the lion is liable to be trapped, whereas the fox cannot ward off wolves. One needs, then, to be a fox to recognise traps, and a lion to frighten away wolves. Those who rely merely upon a lion's strength do not understand matters.

Therefore, a prudent ruler cannot keep his word, nor should he, when such fidelity would damage him, and when the reasons that made him promise are no longer relevant. This advice would not be sound if all men were upright; but because they are treacherous and would not keep their promises to you, you should not consider yourself bound to keep your promises to them.

Moreover, plausible reasons can always be found for such failure to keep promises. One could give countless modern examples of this, and show how many peace treaties and promises have been rendered null and void by the faithlessness of rulers; and those best able to imitate the fox have succeeded best. But foxiness should be well concealed: one must be a great feigner and dissembler. And men are so naive, and so much dominated by immediate needs, that a skilful deceiver always finds plenty of people who will let themselves be deceived.

I must mention one recent case: Alexander VI was concerned only with deceiving men, and he always found them gullible. No man ever affirmed anything more forcefully or with stronger oaths but kept his word less. Nevertheless, his deceptions were always effective, because he well understood the naivety of men.

A ruler, then, need not actually possess all the above-mentioned qualities, but he must certainly seem to. Indeed, I shall be so bold as to say that having and always cultivating them is harmful, whereas seeming to have them is useful; for instance, to seem merciful, trustworthy, humane, upright and devout, and also to be so. But if it becomes necessary to refrain, you must be prepared to act in the opposite way, and be capable of doing it. And it must be understood that a ruler, and especially a new ruler, cannot always act in ways that are considered good because, in order to maintain his power, he is often forced to act treacherously, ruthlessly or inhumanely, and disregard the precepts of religion. Hence, he must be prepared to vary his conduct as the winds of fortune and changing circumstances constrain him and, as I said before, not deviate from right conduct if possible, but be capable of entering upon the path of wrongdoing when this becomes necessary.

A ruler, then, should be very careful that everything he says is replete with the five above-named qualities: to those who see and hear him, he should seem to be exceptionally merciful, trustworthy, upright, humane and devout. And it is most necessary of all to seem devout. In these matters, most men judge more by their eyes than by their hands. For everyone is capable of seeing you, but few can touch you. Everyone can see what you appear to be, whereas few have direct experience of what you really are; and those few will not dare to challenge the popular view, sustained as it is by the majesty of the ruler's position. With regard to all human actions, and especially those of rulers, who cannot be called to account, men pay attention to the outcome. If a ruler, then, contrives to conquer, and to preserve the state, the means will always be judged to be honourable and be praised by everyone. For the common people are impressed by appearances and results. Everywhere the common people are the vast majority, and the few are isolated when the majority and the government are at one. One present-day ruler, whom it is well to leave unnamed,[20] is always preaching peace and trust, although he is really very hostile to both; and if he had practised them he would have lost either reputation or power several times over.

## Chapter XXI

### *How a ruler should act in order to gain reputation*

Nothing enables a ruler to gain more prestige than undertaking great campaigns and performing unusual deeds. In our own times Ferdinand of Aragon, the present King of Spain is a notable example. He might almost be called a new ruler because, from being a weak king, he has become the most famous and glorious king in Christendom. And if his achievements are examined, they will all be found to be very remarkable, and some of them quite extraordinary. This man attacked Granada[21] at the beginning of his reign, and this campaign laid the foundations of his state. First of all, he began this campaign when things were quiet and when he was not afraid of being opposed: he kept the minds of the barons of Castile occupied with that war, so that they would not plan any revolts. And he meanwhile was acquiring prestige, and increasing his hold over them before they were even aware of the fact. He was able to maintain armies with money from the Church[22] and from his subjects, and during that long war he was able to develop a powerful army, whose achievements have subsequently brought him so much honour.

---

[20] [Ferdinand the Catholic. In the very next chapter, M. discusses Ferdinand openly. —J.M.P.]

[21] [The Moorish kingdom in Southern Spain.]

[22] [The war against this Muslim kingdom was seen as a crusade.]

Moreover, in order to undertake even greater campaigns, he continued to make use of religion, resorting to a cruel and apparently pious policy of unexampled wretchedness: that of hunting down the Moors and driving them out of his Kingdom. Using this same cloak,[23] he attacked Africa; he invaded Italy; and recently he has attacked France. Thus he has always plotted and achieved great things, which have never failed to keep his subjects in a state of suspense and amazement, as they await their outcome. And these deeds of his have followed one another so quickly that nobody has had enough time to be able to initiate a revolt against him.

It is also very beneficial for a ruler to perform very unusual deeds within his kingdom, such as those recorded about messer Bernabò, the ruler of Milan. When it happens that someone does something extraordinary (whether good or bad) in social or political life, he should hit on some way of rewarding or punishing him that will be much talked about. Above all, a ruler must contrive to achieve through all his actions the reputation of being a great man of outstanding intelligence.

A ruler is also highly regarded if he is either a true ally or an outright enemy, that is, if he unhesitatingly supports one ruler against another. This policy is always better than remaining neutral, since if two powerful rulers near you come to blows, either the eventual victor will become a threat to you, or he will not. In either situation, it will always be wiser to intervene in favour of one side and fight strongly. For in the former situation, if you do not declare yourself, you will always be liable to be despoiled by the victor (which would please and satisfy the loser), and you will deservedly be defenceless and friendless. For the victor does not want unreliable allies who did not help him when he was hard pressed; and the loser will not show you any favour, because you did not want to run the risk of sharing his fate by assisting him militarily.

Antiochus invaded Greece, invited there by the Aetolians in order to drive out the Romans. Antiochus sent envoys to the Achaeans, who were allies of the Romans, to advise them to remain neutral. On the other hand, the Romans exhorted them to take up arms on their behalf. This matter was discussed at a meeting of the Achaeans at which the envoy of Antiochus exhorted them to remain neutral. To this the Roman envoy replied: *"Quod autem isti dicunt non interponendi vos bello, nihil magis alienum rebus vestris est; sine gratia, sine dignitate, praemium victoris eritis."*[24]

---

[23] [Using religion as a pretext.]

[24] [Livy, XXXV, 49: "As for what they tell you, that it is better for you not to intervene in the war, nothing could be further from your interests; lacking help and dignity, you would be the prize of the victor." The first part of the quotation is somewhat different from what Livy wrote.]

A ruler who is not an ally will always want you to remain neutral, whereas one who is your ally will always want your armed support. In order to avoid present dangers, irresolute rulers usually prefer to remain neutral, and very often this is their undoing. However, let us assume that you strongly support one of the parties, who then emerges victorious: even if he is powerful and you are at his mercy, he is beholden to you and friendship is established between you. And men are never so dishonourable that they would attack you in such circumstances, and display so much ingratitude. Moreover, victories are never so decisive that the victor does not need to be careful, and especially about acting justly. But if the ruler whom you help loses, he will show gratitude to you and will help you as far as he can; thus you become an ally in a cause that may flourish again.

In the second situation (when the rulers fighting each other cannot be a threat to you), it is wiser still to intervene: because you will contribute to the downfall of one ruler, and are helped by another ruler who, if he had been wise, would have saved him; and if together you win, the ruler whom you help will be at your mercy. (And it is certainly to be expected that he will overcome his enemy, since he has your help.)

Here it should be observed that a ruler should be careful never to ally himself with a ruler who is more powerful than himself in order to attack other powers, unless he is forced to, as has been said above. For if you are victorious together, you will be at his mercy, and rulers should do their best to avoid being at the mercy of other powers. The Venetians allied themselves with France against the Duke of Milan; they could have avoided this alliance, and the outcome was their downfall. But if it is not possible to avoid such a commitment (as happened to the Florentines, when the Pope and the King of Spain launched an attack against Lombardy), a ruler should then become involved for the reasons previously mentioned.

No government should ever believe that it is always possible to follow safe policies. Rather, it should be realised that all courses of action involve risks: for it is in the nature of things that when one tries to avoid one danger another is always encountered. But prudence consists in knowing how to assess the dangers, and to choose the least bad course of action as being the right one to follow.

A ruler should also show himself a lover of talent,[25] and honour those who excel in any art. Moreover, he should encourage the citizens to follow quietly their ordinary occupations, both in trade and agriculture and every other kind, so that one man is not afraid to improve or increase his possessions for fear that they will be

---

[25] [*virtú*, which here denotes primarily artistic and literary talents.]

taken from him, and another does not hesitate to begin to trade for fear of the taxes that will be levied. Rather, he should offer rewards to anyone who wants to do such things, and to anyone who seeks in any way to improve his city or country. Furthermore, at appropriate times of the year, he should keep the people entertained with feasts and spectacles. And since every city is divided into guilds or family groups he should pay due attention to these groups, meeting them from time to time, and performing acts that display his own affability and munificence. But he should always be careful to preserve the prestige of his office, for this is something that should never be diminished.

## Chapter XXV

### How much power fortune has over human affairs, and how it should be resisted

I am not unaware that many have thought, and many still think, that the affairs of the world are so ruled by fortune and by God that the ability of men cannot control them. Rather, they think that we have no remedy at all; and therefore it could be concluded that it is useless to sweat much over things, but let them be governed by fate. This opinion has been more popular in our own times because of the great changes that have taken place and are still to be seen even now, which could hardly have been predicted. When I think about this, I am sometimes inclined, to some extent, to share this opinion. Nevertheless, so as not to eliminate human freedom, I am disposed to hold that fortune is the arbiter of half our actions, but that it lets us control roughly the other half.[26]

I compare fortune to one of those dangerous rivers that, when they become enraged, flood the plains, destroy trees and buildings, move earth from one place and deposit it in another. Everyone flees before it, everyone gives way to its thrust, without being able to halt it in any way. But this does not mean that, when the river is not in flood, men are unable to take precautions, by means of dykes and dams, so that when it rises next time, it will either not overflow its banks or, if it does, its force will not be so uncontrolled or damaging.

---

[26] [The power of *fortuna* varies according to how much *virtú* there is in a country. Germany, Spain and France were well equipped in this respect, whereas Italy was not.]

The same happens with fortune, which shows its powers where no force has been organised to resist it, and therefore strikes in the places where it knows that no dykes or dams have been built to restrain it. And if you consider Italy, which has been the seat of these changes, and which has given rise to them, you will see a countryside devoid of any embankments or defences. If it had been protected by proper defences, like Germany, Spain and France, the flood would not have caused such great changes or it would not have occurred at all. But I have said enough in general terms about resisting fortune.

Considering the matter in more detail, I would observe that one sees a ruler flourishing today and ruined tomorrow, without his having changed at all in character or qualities. I believe this is attributable, first, to the cause previously discussed at length, namely, that a ruler who trusts entirely to luck comes to grief when his luck runs out. Moreover, I believe that we are successful when our ways are suited to the times and circumstances, and unsuccessful when they are not. For one sees that, in the things that lead to the end which everyone aims at, that is, glory and riches, men proceed in different ways: one man cautiously, another impetuously; one man forcefully, another cunningly; one man patiently, another impatiently, and each of these different ways of acting can be effective. On the other hand, of two cautious men, one may achieve his aims and the other fail. Again, two men may both succeed, although they have different characters, one acting cautiously and the other impetuously. The reason for these different outcomes is whether their ways of acting conform with the conditions in which they operate. Consequently, as I have said, two men, acting differently, may achieve the same results; and if two men act in the same way, one may succeed and the other fail. From this, again, arise changes in prosperity; because if a man acts cautiously and patiently, and the times and circumstances change in ways for which his methods are appropriate, he will be successful. But if the times and circumstances change again, he will come to grief, because he does not change his methods. And one does not find men who are so prudent that they are capable of being sufficiently flexible: either because our natural inclinations are too strong to permit us to change, or because, having always fared well by acting in a certain way, we do not think it a good idea to change our methods. Therefore, if it is necessary for a cautious man to act expeditiously, he does not know how to do it; this leads to his failure. But if it were possible to change one's character to suit the times and circumstances, one would always be successful.

Pope Julius II always acted impetuously, and found the times and circumstances so suited to his ways that he was always successful. Consider the first expedition he made to Bologna, while messer Giovanni Bentivoglio was still alive. The Venetians were opposed to it, and so was the King of Spain; there were also discussions with the King of France about such an enterprise. Nevertheless, acting with his usual indomitable spirit and impetuosity, he led the expedition personally. This initiative caught the King of Spain and the Venetians off guard and constrained them to be passive spectators, the latter through fear and the former because of his desire to recover the whole of the Kingdom of Naples. On the other hand, Julius involved the King of France: for that King saw the Pope moving and, because he wanted to cultivate the Pope's friendship with a view to reducing the power of Venice, he decided that he could not refuse him troops without offending him very openly. With this swift initiative, then, Julius achieved what no other pope, acting with consummate prudence, could have attained. If he had not left Rome until everything had been agreed and settled, as any other pope would have done, he would never have succeeded. For the King of France would have contrived to find countless excuses, and the others would have produced countless reasons why the Pope should hesitate. I shall not discuss his other actions, which were similar in character, and all turned out well for him. The shortness of his pontificate did not permit him to taste of failure. But if circumstances had changed so that it was imperative to act cautiously, he would have been undone; for he would never have deviated from the methods that were natural to him.

I conclude, then, that since circumstances vary and men when acting lack flexibility, they are successful if their methods match the circumstances and unsuccessful if they do not. I certainly think that it is better to be impetuous than cautious, because fortune is a woman, and if you want to control her, it is necessary to treat her roughly. And it is clear that she is more inclined to yield to men who are impetuous than to those who are calculating. Since fortune is a woman, she is always well disposed towards young men, because they are less cautious and more aggressive, and treat her more boldly.

## Chapter XXVI

### Exhortation to liberate Italy from the barbarian yoke

Bearing in mind all the matters previously discussed, I ask myself whether the present time is appropriate for welcoming a new ruler in Italy, and whether there is matter that provides an opportunity for a far-seeing and able man to mould it into a form that will bring honour to him and benefit all its inhabitants. It seems to me that so many things are propitious for a new ruler that I am not aware that there has ever been a more appropriate time than this.

I have maintained that the Israelites had to be enslaved in Egypt before the ability of Moses could be displayed, the Persians had to be oppressed by the Medes before Cyrus's greatness of spirit could be revealed, and the Athenians in disarray before the magnificent qualities of Theseus could be demonstrated. Likewise, in order for the valour and worth of an Italian spirit to be recognised, Italy had to be reduced to the desperate straits in which it now finds itself: more enslaved than the Hebrews, more oppressed than the Persians, more scattered than the Athenians, without an acknowledged leader, and without order or stability, beaten, despoiled, lacerated, overrun, in short, utterly devastated. And although recently a spark was revealed in one man that might have led one to think that he was ordained by God to achieve her redemption, yet it was seen that he was struck down by misfortune at the highest point of his career.[27] Thus, remaining almost lifeless, Italy is waiting for someone to heal her wounds, and put an end to the ravaging of Lombardy, to the extortions in the Kingdom of Naples and Tuscany, and to cure the sores that have been festering for so long. Look how Italy beseeches God to send someone to rescue it from the cruel and arrogant domination of the foreigners. Again, see how ready and willing she is to rally to a standard, if only there is someone to lead the way.

There is no one in whom Italy can now place any hope except your illustrious family which (because it is successful and talented, and favoured by God and by the Church, of which it is now head)[28] can take the lead in saving her. It will not be very difficult, if you bear in mind the deeds and lives of the men named above. Although they were exceptional and remarkable men, they were still only human, and all of them had less favourable opportunities than the one that now exists, for their causes were not more righteous than this one, nor easier, nor more favoured by God. This is a very righteous cause: "*iustum enim est bellum quibus necessarium, et pia arma ubi nulla nisi in armis spes est.*"[29] Circumstances are now very favourable indeed, and the difficulties to be confronted cannot be

---

[27] [Probably a reference to Cesare Borgia.]

[28] [Giovanni de' Medici had become Pope Leo X in March 1513.]

[29] [Livy, IX, I: "necessary wars are just wars, and when there is no other hope except in arms, they too become holy."]

very great when the circumstances are propitious, if only your family will imitate the methods of the men I have proposed as exemplars. Moreover, very unusual events, which are signs from God, have recently been observed here: the sea has opened; a cloud has shown you the way; water has flowed from the rock; manna has rained down here.[30] Everything points to your future greatness. But you must play your part, for God does not want to do everything, in order not to deprive us of our freedom and the glory that belong to us.

It is not very surprising that none of the Italians previously mentioned[31] was able to achieve what it is hoped your illustrious family will achieve, or that in all the great changes that have occurred in Italy and all the military campaigns, it always seems as if Italian military skill and valour no longer exist.

The reason for this is that our old military practices were unsound, and there has been nobody capable of devising new ones. Nothing brings so much honour to a new ruler as new laws and new practices that he has devised. Such things, if they are solidly based and conduce to achieving greatness, will make him revered and admired; and in Italy there is no lack of matter to shape into any form.

Here individuals have great skill and valour; it is the leaders who lack these qualities. Look how in duels and combats between several men Italians are superior in strength, skill and resourcefulness. But when it comes to fighting in armies, they do not distinguish themselves. And all this stems from the weakness of the leaders: those who are capable are not followed, and everyone thinks that he knows best. Until now nobody has had sufficient ability or luck to succeed in imposing himself to such an extent that the other leaders have recognised his superiority. The outcome has been that, for a long time, in all the wars that have been fought during the last twenty years, any armies composed only of Italian troops have always fared badly. What happened on the Taro, and at Alessandria, Capua, Genoa, Vailà, Bologna and Mestre[32] all confirm this judgment.

---

[30] [All these images recall the journey of the Israelites from Egypt to the Promised Land.]

[31] [E.g., Francesco Sforza and Cesare Borgia.]

[32] [M. alludes to the battle of Fornovo, on the river Taro (1495), where Charles VIII's army succeeded in escaping, and returned to France; Alessandria was conquered by the French in 1499; Capua was sacked by the French in 1501; Genoa surrendered to the French in 1507; Bologna was taken by the French in 1511; Mestre was destroyed by the Spaniards in 1513.]

If your illustrious family, then, wants to emulate those great men[33] who saved their countries, it is essential above all else, as a sound basis for every campaign, to form an army composed of your own men, for there can be no soldiers more loyal, more reliable or better. Even if each of these soldiers individually is brave, they will combine to form a better fighting force if they are led by their own ruler, and honoured and well treated by him. Hence, if Italian skill and courage is to protect us from foreign enemies, it is essential to form an army of this kind.

Although the Swiss and Spanish infantry are considered very formidable, both have weaknesses, so a different kind of army could not only fight them, but be confident of defeating them. For the Spaniards are very vulnerable against cavalry, and the Swiss lack confidence against infantry that fight as strongly as they do themselves. Thus, it has been seen, and experience will confirm it, that the Spaniards are very vulnerable against the French cavalry, and the Swiss have a fatal weakness against the Spanish infantry. And although there is no proof of the latter weakness, some evidence is provided by the battle of Ravenna, when the Spanish infantry fought against the German battalions, which fight in the same way as the Swiss. In this battle, the Spaniards, using their agility and helped by their use of bucklers,[34] penetrated under the long German pikes, and were able to inflict great damage. The Germans were unable to repel them, and if the cavalry had not attacked the Spaniards, the Germans would all have been killed. Once the weaknesses of both the Spanish and the Swiss infantry are recognised, then, it will be possible to form a new kind of infantry, which should be able to resist cavalry charges and not be intimidated by infantry. It will be possible to do this by the right choice of weapons and by changing battle formations. It is the introduction of such new methods of fighting that enhances the reputation of a new ruler, establishing him as a great leader.

This opportunity to provide Italy with a liberator, then, after such a long time, must not be missed. I have no doubt at all that he would be received with great affection in all those regions that have been inundated by the foreign invasions, as well as with a great thirst for revenge, with resolute fidelity, with devotion and with tears of gratitude. What gate would be closed to him? What people

---

[33] [Moses, Theseus and Cyrus.]

[34] ["Small round shields usually held by a handle" (*C.O.D.*).]

# DISCOURSES ON THE FIRST TEN BOOKS OF TITUS LIVIUS[1]

## → FIRST BOOK ←

### Introduction

Although the envious nature of men, so prompt to blame and so slow to praise, makes the discovery and introduction of any new principles and systems as dangerous almost as the exploration of unknown seas and continents, yet, animated by that desire which impels me to do what may prove for the common benefit of all, I have resolved to open a new route, which has not yet been followed by any one, and may prove difficult and troublesome, but may also bring me some reward in the approbation of those who will kindly appreciate my efforts.

And if my poor talents, my little experience of the present and insufficient study of the past, should make the result of my labors defective and of little utility, I shall at least have shown the way to others, who will carry out my views with greater ability, eloquence, and judgment, so that if I do not merit praise, I ought at least not to incur censure.

When we consider the general respect for antiquity, and how often—to say nothing of other examples—a great price is paid for some fragments of an antique statue, which we are anxious to possess to ornament our houses with, or to give to artists who strive to imitate them in their own works; and when we see, on the other hand, the wonderful examples which the history of ancient kingdoms and republics presents to us, the prodigies of virtue and of wisdom displayed by the kings, captains, citizens, and legislators who have sacrificed themselves for their country—when we see these, I say, more admired than imitated, or so much neglected that not the least trace of this ancient virtue remains, we cannot but be at the same time as much surprised as afflicted. The more so as in the differences which arise between citizens, or in the maladies to which they are subjected, we see these same people have recourse to the judgments and the remedies prescribed

---

*Discourses on the First Ten Books of Titus Livius*, by Niccolò Machiavelli, translated by Christian E. Detmold (1882).

[1] [The *Discourses* is a commentary on the first ten books of Titus Livy's *History of Rome*. Livy lived from 57 to 24 B.C. — J.M.P.]

by the ancients. The civil laws are in fact nothing but decisions given by their jurisconsults, and which, reduced to a system, direct our modern jurists in their decisions. And what is the science of medicine, but the experience of ancient physicians, which their successors have taken for their guide? And yet to found a republic, maintain states, to govern a kingdom, organize an army, conduct a war, dispense justice, and extend empires, you will find neither prince, nor republic, nor captain, nor citizen, who has recourse to the examples of antiquity! This neglect, I am persuaded, is due less to the weakness to which the vices of our education have reduced the world, than to the evils caused by the proud indolence which prevails in most of the Christian states, and to the lack of real knowledge of history, the true sense of which is not known, or the spirit of which they do not comprehend. Thus the majority of those who read it take the pleasure only in the variety of the events which history relates, without ever thinking of imitating the noble actions, deeming that not only difficult, but impossible; as though heaven, the sun, the elements, and men had changed the order of their motions and power, and were different from what they were in ancient times.

Wishing, therefore, so far as in me lies, to draw mankind from this error, I have thought it proper to write upon those books of Titus Livius that have come to us entire despite the malice of time; touching upon all those matters which, after a comparison between the ancient and modern events, may seem to me necessary to facilitate their proper understanding. In this way those who read my remarks may derive those advantages which should be the aim of all study of history; and although the undertaking is difficult, yet, aided by those who have encouraged me in this attempt, I hope to carry it sufficiently far, so that but little may remain for others to carry it to its destined end.

## Chapter 1

### Of the Beginnings of Cities in General, and Especially that of the City of Rome

Those who read what the beginning of Rome was, and what her lawgivers and her organization, will not be astonished that so much virtue should have maintained itself during so many centuries; and that so great an empire should have sprung from it afterwards. To speak first of her origin, we will premise that all cities are founded either by natives of the country or by strangers. The little security which the natives found in living dispersed; the impossibility for each to resist isolated, either because of the situation or because of their small number, the attacks of any enemy that might present himself; the difficulty of uniting in time for defence at his approach, and the necessity of abandoning the greater number of their re-treats, which quickly became a prize to the assailant,—such were the motives that caused the first inhabitants of a country to build cities for the purpose of escaping these dangers. They resolved, of their own accord, or by the advice of some one who had most authority amongst them, to live together in some place of their selection that might offer them greater conveniences and greater facility of defence. Thus, amongst many others were Athens and Venice; the first was built under the authority of Theseus, who had gathered the dispersed inhabitants; and the second owed its origin to the fact that several tribes had taken refuge on the little islands situated at the head of the Adriatic Sea, to escape from war, and from the Barbarians who after the fall of the Roman Empire had overrun Italy. These refugees of themselves, and without any prince to govern them, began to live under such laws as seemed to them best suited to maintain their new state. In this they succeeded, happily favored by the long peace, for which they were in-debted to their situation upon a sea without issue, where the people that ravaged Italy could not harass them, being without any ships. Thus from that small beginning they attained that degree of power in which we see them now.

The second case is when a city is built by strangers; these may be either freemen, or subjects of a republic or of a prince, who, to relieve their states from an exces-sive population, or to defend a newly acquired territory which they wish to preserve without expense, send colonies there. The Romans founded many cities in this way within their empire. Sometimes cities are built by a prince, not for the purpose of living there, but merely as monuments to his glory, such was Alexandria, built by Alexander the Great. But as all these cities are at their very origin deprived of lib-erty, they rarely succeed in making great progress, or in being counted amongst the great powers. Such was the origin of Florence; for it was built either by the soldiers of Sylla, or perhaps by the inhabitants of Mount Fiesole, who, trusting to the long peace that prevailed in the reign of Octavian, were attracted to the plains along the Arno. Florence, thus built under the Roman Empire, could in the beginning have no growth except what depended on the will of its master.

The founders of cities are independent when they are people who, under the lead-ership of some prince, or by themselves, have been obliged to fly from pestilence, war, or famine, that was desolating their native country, and are seeking a new home. These either inhabit the cities of the country of which they take possession, as Moses did; or they build new ones, as was done by Aeneas. In such case we are able to appreciate the talents of the founder and the success of his work, which is more or less remarkable according as he, in founding the city, displays more or less wisdom and skill. Both the one and the other are recognized by the selection of the place where he has located the city, and by the nature of the laws which he establishes in it. And as men work either from necessity or from choice, and as it has been observed that virtue has more sway where labor is the result of necessity rather than of choice, it is a matter of consideration whether it might not be better to select for the establishment of a city a sterile region, where the people, compelled by necessity to be industrious, and therefore less given to idleness, would be more united, and less exposed by the poverty of the country to occasions for discord; as was the case with Ragusa, and several other cities that were built upon an ungrateful soil. Such a selection of site would doubtless be more useful and wise if men were content with what they possess, and did not desire to exercise command over others.

Now, as people cannot make themselves secure except by being powerful, it is necessary in the founding of a city to avoid a sterile country. On the contrary, a city should be placed rather in a region where the fertility of the soil affords the means of becoming great, and of acquiring strength to repel all who might attempt to attack it, or oppose the development of its power. As to the idleness which the fertility of a country tends to encourage, the laws should compel men to labor where the sterility of the soil does not do it; as was done by those skilful and sagacious legislators who have inhabited very agreeable and fertile countries, such as are apt to make men idle and unfit for the exercise of valor. These by way of an offset to the pleasures and softness of the climate, imposed upon their soldiers the rigors of a strict discipline and severe exercises, so that they became better warriors than what nature produces in the harshest climates and most sterile countries. Amongst these legislators we may cite the founders of the kingdom of Egypt: despite the charms of the climate, the severity of the institutions there formed excellent men; and if great antiquity had not buried their names in oblivion, we should see that they deserved more praise than Alexander the Great and many others of more recent memory. And whoever has examined the government of the Pachas of Egypt and the discipline of their Mameluke militia before it was destroyed by the Sultan Selim of Turkey, will have seen how much they dreaded idleness, and by what variety of exercises and by what severe laws they prevented in their soldiers that effeminacy which is the natural fruit of the softness of their climate.

I say, then, that for the establishment of a city it is wisest to select the most fertile spot, especially as the laws can prevent the ill effects that would otherwise result from that very fertility.

When Alexander the Great wished to build a city that should serve as a monument to his glory, his architect, Dinocrates, pointed out to him how he could build a city on Mount Athos, which place he said, besides being very strong, could be so arranged as to give the city the appearance of the human form, which would make it a wonder worthy of the greatness of its founder. Alexander having asked him what the inhabitants were to live upon, he replied, "That I have not thought of"; at which Alexander smiled, and, leaving Mount Athos as it was, he built Alexandria, where the inhabitants would be glad to remain on account of the richness of the country and the advantages which the proximity of the Nile and the sea afforded them.

If we accept the opinion that Aeneas was the founder of Rome, then we must count that city as one of those built by strangers; but if Romulus is taken as its founder, then must it be classed with those built by the natives of the country. Either way it will be seen that Rome was from the first free and independent; and we shall also see (as we shall show further on) to how many privations the laws of Romulus, of Numa, and of others subjected its inhabitants; so that neither the fertility of the soil, nor the proximity of the sea, nor their many victories, nor the greatness of the Empire, could corrupt them during several centuries, and they maintained there more virtues than have ever been seen in any other republic.

The great things which Rome achieved, and of which Titus Livius has preserved the memory, have been the work either of the government or of private individuals; and as they relate either to the affairs of the interior or of the exterior, I shall begin to discourse of those internal operations of the government which I believe to be most noteworthy, and shall point out their results. This will be the subject of the discourses that will compose this First Book, or rather First Part.

### Chapter 2

### *Of the Different Kinds of Republics, and of What Kind the Roman Republic Was*

I will leave aside what might be said of cities which from their very birth have been subject to a foreign power, and will speak only of those whose origin has been independent, and which from the first governed themselves by their own laws, whether as republics or as principalities, and whose constitution and laws have differed as their origin. Some have had at the very beginning, or soon after, a legislator, who, like Lycurgus with the Lacedaemonians, gave them by a single act all the laws they needed. Others have owed theirs to chance and to events, and have received their laws at different times, as Rome did. It is great good fortune for a republic to have a legislator sufficiently wise to give her laws so regulated that, without the necessity of correcting them, they afford security to those who live under them. Sparta observed her laws for more than eight hundred years without altering them and without experiencing a single dangerous disturbance. Unhappy, on the contrary, is that republic which, not having at the beginning fallen into the hands of a sagacious and skilful legislator, is herself obliged to reform her laws. More unhappy still is that republic which from the first has diverged from a good constitution. And that republic is furthest from it whose vicious institutions impede her progress, and make her leave the right path that leads to a good end; for those who are in that condition can hardly be brought into the right road.

Those republics, on the other hand, that started without having even a perfect constitution, but made a fair beginning, and are capable of improvement,—such republics, I say, may perfect themselves by the aid of events. It is very true, however, that such reforms are never effected without danger, for the majority of men never willingly adopt any new law tending to change the constitution of the state, unless the necessity of the change is clearly demonstrated; and as such a necessity cannot make itself felt without being accompanied with danger, the republic may easily be destroyed before having perfected its constitution. That of Florence is a complete proof of this: reorganized after the revolt of Arezzo, in 1502, it was overthrown after the taking of Prato, in 1512.

Having proposed to myself to treat of the kind of government established at Rome, and of the events that led to its perfection, I must at the beginning observe that some of the writers on politics distinguished three kinds of government, viz. the monarchical, the aristocratic, and the democratic; and maintain that the legislators of a people must choose from these three the one that seems to them most suitable. Other authors, wiser according to the opinion of many, count six kinds of governments, three of which are very bad, and three good in themselves, but so liable to be corrupted that they become absolutely bad. The three good ones are those which we have just named; the three bad ones result from the degradation of the other three, and each of them resembles its corresponding original, so that the transition from the one to the other is very easy. Thus monarchy becomes tyranny; aristocracy degenerates into oligarchy; and the popular government lapses readily into licentiousness. So that a legislator who gives to a state which he founds, either of these three forms of government, constitutes it but for a brief time; for no precautions can prevent either one of the three that are reputed good, from degenerating into its opposite kind; so great are in these the attractions and resemblances between the good and the evil.

Chance has given birth to these different kinds of governments amongst men; for at the beginning of the world the inhabitants were few in number, and lived for a time dispersed, like beasts. As the human race increased, the necessity for uniting themselves for defence made itself felt; the better to attain this object, they chose the strongest and most courageous from amongst themselves and placed him at their head, promising to obey him. Thence they began to know the good and the honest, and to distinguish them from the bad and vicious; for seeing a man injure his benefactor aroused at once two sentiments in every heart, hatred against the ingrate and love for the benefactor. They blamed the first, and on the contrary honored those the more who showed themselves grateful, for each felt he in turn might be subject to a like wrong; and to prevent similar evils, they set to work to make laws, and to institute punishments for those who contravened them. Such was the origin of justice. This caused them, when they had afterwards to choose a prince, neither to look to the strongest nor bravest, but to the wisest and most just. But when they began to make sovereignty hereditary and non-elective, the children quickly degenerated from their fathers; and, so far from trying to equal their virtues, they considered that a prince had nothing else to do than to excel all the rest in luxury, indulgence, and every other variety of pleasure. The prince consequently soon drew upon himself the general hatred. An object of hatred, he naturally felt fear; fear in turn dictated to him precautions and wrongs, and thus tyranny quickly developed itself. Such were the beginning and causes of disorders, conspiracies, and plots against the sovereigns, set on foot, not by the feeble and timid, but by those citizens who, surpassing the others in grandeur of soul, in wealth, and in courage, could not submit to the outrages and excesses of their princes.

Under such powerful leaders the masses armed themselves against the tyrant, and, after having rid themselves of him, submitted to these chiefs as their liberators. These, abhorring the very name of prince, constituted themselves a new government; and at first, bearing in mind the past tyranny, they governed in strict accordance with the laws which they had established themselves; preferring public interests to their own, and to administer and protect with greatest care both public and private affairs. The children succeeded their fathers, and ignorant of the changes of fortune, having never experienced its reverses, and indisposed to remain content with this civil equality, they in turn gave themselves up to cupidity, ambition, libertinage, and violence, and soon caused the aristocratic government to degenerate into an oligarchic tyranny, regardless of all civil rights. They soon, however, experienced the same fate as the first tyrant; the people, disgusted with their government, placed themselves at the command of whoever was willing to attack them, and this disposition soon produced an avenger, who was sufficiently well seconded to destroy them. The memory of the prince and the wrongs committed by him being still fresh in their minds, and having overthrown the oligarchy, the people were not willing to return to the government of a prince. A popular government was therefore resolved upon, and it was so organized that the authority should not again fall into the hands of a prince or a small number of nobles. And as all governments are at first looked up to with some degree of reverence, the popular state also maintained itself for a time, but which was never of long duration, and lasted generally only about as long as the generation that had established it; for it soon ran into that kind of license which inflicts injury upon public as well as private interests. Each individual only consulted his own passions, and a thousand acts of injustice were daily committed, so that, constrained by necessity, or directed by the counsels of some good man, or for the purpose of escaping from this anarchy, they returned anew to the government of a prince, and from this they generally lapsed again into anarchy, step by step, in the same manner and from the same causes as we have indicated.

Such is the circle which all republics are destined to run through. Seldom, however, do they come back to the original form of government, which results from the fact that their duration is not sufficiently long to be able to undergo these repeated changes and preserve their existence. But it may well happen that a republic lacking strength and good counsel in its difficulties becomes subject after a while to some neighboring state, that is better organized than itself; and if such is not the case, then they will be apt to revolve indefinitely in the circle of revolutions. I say, then, that all kinds of government are defective; those three which we have qualified as good because they are too short-lived, and the three bad ones because of their inherent viciousness. Thus sagacious legislators, knowing the vices of each of these systems of government by themselves, have chosen one that should partake of all of them, judging that to be the most stable and solid. In fact, when there is combined under the same constitution a prince, a nobility, and the power of the people, then these three powers will watch and keep each other reciprocally in check.

Amongst those justly celebrated for having established such a constitution, Lycurgus beyond doubt merits the highest praise. He organized the government of Sparta in such manner that, in giving to the king, the nobles, and the people each their portion of authority and duties, he created a government which maintained itself for over eight hundred years in the most perfect tranquility, and reflected infinite glory upon this legislator. On the other hand, the constitution given by Solon to the Athenians, by which he established only a popular government, was of such short duration that before his death he saw the tyranny of Pisistratus arise. And although forty years afterwards the heirs of the tyrant were expelled, so that Athens recovered her liberties and restored the popular government according to the laws of Solon, yet it did not last over a hundred years; although a number of laws that had been overlooked by Solon were adopted, to maintain the government against the insolence of the nobles and the license of the populace. The fault he had committed in not tempering the power of the people and that of the prince and his nobles, made the duration of the government of Athens very short, as compared with that of Sparta.

But let us come to Rome. Although she had no legislator like Lycurgus, who constituted her government, at her very origin, in a manner to secure her liberty for a length of time, yet the disunion which existed between the Senate and the people produced such extraordinary events, that chance did for her what the laws had failed to do. Thus, if Rome did not attain the first degree of happiness, she at least had the second. Her first institutions were doubtless defective, but they were not in conflict with the principles that might bring her to perfection. For Romulus and all the other kings gave her many and good laws, well suited even to a free people; but as the object of these princes was to found a monarchy, and not a republic, Rome, upon becoming free, found herself lacking all those institutions that are most essential to liberty, and which her kings had not established. And although these kings lost their empire, for the reasons and in the manner which we have explained, yet those who expelled them appointed immediately two consuls in place of the king;

and thus it was found that they had banished the title of king from Rome, but not the regal power. The government, composed of Consuls and a Senate, had but two of the three elements of which we have spoken, the monarchical and the aristocratic; the popular power was wanting. In the course of time, however, the insolence of the nobles, produced by the causes which we shall see further on, induced the people to rise against the others. The nobility, to save a portion of their power, were forced to yield a share of it to the people; but the Senate and the Consuls retained sufficient to maintain their rank in the state. It was then that the Tribunes of the people were created, which strengthened and confirmed the republic, being now composed of the three elements of which we have spoken above. Fortune favored her, so that, although the authority passed successively from the kings and nobles to the people, by the same degrees and for the same reasons that we have spoken of, yet the royal authority was never entirely abolished to bestow it upon the nobles; and these were never entirely deprived of their authority to give it to the people; but a combination was formed of the three powers, which rendered the constitution perfect, and this perfection was attained by the disunion of the Senate and the people, as we shall more fully show in the following....

## Chapter 3

### Of the Events that Caused the Creation of Tribunes in Rome; Which Made the Republic More Perfect

All those who have written upon civil institutions demonstrate (and history is full of examples to support them) that whoever desires to found a state and give it laws, must start with assuming that all men are bad and ever ready to display their vicious nature, whenever they may find occasion for it. If their evil disposition remains concealed for a time, it must be attributed to some unknown reason; and we must assume that it lacked occasion to show itself; but time, which has been said to be the father of all truth, does not fail to bring it to light. After the expulsion of the Tarquins the greatest harmony seemed to prevail between the Senate and the people. The nobles seemed to have laid aside all their haughtiness and assumed popular manners, which made them supportable even to the lowest of the citizens. The nobility played this role so long as the Tarquins lived, without their motive being divined; for they feared the Tarquins, and also lest the ill-treated people might side with them. Their party therefore assumed all possible gentleness in their manners towards the people. But so soon as the death of the Tarquins had relieved them of their apprehensions, they began to vent upon the people all the venom they had so long retained within their breasts, and lost no opportunity to outrage them in every possible way; which is one of the proofs of the argument we have advanced, that men act right only upon compulsion; but from the moment that they have the option and liberty to commit wrong with impunity, then they never fail to carry confusion and disorder everywhere. It is this that has caused it to be said that poverty and hunger make men industrious, and that the law makes men good; and if fortunate circumstances cause good to be done without constraint, the law may be dispensed with. But when such happy influence is lacking, then the law immediately becomes necessary. Thus the nobles, after the death of the Tarquins, being no longer under the influence that had restrained them, determined to establish a new order of things, which had the same effect as the misrule of the Tarquins during their existence; and therefore, after many troubles, tumults, and dangers occasioned by the excesses which both the nobles and the people committed, they came, for the security of the people, to the creation of the Tribunes, who were endowed with so many prerogatives, and surrounded with so much respect, that they formed a powerful barrier between the Senate and the people, which curbed the insolence of the former.

## Chapter 4

### The Disunion of the Senate and the People Renders the Republic of Rome Powerful and Free

I shall not pass over in silence the disturbances that occurred in Rome from the time of the death of the Tarquins to that of the creation of the Tribunes; and shall afterwards refute the opinion of those who claim that the Roman republic has always been a theatre of turbulence and disorder, and that if its extreme good fortune and the military discipline had not supplied the defects of her constitution, she would have deserved the lowest rank amongst the republics.

It cannot be denied that the Roman Empire was the result of good fortune and military discipline; but it seems to me that it ought to be perceived that where good discipline prevails there also will good order prevail, and good fortune rarely fails to follow in their train. Let us, however, go into details upon this point. I maintain that those who blame the quarrels of the Senate and the people of Rome condemn that which was the very origin of liberty, and that they were probably more impressed by the cries and noise which these disturbances occasioned in the public places, than by the good effect which they produced; and that they do not consider that in every republic there are two parties, that of the nobles and that of the people; and all the laws that are favorable to liberty result from the opposition of these parties to each other, as may easily be seen from the events that occurred in Rome. From the time of the Tarquins to that of the Gracchi, that is to say, within the space of over three hundred years, the differences between these parties caused but very few exiles, and cost still less blood; they cannot therefore be regarded as having been very injurious and fatal to a republic, which during the course of so many years saw on this account only eight or ten of its citizens sent into exile, and but a very small number put to death, and even but a few condemned to pecuniary fines. Nor can we regard a republic as disorderly where so many virtues were seen to shine. For good examples are the result of good education, and good education is due to good laws; and good laws in their turn spring from those very agitations which have been so inconsiderately condemned by many. For whoever will carefully examine the result of these agitations will find that they have neither caused exiles nor any violence prejudicial to the general good, and will be convinced even that they have given rise to laws that were to the advantage of public liberty. And if it be said that these are strange means,—to hear constantly the cries of the people furious against the Senate, and of a Senate declaiming against the people, to see the populace rush tumultuously through the streets, close their houses, and even leave the city of Rome,—I reply, that all these things can alarm only those who read of them, and that every free state ought to afford the people the opportunity of giving vent, so to say, to their ambition; and above all those republics which on important occasions have to avail themselves of this very people. Now such were the means employed at Rome; when the people wanted to obtain a law, they resorted to some of the extremes of which we have just spoken, or they refused to enroll themselves to serve in the wars, so that the Senate was obliged to satisfy them in some measure. The demands of a free people are rarely pernicious to their liberty; they are generally inspired by oppressions, experienced or apprehended; and if their fears are ill founded, resort is had to public assemblies where the mere eloquence of a single good and respectable man will make them sensible of their error, "The people," says Cicero, "although ignorant, yet are capable of appreciating the truth, and yield to it readily when it is presented to them by a man whom they esteem worthy of their confidence."

One should show then more reserve in blaming the Roman government, and consider that so many good effects, which originated in that republic, cannot but result from very good causes. If the troubles of Rome occasioned the creation of Tribunes, then they cannot be praised too highly; for besides giving to the people a share in the public administration, these Tribunes were established as the most assured guardians of Roman liberty, as we shall see in the following chapter.

## Chapter 6

### Whether It was Possible to Establish in Rome a Government Capable of Putting an End to the Enmities Existing Between the Nobles and the People

We have discussed above the effects of the quarrels between the people and the Senate. These same differences having continued to the time of the Gracchi, when they became the cause of the loss of liberty, one might wish that Rome had done the great things we have admired, without bearing within her bosom such cause of discords. It seems to me therefore important to examine whether it was possible to establish a government in Rome that could prevent all these misunderstandings; and to do this well, we must necessarily recur to those republics that have maintained their liberties without such enmities and disturbances; we must examine what the form of their government was, and whether that could have been introduced in Rome.

In Sparta we have an example amongst the ancients, and in Venice amongst the moderns; to both these states I have already referred above. Sparta had a king and a senate, few in number, to govern her; Venice did not admit these distinctions, and gave the name of gentlemen to all who were entitled to have a part in the administration of the government. It was chance rather than foresight which gave to the latter this form of government; for having taken refuge on those shallows where the city now is, for the reasons mentioned above, the inhabitants soon became sufficiently numerous to require a regular system of laws. They consequently established a government, and assembled frequently in council to discuss the interests of the city. When it seemed to them that they were sufficiently numerous to govern themselves, they barred the way to a share in the government to the newly arrived who came to live amongst them; and finding in the course of time that the number of the latter increased sufficiently to give reputation to those who held the government in their hands, they designated the latter by the title of "gentlemen," and the others were called the popular class. This form of government had no difficulty in establishing and maintaining itself without disturbances; for at the moment of its origin all those who inhabited Venice had the right to participate in the government, so that no one had cause to complain. Those who afterwards came to live there, finding the government firmly established, had neither a pretext for, nor the means of, creating disturbances. They had no cause, for the reason that they had not been deprived of anything; and they lacked the means, because they were kept in check by those who held the government, and who did not employ them in any affairs that might tempt them to seize authority. Besides, the newcomers in Venice were not sufficiently numerous to have produced a disproportion between the governing and the governed, for the number of nobles equalled or exceeded that of the others; and thus for these reasons Venice could establish and preserve that form of government.

Sparta, as I have said, being governed by a king and a limited senate, could maintain itself also for a long time, because there were but few inhabitants, and strangers were not permitted to come in; besides, the laws of Lycurgus had obtained such influence that their observance prevented even the slightest pretext for trouble. It was also the easier for the citizens to live in union, as Lycurgus had established equality in fortunes and inequality in conditions; for an equal poverty prevailed there, and the people were the less ambitious, as the offices of the government were given but to a few citizens, the people being excluded from them; and the nobles in the exercise of their functions did not treat the people sufficiently ill to excite in them the desire of exercising them themselves. This last advantage was due to the kings of Sparta; for being placed in this government, as it were, between the two orders, and living in the midst of the nobility, they had no better means of maintaining their authority than to protect the people against all injustice; whence these neither feared nor desired authority, and consequently there was no motive for any differences between them and the nobles, nor any cause for disturbances; and thus they could live for a long time united. Two principal causes, however, cemented this union: first, the inhabitants of Sparta were few in number, and therefore could be governed by a few; and the other was, that, by not permitting strangers to establish themselves in the republic, they had neither opportunity of becoming corrupt, nor of increasing their population to such a degree that the burden of government became difficult to the few who were charged with it.

In examining now all these circumstances, we see that the legislators of Rome had to do one of two things to assure to their republic the same quiet as that enjoyed by the two republics of which we have spoken; namely, either not to employ the people in the armies, like the Venetians, or not to open the doors to strangers, as had been the case in Sparta. But the Romans in both took just the opposite course, which gave to the people greater power and infinite occasion for disturbances. But if the republic had been more tranquil, it would necessarily have resulted that she would have been more feeble, and that she would have lost with her energy also the ability of achieving that high degree of greatness to which she attained; so that to have removed the cause of trouble from Rome would have been to deprive her of her power of expansion. And thus it is seen in all human affairs, upon careful examination, that you cannot avoid one inconvenience without incurring another. If therefore you wish to make a people numerous and warlike, so as to create a great empire, you will have to constitute it in such manner as will cause you more difficulty in managing it; and if you keep it either small or unarmed, and you acquire other dominions, you will not be able to hold them, or you will become so feeble that you will fall a prey to whoever attacks you. And therefore in all our decisions we must consider well what presents the least inconveniences, and then choose the best, for we shall never find any course entirely free from objections. Rome then might, like Sparta, have created a king for life, and established a limited senate; but with her desire to become a great empire, she could not, like Sparta, limit the number of her citizens; and therefore a king for life and a limited senate would have been of no benefit to her so far as union was concerned. If any one therefore wishes to establish an entirely new republic, he will have to consider whether he wishes to have her expand in power and dominion like Rome, or whether he intends to confine her within narrow limits. In the first case, it will be necessary to organize her as Rome was, and submit to dissensions and troubles as best he may; for without a great number of men, and these well armed, no republic can ever increase. In the second case, he may organize her like Sparta and Venice; but as expansion is the poison of such republics, he must by every means in his power prevent her from making conquests, for such acquisitions by a feeble republic always prove their ruin, as happened to both Sparta and Venice; the first of which, having subjected to her rule nearly all Greece, exposed its feeble foundations at the slightest accident, for when the rebellion of Thebes occurred, which was led by Pelopidas, the other cities of Greece also rose up and almost ruined Sparta.

In like manner, Venice, having obtained possession of a great part of Italy, and the most of it not by war, but by means of money and fraud, when occasion came for her to give proof of her strength, she lost everything in a single battle. I think, then, that to found a republic which should endure a long time it would be best to organize her internally like Sparta, or to locate her, like Venice, in some strong place; and to make her sufficiently powerful, so that no one could hope to overcome her readily, and yet on the other hand not so powerful as to make her formidable to her neighbors. In this wise she might long enjoy her independence. For there are but two motives for making war against a republic: one, the desire to subjugate her; the other, the apprehension of being subjugated by her. The two means which we have indicated remove, as it were, both these pretexts for war; for if the republic is difficult to be conquered, her defences being well organized, as I presuppose, then it will seldom or never happen that any one will venture upon the project of conquering her. If she remains quiet within her limits, and experience shows that she entertains no ambitious projects, the fear of her power will never prompt any one to attack her; and this would even be more certainly the case if her constitution and laws prohibited all aggrandizement. And I certainly think that if she could be kept in this equilibrium it would be the best political existence, and would insure to any state real tranquility. But as all human things are kept in a perpetual movement, and can never remain stable, states naturally either rise or decline, and necessity compels them to many acts to which reason will not influence them; so that, having organized a republic competent to maintain herself without expanding, still, if forced by necessity to extend her territory, in such case we shall see her foundations give way and herself quickly brought to ruin. And thus, on the other hand, if Heaven favors her so as never to be involved in war, the continued tranquility would enervate her, or provoke internal dissensions, which together, or either of them separately, will be apt to prove her ruin. Seeing then the impossibility of establishing in this respect a perfect equilibrium, and that a precise middle course cannot be maintained, it is proper in the organization of a republic to select the most honorable course, and to constitute her so that, even if necessity should oblige her to expand, she may yet be able to preserve her acquisitions. To return now to our first argument, I believe it therefore necessary rather to take the constitution of Rome as a model than that of any other republic (for I do not believe that a middle course between the two can be found,) and to tolerate the differences that will arise between the Senate and the people as an unavoidable inconvenience in achieving greatness like that of Rome. Besides the other reasons alleged, which demonstrate the creation and authority of the Tribunes to have been necessary for the protection of liberty, it is easy to see the advantage which a republic must derive from the faculty of accusing, which amongst others was bestowed upon the Tribunes, as will be seen....

## Chapter 9

### *To Found a New Republic, or to Reform Entirely the Old Institutions of an Existing One, Must be the Work of One Man Only*

It may perhaps appear to some that I have gone too far into the details of Roman history before having made any mention of the founders of that republic, or of her institutions, her religion, and her military establishment. Not wishing, therefore, to keep any longer in suspense the desires of those who wish to understand these matters, I say that many will perhaps consider it an evil example that the founder of a civil society, as Romulus was, should first have killed his brother, and then have consented to the death of Titus Tatius, who had been elected to share the royal authority with him; from which it might be concluded that the citizens, according to the example of their prince, might, from ambition and the desire to rule, destroy those who attempt to oppose their authority. This opinion would be correct, if we do not take into consideration the object which Romulus had in view in committing that homicide. But we must assume, as a general rule, that it never or rarely happens that a republic or monarchy is well constituted, or its old institutions entirely reformed, unless it is done by only one individual; it is even necessary that he whose mind has conceived such a constitution should be alone in carrying it into effect. A sagacious legislator of a republic, therefore, whose object is to promote the public good, and not his private interests, and who prefers his country to his own successors, should concentrate all authority in himself; and a wise mind will never censure any one for having employed any extraordinary means for the purpose of establishing a kingdom or constituting a republic. It is well that, when the act accuses him, the result should excuse him; and when the result is good, as in the case of Romulus, it will always absolve him from blame. For he is to be reprehended who commits violence for the purpose of destroying, and not he who employs it for beneficent purposes. The lawgiver should, however, be sufficiently wise and virtuous not to leave this authority which he has assumed either to his heirs or to any one else; for mankind, being more prone to evil than to good, his successor might employ for evil purposes the power which he had used only for good ends. Besides, although one man alone should organize a government, yet it will not endure long if the administration of it remains on the shoulders of a single individual; it is well, then, to confide this to the charge of many, for thus it will be sustained by the many. Therefore, as the organization of anything cannot be made by many, because the divergence of their opinions hinders them from agreeing as to what is best, yet, when once they do understand it, they will not readily agree to abandon it. That Romulus deserves to be excused for the death of his brother and that of his associate, and that what he had done was for the general good, and not for the gratification of his own ambition, is proved by the fact that he immediately instituted a Senate with which to consult, and according to the opinions of which he might form his resolutions. And on carefully considering the authority which Romulus reserved for himself, we see that all he kept was the command of the army in case of war, and the power of convoking the Senate. This was seen when Rome became free, after the expulsion of the Tarquins, when there was no other innovation made upon the existing order of things than the substitution of two Consuls, appointed annually, in place of an hereditary king; which proves clearly that all the original institutions of that city were more in conformity with the requirements of a free and civil society than with an absolute and tyrannical government.

The above views might be corroborated by any number of examples, such as those of Moses, Lycurgus, Solon, and other founders of monarchies and republics, who were enabled to establish laws suitable for the general good only by keeping for themselves an exclusive authority; but all these are so well known that I will not further refer to them. I will adduce only one instance, not so celebrated, but which merits the consideration of those who aim to become good legislators: it is this. Agis, king of Sparta, desired to bring back the Spartans to the strict observance of the laws of Lycurgus, being convinced that, by deviating from them, their city had lost much of her ancient virtue, and consequently her power and dominion; but the Spartan Ephores had him promptly killed, as one who attempted to make himself a tyrant. His successor, Cleomenes, had conceived the same desire, from studying the records and writings of Agis, which he had found, and which explained his aims and intentions. Cleomenes was convinced that he would be unable to render this service to his country unless he possessed sole authority; for he judged that, owing to the ambitious nature of men, he could not promote the interests of the many against the will of the few; and therefore he availed of a convenient opportunity to have all the Ephores slain, as well as all such others as might oppose his project, after which he restored the laws of Lycurgus entirely. This course was calculated to resuscitate the greatness of Sparta, and to give Cleomenes a reputation equal to that of Lycurgus, had it not been for the power of the Macedonians and the weakness of the other Greek republics. For being soon after attacked by the Macedonians, and Sparta by herself being inferior in strength, and there being no one whom he could call to his aid, he was defeated; and thus his project, so just and laudable, was never put into execution. Considering, then, all these things, I conclude that, to found a republic, one must be alone; and that Romulus deserves to be absolved from, and not blamed for, the death of Remus and of Tatius.

## Chapter 10

### In Proportion as the Founders of a Republic or Monarchy are Entitled to Praise, So Do the Founders of a Tyranny Deserve Execration

Of all men who have been eulogized, those deserve it most who have been the authors and founders of religions; next come such as have established republics or kingdoms. After these the most celebrated are those who have commanded armies, and have extended the possessions of their kingdom or country. To these may be added literary men, but, as these are of different kinds, they are celebrated according to their respective degrees of excellence. All others—and their number is infinite—receive such share of praise as pertains to the exercise of their arts and professions. On the contrary, those are doomed to infamy and universal execration who have destroyed religions, who have overturned republics and kingdoms, who are enemies of virtue, of letters, and of every art that is useful and honorable to mankind. Such are the impious and violent, the ignorant, the idle, the vile and degraded. And there are none so foolish or so wise, so wicked or so good, that, in choosing between these two qualities, they do not praise what is praiseworthy and blame that which deserves blame. And yet nearly all men, deceived by a false good and a false glory, allow themselves voluntarily or ignorantly to be drawn towards those who deserve more blame than praise. Such as by the establishment of a republic or kingdom could earn eternal glory for themselves incline to tyranny, without perceiving how much glory, how much honor, security, satisfaction, and tranquility of mind, they forfeit; and what infamy, disgrace, blame, danger, and disquietude they incur. And it is impossible that those who have lived as private citizens in a republic, or those who by fortune or courage have risen to be princes of the same, if they were to read history or take the records of antiquity for example, should not prefer Scipio to Caesar; and that those who were (originally) princes should not rather choose to be like Agesilaus, Timoleon, and Dion, than Nabis, Phalaris, and Dionysius; for they would then see how thoroughly the latter were despised, and how highly the former were appreciated. They would furthermore see that Timoleon and the others had no less authority in their country than Dionysius and Phalaris, but that they enjoyed far more security, and for a much greater length of time. Nor let any one be deceived by the glory of that Caesar who has been so much celebrated by writers; for those who praised him were corrupted by his fortune, and frightened by the long duration of the empire that was maintained under his name, and which did not permit writers to speak of him with freedom. And if any one wishes to know what would have been said of him if writers had been free to speak their minds, let them read what Catiline said of him. Caesar is as much more to be condemned, as he who commits an evil deed is more guilty than he who merely has the evil intention. He will also see how highly Brutus was eulogized; for, not being allowed to blame Caesar on account of his power, they extolled his enemy. Let him also note how much more praise those Emperors merited who, after Rome became an empire, conformed to the laws like good princes, than those who took the opposite course; and he will see that Titus, Nerva, Trajan, Hadrian, Antoninus, and Marcus Aurelius did not require the Praetorians nor the multitudinous legions to defend them, because they were protected by their own good conduct, the good will of the people, and by the love of the Senate. He will furthermore see that neither the Eastern nor the Western armies sufficed to save Caligula, Nero, Vitellius, and so many other wicked Emperors, from the enemies which their bad conduct and evil lives had raised up against them.

And if the history of these men were carefully studied, it would prove an ample guide to any prince, and serve to show him the way to glory or to infamy, to security or to perpetual apprehension. For of the twenty-six Emperors that reigned from the time of Caesar to that of Maximinius, sixteen were assassinated, and ten only died a natural death; and if, amongst those who were killed, there were one or two good ones, like Galba and Pertinax, their death was the consequence of the corruption which their predecessors had engendered amongst the soldiers. And if amongst those who died a natural death there were some wicked ones, like Severus, it was due to their extraordinary good fortune and courage, which two qualities rarely fall to the lot of such men. He will furthermore learn from the lessons of that history how an empire should be organized properly; for all the Emperors that succeeded to the throne by inheritance, except Titus, were bad, and those who became Emperors by adoption were all good, such as the five from Nero to Marcus Aurelius; and when the Empire became hereditary, it came to ruin. Let any prince now place himself in the times from Nerva to Marcus Aurelius, and let him compare them with those that preceded and followed that period, and let him choose in which of the two he would like to have been born, and in which he would like to have reigned. In the period under the good Emperors he will see the prince secure amidst his people, who are also living in security; he will see peace and justice prevail in the world, the authority of the Senate respected, the magistrates honored, the wealthy citizens enjoying their riches, nobility and virtue exalted, and everywhere will he see tranquility and well-being. And on the other hand he will behold all animosity, license, corruption, and all noble ambition extinct. During the period of the good Emperors he will see that golden age when every one could hold and defend whatever opinion he pleased; in fine, he will see the triumph of the world, the prince surrounded with reverence and glory, and beloved by his people, who are happy in their security. If now he will but glance at the times under the other Emperors, he will behold the atrocities of war, discords and sedition, cruelty in peace as in war, many princes massacred, many civil and foreign wars, Italy afflicted and overwhelmed by fresh misfortunes, and her cities ravaged and ruined; he will see Rome in ashes, the Capital pulled down by her own citizens, the ancient temples desolate, all religious rites and ceremonies corrupted, and the city full of adultery; he will behold the sea covered with ships full of flying exiles, and the shores stained with blood. He will see innumerable cruelties in Rome, and nobility, riches, and honor, and above all virtue, accounted capital crimes. He will see informers rewarded, servants corrupted against their masters, the freedmen arrayed against their patrons, and those who were without enemies betrayed and oppressed by their friends. And then will he recognize what infinite obligations Rome, Italy, and the whole world owed to Caesar. And surely, if he be a man, he will be shocked at the thought of re-enacting those evil times, and be fired with an intense desire to follow the example of the good. And truly, if a prince be anxious for glory and the good opinion of the world, he should rather wish to possess a corrupt city, not to ruin it wholly like Caesar, but to reorganize it like Romulus. For certainly the heavens cannot afford a man a greater opportunity of glory, nor could men desire a better one. And if for the proper organization of a city it should be necessary to abolish the principality, he who had failed to give her good laws for the sake of preserving his rank may be entitled to some excuse; but there would be none for him who had been able to organize the city properly and yet preserve the sovereignty. And, in fine, let him to whom Heaven has vouchsafed such an opportunity reflect that there are two ways open to him; one that will enable him to live securely and insure him glory after death, and the other that will make his life one of constant anxiety, and after death consign him to eternal infamy.

## Chapter 11

### Of the Religion of the Romans

Although the founder of Rome was Romulus, to whom like a daughter, she owed her birth and her education, yet the gods did not judge the laws of this prince sufficient for so great an empire, and therefore inspired the Roman Senate to elect Numa Pompilius as his successor, so that he might regulate all those things that had been omitted by Romulus. Numa, finding a very savage people, and wishing to reduce them to civil obedience by the arts of peace, had recourse to religion as the most necessary and assured support of any civil society; and he established it upon such foundations that for many centuries there was nowhere more fear of the gods than in that republic, which greatly facilitated all the enterprises which the Senate or its great men attempted. Whoever will examine the actions of the people of Rome as a body, or of many individual Romans, will see that these citizens feared much more to break an oath than the laws, like men who esteem the power of the gods more than that of men. This was particularly manifested in the conduct of Scipio and Manlius Torquatus; for after the defeat which Hannibal had inflicted upon the Romans at Cannae many citizens had assembled together, and, frightened and trembling, agreed to leave Italy and fly to Sicily. When Scipio heard of this, he went to meet them, and with his drawn sword in hand he forced them to swear not to abandon their country. Lucius Manlius, father of Titus Manlius, who was afterwards called Torquatus, had been accused by Marcus Pomponius, one of the Tribunes of the people. Before the day of judgment Titus went to Marcus and threatened to kill him if he did not promise to withdraw the charges against his father; he compelled him to take an oath, and Marcus, although having sworn under the pressure of fear, withdrew the accusation against Lucius. And thus those citizens, whom neither the love of country nor the laws could have kept in Italy, were retained there by an oath that had been forced upon them by compulsion; and the Tribune Pomponius disregarded the hatred which he bore to the father, as well as the insult offered him by the son for the sake of complying with his oath and preserving his honor; which can be ascribed to nothing else than the religious principles which Numa had instilled into the Romans. And whoever reads Roman history attentively will see in how great a degree religion served in the command of the armies, in uniting the people and keeping them well conducted, and in covering the wicked with shame. So that if the question were discussed whether Rome was more indebted to Romulus or to Numa, I believe that the highest merit would be conceded to Numa; for where religion exists it is easy to introduce armies and discipline, but where there are armies and no religion it is difficult to introduce the latter. And although we have seen that Romulus could organize the Senate and establish other civil and military institutions without the aid of divine authority, yet it was very necessary for Numa, who feigned that he held converse with a nymph, who dictated to him all that he wished to persuade the people to; and the reason for all this was that Numa mistrusted his own authority, lest it should prove insufficient to enable him to introduce new and unaccustomed ordinances in Rome. In truth, there never was any remarkable lawgiver amongst any people who did not resort to divine authority, as otherwise his laws would not have been accepted by the people; for there are many good laws, the importance of which is known to the sagacious lawgiver, but the reasons for which are not sufficiently evident to enable him to persuade others to submit to them; and therefore do wise men, for the purpose of removing this difficulty, resort to divine authority. Thus did Lycurgus and Solon, and many others who aimed at the same thing.

The Roman people, then, admiring the wisdom and goodness of Numa, yielded in all things to his advice. It is true that those were very religious times, and the people with whom Numa had to deal were very untutored and superstitious, which made it easy for him to carry out his designs, being able to impress upon them any new form. And doubtless, if any one wanted to establish a republic at the present time, he would find it much easier with the simple mountaineers, who are almost without any civilization, than with such as are accustomed to live in cities, where civilization is already corrupt; as a sculptor finds it easier to make a fine statue out of a crude block of marble than out of a statue badly begun by another. Considering then, all these things, I conclude that the religion introduced by Numa into Rome was one of the chief causes of the prosperity of that city; for this religion gave rise to good laws, and good laws bring good fortune, and from good fortune results happy success in all enterprises. And as the observance of divine institutions is the cause of the greatness of republics, so the disregard of them produces their ruin; for where the fear of God is wanting, there the country will come to ruin, unless it be sustained by the fear of the prince, which may temporarily supply the want of religion. But as the lives of princes are short, the kingdom will of necessity perish as the prince falls in virtue. Whence it comes that kingdoms which depend entirely upon the virtue of one man endure but for a brief time, for his virtue passes away with his life, and it rarely happens that it is renewed in his successor, as Dante so wisely says:—

> 'Tis seldom human wisdom descends from sire to son;
> Such is the will of Him who gave it,
> That at his hands alone we may implore the boon.

The welfare, then, of a republic or a kingdom does not consist in having a prince who governs it wisely during his lifetime, but in having one who will give it such laws that it will maintain itself even after his death. And although untutored and ignorant men are more easily persuaded to adopt new laws or new opinions, yet that does not make it impossible to persuade civilized men who claim to be enlightened. The people of Florence are far from considering themselves ignorant and benighted, and yet Brother Girolamo Savonarola succeeded in persuading them that he held converse with God. I will not pretend to judge whether it was true or not, for we must speak with all respect of so great a man; but I may well say that an immense number believed it, without having seen any extraordinary manifestations that should have made them believe it; but it was the purity of his life, the doctrines he preached, and the subjects he selected for his discourses, that sufficed to make the people have faith in him. Let no one, then, fear not to be able to accomplish what others have done, for all men (as we have said in our Preface) are born and live and die in the same way, and therefore resemble each other.

## Chapter 12

### The Importance of Giving Religion a Prominent Influence in a State, and How Italy was Ruined Because She Failed in this Respect Through the Conduct of the Church of Rome

Princes and republics who wish to maintain themselves free from corruption must above all things preserve the purity of all religious observances, and treat them with proper reverence; for there is no greater indication of the ruin of a country than to see religion condemned. And this is easily understood, when we know upon what the religion of a country is founded; for the essence of every religion is based upon some one main principle. The religion of the Gentiles had for its foundation the responses of the oracles, and the tenets of the augurs and aruspices; upon these alone depended all their ceremonies, rites, and sacrifices. For they readily believed that the Deity which could predict their future good or ill was also able to bestow it upon them. Thence arose their temples, their sacrifices, their supplications, and all the other ceremonies; for the oracle of Delphos, the temple of Jupiter Ammon, and other celebrated oracles, kept the world in admiration and devoutness. But when these afterwards began to speak only in accordance with the wishes of the princes, and their falsity was discovered by the people, then men became incredulous, and disposed to disturb all good institutions. It is therefore the duty of princes and heads of republics to uphold the foundations of the religion of their countries, for then it is easy to keep their people religious, and consequently well conducted and united. And therefore everything that tends to favor religion (even though it were believed to be false) should be received and availed of to strengthen it; and this should be done the more, the wiser the rulers are, and the better they understand the natural course of things. Such was, in fact, the practice observed by sagacious men; which has given rise to the belief in the miracles that are celebrated in religions, however false they may be. For the sagacious rulers have given these miracles increased importance, no matter whence or how they originated; and their authority afterwards gave them credence with the people. Rome had many such miracles; and one of the most remarkable was that which occurred when the Roman soldiers sacked the city of Veii; some of them entered the temple of Juno, and, placing themselves in front of her statue, said to her, "Will you come to Rome?" Some imagined that they observed the statue make a sign of assent, and others pretended to have heard her reply, "Yes." Now these men, being very religious, as reported by Titus Livius, and having entered the temple quietly, they were filled with devotion and reverence, and might really have believed that they had heard a reply to their question, such as perhaps they could have presupposed. But this opinion and belief was favored and magnified by Camillus and the other Roman chiefs.

And certainly, if the Christian religion had from the beginning been maintained according to the principles of its founder, the Christian states and republics would have been much more united and happy than what they are. Nor can there be a greater proof of its decadence than to witness the fact that the nearer people are to the Church of Rome, which is the head of our religion, the less religious are they. And whoever examines the principles upon which that religion is founded, and sees how widely different from those principles its present practice and application are, will judge that her ruin or chastisement is near at hand. But as there are some of the opinion that the well-being of Italian affairs depends upon the Church of Rome, I will present such arguments against that opinion as occur to me; two of which are most important, and cannot according to my judgment be controverted. The first is, that the evil example of the court of Rome has destroyed all piety and religion in Italy, which brings in its train infinite improprieties and disorders; for as we may presuppose all good where religion prevails, so where it is wanting we have the right to suppose the very opposite. We Italians then owe to the Church of Rome and to her priests our having become irreligious and bad; but we owe her a still greater debt, and one that will be the cause of our ruin, namely, that the Church has kept and still keeps our country divided. And certainly a country can never be united and happy, except when it obeys wholly one government, whether a republic or a monarchy, as is the case in France and in Spain; and the sole cause why Italy is not in the same condition, and is not governed by either one republic or one sovereign, is the Church; for having acquired and holding a temporal dominion, yet she has never had sufficient power or courage to enable her to seize the rest of the country and make herself sole sovereign of all Italy. And on the other hand she has not been so feeble that the fear of losing her temporal power prevented her from calling in the aid of a foreign power to defend her against such others as had become too powerful in Italy; as was seen in former days by many sad experiences, when through the intervention of Charlemagne she drove out the Lombards, who were masters of nearly all Italy; and when in our times she crushed the power of the Venetians by the aid of France, and afterwards with the assistance of the Swiss drove out in turn the French. The Church, then, not having been powerful enough to be able to master all Italy, nor having permitted any other power to do so, has been the cause why Italy has never been able to unite under one head, but has always remained under a number of princes and lords, which occasioned her so many dissensions and so much weakness that she became a prey not only to the powerful barbarians, but of whoever chose to assail her. This we other Italians owe to the Church of Rome, and to none other. And any one, to be promptly convinced by experiment of the truth of all this, should have the power to transport the court of Rome to reside, with all the power it has in Italy, in the midst of the

Swiss, who of all peoples nowadays live most according to their ancient customs so far as religion and their military system are concerned; and he would see in a very little while that the evil habits of that court would create more confusion in that country than anything else that could ever happen there.

## → THIRD BOOK ←

### Chapter 1

### *To Insure a Long Existence to Religious Sects or Republics, It is Necessary Frequently to Bring Them Back to Their Original Principles*

There is nothing more true than that all the things of this world have a limit to their existence; but those only run the entire course ordained for them by Heaven that do not allow their body to become disorganized, but keep it unchanged in the manner ordained, or if they change it, so do it that it shall be for their advantage, and not to their injury. And as I speak here of mixed bodies, such as republics or religious sects, I say that those changes are beneficial that bring them to their original principles. And those are the best-constituted bodies, and have the longest existence, which possess the intrinsic means of frequently renewing themselves, or such as obtain this renovation in consequence of some extrinsic accidents. And it is a truth clearer than light that, without such renovation, these bodies cannot continue to exist; and the means of renewing them is to bring them back to their original principles. For, as all religious republics and monarchies must have within themselves some goodness, by means of which they obtain their first growth and reputation, and as in the process of time this goodness becomes corrupted, it will of necessity destroy the body unless something intervenes to bring it back to its normal condition. Thus, the doctors of medicine say, in speaking of the human body, that "every day some ill humors gather which must be cured."

This return of a republic to its original principles is either the result of extrinsic accident or of intrinsic prudence. As an instance of the first, we have seen how necessary it was that Rome should be taken by the Gauls, as a means of her renovation or new birth; so that, being thus born again, she might take new life and vigor, and might resume the proper observance of justice and religion, which were becoming corrupt. This is clearly seen from the history of Livius, where he shows that, in calling out her army against the Gauls, and in the creation of Tribunes with consular powers, the Romans observed no religious ceremonies whatsoever. In the same way they not only did not deprive the three Fabii of their rank for having, "contrary to the law of nations," fought against the Gauls, but actually raised them to the dignity of Tribunes. And we may readily presume that they made less account of the good institutions and laws established by Romulus and other wise princes, than what was reasonable and necessary to preserve their liberties. It needed, then, this blow from without to revive the observance of all the institutions of the state, and to show to the Roman people, not only the necessity of maintaining religion and justice, but also of honoring their good citizens and making more account of their virtue than of the ease and indulgence of which their energy and valor seemed to deprive them. This admonition succeeded completely; for no sooner was Rome retaken from the Gauls than they renewed all their religious institutions, punished the Fabii for having fought the Gauls contrary to the law of nations; and then they appreciated so highly the valor and excellence of Camillus that the Senate and the other orders in the state laid aside all envy and jealousy, and confided to him all the burden of the affairs of the republic.

It is necessary then (as has been said) for men who live associated together under some kind of regulations often to be brought back to themselves, so to speak, either by external or internal occurrences. As to the latter, they are either the result of a law, that obliges the citizens of the association often to render an account of their conduct; or some man of superior character arises amongst them, whose noble example and virtuous actions will produce the same effect as such a law. This good then in a republic is due either to the excellence of some one man, or to some law; and as to the latter, the institution that brought the Roman republic back to its original principles was the creation of the Tribunes of the people, and all the other laws that tended to repress the insolence and ambition of men. But to give life and vigor to those laws requires a virtuous citizen, who will courageously aid in their execution against the power of those who transgress them.

The most striking instances of such execution of the laws, anterior to the capture of Rome by the Gauls, were the death of the sons of Brutus, that of the Decemvirs, and that of the corn-dealer, Spurius Maelius; and after the taking of Rome by the Gauls, the death of Manlius Capitolinus, that of the son of Manlius Torquatus, the punishment inflicted by Papirius Cursor upon his master of cavalry, Fabius, and the accusation of the Scipios. As these were extreme and most striking cases they caused on each occasion a return of the citizens to the original principles of the republic; and when they began to be more rare, it also began to afford men more latitude in becoming corrupt, and the execution of the laws involved more danger and disturbances. It would be desirable therefore that not more than ten years should elapse between such executions, for in the long course of time men begin to change their customs, and to transgress the laws; and unless some case occurs that recalls the punishment to their memory and revives the fear in their hearts, the delinquents will soon become so numerous that they cannot be punished without danger.

In relation to this subject it was said by the magistrates who governed Florence from the year 1434 until 1494 that it was necessary every five years to resume the government, and that otherwise it would be difficult to maintain it. By "resuming the government" they meant to strike the people with the same fear and terror as they did when they first assumed the government, and when they had inflicted the extremist punishment upon those who, according to their principles, had conducted themselves badly. But as the recollection of these punishments fades from men's minds, they become emboldened to make new attempts against the government, and to speak ill of it, and therefore it is necessary to provide against this, by bringing the government back to its first principles. Such a return to first principles in a republic is sometimes caused by the simple virtues of one man, without depending upon any law that incites him to the infliction of extreme punishments; and yet his good example has such an influence that the good men strive to imitate him, and the wicked are ashamed to lead a life so contrary to his example. Those particularly, who in Rome effected such beneficial results were Horatius Cocles, Scaevola, Fabricius, the two Decii, Regulus Attilius, and some others, who by their rare and virtuous example produced the same effect upon the Romans as laws and institutions would have done. And certainly if at least some such signal punishments as described above, or noble examples, had occurred in Rome every ten years, that city never would have become so corrupt; but as both became more rare, corruption increased more and more. In fact, after Marcus Regulus we find not a single instance of such virtuous example; and although the two Catos arose, yet there was so long an interval between Regulus and them, and between the one Cato and the other, and they were such isolated instances, that their example could effect but little good; and especially the latter Cato found the citizens of Rome already so corrupt that he utterly failed to improve them by his example. Let this suffice so far as regards republics.

Now with regard to religions we shall see that revivals are equally necessary, and the best proof of this is furnished by our own, which would have been entirely lost had it not been brought back to its pristine principles and purity by Saint Francis and Saint Dominic; for by their voluntary poverty and the example of the life of Christ, they revived the sentiment of religion in the hearts of men, where it had become almost extinct. The new orders which they established were so severe and powerful that they became the means of saving religion from being destroyed by the licentiousness of the prelates and heads of the Church. They continued themselves to live in poverty; and by means of confessions and preachings they obtained so much influence with the people, that they were able to make them understand that it was wicked even to speak ill of wicked rulers, and that it is proper to render them obedience and to leave the punishment of their errors to God. And thus these wicked rulers do as much evil as they please, because they do not fear a punishment which they do not see nor believe. This revival of religion then by Saint Francis and Saint Dominic has preserved it and maintains it to this day. Monarchies also have need of renewal, and to bring their institutions back to first principles. The kingdom of France shows us the good effects of such renewals; for this monarchy more than any other is governed by laws and ordinances. The Parliaments, and mainly that of Paris, are the conservators of these laws and institutions, which are renewed by them from time to time, by executions against some of the princes of the realm, and at times even by decisions against the king himself. And thus this kingdom has maintained itself up to the present time by its determined constancy in repressing the ambition of the nobles; for if it were to leave them unpunished, the disorders would quickly multiply, and the end would doubtless be either that the guilty could no longer be punished without danger, or that the kingdom itself would be broken up.

We may conclude, then, that nothing is more necessary for an association of men, either as a religious sect, republic, or monarchy, than to restore to it from time to time the power and reputation which it had in the beginning, and to strive to have either good laws or good men to bring about such a result, without the necessity of the intervention of any extrinsic force. For although such may at times be the best remedy, as in the case of Rome (when captured by the Gauls), yet it is so dangerous that it is in no way desirable....

# THOMAS HOBBES

*Thomas Hobbes (1588–1679) was born prematurely in Wiltshire during the time of the threat to England posed by the Spanish Armada. He once wrote that "my Mother bore twins, myself and fear." He was a very bright child and was sent to Oxford at the age of 14. He was neither impressed by the dominant Aristotelianism in the curriculum nor by the extracurricular activity at Oxford, which he called "the haunt of debauchery." He did graduate and was recommended to the Cavendish family as a secretary and tutor. Most of his life was spent in their employ. The Puritan civil war that began in 1642 caused Hobbes to flee to the Continent, where he briefly tutored the young Charles II. After the publication of* The Leviathan, *Cromwell allowed Hobbes to return to England, and after the Stuart Restoration, Hobbes received a small pension until his death at 91 years of age.*

*Hobbes was fascinated by the new physical science of such thinkers as Bacon, Kepler, Descartes, and Galileo. He was particularly struck by the axiomatic reasoning found in Euclid's geometry. He wrote on a wide variety of subjects, ranging from the Greek historian Thucydides to mathematics. He composed a major three-volume work incorporating his system of thought:* De Corpore (Concerning the Body), De Homine (Concerning Man), *and* De Cive (Concerning the Citizen). *However, his most famous work and, by general agreement, the greatest masterpiece of political philosophy in English is* The Leviathan. *It was published in 1651, while Hobbes was still in exile.*

— J.M.P.

# THE LEVIATHAN

## Or the Matter, Forme and Power
## of a Commonwealth, Ecclesiasticall and Civil

### Author's Introduction

Nature, the art whereby God hath made and governs the world, is by the *art* of man, as in many other things, so in this also imitated, that it can make an artificial animal. For seeing life is but a motion of limbs, the beginning whereof is in some principal part within; why may we not say, that all *automata* (engines that move themselves by springs and wheels as doth a watch) have an artificial life? For what is the *heart*, but a *spring;* and the *nerves*, but so many strings; and the *joints,* but so many *wheels,* giving motion to the whole body, such as was intended by the artificer? *Art* goes yet further, imitating that rational and most excellent work of nature, *man.* For by art is created that great LEVIATHAN called a COMMONWEALTH, or STATE, in Latin CIVITAS, which is but an artificial man; though of greater stature and strength than the natural, for whose protection and defence it was intended; and in which the *sovereignty* is an artificial *soul,* as giving life and motion to the whole body; the *magistrates,* and other *officers* of judicature and execution, artificial *joints, reward* and *punishment,* by which fastened to the seat of the sovereignty every joint and member is moved to perform his duty, are the *nerves,* that do the same in the body natural; the *strength, salus populi,* the *people's safety,* its *business; counsellors,* by whom all things needful for it to know are suggested unto it, are the *memory, equity,* and *laws,* an artificial *reason* and *will; concord, health; sedition, sickness;* and *civil war, death.* Lastly, the *pacts* and *covenants,* by which the parts of this body politic were at first made, set together, and united, resemble that *fiat,* or the *let us make man,* pronounced by God in the creation.

To describe the nature of this artificial man, I will consider

First, the *matter* thereof, and the *artificer;* both which is *man.*

Secondly, *how,* and by what *covenants* it is made; what are the *rights* and just *power* or *authority* of a *sovereign;* and what it is that *preserveth* and *dissolveth* it.

Thirdly, what is a *Christian commonwealth.*

Lastly, what is the *kingdom of darkness.*

Concerning the first, there is a saying much usurped of late, that *wisdom* is acquired, not by reading of *books,* but of *men.* Consequently whereunto, those persons, that for the most part give no other proof of being wise, take great delight to show that they think they have read in men, by uncharitable censures of one another behind their backs. But there is another saying not of late understood, by which they might learn truly to read one another, if they would take the pains; that is, *nosce teipsum, read thyself:* which was not meant, as it is now used, to countenance either the barbarous state of men in power, towards their inferiors; or to encourage men of low degree, to a saucy behaviour towards their betters; but to teach us, that for the similitude of the thoughts and passions of one man, to the thoughts and passions of another, whosoever looketh into himself, and considereth what he doth, when he does *think, opine, reason, hope, fear,* &c. and upon what grounds; he shall thereby read and know, what are the thoughts and passions of all other men upon the like occasions. I say the similitude of *passions,* which are the same in all men, *desire, fear, hope,* &c.; not the similitude of the *objects* of the passions, which are the things *desired, feared, hoped,* &c.: for these the constitution individual, and particular education, do so vary, and they are so easy to be kept from our knowledge, that the characters of man's heart, blotted and confounded as they are with dissembling, lying, counterfeiting, and erroneous doctrines, are legible only to him that searcheth hearts. And though by men's actions we do discover their design sometimes; yet to do it without comparing them with our own, and distinguishing all circumstances, by which the case may come to be altered, is to decipher without a key, and be for the most part deceived, by too much trust, or by too much diffidence; as he that reads, is himself a good or evil man.

But let one man read another by his actions never so perfectly, it serves him only with his acquaintances, which are but few. He that is to govern a whole nation, must read in himself, not this or that particular man; but mankind: which though it be hard to do, harder than to learn any language or science; yet when I shall have set down my own reading orderly, and perspicuously, the pains left another will be only to consider, if he also find not the same in himself. For this kind of doctrine admitteth no other demonstration.

# ❧ THE FIRST PART ❧
## Of Man

### *Chapter 1*

### *Of Sense*

**Sense.** Concerning the thoughts of man, I will consider them first singly, and afterwards in train, or dependence upon one another. Singly, they are every one a *representation* or *appearance,* of some quality, or other accident of a body without us, which is commonly called an *object.* Which object worketh on the eyes, ears, and other parts of a man's body; and by diversity of working, produceth diversity of appearances.

The original of them all, is that which we call SENSE, for there is no conception in a man's mind, which hath not at first, totally, or by parts, been begotten upon the organs of sense. The rest are derived from that original.

To know the natural cause of sense, is not very necessary to the business now in hand; and I have elsewhere written of the same at large. Nevertheless, to fill each part of my present method, I will briefly deliver the same in this place.

The cause of sense, is the external body, or object, which presseth the organ proper to each sense, either immediately, as in the taste and touch; or mediately, as in seeing, hearing, and smelling; which pressure, by the mediation of the nerves, and other strings and membranes of the body, continued inwards to the brain and heart, causeth there a resistance, or counter-pressure, or endeavour of the heart to deliver itself, which endeavour, because *outward,* seemeth to be some matter without. And this *seeming,* or *fancy,* is that which men call *sense;* and consisteth, as to the eye, in a *light,* or *colour figured;* to the ear, in a *sound;* to the nostril, in an *odour;* to the tongue and palate, in a *savour;* and to the rest of the body, in *heat, cold, hardness, softness,* and such other qualities as we discern by *feeling.* All which qualities, called *sensible,* are in the object, that causeth them, but so many several motions of the matter, by which it presseth our organs diversely. Neither in us that are pressed, are they any thing else, but divers motions; for motion produceth nothing but motion. But their appearance to us is fancy, the same waking, that dreaming. And as pressing, rubbing, or striking the eye, makes us fancy a light; and pressing the ear, produceth a din; so do the bodies also we see, or hear, produce the same by their strong, though unobserved action. For if those colours and sounds were in the bodies, or objects that cause them, they could not be severed from them, as by glasses, and in echoes by reflection, we see they are; where we know the thing we see is in one place, the appearance in another. And though at some certain distance, the real and very object seem invested with the fancy it begets in us; yet still the object is one thing, the image or fancy is another. So that sense, in all cases, is nothing else but original fancy, caused, as I have said, by the pressure, that is, by the motion, of external things upon our eyes, ears, and other organs thereunto ordained.

But the philosophy-schools, through all the universities of Christendom, grounded upon certain texts of Aristotle, teach another doctrine, and say, for the cause of *vision,* that the thing seen, sendeth forth on every side a *visible species,* in English, a *visible show, apparition,* or *aspect,* or *a being seen;* the receiving whereof into the eye, is *seeing.* And for the cause of *hearing,* that the thing heard, sendeth forth an *audible species,* that is an *audible aspect,* or *audible being seen;* which entering at the ear, maketh *hearing.* Nay, for the cause of *understanding* also, they say the thing understood, sendeth forth an *intelligible species,* that is, an *intelligible being seen;* which, coming into the understanding, makes us understand. I say not this, as disproving the use of universities; but because I am to speak hereafter of their office in a commonwealth, I must let you see on all occasions by the way, what things would be amended in them; amongst which the frequency of insignificant speech is one.

## Chapter 4

### Of Speech

**Original of Speech.**  The invention of *printing,* though ingenious, compared with the invention of *letters,* is no great matter. But who was the first that found the use of letters, is not known. He that first brought them into Greece, men say was Cadmus, the son of Agenor, king of Phoenicia. A profitable invention for continuing the memory of time past, and the conjunction of mankind, dispersed into so many, and distant regions of the earth; and withal difficult, as proceeding from a watchful observation of the divers motions of the tongue, palate, lips, and other organs of speech; whereby to make as many differences of characters, to remember them. But the most noble and profitable invention of all other, was that of SPEECH, consisting of *names* or *appellations,* and their connexion; whereby men register their thoughts; recall them when they are past; and also declare them one to another for mutual utility and conversation; without which, there had been amongst men, neither commonwealth, nor society, nor contract, nor peace, no more than amongst lions, bears, and wolves. The first author of *speech* was God himself, that instructed Adam how to name such creatures as he presented to his sight; for the Scripture goeth no further in this matter. But this was sufficient to direct him to add more names, as the experience and use of the creatures should give him occasion; and to join them in such manner by degrees, as to make himself understood; and so by succession of time, so much language might be gotten, as he had found use for; though not so copious, as an orator or philosopher has need of: for I do not find any thing in the Scripture, out of which, directly or by consequence, can be gathered, that Adam was taught the names of all figures, numbers, measures, colours, sounds, fancies, relations; much less the names of words and speech, as *general, special, affirmative, negative, interrogative, optative, infinitive,* all which are useful; and least of all, of *entity, intentionality, quiddity,* and other insignificant words of the school....

**The use of speech.** The general use of speech, is to transfer our mental discourse, into verbal; or the train of our thoughts, into a train of words; and that for two commodities, whereof one is the registering of the consequences of our thoughts; which being apt to slip out of our memory, and put us to a new labour, may again be recalled, by such words as they were marked by. So that the first use of names is to serve for *marks,* or *notes* of remembrance. Another is, when many use the same words, to signify, by their connexion and order, one to another, what they conceive, or think of each matter; and also what they desire, fear, or have any other passion for. And for this use they are called *signs.* Special uses of speech are these; first, to register, what by cogitation, we find to be the cause of any thing, present or past; and what we find things present and past may produce, or effect; which in sum, is acquiring of arts. Secondly, to show to others that knowledge which we have attained, which is, to counsel and teach one another. Thirdly, to make known to others our wills and purposes, that we may have the mutual help of one another. Fourthly, to please and delight ourselves and others, by playing with our words, for pleasure or ornament, innocently....

**Names, proper and common. Universal.** Of names, some are *proper,* and singular to one only thing, as *Peter, John, this man, this tree;* and some are *common* to many things, *man, horse, tree;* every of which, though but one name, is nevertheless the name of divers particular things; in respect of all which together, it is called an *universal;* there being nothing in the world universal but names; for the things named are every one of them individual and singular.

One universal name is imposed on many things, for their similitude in some quality, or other accident; and whereas a proper name bringeth to mind one thing only, universals recall any one of those many.

And of names universal, some are of more, and some of less extent; the larger comprehending the less large; and some again of equal extent, comprehending each other reciprocally. As for example: the name *body* is of larger signification than the word *man,* and comprehendeth it; and the names *man* and *rational,* are of equal extent, comprehending mutually one another. But here we must take notice, that by a name is not always understood, as in grammar, one only word; but sometimes, by circumlocution, many words together. For all these words, *he that in his actions observeth the laws of his country,* make but one name, equivalent to this one word, *just.*

By this imposition of names, some of larger, some of stricter signification, we turn the reckoning of the consequences of things imagined in the mind, into a reckoning of the consequences of appellations. For example: a man that hath no use of speech at all, such as is born and remains perfectly deaf and dumb, if he set before his eyes a triangle, and by it two right angles, such as are the corners of a square figure, he may, by meditation, compare and find, that the three angles of that triangle, are equal to those two right angles that stand by it. But if another triangle be shown him, different in shape from the former, he cannot know, without a new labour, whether the three angles of that also be equal to the same. But he that hath the use of words, when he observes, that such equality was consequent, not to the length of the sides, nor to any other particular thing in his triangle; but only to this, that the sides were straight, and the angles three; and that that was all, for which he named it a triangle; will boldly conclude universally, that such equality of angles is in all triangles whatsoever; and register his invention in these general terms, *every triangle hath its three angles equal to two right angles.* And thus the consequence found in one particular, comes to be registered and remembered, as a universal rule, and discharges our mental reckoning, of time and place, and delivers us from all labour of the mind, saving the first, and makes that which was found true *here,* and *now,* to be true in *all times* and *places....*

When two names are joined together into a consequence, or affirmation, as thus, *a man is a living creature;* or thus, *if he be a man, he is a living creature;* if the latter name, *living creature* signify all that the former name *man* signifieth, then the affirmation, or consequence, is *true;* otherwise false. For *true* and *false* are attributes of speech, not of things. And where speech is not, there is neither *truth* nor *falsehood; error* there may be, as when we expect that which shall not be, or suspect what has not been; but in neither case can a man be charged with untruth.

**Necessity of definitions.** Seeing then that truth consisteth in the right ordering of names in our affirmations, a man that seeketh precise truth had need to remember what every name he uses stands for, and to place it accordingly, or else he will find himself entangled in words, as a bird in lime twigs, the more he struggles the more belimed. And therefore in geometry, which is the only science that it hath pleased God hitherto to bestow on mankind, men begin at settling the significance of their words; which settling of significations they call *definitions,* and place them in the beginning of their reckoning.

By this it appears how necessary it is for any man that aspires to true knowledge, to examine the definitions of former authors; and either to correct them, where they are negligently set down, or to make them himself. For the errors of definitions multiply themselves according as the reckoning proceeds, and lead men into absurdities, which at last they see, but cannot avoid, without reckoning anew from the beginning, in which lies the foundation of their errors. From whence it happens, that they which trust to books do as they that cast up many little sums into a greater, without considering whether those little sums were rightly cast up or not; and at last finding the error visible, and not mistrusting their first grounds, know not which way to clear themselves, but spend time in fluttering over their books; as birds that entering by the chimney, and finding themselves enclosed in a chamber, flutter at the false light of a glass window, for want of wit to consider which way they came in. So that in the right definition of names lies the first use of speech; which is the acquisition of science: and in wrong, or no definitions, lies the first abuse; from which proceed all false and senseless tenets; which make those men that take their instruction from the authority of books, and not from their own meditation, to be as much below the condition of ignorant men, as men endued with true science are above it. For between true science and erroneous doctrines, ignorance is in the middle. Natural sense and imagination are not subject to absurdity. Nature itself cannot err; and as men abound in copiousness of language, so they become more wise, or more mad than ordinary. Nor is it possible without letters for any man to become either excellently wise, or, unless his memory be hurt by disease or ill constitution of organs, excellently foolish. For words are wise men's counters, they do but reckon by them; but they are the money of fools, that value them by the authority of an Aristotle, a Cicero, or a Thomas, or any other doctor whatsoever, if but a man....

**Inconstant names.** The names of such things as affect us, that is, which please and displease us, because all men be not alike affected with the same thing, nor the same man at all times, are in the common discourses of men of *inconstant* signification. For seeing all names are imposed to signify our conceptions, and all our affections are but conceptions, when we conceive the same things differently, we can hardly avoid different naming of them. For though the nature of that we conceive, be the same; yet the diversity of our reception of it, in respect of different constitutions of body, and prejudices of opinion, gives every thing a tincture of our different passions. And therefore in reasoning a man must take heed of words; which besides the signification of what we imagine of their nature, have a signi-fication also of the nature, disposition, and interest of the speaker; such as are the names of virtues and vices; for one man calleth *wisdom*, what another cal-leth *fear;* and one *cruelty*, what another *justice;* one *prodigality,* what another *mag-nanimity;* and one *gravity,* what another *stupidity,* &c. And therefore such names can never be true grounds of any ratiocination. No more can metaphors, and tropes of speech: but these are less dangerous, because they profess their con-stancy; which the other do not.

## Chapter 6

### Of the Interior Beginnings of Voluntary Motions, Commonly Called the Passions; and the Speeches by Which They are Expressed

**Motion, vital and animal. Endeavour.** There be in animals, two sorts of *motions* peculiar to them: one called *vital;* begun in generation, and continued without in-terruption through their whole life; such as are the *course* of the *blood,* the *pulse,* the *breathing,* the *concoction, nutrition, excretion,* &c., to which motions there needs no help of imagination: the other is *animal motion,* otherwise called *voluntary motion;* as to *go,* to *speak,* to *move* any of our limbs, in such manner as is first fancied in our minds. That sense is motion in the organs and interior parts of man's body, caused by the action of the things we see, hear, &c.; and that fancy is but the relics of the same motion, remaining after sense, has been already said in the first and second chapters. And because *going, speaking,* and the like voluntary motions, depend always upon a precedent thought of *whither, which way,* and *what;* it is evident, that the imagination is the first internal beginning of all voluntary motion. And although unstudied men do not conceive any motion at all to be there, where the thing moved is invisible; or the space it is moved in is, for the shortness of it, insensible; yet that doth not hinder, but that such motions are. For let a space be never so little, that which is moved over a greater space, whereof that little one is part, must first be moved over that. These small beginnings of motion, within the body of man, before they appear in walking, speaking, striking, and other visible actions, are commonly called ENDEAVOUR.

**Appetite. Desire. Hunger. Thirst. Aversion.** This endeavour, when it is toward something which causes it, is called APPETITE, or DESIRE; the latter, being the general name; and the other oftentimes restrained to signify the desire of food, namely *hunger* and *thirst.* And when the endeavour is fromward something, it is generally called AVERSION. These words, *appetite* and *aversion,* we have from the Latins; and they both of them signify the motions, one of approaching, the other of retiring. So also do the Greek words for the same…. For nature itself does often press upon men those truths, which afterwards, when they look for somewhat beyond nature, they stumble at. For the Schools find in mere appetite to go, or move, no actual motion at all: but because some motion they must acknowledge, they call it metaphorical motion; which is but an absurd speech: for though words may be called metaphorical; bodies and motions can not.

**Love. Hate.** That which men desire, they are also said to LOVE: and to HATE those things for which they have aversion. So that desire and love are the same thing; save that by desire, we always signify the absence of the object; by love, most commonly the presence of the same. So also by aversion, we signify the absence; and by hate, the presence of the object.

**Contempt.** Of appetites and aversions, some are born with men; as appetite of food, appetite of excretion, and exoneration, which may also and more properly be called aversions, from somewhat they feel in their bodies; and some other appetites, not many. The rest which are appetites of particular things, proceed from experience, and trial of their effects upon themselves or other men. For of things we know not at all, or believe not to be, we can have no further desire, than to taste and try. But aversion we have for things, not only which we know have hurt us, but also that we do not know whether they will hurt us, or not.

Those things which we neither desire, nor hate, we are said to *contemn;* CONTEMPT being nothing else but an immobility, or contumacy of the heart, in resisting the action of certain things; and proceeding from that the heart is already moved otherwise, by other more potent objects; or from want of experience of them.

And because the constitution of a man's body is in continual mutation, it is impossible that all the same things should always cause in him the same appetites, and aversions: much less can men consent, in the desire of almost any one and the same object.

**Good. Evil.** But whatsoever is the object of any man's appetite or desire, that is it which he for his part calleth *good:* and the object of his hate and aversion, *evil;* and of his contempt, *vile* and *inconsiderable.* For these words of good, evil, and contemptible, are ever used with relation to the person that useth them: there being nothing simply and absolutely so; nor any common rule of good and evil, to be taken from the nature of the objects themselves; but from the person of the man, where there is no commonwealth; or, in a commonwealth, from the person that representeth it; or from an arbitrator or judge, whom men disagreeing shall by consent set up, and make his sentence the rule thereof....

These simple passions called *appetite, desire, love, aversion, hate, joy,* and *grief,* have their names for divers considerations diversified. As first, when they one succeed another, they are diversely called from the opinion men have of the likelihood of attaining what they desire. Secondly, from the object loved or hated. Thirdly, from the consideration of many of them together. Fourthly, from the alteration or succession itself.

**Hope.** For *appetite,* with an opinion of attaining, is called HOPE.

**Despair.** The same, without such opinion, DESPAIR.

**Fear.** *Aversion,* with the opinion of HURT from the object, FEAR.

**Courage.** The same, with hope of avoiding that hurt by resistance, COURAGE.

**Anger.** Sudden *courage,* ANGER.

**Confidence.** Constant *hope,* CONFIDENCE of ourselves.

**Diffidence.** Constant *despair,* DIFFIDENCE of ourselves.

**Indignation.** *Anger* for great hurt done to another, when we conceive the same to be done by injury, INDIGNATION.

**Benevolence. Good nature.** *Desire* of good to another, BENEVOLENCE, GOOD WILL, CHARITY. If to man generally, GOOD NATURE.

**Covetousness.** *Desire* of riches, COVETOUSNESS; a name used always in signification of blame; because men contending for them, are displeased with one another attaining them; though the desire in itself, be to be blamed, or allowed, according to the means by which these riches are sought.

**Ambition.** *Desire* of office, or precedence, AMBITION: a name used also in the worse sense, for the reason before mentioned.

**Pusillanimity.** *Desire* of things that conduce but a little to our ends, and fear of things that are but of little hindrance, PUSILLANIMITY.

**Magnanimity.** *Contempt* of little helps and hindrances, MAGNANIMITY.

**Valour.** *Magnanimity,* in danger of death or wounds, VALOUR, FORTITUDE.

**Liberality.** *Magnanimity* in the use of riches, LIBERALITY.

**Miserableness.** *Pusillanimity* in the same, WRETCHEDNESS, MISER-ABLENESS, or PARSIMONY; as it is liked or disliked.

**Kindness.** *Love* of persons for society, KINDNESS.

**Natural lust.** *Love* of persons for pleasing the sense only, NATURAL LUST.

**Luxury.** *Love* of the same, acquired from rumination, that is, imagination of pleasure past, LUXURY.

**The passion of love. Jealousy.** *Love* of one singularly, with desire to be singularly beloved, THE PASSION OF LOVE. The same, with fear that the love is not mutual, JEALOUSY.

**Revengefulness.** *Desire,* by doing hurt to another, to make him condemn some fact of his own, REVENGEFULNESS.

**Curiosity.** *Desire* to know why, and how, CURIOSITY; such as is in no living creature but *man:* so that man is distinguished, not only by his reason, but also by this singular passion from other *animals;* in whom the appetite of food, and other pleasures of sense, by predominance, take away the care of knowing causes; which is a lust of the mind, that by a perseverance of delight in the continual and indefatigable generation of knowledge, exceedeth the short vehemence of any carnal pleasure.

**Religion. Superstition. True religion.** *Fear* of power invisible, feigned by the mind, or imagined from tales publicly allowed, RELIGION; not allowed, SUPERSTITION. And when the power imagined, is truly such as we imagine, TRUE RELIGION....

**Deliberation.** When in the mind of man, appetites, and aversions, hopes, and fears, concerning one and the same thing, arise alternately; and divers good and evil consequences of the doing, or omitting the thing propounded, come successively into our thoughts; so that sometimes we have an appetite to it; sometimes an aversion from it; sometimes hope to be able to do it; sometimes despair, or fear to attempt it; the whole sum of desires, aversions, hopes and fears continued till the thing be either done, or thought impossible, is that we call DELIBERATION.

Therefore of things past, there is no *deliberation;* because manifestly impossible to be changed: nor of things known to be impossible, or thought so; because men know, or think such deliberation vain. But of things impossible, which we think possible, we may deliberate; not knowing it is in vain. And it is called *deliberation;* because it is a putting an end to the *liberty* we had of doing, or omitting, according to our own appetite, or aversion.

This alternate succession of appetites, aversions, hopes and fears, is no less in other living creatures than in man: and therefore beasts also deliberate.

Every *deliberation* is then said to *end,* when that whereof they deliberate, is either done, or thought impossible; because till then we retain the liberty of doing, or omitting; according to our appetite, or aversion.

**The will.**  In *deliberation,* the last appetite, or aversion, immediately adhering to the action, or to the omission thereof, is that we call the WILL; the act, not the faculty, of *willing.* And beasts that have *deliberation,* must necessarily also have *will.* The definition of the *will,* given commonly by the Schools, that it is a *rational appetite,* is not good. For if it were, then could there be no voluntary act against reason. For a *voluntary act* is that, which proceedeth from the *will,* and no other. But if instead of a rational appetite, we shall say an appetite resulting from a precedent deliberation, then the definition is the same that I have given here. *Will* therefore *is the last appetite in deliberating.* And though we say in common discourse, a man had a will once to do a thing, that nevertheless he forbore to do; yet that is properly but an inclination, which makes no action voluntary; because the action depends not of it, but of the last inclination, or appetite. For if the intervenient appetites, make any action voluntary; then by the same reason all intervenient aversions, should make the same action involuntary; and so one and the same action, should be both voluntary and involuntary.

By this it is manifest, that not only actions that have their beginning from covetousness, ambition, lust, or other appetites to the thing propounded; but also those that have their beginning from aversion, or fear of those consequences that follow the omission, are *voluntary actions....*

**Felicity.**  *Continual success* in obtaining those things which a man from time to time desireth, that is to say, continual prospering, is that men call FELICITY;

I mean the felicity of this life. For there is no such thing as perpetual tranquillity of mind, while we live here; because life itself is but motion, and can never be without desire, nor without fear, no more than without sense. What kind of felicity God hath ordained to them that devoutly honour Him, a man shall no sooner know, than enjoy; being joys, that now are as incomprehensible, as the word of Schoolmen *beatifical vision* is unintelligible....

## Chapter 10

### Of Power, Worth, Dignity, Honour, and Worthiness

**Power.** The POWER *of a man,* to take it universally, is his present means, to obtain some future apparent good; and is either *original* or *instrumental.*

*Natural power,* is the eminence of the faculties of body, or mind: as extraordinary strength, form, prudence, arts, eloquence, liberality, nobility. *Instrumental* are those powers, which acquired by these, or by fortune, are means and instruments to acquire more: as riches, reputation, friends, and the secret working of God, which men call good luck. For the nature of power, is in this point, like to fame, increasing as it proceeds; or like the motion of heavy bodies, which the further they go, make still the more haste.

The greatest of human powers, is that which is compounded of the powers of most men, united by consent, in one person, natural, or civil, that has the use of all their powers depending on his will; such as is the power of a commonwealth: or depending on the wills of each particular; such as is the power of a faction or of divers factions leagued. Therefore to have servants, is power; to have friends, is power: for they are strengths united.

Also riches joined with liberality, is power; because it procureth friends, and servants: without liberality, not so; because in this case they defend not; but expose men to envy, as a prey.

Reputation of power, is power; because it draweth with it the adherence of those that need protection.

So is reputation of love of a man's country, called popularity, for the same reason.

Also, what quality soever maketh a man beloved, or feared of many; or the reputation of such quality, is power; because it is a means to have the assistance, and service of many.

Good success is power; because it maketh reputation of wisdom, or good fortune; which makes men either fear him, or rely on him.

Affability of men already in power, is increase of power; because it gaineth love.

Reputation of prudence in the conduct of peace or war, is power; because to prudent men, we commit the government of ourselves, more willingly than to others.

Nobility is power, not in all places, but only in those commonwealths, where it has privileges: for in such privileges, consisteth the power.

Eloquence is power, because it is seeming prudence.

Form is power; because being a promise of good, it recommendeth men to the favour of women and strangers.

The sciences, are small power; because not eminent; and therefore, not acknowledged in any man; nor are at all, but in a few, and in them, but of a few things. For science is of that nature, as none can understand it to be, but such as in a good measure have attained it.

Arts of public use, as fortification, making of engines, and other instruments of war; because they confer to defence, and victory, are power: and though the true mother of them, be science, namely the mathematics; yet, because they are brought into the light, by the hand of the artificer, they be esteemed, the midwife passing with the vulgar for the mother, as his issue.

**Worth.** The *value,* or WORTH of a man, is as of all other things, his price; that is to say, so much as would be given for the use of his power: and therefore is not absolute; but a thing dependant on the need and judgment of another. An able conductor of soldiers, is of great price in time of war present, or imminent; but in peace not so. A learned and uncorrupt judge, is much worth in time of peace; but not so much in war. And as in other things, so in men, not the seller, but the buyer determines the price. For let a man, as most men do, rate themselves at the highest value they can; yet their true value is no more than it is esteemed by others.

The manifestation of the value we set on one another, is that which is commonly called honouring, and dishonouring. To value a man at a high rate, is to *honour* him; at a low rate, is to *dishonour* him. But high, and low, in this case, is to be understood by comparison to the rate that each man setteth on himself....

## Chapter 11

### Of the Difference of Manners

**What is here meant by manners.** By MANNERS, I mean not here, decency of behaviour; as how one should salute another, or how a man should wash his mouth, or pick his teeth before company, and such other points of the *small* *morals;* but those qualities of mankind, that concern their living together in peace, and unity. To which end we are to consider, that the felicity of this life, consisteth not in the repose of a mind satisfied. For there is no such *finis ultimus,* utmost aim, nor *summum bonum,* greatest good, as is spoken of in the books of the old moral philosophers. Nor can a man any more live, whose desires are at an end, than he, whose senses and imaginations are at a stand. Felicity is a continual progress of the desire, from one object to another; the attaining of the former, being still but the way to the latter. The cause whereof is, that the object of man's desire, is not to enjoy once only, and for one instant of time; but to assure for ever, the way of his future desire. And therefore the voluntary actions, and inclinations of all men, tend, not only to the procuring, but also to the assuring of a contented life; and differ only in the way: which ariseth partly from the diversity of passions, in divers men; and partly from the difference of the knowledge, or opinion each one has of the causes, which produce the effect desired.

**A restless desire of power in all men.** So that in the first place, I put for a general inclination of all mankind, a perpetual and restless desire of power after power, that ceaseth only in death. And the cause of this, is not always that a man hopes for a more intensive delight, than he has already attained to; or that he cannot be content with a moderate power: but because he cannot assure the power and means to live well, which he hath present, without the acquisition of more. And from hence it is, that kings, whose power is greatest, turn their endeavours to the assuring it at home by laws, or abroad by wars: and when that is done, there succeedeth a new desire; in some, of fame from new conquest; in others, of ease and sensual pleasure; in others, of admiration, or being flattered for excellence in some art, or other ability of the mind.

**Love of contention from competition.** Competition of riches, honour, command, or other power, inclineth to contention, enmity, and war: because the way of one competitor, to the attaining of his desire, is to kill, subdue, supplant, or repel the other. Particularly, competition of praise, inclineth to a reverence of antiquity. For men contend with the living, not with the dead; to these ascribing more than due, that they may obscure the glory of the other.

**Civil obedience from love of ease. From fear of death, or wounds.** Desire of ease, and sensual delight, disposeth men to obey a common power: because by such desires, a man doth abandon the protection that might be hoped for from his own industry, and labour. Fear of death, and wounds, disposeth to the same;

and for the same reason. On the contrary, needy men, and hardy, not contented with their present condition; as also, all men that are ambitious of military command, are inclined to continue the causes of war; and to stir up trouble and sedition: for there is no honour military but by war; nor any such hope to mend an ill game, as by causing a new shuffle.

**And from love of arts.** Desire of knowledge, and arts of peace, inclineth men to obey a common power: for such desire, containeth a desire of leisure; and consequently protection from some other power than their own.

**Love of virtue from love of praise.** Desire of praise, disposeth to laudable actions, such as please them whose judgment they value; for of those men whom we contemn, we contemn also the praises. Desire of fame after death does the same. And though after death, there be no sense of the praise given us on earth, as being joys, that are either swallowed up in the unspeakable joys of Heaven, or extinguished in the extreme torments of hell: yet is not such fame vain; because men have a present delight therein, from the foresight of it, and of the benefit that may redound thereby to their posterity; which though they now see not, yet they imagine; and any thing that is pleasure to the sense, the same also is pleasure in the imagination.

**Hate, from difficulty of requiting great benefits.** To have received from one, to whom we think ourselves equal, greater benefits than there is hope to requite, disposeth to counterfeit love; but really secret hatred; and puts a man into the estate of a desperate debtor, in that in declining the sight of his creditor, tacitly wishes him there, where he might never see him more. For benefits oblige, and obligation is thraldom; and unrequitable obligation perpetual thraldom; which is to one's equal, hateful. But to have received benefits from one, whom we acknowledge for superior, inclines to love; because the obligation is no new depression; and cheerful acceptation, which men call *gratitude,* is such an honour done to the obliger, as is taken generally for retribution. Also to receive benefits, though from an equal, or inferior, as long as there is hope of requital, disposeth to love: for in the intention of the receiver, the obligation is of aid and service mutual; from whence proceedeth an emulation of who shall exceed in benefiting; the most noble and profitable contention possible; wherein the victor is pleased with his victory, and the other revenged by confessing it.

**And from conscience of deserving to be hated.** To have done more hurt to a man, than he can, or is willing to expiate, inclineth the doer to hate the sufferer. For he must expect revenge, or forgiveness; both which are hateful....

## Chapter 12

### Of Religion

**Religion in man only.** Seeing there are no signs, nor fruit of *religion,* but in man only; there is no cause to doubt, but that the seed of *religion,* is also only in man; and consisteth in some peculiar quality, or at least in some eminent degree thereof, not to be found in any other living creatures.

**First, from his desire of knowing causes.** And first, it is peculiar to the nature of man, to be inquisitive into the causes of the events they see, some more, some less; but all men so much, as to be curious in the search of the causes of their own good and evil fortune.

**From the consideration of the beginning of things.** Secondly, upon the sight of any thing that hath a beginning, to think also it had a cause, which determined the same to begin, then when it did, rather than sooner or later.

**From his observation of the sequel of things.** Thirdly, whereas there is no other felicity of beasts, but the enjoying of their quotidian food, ease, and lusts; as having little or no foresight of the time to come, for want of observation, and memory of the order, consequence, and dependence of the things they see; man observeth how one event hath been produced by another; and remembereth in them antecedence and consequence; and when he cannot assure himself of the true causes of things, (for the causes of good and evil fortune for the most part are invisible,) he supposes causes of them, either such as his own fancy suggesteth; or trusteth the authority of other men, such as he thinks to be his friends, and wiser than himself.

**The natural cause of religion, the anxiety of the time to come.** The two first, make anxiety. For being assured that there be causes of all things that have arrived hitherto, or shall arrive hereafter; it is impossible for a man, who continually endeavoureth to secure himself against the evil he fears, and procure the good he desireth, not to be in a perpetual solicitude of the time to come so that every man, especially those that are over provident, are in a state like to that of Prometheus. For as Prometheus, which interpreted, is, *the prudent man,* was bound to the hill Caucasus, a place of large prospect, where, an eagle feeding on his liver, devoured in the day, as much as was repaired in the night: so that man, which looks too far before him, in the care of future time, hath his heart all the day long, gnawed on by fear of death, poverty, or other calamity; and has no repose, nor pause of his anxiety, but in sleep.

**Which makes them fear the power of invisible things.** This perpetual fear, always accompanying mankind in the ignorance of causes, as it were in the dark, must needs have for object something. And therefore when there is nothing to be seen, there is nothing to accuse, either of their good, or evil fortune, but some *power,* or agent *invisible:* in which sense perhaps it was, that some of the old poets said, that the gods were at first created by human fear: which spoken of the gods, that is to say, of the many gods of the Gentiles, is very true. But the acknowledging of one God, eternal, infinite, and omnipotent, may more easily be derived, from the desire men have to know the causes of natural bodies, and their several virtues, and operations; than from the fear of what was to befall them in time to come. For he that from any effect he seeth come to pass, should reason to the next and immediate cause thereof, and from thence to the cause of that cause, and plunge himself profoundly in the pursuit of causes; shall at last come to this, that there must be, as even the heathen philosophers confessed, one first mover; that is, a first, and an eternal cause of all things; which is that which men mean by the name of God: and all this without thought of their fortune; the solicitude whereof, both inclines to fear, and hinders them from the search of the causes of other things; and thereby gives occasion of feigning of as many gods, as there be men that feign them....

**But honour them as they honour men.** Thirdly, for the worship which naturally men exhibit to powers invisible, it can be no other, but such expressions of their reverence, as they would use towards men; gifts, petitions, thanks, submission of body, considerate addresses, sober behaviour, premeditated words, swearing, that is, assuring one another of their promises, by invoking them. Beyond that reason suggesteth nothing; but leaves them either to rest there; or for further ceremonies, to rely on those they believe wiser than themselves....

**Four things, natural seeds of religion.** And in these four things, opinion of ghosts, ignorance of second causes, devotion towards what men fear, and taking of things casual for prognostics, consisteth the natural seed of *religion;* which by reason of the different fancies, judgments, and passions of several men, hath grown up into ceremonies so different, that those which are used by one man, are for the most part ridiculous to another.

**Made different by culture.** For these seeds have received culture from two sorts of men. One sort have been they, that have nourished, and ordered them, according to their own invention. The other have done it, by God's commandment, and direction: but both sorts have done it, with a purpose to make those men that relied on them, the more apt to obedience, laws, peace, charity, and civil society. So that the religion of the former sort, is a part of human politics; and teacheth part of the duty which earthly kings require of their subjects. And the religion of the latter sort is divine politics; and containeth precepts to those that have yielded themselves subjects in the kingdom of God. Of the former sort, were all the founders of commonwealths, and the lawgivers of the Gentiles: of the latter sort, were Abraham, Moses, and our blessed Saviour; by whom have been derived unto us the laws of the kingdom of God.

**The absurd opinion of Gentilism.** And for that part of religion, which consisteth in opinions concerning the nature of powers invisible, there is almost nothing that has a name, that has not been esteemed amongst the Gentiles, in one place or another, a god, or devil; or by their poets feigned to be inanimated, inhabited, or possessed by some spirit or other....

The same authors of the religion of the Gentiles, observing the second ground for religion, which is men's ignorance of causes; and thereby their aptness to attribute their fortune to causes, on which there was no dependence at all apparent, took occasion to obtrude on their ignorance, instead of second causes, a kind of second and ministerial gods; ascribing the cause of fecundity, to Venus; the cause of arts, to Apollo; of subtlety and craft, to Mercury; of tempests and storms, to Æolus; and of other effects, to other gods; insomuch as there was amongst the heathen almost as great variety of gods, as of business.

And to the worship, which naturally men conceived fit to be used towards their gods, namely, oblations, prayers, thanks, and the rest formerly named; the same legislators of the Gentiles have added their images, both in picture, and sculpture; that the more ignorant sort, that is to say, the most part or generality of the people, thinking the gods for whose representation they were made, were really included, and as it were housed within them, might so much the more stand in fear of them: and endowed them with lands, and houses, and officers, and revenues, set apart from all other human uses; that is, consecrated, and made holy to those their idols; as caverns, groves, woods, mountains, and whole islands; and have attributed to them, not only the shapes, some of men, some of beasts, some of monsters; but also the faculties, and passions of men and beasts: as sense, speech, sex, lust, generation, and this not only by mixing one with another, to propagate the kind of gods; but also by mixing with men, and women, to beget mongrel gods, and but inmates of heaven, as Bacchus, Hercules, and others; besides anger, revenge, and other passions of living creatures, and the actions proceeding from them, as fraud, theft, adultery, sodomy, and any vice that may be taken for an effect of power, or a cause of pleasure; and all such vices, as amongst men are taken to be against law, rather than against honour.

Lastly, to the prognostics of time to come; which are naturally, but conjectures upon experience of time past; and supernaturally, divine revelation; the same authors of the religion of the Gentiles, partly upon pretended experience, partly upon pretended revelation, have added innumerable other superstitious ways of divination; and made men believe they should find their fortunes, sometimes in the ambiguous or senseless answers of the priests at Delphi, Delos, Ammon, and other famous oracles; which answers, were made ambiguous by design, to own the event both ways; or absurd, by the intoxicating vapour of the place, which is very frequent in sulphurous caverns....

**The designs of the authors of the religion of the heathen.** And therefore the first founders, and legislators of commonwealths among the Gentiles, whose ends were only to keep the people in obedience, and peace, have in all places taken care; first, to imprint in their minds a belief, that those precepts which they gave concerning religion, might not be thought to proceed from their own device, but from the dictates of some god, or other spirit; or else that they themselves were of a higher nature than mere mortals, that their laws might the more easily be received: so Numa Pompilius pretended to receive the ceremonies he instituted amongst the Romans, from the nymph Egeria: and the first king and founder of the kingdom of Peru, pretended himself and his wife to be the children of the Sun; and Mahomet, to set up his new religion, pretended to have conferences with the Holy Ghost, in form of a dove. Secondly, they have had a care, to make it believed, that the same things were displeasing to the gods, which were forbidden by the laws. Thirdly, to prescribe ceremonies, supplications, sacrifices, and festivals, by which they were to believe, the anger of the gods might be appeased; and that ill success in war, great contagions of sickness, earthquakes, and each man's private misery, came from the anger of the gods, and their anger from the neglect of their worship, or the forgetting, or mistaking some point of the ceremonies required. And though amongst the ancient Romans, men were not forbidden to deny, that which in the poets is written of the pains, and pleasures after this life: which divers of great authority, and gravity in that state have in their harangues openly derided; yet that belief was always more cherished, than the contrary.

And by these, and such other institutions, they obtained in order to their end, which was the peace of the commonwealth, that the common people in their misfortunes, laying the fault on neglect, or error in their ceremonies, or on their own disobedience to the laws, were the less apt to mutiny against their governors; and being entertained with the pomp, and pastime of festivals, and public games, made in honour of the gods, needed nothing else but bread to keep them from discontent, murmuring, and commotion against the state. And therefore the Romans, that had conquered the greatest part of the then known world, made no scruple of tolerating any religion whatsoever in the city of Rome itself; unless it had something in it, that could not consist with their civil government; nor do we read, that any religion was there forbidden, but that of the Jews; who, being the peculiar kingdom of God, thought it unlawful to acknowledge subjection to any mortal king or state whatsoever. And thus you see how the religion of the Gentiles was a part of their policy....

## Chapter 13

### Of the Natural Condition of Mankind as Concerning Their Felicity and Misery

**Men by nature equal.**  Nature hath made men so equal, in the faculties of the body, and mind; as that though there be found one man sometimes manifestly stronger in body, or of quicker mind than another; yet when all is reckoned together, the difference between man, and man, is not so considerable, as that one man can thereupon claim to himself any benefit, to which another may not pretend, as well as he. For as to the strength of body, the weakest has strength enough to kill the strongest, either by secret machination, or by confederacy with others, that are in the same danger with himself.

And as to the faculties of the mind, setting aside the arts grounded upon words, and especially that skill of proceeding upon general, and infallible rules, called science; which very few have, and but in few things; as being not a native faculty, born with us; nor attained, as prudence, while we look after somewhat else, I find yet a greater equality amongst men, than that of strength. For prudence, is but experience, which equal time, equally bestows on all men, in those things they equally apply themselves unto. That which may perhaps make such equality incredible, is but a vain conceit of one's own wisdom, which almost all men think they have in a greater degree, than the vulgar; that is, than all men but themselves, and a few others, whom by fame, or for concurring with themselves, they approve. For such is the nature of men, that howsoever they may acknowledge many others to be more witty, or more eloquent, or more learned; yet they will hardly believe there be many so wise as themselves; for they see their own wit at hand, and other men's at a distance. But this proveth rather that men are in that point equal, than unequal. For there is not ordinarily a greater sign of the equal distribution of any thing, than that every man is contented with his share.

**From equality proceeds diffidence.** From this equality of ability, ariseth equality of hope in the attaining of our ends. And therefore if any two men desire the same thing, which nevertheless they cannot both enjoy, they become enemies; and in the way to their end, which is principally their own conservation, and sometimes their delectation only, endeavour to destroy, or subdue one another. And from hence it comes to pass, that where an invader hath no more to fear, than another man's single power; if one plant, sow, build, or possess a convenient seat, others may probably be expected to come prepared with forces united, to dispossess, and deprive him, not only of the fruit of his labour, but also of his life, or liberty. And the invader again is in the like danger of another.

**From diffidence war.** And from this diffidence of one another, there is no way for any man to secure himself, so reasonable, as anticipation; that is, by force, or wiles, to master the persons of all men he can, so long, till he see no other power great enough to endanger him: and this is no more than his own conservation requireth, and is generally allowed. Also because there be some, that taking pleasure in contemplating their own power in the acts of conquest, which they pursue farther than their security requires; if others, that otherwise would be glad to be at ease within modest bounds, should not by invasion increase their power, they would not be able, long time, by standing only on their defence, to subsist. And by consequence, such augmentation of dominion over men being necessary to a man's conservation, it ought to be allowed him.

Again, men have no pleasure, but on the contrary a great deal of grief, in keeping company, where there is no power able to over-awe them all. For every man looketh that his companion should value him, at the same rate he sets upon himself: and upon all signs of contempt, or undervaluing, naturally endeavours, as far as he dares, (which amongst them that have no common power to keep them in quiet, is far enough to make them destroy each other), to extort a greater value from his contemners, by damage; and from others, by the example.

So that in the nature of man, we find three principal causes of quarrel. First, competition; secondly, diffidence; thirdly, glory.

The first, maketh men invade for gain; the second, for safety; and the third, for reputation. The first use violence, to make themselves masters of other men's persons, wives, children, and cattle; the second, to defend them; the third, for trifles, as a word, a smile, a different opinion, and any other sign of undervalue, either direct in their persons, or by reflection in their kindred, their friends, their nation, their profession, or their name.

**Out of civil states, there is always war of every one against every one.** Hereby it is manifest, that during the time men live without a common power to keep them all in awe, they are in that condition which is called war; and such a war, as is of every man, against every man. For WAR, consisteth not in battle only, or the act of fighting; but in a tract of time, wherein the will to contend by battle is sufficiently known: and therefore the notion of *time,* is to be considered in the nature of war; as it is in the nature of weather. For as the nature of foul weather, lieth not in a shower or two of rain; but in an inclination thereto of many days together: so the nature of war, consisteth not in actual fighting; but in the known disposition thereto, during all the time there is no assurance to the contrary. All other time is PEACE.

**The incommodities of such a war.** Whatsoever therefore is consequent to a time of war, where every man is enemy to every man; the same is consequent to the time, wherein men live without other security, than what their own strength, and their own invention shall furnish them withal. In such condition, there is no place for industry; because the fruit thereof is uncertain: and consequently no culture of the earth; no navigation, nor use of the commodities that may be imported by sea; no commodious building; no instruments of moving, and removing, such things as require much force; no knowledge of the face of the earth; no account of time; no arts; no letters; no society; and which is worst of all, continual fear, and danger of violent death; and the life of man, solitary, poor, nasty, brutish, and short.

It may seem strange to some man, that has not well weighed these things; that nature should thus dissociate, and render men apt to invade, and destroy one another: and he may therefore, not trusting to this inference, made from the passions, desire perhaps to have the same confirmed by experience. Let him therefore consider with himself, when taking a journey, he arms himself, and seeks to go well accompanied; when going to sleep, he locks his doors; when even in his house he locks his chests; and this when he knows there be laws, and public officers, armed, to revenge all injuries shall be done him; what opinion he has of his fellow-subjects, when he rides armed; of his fellow citizens, when he locks his doors; and of his children, and servants, when he locks his chests. Does he not there as much accuse mankind by his actions, as I do by my words? But neither of us accuse man's nature in it. The desires, and other passions of man, are in themselves no sin. No more are the actions, that proceed from those passions, till they know a law that forbids them: which till laws be made they cannot know: nor can any law be made, till they have agreed upon the person that shall make it.

It may peradventure be thought, there was never such a time, nor condition of war as this; and I believe it was never generally so, over all the world: but there are many places, where they live so now. For the savage people in many places of America, except the government of small families, the concord whereof dependeth on natural lust, have no government at all; and live at this day in that brutish manner, as I said before. Howsoever, it may be perceived what manner of life there would be, where there were no common power to fear, by the manner of life, which men that have formerly lived under a peaceful government, use to degenerate into, in a civil war.

But though there had never been any time, wherein particular men were in a condition of war one against another; yet in all times, kings, and persons of sovereign authority, because of their independency, are in continual jealousies, and in the state and posture of gladiators; having their weapons pointing, and their eyes fixed on one another; that is, their forts, garrisons, and guns upon the frontiers of their kingdoms; and continual spies upon their neighbours; which is a posture of war. But because they uphold thereby, the industry of their subjects; there does not follow from it, that misery, which accompanies the liberty of particular men.

**In such a war nothing is unjust.** To this war of every man, against every man, this also is consequent; that nothing can be unjust. The notions of right and wrong, justice and injustice have there no place. Where there is no common power, there is no law: where no law, no injustice. Force, and fraud, are in war the two cardinal virtues. Justice, and injustice are none of the faculties neither of the body, nor mind. If they were, they might be in a man that were alone in the world, as well as his senses, and passions. They are qualities, that relate to men in society, not in solitude. It is consequent also to the same condition, that there be no propriety, no dominion, no *mine* and *thine* distinct; but only that to be every man's, that he can get: and for so long, as he can keep it. And thus much for the ill condition, which man by mere nature is actually placed in; though with a possibility to come out of it, consisting partly in the passions, partly in his reason.

**The passions that incline men to peace.** The passions that incline men to peace, are fear of death; desire of such things as are necessary to commodious living; and a hope by their industry to obtain them. And reason suggesteth convenient articles of peace, upon which men may be drawn to agreement. These articles, are they, which otherwise are called the Laws of Nature: whereof I shall speak more particularly, in the two following chapters.

## Chapter 14

### Of the First and Second Natural Laws, and of Contracts

**Right of nature what.** The RIGHT OF NATURE, which writers commonly call *jus naturale,* is the liberty each man hath, to use his own power, as he will himself, for the preservation of his own nature; that is to say, of his own life; and consequently, of doing any thing, which in his own judgment, and reason, he shall conceive to be the aptest means thereunto.

**Liberty what.** By LIBERTY, is understood, according to the proper signification of the word, the absence of external impediments: which impediments, may oft take away part of a man's power to do what he would; but cannot hinder him from using the power left him, according as his judgment, and reason shall dictate to him.

**A law of nature what. Difference of right and law.** A LAW OF NATURE, *lex naturalis,* is a precept or general rule, found out by reason, by which a man is forbidden to do that, which is destructive of his life, or taketh away the means of preserving the same; and to omit that, by which he thinketh it may be best preserved. For though they that speak of this subject, use to confound *jus,* and *lex,* *right* and *law:* yet they ought to be distinguished; because RIGHT, consisteth in liberty to do, or to forbear: whereas LAW, determineth, and bindeth to one of them: so that law, and right, differ as much, as obligation, and liberty; which in one and the same matter are inconsistent.

**Naturally every man has right to every thing. The fundamental law of nature.** And because the condition of man, as hath been declared in the precedent chapter, is a condition of war of every one against every one; in which case every one is governed by his own reason; and there is nothing he can make use of, that may not be a help unto him, in preserving his life against his enemies; it followeth, that in such a condition, every man has a right to every thing; even to one another's body. And therefore, as long as this natural right of every man to every thing endureth, there can be no security to any man, how strong or wise soever he be, of living out the time, which nature ordinarily alloweth men to live. And consequently it is a precept, or general rule of reason, *that every man, ought to endeavour peace, as far as he has hope of obtaining it; and when he cannot obtain it, that he may seek, and use, all helps, and advantages of war.* The first branch of which rule, containeth the first, and fundamental law of nature; which is, *to seek peace, and follow it.* The second, the sum of the right of nature; which is, *by all means we can, to defend ourselves.*

**The second law of nature.** From this fundamental law of nature, by which men are commanded to endeavour peace, is derived this second law; *that a man be willing, when others are so too, as far-forth, as for peace, and defence of himself he shall think it necessary, to lay down this right to all things; and be contented with so much liberty against other men, as he would allow other men against himself.* For as long as every man holdeth this right, of doing any thing he liketh; so long are all men in the condition of war. But if other men will not lay down their right, as well as he; then there is no reason for any one to divest himself of his: for that were to expose himself to prey, which no man is bound to, rather than to dispose himself to peace. This is that law of the Gospel; *whatsoever you require that others should do to you, that do ye to them.* And that law of all men, *quod tibi fieri non vis, alteri ne feceris....*[1]

**Not all rights are alienable.** Whensoever a man transferreth his right, or renounceth it; it is either in consideration of some right reciprocally transferred to himself; or for some other good he hopeth for thereby. For it is a voluntary act: and of the voluntary acts of every man, the object is some *good to himself.* And therefore there be some rights, which no man can be understood by any words, or other signs, to have abandoned, or transferred. As first a man cannot lay down the right of resisting them, that assault him by force, to take away his life; because he cannot be understood to aim thereby, at any good to himself. The same may be said of wounds, and chains, and imprisonment; both because there is no benefit consequent to such patience; as there is to the patience of suffering another

---

1 ["What you do not want done to yourself, do not do to others."— J.M.P.]

to be wounded, or imprisoned: as also because a man cannot tell, when he seeth men proceed against him by violence whether they intend his death or not. And lastly the motive, and end for which this renouncing, and transferring of right is introduced, is nothing else but the security of a man's person, in his life, and in the means of so preserving life, as not to be weary of it. And therefore if a man by words, or other signs, seem to despoil himself of the end, for which those signs were intended; he is not to be understood as if he meant it, or that it was his will; but that he was ignorant of how such words and actions were to be interpreted.

**Contract what.** The mutual transferring of right, is that which men call CONTRACT....

**Covenants of mutual trust, when invalid.** If a covenant be made, wherein neither of the parties perform presently, but trust one another; in the condition of mere nature, which is a condition of war of every man against every man, upon any reasonable suspicion, it is void: but if there be a common power set over them both, with right and force sufficient to compel performance, it is not void. For he that performeth first, has no assurance the other will perform after; because the bonds of words are too weak to bridle men's ambition, avarice, anger, and other passions, without the fear of some coercive power; which in the condition of mere nature, where all men are equal, and judges of the justness of their own fears, cannot possibly be supposed. And therefore he which performeth first does but betray himself to his enemy; contrary to the right, he can never abandon, of defending his life, and means of living.

But in a civil estate, where there is a power set up to constrain those that would otherwise violate their faith, that fear is no more reasonable; and for that cause, he which by the covenant is to perform first, is obliged so to do....

**Covenants extorted by fear are valid.** Covenants entered into by fear, in the condition of mere nature, are obligatory. For example, if I covenant to pay a ransom, or service for my life, to an enemy; I am bound by it: for it is a contract, wherein one receiveth the benefit of life; the other is to receive money, or service for it; and consequently, where no other law, as in the condition of mere nature, forbiddeth the performance, the covenant is valid. Therefore prisoners of war, if trusted with the payment of their ransom, are obliged to pay it: and if a weaker prince, make a disadvantageous peace with a stronger, for fear; he is bound to keep it; unless, as hath been said before, there ariseth some new, and just cause of fear, to renew the war. And even in commonwealths, if I be forced to redeem myself from a thief by promising him money, I am bound to pay it, till the civil law discharge me. For whatsoever I may lawfully do without obligation, the same I may lawfully covenant to do through fear; and what I lawfully covenant, I cannot lawfully break....

**A man's covenant not to defend himself is void.** A covenant not to defend myself from force, by force, is always void. For, as I have showed before, no man can transfer, or lay down his right to save himself from death, wounds, and imprisonment, the avoiding whereof is the only end of laying down any right; and therefore the promise of not resisting force, in no covenant transferreth any right; nor is obliging. For though a man may covenant thus, *unless I do so, or so, kill me;* he cannot covenant thus, *unless I do so, or so, I will not resist you, when you come to kill me.* For man by nature chooseth the lesser evil, which is danger of death in resisting; rather than the greater, which is certain and present death in not resisting. And this is granted to be true by all men, in that they lead criminals to execution, and prison, with armed men, notwithstanding that such criminals have consented to the law, by which they are condemned....

**The end of an oath. The form of an oath.** The force of words, being, as I have formerly noted, too weak to hold men to the performance of their covenants; there are in man's nature, but two imaginable helps to strengthen it. And those are either a fear of the consequence of breaking their word; or a glory, or pride in appearing not to need to break it. This latter is a generosity too rarely found to be presumed on, especially in the pursuers of wealth, command, or sensual pleasure; which are the greatest part of mankind. The passion to be reckoned upon, is fear; whereof there be two very general objects: one, the power of spirits invisible; the other, the power of those men they shall therein offend. Of these two, though the former be the greater power, yet the fear of the latter is commonly the greater fear....

## Chapter 15

### Of Other Laws of Nature

**The third law of nature, justice.** From that law of nature, by which we are obliged to transfer to another, such rights, as being retained, hinder the peace of mankind, there followeth a third; which is this, *that men perform their covenants made:* without which, covenants are in vain, and but empty words; and the right of all men to all things remaining, we are still in the condition of war.

**Justice and injustice what.** And in this law of nature, consisteth the fountain and original of JUSTICE. For where no covenant hath preceded, there hath no right been transferred, and every man has right to every thing; and consequently, no action can be unjust. But when a covenant is made, then to break it is *unjust:* and the definition of INJUSTICE, is no other than *the not performance of covenant.* And whatsoever is not unjust, *is just.*

**Justice and propriety begin with the constitution of commonwealth.** But because covenants of mutual trust, where there is a fear of not performance on either part, as hath been said in the former chapter, are invalid; though the original of justice be the making of covenants; yet injustice actually there can be none, till the cause of such fear be taken away; which while men are in the natural condition of war, cannot be done. Therefore before the names of just, and unjust can have place, there must be some coercive power, to compel men equally to the performance of their covenants, by the terror of some punishment, greater than the benefit they expect by the breach of their covenant; and to make good that propriety, which by mutual contract men acquire, in recompense of the universal right they abandon: and such power there is none before the erection of a commonwealth. And this is also to be gathered out of the ordinary definition of justice in the Schools: for they say, that *justice is the constant will of giving to every man his own.* And therefore where there is no *own,* that is no propriety, there is no injustice; and where there is no coercive power erected, that is, where there is no commonwealth, there is no propriety; all men having right to all things: therefore where there is no commonwealth, there nothing is unjust. So that the nature of justice, consisteth in keeping of valid covenants: but the validity of covenants begins not but with the constitution of a civil power, sufficient to compel men to keep them: and then it is also that propriety begins.

**Justice not contrary to reason.** The fool hath said in his heart, there is no such thing as justice; and sometimes also with his tongue; seriously alleging, that every man's conservation, and contentment, being committed to his own care, there could be no reason, why every man might not do what he thought conduced thereunto: and therefore also to make, or not make; keep, or not keep covenants, was not against reason, when it conduced to one's benefit. He does not therein deny, that there be covenants; and that they are sometimes broken, sometimes kept; and that such breach of them may be called injustice, and the observance of them justice: but he questioneth, whether injustice, taking away the fear of God, for the same fool hath said in his heart there is no God, may not sometimes stand with that reason, which dictateth to every man his own good; and particularly then, when it conduceth to such a benefit, as shall put a man in a condition, to neglect not only the dispraise, and revilings, but also the power of other men. The kingdom of God is gotten by violence: but what if it could be gotten by unjust violence? were it against reason so to get it, when it is impossible to receive hurt by it? and if it be not against reason, it is not against justice; or else justice is not to be approved for good. From such reasoning as this, successful wickedness hath obtained the name of virtue: and some that in all other things have disallowed the violation of faith; yet have allowed it, when it is for the getting of a kingdom. And the heathen that believed, that Saturn was deposed by his son Jupiter, believed nevertheless the same Jupiter to be the avenger of injustice: somewhat like to a piece of law in Coke's *Commentaries on Littleton;* where he says, if the right heir of the crown be attainted of treason; yet the crown shall descend to him, and *eo instante* the attainder be void: from which instances a man will be very prone to infer; that when the heir apparent of a kingdom, shall kill him that is in possession, though his father; you may call it injustice, or by what other name you will; yet it can never be against reason, seeing all the voluntary actions of men tend to the benefit of themselves; and those actions are most reasonable, that conduce most to their ends. This specious reasoning is nevertheless false.

For the question is not of promises mutual, where there is no security of performance on either side; as when there is no civil power erected over the parties promising; for such promises are no covenants: but either where one of the parties has performed already; or where there is a power to make him perform; there is the question whether it be against reason, that is, against the benefit of the other to perform, or not. And I say it is not against reason. For the manifestation whereof, we are to consider; first, that when a man doth a thing, which notwithstanding any thing can be foreseen, and reckoned on, tendeth to his own destruction, howsoever some accident which he could not expect, arriving may turn it to his benefit; yet such events do not make it reasonably or wisely done. Secondly, that in a condition of war, wherein every man to every man, for want of a common power to keep them all in awe, is an enemy, there is no man who can hope by his own strength, or wit, to defend himself from destruction, without the help of confederates; where every one expects the same defence by the confederation, that any one else does: and therefore he which declares he thinks it reason to deceive those that help him, can in reason expect no other means of safety, than what can be had from his own single power. He therefore that breaketh his covenant, and consequently declareth that he thinks he may with reason do so, cannot be received into any society, that unite themselves for peace and defence, but by the error of them that receive him; nor when he is received, be retained in it, without seeing the danger of their error; which errors a man cannot reasonably reckon upon as the means of his security: and therefore if he be left, or cast out of society, he perisheth; and if he live in society, it is by the errors of other men, which he could not foresee, nor reckon upon; and consequently against the reason of his preservation; and so, as all men that contribute not to his destruction, forbear him only out of ignorance of what is good for themselves.

As for the instance of gaining the secure and perpetual felicity of heaven, by any way; it is frivolous: there being but one way imaginable; and that is not breaking, but keeping of covenant.

And for the other instance of attaining sovereignty by rebellion; it is manifest, that though the event follow, yet because it cannot reasonably be expected, but rather the contrary; and because by gaining it so, others are taught to gain the same in like manner, the attempt thereof is against reason. Justice therefore, that is to say, keeping of covenant, is a rule of reason, by which we are forbidden to do any thing destructive to our life; and consequently a law of nature.

There be some that proceed further; and will not have the law of nature, to be those rules which conduce to the preservation of man's life on earth; but to the attaining of an eternal felicity after death; to which they think the breach of covenant may conduce; and consequently be just and reasonable; such are they that think it a work of merit to kill, or depose, or rebel against, the sovereign power constituted over them by their own consent. But because there is no natural knowledge of man's estate after death; much less of the reward that is then to be given to breach of faith; but only a belief grounded upon other men's saying, that they know it supernaturally, or that they know those, that knew them, that knew others, that knew it supernaturally; breach of faith cannot be called a precept of reason, or nature....

## ⊹ THE SECOND PART ⊱

### Of Commonwealth

### *Chapter 16*

### *Of Persons, Authors, and Things Personated*

**A person what.** A person, is he, *whose words or actions are considered, either as his own, or as representing the words or actions of another man, or of any other thing, to whom they are attributed, whether truly or by fiction.*

**Person natural, and artificial.** When they are considered as his own, then is he called a *natural person:* and when they are considered as representing the words and actions of another, then is he a *feigned* or *artificial person.*

**The word person, whence.** The word person is Latin ..., which signifies the *face,* as *persona* in Latin signifies the *disguise,* or *outward appearance* of a man, counterfeited on the stage; and sometimes more particularly that part of it, which disguiseth the face, as a mask or vizard: and from the stage, hath been translated to any representer of speech and action, as well in tribunals, as theatres. So that a *person,* is the same that an *actor* is, both on the stage and in common conversation; and to *personate,* is to *act,* or *represent* himself, or another; and he that acteth another, is said to bear his person, or act in his name; in which sense Cicero useth it where he says, *Unus sustineo tres personas; mei, adversarii, et judicis:* I bear three persons; my own, my adversary's, and the judge's; and is called in divers occasions, diversely; as a *representer,* or *representative,* a *lieutenant,* a *vicar,* an *attorney,* a *deputy,* a *procurator,* an *actor,* and the like.

**Actor. Author. Authority.** Of persons artificial, some have their words and actions *owned* by those whom they represent. And then the person is the *actor;* and he that owneth his words and actions, is the AUTHOR: in which case the actor acteth by authority. For that which in speaking of goods and possessions, is called an *owner,* and in Latin *dominus,* ... speaking of actions, is called author. And as the right of possession, is called dominion; so the right of doing any action, is called AUTHORITY. So that by authority, is always understood a right of doing any act; and *done by authority,* done by commission, or licence from him whose right it is.

**Covenants by authority, bind the author.** From hence it followeth, that when the actor maketh a covenant by authority, he bindeth thereby the author, no less than if he had made it himself; and no less subjecteth him to all the consequences of the same. And therefore all that hath been said formerly, (chapter 14) of the nature of covenants between man and man in their natural capacity, is true also when they are made by their actors, representers, or procurators, that have authority from them, so far forth as is in their commission, but no further.

And therefore he that maketh a covenant with the actor, or representer, not knowing the authority he hath, doth it at his own peril. For no man is obliged by a covenant, whereof he is not author; nor consequently by a covenant made against, or beside the authority he gave.

**But not the actor.** When the actor doth any thing against the law of nature by command of the author, if he be obliged by former covenant to obey him,

325

not he, but the author breaketh the law of nature; for though the action be against the law of nature; yet it is not his: but contrarily, to refuse to do it, is against the law of nature, that forbiddeth breach of covenant.

**The authority is to be shown.** And he that maketh a covenant with the author, by mediation of the actor, not knowing what authority he hath, but only takes his word; in case such authority be not made manifest unto him upon demand, is no longer obliged: for the covenant made with the author, is not valid, without his counter-assurance. But if he that so covenanteth, knew beforehand he was to expect no other assurance, than the actor's word; then is the covenant valid; because the actor in this case maketh himself the author. And therefore, as when the authority is evident, the covenant obligeth the author, not the actor; so when the authority is feigned, it obligeth the actor only; there being no author but himself.

**Things personated, inanimate.** There are few things, that are incapable of being represented by fiction. Inanimate things, as a church, an hospital, a bridge, may be personated by a rector, master, or overseer. But things inanimate, cannot be authors, nor therefore give authority to their actors: yet the actors may have authority to procure their maintenance, given them by those that are owners, or governors of those things. And therefore, such things cannot be personated, before there be some state of civil government.

**Irrational.** ikewise children, fools, and madmen that have no use of reason, may be personated by guardians, or curators; but can be no authors, during that time, of any action done by them, longer than, when they shall recover the use of reason, they shall judge the same reasonable. Yet during the folly, he that hath right of governing them, may give authority to the guardian. But this again has no place but in a state civil, because before such estate, there is no dominion of persons.

**False gods.** An idol, or mere figment of the brain, may be personated; as were the gods of the heathen: which by such officers as the state appointed, were personated, and held possessions, and other goods, and rights, which men from time to time dedicated, and consecrated unto them. But idols cannot be authors: for an idol is nothing. The authority proceeded from the state: and therefore before introduction of civil government, the gods of the heathen could not be personated.

**The true God.** The true God may be personated. As he was; first, by Moses; who governed the Israelites, that were not his, but God's people, not in his own name, with *hoc dicit Moses;* but in God's name, with *hoc dicit Dominus.* Secondly, by the Son of man, his own Son, our blessed Saviour Jesus Christ, that came to reduce the Jews, and induce all nations into the kingdom of his father; not as of himself, but as sent from his father. And thirdly, by the Holy Ghost, or Comforter, speaking, and working in the Apostles: which Holy Ghost, was a Comforter that came not of himself; but was sent, and proceeded from them both.

**A multitude of men, how one person.** A multitude of men, are made *one* person, when they are by one man, or one person, represented; so that it be done with the consent of every one of that multitude in particular. For it is the *unity* of the representer, not the *unity* of the represented, that maketh the person *one*. And it is the representer that beareth the person, and but one person: and *unity,* cannot otherwise be understood in multitude.

**Every one is author.** And because the multitude naturally is not *one,* but *many;* they cannot be understood for one; but many authors, of every thing their representative saith, or doth in their name; every man giving their common representer, authority from himself in particular; and owning all the *actions the representer doth,* in case they give him authority without stint: otherwise, when they limit him in what, and how far he shall represent them, none of them owneth more that they gave him commission to act.

**An actor may be many men made one by plurality of voices.** And if the representative consist of many men, the voice of the greater number, must be considered as the voice of them all. For if the lesser number pronounce, for example, in the affirmative, and the greater in the negative, there will be negatives more than enough to destroy the affirmatives; and thereby the excess of negatives, standing uncontradicted, are the only voice the representative hath.

**Representatives, when the number is even, unprofitable.** And a representative of even number, especially when the number is not great, whereby the contradictory voices are oftentimes mute, and incapable of action. Yet in some cases contradictory voices equal in number, may determine a question; as in condemning, or absolving, equality of votes, even in that they condemn not, do absolve; but not on the contrary condemn, in that they absolve not. For when a cause is heard; not to condemn, is to absolve: but on the contrary, to say that not absolving, is condemning, is not true. The like it is in a deliberation of executing presently, or deferring till another time: for when the voices are equal, the not decreeing execution, is a decree of dilation.

**Negative voice.** Or if the number be odd, as three, or more, men or assemblies; whereof every one has by a negative voice, authority to take away the effect of all the affirmative voices of the rest, this number is no representative; because by the diversity of opinions, and interests of men, it becomes oftentimes, and in cases of the greatest consequence, a mute person, and unapt, as for many things else, so for the government of a multitude, especially in time of war.

Of authors there be two sorts. The first simply so called; which I have before defined to be him, that owneth the action of another simply. The second is he, that owneth an action, or covenant of another conditionally; that is to say, he undertaketh to do it, if the other doth it not, at, or before a certain time. And these authors conditional, are generally called SURETIES, in Latin, *fidejussores,* and *sponsores;* and particularly for debt, *praedes;* and for appearance before a judge, or magistrate, *vades.*

## Chapter 17

### Of the Causes, Generation, and Definition of a Commonwealth

**The end of commonwealth, particular security.** The final cause, end, or design of men, who naturally love liberty, and dominion over others, in the introduction of that restraint upon themselves, in which we see them live in commonwealths, is the foresight of their own preservation, and of a more contented life thereby; that is to say, of getting themselves out from that miserable condition of war, which is necessarily consequent, as hath been shown (chapter 13), to the natural passions of men, when there is no visible power to keep them in awe, and tie them by fear of punishment to the performance of their covenants, and observation of those laws of nature set down in the fourteenth and fifteenth chapters.

**Which is not to be had from the law of nature.** For the laws of nature, as *justice, equality, modesty, mercy,* and, in sum, *doing to others, as we would be done to,* of themselves, without the terror of some power, to cause them to be observed, are contrary to our natural passions, that carry us to partiality, pride, revenge, and the like. And covenants, without the sword, are but words, and of no strength to secure a man at all. Therefore notwithstanding the laws of nature (which every one hath then kept, when he has the will to keep them, when he can do it safely) if there be no power erected or not great enough for our security; every man will, and may lawfully rely on his own strength and art, for caution against all other men. And in all places, where men have lived by small families, to rob and spoil one another, has been a trade, and so far from being reputed against the law of nature, that the greater spoils they gained, the greater was their honour; and men observed no other laws therein, but the laws of honour; that is, to abstain from cruelty, leaving to men their lives, and instruments of husbandry. And as small families did then; so now do cities and kingdoms which are but greater families, for their own security, enlarge their dominions, upon all pretenses of danger, and fear of invasion, or assistance that may be given to invaders, and endeavour as much as they can, to subdue, or weaken their neighbours, by open force, and secret arts, for want of other caution, justly; and are remembered for it in after ages with honour.

**Nor from the conjunction of a few men or families.**  Nor is it the joining together of a small number of men, that gives them this security; because in small numbers, small additions on the one side or the other, make the advantage of strength so great, as is sufficient to carry the victory; and therefore gives encouragement to an invasion. The multitude sufficient to confide in for our security, is not determined by any certain number, but by comparison with the enemy we fear; and is then sufficient, when the odds of the enemy is not of so visible and conspicuous moment, to determine the event of war, as to move him to attempt.

**Nor from a great multitude, unless directed by one judgment.**  And be there never so great a multitude; yet if their actions be directed according to their particular judgments, and particular appetites, they can expect thereby no defence, nor protection, neither against a common enemy, nor against the injuries of one another. For being distracted in opinions concerning the best use and application of their strength, they do not help but hinder one another; and reduce their strength by mutual opposition to nothing: whereby they are easily, not only subdued by a very few that agree together; but also when there is no common enemy, they make war upon each other, for their particular interests. For if we could suppose a great multitude of men to consent in the observation of justice, and other laws of nature, without a common power to keep them all in awe; we might as well suppose all mankind to do the same; and then there neither would be, nor need to be any civil government, or commonwealth at all; because there would be peace without subjection.

**And that continually.**  Nor is it enough for the security, which men desire should last all the time of their life, that they be governed, and directed by one judgment, for a limited time; as in one battle, or one war. For though they obtain a victory by their unanimous endeavour against a foreign enemy; yet afterwards, when they have no common enemy, or he that by one part is held for an enemy, is by another part held for a friend, they must needs by the difference of their interests dissolve, and fall again into a war amongst themselves.

**Why certain creatures without reason, or speech, do nevertheless live in society, without any coercive power.** It is true, that certain living creatures, as bees, and ants, live sociably one with another, which are therefore by Aristotle numbered amongst political creatures; and yet have no other direction, than their particular judgments and appetites; nor speech, whereby one of them can signify to another, what he thinks expedient for the common benefit: and therefore some man may perhaps desire to know, why mankind cannot do the same. To which I answer,

First, that men are continually in competition for honour and dignity, which these creatures are not; and consequently amongst men there ariseth on that ground, envy and hatred, and finally war; but amongst these not so.

Secondly, that amongst these creatures, the common good differeth not from the private; and being by nature inclined to their private they procure thereby the common benefit. But man, whose joy consisteth in comparing himself with other men, can relish nothing but what is eminent.

Thirdly, that these creatures, having not, as man, the use of reason, do not see, nor think they see any fault, in the administration of their common business; whereas amongst men, there are very many, that think themselves wiser, and abler to govern the public, better than the rest; and these strive to reform and innovate, one this way, another that way; and thereby bring it into distraction and civil war.

Fourthly, that these creatures though they have some use of voice, in making known to one another their desires, and other affections; yet they want that art of words, by which some men can represent to others, that which is good, in the likeness of evil; and evil, in the likeness of good; and augment, or diminish the apparent greatness of good and evil; discontenting men, and troubling their peace at their pleasure.

Fifthly, irrational creatures cannot distinguish between *injury,* and *damage;* and therefore as long as they be at ease, they are not offended with their fellows: whereas man is then most troublesome, when he is most at ease: for then it is that he loves to shew his wisdom, and control the actions of them that govern the commonwealth.

Lastly, the agreement of these creatures is natural; that of men, is by covenant only, which is artificial: and therefore it is no wonder if there be somewhat else required, besides covenant, to make their agreement constant and lasting; which is a common power, to keep them in awe, and to direct their actions to the common benefit.

**The generation of a commonwealth. The definition of a commonwealth.** The only way to erect such a common power, as may be able to defend them from the invasion of foreigners, and the injuries of one another, and thereby to se-cure them in such sort, as that by their own industry, and by the fruits of the earth, they may nourish themselves and live contentedly; is, to confer all their power and strength upon one man, or upon one assembly of men, that may re-duce all their wills, by plurality of voices, unto one will: which is as much as to say, to appoint one man, or assembly of men, to bear their person; and every one to own, and acknowledge himself to be author of whatsoever he that so beareth their person, shall act, or cause to be acted, in those things which concern the common peace and safety; and therein to submit their wills, every one to his will, and their judgments, to his judgment. This is more than consent, or concord; it is a real unity of them all, in one and the same person, made by covenant of every man with every man, in such manner, as if every man should say to every man, *I authorize and give up my right of governing myself, to this man, or to this assembly of men, on this condition, that thou give up thy right to him, and authorize all his actions in like manner.* This done, the multitude so united in one person, is called a COMMONWEALTH, in Latin CIVITAS. This is the generation of that great LEVIATHAN, or rather, to speak more reverently, of that *mortal god,* to which we owe under the *immortal God,* our peace and defence. For by this authority, given him by particular man in the commonwealth, he hath the use of so much power and strength conferred on him, that by terror thereof, he is enabled to form the wills of them all, to peace at home, and mutual aid against their enemies abroad. And in him consisteth the essence of the commonwealth; which, to define it, is *one person, of whose acts a great multitude, by mutual covenants one with another, have made themselves every one the author, to the end he may use the strength and means of them all, as he shall think expedient, for their peace and common defence.*

**Sovereign, and subject, what.** And he that carrieth this person, is called SOV-EREIGN, and said to have *sovereign power;* and every one besides, his SUBJECT.

The attaining to this sovereign power, is by two ways. One, by natural force; as when a man maketh his children, to submit themselves, and their children to his government, as being able to destroy them if they refuse; or by war subdueth his enemies to his will, giving them their lives on that condition. The other, is when men agree amongst themselves, to submit to some man, or assembly of men, voluntarily, on confidence to be protected by him against all others. This lat-ter, may be called a political commonwealth, or commonwealth by *institution;* and the former, a commonwealth by acquisition. And first, I shall speak of a commonwealth by institution.

## Chapter 18

### Of the Rights of Sovereigns by Institution

**The act of instituting a commonwealth, what.** A *commonwealth* is said to be *instituted*, when a *multitude* of men do agree, and *covenant, every one, with every one*, that to whatsoever *man*, or *assembly of men*, shall be given by the major part, the *right* to *present* the person of them all, that is to say, to be their *representative*; every one, as well he that *voted for it*, as he that *voted against it*, shall *authorize* all the actions and judgments, of that man, or assembly of men, in the same manner, as if they were his own, to the end, to live peaceably amongst themselves, and be protected against other men.

**The consequences to such institutions, are:** From this institution of a commonwealth are derived all the *rights,* and *faculties* of him, or them, on whom the sovereign power is conferred by the consent of the people assembled.

**1. The subjects cannot change the form of government.** First, because they covenant, it is to be understood, they are not obliged by former covenant to any thing repugnant hereunto. And consequently they that have already instituted a commonwealth, being thereby bound by covenant, to own the actions, and judgments of one, cannot lawfully make a new covenant, amongst themselves, to be obedient to any other, in any thing whatsoever, without his permission. And therefore, they that are subjects to a monarch, cannot without his leave cast off monarchy, and return to the confusion of a disunited multitude; nor transfer their person from him that beareth it, to another man, or other assembly of men: for they are bound, every man to every man, to own, and be reputed author of all, that he that already is their sovereign, shall do, and judge fit to be done: so that any one man dissenting, all the rest should break their covenant made to that man, which is injustice: and they have also every man given the sovereignty to him that beareth their person; and therefore if they depose him, they take from him that which is his own, and so again it is injustice. Besides, if he that attempteth to depose his sovereign, be killed, or punished by him for such attempt, he is author of his own punishment, as being by the institution, author of all his sovereign shall do: and because it is injustice for a man to do any thing, for which he may be punished by his own authority, he is also upon that title, unjust. And whereas some men have pretended for their disobedience to their sovereign, a new covenant, made, not with men, but with God; this also is unjust: for there is no covenant with God, but by mediation of somebody that representeth God's person; which none doth but

God's lieutenant, who hath the sovereignty under God. But this pretence of covenant with God, is so evident a lie, eve in the pretenders' own consciences, that it is not only an act of an unjust, but also of a vile, and unmanly disposition.

**2. Sovereign power cannot be forfeited.** Secondly, because the right of bearing the person of them all, is given to him they make sovereign, by covenant only of one to another, and not of him to any of them; there can happen no breach of covenant on the part of the sovereign; and consequently none of his subjects, by any pretence of forfeiture, can be freed from his subjection. That he which is made sovereign maketh no covenant with his subjects beforehand, is manifest; because either he must make it with the whole multitude, as one party to the covenant; or he must make a several covenant with every man. With the whole, as one party, it is impossible; because as yet they are not one person: and if he make so many several covenants as there be men, those covenants after he hath the sovereignty are void; because what act soever can be pretended by any one of them for breach thereof, is the act both of himself, and of all the rest, because done in the person, and by the right of every one of them in particular. Besides, if any one, or more of them, pretend a breach of the covenant made by the sovereign as his institution; and others, or one other of his subjects, or himself alone, pretend there was no such breach, there is in this case, no judge to decide the controversy; it returns therefore to the sword again; and every man recovereth the right of protecting himself by his own strength, contrary to the design they had in the institution. It is therefore in vain to grant sovereignty by way of precedent covenant. The opinion that any monarch receiveth his power by covenant, that is to say, on condition, proceedeth from want of understanding this easy truth, that covenants being but words and breath, have no force to oblige, contain, constrain, or protect any man, but what it has from the public sword; that is, from the untied hands of that man, or assembly of men that hath the sovereignty, and whose actions are avouched by them all, and performed by the strength of them all, in him united. But when an assembly of men is made sovereign; then no man imagineth any such covenant to have passed in the institution; for no man is so dull as to say, for example, the people of Rome made a covenant with the Romans, to hold the sovereignty on such or such conditions; which not performed, the Romans might lawfully depose the Roman people. That men see not the reason to be alike in a monarchy, and in a popular government, proceedeth from the ambition of some, that are kinder to the government of an assembly, whereof they may hope to participate, than of monarchy, which they despair to enjoy.

**3. No man can without injustice protest against the institution of the sovereign declared by the major part.** Thirdly, because the major part hath by consenting voices declared a sovereign; he that dissented must now consent with the rest; that is, be contented to avow all the actions he shall do, or else justly be destroyed by the rest. For if he voluntarily entered into the congregation of them that were assembled, he sufficiently declared thereby his will, and therefore tacitly covenanted, to stand to what the major part should ordain: and therefore if he refuse to stand thereto, or make protestation against any of their decrees, he does contrary to his covenant, and therefore unjustly. And whether he be of the congregation, or not; and whether his consent be asked, or not, he must either submit to their decrees, or be left in the condition of war he was in before; wherein he might without injustice be destroyed by any man whatsoever.

**4. The sovereign's actions cannot be justly accused by the subject.** Fourthly, because every subject is by this institution author of all the actions, and judgments of the sovereign instituted; it follows, that whatsoever he doth, it can be no injury to any of his subjects; nor ought he to be by any of them accused of injustice. For he that doth anything by authority from another, doth therein no injury to him by whose authority he acteth: but by this institution of a commonwealth, every particular man is author of all the sovereign doth: and consequently he that complaineth of injury from his sovereign, complaineth of that whereof he himself is author; and therefore ought not to accuse any man but himself, no nor himself of injury; because to do injury to one's self, is impossible. It is true that they that have sovereign power may commit iniquity; but not injustice, or injury in the proper signification.

**5. Whatsoever the sovereign doth is unpunishable by the subject.** Fifthly, and consequently to that which was said last, no man that hath sovereign power can justly be put to death, or otherwise in any manner by his subjects punished. For seeing every subject is author of the actions of his sovereign; he punisheth another for the actions committed by himself.

**6. The sovereign is judge of what is necessary for the peace and defence of his subjects.** And because the end of this institution, is the peace and defence of them all; and whosoever has right to the end, has right to the means; it belongeth of right, to whatsoever man, or assembly that hath the sovereignty, to be judge both of the means of peace and defence, and also of the hindrances, and disturbances of the same; and to do whatsoever he shall think necessary to be done, both beforehand, for the preserving of peace and security, by prevention of discord at home, and hostility from abroad; and, when peace and security are lost, for the recovery of the same. And therefore,

**And judge of what doctrines are fit to be taught them.** Sixthly, it is annexed to the sovereignty, to be judge of what opinions and doctrines are averse, and what conducing to peace; and consequently, on what occasions, how far, and what men are to be trusted withal, in speaking to multitudes of people; and who shall examine the doctrines of all books before they be published. For the actions of men proceed from their opinions; and in the well-governing of opinions, consisteth the well-governing of men's actions, in order to their peace, and concord. And though in matter of doctrine, nothing ought to be regarded but the truth; yet this is not repugnant to regulating the same by peace. For doctrine repugnant to peace, can no more be true, than peace and concord can be against the law of nature. It is true, that in a commonwealth, where by the negligence, or unskilfulness of governors, and teachers, false doctrines are by time generally received; the contrary truths may be generally offensive. Yet the most sudden, and rough busling in of a new truth, that can be, does never break the peace, but only sometimes awake the war. For those men that are so remissly governed, that they dare take up arms to defend, or introduce an opinion, are still in war; and their condition not peace, but only a cessation of arms for fear of one another; and they live, as it were, in the precincts of battle continually. It belongeth therefore to him that hath the sovereign power, to be judge, or constitute all judges of opinions and doctrines, as a thing necessary to peace; thereby to prevent discord and civil war.

**7. The right of making rules; whereby the subjects may every man know what is so his own, as no other subject can without injustice take it from him.** Seventhly, is annexed to the sovereignty, the whole power of prescribing the rules, whereby every man may know, what goods he may enjoy, and what actions he may do, without being molested by any of his fellow-subjects; and this is it men call *propriety*. For before constitution of sovereign power, as hath already been shown, all men had right to all things; which necessarily causeth war: and therefore this propriety, being necessary to peace, and depending on sovereign power, is the act of that power, in order to the public peace. These rules of propriety, or *meum* and *tuum*, and *of good, evil, lawful,* and *unlawful* in the actions of subjects, are the civil laws; that is to say, the laws of each commonwealth in particular; though the name of civil law be now restrained to the ancient civil laws of the city of Rome; which being the head of a great part of the world, her laws at that time were in these parts the civil law.

**8. To him also belongeth the right of judicature and decision of controversy.** Eighthly, is annexed to the sovereignty, the right of judicature; that is to say, of hearing and deciding all controversies, which may arise concerning law, either civil, or natural; or concerning fact. For without the decision of controversies, there is no protection of one subject, against the injuries of another; the laws concerning *meum* and *tuum* are in vain; and to every man remaineth, from the natural and necessary appetite of his own conservation, the right of protecting himself by his private strength, which is the condition of war, and contrary to the end for which every commonwealth is instituted.

**9. And of making war, and peace, as he shall think best.** Ninthly, is annexed to the sovereignty, the right of making war and peace with other nations, and commonwealths; that is to say, of judging when it is for the public good, and how great forces are to be assembled, armed, and paid for that end; and to levy money upon the subjects, to defray the expenses thereof. For the power by which the people are to be defended, consisteth in their armies; and the strength of an army, in the union of their strength under one command; which command the sovereign instituted, therefore hath; because the command of the *militia*, without other institution, maketh him that hath it sovereign. And therefore whosoever is made general of an army, he that hath the sovereign power is always generalissimo.

**10. And of choosing all counsellors and ministers, both of peace and war.** Tenthly, is annexed to the sovereignty, the choosing of all counsellors, ministers, magistrates, and officers, both in peace, and war. For seeing the sovereign is charged with the end, which is the common peace and defence, he is understood to have power to use such means, as he shall think most fit for his discharge.

**11. And of rewarding and punishing, and that (where no former law hath determined the measure of it) arbitrarily.** Eleventhly, to the sovereign is committed the power of rewarding with riches, or honour, and of punishing with corporal or pecuniary punishment, or with ignominy, every subject according to the law he hath formerly made; or if there be no law made, according as he shall judge most to conduce to the encouraging of men to serve the commonwealth, or deterring of them from doing disservice to the same.

**12. And of honour and order.** Lastly, considering what value men are naturally apt to set upon themselves; what respect they look for from others; and how little they value other men; from whence continually arise amongst them, emulation, quarrels, factions, and at last war, to the destroying of one another, and diminution of their strength against a common enemy; it is necessary that there be laws of honour, and a public rate of the worth of such men as have deserved, or are able to deserve well of the commonwealth; and that there be force in the hands of some or other, to put those laws in execution. But it hath already been shown, that not only the whole *militia*, or forces of the commonwealth; but also the judicature of all controversies, is annexed to the sovereignty. To the sovereign therefore it belongeth also to give titles of honour; and to appoint what order of place, and dignity, each man shall hold; and what signs of respect, in public or private meetings, they shall give to one another....

**Sovereign power not so hurtful as the want of it, and the hurt proceeds for the greatest part from not submitting readily to a less.** But a man may here object, that the condition of subjects is very miserable; as being obnoxious to the lusts, and other irregular passions of him, or them that have so unlimited a power in their hands. And commonly they that live under a monarch, think it the fault of monarchy; and they that live under the government of democracy, or other sovereign assembly, attribute all the inconvenience to that form of commonwealth; whereas the power in all forms, if they be perfect enough to protect them, is the same: not considering that the state of man can never be without some incommodity or other; and that the greatest, that in any form of government can possibly happen to the people in general, is scarce sensible in respect of the miseries, and horrible calamities, that accompany a civil war, or that dissolute condition of masterless men, without subjection to laws, and a coercive power to tie their hands from rapine and revenge: nor considering that the greatest pressure of sovereign governors, proceedeth not from any delight, or profit they can expect in the damage or weakening of their subjects, in whose vigour, consisteth their own strength and glory; but in the restiveness of themselves, that unwillingly contributing to their own defence, make it necessary for their governors to draw from them what they can in time of peace, that they may have means on any emergent occasion, or sudden need, to resist, or take advantage on their enemies. For all men are by nature provided of notable multiplying glasses, that is their passions and self-love, through which, every little payment appeareth a great grievance; but are destitute of those prospective glasses, namely moral and civil science, to see afar off the miseries that hang over them, and cannot without such payments be avoided.

## Chapter 21

### Of the Liberty of Subjects

**Liberty, what.** LIBERTY, or FREEDOM, signifieth, properly, the absence of opposition; by opposition, I mean external impediments of motion; and may be applied no less to irrational, and inanimate creatures, than to rational. For whatsoever is so tied, or environed, as it cannot move but within a certain space, which space is determined by the opposition of some external body, we say it hath not liberty to go further. And so of all living creatures, whilst they are imprisoned, or restrained, with walls, or chains; and of the water whilst it is kept in by banks, or vessels, that otherwise would spread itself into a larger space, we use to say, they are not at liberty, to move in such manner, as without those external impediments they would. But when the impediment of motion, is in the constitution of the thing itself, we use not to say; it wants the liberty; but the power to move; as when a stone lieth still, or a man is fastened to his bed by sickness.

**What it is to be free.** And according to this proper, and generally received meaning of the word, a FREEMAN, *is he that in those things, which by his strength and wit he is able to do, is not hindered to do what he has a will to.* But when the words *free,* and *liberty,* are applied to any thing but *bodies,* they are abused; for that which is not subject to motion, is not subject to impediment: and therefore, when it is said, for example, the way is free, no liberty of the way is signified, but of those that walk in it without stop. And when we say a gift is free, there is not meant any liberty of the gift, but of the giver, that was not bound by any law or covenant to give it. So when we *speak freely,* it is not the liberty of voice, or pronunciation, but of the man, whom no law hath obliged to speak otherwise than he did. Lastly, from the use of the word *free-will,* no liberty can be inferred of the will, desire, or inclination, but the liberty of the man; which consisteth in this, that he finds no stop, in doing what he has the will, desire, or inclination to do.

**Fear and liberty consistent.** Fear and liberty are consistent; as when a man throweth his goods into the sea for *fear* the ship should sink, he doth it nevertheless very willingly, and may refuse to do it if he will: it is therefore the action of one that was *free:* so a man sometimes pays his debt, only for *fear* of imprisonment, which because nobody hindered him from detaining, was the action of a man at *liberty.* And generally all actions which men do in commonwealths, for *fear* of the law, are actions, which the doers had *liberty* to omit.

**Liberty and necessity consistent.** *Liberty,* and *necessity* are consistent: as in the water, that hath not only *liberty,* but a *necessity* of descending by the channel; so likewise in the actions which men voluntarily do: which, because they proceed from their will, proceed from *liberty;* and yet, because every act of man's will, and every desire, and inclination proceedeth from some cause, and that from another cause, in a continual chain, whose first link is in the hand of God the first of all causes, proceed from *necessity.* So that to him that could see the connexion of those causes, the *necessity* of all men's voluntary actions, would appear manifest. And therefore God, that seeth, and disposeth all things, seeth also that the *liberty* of man in doing what he will, is accompanied with the *necessity* of doing that which God will, and no more, nor less. For though men may do many things, which God does not command, nor is therefore author of them; yet they can have no passion, nor appetite to any thing, of which appetite God's will is not the cause. And did not his will assure the *necessity* of man's will, and consequently of all that on man's will dependeth, the *liberty* of men would be a contradiction, and impediment to the omnipotence and *liberty* of God. And this shall suffice, as to the matter in hand, of that natural *liberty,* which only is properly called *liberty....*

**Liberty of subjects how to be measured.** To come now to the particulars of the true liberty of a subject; that is to say, what are the things, which though commanded by the sovereign, he may nevertheless, without injustice, refuse to do; we are to consider, what rights we pass away, when we make a commonwealth; or, which is all one, what liberty we deny ourselves, by owning all the actions, without exception, of the man, or assembly we make our sovereign. For in the act of our *submission,* consisteth both our *obligation,* and our *liberty;* which must therefore be inferred by arguments taken from thence; there being no obligation on any man, which ariseth not from some act of his own; for all men equally, are by nature free. And because such arguments, must either be drawn from the express words, *I authorize all his actions,* or from the intention of him that submitteth himself to his power, which intention is to be understood by the end for which he so submitteth; the obligation, and liberty of the subject, is to be derived, either from those words, or others equivalent; or else from the end of the institution of sovereignty, namely, the peace of the subjects within themselves, and their defence against a common enemy.

**Subjects have liberty to defend their own bodies, even against them that lawfully invade them.** First therefore, seeing sovereignty by institution, is by covenant of every one to every one; and sovereignty by acquisition, by covenants of the vanquished to the victor, or child to the parent; it is manifest, that every subject has liberty in all those things, the right whereof cannot by covenant be transferred. I have shewn before in the 14th chapter, that covenants, not to defend a man's own body, are void. Therefore,

**Are not bound to hurt themselves.** If the sovereign command a man, though justly condemned, to kill, wound, or maim himself; or not to resist those that assault him; or to abstain from the use of food, air, medicine, or any other thing, without which he cannot live; yet hath that man the liberty to disobey.

If a man be interrogated by the sovereign, or his authority, concerning a crime done by himself, he is not bound, without assurance of pardon, to confess it; because no man, as I have shown in the same chapter, can be obliged by covenant to accuse himself.

Again, the consent of a subject to sovereign power, is contained in these words, *I authorize, or take upon me, all his actions;* in which there is no restriction at all, of his own former natural liberty: for by allowing him to *kill me,* I am not bound to kill myself when he commands me. It is one thing to say, *kill me, or my fellow, if you please;* another thing to say, *I will kill myself, or my fellow.* It followeth therefore, that

No man is bound by these words themselves, either to kill himself, or any other man; and consequently, that the obligation a man may sometimes have, upon the command of the sovereign to execute any dangerous, or dishonourable office, dependeth not on the words of our submission; but on the intention, which is to be understood by the end thereof. When therefore our refusal to obey, frustrates the end for which the sovereignty was ordained; then there is no liberty to refuse: otherwise there is.

**Nor to warfare, unless they voluntarily undertake it.** Upon this ground, a man that is commanded as a soldier to fight against the enemy, though his sovereign have right enough to punish his refusal with death, may nevertheless in many cases refuse, without injustice; as when he substituteth a sufficient soldier in his place: for in this case he deserteth not the service of the commonwealth. And there is allowance to be made for natural timorousness; not only to women, of whom no such dangerous duty is expected, but also to men of feminine courage. When armies fight, there is on one side, or both, a running away; yet when they do it not out of treachery, but fear, they are not esteemed to do it unjustly, but dishonourably. For the same reason, to avoid battle, is not injustice, but cowardice. But he that enrolleth himself a soldier, or taketh imprest money, taketh away the excuse of a timorous nature; and is obliged, not only to go to the battle, but also not to run from it, without his captain's leave. And when the defence of the commonwealth, requireth at once the help of all that are able to bear arms, every one is obliged; because otherwise the institution of the commonwealth, which they have not the purpose, or courage to preserve, was in vain.

To resist the sword of the commonwealth, in defence of another man, guilty, or innocent, no man hath liberty; because such liberty takes away from the sovereign, the means of protecting us; and is therefore destructive of the very essence of government. But in case a great many men together, have already resisted the sovereign power unjustly, or committed some capital crime, for which every one of them expecteth death, whether have they not the liberty then to join together, and assist, and defend one another? Certainly they have: for they but defend their lives, which the guilty man may as well do, as the innocent. There was indeed injustice in the first breach of their duty; their bearing of arms subsequent to it, though it be to maintain what they have done, is no new unjust act. And if it be only to defend their persons, it is not unjust at all. But the offer of pardon taketh from them, to whom it is offered, the plea of self-defence, and maketh their perseverance in assisting, or defending the rest, unlawful.

**The greatest liberty of subjects, dependeth on the silence of the law.** As for other liberties, they depend on the silence of the law. In cases where the sovereign has prescribed no rule, there the subject hath the liberty to do, or forbear, according to his own discretion. And therefore such liberty is in some places more, and in some less; and in some times more, in other times less, according as they that have the sovereignty shall think most convenient. As for example, there was a time, when in England a man might enter into his own land, and dispossess such as wrongfully possessed it, by force. But in aftertimes, that liberty of forcible entry, was taken away by a statute made, by the king, in parliament. And in some places of the world, men have the liberty of many wives: in other places, such liberty is not allowed....

**In what cases subjects are absolved of their obedience to their sovereign.** The obligation of subjects to the sovereign, is understood to last as long, and no longer, than the power lasteth, by which he is able to protect them. For the right men have by nature to protect themselves, when none else can protect them, can by no covenant be relinquished. The sovereignty is the soul of the commonwealth; which once departed from the body, the members do no more receive their motion from it. The end of obedience is protection; which, wheresoever a man seeth it, either in his own, or in another's sword, nature applieth his obedience to it, and his endeavour to maintain it. And though sovereignty, in the intention of them that make it, be immortal; yet is it in its own nature, not only subject to violent death, by foreign war; but also through the ignorance, and passions of men, it hath in it, from the very institution, many seeds of a natural mortality, by intestine discord....

## Chapter 26

### Of Civil Laws

**Civil law, what.** By civil laws, I understand the laws, that men are therefore bound to observe, because they are members, not of this, or that commonwealth in particular, but of a commonwealth. For the knowledge of particular laws belongeth to them, that profess the study of the laws of their several countries; but the knowledge of civil law in general, to any man. The ancient law of Rome was called their *civil law,* from the word *civitas,* which signifies a commonwealth: and those countries, which having been under the Roman empire, and governed by that law, retain still such part thereof as they think fit, call that part the civil law, to distinguish it from the rest of their own civil laws. But that is not it I intend to speak of here; my design being not to show what is law here, and there; but what is law; as Plato, Aristotle, Cicero, and divers others have done, without taking upon them the profession of the study of the law.

And first it is manifest, that law in general, is not counsel, but command; nor a command of any man to any man; but only of him, whose command is addressed to one formerly obliged to obey him. And as for civil law, it addeth only the name of the person commanding, which is *persona civitatis,* the person of the commonwealth.

Which considered, I define civil law in this manner. CIVIL LAW, *is to every subject, those rules, which the commonwealth hath commanded him, by word, writing, or other sufficient sign of the will, to make use of, for the distinction of right, and wrong; that is to say, of what is contrary, and what is not contrary to the rule.*

In which definition, there is nothing that is not at first sight evident. For every man seeth, that some laws are addressed to all the subjects in general; some to particular provinces; some to particular vocations; and some to particular men; and are therefore laws, to every of those to whom the command is directed, and to none else. As also, that laws are the rules of just, and unjust; nothing being reputed unjust, that is not contrary to some law. Likewise, that none can make laws but the commonwealth; because our subjection is to the commonwealth only: and that commands, are to be signified by sufficient signs; because a man knows not otherwise how to obey them. And therefore, whatsoever can from this definition by necessary consequence be deduced, ought to be acknowledged for truth. Now I deduce from it this that followeth.

**The sovereign is legislator.** 1. The legislator in all commonwealths, is only the sovereign, be he one man, as in a monarchy, or one assembly of men, as in a democracy, or aristocracy. For the legislator is he that maketh the law. And the commonwealth only prescribes, and commandeth the observation of those rules, which we call law: therefore the commonwealth is the legislator. But the commonwealth is no person, nor has capacity to do any thing, but by the representative, that is, the sovereign; and therefore the sovereign is the sole legislator. For the same reason, none can abrogate a law made, but the sovereign; because a law is not abrogated, but by another law, that forbiddeth it to be put in execution.

**And not subject to civil law.** 2. The sovereign of a commonwealth, be it an assembly, or one man, is not subject to the civil laws. For having power to make, and repeal laws, he may when he pleaseth, free himself from that subjection, by repealing those laws that trouble him, and making of new; and consequently he was free before. For he is free, that can be free when he will: nor is it possible for any person to be bound to himself; because he that can bind, can release; and therefore he that is bound to himself only, is not bound.

**Use, a law not by virtue of time, but of the sovereign's consent.** 3. When long use obtaineth the authority of a law, it is not the length of time that maketh the authority, but the will of the sovereign signified by his silence, for silence is sometimes an argument of consent; and it is no longer law, than the sovereign shall be silent therein. And therefore if the sovereign shall have a question of right grounded, not upon his present will, but upon the laws formerly made; the length of time shall bring no prejudice to his right; but the question shall be judged by equity. For many unjust actions, and unjust sentences, go uncontrolled a longer time than any man can remember. And our lawyers account no customs law, but such as are reasonable, and that evil customs are to be abolished. But the judgment of what is reasonable, and of what is to be abolished, belongeth to him that maketh the law, which is the sovereign assembly, or monarch.

**The law of nature, and the civil law contain each other.** 4. The law of nature, and the civil law, contain each other, and are of equal extent. For the laws of nature, which consist in equity, justice, gratitude, and other moral virtues on these depending, in the condition of mere nature, as I have said before in the end of the fifteenth chapter, are not properly law, but qualities that dispose men to peace and obedience. When a commonwealth is once settled, then are they actually laws, and not before; as being then the commands of the commonwealth; and therefore also civil laws: for it is the sovereign power that obliges men to obey them. For in the differences of private men, to declare, what is equity, what is justice, and what is moral virtue, and to make them binding, there is need of the ordinances of sovereign power, and punishments to be ordained for such as shall break them; which ordinances are therefore part of the civil law. The law of nature therefore is a part of the civil law in all commonwealths of the world. Reciprocally also, the civil law is a part of the dictates of nature. For justice, that is to say, performance of covenant, and giving to every man his own, is a dictate of the law of nature. But every subject in a commonwealth, hath covenanted to obey the civil law; either one with another, as when they assemble to make a common representative, or with the representative itself one by one, when subdued by the sword they promise obedience, that they may receive life; and therefore obedience to the civil law is part also of the law of nature. Civil, and natural law are not different kinds, but different parts of law; whereof one part being written, is called civil, the other unwritten, natural. But the right of nature, that is, the natural liberty of man, may by the civil law be abridged, and restrained: nay, the end of making laws, is no other, but such restraint; without the which there cannot possibly be any peace. And law was brought into the world for nothing else, but to limit the natural liberty of particular men, in such manner, as they might not hurt, but assist one another, and join together against a common enemy....

## Chapter 29

### Of those Things that Weaken, or Tend to the Dissolution of a Commonwealth

**Dissolution of commonwealths proceedeth from their imperfect institution.** Though nothing can be immortal, which mortals make; yet, if men had the use of reason they pretend to, their commonwealth might be secured, at least from perishing by internal diseases. For by the nature of their institution, they are designed to live, as long as mankind, or as the laws of nature, or as justice itself, which gives them life. Therefore when they come to be dissolved, not by external violence, but intestine disorder, the fault is not in men, as they are the *matter;* but as they are the *makers,* and orderers of them. For men, as they become at last weary of irregular jostling, and hewing one another, and desire with all their hearts, to conform themselves into one firm and lasting edifice: so for want, both of the art of making fit laws, to square their actions by, and also of humility, and patience, to suffer the rude and cumbersome points of their present greatness to be taken off, they cannot without the help of a very able architect, be compiled into any other than a crazy building, such as hardly lasting out their own time, must assuredly fall upon the heads of their posterity.

Amongst the *infirmities* therefore of a commonwealth, I will reckon in the first place, those that arise from an imperfect institution, and resemble the diseases of a natural body, which proceed from a defectuous procreation.

**Want of absolute power.** Of which, this is one, *that a man to obtain a kingdom, is sometimes content with less power, than to the peace, and defence of the commonwealth is necessarily required.* From whence it cometh to pass, that when the exercise of the power laid by, is for the public safety to be resumed, it hath the resemblance of an unjust act; which disposeth great numbers of men, when occasion is presented, to rebel; in the same manner as the bodies of children, gotten by diseased parents, are subject either to untimely death, or to purge the ill quality, derived from their vicious conception, by breaking out into biles and scabs. And when kings deny themselves some such necessary power, it is not always, though sometimes, out of ignorance of what is necessary to the office they undertake; but many times out of a hope to recover the same again at their pleasure. Wherein they reason not well; because such as will hold them to their promises, shall be maintained against them by foreign commonwealths; who in order to the good of their own subjects let slip few occasions to *weaken* the estate of their neighbours. So was Thomas Becket, archbishop of Canterbury, supported against Henry the Second, by the Pope; the subjection of ecclesiastics to the commonwealth, having been dispensed with by William the Conqueror at his reception, when he took an oath, not to infringe the liberty of the church. And so were the barons, whose power was by William Rufus, to have their help in transferring the succession from his elder brother to himself, increased to a degree inconsistent with the sovereign power, maintained in their rebellion against king John, by the French....

**Private judgment of good and evil.** In the second place, I observe the *diseases* of a commonwealth, that proceed from the poison of seditious doctrines, whereof one is, *that every private man is judge of good and evil actions.* This is true in the condition of mere nature, where there are no civil laws; and also under civil government, in such cases as are not determined by the law. But otherwise, it is manifest, that the measure of good and evil actions, is the civil law; and the judge the legislator, who is always representative of the commonwealth. From this false doctrine, men are disposed to debate with themselves, and dispute the commands of the commonwealth; and afterwards to obey, or disobey them, as in their private judgments they shall think fit; whereby the commonwealth is distracted and *weakened.*

**Erroneous conscience.** Another doctrine repugnant to civil society, is, *that whatsoever a man does against his conscience, is sin;* and it dependeth on the presumption of making himself judge of good and evil. For a man's conscience, and his judgment is the same thing, and as the judgment, so also the conscience may be erroneous. Therefore, though he that is subject to no civil law, sinneth in all he does against his conscience, because he has no other rule to follow but his own reason; yet it is not so with him that lives in a commonwealth; because the law is the public conscience, by which he hath already undertaken to be guided. Otherwise in such diversity, as there is of private consciences, which are but private opinions, the commonwealth must needs be distracted, and no man dare to obey the sovereign power, further than it shall seem good in his own eyes.

**Pretence of inspiration.** It hath been also commonly taught, *that faith and sanctity, are not to be attained by study and reason, but by supernatural inspiration, or infusion.* Which granted, I see not why any man should render a reason of his faith; or why every Christian should not be also a prophet; or why any man should take the law of his country, rather than his own inspiration, for the rule of his action. And thus we fall again in the fault of taking upon us to judge of good and evil; or to make judges of it, such private men as pretend to be supernaturally inspired, to the dissolution of all civil government. Faith comes by hearing, and hearing by those accidents, which guide us into the presence of them that speak to us; which accidents are all contrived by God Almighty; and yet are not supernatural, but only, for the great number of them that concur to every effect, unobservable. Faith and sanctity, are indeed not very frequent; but yet they are not miracles, but brought to pass by education, discipline, correction, and other natural ways, by which God worketh them in his elect, at such times as he thinketh fit. And these three opinions, pernicious to peace and government, have in this part of the world, proceeded chiefly from the tongues, and pens of unlearned divines, who joining the words of Holy Scripture together, otherwise than is agreeable to reason, do what they can, to make men think, that sanctity and natural reason, cannot stand together.

**Subjecting the sovereign power to civil laws.** A fourth opinion, repugnant to the nature of a commonwealth, is this, *that he that hath the sovereign power is subject to the civil laws.* It is true, that sovereigns are all subject to the laws of nature; because such laws be divine, and cannot by any man, or commonwealth be abrogated. But to those laws which the sovereign himself, that is, which the commonwealth maketh, he is not subject. For to be subject to laws, is to be subject to the commonwealth, that is to the sovereign representative, that is to himself; which is not subjection, but freedom from the laws. Which error, because it setteth the laws above the sovereign, setteth also a judge above him, and a power to punish him; which is to make a new sovereign; and again for the same reason a third, to punish the second; and so continually without end, to the confusion, and dissolution of the commonwealth.

**Attributing of absolute propriety to subjects.** A fifth doctrine, that tendeth to the dissolution of a commonwealth, is, *that every private man has an absolute propriety in his goods; such, as excludeth the right of the sovereign.* Every man has indeed a propriety that excludes the right of every other subject: and he has it only from the sovereign power; without the protection whereof, every other man should have equal right to the same. But if the right of the sovereign also be excluded, he cannot perform the office they have put him into; which is, to defend them both from foreign enemies, and from the injuries of one another; and consequently there is no longer a commonwealth.

And if the propriety of subjects, exclude not the right of the sovereign representative to their goods; much less to their offices of judicature, or execution, in which they represent the sovereign himself.

**Dividing of the sovereign power.** There is a sixth doctrine, plainly, and directly against the essence of a commonwealth; and it is this, *that the sovereign power may be divided.* For what is it to divide the power of a commonwealth, but to dissolve it; for powers divided mutually destroy each other. And for these doctrines, men are chiefly beholding to some of those, that making profession of the laws, endeavour to make them depend upon their own learning, and not upon the legislative power....

**The opinion that there be more sovereigns than one in the commonwealth.**
As there have been doctors, that hold there be three souls in a man; so there be also that think there may be more souls, that is, more sovereigns, than one, in a commonwealth; and set up a *supremacy* against the *sovereignty; canons* against *laws;* and a *ghostly authority* against the *civil;* working on men's minds, with words and distinctions, that of themselves signify nothing, but betray by their obscurity; that there walketh, as some think, invisibly another kingdom, as it were a kingdom of fairies, in the dark. Now seeing it is manifest, that the civil power, and the power of the commonwealth is the same thing; and that supremacy, and the power of making canons, and granting facilities, implieth a commonwealth; it followeth, that where one is sovereign, another supreme; where one can make laws, and another make canons; there must needs be two commonwealths, of one and the same subjects; which is a kingdom divided in itself, and cannot stand. For notwithstanding the insignificant distinction of *temporal,* and *ghostly,* they are still two kingdoms, and every subject is subject to two masters. For seeing the *ghostly* power challengeth the right to declare what is sin, it challengeth by consequence to declare what is law, sin being nothing but the transgression of the law; and again, the civil power challenging to declare what is law, every subject must obey two masters, who both will have their commands be observed as law; which is impossible. Or, if it be but one kingdom, either the *civil,* which is the power of the commonwealth, must be subordinate to the *ghostly,* and then there is no sovereignty but the *ghostly;* or the *ghostly* must be subordinate to the *temporal,* and then there is no *supremacy* but the *temporal.* When therefore these two powers oppose one another, the commonwealth cannot but be in great danger of civil war and dissolution. For the *civil* authority being more visible, and standing in the clearer light of natural reason, cannot choose but draw to it in all times a very considerable part of the people: and the *spiritual,* though it stand in the darkness of School distinctions, and hard words, yet because the fear of darkness and ghosts, is greater than other fears, cannot want a party sufficient to trouble, and sometimes to destroy a commonwealth. And this is a disease which not unfitly may be compared to the epilepsy or falling sickness, which the Jews took to be one kind of possession by spirits, in the body natural. For as in this disease, there is an unnatural spirit, or wind in the head that obstructeth the roots of the nerves, and moving them violently, taketh away the motion which naturally they should have from the power of the soul in the brain, and thereby causeth violent, and irregular motions, which men call convulsions, in the parts; insomuch as he that is seized therewith, falleth down

sometimes into the water, and sometimes into the fire, as a man deprived of his senses; so also in the body politic, when the spiritual power, moveth the members of a commonwealth, by the terror of punishments, and hope of rewards, which are the nerves of it, otherwise than by the civil power, which is the soul of the commonwealth, they ought to be moved; and by strange, and hard words suffocates their understanding, it must needs thereby distract the people and either overwhelm the commonwealth with oppression, or cast it into the fire of a civil war.

**Mixed government.** Sometimes also in the merely civil government, there be more than one soul; as when the power of levying money, which is the nutritive faculty, has depended on a general assembly; the power of conduct and command, which is the motive faculty, on one man; and the power of making laws, which is the rational faculty, on the accidental consent, not only of those two, but also of a third; this endangereth the commonwealth, sometimes for want of consent to good laws: but most often for want of such nourishment, as is necessary to life, and motion. For although few perceive, that such government, is not government, but division of the commonwealth into three factions, and call it mixed monarchy; yet the truth is, that it is not one independent commonwealth, but three independent factions; nor one representative person, but three. In the kingdom of God, there may be three persons independent, without breach of unity in God that reigneth; but where men reign, that be subject to diversity of opinions, it cannot be so. And therefore if the king bear the person of the people, and the general assembly bear also the person of the people, and another assembly bear the person of a part of the people, they are not one person, nor one sovereign, but three persons, and three sovereigns.

To what disease in the natural body of man, I may exactly compare this irregularity of a commonwealth, I know not. But I have seen a man, that had another man growing out of his side, with a head, arms, breast, and stomach, of his own; if he had had another man growing out of his other side, the comparison might then have been exact....

## Chapter 31

### Of the Kingdom of God by Nature

... **The conclusion of the second part.** And thus far concerning the constitution, nature, and right of sovereigns, and concerning the duty of subjects, derived from the principles of natural reason. And now, considering how different this doctrine is, from the practice of the greatest part of the world, especially of these western parts, that have received their moral learning from Rome and Athens; and how much depth of moral philosophy is required, in them that have the administration of the sovereign power; I am at the point of believing this my labour, as useless, as the commonwealth of Plato. For he also is of opinion that it is impossible for the disorders of state, and change of governments by civil war, ever to be taken away, till sovereigns be philosophers. But when I consider again, that the science of natural justice, is the only science necessary for sovereigns and their principal ministers; and that they need not be charged with the sciences mathematical, as by Plato they are, farther than by good laws to encourage men to the study of them; and that neither Plato, nor any other philosopher hitherto, hath put into order, and sufficiently or probably proved all the theorems of moral doctrine, that men may learn thereby, both how to govern, and how to obey; I recover some hope, that one time or other, this writing of mine may fall into the hands of a sovereign, who will consider it himself, (for it is short, and I think clear,) without the help of any interested, or envious interpreter; and by the exercise of entire sovereignty, in protecting the public teaching of it, convert this truth of speculation, into the utility of practice.

[*There are two remaining parts of* The Leviathan: *The Third Part, Of a Christian Commonwealth; and The Fourth Part, Of the Kingdom of Darkness. These two parts account for almost half of the book. In the Third Part Hobbes is anxious to demonstrate that the Church's authority cannot be used to infringe the power of the state and that Christian doctrine, properly understood, is consistent with the teachings of* The Leviathan. *The Fourth Part contains a vigorous and scathing attack on any misinterpretations of scripture and theology which lead to an undermining of the position of the civil ruler. Neither conscience nor the Bible, Hobbes argues, can be "repugnant to Civill Society." Hobbes presents essentially an Erastian position on Church-State relations: that is, that the Church and religion are subservient to the civil authority in external matters.* —J.M.P.]

# JOHN LOCKE

*John Locke (1632-1704) was the son of a Puritan lawyer who fought for Parliament against King Charles I. Because of his father's role as a captain in Cromwell's forces, the local member of Parliament nominated the 15-year-old son to a place at the prestigious Westminster School in London. At the age of 20 Locke won a scholarship to Oxford. While there, his friendship with the chemist Robert Boyle and other scientists led him to an appreciation of the new science. He received his Master of Arts degree in 1658 and became for a short period a tutor in Greek. From 1661 to 1667 he pursued a diplomatic career. He then returned to Oxford in order to become a physician. A year later he obtained a post as secretary and physician to a powerful Whig, Lord Ashley, later Earl of Shaftesbury. For the rest of his life Locke was active in public affairs. Shaftesbury had plotted against the Stuarts, and in 1683 he had to flee to Holland. Locke quickly followed. After the Glorious Revolution in 1688, Locke returned to England. He held several governmental positions and continued to write until his death at the age of 72.*

*Locke wrote essays on theology, economics, education, and various public policy questions of his day. The chief works for understanding his political philosophy are* Two Treatises of Government *(1689),* An Essay Concerning Human Understanding *(1689),* Letter on Toleration *(1689), and* Essays on the Law of Nature *(1660). Locke, who was always cautious, did not publicly acknowledge authorship of* Two Treatises of Government. The First Treatise *was an attack on the divine right of Kings, as expounded in Sir Robert Filmer's* Patriarcha. *In* The Second Treatise *Locke justified the right of a people to change governments. Since* Two Treatises of Government *was published just after the Glorious Revolution, it was widely acclaimed. Locke became known as "the philosopher of the revolution," although there is ample evidence that they were written well before the revolution.*

— J.M.P.

# TWO TREATISES OF GOVERNMENT

## *The Second Treatise—An Essay Concerning the True Origin, Extent and End of Civil Government*

### ⇾ BOOK II ⇽
### *Chapter I*

**1.** It having been shown in the foregoing discourse

> That Adam had not either by natural right of fatherhood, or by positive donation from God, any such authority over his children, or dominion over the world as is pretended.

> That if he had, his heirs, yet, had no right to it.

> That if his heirs had, there being no law of Nature nor positive law of God that determines, which is the right heir in all cases that may arise, the right of succession, and consequently of bearing rule, could not have been certainly determined.

> That if even that had been determined, yet the knowledge of which is the eldest line of Adam's posterity, being so long since utterly lost, that in the races of mankind and families of the world, there remains not to one above another, the least pretence to be the eldest house, and to have the right of inheritance.

All these premises having, as I think, been clearly made out, it is impossible that the rulers now on Earth, should make any benefit, or derive any the least shadow of authority from that, which is held to be the fountain of all power, Adam's private dominion and paternal jurisdiction, so that, he that will not give just occasion, to think that all government in the world is the product only of force and violence, and that men live together by no other rules but that of beasts, where the strongest carries it, and so lay a foundation for perpetual disorder and mischief, tumult, sedition and rebellion, (things that the followers of that hypothesis so loudly cry out against) must of necessity find out another rise of government, another original of political power, and another way of designing and knowing the persons that have it, then what Sir Robert Filmer has taught us.

**2.** To this purpose, I think it may not be amiss, to set down what I take to be political power. That the power of a magistrate over a subject, may be distinguished from that of a father over his children, a master over his servant, a husband over his wife, and a lord over his slave. All which distinct powers happening sometimes together in the same man, if he be considered under these different relations, it may help us to distinguish these powers one from another, and show the difference between a ruler of a commonwealth, a father of a family, and a captain of a galley.

**3.** Political power then I take to be a right of making laws with penalties of death, and consequently all less penalties, for the regulating and preserving of property, and of employing the force of the community, in the execution of such laws, and in the defence of the commonwealth from foreign injury, and all this only for the public good.

## Chapter II

### Of the State of Nature

**4.** To understand political power right, and derive it from its original, we must consider what state all men are naturally in, and that is, a state of perfect freedom to order their actions, and dispose of their possessions, and persons as they think fit, within the bounds of the law of Nature, without asking leave, or depending upon the will of any other man.

A state also of equality, wherein all the power and jurisdiction is reciprocal, no one having more than another: there being nothing more evident, than that creatures of the same species and rank promiscuously born to all the same advantages of Nature, and the use of the same faculties, should also be equal one amongst another without subordination or subjection, unless the Lord and Master of them all, should by any manifest declaration of his will set one above another, and confer on him by an evident and clear appointment an undoubted right to dominion and sovereignty.

**5.** This equality of men by Nature, the judicious Hooker[1] looks upon as so evident in itself, and beyond all question, that he makes it the foundation of that

---

[1] [Richard Hooker (1554-1660), an Anglican thelogian, wrote the *Ecclesiastical Policy*, which presented a careful and sustained criticism of Puritanism and a moderate defence of the Anglican-Royalist tradition —J.M.P.]

obligation to mutual love amongst men, on which he builds the duties they owe one another, and from whence he derives the great maxims of justice and charity. His words are:

"The like natural inducement, has brought men to know that it is no less their duty, to love others than themselves, for seeing those things which are equal, must needs all have one measure; If I cannot but wish to receive good, even as much as every man's hands, as any man can wish unto his own soul, how should I look to have any part of my desire herein satisfied, unless my self be careful to satisfy the like desire, which is undoubtedly in other men, being of one and the same nature? to have any thing offered them repugnant to this desire, must needs in all respects grieve them as much as me, so that if I do harm, I must look to suffer, there being no reason that others should show greater measure of love to me, than they have by me, showed unto them; my desire therefore to be loved of my equals in nature, as much as possible may be, imposes upon me a natural duty of bearing to them, fully the like affection; From which relation of equality between ourselves and them, that are as ourselves, what several rules and canons, natural reason has drawn for direction of life, no man is ignorant." *Eccl. Pol. Lib. 1.*

**6.** But though this be a state of liberty, yet it is not a state of licence, though man in that state have an uncontrollable liberty, to dispose of his person or possessions, yet he has not liberty to destroy himself, or so much as any creature in his possession, but where some nobler use, than its bare preservation calls for it. The state of Nature has a law of Nature to govern it, which obliges every one: and reason, which is that law, teaches all mankind, who will but consult it, that being all equal and independent, no one ought to harm another in his life, health, liberty, or possessions. For men being all the workmanship of one Omnipotent, and infinitely wise Maker; all the servants of one Sovereign Master, sent into the world by his order and about his business; they are his property, whose workmanship they are, made to last during his, not one another's pleasure. And being furnished with like faculties, sharing all in one community of Nature, there cannot be supposed any such subordination among us, that may authorize us to destroy one another, as if we were made for one another's uses, as the inferior ranks of creatures are for ours. Every one as he is bound to preserve himself, and not to quit his station willfully; so by the like reason when his own preservation comes not in competition, ought he, as much as he can, to preserve the rest of mankind, and may not unless it be to do justice on an offender, take away, or impair the life, or what tends to the preservation of the life, liberty, health, limb or goods of another.

**7.** And that all men may be restrained from invading others' rights, and from doing hurt to one another, and the law of Nature be observed, which wills the peace and preservation of all mankind, the execution of the law of Nature is in that state, put into every man's hands, whereby every one has a right to punish the transgressors of that law to such a degree, as may hinder its violation. For the law of Nature would, as all other laws that concern men in this world, be in vain, if there were no body that in the state of Nature, had a power to execute that law, and thereby preserve the innocent and restrain offenders, and if any one in the state of Nature may punish another, for any evil he has done, every one may do so. For in that state of perfect equality, where naturally there is no superiority or jurisdiction of one, over another, what any may do in prosecution of that law, every one must needs have a right to do.

**8.** And thus in the state of Nature, one man comes by a power over another; but yet no absolute or arbitrary power, to use a criminal when he has got him in his hands, according to the passionate heats, or boundless extravagancy of his own will, but only to retribute to him, so far as calm reason and conscience dictates, what is proportionate to his transgression, which is so much as may serve for reparation and restraint. For these two are the only reasons, why one man may lawfully do harm to another, which is that we call punishment. In transgressing the law of Nature, the offender declares himself to live by another rule, than that of reason and common equity, which is that measure God has set to the actions of men, for their mutual security: and so he becomes dangerous to mankind, the tie, which is to secure them from injury and violence, being slighted and broken by him. Which being a trespass against the whole species, and the peace and safety of it, provided for by the law of Nature, every man upon this score, by the right he has to preserve mankind in general, may restrain, or where it is necessary, destroy things noxious to them, and so may bring such evil on any one, who has transgressed that law, as may make him repent the doing of it, and thereby deter him, and by his example others, from doing the like mischief. And in this case, and upon this ground, every man has a right to punish the offender, and be executioner of the law of Nature.

**14.** It is often asked as a mighty objection, Where are, or ever were, there any men in such a state of Nature? To which it may suffice as an answer at present; that since all princes and rulers of independent governments all through the world, are in a state of Nature, it is plain the world never was, nor ever will be, without numbers of men in that state. I have named all governors of independent communities, whether they are, or are not, in league with others: for it is not every compact that puts an end to the state of Nature between men, but only this one of agreeing together mutually to enter into one community, and make one body politic; other promises and compacts, men may make one with another, and yet still be in the state of Nature. The promises and bargains for truck, &c. between the two men in the desert island, mentioned by Garcilasso de la Vega, in his history of Peru, or between a Swiss and an Indian, in the woods of America, are binding to them, though they are perfectly in a state of Nature, in reference to one another. For truth and keeping of faith belongs to men, as men, and not as members of society.

**15.** To those that say, There were never any men in the state of Nature; I will not only oppose the authority of the judicious Hooker, *Eccl. Pol. Lib. I. Sect. 10.* where he says, "The laws which have been hitherto mentioned, i.e. the laws of Nature, do bind men, although they have never any settled fellowship, never any solemn agreement amongst themselves what to do or not to do, but for as much as we are not by ourselves sufficient to furnish ourselves with competent store of things, needful for such a life, as our Nature does desire, a life, fit for the dignity of man; therefore to supply those defects and imperfections which are in us, as living singly and solely by ourselves, we are naturally induced to seek communion and fellowship with others, this was the cause of men uniting themselves, at first in political societies." But I moreover affirm, that all men are naturally in that state, and remain so, till by their own consents they make themselves members of some political society; and I doubt not in the sequel of this discourse, to make it very clear.

## Chapter III

### Of the State of War

**16.** The state of war is a state of enmity and destruction; and therefore declaring by word or action, not a passionate and hasty, but a sedate settled design, upon another man's life, puts him in a state of war with him against whom he has declared such an intention, and so has exposed his life to the other's power to be taken away by him, or any one that joins with him in his defence, and espouses his quarrel: it being reasonable and just I should have a right to destroy that which threatens me with destruction. For by the fundamental law of Nature, man being to be preserved, as much as possible, when all cannot be preserved, the safety of the innocent is to be preferred; and one may destroy a man who makes war upon him, or has discovered an enmity to his being, for the same reason, that he may kill a wolf or a lion; because such men are not under the ties of the common law of reason, have no other rule, but that of force and violence, and so may be treated as beasts of prey, those dangerous and noxious creatures, that will be sure to destroy him, whenever he falls into their power.

**17.** And hence it is, that he who attempts to get another man into his absolute power, does thereby put himself into a state of war with him; it being to be understood as a declaration of a design upon his life. For I have reason to conclude, that he who would get me into his power without my consent, would use me as he pleased, when he had a fancy to it: for no body can desire to have me in his absolute power, unless it be to compel me by force to that, which is against the right of my freedom, i.e. make me a slave. To be free from such force is the only security of my preservation: and reason bids me look on him, as an enemy to my preservation, who would take away that freedom, which is the fence to it: so that he who makes an attempt to enslave me, thereby puts himself into a state of war with me. He that in the state of Nature, would take away the freedom, that belongs to any one in that state, must necessarily be supposed to have a design to take away every thing else, that freedom being the foundation of all the rest: as he that in the state of society, would take away the freedom belonging to those of that society or commonwealth, must be supposed to design to take away from them every thing else, and so be looked on as in a state of war.

**18.** This makes it lawful for a man to kill a thief, who had not in the least hurt him, nor declared any design upon his life, any farther than by the use of force, so to get him in his power, as to take away his money, or what he pleases from him: because using force, where he has no right, to get me into his power, let his pretence be what it will, I have no reason to suppose, that he, who would take away my liberty, would not when he had me in his power, take away everything else. And therefore it is lawful for me to treat him, as one who has put himself into a state of war with me, i.e. kill him if I can; for to that hazard does he justly expose himself, whoever introduces a state of war, and is aggressor in it.

**19.** And here we have the plain difference between the state of Nature, and the state of war, which however some men have confounded, are as far distant, as a state of peace, good will, mutual assistance, and preservation, and a state of enmity, malice, violence, and mutual destruction are one from another. Men living together according to reason, without a common superior on Earth, with authority to judge between them, is properly the state of Nature. But force, or a declared design of force upon the person of another, where there is no common superior on Earth to appeal to for relief, is the state of war: and it is the want of such an appeal gives a man the right of war even against an aggressor, though he be in society and a fellow subject. Thus a thief, whom I cannot harm but by appeal to the law, for having stolen all that I am worth, I may kill, when he sets on me to rob me, but of my horse or goat: because the law, which was made for my preservation, where it cannot interpose to secure my life from present force, which if lost, is capable of no reparation, permits me my own defence, and the right of war, a liberty to kill the aggressor, because the aggressor allows not time to appeal to our common judge, nor the decision of the law, for remedy in a case, where the mischief may be irreparable. Want of a common judge with authority, puts all men in a state of Nature; force without right, upon a man's person, makes a state of war, both where there is, and is not, a common judge.

**20.** But when the actual force is over, the state of war ceases between those that are in society, and are equally on both sides subjected to the fair determination of the law; because then there lies open the remedy of appeal for the past injury, and to prevent future harm: but where no such appeal is, as in the state of Nature, for want of positive laws, and judges with authority to appeal to, the state of war once begun, continues, with a right to the innocent party, to destroy the other whenever he can, until the aggressor offers peace, and desires reconciliation on such terms, as may repair any wrongs he has already done, and secure the innocent for the future: nay where an appeal to the law, and constituted judges lies open, but the remedy is denied by a manifest perverting of justice, and a barefaced wresting of the laws, to protect or indemnify the violence or injuries of some men, or party of men, there it is hard to imagine any thing but a state of war. For wherever violence is used, and injury done, though by hands appointed to administer justice, it is still violence and injury, however coloured with the name, pretences, or forms of law, the end whereof being to protect and redress the innocent, by an unbiased application of it, to all who are under it; wherever that is not *bona fide* done, war is made upon the sufferers, who having no appeal on Earth to right them, they are left to the only remedy in such cases, an appeal to heaven.

## Chapter IV

## Of Slavery

**22.** The natural liberty of man is to be free from any superior power on Earth, and not to be under the will or legislative authority of man, but to have only the law of Nature for his rule. The liberty of man, in society, is to be under no other legislative power, but that established, by consent, in the commonwealth, nor under the dominion of any will, or restraint of any law, but what the legislative shall enact, according to the trust put in it. Freedom then is not what Sir R. F. [Richard Filmer] tells us, *O.A. 55* [224]. A liberty for every one to do what he lists, to live as he pleases, and not to be tied by any laws: but freedom of men under government, is, to have a standing rule to live by, common to every one of that society, and made by the legislative power erected in it; a liberty to follow my own will in all things, where the rule prescribes not; and not to be subject to the inconstant, uncertain, unknown, arbitrary will of another man. As freedom of Nature is to be under no other restraint but the law of Nature.

**23.** This freedom from absolute, arbitrary power, is so necessary to, and closely joined with a man's preservation, that he cannot part with it, but by what forfeits his preservation and life together. For a man, not having the power of his own life, cannot, by compact, or his own consent, enslave himself to anyone, nor put himself under the absolute, arbitrary power of another, to take away his life, when he pleases. Nobody can give more power than he has himself; and he that cannot take away his own life, cannot give another power over it. Indeed having, by his fault, forfeited his own life, by some act that deserves death; he, to whom he has forfeited it, may (when he has him in his power) delay to take it, and make use of him to his own service, and he does him no injury by it. For, whenever he finds the hardship of his slavery out-weigh the value of his life, it is in his power, by resisting the will of his master, to draw on himself the death he desires.

**24.** This is the perfect condition of slavery, which is nothing else, but the state of war continued, between a lawful conqueror, and a captive. For, if once compact enter between them, and make an agreement for a limited power on the one side, and obedience on the other, the state of war and slavery ceases, as long as the compact endures. For, as has been said, no man can, by agreement, pass over to another that which he has not in himself, a power over his own life.

I confess, we find among the Jews, as well as other nations, that men did sell themselves; but, it is plain, this was only to drudgery, not to slavery. For, it is evident, the person sold was not under an absolute, arbitrary, despotic power. For the master could not have power to kill him, at any time, whom, at a certain time, he was obliged to let go free out of his service: and the master of such a servant was so far from having an arbitrary power over his life, that he could not, at pleasure, so much as maim him, but the loss of an eye, or tooth, set him free, *Exod.* XXI.

## Chapter V

## Of Property

**25.** Whether we consider natural reason, which tells us, that men, being once born, have a right to their preservation, and consequently to meat and drink, and such other things, as Nature affords for their subsistence: or revelation, which gives us an account of those grants God made of the world to Adam, and to Noah, and his sons, it is very clear, that God, as King David says, *Psal.* CXV, xvi. has given the Earth to the children of men, given it to mankind in common. But this being supposed, it seems to some a very great difficulty, how any one should ever come to have a property in anything: I will not content myself to answer, that if it be difficult to make out property, upon a supposition, that God gave the world to Adam and his posterity in common; it is impossible that any man, but one universal monarch, should have any property, upon a supposition, that God gave the world to Adam, and his heirs in succession, exclusive of all the rest of his posterity. But I shall endeavour to show, how men might come to have a property in several parts of that which God gave to mankind in common, and that without any express compact of all the commoners.

**26.** God, who has given the world to men in common, has also given them reason to make use of it, to the best advantage of life, and convenience. The Earth, and all that is therein, is given to men for the support and comfort of their being. And though all the fruits it naturally produces, and beasts it feeds, belong to mankind in common, as they are produced by the spontaneous hand of Nature; and nobody has originally a private dominion, exclusive of the rest of mankind, in any of them, as they are thus in their natural state: yet being given for the use of men, there must of necessity be a means to appropriate them some way or other before they can be of any use, or at all beneficial to any particular man. The fruit, or venison, which nourishes the wild Indian, who knows no inclosure, and is still a tenant in common, must be his, and so his, i.e. a part of him, that another can no longer have any right to it, before it can do him any good for the support of his life.

**27.** Though the Earth, and all inferior creatures be common to all men, yet every man has a property in his own person. This nobody has any right to but himself. The labour of his body, and the work of his hands, we may say, are properly his. Whatsoever then he removes out of the state that Nature has provided, and left it in, he has mixed his labour with, and joined to it something that is his own, and thereby makes it his property. It being by him removed from the common state Nature placed it in, has by his labour something annexed to it, that excludes the common right of other men. For this labour being the unquestionable property of the labourer, no man but he can have a right to what that is once joined to, at least where there is enough, and as good left in common for others.

**28.** He that is nourished by the acorns he picked up under an oak, or the apples he gathered from the trees in the wood, has certainly appropriated them to himself. Nobody can deny but the nourishment is his. I ask then, When did they begin to be his? When he digested? Or when he eat? Or when he boiled? Or when he brought them home? Or when he picked them up? And it is plain, if the first gathering made them not his, nothing else could. That labour put a distinction between them and common. That added something to them more than Nature, the common mother of all, had done; and so they became his private right. And will any one say he had no right to those acorns or apples he thus appropriated, because he had not the consent of all mankind to make them his? Was it a robbery thus to assume to himself what belonged to all in common? If such a consent as that was necessary, man had starved, notwithstanding the plenty God had given him. We see in commons, which remain so by compact, that it is the taking any part of what is common, and removing it out of the state Nature leaves it in, which begins the property; without which the common is of no use. And the taking of this or that part does not depend on the express consent of all the commoners. Thus the grass my horse has bit; the turfs my servant has cut; and the ore I have dug in any place where I have a right to them in common with others, become my property, without the assignation or consent of any body. The labour that was mine, removing them out of the common state they were in, has fixed my property in them.

**31.** It will perhaps be objected to this, that if gathering the acorns, or other fruits of the earth, &c. makes a right to them, then any one may ingross as much as he will. To which I answer, not so. The same law of Nature, that does by this means give us property, does also bound that property too. God has given us all things richly, *1 Tim.* vi. 17. is the voice of reason confirmed by inspiration. But how far has he given it us? To enjoy. As much as any one can make use of to any advantage of life before it spoils; so much he may by his labour fix a property in. Whatever is beyond this, is more than his share, and belongs to others. Nothing was made by God for man to spoil or destroy. And thus considering the plenty of natural provisions there was a long time in the world, and the few spenders, and to how small a part of that provision the industry of one man could extend itself, and ingross it to the prejudice of others; especially keeping within the bounds, set by reason of what might serve for his use; there could be then little room for quarrels or contentions about property so established.

**32.** But the chief matter of property being now not the fruits of the Earth, and the beasts that subsist on it, but the Earth itself; as that which takes in and carries with it all the rest: I think it is plain, that property in that too is acquired as the former. As much land as a man tills, plants, improves, cultivates, and can use the product of, so much is his property. He by his labour does, as it were, inclose it from the common. Nor will it invalidate his right to say, everybody else has an equal title to it; and therefore he cannot appropriate, he cannot inclose, without the consent of all his fellow commoners, all mankind. God, when he gave the world in common to all mankind, commanded man also to labour, and the penury of his condition required it of him. God and his reason commanded him to subdue the Earth, i.e. improve it for the benefit of life, and therein lay out something upon it that was his own, his labour. He that in obedience to this command of God, subdued, tilled and sowed any part of it, thereby annexed to it something that was his property, which another had no title to, nor could without injury take from him.

**33.** Nor was this appropriation of any parcel of land, by improving it, any prejudice to any other man, since there was still enough, and as good left; and more than the yet unprovided could use. So that in effect, there was never the less left for others because of his enclosure for himself. For he that leaves as much as another can make use of, does as good as take nothing at all. Nobody could think himself injured by the drinking of another man, though he took a good draught, who had a whole river of the same water left him to quench his thirst. And the case of land and water, where there is enough of both, is perfectly the same.

**37.** This is certain, that in the beginning, before the desire of having more than men needed, had altered the intrinsic value of things, which depends only on their usefulness to the life of man; or [men] had agreed, that a little piece of yellow metal, which would keep without wasting or decay, should be worth a great piece of flesh, or a whole heap of corn; though men had a right to appropriate, by their labour, each one to himself, as much of the things of Nature, as he could use: yet this could not be much, nor to the prejudice of others, where the same plenty was still left, to those who would use the same industry. To which let me add, that he who appropriates land to himself by his labour, does not lessen but increase the common stock of mankind. For the provisions serving to the support of humane life, produced by one acre of inclosed and cultivated land, are (to speak much within compass) ten times more, than those, which are yielded by an acre of Land, of an equal richness, lying waste in common. And therefore he, that incloses land and has a greater plenty of the conveniencies of life from ten acres, than he could have from an hundred left to Nature, may truly be said, to give ninety acres to mankind. For his labour now supplies him with provisions out of ten acres, which were but the product of an hundred lying in common. I have here rated the improved land very low in making its product but as ten to one, when it is much nearer an hundred to one. For I ask whether in the wild woods and uncultivated waste of America left to Nature, without any improvement, tillage or husbandry, a thousand acres will yield the needy and wretched inhabitants as many conveniencies of life as ten acres of equally fertile land do in Devonshire where they are well cultivated?

Before the appropriation of land, he who gathered as much of the wild fruit, killed, caught, or tamed, as many of the beasts as he could; he that so employed his pains about any of the spontaneous products of Nature, as any way to alter them, from the state which Nature put them in, by placing any of his labour on them, did thereby acquire a property in them: but if they perished, in his possession, without their due use; if the fruits rotted, or the venison putrefied, before he could spend it, he offended against the common law of Nature, and was liable to be punished; he invaded his neighbour's share, for he had no right, further than his use called for any of them, and they might serve to afford him conveniencies of life.

**38.** The same measures governed the possession of land too: whatsoever he tilled and reaped, laid up and made use of, before it spoiled, that was his peculiar right; whatsoever he enclosed, and could feed, and make use of, the cattle and produce was also his. But if either the grass of his inclosure rotted on the ground, or the fruits of his planting perished without gathering, and laying up, this part of the Earth, notwithstanding his inclosure, was still to be looked on as waste, and might be the possession of any other. Thus, at the beginning, Cain might take as much ground as he could till, and make it his own land, and yet leave enough to Abel's sheep to feed on; a few acres would serve for both their possessions. But as families increased, and industry enlarged their stocks, their possessions enlarged with the need of them; but yet it was commonly without any fixed property in the ground they made use of, till they incorporated, settled themselves together, and built cities, and then, by consent, they came in time, to set out the bounds of their distinct territories, and agree on limits between them and their neighbours, and by laws within themselves, settled the properties of those of the same society. For we see, that in that part of the world which was first inhabited, and therefore like to be best peopled, even as low down as Abraham's time, they wandered with their flocks, and their herds, which was their substance, freely up and down; and this Abraham did, in a country where he was a stranger. Whence it is plain, that at least, a great part of the land lay in common; that the inhabitants valued it not, nor claimed property in any more than they made use of. But when there was not room enough in the same place, for their herds to feed together, they, by consent, as Abraham and Lot did, *Gen.* xiii. 5. separated and enlarged their pasture, where it best liked them. And for the same reason Esau went from his father, and his brother, and planted in Mount Seir, *Gen.* xxxvi. 6.

**39.** And thus, without supposing any private dominion, and property in Adam, over all the world, exclusive of all other men, which can no way be proved, nor any one's property be made out from it; but supposing the world given as it was to the children of men in common, we see how labour could make men distinct titles to several parcels of it, for their private uses; wherein there could be no doubt of right, no room for quarrel.

**40.** Nor is it so strange, as perhaps before consideration it may appear, that the property of labour should be able to over-balance the community of land. For it is labour indeed that puts the difference of value on everything; and let any one consider, what the difference is between an acre of land planted with tobacco, or sugar, sown with wheat or barley; and an acre of the same land lying in common, without any husbandry upon it, and he will find, that the improvement of labour makes the far greater part of the value. I think it will be but a very modest computation to say, that of the products of the Earth useful to the life of man 9/10 are the effects of labour: nay, if we will rightly estimate things as they come to our use, and cast up the several expenses about them, what in them is purely owing to Nature, and what to labour, we shall find, that in most of them 99/100 are wholly to be put on the account of labour.

**41.** There cannot be a clearer demonstration of any thing, than several nations of the Americans are of this, who are rich in land, and poor in all the comforts of life; whom Nature having furnished as liberally as any other people, with the materials of plenty, i.e. a fruitful soil, apt to produce in abundance, what might serve for food, raiment, and delight; yet for want of improving it by labour, have not one hundredth part of the conveniencies we enjoy: and a king of a large fruitful territory there feeds, lodges, and is clad worse than a day labourer in England.

**42.** To make this a little clearer, let us but trace some of the ordinary provisions of life, through their several progresses, before they come to our use, and see how much they receive of their value from humane industry. Bread, wine and cloth, are things of daily use, and great plenty, yet notwithstanding, acorns, water, and leaves, or skins, must be our bread, drink and clothing, did not labour furnish us with these more useful commodities? For whatever bread is more worth than acorns, wine than water, and cloth or silk than leaves, skins, or moss, that is wholly owing to labour and industry. The one of these being the food and raiment which unassisted Nature furnishes us with; the other provisions which our industry and pains prepare for us, which how much they exceed the other in value, when any one has computed, he will then see, how much labour makes the far greatest part of the value of things, we enjoy in this world: and the ground which produces the materials, is scarce to be reckoned in, as any, or at most, but a very small, part of it; so little, that even amongst us, land that is left wholly to Nature, that has no improvement of pasturage, tillage, or planting, is called, as indeed it is, waste; and we shall find the benefit of it amount to little more than nothing. This shows, how much numbers of men are to be preferred to largesse of dominions, and that the increase of lands and the right employing of them is the great art of government. And that prince who shall be so wise and godlike as by established laws of liberty to secure protection and encouragement to the honest industry of mankind against the oppression of power and narrowness of party will quickly be too hard for his neighbours. But this bye the bye. To return to the argument in hand.

**43.** An acre of land that bears here twenty bushels of wheat, and another in America, which, with the same husbandry, would do the like, are without doubt, of the same natural, intrinsic value. But yet the benefit mankind receives from the one, in a year, is worth £5 and from the other possibly not worth a penny, if all the profit an Indian received from it were to be valued, and sold here; at least, I may truly say, not 1/1000. It is labour then which puts the greatest part of value upon land, without which it would scarcely be worth anything: it is to that we owe the greatest part of all its useful products: for all that the straw, bran, bread, of that acre of wheat, is more worth than the product of an acre of as good land, which lies waste, is all the effect of labour. For it is not barely the plough-man's pains, the reaper's and thresher's toil, and the baker's sweat, is to be counted into the bread we eat; the labour of those who broke the oxen, who dug and wrought the iron and stones, who felled and framed the timber employed about the plough, mill, oven, or any other utensils, which are a vast number, requisite to this corn, from its being seed to be sown to its being made bread, must all be charged on the account of labour, and received as an effect of that: Nature and the Earth furnished only the almost worthless materials, as in themselves. It would be a strange catalogue of things, that industry provided and made use of, about every loaf of bread, before it came to our use, if we could trace them; iron, wood, leather, bark, timber, stone, bricks, coals, lime, cloth, dying-drugs, pitch, tar, masts, ropes, and all the materials made use of in the ship, that brought any of the commodities made use of by any of the workmen, to any part of the work, all which, it would be almost impossible, at least too long, to reckon up.

**44.** From all which it is evident, that though the things of Nature are given in common, yet man (by being master of himself, and proprietor of his own person, and the actions or labour of it) had still in himself the great foundation of property; and that which made up the great part of what he applied to the support or comfort of his being, when invention and arts had improved the conveniencies of life, was perfectly his own, and did not belong in common to others.

**46.** The greatest part of things really useful to the life of man, and such as the necessity of subsisting made the first commoners of the world look after, as it does the Americans now, are generally things of short duration; such as, if they are not consumed by use, will decay and perish of themselves: gold, silver, and diamonds, are things, that fancy or agreement has put the value on, more than real use, and the necessary support of life. Now of those good things which Nature has provided in common, every one had a right (as has been said) to as much as he could use, and had a property in all that he could affect with his labour: all that his industry could extend to, to alter from the state Nature had put it in, was his. He that gathered a hundred bushels of acorns or apples, had thereby a property in them; they were his goods as soon as gathered. He was only to look that he used them before they spoiled; else he took more than his share, and robbed others. And indeed it was a foolish thing, as well as dishonest, to hoard up more than he could make use of. If he gave away a part to any body else, so that it perished not uselessly in his possession, these he also made use of. And if he also bartered away plums that would have rotted in a week, for nuts that would last good for his eating a whole year, he did no injury; he wasted not the common stock; destroyed no part of the portion of goods that belonged to others, so long as nothing perished uselessly in his hands. Again, if he would give us nuts for a piece of metal, pleased with its colour; or exchanged his sheep for shells, or wool for a sparkling pebble or a diamond, and keep those by him all his life, he invaded not the right of others, he might heap up as much of these durable things as he pleased; the exceeding of the bounds of his just property not lying in the largeness of his possession, but the perishing of any thing uselessly in it.

47. And thus came in the use of money, some lasting thing that men might keep without spoiling, and that by mutual consent men would take in exchange for the truly useful, but perishable supports of life.

48. And as different degrees of industry were apt to give men possessions in different proportions, so this invention of money gave them the opportunity to continue to enlarge them. For supposing an island, separated from all possible commerce with the rest of the world, wherein there were but a hundred families, but there were sheep, horses and cows, with other useful animals, wholesome fruits, and land enough for corn for a hundred thousand times as many, but nothing in the island, either because of its commonness, or perishableness, fit to supply the place of money: what reason could any one have there to enlarge his possessions beyond the use of his family, and a plentiful supply to its consumption, either in what their own industry produced, or they could barter for like perishable, useful commodities, with others? Where there is not something both lasting and scarce, and so valuable to be hoarded up, there men will not be apt to enlarge

their possessions of land, were it never so rich, never so free for them to take. For I ask, what would a man value ten thousand, or an hundred thousand acres of excellent land, ready cultivated, and well stocked too with cattle, in the middle of the in-land parts of America, where he had no hopes of commerce with other parts of the world, to draw money to him by the sale of the product? It would not be worth the inclosing, and we should see him give up again to the wild common of Nature, whatever was more than would supply the conveniencies of life to be had there for him and his family.

**49.** Thus in the beginning all the world was America, and more so than that is now; for no such thing as money was anywhere known. Find out something that has the use and value of money amongst his neighbours, you shall see the man will begin presently to enlarge his possessions.

**50.** But since gold and silver, being little useful to the life of man in proportion to food, raiment, and carriage, has its value only from the consent of men, whereof labour yet makes, in great part, the measure, it is plain, that men have agreed to disproportionate and unequal possession of the Earth, they having by a tacit and voluntary consent found out a way, how a man may fairly possess more land than he himself can use the product of, by receiving in exchange for the surplus, gold and silver, which may be hoarded up without injury to any one, those metals not spoiling or decaying in the hands of the possessor. This partage of things, in an inequality of private possessions, men have made practicable out of the bounds of society, and without compact, only by putting a value on gold and silver and tacitly agreeing in the use of money. For in governments the laws regulate the right of property, and the possession of land is determined by positive constitutions.

**51.** And thus, I think, it is very easy to conceive without any difficulty, how labour could at first begin a title of property in the common things of Nature, and how the spending it upon our uses bounded it. So that there could then be no reason of quarrelling about title, nor any doubt about the largeness of possession it gave. Right and convenience went together; for as a man had a right to all he could employ his labour upon, so he had no temptation to labour for more than he could make use of. This left no room for controversy about the title, nor for encroachment on the right of others; what portion a man carved to himself, was easily seen; and it was useless as well as dishonest to carve himself too much, or take more than he needed.

*Chapter VI*

*Of Paternal Power*

**54.** Though I have said above, Chapter II, that all men by Nature are equal, I cannot be supposed to understand all sorts of equality: age or virtue may give men a just precedence: excellency of parts and merit may place others above the common level: birth may subject some, and alliance or benefits others, to pay an observance to those to whom Nature, gratitude or other respects may have made it due; and yet all this consists with the equality, which all men are in, in respect of jurisdiction or dominion one over another, which was the equality I there spoke of, as proper to the business in hand, being that equal right that every man has, to his natural freedom, without being subjected to the will or authority of any other man.

**55.** Children, I confess are not born in this full state of equality, though they are born to it. Their parents have a sort of rule and jurisdiction over them when they come into the world, and for some time after, but it is but a temporary one. The bonds of this subjection are like the swaddling cloths they are wrapped up in, and supported by, in the weakness of their infancy. Age and reason as they grow up, loosen them till at length they drop quite off, and leave a man at his own free disposal.

**56.** Adam was created a perfect man, his body and mind in full possession of their strength and reason, and so was capable from the first instant of his being to provide for his own support and preservation, and govern his actions according to the dictates of the law of reason which God had implanted in him. From him the world is peopled with his descendants, who are all born infants, weak and helpless, without knowledge or understanding. But his off-spring having another way of entrance into improvement of growth and age has removed them, Adam and Eve, and after them all parents were by the law of Nature, under an obligation to preserve, nourish, and educate the children, they had begotten, not as their own workmanship, but the workmanship of their own Maker, the Almighty, to whom they were to be accountable for them.

**57.** The law that was to govern Adam, was the same that was to govern all his posterity, the law of reason. But this off-spring having another way of entrance into the world, different from him, by a natural birth, that produced them ignorant and without the use of reason, they were not presently under that law: for nobody can be under a law, which is not promulgated to him; and this law being promulgated or made known by reason only, he that is not come to the use of his reason cannot be said to be under this law; Adam's children being not presently as soon as born, under this law of reason were not presently free. For law, in its true notion, is not so much the limitation as the direction of a free and intelligent agent to his proper interest, and prescribes no farther than is for the general good of those under that law. Could they be happier without it, the law, as an useless thing would of itself vanish; and that ill deserves the name of confinement which hedges us in only from bogs and precipices. So that, however it may be mistaken, the end of law is not to abolish or restrain, but to preserve and enlarge freedom: for in all the states of created beings capable of laws, where there is no law, there is no freedom. For liberty is to be free from restraint and violence from others which cannot be, where there is no law: but freedom is not, as we are told, a liberty for every man to do what he lists: (for who could be free, when every other man's humour might domineer over him?) but a liberty to dispose, and order, as he lists, his person, actions, possessions, and his whole property, within the allowance of those laws under which he is; and therein not to be subject to the arbitrary will of another, but freely follow his own.

**58.** The power, then, that parents have over their children, arises from that duty which is incumbent on them, to take care of their off-spring, during the imperfect state of childhood. To inform the mind, and govern the actions of their yet ignorant nonage, till reason shall take its place, and ease them of that trouble, is what the children want, and the parents are bound to. For God having given man an understanding to direct his actions, has allowed him a freedom of will, and liberty of acting, as properly belonging thereunto, within the bounds of that law he is under. But whilst he is in an estate, wherein he has not understanding of his own to direct his will, he is not to have any will of his own to follow: he that understands for him, must will for him too; he must prescribe to his will, and regulate his actions; but when he comes to the estate that made his father a freeman, the son is a freeman too.

**59.** This holds in all the laws a man is under, whether natural or civil. Is a man under the law of Nature? What made him free of that law? What gave him a free disposing of his property according to his own will, within the compass of that law? I answer; state of maturity wherein he might be supposed capable to know that law, that so he might keep his actions within the bounds of it. When he has acquired that state, he is presumed to know how far that law is to be his guide, and how far he may make use of his freedom, and so comes to have it; till then, somebody else must guide him, who is presumed to know how far the law allows a liberty. If such a state of reason, such an age of discretion made him free, the same shall make his son free too. Is a man under the law of England? What made him free of that law? That is, to have the liberty to dispose of his actions and possessions according to his own will, within the permission of that law? A capacity of knowing that law. Which is supposed by that law, at the age of one and twenty years, and in some cases sooner. If this made the father free, it shall make the son free too. Till then we see the law allows the son to have no will, but he is to be guided by the will of his father or guardian, who is to understand for him. And if the father die, and fail to substitute a deputy in this trust, if he has not provided a tutor to govern his son during his minority, during his want of understanding, the law takes care to do it; some other must govern him, and be a will to him, till he has attained to a state of freedom, and his understanding be fit to take the government of his will. But after that, the father and son are equally free as much as tutor and pupil after nonage; equally subjects of the same law together, without any dominion left in the father over the life, liberty, or estate of his son, whether they be only in the state and under the law of Nature, or under the positive laws of an established government.

**60.** But if through defects that may happen out of the ordinary course of Nature, any one comes not to such a degree of reason, wherein he might be supposed capable of knowing the law, and so living within the rules of it, he is never capable of being a free man, he is never let loose to the disposal of his own will (because he knows no bounds to it, has not understanding, its proper guide) but is continued under the tuition and government of others, all the time his own understanding is incapable of that charge. And so lunatics and idiots are never set free from the government of their parents....

**61.** Thus we are born free, as we are born rational; not that we have actually the exercise of either: age that brings one, brings with it the other too. And thus we see how natural freedom and subjection to parents may consist together, and are both founded on the same principle. A child is free by his father's title, by his father's understanding, which is to govern him, till he has it of his own....

**63.** The freedom then of man and liberty of acting according to his own will, is grounded on his having reason, which is able to instruct him in that law he is to govern himself by, and make him know how far he is left to the freedom of his own will. To turn him loose to an unrestrained liberty, before he has reason to guide him, is not allowing him the privilege of his nature, to be free; but to thrust him out amongst brutes, and abandon him to a state as wretched, and as much beneath that of a man, as theirs. This is that which puts the authority into the parents' hands to govern the minority of their children. God has made it their business to employ this care on their off-spring, and has placed in them suitable inclinations of tenderness and concern to temper this power, to apply it as his wisdom designed it, to the children's good, as long as they should need to be under it.

## Chapter VII

### Of Political or Civil Society

**77.** God having made man such a creature, that, in his own judgment, it was not good for him to be alone, put him under strong obligations of necessity, convenience, and inclination to drive him into society, as well as fitted him with understanding and language to continue and enjoy it. The first society was between man and wife, which gave beginning to that between parents and children; to which, in time, that between master and servant came to be added: and though all these might, and commonly did meet together, and make up but one family, wherein the master or mistress of it had some sort of rule proper to a family; each of these, or all together came short of political society, as we shall see, if we consider the different ends, ties, and bounds of each of these.

**85.** Master and servant are names as old as history, but given to those of far different condition; for a freeman makes himself a servant to another, by selling him for a certain time, the service he undertakes to do, in exchange for wages he is to receive: and though this commonly puts him into the family of his master, and under the ordinary discipline thereof; yet it gives the master but a temporary power over him, and no greater, than what is contained in the contract between them. But there is another sort of servants, which by a peculiar name we call slaves, who being captives taken in a just war, are by the right of Nature subjected to the absolute dominion and arbitrary power of their masters. These men having, as I say, forfeited their lives, and with it their liberties, and lost their estates; and being in the state of slavery, not capable of any property, cannot in that state be considered as any part of civil society; the chief end whereof is the preservation of property.

**87.** Man being born, as has been proved, with a title to perfect freedom, and an uncontrolled enjoyment of all the rights and privileges of the law of Nature, equally with any other man, or number of men in the world, has by nature a power, not only to preserve his property, that is, his life, liberty and estate, against the injuries and attempts of other men; but to judge of, and punish the breaches of that law in others, as he is persuaded the offence deserves, even with death itself, in crimes where the heinousness of the fact, in his opinion, requires it. But because no political society can be, nor subsist without having in itself the power to preserve the property, and in order thereunto punish the offences of all those of that society; there, and there only is political society, where every one of the members has quitted this natural power, resigned it up into the hands of the community in all cases that exclude him not from appealing for protection to the law established by it. And thus all private judgment of every particular member being excluded, the community comes to be umpire, by settled standing rules, indifferent, and the same to all parties; and by men having authority from the community, for the execution of those rules, decides all the differences that may happen between any members of that society, concerning any matter of right; and punishes those offences, which any member has committed against the society, with such penalties as the law has established: whereby it is easier to discern who are, and who are not, in political society together. Those who are united into one body, and have a common established law and judicature to appeal to, with authority to decide controversies between them, and punish offenders, are in civil society one with another: but those who have no such common appeal, I mean on Earth, are still in the state of Nature, each being, where there is no other, judge for himself, and executioner; which is, as I have before shown it, the perfect state of Nature.

**88.** And thus the commonwealth comes by a power to set down, what punishment shall belong to the several transgressions which they think worthy of it, committed amongst the members of that society—which is the power of making laws—as well as it has the power to punish any injury done unto any of its members, by any one that is not of it—which is the power of war and peace—and all this for the preservation of the property of all the members of that society, as far as is possible. But though every man who has entered into civil society, and is become a member of any commonwealth, has thereby quitted his power to punish offences against the law of Nature, in prosecution of his own private judgment; yet with the judgment of offences which he has given up to the legislative in all cases, where he can appeal to the magistrate, he has given a right to the commonwealth to employ his force, for the execution of the judgments of the commonwealth, whenever he shall be called to it; which indeed are his own judgments, they being made by himself, or his representative. And herein we have the original of the legislative and executive power of civil society, which is to judge by standing laws how far offences are to be punished, when committed within the commonwealth; and also to determine by occasional judgments founded on the present circumstances of the fact, how far injuries from without are to be vindicated, and in both these to employ all the force of all the members when there shall be need.

89. Wherever therefore any number of men are so united into one society, as to quit everyone his executive power of the law of Nature, and to resign it to the public, there and there only is a political, or civil society. And this is done wherever any number of men, in the state of Nature, enter into society to make one people, one body politic under one supreme government, or else when anyone joins himself to, and incorporates with any government already made. For hereby he authorizes the society, or which is all one, the legislative thereof to make laws for him as the public good of the society shall require; to the execution whereof, his own assistance (as to his own decrees) is due. And this puts men out of a state of Nature into that of a commonwealth, by setting up a judge on Earth, with authority to determine all the controversies, and redress the injuries, that may happen to any member of the commonwealth; which judge is the legislative, or magistrates appointed by it. And wherever there are any number of men, however associated, that have no such decisive power to appeal to, there they are still in the state of Nature.

90. Hence it is evident, that absolute monarchy, which by some men is counted the only government in the world, is indeed inconsistent with civil society, and so can be no form of civil government at all. For the end of civil society, being to avoid, and remedy those inconveniencies of the state of Nature, which necessarily follow from every man's being judge in his own case, by setting up a known authority, to which everyone of that society may appeal upon any injury received, or controversy that may arise, and which everyone of the society ought to obey; wherever any persons are, who have not such an authority to appeal to, for the decision of any difference between them, there those persons are still in the state of Nature. And so is every absolute prince in respect of those who are under his dominion.

91. For he being supposed to have all, both legislative and executive power in himself alone, there is no judge to be found, no appeal lies open to anyone, who may fairly, and indifferently, and with authority decide, and from whose decision relief and redress may be expected of any injury or inconvenience, that may

be suffered from the prince or by his order: so that such a man, however entitled, czar, or grand signior, or how you please, is as much in the state of Nature, with all under his dominion, as he is with the rest of mankind. For wherever any two are, who have no standing rule, and common judge to appeal to on Earth for the determination of controversies of right between them, there they are still in the state of Nature, and under all the inconveniencies of it, with only this woeful difference to the subject, or rather slave of an absolute prince: that whereas, in the ordinary state of Nature, he has a liberty to judge of his right, and according to the best of his power, to maintain it; now whenever his property is invaded by the will and order of his monarch, he has not only no appeal, as those in society ought to have, but as if he were degraded from the common state of rational creatures, is denied a liberty to judge of, or to defend his right, and so is exposed to all the misery and inconveniencies that a man can fear from one, who being in the unrestrained state of Nature, is yet corrupted with flattery, and armed with power.

## Chapter VIII

## Of the Beginning of Political Societies

**95.** Men being, as has been said, by Nature, all free, equal and independent, no one can be put out of this estate, and subjected to the political power of another, without his own consent. The only way whereby any one divests himself of his natural liberty, and puts on the bonds of civil society is by agreeing with other men to join and unite into a community, for their comfortable, safe, and peaceable living one amongst another, in a secure enjoyment of their properties, and a greater security against any that are not of it. This any number of men may do, because it injures not the freedom of the rest; they are left as they were in the liberty of the state of Nature. When any number of men have so consented to make one community or government, they are thereby presently incorporated, and make one body politic, wherein the majority have a right to act and conclude the rest.

**96.** For when any number of men have, by the consent of every individual, made a community, they have thereby made that community one body, with a power to act as one body, which is only by the will and determination of the majority. For that which acts any community, being only the consent of the individuals of it, and it being necessary to that which is one body to move one way; it is necessary the body should move that way whither the greater force carries it, which is the consent of the majority: or else it is impossible it should act or continue one body, one community, which the consent of every individual that united into it, agreed that it should; and so every one is bound by that consent to be concluded by the majority. And therefore we see that in assemblies empowered to act by positive laws where no number is set by that positive law which empowers them, the act of the majority passes for the act of the whole, and of course determines, as having by the law of Nature and reason, the power of the whole.

**97.** And thus every man, by consenting with others to make one body politic under one government, puts himself under an obligation to every one of that society, to submit to the determination of the majority, and to be concluded by it; or else this original compact, whereby he with others incorporates into one society, would signify nothing, and be no compact, if he be left free, and under no other ties, than he was in before in the state of Nature. For what appearance would there be of any compact? What new engagement if he were no farther tied by any decrees of the society, than he himself thought fit, and did actually consent to? This would be still as great a liberty, as he himself had before his compact, or any one else in the state of Nature has, who may submit himself and consent to any acts of it if he thinks fit.

**98.** For if the consent of the majority shall not in reason, be received, as the act of the whole, and conclude every individual; nothing but the consent of every individual can make any thing to be the act of the whole: but such a consent is next impossible ever to be had, if we consider the infirmities of health, and avocations of business, which in a number, though much less than that of a commonwealth, will necessarily keep many away from the public assembly. To which if we add the variety of opinions, and contrariety of interests, which unavoidably happen in all collections of men, the coming into society upon such terms, would be only like Cato's coming into the theatre, only to go out again. Such a constitution as this would make the mighty *Leviathan* of a shorter duration, than the feeblest creatures; and not let it outlast the day it was born in: which cannot be supposed till we can think, that rational creatures should desire and constitute societies only to be dissolved. For where the majority cannot conclude the rest, there they cannot act as one body, and consequently will be immediately dissolved again.

**99.** Whosoever therefore out of a state of Nature unite into a community, must be understood to give up all the power, necessary to the ends for which they unite into society, to the majority of the community, unless they expressly agreed in any number greater than the majority. And this is done by barely agreeing to unite into one political society, which is all the compact that is, or needs be, between the individuals, that enter into, or make up a commonwealth. And thus that, which begins and actually constitutes any political society, is nothing but the consent of any number of freemen capable of a majority to unite and incorporate into such a society. And this is that, and that only, which did, or could give beginning to any lawful government in the world.

**119.** Every man being, as has been shown, naturally free, and nothing being able to put him into subjection to any earthly power, but only his own consent; it is to be considered, what shall be understood to be a sufficient declaration of a man's consent, to make him subject to the laws of any government. There is a common distinction of an express and a tacit consent, which will concern our present case. Nobody doubts that an express consent, of any man, entering into any society, makes him a perfect member of that society, a subject of that government. The difficulty is, what ought to be looked upon as a tacit consent, and how far it binds, i.e. how far anyone shall be looked on to have consented, and thereby submitted to any government, where he has made no expressions of it at all. And to this I say, that every Man, that has any possession, or enjoyment, of any part of the dominions of any government, does thereby give his tacit consent, and is as far forth obliged to obedience to the laws of that government, during such enjoyment, as any one under it; whether this his possession be of land, to him and his heirs for ever, or a lodging only for a week; or whether it be barely travelling freely on the highway; and in effect, it reaches as far as the very being, of any one within the territories of that government.

**120.** To understand this the better, it is fit to consider, that every man, when he, at first, incorporates himself into any commonwealth, he, by his uniting himself thereunto, annexed also, and submits to the community those possessions, which he has, or shall acquire, that do not already belong to any other government. For it would be a direct contradiction, for any one, to enter into society with others for the securing and regulating of property: and yet to suppose his land, whose property is to be regulated by the laws of the society, should be exempt from the jurisdiction of that government, to which he himself the proprietor of the land, is a subject. By the same act therefore, whereby any one unites his person, which was before free, to any commonwealth; by the same he unites his possessions, which were before free, to it also; and they become, both of them, person and possession, subject to the government and dominion of that commonwealth, as long as it has a being. Whoever therefore, from thenceforth, by inheritance, purchase, permission, or otherwise enjoys any part of the land, so annexed to, and under the government of that commonwealth, must take it with the condition it is under; that is, of submitting to the government of the commonwealth, under whose jurisdiction it is, as far forth, as any subject of it.

**121.** But since the government has a direct jurisdiction only over the land, and reaches the possessor of it, (before he has actually incorporated himself in the society) only as he dwells upon, and enjoys that: the obligation any one is under, by virtue of such enjoyment, to submit to the government, begins and ends with the enjoyment; so that whenever the owner, who has given nothing but such a tacit consent to the government, will, by donation, sale, or otherwise, quit the said possession, he is at liberty to go and incorporate himself into any other commonwealth, or to agree with others to begin a new one, *in vacuis locis,* in any part of the world, they can find free and unpossessed: whereas he that has once, by actual agreement, and any express declaration, given his consent to be of any commonweal, is perpetually and indispensably obliged to be and remain unalterably a subject to it, and can never be again in the liberty of the state of Nature; unless by any calamity, the government he was under, comes to be dissolved; or else by some public act cuts him off from being any longer a member of it.

**122.** But submitting to the laws of any country, living quietly, and enjoying privileges and protection under them, makes not a man a member of that society: this is only a local protection and homage due to, and from all those, who, not being in a state of war, come within the territories belonging to any government, to all parts whereof the force of its law extends. But this no more makes a man a member of that society, a perpetual subject of that commonwealth, than it would make a man a subject to another in whose family he found it convenient to abide for some time; though, whilst he continued in it, he were obliged to comply with the laws, and submit to the government he found there. And thus we see, that foreigners, by living all their lives under another government, and enjoying the privileges and protection of it, though they are bound, even in conscience, to submit to its administration, as far forth as any denison; yet do not thereby come to be subjects or members of that commonwealth. Nothing can make any man so, but his actually entering into it by positive engagement, and express promise and compact. This is that, which I think, concerning the beginning of political societies, and that consent which makes any one a member of any commonwealth.

*Chapter IX*

*Of the Ends of Political Society and Government*

**123.** If man in the state of Nature be so free, as has been said; if he be absolute lord of his own person and possessions, equal to the greatest and subject to nobody, why will he part with his freedom? Why will he give up this empire, and subject himself to the dominion and control of any other power? To which it is obvious to answer, that though in the state of Nature he has such a right, yet the enjoyment of it is very uncertain, and constantly exposed to the invasion of others. For all being kings as much as he, every man his equal, and the greater part no strict observers of equity and justice, the enjoyment of the property he has in this state is very unsafe, very insecure. This makes him willing to quit a condition, which however free, is full of fears and continual dangers: and it is not without reason, that he seeks out, and is willing to join in society with others who are already united, or have a mind to unite for the mutual preservation of their lives, liberties and estates, which I call by the general name, property.

**124.** The great and chief end therefore, of men's uniting into commonwealths, and putting themselves under government, is the preservation of their property. To which in the state of Nature there are many things wanting.

First, there wants an established, settled, known law, received and allowed by common consent to be the standard of right and wrong, and the common measure to decide all controversies between them. For though the law of Nature be plain and intelligible to all rational creatures; yet men being biassed by their interest, as well as ignorant for want of study of it, are not apt to allow it as a law binding to them in the application of it to their particular cases.

**125.** Secondly, in the state of Nature there wants a known and indifferent judge, with authority to determine all differences according to the established law. For everyone in that state being both judge and executioner of the law of Nature, men being partial to themselves, passion and revenge is very apt to carry them too far, and with too much heat, in their own cases; as well as negligence, and unconcernedness, to make them too remiss, in other men.

**126.** Thirdly, in the state of Nature there often wants power to back and support the sentence when right, and to give it due execution. They who by any injustice offended, will seldom fail, where they are able, by force to make good their injustice: such resistance many times makes the punishment dangerous, and frequently destructive, to those who attempt it.

**127.** Thus mankind, notwithstanding all the privileges of the state of Nature, being but in an ill condition, while they remain in it, are quickly driven into society. Hence it comes to pass, that we seldom find any number of men live any time together in this state. The inconveniencies, that they are therein exposed to, by the irregular and uncertain exercise of the power every man has of punishing the transgressions of others, make them take sanctuary under the established law of government, and therein seek the preservation of their property. It is this makes them so willingly give up every one his single power of punishing to be exercised by such alone as shall be appointed to it amongst them; and by such rules as the community, or those authorised by them to that purpose, shall agree on. And in this we have the original right and rise of both the legislative and executive power, as well as of the governments and societies themselves.

**131.** But though men when they enter into society, give up the equality, liberty, and executive power they had in the state of Nature, into the hands of the society, to be so far disposed of by the legislative, as the good of the society shall require; yet it being only with an intention in every one the better to preserve himself his liberty and property; (for no rational creature can be supposed to change his condition with an intention to be worse) the power of the society, or legislative constituted by them, can never be supposed to extend farther than the common good; but is obliged to secure every one's property by providing against those three defects above-mentioned, that made the state of Nature so unsafe and uneasy. And so whoever has the legislative or supreme power of any commonwealth, is bound to govern by established standing laws, promulgated and known to the people, and not by extemporary decrees; by indifferent and upright judges, who are to decide controversies by those laws; and to employ the force of the community at home, only in the execution of such laws, or abroad to prevent or redress foreign injuries, and secure the community from inroads and invasion. And all this to be directed to no other end, but the peace, safety, and public good of the people.

## Chapter X

### Of the Forms of a Commonwealth

**132.** The majority having, as has been shown, upon men first uniting into society, the whole power of the community, naturally in them, may employ all that power in making laws for the community from time to time, and executing those laws by officers of their own appointing; and then the form of the government is a perfect democracy: or else may put the power of making laws into the hands of a few select men, and their heirs or successors; and then it is an oligarchy: or else into the hands of one man, and then it is a monarchy: if to him and his heirs, it is an hereditary monarchy: if to him only for life, but upon his death the power only of nominating a successor to return to them; an elective monarchy. And so accordingly of these the community may make compounded and mixed forms of government, as they think good. And if the legislative power be at first given by the majority to one or more persons only for their lives, or any limited time, and then the supreme power to revert to them again; when it is so reverted, the community may dispose of it again anew into what hands they please, and so constitute a new form of government. For the form of government depending upon the placing the supreme power, which is the legislative, it being impossible to conceive that an inferior power should prescribe to a superior, or any but the supreme make laws, according as the power of making laws is placed, such is the form of the commonwealth.

**133.** By commonwealth, I must be understood all along to mean, not a democracy, or any form of government, but any independent community which the Latins signified by the word *civitas,* to which the word which best answers in our language, is commonwealth, and most properly expresses such a society of men, which community or city in English does not, for there may be subordinate communities in a government; and city amongst us has a quite different notion from commonwealth: and therefore to avoid ambiguity, I crave leave to use the word commonwealth in that sense, in which I find it used by King James the First, and I take it to be its genuine signification; which if anybody dislike, I consent with him to change it for a better.

## Chapter XI

### Of the Extent of the Legislative Power

**134.** The great end of men entering into society, being the enjoyment of their properties in peace and safety, and the great instrument and means of that being the laws established in that society; the first and fundamental positive law of all commonwealths, is the establishing of the legislative power; as the first and fundamental natural law, which is to govern even the legislative itself, is the preservation of the society, and (as far as will consist with the public good) of every person in it. This legislative is not only the supreme power of the commonwealth, but sacred and unalterable in the hands where the community have once placed it; nor can any edict of anybody else, in what form soever conceived, or by what power soever backed, have the force and obligation of a law, which has not its sanction from that legislative, which the public has chosen and appointed. For without this the law could not have that, which is absolutely necessary to its being a law, the consent of the society, over whom nobody can have a power to make laws, but by their own consent, and by authority received from them; and therefore all the obedience, which by the most solemn ties anyone can be obliged to pay, ultimately terminates in this supreme power, and is directed by those laws which it enacts: nor can any oaths to any foreign power whatsoever, or any domestic subordinate power, discharge any member of the society from his obedience to the legislative, acting pursuant to their trust, nor oblige him to any obedience contrary to the laws so enacted, or farther than they do allow; it being ridiculous to imagine one can be tied ultimately to obey any power in the society, which is not the supreme.

**135.** Though the legislative, whether placed in one or more, whether it be always in being, or only by intervals, though it be the supreme power in every commonwealth; yet,

First, it is not, nor can possibly be absolutely arbitrary over the lives and fortunes of the people. For it being but the joint power of every member of the society given up to that person, or assembly, which is legislator, it can be no more than those persons had in a state of Nature before they entered into society, and gave up to the community. For nobody can transfer to another more power than he has in himself; and nobody has an absolute arbitrary power over himself, or over any other, to destroy his own life, or take away the life or property of another. A man, as has been proved, cannot subject himself to the arbitrary power of another; and having in the state of Nature no arbitrary power over the life, liberty, or possession of another, but only so much as the law of Nature gave him for the preservation of himself, and the rest of mankind; this is all he does, or can give up to the commonwealth, and by it to the legislative power, so that the legislative can have no more than this. Their power in the utmost bounds of it, is limited to the public good of the society. It is a power, that has no other end but preservation, and therefore can never have a right to destroy, enslave, or designedly to impoverish the subjects. The obligations of the law of Nature, cease not in society but only in many cases are drawn closer, and have by humane laws known penalties annexed to them, to enforce their observation. Thus the law of Nature stands as an eternal rule to all men, legislators as well as others. The rules that they make for other men's actions, must, as well as their own and other men's actions, be conformable to the law of Nature, i.e. to the will of God, of which that is a declaration, and the fundamental law of Nature being the preservation of mankind, no humane sanction can be good, or valid against it.

**136.** Secondly, the legislative, or supreme authority, cannot assume to itself a power to rule by extemporary arbitrary decrees, but is bound to dispense justice, and decide the rights of the subject by promulgated standing laws, and known authorised judges. For the law of Nature being unwritten, and so no where to be found but in the minds of men, they who through passion or interest shall mis-cite, or misapply it, cannot so easily be convinced of their mistake where there is no established judge: and so it serves not, as it ought, to determine the rights, and fence the properties of those that live under it, especially where every one is judge, interpreter, and executioner of it too, and that in his own case: and he that has right on his side, having ordinarily but his own single strength, has not force enough to defend himself from injuries, or to punish delinquents. To avoid these inconveniencies which disorder men's properties in the state of Nature, men unite into societies, that they may have the united strength of the whole society to secure and defend their properties, and may have standing rules to bound it, by which every one may know what is his. To this end it is that men give up all their natural power to the society which they enter into, and the community put the legislative power into such hands as they think fit, with this trust, that they shall be governed by declared laws, or else their peace, quiet, and property will still be at the same uncertainty, as it was in the state of Nature.

**137.** Absolute arbitrary power, or governing without settled standing laws, can neither of them consist with the ends of society and government, which men would not quit the freedom of the state of Nature for, and tie themselves up under, were it not to preserve their lives, liberties and fortunes; and by stated rules of right and property to secure their peace and quiet. It cannot be supposed that they should intend, had they a power so to do, to give to anyone, or more, an absolute arbitrary power over their persons and estates, and put a force into the magistrates hand to execute his unlimited will arbitrarily upon them: this were to put themselves into a worse condition than the state of Nature, wherein they had a liberty to defend their right against the injuries of others, and were upon equal terms of force to maintain it, whether invaded by a single man, or many in combination. Whereas by supposing they have given up themselves to the absolute arbitrary power and will of a legislator, they have disarmed themselves, and armed him, to make a prey of them when he pleases. He being in a much worse condition who is exposed to the arbitrary power of one man, who has the command of 100,000 than he that is exposed to the arbitrary power of 100,000 single men: nobody being secure, that his will, who has such a command, is better, than that of other men, though his force be 100,000 times stronger. And therefore whatever form the commonwealth is under, the ruling power ought to govern by declared and received laws, and not by extemporary dictates and undetermined resolutions. For then mankind will be in a far worse condition, than in the state of Nature, if they shall have armed one or a few men with the joint power of a multitude, to force them to obey at pleasure the exorbitant and unlimited decrees of their sudden thoughts, or unrestrained, and till that moment unknown wills without having any measures set down which may guide and justify their actions. For all the power the government has, being only for the good of the society, as it ought not to be arbitrary and at pleasure, so it ought to be exercised by established and promulgated laws: that both the people may know their duty, and be safe and secure within the limits of the law, and the rulers too kept within their due bounds, and not to be tempted, by the power they have in their hands, to employ it to such purposes, and by such measures, as they would not have known, and own not willingly.

**138.** Thirdly, the supreme power cannot take from any man any part of his property without his own consent. For the preservation of property being the end of government, and that for which men enter into society, it necessarily supposes and requires, that the people should have property, without which they must be supposed to lose that by entering into society, which was the end for which they entered into it, too gross an absurdity for any man to own. Men therefore in society having property, they have such a right to the goods, which by the law of the community are theirs, that nobody has a right to take their substance, or any part of it from them, without their own consent; without this, they have no property at all. For I have truly no property in that, which another can by right take from me, when he pleases, against my consent. Hence it is a mistake to think, that the supreme or legislative power of any commonwealth, can do what it will, and dispose of the estates of the subject arbitrarily, or take any part of them at pleasure. This is not much to be feared in governments where the legislative consists, wholly or in part, in assemblies which are variable, whose members upon the dissolution of the assembly, are subjects under the common laws of their country, equally with the rest. But in governments, where the legislative is in one lasting assembly always in being, or in one man, as in absolute monarchies, there is danger still, that they will think themselves to have a distinct interest, from the rest of the community; and so will be apt to increase their own riches and power, by taking, what they think fit, from the people. For a man's property is not at all secure, though there be good and equitable laws to set the bounds of it, between him and his fellow subjects, if he who commands those subjects, have power to take from any private man, what part he pleases of his property, and use and dispose of it as he thinks good.

**140.** It is true, governments cannot be supported without great charge, and it is fit every one who enjoys his share of the protection, should pay out of his estate his proportion for the maintenance of it. But still it must be with his own consent, i.e. the consent of the majority, giving it either by themselves, or their representatives chosen by them. For if any one shall claim a power to lay and levy taxes on the people, by his own authority, and without such consent of the people, he thereby invades the fundamental law of property, and subverts the end of government. For what property have I in that which another may by right take, when he pleases to himself?

**141.** Fourthly, the legislative cannot transfer the power of making laws to any other hands. For it being but a delegated power from the people, they, who have it, cannot pass it over to others. The people alone can appoint the form of the commonwealth, which is by constituting the legislative, and appointing in whose hands that shall be. And when the people have said, we will submit to rules, and be governed by laws made by such men, and in such forms, nobody else can say other men shall make laws for them; nor can the people be bound by any laws but such as are enacted by those, whom they have chosen, and authorised to make laws for them. The power of the legislative being derived from the people by a positive voluntary grant and institution, can be no other, than what that positive grant conveyed, which being only to make laws, and not to make legislators, the legislative can have no power to transfer their authority of making laws, and place it in other hands.

## Chapter XII

## *Of the Legislative, Executive, and Federative Power of the Commonwealth*

**143.** The legislative power is that which has a right to direct how the force of the commonwealth shall be employed for preserving the community and the members of it. But because those laws which are constantly to be executed, and whose force is always to continue, may be made in a little time; therefore there is no need, that the legislative should be always in being, not having always business to do. And because it may be too great a temptation to humane frailty apt to grasp at power, for the same persons who have the power of making laws, to have also in their hands the power to execute them, whereby they may exempt themselves from obedience to the laws they make, and suit the law, both in its making and execution, to their own private advantage, and thereby come to have a distinct interest from the rest of the community, contrary to the end of society and government: therefore in well ordered commonwealths, where the good of the whole is so considered, as it ought, the legislative power is put into the hands of divers persons who duly assembled, have by themselves, or jointly with others, a power to make laws, which when they have done, being separated again, they are themselves subject to the laws, they have made; which is a new and near tie upon them, to take care, that they make them for the public good.

**144.** But because the laws, that are at once, and in a short time made, have a constant and lasting force, and need a perpetual execution, or an attendance thereunto: therefore it is necessary there should be a power always in being, which should see to the execution of the laws that are made, and remain in force. And thus the legislative and executive power come often to be separated.

**145.** There is another power in every commonwealth, which one may call natural, because it is that which answers to the power every man naturally had before he entered into society. For though in a commonwealth the members of it are distinct persons still in reference to one another, and as such are governed by the laws of the society; yet in reference to the rest of mankind, they make one body, which is, as every member of it before was, still in the state of Nature with the rest of mankind. Hence it is, that the controversies that happen between any man of the society with those that are out of it, are managed by the public; and an injury done to a member of their body, engages the whole in the reparation of it. So that under this consideration, the whole community is one body in the state of Nature, in respect of all other states or persons out of its community.

**146.** This therefore contains the power of war and peace, leagues and alliances, and all the transactions, with all persons and communities without the commonwealth, and may be called federative, if anyone pleases. So the thing be understood, I am indifferent as to the name.

**147.** These two powers, executive and federative, though they be really distinct in themselves, yet one comprehending the execution of the municipal laws of the society within itself, upon all that are parts of it; the other the management of the security and interest of the public without, with all those that it may receive benefit or damage from, yet they are always almost united. And though this federative power in the well or ill management of it be of great amount to the commonwealth, yet it is much less capable to be directed by antecedent, standing, positive laws, than the executive; and so must necessarily be left to the prudence and wisdom of those whose hands it is in, to be managed for the public good. For the laws that concern subjects one amongst another, being to direct their actions, may well enough precede them. But what is to be done in reference to foreigners, depending much upon their actions, and the variation of designs and interests, must be left in great part to the prudence of those who have this power committed to them, to be managed by the best of their skill, for the advantage of the commonwealth.

**148.** Though, as I said, the executive and federative power of every community be really distinct in themselves, yet they are hardly to be separated, and placed, at the same time, in the hands of distinct persons. For both of them requiring the force of the society for their exercise, it is almost impracticable to place the force of the commonwealth in distinct, and not subordinate hands; or that the executive and federative power should be placed in persons that might act separately, whereby the force of the public would be under different commands: which would be apt sometime or other to cause disorder and ruin.

## Chapter XIII

### Of the Subordination of the Powers of the Commonwealth

**149.** Though in a constituted commonwealth, standing upon its own basis, and acting according to its own nature, that is, acting for the preservation of the community, there can be but one supreme power, which is the legislative, to which all the rest are and must be subordinate, yet the legislative being only a fiduciary power to act for certain ends, there remains still in the people a supreme power to remove or alter the legislative, when they find the legislative act contrary to the trust reposed in them. For all power given with trust for the attaining an end, being limited by that end, whenever that end is manifestly neglected, or opposed, the trust must necessarily be forfeited, and the power devolve into the hands of those that gave it, who may place it anew where they shall think best for their safety and security. And thus the community perpetually retains a supreme power of saving themselves from the attempts and designs of anybody, even of their legislators, whenever they shall be so foolish, or so wicked, as to lay and carry on designs against the liberties and properties of the subject. For no man, or society of men, having a power to deliver up their preservation, or consequently the means of it, to the absolute will and arbitrary dominion of another; whenever any one shall go about to bring them into such a slavish condition, they will always have a right to preserve what they have not a power to part with; and to rid themselves of those who invade this fundamental, sacred, and unalterable law of self-preservation, for which they entered into society. And thus the community may be said in this respect to be always the supreme power, but not as considered under any form of government, because this power of the people can never take place till the government be dissolved.

[*In Chapter XIV ("Of Prerogative"), Locke argues that "it is fit that the laws themselves should in some cases give way to the executive power, or rather to this fundamental law of nature and government, viz. that as much as may be, all the members of the society are to be preserved." He adds that the prerogative power is derived from the "peoples permitting their rulers to do several things of their own free choice, where the law was silent, and sometimes too against the direct letter of the law, for the public good; and their acquiescing in it when so done."*

*Chapter XV ("Of Paternal, Political, and Despotical Power," considered together) contains definitions of these terms. Paternal power is that which parents have over children "till they come to the use of reason." Political power exists in the state of Nature and is "given up into the hands of society, and therein to the governors whom the society has set over itself...." Despotical power is an absolute and arbitrary power "one man has over another, to take away his life, whenever he pleases." It is not given by Nature or compact. —J.M.P.*]

### Chapter XVI

### Of Conquest

**175.** Though governments can originally have no other rise than that before mentioned, nor polities be founded on any thing but the consent of the people; yet such has been the disorders ambition has filled the world with, that in the noise of war, which makes so great a part of the history of mankind, this consent is little taken notice of: and therefore many have mistaken the force of arms, for the consent of the people; and reckon conquest as one of the originals of government. But conquest is as far from setting up any government, as demolishing an house is from building a new one in the place. Indeed it often makes way of a new frame of a commonwealth, by destroying the former; but, without the consent of the people, can never erect a new one.

**177.** But supposing victory favours the right side, let us consider a conqueror in a lawful war, and see what power he gets, and over whom.

First, it is plain he gets no power by his conquest over those that conquered with him. They that fought on his side cannot suffer by the conquest, but must at least be as much freemen as they were before. And most commonly they serve upon terms, and on condition to share with their leader, and enjoy a part of the spoil, and other advantages that attend the conquering sword: or at least have a part of the subdued country bestowed upon them. And the conquering people are not, I hope, to be slaves by conquest, and wear their laurels only to show they are sacrifices to their leader's triumph. They that found absolute monarchy upon the title of the sword, make their heroes, who are the founders of such monarchies, arrant draw-can-sirs, and forget they had any officers and soldiers that fought on their side in the battles they won, or assisted them in the subduing, or shared in possessing the countries they mastered. We are told by some, that the English monarchy is founded in the Norman Conquest, and that our princes have thereby a title to absolute dominion: which if it were true, (as by history it appears otherwise) and that William had a right to make war on this island; yet his dominion by conquest could reach no farther, than to the Saxons and Britains that were then inhabitants of the country. The Normans that came with him, and helped to conquer, and all descended from them are freemen and no subjects by conquest; let that give what dominion it will. And if I, or anybody else, shall claim freedom, as derived from them, it will be very hard to prove the contrary: and it is plain, the law that has made no distinction between the one and the other, intends not there should be any difference in their freedom or privileges.

**178.** But supposing, which seldom happens, that the conquerors and conquered never incorporate into one people, under the same laws and freedom. Let us see next what power a lawful conqueror has over the subdued; and that I say is purely despotical. He has an absolute power over the lives of those, who by an unjust war have forfeited them; but not over the lives or fortunes of those, who engaged not in the war, nor over the possessions even of those, who were actually engaged in it.

**179.** Secondly, I say then the conqueror gets no power but only over those, who have actually assisted, concurred or consented to that unjust force, that is used against him. For the people having given to their governors no power to do an unjust thing, such as is to make an unjust war—for they never had such a power in themselves—they ought not to be charged, as guilty of the violence and injustice that is committed in an unjust war, any farther, than they actually abet it; no more, than they are to be thought guilty of any violence or oppression their governors should use upon the people themselves, or any part of their fellow subjects, they having empowered them no more to the one, than to the other....

**180.** Thirdly, the power a conqueror gets over those he overcomes in a just war, is perfectly despotical: he has an absolute power over the lives of those, who by putting themselves in a state of war, have forfeited them; but he has not thereby a right and title to their possessions. This I doubt not, but at first sight will seem a strange doctrine, it being so quite contrary to the practice of the world; there being nothing more familiar in speaking of the dominion of countries, than to say, such an one conquered it. As if conquest, without any more ado, conveyed a right of possession. But when we consider, that the practice of the strong and powerful, how universal soever it may be, is seldom the rule of right, however it be one part of the subjection of the conquered, not to argue against the conditions, cut out to them by the conquering sword.

**181.** Though in all war there be usually a complication of force and damage, and the aggressor seldom fails to harm the estate, when he uses force against the persons of those he makes war upon; yet it is the use of force only, that puts a man into the state of war. For whether by force he begins the injury, or else having quietly, and by fraud, done the injury, he refuses to make reparation, and by force maintains it, (which is the same thing as at first to have done it by force) it is the unjust use of force that makes the war. For he that breaks open my house, and violently turns me out of doors; or having peaceably got in, by force keeps me out, does in effect the same thing; supposing we are in such a state, that we have no common judge on Earth, whom I may appeal to, and to whom we are both obliged to submit: for of such I am now speaking. It is the unjust use of force then, that puts a man into the state of war with another, and thereby he, that is guilty of it, makes a forfeiture of his life. For quitting reason, which is the rule given between man and man, and using force the way of beasts, he becomes liable to be destroyed by him he uses force against, as any savage ravenous beast, that is dangerous to his being.

**183.** Let the conqueror have as much justice on his side, as could be supposed, he has no right to seize more than the vanquished could forfeit; his life is at the victor's mercy, and his service and goods he may appropriate to make himself reparation; but he cannot take the goods of his wife and children; they too had a title to the goods he enjoyed, and their shares in the estate he possessed. For example, I in the state of Nature (and all commonwealths are in the state of Nature one with another) have injured another man, and refusing to give satisfaction, it comes to a state of war, wherein my defending by force, what I had gotten unjustly, makes me the aggressor. I am conquered: my life, it is true, as forfeit, is at mercy, but not my wife's and children's. They made not the war, nor assisted in it. I could not forfeit their lives, they were not mine to forfeit. My wife had a share in my estate, that neither could I forfeit. And my children also, being born of me, had a right to be maintained out of my labour or substance. Here then is the case; the conqueror has a title to reparation for damages received, and the children have a title to their father's estate for their subsistence. For as to the wife's share, whether her own labour or compact gave her a title to it, it is plain, her husband could not forfeit what was hers. What must be done in the case? I answer; the fundamental law of Nature being, that all, as much as may be, should be preserved, it follows, that if there be not enough fully to satisfy both, viz. for the conqueror's losses, and the children's maintenance, he that has, and to spare, must remit something of his full satisfaction, and give way to the pressing and preferable title of those, who are in danger to perish without it.

**190.** Every man is born with a double right: first, a right of freedom to his person, which no other man has a power over, but the free disposal of it lies in himself. Secondly, a right, before any other man, to inherit, with his brethren, his father's goods.

**191.** By the first of these, a man is naturally free from subjection to any government, though he be born in a place under its jurisdiction. But if he disclaim the lawful government of the country he was born in, he must also quit the right that belonged to him by the laws of it, and the possessions there descending to him from his ancestors, if it were a government made by their consent.

**192.** By the second, the inhabitants of any country, who are descended, and derive a title to their estates from those, who are subdued, and had a government forced upon them against their free consents, retain a right to the possession of their ancestors', though they consent not freely to the government, whose hard conditions were by force imposed on the possessors of that country. For the first conqueror never having had a title to the land of that country, the people who are the descendants of, or claim under those, who were forced to submit to the yoke of a government by constraint, have always a right to shake it off, and free themselves from the usurpation, or tyranny, which the sword has brought in upon them till their rulers put them under such a frame of government, as they willingly, and of choice consent to. Who doubts but the Grecian Christians, descendants of the ancient possessors of that country, may justly cast off the Turkish yoke which they have so long groaned under whenever they have a power to do it? For no government can have a right to obedience from a people who have not freely consented to it: which they can never be supposed to do, till either they are put in a full state of liberty to choose their government and governors, or at least till they have such standing laws, to which they have by themselves or their representatives, given their free consent, and also till they are allowed their due property, which is so to be proprietors of what they have, that nobody can take away any part of it without their consent, without which, men under any government are not in the state of freemen, but are direct slaves under the force of war.

**196.** The short of the case in conquest is this. The conqueror, if he have a just cause, has a despotical right over the persons of all, that actually aided, and concurred in the war against him, and a right to make up his damage and cost out of their labour and estates, so he injure not the right of any other. Over the rest of the people, if there were any that consented not to the war, and over the children of the captives themselves, or the possessions of either he has no power; and so can have, by virtue of conquest, no lawful title himself to dominion over them, or derive it to his posterity; but is an aggressor, if he attempts upon their properties, and thereby puts himself in a state of war against them; and has no better a right of principality, he, nor any of his successors, than Hingar, or Hubba the Danes had here in England; or Spartacus, had he conquered Italy would have had; which is to have their yoke cast off, as soon as God shall give those under their subjection courage and opportunity to do it….

## Chapter XVII

### Of Usurpation

**197.** As conquest may be called a foreign usurpation, so *usurpation* is a kind of domestic conquest, with this difference, that an usurper can never have right on his side, it being no *usurpation* but where one is got into the *possession of what another has right to*. This, so far as it is usurpation, is a change only of persons, but not of the forms and rules of the government: for if the usurper extend his power beyond what of right belonged to the lawful princes, or governors of the commonwealth, 'tis *tyranny* added to usurpation.

**198.** In all lawful governments the designation of the persons who are to bear rule, is as natural and necessary a part as the form of the government itself, and is that which had its establishment originally from the people. Hence all commonwealths with the form of government established, have rules also of appointing those, who are to have any share in the public authority; and settled methods of conveying the right to them. For the anarchy is much alike to have no form of government at all; or to agree that it shall be monarchical, but to appoint no way to know or design the person that shall have the power and be the monarch. Whoever gets into the exercise of any part of the power, by other ways, than what the laws of the community have prescribed, has no right to be obeyed, though the form of the commonwealth be still preserved; since he is not the person the laws have appointed, and consequently not the person the people have consented to. Nor can such as *usurper*, or any deriving from him, ever have a title, till the people are both at liberty to consent, and have actually consented to allow, and confirm in him, the power he hath till then usurped.

## Chapter XVIII

## Of Tyranny

**199.** As usurpation is the exercise of power, which another has a right to; so tyranny is the exercise of power beyond right, which nobody can have a right to. And this is making use of the power any one has in his hands; not for the good of those, who are under it, but for his own private separate advantage. When the governor, however entitled, makes not the law, but his will, the rule; and his commands and actions are not directed to the preservation of the properties of his people, but the satisfaction of his own ambition, revenge, covetousness, or any other irregular passion.

**201.** It is a mistake to think this fault is proper only to monarchies; other forms of government are liable to it, as well as that. For where ever the power that is put in any hands for the government of the people, and the preservation of their properties, is applied to other ends, and made use of to impoverish, harass, or subdue them to the arbitrary and irregular commands of those that have it: there it presently becomes tyranny, whether those that thus use it are one or many. Thus we read of the thirty tyrants at Athens, as well as one at Syracuse; and the intolerable dominion of the Decemviri at Rome was nothing better.

**202.** Wherever law ends tyranny begins, if the law be transgressed to another's harm. And whosoever in authority exceeds the power given him by the law, and makes use of the force he has under his command, to compass that upon the subject, which the law allows not, ceases in that to be a magistrate, and acting without authority, may be opposed, as any other man, who by force invades the right of another. This is acknowledged in subordinate magistrates. He that has authority to seize my person in the street, may be opposed as a thief and a robber, if he endeavors to break into my house to execute a writ, notwithstanding that I know he has such a warrant, and such a legal authority as will empower him to arrest me abroad. And why this should not hold in the highest, as well as in the most inferior magistrate, I would gladly be informed. Is it reasonable that the eldest brother, because he has the greatest part of his father's estate, should thereby have a right to take away any of his younger brothers' portions? Or that a rich man, who possessed a whole country, should from thence have a right to seize, when he pleased, the cottage and garden of his poor neighbour? The being rightfully possessed of great power and riches exceedingly beyond the greatest part of the sons of Adam, is so far from being an excuse, much less a reason, for rapine, and oppression, which the damaging another without authority is, that it is a great aggravation of it. For the exceeding the bounds of authority is no more a right in a great, than a petty officer; no more justifiable in a king, than a constable. But is so much the worse in him, in that he has more trust put in him, has already a much greater share than the rest of his brethren, and is supposed from the advantages of education, employment and counsellors to be more knowing in the measures of right and wrong.

**203.** May the commands then of a prince be opposed? May he be resisted as often as any one shall find himself aggrieved, and but imagine he has not right done him? This will unhinge and overturn all polities, and instead of government and order leave nothing but anarchy and confusion.

**204.** To this I answer: that force is to be opposed to nothing, but to unjust and unlawful force; whoever makes any opposition in any other case, draws on himself a just condemnation both from God and man; and so no such danger or confusion will follow, as is often suggested. For,

**205.** First, as in some countries, the person of the prince by the law is sacred; and so whatever he commands, or does, his person is still free from all question or violence, not liable to force, or any judicial censure or condemnation. But yet opposition may be made to the illegal acts of any inferior officer, or other commissioned by him; unless he will by actually putting himself into a state of war with his people, dissolve the government, and leave them to that defence, which belongs to every one in the state of Nature. For of such things who can tell what the end will be? And a neighbour kingdom has showed the world an odd example. In all other cases the sacredness of the person exempts him from all inconveniencies whereby he is secure, whilst the government stands, from all violence and harm whatsoever; than which there cannot be a wiser constitution. For the harm he can do in his own person, not being likely to happen often, nor to extend itself far; nor being able by his single strength to subvert the laws, nor oppressed the body of the people, should any prince have so much weakness and ill nature as to be willing to do it, the inconvenience of some particular mischiefs, that may happen sometimes, when a heady prince comes to the throne, are well recompensed, by the peace of the public, and security of the government, in the person of the chief magistrate, thus set out of the reach of danger: it being safer for the body, that some few private men should be sometimes in danger to suffer, than that the head of the republic should be easily, and upon slight occasion exposed.

**206.** Secondly, but this privilege, belonging only to the king's person, hinders not, but they may be questioned, opposed, and resisted, who use unjust force, though they pretend a commission from him, which the law authorizes not. As is plain the case of him, that has the king's writ to arrest a man, which is a full commission from the king; and yet he that has it cannot break open a man's house to do it, nor execute this command of the king upon certain days, nor in certain places, though this commission have no such exception in it, but they are the limitations of the law, which if anyone transgress, the king's commission excuses him not. For the king's authority being given him only by the law, he cannot empower any one to act against the law, or justify him, by his commission in so doing....

**207.** Thirdly, supposing a government wherein the person of the chief magistrate is not thus sacred; yet this doctrine of the lawfulness of resisting all unlawful exercises of his power, will not upon every slight occasion endanger him, or embroil the government. For where the injured party may be relieved, and his damages repaired by appeal to the law, there can be no pretence for force, which is only to be used, where a man is intercepted from appealing to the law. For nothing is to be accounted hostile force, but where it leaves not the remedy of such an appeal. And it is such force alone, that puts him that uses it into a state of war, and makes it lawful to resist him. A man with a sword in his hand demands my purse in the highway, when perhaps I have not 12d. in my pocket; this man I may lawfully kill. To another I deliver 100l to hold only whilst I alight, which he refuses to restore me, when I am got up again, but draws his sword to defend the possession of it by force, if I endeavour to retake it. The mischief this man does me, is a hundred, or possibly a thousand times more, than the other perhaps intended me, (whom I killed before he really did me any) and yet I might lawfully kill the one, and cannot so much as hurt the other lawfully. The reason whereof is plain; because the one using force, which threatened my life, I could not have time to appeal to the law to secure it: and when it was gone, it was too late to appeal. The law could not restore life to my dead carcass: the loss was irreparable; which to prevent, the law of Nature gave me a right to destroy him, who had put himself into a state of war with me, and threatened my destruction. But in the other case, my life not being in danger, I may have the benefit of appealing to the law, and have reparation for my 100l that way.

**208.** Fourthly, but if the unlawful acts done by the magistrate, be maintained (by the power he has got) and the remedy which is due by law, be by the same power obstructed; the right of resisting, even in such manifest acts of tyranny, will not suddenly, or on slight occasions, disturb the government. For if it reach no farther than some private men's cases, though they have a right to defend themselves, and to recover by force, what by unlawful force is taken from them; yet the right to do so, will not easily engage them in a contest, wherein they are sure to perish; it being as impossible for one or a few oppressed men to disturb the government, where the body of the people do not think themselves concerned in it, as for a raving mad man, or heady malcontent to overturn a well-settled state; the people being as little apt to follow the one, as the other.

**209.** But if either these illegal acts have extended to the majority of the people; or, if the mischief and oppression has lit only on some few, but in such cases, as the precedent, and consequences seem to threaten all, and they are persuaded in their consciences, that their laws, and with them their estates, liberties, and lives are in danger, perhaps their religion too, how they will be hindered from resisting illegal force, used against them, I cannot tell. This is an inconvenience, I confess, that attends all governments whatsoever, when the governors have brought it to this pass, to be generally suspected of their people; the most dangerous state which they can possibly put themselves in: wherein they are the less to be pitied, because it is so easy to be avoided; it being as impossible for a governor, if he really means the good of his people, and the preservation of them and their laws together, not to make them see and feel it; as it is for the father of a family, not to let his children see he loves, and takes care of them.

## Chapter XIX

### Of the Dissolution of Government

**211.** He that will with any clearness speak of the dissolution of government, ought, in the first place to distinguish between the dissolution of the society, and the dissolution of the government. That which makes the community, and brings men out of the loose state of Nature, into one politic society, is the agreement which every one has with the rest to incorporate, and act as one body, and so be one distinct commonwealth. The usual, and almost only way whereby this union is dissolved, is the inroad of foreign force making a conquest upon them. For in that case, (not being able to maintain and support themselves, as one entire and independent body) the union belonging to that body which consisted therein, must necessarily cease, and so every one return to the state he was in before, with a liberty to shift for himself, and provide for his own safety as he thinks fit in some other society. Whenever the society is dissolved, it is certain the government of that society cannot remain. Thus conquerors' swords often cut up governments by the roots, and mangle societies to pieces, separating the subdued or scattered multitude from the protection of, and dependence on that society which ought to have preserved them from violence. The world is too well instructed in, and too forward to allow of this way of dissolving of governments to need any more to be said of it: and there wants not much argument to prove, that where the society is dissolved, the government cannot remain; that being as impossible, as for the frame of an house to subsist when the materials of it are scattered, and dissipated by a whirlwind, or jumbled into a confused heap by an earthquake.

**212.** Besides this overturning from without, governments are dissolved from within.

First, when the legislative is altered. Civil society being a state of peace, amongst those who are of it, from whom the state of war is excluded by the umpirage, which they have provided in their legislative, for the ending all differences, that may arise amongst any of them, it is in their legislative, that the members of a commonwealth are united, and combined together into one coherent living body. This is the soul that gives form, life, and unity to the commonwealth: from hence the several members have their mutual influence, sympathy, and connection: and therefore when the legislative is broken, or dissolved, dissolution and death follows. For the essence and union of the society consisting in having one will, the legislative, when once established by the majority, has the declaring, and as it were keeping of that will. The constitution of the legislative is the first and fundamental act of society, whereby provision is made for the continuation of their union, under the direction of persons, and bonds of laws made by persons authorized thereunto, by the consent and appointment of the people, without which no one man, or number of men, amongst them, can have authority of making laws, that shall be binding to the rest. When any one, or more, shall take upon them to make laws, whom the people have not appointed so to do, they make laws without authority, which the people are not therefore bound to obey; by which means they come again to be out of subjection, and may constitute to themselves a new legislative, as they think best, being in full liberty to resist the force of those, who without authority would impose any thing upon them. Every one is at the disposal of his own will, when those who had by the delegation of the society, the declaring of the public will, are excluded from it, and others usurp the place who have no such authority or delegation.

**221.** There is therefore, secondly, another way whereby governments are dissolved, and that is; when the legislative, or the prince, either of them act contrary to their trust.

First, the legislative acts against the trust reposed in them, when they endeavour to invade the property of the subject, and to make themselves, or any part of the community, masters, or arbitrary disposers of the lives, liberties, or fortunes of the people.

**222.** The reason why men enter into society, is the preservation of their property; and the end why they choose and authorize a legislative, is, that there may be laws made, and rules set as guards and fences to the properties of all the members of the society, to limit the power, and moderate the dominion of every part and member of the society. For since it can never be supposed to be the will of the society, that the legislative should have a power to destroy that, which every one designs to secure, by entering into society, and for which the people submitted themselves to the legislators of their own making; whenever the legislators endeavour to take away, and destroy the property of the people, or to reduce them to slavery under arbitrary power, they put themselves into a state of war with the people, who are thereupon absolved from any further obedience, and are left to the common refuge, which God has provided for all men, against force and violence. Whensoever therefore the legislative shall transgress this fundamental rule of society; and either by ambition, fear, folly or corruption, endeavour to grasp themselves, or put into the hands of any other an absolute power over the lives, liberties, and estates of the people; by this breach of trust they forfeit the power, the people had put into their hands, for quite contrary ends, and it devolves to the people, who have a right to resume their original liberty, and, by the establishment of a new legislative (such as they shall think fit) provide for their own safety and security, which is the end for which they are in society....

**223.** To this perhaps it will be said, that the people being ignorant, and always discontented, to lay the foundation of government in the unsteady opinion, and uncertain humour of the people, is to expose it to certain ruin; and no government will be able long to subsist, if the people may set up a new legislative, whenever they take offence at the old one. To this, I answer: Quite the contrary. People are not so easily got out of their old forms, as some are apt to suggest. They are hardly to be prevailed with to amend the acknowledged faults, in the frame they have been accustomed to. And if there be any original defects, or adventitious ones introduced by time, or corruption; it is not an easy thing to get them changed, even when all the world sees there is an opportunity for it. This slowness and aversion in the people to quit their old constitutions, has, in the many revolutions which have been seen in this kingdom, in this and former ages, still kept us to, or, after some interval of fruitless attempts, still brought us back again to our old legislative of king, lords and commons: and whatever provocations have made the crown be taken from some of our princes' heads, they never carried the people so far, as to place it in another line.

**224.** But 'twill be said, this hypothesis lays a ferment for frequent rebellion. To which I answer,

First, no more than any other hypothesis. For when the people are made miserable, and find themselves exposed to the ill usage of arbitrary power, cry up their governors, as much as you will for sons of Jupiter, let them be sacred and divine, descended or authorized from heaven; give them out for whom or what you please, the same will happen. The people generally ill treated, and contrary to right, will be ready upon any occasion to ease themselves of a burden that sits heavy upon them. They will wish and seek for the opportunity, which, in the change, weakness, and accidents of human affairs, seldom delays long to offer itself. He must have lived but a little while in the world, who has not seen examples of this in his time; and he must have read very little, who cannot produce examples of it in all sorts of governments in the world.

**225.** Secondly, I answer, such revolutions happen not upon every little mismanagement in public affairs. Great mistakes in the ruling part, many wrong and inconvenient laws, and all the slips of human frailty will be born by the people, without mutiny or murmur. But if a long train of abuses, prevarications, and artifices, all tending the same way, make the design visible to the people, and they cannot but feel, what they lie under, and see, whither they are going; it is not to be wondered, that they should then rouse themselves, and endeavour to put the rule into such hands, which may secure to them the ends for which government was at first erected; and without which, ancient names, and specious forms, are so far from being better, that they are much worse, than the state of Nature, or pure anarchy; the inconveniencies being all as great and as near, but the remedy farther off and more difficult.

**226.** Thirdly, I answer, that this doctrine of a power in the people of providing for their safety anew by a new legislative, when their legislators have acted contrary to their trust, by invading their property, is the best fence against rebellion, and the most probable means to hinder it. For rebellion being an opposition, not to persons, but authority, which is founded only in the constitutions and laws of the government; those, whoever they be, who by force break through, and by force justify their violation of them, are truly and properly rebels. For when men by entering into society and civil government, have excluded force, and introduced laws for the preservation of property, peace, and unity amongst themselves; those who set up force again in opposition to the laws, do *rebellare,* that is, bring back again the state of war, and are properly rebels: which they who are in power (by the pretence they have to authority, the temptation of force they have in their hands, and the flattery of those about them) being likeliest to do; the most proper way to prevent the evil, is to show them the danger and injustice of it, who are under the greatest temptation to run into it.

**227.** In both the aforementioned cases, when either the legislative is changed, or the legislators act contrary to the end for which they were constituted; those who are guilty are guilty of rebellion. For if anyone by force takes away the established legislative of any society, and the laws by them made pursuant to their trust, he thereby takes away the umpirage, which every one had consented to, for a peaceable decision of all their controversies, and a bar to the state of war amongst them. They, who remove, or change the legislative, take away this decisive power, which nobody can have, but by the appointment and consent of the people; and so destroying the authority, which the people did, and nobody else can set up, and introducing a power, which the people has not authorized, they actually introduce a state of war, which is that of force without authority: and thus by removing the legislative established by the society (in whose decisions the people acquiesced and united, as to that of their own will) they untie the knot, and expose the people anew to the state of war. And if those, who by force take away the legislative, are rebels, and legislators themselves, as has been shown, can be no less esteemed so; when they, who were set up for the protection, and preservation of the people, their liberties and properties, shall by force invade, and endeavor to take them away; and so they putting themselves into a state of war with those, who made them the protectors and guardians of their peace, are properly, and with the greatest aggravation, *rebellantes* rebels.

**240.** Here, it is like, the common question will be made, who shall be judge whether the prince or legislative act contrary to their trust? This, perhaps, ill affected and factious men may spread amongst the people, when the prince only makes use of his due prerogative. To this I reply, the people shall be judge; for who shall be judge whether his trustee or deputy acts well, and according to the trust reposed in him, but he who deputes him, and must, by having deputed him have still a power to discard him, when he fails in his trust? If this be reasonable in particular cases of private men, why should it be otherwise in that of the greatest moment; where the welfare of millions is concerned, and also where the evil, if not prevented, is greater, and the redress very difficult, dear, and dangerous?

**241.** But further, this question, (Who shall be judge?) cannot mean, that there is no judge at all. For where there is no judicature on Earth, to decide controversies, amongst men, God in heaven is judge: He alone, it is true, is judge of the right. But every man is judge for himself, as in all other cases, so in this, whether another has put himself into a state of war with him, and whether he should appeal to the Supreme Judge as Jephtha did.

**242.** If a controversy arise betwixt a prince and some of the people, in a matter where the law is silent, or doubtful, and the thing be of great consequence, I should think the proper umpire, in such a case, should be the body of the people, for in cases where the prince has a trust reposed in him, and is dispensed from the common ordinary rules of the law; there, if any men find themselves aggrieved, and think the prince acts contrary to, or beyond that trust, who so proper to judge as the body of the people, (who, at first, lodged that trust in him) how far they meant it should extend? But if the prince, or whoever they be in the administration, decline that way of determination, the appeal then lies no where but to heaven. Force between either persons, who have no known superior on Earth, or which permits no appeal to a judge on Earth, being properly a state of war, wherein the appeal lies only to heaven, and in that state the injured party must judge for himself, when he will think fit to make use of that appeal, and put himself upon it.

**243.** To conclude, the power that every individual gave the society, when he entered into it, can never revert to the individuals again, as long as the society lasts, but will always remain in the community; because without this, there can be no community, no commonwealth, which is contrary to the original agreement: so also when the society has placed the legislative in any assembly of men, to continue in them and their successors, with direction and authority for providing such successors, the legislative can never revert to the people whilst that government lasts: because having provided a legislative with power to continue for ever, they have given up their political power to the legislative, and cannot resume it. But if they have set limits to the duration of their legislative, and made this supreme power in any person, or assembly, only temporary: or else when by the miscarriages of those in authority, it is forfeited; upon the forfeiture of their rulers, or at the determination of the time set, it reverts to the society, and the people have a right to act as supreme, and continue the legislative in themselves, or erect a new form, or under the old form place it in new hands, as they think good.

---

## F I N I S

# JEAN-JACQUES ROUSSEAU

*Jean-Jacques Rousseau (1712–1778) was born in Switzerland in Calvinist Geneva. His mother died giving birth to him, and he was raised haphazardly by his father until the age of ten. His father, who was of a romantic bent and hot-tempered, became embroiled in a duel and had to flee Geneva. Rousseau was left with relatives and shortly thereafter served as an unhappy apprentice in several jobs. In his* Confessions, *Rousseau tells, with candor and relish, how he left Geneva at the age of 16, lived a Bohemian existence wandering throughout Europe, and became self-educated. In 1742 he arrived in Paris with the ambition to establish himself in Parisian society. His initial efforts were disappointing: he was unsuccessful as a secretary to the French ambassador to Venice; an opera he composed failed, and his musical notation system was rejected. He barely eked out a living copying music. But he did gain a new mistress in Paris, an illiterate laundress to whom he was faithful, in his fashion, for the rest of his life. They had five children together; however, Rousseau placed all of them in a foundling home at birth.*

*Rousseau became suddenly famous in 1749 when he won first prize for his essay, the* First Discourse, *on a question asked by the Academy of Dijon: "Has the progress of the sciences and the arts contributed to corrupt or purify morals?" In contrast with the progressive spirit of the age, Rousseau argued that the rise of civilization had harmed morality. In the following years he wrote many essays and two immensely popular novels,* Héloise *(1760) and* Émile *(1762). His works were mainly on political topics, and were original, widely read, and controversial. In fact, both Geneva and Paris ordered his arrest and burned his books. He was also driven from several other domiciles. He lived in England for a short time in 1766, and in various places in Europe. He was probably mentally ill in his last years. He died in poverty.*

*Almost all of Rousseau's writings contain elements of his political philosophy. The* Social Contract *(1762) is clearly the classic work. Several other writings are also important for understanding his political philosophy: the* First Discourse, *the* Second Discourse *(1755), the* Discourse on Political Economy *(1755),* Émile, Project of a Constitution for Corsica *(1765), and* Considerations on the Government of Poland *(1772).*

—J.M.P.

# SECOND DISCOURSE

## *Discourse on the Origin and Foundations of Inequality Among Men*

### ⇢ FIRST PART ⇠

Important as it may be, in order to judge the natural state of man correctly, to consider him from his origin and examine him, so to speak, in the first embryo of the species, I shall not follow his organic structure through its successive developments. I shall not stop to investigate in the animal system what he could have been at the beginning in order to become at length what he is.... I shall suppose him to have been formed from all time as I see him today: walking on two feet, using his hands as we do ours, directing his gaze on all of nature, and measuring the vast expanse of heaven with his eyes.

Stripping this being, so constituted, of all the supernatural gifts he could have received and of all the artificial faculties he could only have acquired by long progress—considering him, in a word, as he must have come from the hands of nature—I see an animal less strong than some, less agile than others, but all things considered, the most advantageously organized of all. I see him satisfying his hunger under an oak, quenching his thirst at the first stream, finding his bed at the foot of the same tree that furnished his meal; and therewith his needs are satisfied.

The earth, abandoned to its natural fertility and covered by immense forests never mutilated by the axe, offers at every step storehouses and shelters to animals of all species. Men, dispersed among the animals, observe and imitate their industry, and thereby develop in themselves the instinct of the beasts; with the advantage that whereas each species has only its own proper instinct, man—perhaps having none that belongs to him—appropriates them all to himself, feeds himself equally well with most of the diverse foods which the other animals share, and consequently finds his subsistence more easily than any of them can.

Accustomed from infancy to inclemencies of the weather and the rigor of the seasons, trained in fatigue, and forced, naked and without arms, to defend their lives and their prey against other wild beasts, or to escape by outrunning them, men develop a robust and almost unalterable temperament. Children, bringing into the world the excellent constitution of their fathers and fortifying it with the same training that produced it, thus acquire all the vigor of which the human species is capable. Nature treats them precisely as the law of Sparta treated the children of citizens: it renders strong and robust those who are well constituted and makes all the others perish, thereby differing from our societies, in which the State, by making children burdensome to their fathers, kills them indiscriminately before their birth....

Let us ... take care not to confuse savage man with the men we have before our eyes. Nature treats all the animals abandoned to its care with a partiality that seems to show how jealous it is of this right. The horse, the cat, the bull, even the ass, are mostly taller, and all have a more robust constitution, more vigor, more strength and courage in the forest than in our houses. They lose half of these advantages in becoming domesticated, and it might be said that all our cares to treat and feed these animals well end only in their degeneration. It is the same even for man. In becoming sociable and a slave he becomes weak, fearful, servile; and his soft and effeminate way of life completes the enervation of both his strength and his courage. Let us add that between savage and domesticated conditions the difference from man to man must be still greater than that from beast to beast; for animal and man having been treated equally by nature, all the commodities of which man gives himself more than the animals he tames are so many particular causes that make him degenerate more noticeably....

Whatever these origins [of man] may be, from the little care taken by nature to bring men together through mutual needs and to facilitate their use of speech, one at least sees how little it prepared their sociability, and how little it contributed to everything men have done to establish social bonds. In fact, it is impossible to imagine why, in that primitive state, a man would sooner have need of another man than a monkey or a wolf of its fellow creature; nor, supposing this need, what motive could induce the other to provide for it, nor even, in this last case, how they could agree between them on the conditions. I know we are repeatedly told that nothing would have been so miserable as man in that state; and if it is true, as I believe I have proved, that only after many centuries could man have had the desire and opportunity to leave that state, it would be a fault to find with nature and not with him who would have been so constituted by nature. But if I understand properly this term miserable, it is a word that has no meaning or only signifies a painful privation and the suffering of the body or soul. Now I would really like someone to explain to me what type of misery there can be for a free being whose heart is at peace and whose body is healthy? I ask which, civil or natural life, is most liable to become unbearable to those who enjoy it? We see around us practically no people who do not complain of their existence, even many who deprive themselves of it insofar as they have the capacity; and the combination of divine and human laws hardly suffices to stop this disorder. I ask if anyone has ever heard it said that a savage in freedom even dreamed of complaining about life and killing himself. Let it then be judged with less pride on which side true misery lies. Nothing, on the contrary, would have been so miserable as savage man dazzled by enlightenment, tormented by passions, and reasoning about a state different from his own. It was by a very wise providence that his potential faculties were to develop only with the opportunities to exercise them, so that they were neither superfluous and burdensome to him beforehand, nor tardy and useless when needed. He had, in instinct alone, everything necessary for him to live in the state of nature; he has, in a cultivated reason, only what is necessary for him to live in society.

It seems at first that men in that state, not having among themselves any kind of moral relationship or known duties, could be neither good nor evil, and had neither vices nor virtues: unless, taking these words in a physical sense, one calls vices in the individual the qualities that can harm his own preservation, and virtues those that can contribute to it; in which case, it would be necessary to call the most virtuous the one who least resists the simple impulses of nature. But without departing from the ordinary meaning, it is appropriate to suspend the judgment we could make of such a situation and to beware of our prejudices, until one has examined with scale in hand whether there are more virtues than vices among civilized men; or whether their virtues are more advantageous than their vices are deadly; or whether the progress of their knowledge is a sufficient compensation for the harms they do one another as they learn of the good they ought to do; or whether all things considered, they would not be in a happier situation having neither harm to fear nor good to hope for from anyone, rather than subjecting themselves to a universal dependence and obliging themselves to receive everything from those who do not obligate themselves to give them anything.

Above all, let us not conclude with Hobbes that because man has no idea of goodness he is naturally evil; that he is vicious because he does not know virtue; that he always refuses his fellow-men services he does not believe he owes them; nor that, by virtue of the right he reasonably claims to things he needs, he foolishly imagines himself to be the sole proprietor of the whole universe. Hobbes saw very clearly the defect of all modern definitions of natural right; but the consequences he draws from his own definition show that he takes it in a sense which is no less false. Reasoning upon the principles he establishes, this author ought to have said that since the state of nature is that in which care of our self-preservation is the least prejudicial to the self-preservation of others, that state was consequently the best suited to peace and the most appropriate for the human race. He says precisely the opposite, because of having improperly included in the savage man's care of self-preservation the need to satisfy a multitude of passions which are the produce of society and which have made laws necessary. The evil man, he says, is a robust child. It remains to be seen whether savage man is a robust child. Should we grant this to him, what would he conclude from it? That if, when he is robust, this man were as dependent on others as when he is weak, there is no kind of excess to which he would not be inclined: that he would beat his mother when she would be too slow in giving him her breast; that he would strangle one of his young brothers when he would be inconvenienced by him; that he would bite another's leg when he was hit or annoyed by it. But to be robust and to be dependent are two contradictory suppositions in the state of nature. Man is weak when he is dependent, and he is emancipated before he is robust. Hobbes did not see that the same cause that prevents savages from using their reason, as our jurists claim, prevents them at the same time from abusing their faculties, as he himself claims. Thus one could say that savages are not evil precisely because they do not know what it is to be good; for it is neither the growth of enlightenment nor the restraint of law, but the calm of passions and the ignorance of vice which prevent them from doing evil: *Tanto plus in illis proficit vitiorum ignoratio, quam in his cognitio virtutis.* ["So much more does ignorance of vice profit these than knowledge of virtue the others," Justin, *Histories,* II, 2.] There is, besides, another principle which Hobbes did not notice, and which—having been given to man in order to soften, under certain circumstances, the ferocity of his vanity or the desire for self-preservation before the birth of vanity—tempers the ardor he has for his own well-being by an innate repugnance to see his fellow-man suffer. I do not believe I have any contradiction to fear in granting man the sole natural virtue that the most excessive detractor of human virtues was forced to recognize. I speak of pity, a disposition that is appropriate to beings as weak and subject to as many ills as we are; a virtue all the more universal and useful to man because it precedes in him the use of all reflection; and so natural that even beasts sometimes give perceptible signs of it. Without speaking of the tenderness of mothers for their young and of the perils they brave to guard them, one observes daily the repugnance of horses to trample a living body underfoot. An animal does not pass near a dead animal of its species without uneasiness. There are even some animals that give them a kind of sepulcher; and the sad lowing of cattle entering a slaughterhouse announces the impression they receive from the horrible sight that strikes them. One sees with pleasure the author of the *Fable of the Bees*, forced to recognize man as a compassionate and sensitive being, departing from his cold and subtle style in the example he gives in order to offer us the pathetic image of an imprisoned man who sees outside a wild beast tearing a child from his mother's breast, breaking his weak limbs in its murderous teeth, and ripping apart with its claws the palpitating entrails of this child. What horrible agitation must be felt by this witness of an event in which he takes no personal interest! What anguish must he suffer at this sight, unable to bring help to the fainting mother or to the dying child.

Such is the pure movement of nature prior to all reflection. Such is the force of natural pity, which the most depraved morals still have difficulty destroying, since daily in our theaters one sees, moved and crying for the troubles of an unfortunate person, a man who, if he were in the tyrant's place, would aggravate his enemy's torments even more—like bloodthirsty Sulla, so sensitive to ills he had not caused, or like Alexander of Pherae, who did not dare attend the performance of any tragedy lest he be seen moaning with Andromache and Priam, whereas he listened without emotion to the cries of so many citizens murdered daily on his orders....

Mandeville sensed very well that even with all their ethics men would never have been anything but monsters if nature had not given them pity in support of reason; but he did not see that from this quality alone flow all the social virtues he wants to question in men. In fact, what are generosity, clemency, humanity, if not pity applied to the weak, to the guilty, or to the human species in general? Benevolence and even friendship are, rightly understood, the products of a constant pity fixed on a particular object: for is desiring that someone not suffer anything but desiring that he be happy? Even should it be true that commiseration is only a sentiment that puts us in the position of him who suffers—a sentiment that is obscure and strong in savage man, developed but weak in civilized man—what would this idea matter to the truth of what I say, except to give it more force? In fact, commiseration will be all the more energetic as the observing animal identifies himself more intimately with the suffering animal. Now it is evident that this identification must have been infinitely closer in the state of nature than in the state of reasoning. Reason engenders vanity and reflection fortifies it; reason turns man back upon himself, it separates him from all that bothers and afflicts him. Philosophy isolates him; because of it he says in secret, at the sight of a suffering man: Perish if you will, I am safe. No longer can anything except dangers to the entire society trouble the tranquil sleep of the philosopher and tear him from his bed. His fellow-man can be murdered with impunity right under his window; he has only to put his hands over his ears and argue with himself a bit to prevent nature, which revolts within him, from identifying him with the man who is being assassinated. Savage man does not have this admirable talent, and for want of wisdom and reason he is always seen heedlessly yielding to the first sentiment of humanity. In riots or street fights the populace assembles, the prudent man moves away; it is the rabble, the marketwomen, who separate the combatants and prevent honest people from murdering each other.

It is very certain, therefore, that pity is a natural sentiment which, moderating in each individual the activity of love of oneself, contributes to the mutual preservation of the entire species. It carries us without reflection to the aid of those whom we see suffer; in the state of nature, it takes the place of laws, morals, and virtue, with the advantage that no one is tempted to disobey its gentle voice; it will dissuade every robust savage from robbing a weak child or an infirm old man of his hard-won subsistence if he himself hopes to be able to find his own elsewhere. Instead of that sublime maxim of reasoned justice, *Do unto others as you would have them do unto you*, it inspires all men with this other maxim of natural goodness, much less perfect but perhaps more useful than the preceding one: *Do what is good for you with the least possible harm to others*. In a word, it is in this natural sentiment, rather than in subtle arguments, that we must seek the cause of the repugnance every man would feel in doing evil, even independently of the maxims of education. Although it may behoove Socrates and minds of his stamp to acquire virtue through reason, the human race would have perished long ago if its preservation had depended only on the reasonings of its members.

With such inactive passions and such a salutary restraint, men—more untamed than evil, and more attentive to protecting themselves from harm they could receive than tempted to harm others—were not subject to very dangerous quarrels. Since they had no kind of commerce among themselves; since they consequently knew neither vanity, nor consideration, nor esteem, nor contempt; since they did not have the slightest notion of thine and mine, nor any true idea of justice; since they regarded the violences they might suffer as harm easy to redress and not as an insult which must be punished, and since they did not even dream of vengeance, except perhaps mechanically and on the spot, like the dog that bites the stone thrown at him, their disputes would rarely have had bloody consequences had there been no more sensitive subject than food. But I see a more dangerous subject left for me to discuss.

Among the passions that agitate the heart of man, there is an ardent, impetuous one that makes one sex necessary to the other; a terrible passion which braves all dangers, overcomes all obstacles, and which, in its fury, seems fitted to destroy the human race it is destined to preserve. What would become of men, tormented by this unrestrained and brutal rage, without chastity, without modesty, daily fighting over their loves at the price of their blood?

It must first be agreed that the more violent the passions, the more necessary laws are to contain them. But besides the fact that the disorders and crimes these passions cause every day among us show well enough the inadequacy of laws in this regard, it would still be good to examine whether these disorders did not arise with the laws themselves; for then, even should they be capable of repressing these disorders, the very least that ought to be required of the laws is to stop an evil which would not exist without them.

Let us begin by distinguishing between the moral and the physical in the sentiment of love. The physical is that general desire which inclines one sex to unite with the other. The moral is that which determines this desire and fixes it exclusively on a single object, or which at least gives it a greater degree of energy for this preferred object. Now it is easy to see that the moral element of love is an artificial sentiment born of the usage of society, and extolled with much skill and care by women in order to establish their ascendancy and make dominant the sex that ought to obey. This sentiment, founded on certain notions of merit or beauty that a savage is not capable of having, and on comparisons he is not capable of making, must be almost null for him. For as his mind could not form abstract ideas of regularity and proportion, so his heart is not susceptible to the sentiments of admiration and love that, even without its being noticed, arise from the application of these ideas. He heeds solely the temperament he received from nature, and not the taste he has not been able to acquire; any woman is good for him.

Limited solely to that which is physical in love, and fortunate enough to be ignorant of those preferences that irritate its sentiment and augment its difficulties, men must feel the ardors of their temperament less frequently and less vividly, and consequently have fewer and less cruel disputes among themselves. Imagination, which causes so much havoc among us, does not speak to savage hearts. Everyone peaceably waits for the impulsion of nature, yields to it without choice with more pleasure than frenzy; and the need satisfied, all desire is extinguished.

It is therefore incontestable that love itself, like all the other passions, has acquired only in society that impetuous ardor which so often makes it fatal for men; and it is all the more ridiculous to portray savages continually murdering each other to satisfy their brutality as this opinion is directly contrary to experience, and as the Caribs, that of all existing peoples which until now has departed least from the state of nature, are precisely the most peaceful in their loves and the least subject to jealousy, even though they live in a burning hot climate, which always seems to give greater activity to these passions.

Regarding inferences that one could draw, in some species of animals, from the fights of males which bloody our farmyards in all seasons or which make our forests resound with their cries in Spring as they contend for a female, it is necessary to begin by excluding all species in which nature has manifestly established, in the relative power of the sexes, other relations than among us: thus cockfights do not provide an inference for the human species. In species where the proportion is better observed, these fights can have for causes only the scarcity of females with reference to the number of males, or the exclusive intervals during which the female constantly refuses to let the male approach her, which amounts to the first cause; for if each female tolerates the male during only two months of the year, in this respect it is the same as if the number of females were reduced by five-sixths. Now neither of these two cases is applicable to the human species, in which the number of females generally surpasses the number of males, and in which it has never been observed that, even among savages, females, like those of other species, have times of heat and exclusion. Moreover, among some of these animals, since the entire species enters a state of heat at the same time, there comes a terrible moment of general ardor, tumult, disorder, and fighting: a moment that does not take place in the human species, in which love is never periodic. Therefore one cannot conclude from the fights of certain animals for the possession of females that the same thing would happen to man in the state of nature. And even if one could draw that conclusion, as these dissensions do not destroy the other species, one must consider at least that they would not be more fatal to ours; and it is very apparent that they would cause still less havoc in the state of nature than they do in society, particularly in countries where, morals still counting for something, the jealousy of lovers and the vengeance of husbands are a daily cause of duels, murders, and worse things; where the obligation to eternal fidelity serves only to create adulterers; and where even the laws of continence and honor necessarily spread debauchery and multiply abortions.

Let us conclude that wandering in the forests, without industry, without speech, without domicile, without war and without liaisons, with no need of his fellowmen, likewise with no desire to harm them, perhaps never even recognizing anyone individually, savage man, subject to few passions and self-sufficient, had only the sentiments and intellect suited to that state; he felt only his true needs, saw only what he believed he had an interest to see; and his intelligence made no more progress than his vanity. If by chance he made some discovery, he was all the less able to communicate it because he did not recognize even his children. Art perished with the inventor. There was neither education nor progress; the generations multiplied uselessly; and everyone always starting from the same point, centuries passed in all the crudeness of the first ages; the species was already old, and man remained ever a child.

If I have spent so much time on the supposition of this primitive condition, it is because, having ancient errors and inveterate prejudices to destroy, I thought I ought to dig down to the root and show, in the panorama of the true state of nature, how far even natural inequality is from having as much reality and influence in that state as our writers claim.

In fact, it is easy to see that, among the differences that distinguish men, some pass for natural that are uniquely the work of habit and the various types of life men adopt in society. Thus a robust or delicate temperament, and the strength or weakness that depend on it, often come more from the harsh or effeminate way in which one has been raised than from the primitive constitution of bodies. The same is true of strength of mind; and not only does education establish a difference between cultivated minds and those which are not, but it augments the difference among the former in proportion to their culture; for should a giant and a dwarf walk on the same road, every step they both take will give fresh advantage to the giant. Now if one compares the prodigious diversity of educations and types of life that prevail in the different orders of the civil state with the simplicity and uniformity of animal and savage life, in which all nourish themselves on the same foods, live in the same manner, and do exactly the same things, it will be understood how much less the difference between one man and another must be in the state of nature than in society, and how much natural inequality must increase in the human species through instituted inequality.

But even should nature assign as many preferences in the distribution of its gifts as is claimed, what advantage would the most favored draw from them to the prejudice of others in a state of things which permitted almost no sort of relationship among them? Where there is no love, of what use is beauty? What is the use of wit for people who do not speak, and ruse for those who have no dealings? I hear it always repeated that the stronger will oppress the weak. But let someone explain to me what is meant by this word oppression. Some will dominate by violence, the others will groan, enslaved to all their whims. That is precisely what I observe among us; but I do not see how that could be said of savage men, to whom one would even have much trouble explaining what servitude and domination are. A man might well seize the fruits another has gathered, the game he has killed, the cave that served as his shelter; but how will he ever succeed in making himself obeyed? And what can be the chain of dependence among men who possess nothing? If someone chases me from one tree, I am at liberty to go to another; if someone torments me in one place, who will prevent me from going elsewhere? Is there a man whose strength is sufficiently superior to mine and who is, in addition, depraved enough, lazy enough, and wild enough to force me to provide for his subsistence while he remains idle? He must resolve not to lose sight of me for a single moment and to keep me very carefully tied up during his sleep, for fear that I should escape or kill him—that is to say, he is obliged to expose himself voluntarily to much greater trouble than he wants to avoid and gives to me. After all that, should his vigilance relax for a moment, should an unforeseen noise make him turn his head, I take twenty steps in the forest, my chains are broken, and he never in his life sees me again.

Without uselessly prolonging these details, everyone must see that, since the bonds of servitude are formed only from the mutual dependence of men and the reciprocal needs that unite them, it is impossible to enslave a man without first putting him in the position of being unable to do without another; a situation which, as it did not exist in the state of nature, leaves each man there free of the yoke, and renders vain the law of the stronger. After having proved that inequality is barely perceptible in the state of nature, and that its influence there is almost null, it remains for me to show its origin and progress in the successive developments of the human mind. After having shown that *perfectibility*, social virtues, and the other faculties that natural man had received in potentiality could never develop by themselves, that in order to develop they needed the chance combination of several foreign causes which might never have arisen and without which he would have remained eternally in his primitive condition, it remains for me to consider and bring together the different accidents that were able to perfect human reason while deteriorating the species, make a being evil while making him sociable, and from such a distant origin finally bring man and the world to the point where we see them.

I admit that as the events I have to describe could have happened in several ways, I can make a choice only by conjectures. But besides the fact that these conjectures become reasons when they are the most probable that one can draw from the nature of things, and the sole means that one can have to discover the truth, the conclusions I want to deduce from mine will not thereby be conjectural, since, on the principles I have established, one could not conceive of any other system that would not provide me with the same results, and from which I could not draw the same conclusions.

This will excuse me from expanding my reflections concerning the way in which the lapse of time compensates for the slight probability of events; concerning the surprising power of very trivial causes when they act without interruption; concerning the impossibility, on the one hand, for one to destroy certain hypotheses, although on the other one cannot give them the degree of certainty of facts; concerning how, when two facts given as real are to be connected by a series of intermediate facts which are unknown or considered as such, it is up to history, when it exists, to present the facts that connect them; while it is up to philosophy, when history is lacking, to determine similar facts that might connect them; finally, concerning how, with reference to events, similarity reduces the facts to a much smaller number of different classes than is imagined. It is enough for me to offer these objects to the consideration of my judges; it is enough for me to have arranged it so that vulgar readers would have no need to consider them.

## ⸭ SECOND PART ⸭

The first person who, having fenced off a plot of ground, took it into his head to say *this is mine* and found people simple enough to believe him, was the true founder of civil society. What crimes, wars, murders, what miseries and horrors would the human race have been spared by someone who, uprooting the stakes or filling in the ditch, had shouted to his fellow-men: Beware of listening to this impostor; you are lost if you forget that the fruits belong to all and the earth to no one! But it is very likely that by then things had already come to the point where they could no longer remain as they were. For this idea of property, depending on many prior ideas which could only have arisen successively, was not conceived all at once in the human mind. It was necessary to make much progress, to acquire much industry and enlightenment, and to transmit and augment them from age to age, before arriving at this last stage of the state of nature. Therefore let us start further back in time and attempt to assemble from a single point of view this slow succession of events and knowledge in their most natural order.

Man's first sentiment was that of his existence, his first care that of his preservation. The products of the earth furnished him with all the necessary help; instinct led him to make use of them. Hunger and other appetites making him experience by turns various manners of existing, there was one appetite that invited him to perpetuate his species; and this blind inclination, devoid of any sentiment of the heart, produced only a purely animal act. This need satisfied, the two sexes no longer recognized each other, and even the child no longer meant anything to his mother as soon as he could do without her.

Such was the condition of nascent man; such was the life of an animal limited at first to pure sensations and scarcely profiting from the gifts nature offered him, far from dreaming of wresting anything from it. But difficulties soon arose; it was necessary to learn to conquer them. The height of trees, which prevented him from reaching their fruits, the competition of animals that sought to nourish themselves with these fruits, the ferocity of those animals that wanted to take his very life, all obliged him to apply himself to bodily exercises. It was necessary to become agile, fleet in running, vigorous in combat. Natural arms, which are branches of trees and stones, were soon discovered at hand. He learned to surmount nature's obstacles, combat other animals when necessary, fight for his subsistence even with men, or make up for what had to be yielded to the stronger.

In proportion as the human race spread, difficulties multiplied along with men. Differences of soil, climate, and season could force them to admit differences in their ways of life. Barren years, long and hard winters, and scorching summers which consume everything required of them new industry. Along the sea and rivers they invented the fishing line and hook, and became fishermen and eaters of fish. In forests they made bows and arrows, and became hunters and warriors. In cold countries they covered themselves with the skins of beasts they had killed. Lightning, a volcano, or some happy accident introduced them to fire, a new resource against the rigor of winter. They learned to preserve this element, then to reproduce it, and finally to prepare with it meats they previously devoured raw.

This repeated utilization of various beings in relation to himself, and of some beings in relation to others, must naturally have engendered in man's mind perceptions of certain relations. Those relationships that we express by the words large, small, strong, weak, fast, slow, fearful, bold, and other similar ideas, compared when necessary and almost without thinking about it, finally produced in him some sort of reflection, or rather a mechanical prudence that indicated to him the precautions most necessary for his safety.

The new enlightenment that resulted from this development increased his superiority over the other animals by making him aware of his superiority. He practiced setting traps for them; he tricked them in a thousand ways; and although several surpassed him in strength at fighting, or in speed at running, of those which might serve him or hurt him he became with time the master of the former, and the scourge of the latter. Thus the first glance he directed upon himself produced in him the first stirring of pride; thus, as yet scarcely knowing how to distinguish ranks, and considering himself in the first rank as a species, he prepared himself from afar to claim first rank as an individual.

Although his fellow-men were not for him what they are for us, and although he scarcely had more intercourse with them than with other animals, they were not forgotten in his observations. The conformities that time could make him perceive among them, his female, and himself led him to judge of those which he did not perceive; and seeing that they all behaved as he would have done under similar circumstances, he concluded that their way of thinking and feeling conformed entirely to his own. And this important truth, well established in his mind, made him follow, by a premonition as sure as dialectic and more prompt, the best rules of conduct that it was suitable to observe toward them for his advantage and safety.

Taught by experience that love of well-being is the sole motive of human actions, he found himself able to distinguish the rare occasions when common interest should make him count on the assistance of his fellow-men, and those even rarer occasions when competition should make him distrust them. In the first case he united with them in a herd; or at most by some kind of free association that obligated no one and lasted only as long as the passing need that had formed it. In the second case, everyone sought to obtain his own advantage, either by naked force if he believed he could, or by cleverness and cunning if he felt himself to be the weaker.

That is how men could imperceptibly acquire some crude idea of mutual engagements and of the advantages of fulfilling them, but only insofar as present and perceptible interest could require; for foresight meant nothing to them, and far from being concerned about a distant future, they did not even think of the next day. Was it a matter of catching a deer, everyone clearly felt that for this purpose he ought faithfully to keep his post; but if a hare happened to pass within reach of one of them, there can be no doubt that he pursued it without scruple, and that having obtained his prey, he cared very little about having caused his companions to miss theirs.

It is easy to understand that such intercourse did not require a language much more refined than that of crows or monkeys, which group together in approximately the same way. For a long time inarticulate cries, many gestures, and some imitative noises must have composed the universal language; by joining to this in each country a few articulated and conventional sounds—the institution of which, as I have already said, is not too easy to explain—there were particular languages, but crude imperfect ones, approximately like those which various savage nations still have today.

I cover multitudes of centuries like a flash, forced by the time that elapses, the abundance of things I have to say, and the almost imperceptible progress of the beginnings; for the more slowly events followed upon one another, the more quickly they can be described.

These first advances finally put man in a position to make more rapid ones. The more the mind was enlightened, the more industry was perfected. Soon, ceasing to fall asleep under the first tree or to withdraw into caves, they discovered some kinds of hatchets of hard, sharp stones, which served to cut wood, scoop out earth, and make huts from branches they later decided to coat with clay and mud. This was the epoch of a first revolution, which produced the establishment and differentiation of families, and which introduced a sort of property—from which perhaps many quarrels and fights already arose. However, as the stronger were probably the first to make themselves lodgings they felt capable of defending, it is to be presumed that the weak found it quicker and safer to imitate them than to try to dislodge them; and as for those who already had huts, each man must seldom have sought to appropriate his neighbor's, less because it did not belong to him than because it was of no use to him, and because he could not seize it without exposing himself to a lively fight with the family occupying it.

The first developments of the heart were the effect of a new situation, which united husbands and wives, fathers and children in a common habitation. The habit of living together gave rise to the sweetest sentiments known to men: conjugal love and paternal love. Each family became a little society all the better united because reciprocal affection and freedom were its only bonds; and it was then that the first difference was established in the way of life of the two sexes, which until this time had had but one. Women became more sedentary and grew accustomed to tend the hut and the children, while the man went to seek their common subsistence. The two sexes also began, by their slightly softer life, to lose something of their ferocity and vigor. But if each one separately became less suited to combat savage beasts, on the contrary it was easier to assemble in order to resist them jointly.

In this new state, with a simple and solitary life, very limited needs, and the implements they had invented to provide for them, since men enjoyed very great leisure, they used it to procure many kinds of commodities unknown to their fathers; and that was the first yoke they imposed on themselves without thinking about it, and the first source of the evils they prepared for their descendants. For, besides their continuing thus to soften body and mind, as these commodities had lost almost all their pleasantness through habit, and as they had at the same time degenerated into true needs, being deprived of them became much more cruel than possessing them was sweet; and people were unhappy to lose them without being happy to possess them.

At this point one catches a slightly better glimpse of how the use of speech was established or perfected imperceptibly in the bosom of each family; and one can conjecture further how particular causes could have spread language and accelerated its progress by making it more necessary. Great floods or earthquakes surrounded

419

inhabited cantons with water or precipices; revolutions of the globe detached and broke up portions of the continent into islands. One conceives that among men thus brought together and forced to live together, a common idiom must have been formed sooner than among those who wandered freely in the forests on solid ground. Thus it is very possible that after their first attempts at navigation, islanders brought the use of speech to us; and it is at least very probable that society and languages came into being on islands and were perfected there before they were known on the continent.

Everything begins to change its appearance. Men who until this time wandered in the woods, having adopted a more fixed settlement, slowly come together, unite into different bands, and finally form in each country a particular nation, unified by customs and character, not by regulations and laws but by the same kind of life and foods and by the common influence of climate. A permanent proximity cannot fail to engender at length some contact between different families. Young people of different sexes living in neighboring huts; the passing intercourse demanded by nature soon leads to another kind no less sweet and more permanent through mutual frequentation. People grow accustomed to consider different objects and to make comparisons; imperceptibly they acquire ideas of merit and beauty which produce sentiments of preference. By dint of seeing one another, they can no longer do without seeing one another again. A tender and gentle sentiment is gradually introduced into the soul and at the least obstacle becomes an impetuous fury. Jealousy awakens with love; discord triumphs, and the gentlest of the passions receives sacrifices of human blood.

In proportion as ideas and sentiments follow upon one another and as mind and heart are trained, the human race continues to be tamed, contacts spread, and bonds are tightened. People grew accustomed to assembling in front of the huts or around a large tree; song and dance, true children of love and leisure, became the amusement or rather the occupation of idle and assembled men and women. Each one began to look at the others and to want to be looked at himself, and public esteem had a value. The one who sang or danced the best, the handsomest, the strongest, the most adroit, or the most eloquent became the most highly considered; and that was the first step toward inequality and, at the same time, toward vice. From these first preferences were born on one hand vanity and contempt, on the other shame and envy; and the fermentation caused by these new leavens eventually produced compounds fatal to happiness and innocence.

As soon as men had begun to appreciate one another, and the idea of consideration was formed in their minds, each one claimed a right to it, and it was no longer possible to be disrespectful toward anyone with impunity. From this came the first duties of civility, even among savages; and from this any voluntary wrong became an outrage, because along with the harm that resulted from the injury, the offended man saw in it contempt for his person which was often more unbearable than the harm itself. Thus, everyone punishing the contempt shown him by another in a manner proportionate to the importance he accorded himself, vengeances became terrible, and men bloodthirsty and cruel. This is precisely the point reached by most of the savage peoples known to us, and it is for want of having sufficiently distinguished between ideas and noticed how far these peoples already were from the first state of nature that many have hastened to conclude that man is naturally cruel, and that he needs civilization in order to make him gentler. On the contrary, nothing is so gentle as man in his primitive state when, placed by nature at equal distances from the stupidity of brutes and the fatal enlightenment of civil man, and limited equally by instinct and reason to protecting himself from the harm that threatens him, he is restrained by natural pity from harming anyone himself, and nothing leads him to do so even after he has received harm. For, according to the axiom of the wise Locke, *where there is no property, there is no injury.*

But it must be noted that the beginnings of society and the relations already established among men required in them qualities different from those they derived from their primitive constitution; that, morality beginning to be introduced into human actions, and each man, prior to laws, being sole judge and avenger of the offenses he had received, the goodness suitable for the pure state of nature was no longer that which suited nascent society; that it was necessary for punishments to become more severe as the occasions for offense became more frequent; and that it was up to the terror of revenge to take the place of the restraint of laws. Thus although men had come to have less endurance and although natural pity had already undergone some alteration, this period of the development of human faculties, maintaining a golden mean between the indolence of the primitive state and the petulant activity of our vanity, must have been the happiest and most durable epoch. The more one thinks about it, the more one finds that this state was the least subject to revolutions, the best for man, and that he must have come out of it only by some fatal accident, which for the common good ought never to have happened. The example of savages, who have almost all been found at this point, seems to confirm that the human race was made to remain in it always; that this state is the veritable prime of the world; and that all subsequent progress has been in appearance so many steps toward the perfection of the individual, and in fact toward the decrepitude of the species.

As long as men were content with their rustic huts, as long as they were limited to sewing their clothing of skins with thorns or fish bones, adorning themselves with feathers and shells, painting their bodies with various colors, perfecting or embellishing their bows and arrows, carving with sharp stones a few fishing canoes or a few crude musical instruments; in a word, as long as they applied themselves only to tasks that a single person could do and to arts that did not require the cooperation of several hands, they lived free, healthy, good, and happy insofar as they could be according to their nature, and they continued to enjoy among themselves the sweetness of independent intercourse. But from the moment one man needed the help of another, as soon as they observed that it was useful for a single person to have provisions for two, equality disappeared, property was introduced, labor became necessary; and vast forests were changed into smiling fields which had to be watered with the sweat of men, and in which slavery and misery were soon seen to germinate and grow with the crops.

Metallurgy and agriculture were the two arts whose invention produced this great revolution. For the poet it is gold and silver, but for the philosopher it is iron and wheat which have civilized men and ruined the human race. Accordingly, both of these were unknown to the savages of America, who therefore have always remained savage; other peoples even seem to have remained barbarous as long as they practiced one of these arts without the other. And perhaps one of the best reasons why Europe has been, if not earlier, at least more constantly and better civilized than the other parts of the world is that it is at the same time the most abundant in iron and the most fertile in wheat. It is very difficult to guess how men came to know and use iron; for it is not credible that by themselves they thought of drawing the raw material from the mine and giving it the necessary preparations to fuse it before they knew what would result. From another point of view, it is even harder to attribute this discovery to some accidental fire, because mines are formed only in arid spots, stripped of both trees and plants; so that one would say that nature had taken precautions to hide this deadly secret from us. There only remains, therefore, the extraordinary circumstance of some volcano which, by throwing up metallic materials in fusion, would have given observers the idea of imitating this operation of nature. Even so, it is necessary to suppose in them much courage and foresight to undertake such difficult labor and to envisage so far in advance the advantages they could gain from it: all of which hardly suits minds that are not already more trained than theirs must have been.

With regard to agriculture, its principle was known long before its practice was established, and it is hardly possible that men, constantly occupied with obtaining their subsistence from trees and plants, did not rather promptly have an idea of the ways used by nature to grow plants. But their industry probably turned in that direction only very late, either because trees, which along with hunting and fishing provided their food, did not have need of their care; or for want of knowing how to use wheat; or for want of implements to cultivate it; or for want of foresight concerning future need; or, finally, for want of means to prevent others from appropriating the fruit of their labor. Once they became industrious, it is credible that, with sharp stones and pointed sticks, they began by cultivating a few vegetables or roots around their huts long before they knew how to prepare wheat and had the implements necessary for large-scale cultivation. Besides, to devote oneself to that occupation and seed the land, one must be resolved to lose something at first in order to gain a great deal later: a precaution very far from the turn of mind of savage man, who, as I have said, has great difficulty thinking in the morning of his needs for the evening.

The invention of the other arts was therefore necessary to force the human race to apply itself to that of agriculture. As soon as some men were needed to smelt and forge iron, other men were needed to feed them. The more the number of workers was multiplied, the fewer hands were engaged in furnishing the common subsistence, without there being fewer mouths to consume it; and since some needed foodstuffs in exchange for their iron, the others finally found the secret of using iron in order to multiply foodstuffs. From this arose husbandry and agriculture on the one hand, and on the other the art of working metals and multiplying their uses.

From the cultivation of land, its division necessarily followed; and from property once recognized, the first rules of justice. For in order to give everyone what is his, it is necessary that everyone can have something; moreover, as men began to look to the future and as they all saw themselves with some goods to lose, there was not one of them who did not have to fear reprisals against himself for wrongs he might do to another. This origin is all the more natural as it is impossible to conceive of the idea of property arising from anything except manual labor; because one cannot see what man can add, other than his own labor, in order to appropriate things he has not made. It is labor alone which, giving the cultivator a right to the product of the land he has tilled, gives him a right to the soil as a consequence, at least until the harvest, and thus from year to year; which, creating continuous possession, is easily transformed into property. When the ancients, says Grotius[1], gave Ceres the epithet of legislatrix, and gave the name of Thesmaphories to a festival celebrated in her honor, they thereby made it clear that the division of lands produced a new kind of right: that is, the right of property, different from the one which results from natural law.

Things in this state could have remained equal if talents had been equal, and if, for example, the use of iron and the consumption of foodstuffs had always been exactly balanced. But this proportion, which nothing maintained, was soon broken; the stronger did more work; the cleverer turned his to better advantage; the more ingenious found ways to shorten his labor; the farmer had greater need of iron or the blacksmith greater need of wheat; and working equally, the one earned a great deal while the other barely had enough to live. Thus does natural inequality imperceptibly manifest itself along with contrived inequality; and thus do the differences among men, developed by those of circumstances, become more perceptible, more permanent in their effects, and begin to have a proportionate influence over the fate of individuals.

Things having reached this point, it is easy to imagine the rest. I shall not stop to describe the successive invention of the other arts, the progress of languages, the testing and use of talents, the inequality of fortunes, the use or abuse of wealth, nor all the details that follow these, and that everyone can easily fill in. I shall simply limit myself to casting a glance at the human race placed in this new order of things.

Behold all our faculties developed, memory and imagination in play, vanity aroused, reason rendered active, and the mind having almost reached the limit of the perfection of which it is susceptible. Behold all the natural qualities put into action, the rank and fate of each man established, not only upon the quantity of goods and the power to serve or harm, but also upon the mind, beauty, strength, or skill, upon merit or talents. And these qualities being the only ones which

---

[1] [Hugo Crotius (1583-1645), a Dutch jurist and philosopher, wrote on natural rights and utilized the writings of Roman and Stoic thinkers. —J.M.P.]

could attract consideration, it was soon necessary to have them or affect them; for one's own advantage, it was necessary to appear to be other than what one in fact was. To be and to seem to be became two altogether different things; and from this distinction came conspicuous ostentation, deceptive cunning, and all the vices that follow from them. From another point of view, having formerly been free and independent, behold man, due to a multitude of new needs, subjected so to speak to all of nature and especially to his fellow-men, whose slave he becomes in a sense even in becoming their master; rich, he needs their services; poor, he needs their help; and mediocrity cannot enable him to do without them. He must therefore incessantly seek to interest them in his fate, and to make them find their own profit, in fact or in appearance, in working for his. This makes him deceitful and sly with some, imperious and harsh with others, and makes it necessary for him to abuse all those whom he needs when he cannot make them fear him and does not find his interest in serving them usefully. Finally, consuming ambition, the fervor to raise one's relative fortune less out of true need than in order to place oneself above others, inspires in all men a base inclination to harm each other, a secret jealousy all the more dangerous because, in order to strike its blow in greater safety, it often assumes the mask of benevolence: in a word, competition and rivalry on one hand, opposition of interest on the other; and always the hidden desire to profit at the expense of others. All these evils are the first effect of property and the inseparable consequence of nascent inequality.

Before representative signs of wealth had been invented, it could hardly consist of anything except land and livestock, the only real goods men can possess. Now when inheritances had increased in number and extent to the point of covering the entire earth and of all bordering on each other, some of them could no longer be enlarged except at the expense of others; and the supernumeraries, whom weakness or indolence had prevented from acquiring an inheritance in their turn, having become poor without having lost anything—because while everything around them changed they alone had not changed at all—were obliged to receive or steal their subsistence from the hand of the rich; and from that began to arise, according to the diverse characters of the rich and the poor, domination and servitude or violence and rapine. The rich, for their part, had scarcely known the pleasure of domination when they soon disdained all others, and using their old slaves to subdue new ones, they thought only of subjugating and enslaving their neighbors: like those famished wolves which, having once tasted human flesh, refuse all other food and thenceforth want only to devour men.

Thus, as the most powerful or most miserable made of their force or their needs a sort of right to the goods of others, equivalent according to them to the right of property, the destruction of equality was followed by the most frightful disorder; thus the usurpations of the rich, the brigandage of the poor, the unbridled passions of all, stifling natural pity and the as yet weak voice of justice, made man avaricious, ambitious, and evil. Between the right of the stronger and the right of the first occupant there arose a perpetual conflict which ended only in fights and murders. Nascent society gave way to the most horrible state of war: the human race, debased and desolated, no longer able to turn back or renounce the unhappy acquisitions it had made, and working only toward its shame by abusing the faculties that honor it, brought itself to the brink of its ruin.

> *Attonitus novitate mali, divesque, miserque,*
> *Effugere optat opes, et quae modo voverat, odit.*

It is not possible that men should not at last have reflected upon such a miserable situation and upon the calamities overwhelming them. The rich above all must have soon felt how disadvantageous to them was a perpetual war in which they alone paid all the costs, and in which the risk of life was common to all while the risk of goods was theirs alone. Moreover, whatever pretext they might give for their usurpations, they were well aware that these were established only on a precarious and abusive right, and that having been acquired only by force, force could take them away without their having grounds for complaint. Even those enriched by industry alone could hardly base their property upon better titles. In vain might they say: But I built this wall; I earned this field by my labor. Who gave you its dimensions, they might be answered, and by virtue of what do you presume to be paid at our expense for work we did not impose on you? Do you not know that a multitude of your brethren die or suffer from need of what you have in excess, and that you needed express and unanimous consent of the human race to appropriate for yourself anything from common subsistence that exceeded your own? Destitute of valid reasons to justify himself and of sufficient forces to defend himself; easily crushing an individual, but himself crushed by groups of bandits; alone against all, and unable because of mutual jealousies to unite with his equals against enemies united by the common hope of plunder, the rich, pressed by necessity, finally conceived the

---

* "Both rich and poor shocked at their newfound ills, would fly from wealth, and hate what they had sought." Ovid, *Metamorphoses*, XI, 127.

most deliberate project that ever entered the human mind. It was to use in his favor the very forces of those who attacked him, to make his defenders out of his adversaries, inspire them with other maxims, and give them other institutions which were as favorable to him as natural right was adverse.

To this end, after having shown his neighbors the horror of a situation that made them all take up arms against one another, that made their possessions as burdensome as their needs, and in which no one found security in either poverty or wealth, he easily invented specious reasons to lead them to his goal. "Let us unite," he says to them, "to protect the weak from oppression, restrain the ambitious, and secure for everyone the possession of what belongs to him. Let us institute regulations of justice and peace to which all are obliged to conform, which make an exception of no one, and which compensate in some way for the caprices of fortune by equally subjecting the powerful and the weak to mutual duties. In a word, instead of turning our forces against ourselves, let us gather them into one supreme power which governs us according to wise laws, protects and defends all the members of the association, repulses common enemies, and maintains us in an eternal concord."

Far less than the equivalent of this discourse was necessary to win over crude, easily seduced men, who in addition had too many disputes to straighten out among themselves to be able to do without arbiters, and too much avarice and ambition to be able to do without masters for long. All ran to meet their chains thinking they secured their freedom, for although they had enough reason to feel the advantages of a political establishment, they did not have enough experience to foresee its dangers. Those most capable of anticipating the abuses were precisely those who counted on profiting from them; and even the wise saw the necessity of resolving to sacrifice one part of their freedom for the preservation of the other, just as a wounded man has his arm cut off to save the rest of his body.

Such was, or must have been, the origin of society and laws, which gave new fetters to the weak and new forces to the rich, destroyed natural freedom for all time, established forever the law of property and inequality, changed a clever usurpation into an irrevocable right, and for the profit of a few ambitious men henceforth subjected the whole human race to work, servitude, and misery. It is easily seen how the establishment of a single society made that of all the others indispensable, and how, to stand up to the united forces, it was necessary to unite in turn. Societies, multiplying or spreading rapidly, soon covered the entire surface of the earth; and it was no longer possible to find a single corner in the universe where one could free oneself from the yoke and withdraw one's head from the sword, often ill-guided, that every man saw perpetually hanging over his head. Civil right having thus become the common rule of citizens, the law of nature no longer operated except between the various societies, where, under the name law of nations, it was tempered by some tacit conventions in order to make intercourse possible and to take the place of natural commiseration which, losing between one society and another nearly all the force it had between one man and another, no longer dwells in any but a few great cosmopolitan souls, who surmount the imaginary barriers that separate peoples and who, following the example of the sovereign Being who created them, include the whole human race in their benevolence.

The bodies politic, thus remaining in the state of nature with relation to each other, soon experienced the inconveniences that had forced individuals to leave it; and among these great bodies that state became even more fatal than it had previously been among the individuals of whom they were composed. Hence arose the national wars, battles, murders, and reprisals which make nature tremble and shock reason, and all those horrible prejudices which rank the honor of shedding human blood among the virtues. The most decent men learned to consider it one of their duties to murder their fellow-men; at length men were seen to massacre each other by the thousands without knowing why; more murders were committed on a single day of fighting and more horrors in the capture of a single city than were committed in the state of nature during whole centuries over the entire face of the earth. Such are the first effects one glimpses of the division of the human race into different societies....

# ON THE SOCIAL CONTRACT

## ✣ BOOK I ✣

I want to inquire whether there can be a legitimate and reliable rule of administration in the civil order, taking men as they are and laws as they can be. I shall try always to reconcile in this research what right permits with what interest prescribes, so that justice and utility are not at variance....

### *Chapter I*

### *Subject of This First Book*

Man was/is born free, and everywhere he is in chains. One who believes himself the master of others is nonetheless a greater slave than they. How did this change occur? I do not know. What can make it legitimate? I believe I can answer this question.

If I were to consider only force and the effect it produces, I would say that as long as a people is constrained to obey and does so, it does well; as soon as it can shake off the yoke and does so, it does even better. For in recovering its freedom by means of the same right used to steal it, either the people is justified in taking it back, or those who took it away were not justified in doing so. But the social order is a sacred right that serves as a basis for all the others. However, this right does not come from nature; it is therefore based on conventions. The problem is to know what these conventions are. Before coming to that, I should establish what I have just asserted.

### *Chapter II*

### *On the First Societies*

The most ancient of all societies, and the only natural one, is that of the family. Yet children remain bound to the father only as long as they need him for self-preservation. As soon as this need ceases, the natural bond dissolves. The children, exempt from the obedience they owed the father, and the father, exempt from the care he owed the children, all return equally to independence. If they continue to remain united, it is no longer naturally but voluntarily, and the family itself is maintained only by convention.

*On the Social Contract,* by Jean-Jacques Rousseau, edited by Roger D. Masters, translated by Judith R. Masters. New York: St. Martin's Press. Copyright © 1978 by St. Martin's Press. Reprinted by permission.

This common freedom is a consequence of man's nature. His first law is to attend to his own preservation, his first cares are those he owes himself; and as soon as he has reached the age of reason, as he alone is the judge of the proper means of preserving himself, he thus becomes his own master....

## Chapter III

### On the Right of the Strongest

The strongest is never strong enough to be the master forever unless he transforms his force into right and obedience into duty. This leads to the right of the strongest, a right that is in appearance taken ironically and in principle really established. But won't anyone ever explain this word to us? Force is a physical power. I do not see what morality can result from its effects. Yielding to force is an act of necessity, not of will. At most, it is an act of prudence. In what sense could it be a duty?

Let us suppose this alleged right for a moment. I say that what comes of it is nothing but inexplicable confusion. For as soon as force makes right, the effect changes along with the cause. Any force that overcomes the first one succeeds to its right. As soon as one can disobey without punishment, one can do so legitimately, and since the strongest is always right, the only thing to do is to make oneself the strongest. But what is a right that perishes when force ceases? If it is necessary to obey by force, one need not obey by duty, and if one is no longer forced to obey, one is no longer obligated to do so. It is apparent, then, that this word right adds nothing to force. It is meaningless here.

Obey those in power. If that means yield to force, the precept is good, but superfluous; I reply that it will never be violated. All power comes from God, I admit, but so does all illness. Does this mean it is forbidden to call the doctor? If a brigand takes me by surprise at the edge of a woods, must I not only give up my purse by force; am I obligated by conscience to give it even if I could keep it away? After all, the pistol he holds is also a power.

Let us agree, therefore, that might does not make right, and that one is only obligated to obey legitimate powers. Thus my original question still remains.

## Chapter V

### That It is Always Necessary to Go Back to a First Convention

Even if I were to grant everything I have thus far refuted, the proponents of despotism would be no better off. There will always be a great difference between subjugating a multitude and governing a society. If scattered men, however many there may be, are successively enslaved by one individual, I see only a master and slaves; I do not see a people and its leader. It is an aggregation, if you wish, but not an association. It has neither public good nor body politic. That man, even if he had enslaved half the world, is nothing but a private individual. His interest, separate from that of the others, is still nothing but a private interest. If this same man dies, thereafter his empire is left scattered and without bonds, just as an oak tree disintegrates and falls into a heap of ashes after fire has consumed it.

A people, says Grotius[1], can give itself to a king. According to Grotius, a people is therefore a people before it gives itself to a king. This gift itself is a civil act; it presupposes a public deliberation. Therefore, before examining the act by which a people elects a king, it would be well to examine the act by which a people becomes a people. For this act, being necessarily prior to the other, is the true basis of society.

Indeed, if there were no prior convention, what would become of the obligation for the minority to submit to the choice of the majority, unless the election were unanimous; and where do one hundred who want a master get the right to vote for ten who do not? The law of majority rule is itself an established convention, and presupposes unanimity at least once.

## Chapter VI

## On the Social Compact

I assume that men have reached the point where obstacles to their self-preservation in the state of nature prevail by their resistance over the forces each individual can use to maintain himself in that state. Then that primitive state can no longer subsist and the human race would perish if it did not change its way of life.

Now since men cannot engender new forces, but merely unite and direct existing ones, they have no other means of self-preservation except to form, by aggregation, a sum of forces that can prevail over the resistance; set them to work by a single motivation; and make them act in concert.

This sum of forces can arise only from the cooperation of many. But since each man's force and freedom are the primary instruments of his self-preservation, how is he to engage them without harming himself and without neglecting the cares he owes to himself? In the context of my subject, this difficulty can be stated in these terms:

---

[1] [See footnote on page 424.]

"Find a form of association that defends and protects the person and goods of each associate with all the common force, and by means of which each one, uniting with all, nevertheless obeys only himself and remains as free as before." This is the fundamental problem which is solved by the social contract.

The clauses of this contract are so completely determined by the nature of the act that the slightest modification would render them null and void. So that although they may never have been formally pronounced, they are everywhere the same, everywhere tacitly accepted and recognized, until the social compact is violated, at which point each man recovers his original rights and resumes his natural freedom, thereby losing the conventional freedom for which he renounced it.

Properly understood, all of these clauses come down to a single one, namely the total alienation of each associate, with all his rights, to the whole community. For first of all, since each one gives his entire self, the condition is equal for everyone, and since the condition is equal for everyone, no one has an interest in making it burdensome for the others.

Furthermore, as the alienation is made without reservation, the union is as perfect as it can be, and no associate has anything further to claim. For if some rights were left to private individuals, there would be no common superior who could judge between them and the public. Each man being his own judge on some point would soon claim to be so on all; the state of nature would subsist and the association would necessarily become tyrannical or ineffectual.

Finally, as each gives himself to all, he gives himself to no one; and since there is no associate over whom one does not acquire the same right one grants him over oneself, one gains the equivalent of everything one loses, and more force to preserve what one has. If, then, everything that is not of the essence of the social compact is set aside, one will find that it can be reduced to the following terms. *Each of us puts his person and all his power in common under the supreme direction of the general will; and in a body we receive each member as an indivisible part of the whole.*

Instantly, in place of the private person of each contracting party, this act of association produces a moral and collective body, composed of as many members as there are voices in the assembly, which receives from this same act its unity, its common *self*, its life, and its will. This public person, formed thus by the union of all the others, formerly took the name *City*, and now takes that of *Republic* or *body politic*, which its members call *State* when it is passive, *Sovereign* when active, *Power* when comparing it to similar bodies. As for the associates, they collectively take the name

*people*, and individually are called *Citizens* as participants in the sovereign authority, and *Subjects* as subject to the laws of the State. But these terms are often mixed
up and mistaken for one another. It is enough to know how to distinguish them when
they are used with complete precision.

## Chapter VII

### On the Sovereign

This formula shows that the act of association includes a reciprocal engagement
between the public and private individuals, and that each individual, contracting
with himself so to speak, finds that he is doubly engaged, namely toward private
individuals as a member of the sovereign and toward the sovereign as a member
of the State. But the maxim of civil right that no one can be held responsible for
engagements toward himself cannot be applied here, because there is a great difference between being obligated to oneself, or to a whole of which one is a part.

It must further be noted that the public deliberation that can obligate all of the
subjects to the sovereign—due to the two different relationships in which each of
them is considered—cannot for the opposite reason obligate the sovereign toward itself; and that consequently it is contrary to the nature of the body politic
for the sovereign to impose on itself a law it cannot break. Since the sovereign can
only be considered in a single relationship, it is then in the situation of a private
individual contracting with himself. It is apparent from this that there is not,
nor can there be, any kind of fundamental law that is obligatory for the body of
the people, not even the social contract. This does not mean that this body cannot perfectly well enter an engagement toward another with respect to things
that do not violate this contract. For with reference to the foreigner, it becomes
a simple being or individual.

But the body politic or the sovereign, deriving its being solely from the
sanctity of the contract, can never obligate itself, even toward another, to do anything that violates that original act, such as to alienate some part of itself or to
subject itself to another sovereign. To violate the act by which it exists would be
to destroy itself, and whatever is nothing, produces nothing.

As soon as this multitude is thus united in a body, one cannot harm one of the
members without attacking the body, and it is even less possible to harm the body
without the members feeling the effects. Thus duty and interest equally obligate

the two contracting parties to mutual assistance, and the same men should seek to combine in this double relationship all the advantages that are dependent on it.

Now the sovereign, formed solely by the private individuals composing it, does not and cannot have any interest contrary to theirs. Consequently, the sovereign power has no need of a guarantee toward the subjects, because it is impossible for the body ever to want to harm all its members, and we shall see later that it cannot harm any one of them as an individual. The sovereign, by the sole fact of being, is always what it ought to be.

But the same is not true of the subjects in relation to the sovereign, which, despite the common interest, would have no guarantee of the subjects' engagements if it did not find ways to be assured of their fidelity.

Indeed, each individual can, as a man, have a private will contrary to or differing from the general will he has as a citizen. His private interest can speak to him quite differently from the common interest. His absolute and naturally independent existence can bring him to view what he owes the common cause as a free contribution, the loss of which will harm others less than its payment burdens him. And considering the moral person of the State as an imaginary being because it is not a man, he might wish to enjoy the rights of the citizen without wanting to fulfill the duties of a subject, an injustice whose spread would cause the ruin of the body politic.

Therefore, in order for the social compact not to be an ineffectual formula, it tacitly includes the following engagement, which alone can give force to the others: that whoever refuses to obey the general will shall be constrained to do so by the entire body; which means only that he will be forced to be free. For this is the condition that, by giving each citizen to the homeland, guarantees him against all personal dependence; a condition that creates the ingenuity and functioning of the political machine, and alone gives legitimacy to civil engagements which without it would be absurd, tyrannical, and subject to the most enormous abuses.

## Chapter VIII

### On the Civil State

This passage from the state of nature to the civil state produces a remarkable change in man, by substituting justice for instinct in his behavior and giving his actions the morality they previously lacked. Only then, when the voice of duty replaces physical impulse and right replaces appetite, does man, who until that time only considered himself, find himself forced to act upon other principles and to consult his reason before heeding his inclinations. Although in this state he deprives himself of several advantages given him by nature, he gains such great ones, his faculties are exercised and developed, his ideas broadened, his feelings ennobled, and his whole soul elevated to such a point that if the abuses of this new condition did not often degrade him beneath the condition he left, he ought ceaselessly to bless the happy moment that tore him away from it forever, and that changed him from a stupid, limited animal into an intelligent being and a man.

Let us reduce the pros and cons to easily compared terms. What man loses by the social contract is his natural freedom and an unlimited right to everything that tempts him and that he can get; what he gains is civil freedom and the proprietorship of everything he possesses. In order not to be mistaken about these compensations, one must distinguish carefully between natural freedom, which is limited only by the force of the individual, and civil freedom, which is limited by the general will; and between possession, which is only the effect of force or the right of the first occupant, and property, which can only be based on a positive title.

To the foregoing acquisitions of the civil state could be added moral freedom, which alone makes man truly the master of himself. For the impulse of appetite alone is slavery, and obedience to the law one has prescribed for oneself is freedom. But I have already said too much about this topic, and the philosophic meaning of the word *freedom* is not my subject here.

## Chapter IX

### On Real Estate

Each member of the community gives himself to it at the moment of its formation, just as he currently is—both himself and all his force, which includes the goods he possesses. It is not that by this act possession, in changing hands, changes its nature and becomes property in the hands of the sovereign. But as the force of the City is incomparably greater than that of a private individual, public possession is by that very fact stronger and more irrevocable, without being more legitimate, at least as far as foreigners are concerned. For with regard to its members, the State is master of all their goods through the social contract, which serves within the State as the basis of all rights. But with regard to other powers, it is master only through the right of the first occupant, which it derives from the private individuals.

The right of the first occupant, although more real than the right of the strongest, becomes a true right only after the establishment of the right of property. Every man naturally has a right to everything he needs; but the positive act that makes him the proprietor of some good excludes him from all the rest. Once his portion is designated, he should limit himself to it, and no longer has any right to the community's goods. That is why the right of the first occupant, weak in the state of nature, is respectable to every civilized man. In this right, one respects not so much what belongs to others as what does not belong to oneself.

In general, the following conditions are necessary to authorize the right of the first occupant to any land whatsoever. First, that this land not yet be inhabited by anyone. Second, that one occupy only the amount needed to subsist. Third, that one take possession not by a vain ceremony, but by labor and cultivation, the only sign of property that others ought to respect in the absence of legal titles.

Indeed, by granting the right of the first occupant to need and labor, hasn't it been extended as far as possible? Is it impossible to establish limits to this right? Will setting foot on a piece of common ground be sufficient to claim on the spot to be its master? Will having the force to disperse other men for a moment be sufficient to take away forever their right to return? How can a man or a people seize an immense territory and deprive the whole human race of it except through punishable usurpation, since this act takes away from the remaining men the dwelling place and foods that nature gives them in common? When Nunez Balboa, standing on the shore, took possession of the South Sea and all of South America in the name of the crown of Castile, was this enough to dispossess all the inhabitants and exclude all the princes of the world? On that basis such ceremonies multiplied rather ineffectually, and all the Catholic King had to do was to take possession of the entire universe all at once from his study, subsequently eliminating from his empire what had previously been possessed by other princes.

It is understandable how the combined and contiguous lands of private individuals become public territory, and how the right of sovereignty, extending from the subjects to the ground they occupy, comes to include both property and persons, which places those who possess land in a greater dependency and turns even their force into a guarantee of their loyalty. This advantage does not appear to have been well understood by ancient kings who, only calling themselves Kings of the Persians, the Scythians, the Macedonians, seem to have considered themselves leaders of men rather than masters of the country. Today's kings more cleverly call themselves Kings of France, Spain, England, etc. By thus holding the land, they are quite sure to hold its inhabitants.

436

What is extraordinary about this alienation is that far from plundering private individuals of their goods, by accepting them the community thereby only assures them of legitimate possession, changes usurpation into a true right, and use into property. Then, since their rights are respected by all the members of the State and maintained with all its force against foreigners, through a transfer that is advantageous to the public and even more so to themselves, they have, so to speak, acquired all they have given. This paradox is easily explained by the distinction between the rights of the sovereign and of the proprietor to the same resource, as will be seen hereafter.

It can also happen that men start to unite before possessing anything and that subsequently taking over a piece of land sufficient for all, they use it in common or divide it among themselves, either equally or according to proportions established by the sovereign. However this acquisition is made, the right of each private individual to his own resources is always subordinate to the community's right to all, without which there would be neither solidity in the social bond nor real force in the exercise of sovereignty.

I shall end this chapter and this book with a comment that ought to serve as the basis of the whole social system. It is that rather than destroying natural equality, the fundamental compact on the contrary substitutes a moral and legitimate equality for whatever physical inequality nature may have placed between men, and that although they may be unequal in force or in genius, they all become equal through convention and by right.*

## → BOOK II ←

### Chapter I

### That Sovereignty is Inalienable

The first and most important consequence of the principles established above is that the general will alone can guide the forces of the State according to the end for which it was instituted, which is the common good. For if the opposition of private interests made the establishment of societies necessary, it is the agreement

---

*Under bad governments, this equality is only apparent and illusory. It serves merely to maintain the poor man in his misery and the rich in his usurpation. In fact, laws are always useful to those who have possessions and harmful to those who have nothing. It follows from this that the social state is only advantageous to men insofar as they all have something and none of them has anything superfluous.

of these same interests that made it possible. It is what these different interests have in common that forms the social bond, and if there were not some point at which all the interests are in agreement, no society could exist. Now it is uniquely on the basis of this common interest that society ought to be governed.

I say, therefore, that sovereignty, being only the exercise of the general will, can never be alienated, and that the sovereign, which is only a collective being, can only be represented by itself. Power can perfectly well be transferred, but not will.

Indeed, though it is not impossible for a private will to agree with the general will on a given point, it is impossible, at least, for this agreement to be lasting and unchanging. For the private will tends by its nature toward preferences, and the general will toward equality. It is even more impossible for there to be a guarantee of this agreement even should it always exist. It would not be the result of art, but of chance. The sovereign may well say, "I currently want what a particular man wants, or at least what he says he wants." But it cannot say, "What that man will want tomorrow, I shall still want," since it is absurd for the will to tie itself down for the future and since no will can consent to anything that is contrary to the good of the being that wills. Therefore, if the people promises simply to obey, it dissolves itself by that act; it loses the status of a people. The moment there is a master, there is no longer a sovereign, and from then on the body politic is destroyed.

This is not to say that the commands of leaders cannot pass for expressions of the general will, as long as the sovereign, being free to oppose them, does not do so. In such a case, one ought to presume the consent of the people from universal silence. This will be explained at greater length.

## Chapter II

### That Sovereignty is Indivisible

For the same reason that sovereignty is inalienable, it is indivisible. Because either the will is general* or it is not. It is the will of the people as a body, or of only a part. In the first case, this declared will is an act of sovereignty and constitutes law. In the second case, it is merely a private will or an act of magistracy; it is at most a decree....

---

*In order for a will to be general, it is not always necessary for it to be unanimous, but it is necessary that all votes be counted. Any formal exclusion destroys the generality.

## Chapter III

### Whether the General Will Can Err

From the foregoing it follows that the general will is always right and always tends toward the public utility. But it does not follow that the people's deliberations always have the same rectitude. One always wants what is good for oneself, but one does not always see it. The people is never corrupted, but it is often fooled, and only then does it appear to want what is bad.

There is often a great difference between the will of all and the general will. The latter considers only the common interest; the former considers private interest, and is only a sum of private wills. But take away from these same wills the pluses and minuses that cancel each other out,* and the remaining sum of the differences is the general will.

If, when an adequately informed people deliberates, the citizens were to have no communication among themselves, the general will would always result from the large number of small differences, and the deliberation would always be good. But when factions, partial associations at the expense of the whole, are formed, the will of each of these associations becomes general with reference to its members and particular with reference to the State. One can say, then, that there are no longer as many voters as there are men, but merely as many as there are associations. The differences become less numerous and produce a result that is less general. Finally, when one of these associations is so big that it prevails over all the others, the result is no longer a sum of small differences, but a single difference. Then there is no longer a general will, and the opinion that prevails is merely a private opinion.

In order for the general will to be well expressed, it is therefore important that there be no partial society in the State, and that each citizen give only his own opinion.** Such was the unique and sublime system instituted by the great Lycurgus.

---

*"Each interest," says the Marquis d'Argenson, "has different principles. The agreement of two private interests is formed in opposition to the interest of a third." He could have added that the agreement of all interests is formed in opposition to the interest of each. If there were no different interests, the common interest, which would never encounter any obstacle, would scarcely be felt. Everything would run smoothly by itself and politics would cease to be an art.

**"Divisions," says Machiavelli, "sometimes injure and sometimes aid a republic. The injury is done by cabals and factions; the service is rendered by a party which maintains itself without cabals and factions. Since, therefore, it is impossible for the founder of a republic to provide against enmities, he must make the best provision he can against factions." *History of Florence*, Book VII.

If there are partial societies, their number must be multiplied and their inequality prevented, as was done by Solon, Numa, and Servius. These precautions are the only valid means of ensuring that the general will is always enlightened and that the people is not deceived.

## Chapter IV

### On the Limits of the Sovereign Power

If the State or the City is only a moral person whose life consists in the union of its members, and if the most important of its concerns is that of its own preservation, it must have a universal, compulsory force to move and arrange each part in the manner best suited to the whole. Just as nature gives each man absolute power over all his members, the social compact gives the body politic absolute power over all its members, and it is this same power, directed by the general will, which as I have said bears the name sovereignty.

But in addition to the public person, we have to consider the private persons who compose it and whose life and freedom are naturally independent of it. It is a matter, then, of making a clear distinction between the respective rights of the citizens and the sovereign,* and between the duties that the former have to fulfill as subjects and the natural rights to which they are entitled as men.

It is agreed that each person alienates through the social compact only that part of his power, goods, and freedom whose use matters to the community; but it must also be agreed that the sovereign alone is the judge of what matters.

A citizen owes the State all the services he can render it as soon as the sovereign requests them. But the sovereign, for its part, cannot impose on the subjects any burden that is useless to the community. It cannot even will to do so, for under the law of reason nothing is done without a cause, any more than under the law of nature.

The engagements that bind us to the social body are obligatory only because they are mutual, and their nature is such that in fulfilling them one cannot work for someone else without also working for oneself. Why is the general will always right and why do all constantly want the happiness of each, if not because there is no one who does not apply this word each to himself, and does not think

---

*Attentive readers, please do not be in a hurry to accuse me of inconsistency here. I have been unable to avoid it in my terminology, given the poverty of the language. But wait.

of himself as he votes for all? Which proves that the equality of right, and the concept of justice it produces, are derived from each man's preference for himself and consequently from the nature of man; that the general will, to be truly such, should be general in its object as well as in its essence; that it should come from all to apply to all; and that it loses its natural rectitude when it is directed toward any individual, determinate object. Because then, judging what is foreign to us, we have no true principle of equity to guide us.

Indeed, as soon as it is a matter of fact or a particular right concerning a point that has not been regulated by a prior, general convention, the affair is in dispute. It is a lawsuit where the interested private individuals constitute one party and the public the other, but in which I see neither what law must be followed nor what judge should decide. In this case it would be ridiculous to want to turn to an express decision of the general will, which can only be the conclusion of one of the parties and which, for the other party, is consequently only a foreign, private will, showing injustice on this occasion and subject to error. Thus just as a private will cannot represent the general will, the general will in turn changes its nature when it has a particular object: and as a general will it cannot pass judgment on either a man or a fact. When the people of Athens, for example, appointed or dismissed its leaders, awarded honors to one or imposed penalties on another, and by means of a multitude of particular decrees performed indistinguishably all the acts of government, the people then no longer had a general will properly speaking. It no longer acted as sovereign, but as magistrate. This will appear contrary to commonly held ideas, but you must give me time to present my own.

It should be understood from this that what generalizes the will is not so much the number of votes as the common interest that unites them, because in this institution everyone necessarily subjects himself to the conditions he imposes on others, an admirable agreement between interest and justice which confers on common deliberations a quality of equity that vanishes in the discussion of private matters, for want of a common interest that unites and identifies the rule of the judge with that of the party.

However one traces the principle, one always reaches the same conclusion, namely that the social contact established an equality between the citizens such that they all engage themselves under the same conditions and should all benefit from the same rights. Thus by the very nature of the compact, every act of sovereignty, which is to say every authentic act of the general will, obligates or favors all citizens equally, so that the sovereign knows only the nation as a body and makes no distinctions between any of those who compose it. What really is an act of sovereignty then? It is not a convention between a superior and an inferior, but a convention between the body and each of its members. A convention that is legitimate because it has the social contract as a basis, equitable, because it is common to all; useful, because it can have no other object than the general good; and solid, because it has the public force and the supreme power as guarantee. As long as subjects are subordinated only to such conventions, they do not obey anyone, but solely their own will; and to ask how far the respective rights of the sovereign and of citizens extend is to ask how far the latter can engage themselves to one another, each to all and all to each.

It is apparent from this that the sovereign power, albeit entirely absolute, entirely sacred, and entirely inviolable, does not and cannot exceed the limits of the general conventions, and that every man can fully dispose of the part of his goods and freedom that has been left to him by these conventions. So that the sovereign never has the right to burden one subject more than another, because then the matter becomes individual, and its power is no longer competent.

Once these distinctions are acknowledged, it is so false that the social contract involves any true renunciation on the part of private individuals that their situation, by the effect of this contract, is actually preferable to what it was beforehand; and instead of an alienation, they have only exchanged to their advantage an uncertain, precarious mode of existence for another that is better and safer; natural independence for freedom; the power to harm others for their personal safety; and their force, which others could overcome, for a right which the social union makes invincible. Their life itself, which they have dedicated to the State, is constantly protected by it; and when they risk it for the State's defense, what are they then doing except to give back to the State what they have received from it? What are they doing that they did not do more often and with greater danger in the state of nature, when waging inevitable fights they defend at the risk of their life that which preserves it for them? It is true that everyone has to fight, if need be, for the homeland, but also no one ever has to fight for himself. Don't we still gain by risking, for something that gives us security, a part of what we would have to risk for ourselves as soon as our security is taken away?

## Chapter V

### On the Right of Life and Death

It is asked how private individuals who have no right to dispose of their own lives can transfer to the sovereign a right they do not have. This question appears hard to resolve only because it is badly put. Every man has a right to risk his own life in order to preserve it. Has it ever been said that someone who jumps out of a window to escape a fire is guilty of suicide? Has this crime ever even been imputed to someone who dies in a storm, although he was aware of the danger when he set off?

The social treaty has the preservation of the contracting parties as its end. Whoever wants the end also wants the means, and these means are inseparable from some risks, even from some losses. Whoever wants to preserve his life at the expense of others should also give it up for them when necessary. Now the citizen is no longer judge of the risk to which the law wills that he be exposed, and when the prince has said to him, "It is expedient for the State that you should die," he ought to die. Because it is only under this condition that he has lived in safety up to that point, and because his life is no longer only a favor of nature, but a conditional gift of the State.

The death penalty inflicted on criminals can be considered from approximately the same point of view: it is in order not to be the victim of a murderer that a person consents to die if he becomes one. Under this treaty, far from disposing of one's own life, one only thinks of guaranteeing it; and it cannot be presumed that any of the contracting parties is at that time planning to have himself hanged.

Besides, every offender who attacks the social right becomes through his crimes a rebel and traitor to his homeland; he ceases to be one of its members by violating its laws, and he even wages war against it. Then the State's preservation is incompatible with his own, so one of the two must perish; and when the guilty man is put to death, it is less as a citizen than as an enemy. The proceedings and judgment are the proofs and declaration that he has broken the social treaty, and consequently is no longer a member of the State. Now as he had acknowledged himself to be such, at the very least by his residence, he ought to be removed from it by exile as a violator of the compact or by death as a public enemy. For such an enemy is not a moral person but a man, and in this case the right of war is to kill the vanquished.

But it will be said that the condemnation of a criminal is a particular act. Agreed—hence this condemnation is not to be made by the sovereign. It is a right the sovereignty can confer without itself being able to exercise it. All of my ideas fit together, but I can hardly present them simultaneously.

Moreover, frequent corporal punishment is always a sign of weakness or laziness in the government. There is no wicked man who could not be made good for something. One only has the right to put to death, even as an example, someone who cannot be preserved without danger.

With regard to the right to pardon, or to exempt a guilty man from the penalty prescribed by the law and pronounced by the judge, this belongs only to one who is above the judge and the law—which is to say, to the sovereign. Yet its right in this matter is not very clear and the cases in which it is applied are very rare. In a well-governed State, there are few punishments, not because many pardons are given, but because there are few criminals. When the State declines, a high number of crimes guarantees their impunity. Under the Roman Republic, the senate and consuls never tried to pardon. The people itself did not do so, although it sometimes revoked its own judgment. Frequent pardons indicate that crimes will soon have no further need of them, and everyone sees where that leads. But I feel that my heart murmurs and holds back my pen. Let these questions be discussed by the just man who has never transgressed and who never needed pardon himself.

## Chapter VI

## On Law

Through the social compact we have given the body politic existence and life; the issue now is to give it movement and will through legislation. For the original act which forms and unites this body does not thereby determine anything about what it should do to preserve itself.

Whatever is good and in accordance with order is so by the nature of things, independently of human conventions. All justice comes from God; He alone is its source. But if we knew how to receive it from on high, we would need neither government nor laws. There is without doubt a universal justice emanating from reason alone; but to be acknowledged among us, this justice must be reciprocal. Considering things from a human point of view, the laws of justice are ineffectual among men for want of a natural sanction. They merely benefit the wicked man and harm the just, when the latter observes them toward everyone while no one observes them toward him. Therefore, there must be conventions and laws to combine rights with duties and to bring justice back to its object. In the state of nature where everything is in common, I owe nothing to those to whom I have promised nothing; I recognize as belonging to someone else only what is useless to me. It is not the same in the civil state where all rights are fixed by the law.

But what is a law after all? As long as people are satisfied to attach only metaphysical ideas to this word, they will continue to reason without understanding each other, and when they have stated what a law of nature is, they will not thereby have a better idea of what a law of the State is.

I have already said that there is no general will concerning a particular object. Indeed, that particular object is either within the State or outside of the State. If it is outside of the State, a will that is foreign to it is not general in relation to it. And if within the State, that object is part of it. Then a relation between the whole and its parts is formed which makes of them two separate entities, one of which is the part and the other of which is the whole minus that part. But the whole minus a part is not the whole, and for as long as this relationship lasts, there is no whole, but rather two unequal parts. It follows from this that the will of one of them is no longer general in relation to the other.

But when the entire people enacts something concerning the entire people, it considers only itself, and if a relationship is formed then, it is between the whole object viewed in one way and the whole object viewed in another, without any division of the whole. Then the subject matter of the enactment is general like the will that enacts. It is this act that I call a law.

When I say that the object of the laws is always general, I mean that the law considers the subjects as a body and actions in the abstract, never a man as an individual or a particular action. Thus the law can very well enact that there will be privileges, but it cannot confer them on anyone by name. The law can create several classes of citizens, and even designate the qualities determining who has a right to these classes, but it cannot name the specific people to be admitted to them. It can establish a royal government and hereditary succession, but it cannot elect a king or name a royal family. In short, any function that relates to an individual object does not belong to the legislative power.

Given this idea, one sees immediately that it is no longer necessary to ask who should make laws, since they are acts of the general will; nor whether the prince is above the laws, since he is a member of the State; nor whether the law can be unjust, since no one is unjust toward himself; nor how one is free yet subject to the laws, since they merely record our wills.

Furthermore, one sees that since the law combines the universality of the will and that of the object, what any man, whoever he may be, orders on his own authority is not a law. Whatever is ordered even by the sovereign concerning a particular object is not a law either, but rather a decree; nor is it an act of sovereignty, but of magistracy.

I therefore call every State ruled by laws a republic, whatever the form of administration may be, for then alone the public interest governs and the commonwealth really exists. Every legitimate government is republican. I shall explain later what government is.

Laws are properly speaking only the conditions of the civil association. The people that is subject to the laws ought to be their author. Only those who are forming an association have the right to regulate the conditions of the society. But how will they regulate these conditions? Will it be in common accord, by sudden inspiration? Does the body politic have an organ to enunciate its will? Who will give it the necessary foresight to formulate acts and publish them in advance, or how will it pronounce them in time of need? How will a blind multitude, which often does not know what it wants because it rarely knows what is good for it, carry out by itself an undertaking as vast and as difficult as a system of legislation? By itself, the people always wants the good, but by itself it does not always see it. The general will is always right, but the judgment that guides it is not always enlightened. It must be made to see objects as they are, or sometimes as they should appear to be; shown the good path it seeks; safeguarded against the seduction of private wills; shown how to assimilate considerations of time and place; taught to weigh the attraction of present, tangible advantages against the danger of remote, hidden ills. Private individuals see the good they reject; the public wants the good it does not see. All are equally in need of guides. The former must be obligated to make their wills conform to their reason. The latter must be taught to know what it wants. Then public enlightenment results in the union of understanding and will in the social body; hence the complete cooperation of the parts, and finally the greatest force of the whole. From this arises the necessity for a legislator.

## Chapter VII

## On the Legislator

The discovery of the best rules of society suited to nations would require a superior intelligence, who saw all of men's passions yet experienced none of them; who had no relationship at all to our nature yet knew it thoroughly; whose happiness was independent of us, yet who was nevertheless willing to attend to ours; finally one who, preparing for himself a future glory with the passage of time, could work in one century and enjoy the reward in another.* Gods would be needed to give laws to men.

The same reasoning Caligula used with respect to fact was used by Plato with respect to right in defining the civil or royal man he seeks in the *Statesman*. But if it is true that a great prince is a rare man, what about a great legislator? The former only has to follow the model that the latter should propose. The latter is the mechanic who invents the machine; the former is only the workman who puts it together and starts it running. At the birth of societies, says Montesquieu, the leaders of republics create the institutions; thereafter, it is the institutions that form the leaders of republics.

One who dares to undertake the founding of a people should feel that he is capable of changing human nature, so to speak; of transforming each individual, who by himself is a perfect and solitary whole, into a part of a larger whole from which this individual receives, in a sense, his life and his being; of altering man's constitution in order to strengthen it; of substituting a partial and moral existence for the physical and independent existence we have all received from nature. He must, in short, take away man's own forces in order to give him forces that are foreign to him and that he cannot make use of without the help of others. The more these natural forces are dead and destroyed, and the acquired ones great and lasting, the more the institution as well is solid and perfect. So that if each citizen is nothing, and can do nothing, except with all the others, and if the force acquired by the whole is equal or superior to the sum of the natural forces of all the individuals, it may be said that legislation has reached its highest possible point of perfection.

---

*A people only becomes famous when its legislation starts to decline. It is not known for how many centuries the institutions founded by Lycurgus created the happiness of the Spartans before the rest of Greece became aware of them.

The legislator is an extraordinary man in the State in all respects. If he should be so by his genius, he is no less so by his function. It is not magistracy, it is not sovereignty. This function, which constitutes the republic, does not enter into its constitution. It is a particular and superior activity that has nothing in common with human dominion. For if one who has authority over men should not have authority over laws, one who has authority over laws should also not have authority over men. Otherwise his laws, ministers of his passions, would often only perpetuate his injustices, and he could never avoid having private views alter the sanctity of his work.

When Lycurgus gave his homeland laws, he began by abdicating the throne. It was the custom of most Greek cities to entrust the establishment of their laws to foreigners. The modern republics of Italy often imitated this practice. The republic of Geneva did so too, with good results.* During its finest period Rome saw all the crimes of tyranny revived in its midst, and nearly perished as a result of combining legislative authority and sovereign power in the same hands....

*[There are four remaining chapters in Book II. In Chapter VIII Rousseau discusses the political maturity of the different peoples of Europe. He praises Holland and Switzerland but is critical of Russia. He argues in Chapter IX that a state should not be "too large to be well governed nor too small to be self-sustaining." There is "an appropriate ratio," he claims in Chapter X, between the extent of territory and size of people, but, he adds, one "cannot calculate arithmetically a fixed ratio" because there are so many variables. In the last two chapters he explains that legislation and laws should always have as their "principal object[s,] freedom and equality."—J.M.P.]*

## ⇢ BOOK III ⇠

### *Chapter I*

### *On Government in General*

... Let us suppose that the State is composed of ten thousand citizens. The sovereign can only be considered collectively and as a body. But each private individual in his status as a subject is considered as an individual. Thus the sovereign

---

*Those who only consider Calvin as a theologian do not understand the extent of his genius. The drawing up of our wise edicts, in which he played a large part, does him as much honor as his Institutes. Whatever revolution time may bring about in our cult, as long as love of the homeland and liberty is not extinguished among us, the memory of that great man will never cease to be blessed.

is to the subject as ten thousand is to one. Which is to say that the share of each member of the State is only one ten-thousandth of the sovereign authority, even though he is totally subjected to it. If the people is composed of one hundred thousand men, the condition of the subjects does not change, and each is equally under the whole dominion of the laws, while his vote, reduced to one hundred-thousandth, has ten times less influence on their drafting. Thus since the subject always remains one, the ratio of the sovereign to the subject increases in proportion to the number of citizens. From which it follows that the larger the State grows, the less freedom there is.

When I say that the ratio increases, I mean that it grows further away from equality. Thus the greater the ratio in the geometrician's sense, the less relationship there is in the ordinary sense. In the former, the ratio—considered in terms of quantity—is measured by the quotient, and in the latter, the relationship—considered in terms of likeness—is estimated by the similarity.

Now the less relationship there is between private wills and the general will, that is between the mores and the laws, the more repressive force should increase. Thus, in order for the government to be good, it ought to be relatively stronger in proportion as the people is more numerous.

On the other hand, as the enlargement of the State gives those entrusted with the public authority more temptations and means to abuse their power, the more force the government should have to restrain the people, the more the sovereign should have in turn to restrain the government. I am not speaking here of absolute force, but of the relative force of the various parts of the State.

It follows from this double relationship that the continuous proportion between the sovereign, the prince, and the people is no arbitrary idea, but rather a necessary consequence of the nature of the body politic. It also follows that since one of the extremes, namely the people as subject, is fixed and represented by unity, whenever the doubled ratio increases or decreases, the simple ratio increases or decreases similarly; and that consequently the middle term is changed. This shows that there is no unique and absolute constitution of government, but that there can be as many governments of different natures as there are States of different sizes.

If in ridiculing this system, it was said that in order to find this proportional mean and form the body of the government, it is only necessary, according to me, to calculate the square root of the number of people, I would reply that I merely use that number here as an example; that the relationships of which I speak are not measured solely by the number of men, but in general by the quantity of action, which is itself the combined result of a multitude of causes; and moreover that if I momentarily borrow the vocabulary of geometry in order to express myself in fewer words, I am nevertheless not unaware that geometric precision does not exist in moral quantities.

The government is on a small scale what the body politic that contains it is on a large scale. It is a moral person, endowed with certain faculties; active like the sovereign, passive like the State; and that can be broken down into other similar relationships from which a new proportion consequently arises, and still another within this one according to the order of tribunals, until an indivisible middle term is reached; that is, a single leader or supreme magistrate, who can be considered, in the middle of this progression, as the unity between the series of fractions and that of whole numbers.

Without becoming involved in this multiplication of terms, let us be satisfied to consider the government as a new body in the State, distinct from both the people and the sovereign, and intermediate between them.

The essential difference between these two bodies is that the State exists by itself, but the government exists only through the sovereign. Thus the dominant will of the prince is not or should not be anything except the general will or the law; his force is only the public force concentrated in him. As soon as he wants to derive from himself some absolute and independent act, the bond tying the whole together begins to loosen. If it finally came about that the prince had a private will more active than that of the sovereign, and that he used some of the public force at his discretion to obey that private will, so that there were, so to speak, two sovereigns—one by right, the other in fact—at that moment the social union would vanish and the body politic would be dissolved.

However, in order for the body of the government to exist, to have a real life that distinguishes it from the body of the State, and for all its members to be able to act in concert and fulfill the purpose for which it is instituted, it must have a separate self, a sensibility shared by its members, a force or will of its own that leads to its preservation. This separate existence supposes assemblies, councils, power to deliberate and decide, rights, titles, privileges that belong exclusively to the prince and that make the magistrate's status more honorable in proportion as it is more laborious. The difficulties lie in organizing this subordinate whole within the whole in such a way that it does not change the general constitution by strengthening its own; that it always distinguishes between its separate force intended for its own preservation and the public force intended for the preservation of the State; and in short that it is ever ready to sacrifice the government to the people and not the people to the government....

[*Chapters II through XVIII of Book III contain Rousseau's analysis of the advantages and disadvantages of the various forms of government: democracy, aristocracy, monarchy, and mixed. He also relates a variety of "geopolitical" considerations—such as climate, fertility of the land, and foods—to forms of government. He concludes by stressing that the sovereign authority of a state must be its people.—J.M.P.*]

## ⇢ BOOK IV ⇠

### Chapter I

### That the General Will is Indestructible

As long as several men together consider themselves to be a single body, they have only a single will, which relates to their common preservation and the general welfare. Then all the mechanisms of the State are vigorous and simple, its maxims are clear and luminous, it has no tangled, contradictory interests; the common good is clearly apparent everywhere, and requires only good sense to be perceived. Peace, union, and equality are enemies of political subtleties. Upright and simple men are hard to fool because of their simplicity; traps and refined pretexts do not deceive them. They are not even clever enough to be duped. When, among the happiest people in the world, groups of peasants are seen deciding the affairs of State under an oak tree, and always acting wisely, can one help scorning the refinements of other nations, which make themselves illustrious and miserable with so much art and mystery?

A State governed in this way needs very few laws, and to the degree that it becomes necessary to promulgate new ones, this necessity is universally seen. The first to propose them merely states what everyone has already felt, and there is no question of intrigues nor of eloquence to pass into law what each has already resolved to do as soon as he is sure that others will do likewise.

What misleads reasoners, who only see States that have been badly constituted from the beginning, is that they are struck by the impossibility of maintaining similar order in such States. They laugh when they imagine all the nonsense that a clever swindler or an insinuating talker could put over on the people of Paris or

London. They don't know that Cromwell would have been condemned to hard labor by the people of Berne, and the Duc de Beaufort sentenced to the reformatory by the Genevans.

But when the social tie begins to slacken and the State to grow weak; when private interests start to make themselves felt and small societies to influence the large one, the common interest changes and is faced with opponents; unanimity no longer prevails in the votes; the general will is no longer the will of all; contradictions and debates arise and the best advice is not accepted without disputes.

Finally, when the State, close to its ruin, continues to subsist only in an illusory and ineffectual form; when the social bond is broken in all hearts; when the basest interest brazenly adopts the sacred name of the public good, then the general will becomes mute; all—guided by secret motives—are no more citizens in offering their opinions than if the State had never existed, and iniquitous decrees whose only goal is the private interest are falsely passed under the name of laws.

Does it follow from this that the general will is annihilated or corrupted? No, it is always constant, unalterable, and pure. But it is subordinate to others that prevail over it. Each person, detaching his interest from the common interest, sees perfectly well that he cannot completely separate himself from it; but his share of the public misfortune seems like nothing to him compared to the exclusive good that he claims he is getting. With the exception of this private good, he wants the general good in his own interest just as vigorously as anyone else. Even in selling his vote for money, he doesn't extinguish the general will within himself, he evades it. The mistake he makes is to change the state of the question and to answer something other than what he is asked. So that rather than saying through his vote *it is advantageous to the State*, he says *it is advantageous to a given man or to a given party for a given motion to pass*. Thus the law of public order in assemblies is not so much to maintain the general will therein as it is to be sure that it is always questioned and that it always answers....

## Chapter II

### On Voting

… Except for this primitive contract, the vote of the majority always obligates all the others. This is a consequence of the contract itself. But it is asked how a man can be free and forced to conform to wills that are not his own. How can the opponents be free yet subject to laws to which they have not consented?

I reply that the question is badly put. The citizen consents to all the laws, even to those passed against his will, and even to those that punish him when he dares to violate one of them. The constant will of all the members of the State is the general will, which makes them citizens and free.* When a law is proposed in the assembly of the people, what they are being asked is not precisely whether they approve or reject the proposal, but whether it does or does not conform to the general will that is theirs. Each one expresses his opinion on this by voting, and the declaration of the general will is drawn from the counting of the votes. Therefore when the opinion contrary to mine prevails, that proves nothing except that I was mistaken, and what I thought to be the general will was not. If my private will had prevailed, I would have done something other than what I wanted. It is then that I would not have been free.

This presupposes, it is true, that all the characteristics of the general will are still in the majority. When they cease to be, there is no longer any freedom regardless of the side one takes.

In showing earlier how private wills were substituted for the general will in public declarations, I have sufficiently indicated the feasible means of preventing this abuse. I shall discuss this again later. With regard to the proportion of votes needed to declare this will, I have also given the principles on which it can be determined. The difference of a single vote breaks a tie; a single opponent destroys unanimity. But between unanimity and a tie there are several qualified majorities, at any of which the proportion can be established, according to the condition and needs of the body politic.

Two general maxims can serve to regulate these ratios. One, that the more important and serious the deliberations, the closer the winning opinion should be to unanimity. The other, that the more speed the business at hand requires, the smaller the prescribed difference in the division of opinions should be. In deliberations that must be finished on the spot, a majority of a single vote should suffice. The first of these maxims appears more suited to laws; the second, to business matters. However that may be, it is a combination of the two that establishes the proper ratio of the deciding majority.

---

*In Genoa, the word *libertas* can be read on the front of prisons and on convicts' chains in galleys. This application of the motto is noble and just. Indeed, it is only evildoers of all classes who prevent the citizen from being free. In a country where all such men were in galleys, the most perfect freedom would be enjoyed.

[*In Chapters III through VII Rousseau examines the different methods of electing leaders, with particular reference to Roman practices, and the dangers incurred in creating an executive. A dictatorship may be necessary to save the state, but it should be for only "a very short term."* —J.M.P.]

## Chapter VIII

### On Civil Religion

… Among us, the kings of England have established themselves as heads of the church, and the czars have done the same thing. But by this title, they have made themselves not so much the masters as the ministers. They have acquired not so much the right to change it as the power to maintain it. They are not its legislators; they are only its princes. Wherever the clergy constitutes a body,* it is master and legislator in its domain. There are, therefore, two powers, two sovereigns, in England and in Russia just as everywhere else.

Of all Christian authors, the philosopher Hobbes is the only one who correctly saw the evil and the remedy, who dared to propose the reunification of the two heads of the eagle, and the complete return to political unity, without which no State or government will ever be well constituted. But he ought to have seen that the dominating spirit of Christianity was incompatible with his system, and that the interest of the priest would always be stronger than that of the State. It is not so much what is horrible and false in his political theory as what is correct and true that has made it odious.…

Considered in relation to society, which is either general or particular, religion can also be divided into two types, namely the religion of man and that of the citizen. The former, without temples, altars, or rituals, limited to the purely internal cult of the supreme God and to the eternal duties of morality, is the pure and simple religion of the Gospel, true theism, and what may be called natural divine right. The latter, inscribed in a single country, gives it its Gods, its own tutelary patrons. Its dogma, rites, and external cult are prescribed by laws. Outside the

---

*It must be carefully noted that it is not so much formal assemblies, like those in France, that bind the clergy into a body as it is the communion of churches. Communion and ex-communication are the social compact of the clergy, a compact by means of which it will always be master of peoples and kings. All the priests who take communion together are fellow citizens, even though they may come from opposite ends of the earth. This invention is a political masterpiece. The pagan priests had nothing that resembles it, and therefore they never constituted a body of clergymen.

single nation that observes it, everything is considered infidel, foreign, barbarous; it only extends the duties and rights of man as far as its altars. Such were all the religions of the early peoples, to which the name of civil or positive divine right can be given....

The second is good in that it combines the divine cult and love of the laws, and by making the homeland the object of the citizens' prayers, it teaches them that to serve the State is to serve its tutelary God. It is a kind of theocracy in which there ought to be no other pontif than the prince, nor other priests than the magistrates. Then to die for one's country is to be martyred, to violate the laws is to be impious, and to subject a guilty man to public execration is to deliver him to the anger of the Gods: *sacer estod.**

But this religion is bad in that, being based on error and falsehood, it deceives men, makes them credulous, superstitious, and drowns the true cult of divinity in empty ceremonial. It is bad, too, whenever it becomes exclusive and tyrannical and makes a people bloodthirsty and intolerant to the point where it lives only for murder and massacre, and believes it performs a holy act when killing whoever does not accept its Gods. This places such a people in a natural state of war with all others, which is very harmful to its own security.

There remains the religion of man, or Christianity—not that of today, but that of the Gospel, which is totally different from it. Through this saintly, sublime, true religion, men—children of the same God—all acknowledge one another as brothers, and the society that unites them is not even dissolved by death.

But this religion, having no particular relation to the body politic, leaves laws with only their intrinsic force, without adding any other force to them; and because of this, one of the great bonds of particular societies remains without effect. Even worse, far from attaching the citizens' hearts to the State, it detaches them from it as from all worldly things. I know of nothing more contrary to the social spirit....

Christianity is a totally spiritual religion, uniquely concerned with heavenly matters. The Christian's homeland is not of this world. He does his duty, it is true, but he does it with profound indifference for the good or bad outcome of his efforts. As long as he has nothing to reproach himself for, it matters little to him whether things go well or badly here on earth. If the State is flourishing, he barely dares to enjoy the public felicity for fear of becoming proud of his country's glory. If the State declines, he blesses the hand of God that weighs heavily on his people.

---

*"Let him be damned."

In order for the society to be peaceful and for harmony to last, all citizens without exception would have to be equally good Christians. But if unfortunately there is a single ambitious man, a single hypocrite—a Cataline, for example, or a Cromwell—he will very certainly get the better of his pious compatriots. Christian charity makes it hard to think ill of one's neighbor. As soon as he has learned the art of how to trick them through some ruse and seize part of the public authority for himself, he will be a man of constituted dignity; it is God's will to respect him. Soon he is powerful; it is God's will to obey him. Does the depository of this power abuse it? He is the rod with which God punishes His children. It would be against conscience to chase out the usurper, for it would be necessary to disturb the public tranquility, use violence, shed blood. All of that is inconsistent with the gentleness of a Christian. And after all, what does it matter whether one is free or a serf in this vale of tears? The essential thing is to go to heaven, and resignation is but an additional means of doing so.

What if a foreign war breaks out? The citizens march readily to combat; none among them thinks of fleeing; they do their duty, but without passion for victory. They know how to die rather than to win. What does it matter if they are victors or vanquished? Doesn't providence know better than they what is good for them? Imagine how a proud, impetuous, passionate enemy can take advantage of their stoicism! Confront them with those generous and proud peoples consumed by a burning love of glory and homeland; suppose that your Christian republic is face to face with Sparta or Rome. The pious Christians will be beaten, crushed, destroyed before they have had time to look around, or they will owe their salvation only to the scorn their enemies will conceive for them. The oath taken by the soldiers of Fabius was a fine one to my mind. They did not swear to die or to win; they swore to return as victors, and they kept their promise. Christians would never have made such a promise; they would have believed they were tempting God....

Under the pagan Emperors, Christian soldiers were brave. All Christian authors assert this, and I believe it. There was a competition for honor against the pagan troops. As soon as the Emperors were Christians, this emulation ceased, and when the cross chased out the eagle, all Roman valor disappeared.

But setting political considerations aside, let us return to right and determine its principles concerning this important point. The right that the social compact gives the sovereign over the subjects does not exceed, as I have said, the limits of public utility. The subjects, therefore, do not have to account for their opinions to the sovereign, except insofar as these opinions matter to the community. Now it matters greatly to the State that each citizen have a religion that causes him to love his duties; but the dogmas of that religion are of no interest either to the State or to its members; except insofar as these dogmas relate to morality, and to the duties that anyone who professes it is obliged to fulfill toward others. Everyone can have whatever opinions he pleases beyond that, without the sovereign having to know what they are. For since the sovereign has no competence in the other world, whatever the fate of subjects in the life hereafter, it is none of its business, as long as they are good citizens in this one.

There is, therefore, a purely civil profession of faith, the articles of which are for the sovereign to establish, not exactly as religious dogmas, but as sentiments of sociability without which it is impossible to be a good citizen or a faithful subject.* Without being able to obligate anyone to believe them, the sovereign can banish from the State anyone who does not believe them. The sovereign can banish him not for being impious, but for being unsociable; for being incapable of sincerely loving the laws, justice, and of giving his life, if need be, for his duty. If someone who has publicly acknowledged these same dogmas behaves as though he does not believe them, he should be punished with death. He has committed the greatest of crimes: he lied before the laws.

The dogmas of the civil religion ought to be simple, few in number, stated with precision, without explanations or commentaries. The existence of a powerful, intelligent, beneficent, foresighted, and providential divinity; the afterlife; the happiness of the just; the punishment of the wicked; the sanctity of the social contract and the laws. These are the positive dogmas. As for the negative ones, I limit them to a single one: intolerance. It belongs with the cults we have excluded.

Those who make a distinction between civil and theological intolerance are mistaken, in my opinion. These two intolerances are inseparable. It is impossible to live in peace with people whom one believes are damned. To love them would be to hate God who punishes them. They must absolutely be either brought into

---

*In pleading for Cataline, Caesar tried to establish the dogma of the mortality of the soul. To refute him, Cato and Cicero wasted no time philosophizing. They contented themselves with showing that Caesar was speaking as a bad citizen and advancing a doctrine that was pernicious to the State. Indeed, this was what the Roman senate had to judge, and not a question of theology.

the faith or tormented. Wherever theological intolerance exists, it is impossible for it not to have some civil effect; and as soon as it does, the sovereign is no longer sovereign, even over temporal matters. From then on, priests are the true masters; kings are merely their officers.

Now that there is no longer and can never again be an exclusive national religion, one should tolerate all those religions that tolerate others insofar as their dogmas are in no way contrary to the duties of the citizen. But whoever dares to say *there is no salvation outside of the church* should be chased out of the State, unless the State is the church, and the prince is the pontif. Such a dogma is good only in a theocratic government; in any other it is pernicious. The reason for which Henry IV is said to have embraced Roman Catholicism ought to make all honest men—and especially all princes capable of reasoning—leave it.

## Chapter IX

### Conclusion

After setting forth the true principles of political right and trying to found the State on this basis, what remains to be done is to buttress the State by its foreign relations, which would include international law, commerce, the right of war and conquest, public law, alliances, negotiations, treaties, etc. But all that constitutes a new object, too vast for my limited purview. I should always have set my sights closer to myself.

---

## E N D

# GEORG WILHELM FRIEDRICH HEGEL

*Georg Wilhelm Friedrich Hegel (1770–1831) has been judged by many as the greatest philosopher of the nineteenth century, and if the standards used are scope and influence, this judgment would be correct. Neither Karl Marx nor the Danish theologian Soren Kierkegaard can be understood without recourse to Hegel's extraordinarily complex, if not obtuse, writings. Hegel studied theology at the University of Tübingen in Germany, where he received a doctorate (1790) and a certificate in theology (1793). His interest soon broadened to more general philosophical and political problems. He held a variety of teaching posts for the first few years of his career. In 1811 he married a woman 20 years his junior; they had a family of two sons plus an illegitimate son of Hegel's born prior to the marriage. It was apparently a normal middle-class family. The publication of* The Phenomenology of Spirit *(1807) and* The Science of Logic *(1816) provided Hegel with considerable fame and changed the course of his career. He joined the University of Berlin in 1818, and, as his political and philosophical positions became known, his stature increased in the eyes of the Prussian government. He was made Rector of the University in 1830. He died suddenly of cholera in 1831.*

*The essential works for his political philosophy are* The Philosophy of Right *(1821) and the* Introduction to the Philosophy of History. *The latter work, published in 1837, was composed of his lecture notes plus the notes of his students.*

— J.M.P.

# INTRODUCTION TO THE PHILOSOPHY OF HISTORY

The subject of this course of Lectures is the Philosophical History of the World. And by this must be understood, not a collection of general observations respecting it, suggested by the study of its records, and proposed to be illustrated by its facts, but Universal History itself. To gain a clear idea at the outset, of the nature of our task, it seems necessary to begin with an examination of the other methods of treating History. The various methods may be ranged under three heads:

    I. Original History
    II. Reflective History
    III. Philosophical History

## I. Original History

Of the first kind, the mention of one or two distinguished names will furnish a definite type. To this category belong *Herodotus, Thucydides,* and other historians of the same order, whose descriptions are for the most part limited to deeds, events, and states of society, which they have before their eyes, and whose spirit they shared. They simply transferred what was passing the world around them, to the realm of representative intellect. An external phenomenon is thus translated into an internal conception....

Such original historians, then, change the events, the deeds and the states of society with which they are conversant, into an object for the conceptive faculty. The narratives they leave us cannot, therefore, be very comprehensive in their range. Herodotus, Thucydides, Guicciardini, may be taken as fair samples of the class in this respect. What is present and living in their environment, is their proper material. The influences that have formed the writer are identical with those which have moulded the events that constitute the matter of his story. The author's spirit, and that of the actions he narrates, is one and the same. He describes scenes in which he himself has been an actor, or at any rate an interested spectator. It is

*Introduction to the Philosophy of History,* by Georg Wilhelm Friedrich Hegel, from *Hegel Selections,* edited by Jacob Loewenberg. Copyright 1929 Charles Scribner's Sons; copyright renewed © 1957. Reprinted with the permission of Charles Scribner's Sons, an imprint of Macmillan Publishing Company.

**N.B.** The topic headings inserted in the text have been added by J.M.P.

short periods of time, individual shapes of persons and occurrences, single unreflected traits, of which he makes his picture. And his aim is nothing more than the presentation to posterity of an image of events as clear as that which he himself possessed in virtue of personal observation, or life-like descriptions. Reflections are none of his business, for he lives in the spirit of his subject; he has not attained an elevation above it. If, as in Caesar's case, he belongs to the exalted rank of generals or statesmen, it is the prosecution of *his own aims* that constitutes the history.

Such speeches as we find in Thucydides (for example) of which we can positively assert that they are not *bona fide* reports, would seem to make against our statement that a historian of his class presents us no reflected picture; that persons and people appear in his works in *propria persona* [one's own individuality]. Speeches, it must be allowed, are veritable transactions in the human commonwealth; in fact, very gravely influential transactions. It is, indeed, often said, "Such and such things are only talk"; by way of demonstrating their harmlessness. That for which this excuse is brought, may be mere "talk"; and talk enjoys the important privilege of being harmless. But addresses of peoples to peoples, or orations directed to nations and to princes, are integrant constituents of history. Granted that such orations as those of Pericles—that most profoundly accomplished, genuine, noble statesman—were elaborated by Thucydides; it must yet be maintained that they were not foreign to the character of the speaker. In the oration in question, these men proclaim the maxims adopted by their countrymen, and which formed their own character; they record their views of their political relations, and of their moral and spiritual nature; and the principle of their designs and conduct. What the historian puts into their months is no suppositious system of ideas, but an uncorrupted transcript of their intellectual and moral habitudes....

## II. Reflective History

The second kind of history we may call the *reflective*. It is history whose mode of representation is not really confined by the limits of the time to which it relates, but whose spirit transcends the present. In this second order strongly marked variety of species may be distinguished.

**1.** It is the aim of the investigator to gain a view of the entire history of a people or a country, or of the world, in short, what we call *Universal History*. In this case the working up of the historical material is the main point. The workman approaches his task with *his own* spirit; a spirit distinct from that of the element he is to manipulate. Here a very important consideration will be the principles to which the author refers, the bearing and motives of the actions and events which he describes, and those which determine the form of his narrative. Among us Germans this reflective treatment and the display of ingenuity which it occasions, assume a manifold variety of phases. Every writer of history proposes to himself an original method. The English and French confess to general principles of historical composition. Their stand-point is more that of cosmopolitan or of national culture. Among us each labours to invent a purely individual point of view. Instead of writing history, we are always beating our brains to discover how history ought to be written. This first kind of Reflective History is most nearly akin to the preceding, when it has no farther aim than to present the annals of a country complete....

A history which aspires to traverse long periods of time, or to be universal, must indeed forego the attempt to give individual representations of the past as it actually existed. It must foreshorten its pictures by abstractions; and this includes not merely the omission of events and deeds, but whatever is involved in the fact that Thought is, after all, the most trenchant epitomist. A battle, a great victory, a siege, no longer maintains its original proportions, but is put off with a bare mention. When Livy *e.g.* tells us of the wars with the Volsci, we sometimes have the brief announcement: "This year war was carried on with the Volsci."

**2.** A second species of Reflective History is what we may call the Pragmatical. When we have to deal with the Past, and occupy ourselves with a remote world, a Present rises into being for the mind—produced by its own activity, as the reward of its labour. The occurrences are, indeed, various; but the idea which pervades them—their deeper import and connexion—is *one*. This takes the occurrence out of the category of the Past and makes it virtually Present. Pragmatical (didactic) reflections, though in their nature decidedly abstract, are truly and indefeasibly of the Present, and quicken the annals of the dead Past with the life of today. Whether, indeed, such reflections are truly interesting and enlivening, depends on the writer's own spirit. Moral reflections must here be specially noticed,— the moral teaching expected from history; which latter has not unfrequently been treated with a direct view to the former. It may be allowed that examples of virtue elevate the soul, and are applicable in the moral instructions of children for impressing excellence upon their minds. But the destinies of peoples and stages, their interests, relations, and the complicated tissue of their affairs, present quite another field. Rulers, Statesmen, Nations, are wont to be emphatically commended to the teaching which experience offers in history. But what experience and history teach is this,—that peoples and governments never have learned anything from history, or acted on principles deduced from it. Each period is involved in such peculiar circumstances, exhibits a condition of things so strictly idiosyncratic, that its conduct must be regulated by considerations connected with itself, and itself alone. Amid the pressure of great events, a general principle gives no help. It is useless to revert to similar circumstances in the Past. The pallid shades of memory struggle in vain with the life and freedom of the Present. Looked at in this light, nothing can be shallower than the oft-repeated appeal to Greek and Roman examples during the French Revolution. Nothing is more diverse than the genius of those nations and that of our times. Johannes v. Müller, in his Universal History as also in his History of Switzerland, had such moral aims in view. He designed to prepare a body of political doctrines for the instruction of princes, governments and peoples (he formed a special collection of doctrines and reflections,—frequently giving us in his correspondence the exact number of apophthegms which he had compiled in a week); but he cannot reckon this part of his labour as among the best that he accomplished. It is only a thorough, liberal, comprehensive view of historical relations (such *e.g.* as we find in Montesquieu's "Esprit des Loix"), that can give truth and interest to reflections of this order. One Reflective History therefore, supersedes another. The materials are patent to every writer: each is likely enough to believe himself capable of arranging and manipulating them; and we may expect that each will insist upon his own spirit as that of the age in question. Disgusted by such reflective histories, readers have often returned with pleasure to a narrative adopting no particular point of view. These certainly have their value; but for the most part they offer only material for history. We Germans are not content with such. The French, on the other hand, display great genius in reanimating bygone times, and in bringing the past to bear upon the present conditions of things.

**3.** The third form of Reflective History is the *Critical.* This deserves mention as preeminently the mode of treating history, now current in Germany. It is not history itself that is here presented. We might more properly designate it as a History of History; a criticism of historical narratives and an investigation of their truth and credibility. Its peculiarity in point of fact and of intention, consists in the acuteness with which the writer extorts something from the records which was not in the matters recorded. The French have given as much that is profound and judicious in this class of composition. But they have not endeavoured to pass a merely critical procedure for substantial history. They have duly presented their judgments in the form of critical treatises. Among us, the so-called "higher criticism," which reigns supreme in the domain of philology, has also taken possession of our historical literature. This "higher criticism" has been the pretext for introducing all the anti-historical monstrosities that a vain imagination could suggest. Here we have the other method of making the past a living reality; putting subjective fancies in the place of historical data; fancies whose merit is measured by their boldness, that is, the scantiness of the particulars on which they are based, and the peremptoriness with which they contravene the best established facts of history.

**4.** The last species of Reflective History announces its fragmentary character on the very face of it. It adopts an abstract position; yet, since it takes general points of view (*e.g.* as the History of Art, of Law, of Religion) it forms a transition to the Philosophical History of the World. In our time this form of the history of ideas has been more developed and brought into notice. Such branches of national life stand in close relation to the entire complex of a people's annals; and the question of chief importance in relation to our subject is, whether the connexion of the whole is exhibited in its truth and reality, or referred to merely external relations. In the latter case, these important phenomena (Art, Law, Religion, &c.) appear as purely accidental national peculiarities. It must be remarked that, when Reflective History has advanced to the adoption of general points of view, if the position taken is a true one, these are found to constitute—not merely external thread, a superficial series—but are the inward guiding soul of the occurrences and actions that occupy a nation's annals. For, like the soul-conductor Mercury, the Idea is in truth, the leader of peoples and of the World; and Spirit, the rational and necessitated will of that conductor, is and has been the director of the events of the World's History. To become acquainted with Spirit in this its office of guidance, is the object of our present undertaking. This brings us to:

## III. Philosophical History

The third kind of history,—the *Philosophical.* No explanation was needed of the two previous classes; their nature was self-evident. It is otherwise with this last, which certainly seems to require an exposition or justification. The most general definition that can be given, is, that the Philosophy of History means nothing but the *thoughtful consideration of it.* Thought is, indeed, essential to humanity. It is this that distinguishes us from the brutes. In sensation, cognition and intellection; in our instincts and volitions, as far as they are truly human, Thought is an invariable element. To insist upon Thought in this connexion with history, may, however, appear unsatisfactory. In this science it would seem as if Thought must be subordinate to what is given, to the realities of fact; that this is its basis and guide: while Philosophy dwells in the region of self-produced ideas, without reference to actuality. Approaching history thus prepossessed, Speculation might be expected to treat it as a mere passive material; and, so far from leaving it in its native truth, to force it into conformity with a tyrannous idea, and to construe it, as the phrase is, "*a priori.*" But as it is the business of history simply to adopt into its records what is and has been, actual occurrences and transactions; and since it remains true to its character in proportion as it strictly adheres to its data, we seem to have in Philosophy, a process diametrically opposed to that of the historiographer. This contradiction, and the charge consequent brought against speculation, shall be explained and confuted. We do not, however, propose to correct the innumerable special misrepresentations, trite or novel, that are current respecting the aims, the interests, and the modes of treating history, and its relation to Philosophy.

The only Thought which Philosophy brings with it to the contemplation of History, is the simple conception of *Reason;* that Reason is the Sovereign of the World; that the history of the world, therefore, presents us with a rational process. This conviction and intuition is a hypothesis in the domain of history as such. In that of Philosophy it is no hypothesis. It is there proved by speculative cognition, that Reason—and this term may here suffice us, without investigating the relation sustained by the Universe to the Divine Being,—is *Substance*, as well as *Infinite Power;* its own *Infinite Material* underlying all the natural and spiritual life which it originates, as also the *Infinite Form*,—that which sets this Material in motion. On the one hand, Reason is the *substance* of the Universe; *viz.* that by which and in which all reality has its being and subsistence. On the other hand, it is the *Infinite Energy* of the Universe; since Reason is not so powerless as to be incapable of producing anything but a mere ideal, a mere intention—having its place outside reality, nobody knows where; something separate and abstract, in the heads of certain human beings. It is the *infinite complex of things*, their entire Essence and Truth. It is its own material which it commits to its own Active Energy to work up; not needing, as finite action does, the conditions of an external material of given means from which it may obtain its support, and the objects of its activity. It supplies its own nourishment, and is the object of its own operations. While it is exclusively its own basis of existence, and absolute final aim, it is also the energising power realising this aim; developing it not only in the phenomena of the Natural, but also of the Spiritual Universe—the History of the World.

465

That this "Idea" or "Reason" is the *True*, the *Eternal*, the absolutely *powerful* essence; that it reveals itself in the World, and that in that World nothing else is revealed but this and its honour and glory—is the thesis which, as we have said, has been proved in Philosophy, and is here regarded as demonstrated.

In those of my hearers who are not acquainted with Philosophy, I may fairly presume, at least, the existence of a *belief* in Reason, a desire, a thirst for acquaintance with it, in entering upon this course of Lectures. It is, in fact, the wish for rational insight, not the ambition to amass a mere heap of acquirements, that should be presupposed in every case as possessing the mind of the learner in the study of science. If the clear idea of Reason is not already developed in our minds, in beginning the study of Universal History, we should at least have the firm, unconquerable faith that Reason *does* exist there; and that the World of intelligence and conscious volition is not abandoned to change, but must shew itself in the light of the self-cognizant Idea. Yet I am not obliged to make any such preliminary demand upon your faith. What I have said thus provisionally, and what I shall have further to say, is, even in reference to *our* branch of science, not to be regarded as hypothetical, but as a summary view of the whole; the *result of the investigation* we are about to pursue; a result which happens to be known to *me*, because I have traversed the entire field. It is only an inference from the History of the World, that its development has been a rational process; that the history in question has constituted the rational necessary course of the World-Spirit—that Spirit whose nature is always one and the same, but which unfolds this its one nature in the phenomena of the World's existence. This must, as before stated, present itself as the ultimate *result* of History. But we have to take the latter as it is. We must proceed historically—empirically. Among other precautions we must take care not to be misled by professed historians who (especially among the Germans, and enjoying a considerable authority), are chargeable with the very procedure of which they accuse the Philosopher—introducing *a priori* inventions of their own into the records of the Past. It is, for example, a widely current fiction, that there was an original primaeval people, taught immediately by God, endowed with perfect insight and wisdom, possessing a thorough knowledge of all natural laws and spiritual truth; that there have been such or such sacerdotal peoples; or, to mention a more specific averment, that there was a Roman Epos, from which the Roman historians derived the early annals of their city, &c. Authorities of this kind we leave to those talented historians by profession, among whom (in Germany at least) their use is not uncommon.—We might then announce it as the first condition to be observed, that we should faithfully adopt all that is historical. But in such general expressions themselves, as "faithfully" and "adopt," lies the ambiguity. Even the ordinary, the "impartial" historiographer, who believes and professes that he maintains a simply receptive attitude; surrendering himself only to the data supplied him—is by no means passive as regards the exercise of his thinking powers. He brings his categories with him, and sees the phenomena presented to his mental vision, exclusively through these media. And, especially in all that pretends to the name of science, it is indispensable that Reason should not sleep—that reflection should be in full play. To him who looks upon the world rationally, the world in its turn, presents a rational aspect. The relation is mutual. But the various exercises of reflection—the different points of view—the modes of decoding the simple question of the relative importance of events (the first category that occupies the attention of the historian), do not belong to this place.

I will only mention two phases and points of view that concern the generally diffused conviction that Reason has ruled, and is still ruling in the world, and consequently in the world's history; because they give us, at the same time, an opportunity for more closely investigating the question that presents the greatest difficulty, and for indicating a branch of the subject, which will have to be enlarged on in the sequel.

## 1. Reason

One of these points is, that passage in history, which informs us that the Greek Anaxagoras was the first to enunciate the doctrine that *nous*, Understanding generally, or Reason, governs the world. It is not intelligence as self-conscious Reason,—not a Spirit as such that is meant; and we must clearly distinguish these from each other. The movement of the solar system takes place according to unchangeable laws. These laws are Reason, implicit in the phenomena in question. But neither the sun nor the plants, which revolve around it according to these laws, can be said to have any consciousness of them.

A thought of this kind,—that Nature is an embodiment of Reason; that it is unchangeably subordinate to universal laws, appears nowise striking or strange to us. We are accustomed to such conceptions, and find nothing extraordinary in them. And I have mentioned this extraordinary occurrence, partly to shew how history teaches, that ideas of this kind, which may seem trivial to us, have not always been in the world; that on the contrary, such a thought makes an epoch in the annals of human intelligence. Aristotle says of Anaxagoras, as the originator of the thought in question, that he appeared as a sober man among the drunken. Socrates adopted the doctrine from Anaxagoras, and it forthwith became the ruling idea in Philosophy,—except in the school of Epicurus, who ascribed all events to chance. "I was delighted with the sentiment,"—Plato makes Socrates say,—"and hoped I had found a teacher who would shew me Nature in harmony with Reason, who would demonstrate in each particular phenomenon its specific aim, and in the whole, the grand object of the Universe. I would not have surrendered this hope for a great deal. But how very much was I disappointed, when, having zealously applied myself to the writings of Anaxagoras, I found that he adduces only external causes, such as Atmosphere, Ether, Water, and the like." It is evident that the defect which Socrates complains of respecting Anaxagoras's doctrine, does not concern the principle itself, but the shortcoming of the propounder in applying it to Nature in the concrete. Nature is not deduced from that principle; the latter remains in fact a mere abstraction, inasmuch as the former is not comprehended and exhibited as a development of it,—an organisation produced by and from Reason. I wish, at the very outset, to call your attention to the important difference between a conception, a principle, a truth limited to an *abstract* form and its determinate application, and concrete development. This distinction affects the whole fabric of philosophy; and among other bearings of it there is one to which we shall have to revert at the close of our view of Universal History, in investigating the aspect of political affairs in the most recent period.

We have next to notice the rise of this idea—that Reason directs the world—in connexion with a further application of it, well known to us,—in the form, *viz.* of the *religious truth*, that the world is not abandoned to change and external contingent causes, but that a *Providence* controls it. I stated above, that I would not make a demand on your faith, in regard to the principle announced. Yet I might appeal to your belief in it, *in this religious aspect*, if, as a general rule, the nature of philosophical science allowed it to attach authority to presuppositions. To put it in another shape,—this appeal is forbidden, because the science of which we have to treat, proposes itself to furnish the proof (not indeed of the abstract *Truth* of the doctrine, but) of its correctness as compared with facts. The truth, then, that a Providence (that of God) presides over the events of the World—consorts with the proposition in question; for *Divine* Providence is Wisdom, endowed with an infinite Power, which realises its aim, *viz.* the absolute rational design of the World. Reason is Thought conditioning itself with perfect freedom. But a difference—rather a contradiction—will manifest itself, between this belief and our principle, just as was the case in reference to the demand made by Socrates in the case of Anaxagoras's dictum. For that belief is similarly indefinite; it is what is called a belief in a general Providence, and is not followed out in definite application, or displayed in its bearing on the grand total—the entire course of human history. But to *explain* History is to depict the passions of mankind, the genius, the active powers, that play their part on the great stage; and the providentially determined process which these exhibit, constitutes what is generally called the "plan" of Providence. Yet it is this very plan which is supposed to be concealed from our view: which it is deemed presumption, even to wish to recognise. The ignorance of Anaxagoras, as to how intelligence reveals itself in actual existence, was ingenuous. Neither in his consciousness, nor in that of Greece at large, had that thought been further expanded. He had not attained the power to apply his general principle to the concrete, so as to deduce the latter from the former. It was Socrates who took the first step in comprehending the union of the Concrete with the Universal. Anaxagoras, then, did not take up a *hostile* position towards such an application. The common belief in Providence does; at least it opposes the use of the principle on the large scale, and denies the possibility of discerning the plan of Providence. In isolated cases this plan is supposed to be manifest. Pious persons are encouraged to recognise in particular circumstances, something more than mere chance; to acknowledge the guiding hand of God; *e.g.* when help has unexpectedly come to an individual in great perplexity and need. But these instances of providential design are of a limited kind, and concern the accomplishment of nothing more than the desires of the individual in question. But in the History of the World, the *Individuals* we have to do with are *Peoples*; Totalities that are States. We cannot, therefore, be satisfied with what we may call this "peddling" view of Providence, to which the belief alluded to limits itself. Equally unsatisfactory is the merely abstract, undefined belief in a Providence, when that belief is not brought to bear upon the details of the process which it conducts. On the contrary our earnest endeavour must be directed to the recognition of the ways of Providence, the means it uses, and the historical phenomena in which it manifests itself; and we must shew their connexion with the general principle above mentioned. But in noticing the recognition of the plan of Divine Providence generally, I have implicitly touched upon a prominent question of the day; *viz.* that of the possibility of knowing God: or rather— since public opinion has ceased to allow it to be a matter of *question*—the *doctrine* that it is impossible to know God. In direct contravention of what is commanded in holy Scripture as the highest duty,—that we should not merely love, but *know*

469

God,—the prevalent dogma involves the denial of what is there said; *viz.* that it is the Spirit (*der Geist*) that leads into Truth, knows all things, penetrates even into the deep things of the Godhead. While the Divine Being is thus placed beyond our knowledge, and outside the limit of all human things, we have the convenient licence of wandering as far as we list, in the direction of our own fancies. We are freed from the obligation to refer to our knowledge to the Divine and True. On the other hand, the vanity and egotism which characterise it, find, in this false position, ample justification; and the pious modesty which puts far from it the knowledge of God, can well estimate how much furtherance thereby accrues to its own wayward and vain strivings. I have been unwilling to leave out of sight the connexion between our thesis—that Reason governs and has governed the World—and the question of the possibility of a knowledge of God, chiefly that I might not lose the opportunity of mentioning the imputation against Philosophy of being shy of noticing religious truths, or of having occasion to be so; in which is insinuated the suspicion that it has anything but a clear conscience in the presence of these truths. So far from this being the case, the fact is, that in recent times Philosophy has been obliged to defend the domain of religion against the attacks of several theological systems. In the Christian religion God has revealed Himself,—that is, he has given us to understand what He is; so that He is no longer a concealed or secret existence. And this possibility of knowing Him, thus afforded us, renders such knowledge a duty. God wishes no narrow-hearted souls or empty heads for his children; but those whose spirit is of itself indeed, poor, but rich in the knowledge of Him; and who regard this knowledge of God as the only valuable possession. That development of the thinking spirit, which has resulted from the revelation of the Divine Being as its original basis, must ultimately advance to the *intellectual* comprehension of what was presented in the first instances, to *feeling* and *imagination*. The time must eventually come for understanding that rich product of active Reason, which the History of the World offers to us. It was for a while the fashion to profess admiration for the wisdom of God, as displayed in animals, plants, and isolated occurrences. But, if it be allowed that Providence manifests itself in such objects and forms of existence, why not also in Universal History? This is deemed too great a matter to be thus regarded. But Divine Wisdom, *i.e.* Reason, is one and the same in the great as in the little; and we must not imagine God to be too weak to exercise his wisdom on the grand scale. Our intellectual striving aims at realising the conviction that what was *intended* by eternal wisdom, is actually *accomplished* in the domain of existent, active Spirit, as well as in that of mere Nature.

Our mode of treating the subject is, in this aspect, a Theodicaea,—a justification of the ways of God,—which Leibnitz attempted metaphysically, in his method, *i.e.* in indefinite abstract categories,—so that the ill that is found in the world may be comprehended, and the thinking Spirit reconciled with the fact of the existence of evil. Indeed, nowhere is such a harmonising view more pressingly demanded than in Universal History; and it can be attained only by recognising the *positive* existence, in which that negative element is a subordinate, and vanquished nullity. On the one hand, the ultimate design of the World must be perceived; and, on the other hand, the fact that this design has been actually realised in it, and that evil has not been able permanently to assert a competing position. But this conviction involves much more than the mere belief in a superintending *nous* or in "Providence." "Reason," whose sovereignty over the World has been maintained, is as indefinite a term as "Providence," supposing the term to be used by those who are unable to characterise it distinctly,—to shew wherein it consists, so as to enable us to decide whether a thing is rational or irrational. An adequate definition of Reason is the first desideratum; and whatever boast may be made of strict adherence to it in explaining phenomena,—without such a definition we get no farther than mere words. With these observations we may proceed to the second point of view that has to be considered in this Introduction.

## 2. *Ultimate Design*

The enquiry into the *essential destiny* of Reason—as far as it is considered in reference to the World—is identical with the question, *what is the ultimate design of the World?* And the expression implies that that design is destined to be realized. Two points of consideration suggest themselves: first, the *import* of this design—its abstract definition; and secondly, its *realisation*.

It must be observed at the outset, that the phenomenon we investigate—Universal History—belongs to the realm of *Spirit*. The term "World," includes both physical and physical Nature. Physical Nature also plays its part in the World's History, and attention will have to be paid to the fundamental natural relations thus involved. But Spirit, and the course of its development, is our substantial object. Our task does not require us to contemplate Nature as a Rational System in itself—though in its own proper domain it proves itself such—but simply in its relation to *Spirit*. On the stage on which we are observing it,—Universal History—Spirit displays itself in its most concrete reality. Notwithstanding this (or rather for the very purpose of comprehending the *general* principles which this, its form of *concrete reality*, embodies) we must premise some abstract characteristics of the *nature of spirit*. Such an explanation, however, cannot be given here under any other form than that of bare assertion. The present is not the occasion for unfolding the idea of Spirit speculatively; for whatever has a place in an Introduction, must, as already observed, be taken as simply historical; something assumed as having been explained and proved elsewhere; or whose demonstration awaits the sequel of the Science of History itself.

We have therefore to mention here:

(1) The abstract characteristics of the nature of Spirit.

(2) What means Spirit uses in order to realise its Idea.

(3) Lastly, we must consider the shape which the perfect embodiment of Spirit assumes—the State.

### (1) THE NATURE OF SPIRIT

The nature of Spirit may be understood by a glance at its direct opposite—*Matter*. As the essence of Matter is Gravity, so, on the other hand, we may affirm that the substance, the essence of Spirit is Freedom. All will readily assent to the doctrine that Spirit, among other properties, is also endowed with Freedom; but philosophy teaches that all the qualities of Spirit exist only through Freedom; that all are but means for attaining Freedom; that all seek and produce this and this alone. It is a result of speculative Philosophy, that Freedom is the sole truth of Spirit. Matter possesses gravity in virtue of its tendency towards a central point. It is essentially composite; consisting of parts that *exclude* each other. It seeks its Unity; and therefore exhibits itself as self-destructive, as verging towards its opposite [an indivisible point]. If it could attain this, it would be Matter no longer, it would have perished. It strives after the realisation of its Idea; for in Unity it exists *ideally*. Spirit, on the contrary, may be defined as that which has its centre in itself. It has not a unity outside itself, but has already found it; it exists *in* and *with itself*. Matter has its essence out of itself; Spirit is *self-contained existence* (*Bei-sich-selbst-seyn*). Now this is Freedom, exactly. For if I am dependent, my being is referred to something else which I am not; I cannot exist independently of something external. I am free, on the contrary, when my existence depends upon myself. This self-contained existence of Spirit is none other than self-consciousness—consciousness of one's own being. Two things must be distinguished in consciousness; first, the fact *that I know;* secondly, *what I know.* In *self* consciousness these are merged in one; for Spirit *knows itself.* It involves an appreciation of its own nature, as also an energy enabling it to realise itself; to make itself *actually* that which it is *potentially.* According to this abstract definition it may be said of Universal History, that it is the exhibition of Spirit in the process of working out the knowledge of that which it is potentially. And as the germ bears in itself the whole nature of the tree, and the taste and form of its fruits, so do the first traces of Spirit virtually contain the whole of that History. The Orientals have not attained the knowledge that Spirit—Man *as such*—is free; and because they do not know this they are not free. They only know that *one is free.* But on this very account, the freedom of that one is only caprice; ferocity—brutal recklessness or passion, or a mildness and tameness of the desires, which is itself only an accident of Nature— mere caprice like the former. —That *one* is therefore only a Despot; not a *free* man. The consciousness of Freedom first arose among the Greeks, and therefore they were free; but they, and the Romans likewise, knew only that *some* are free,— not man as such. Even Plato and Aristotle did not know this. The Greeks, therefore, had slaves; and their whole life and the maintenance of their splendid liberty, was implicated with the institution of slavery: a fact moreover, which made that liberty on the one hand only an accidental, transient and limited growth; on the other hand, constituted it a rigorous thraldom of our common nature—of the Human. The German nations, under the influence of Christianity, were the first to attain the consciousness, that man, as man, is free: that it is the *freedom* of Spirit which constitutes its essence. This consciousness arose first in religion, the inmost region of Spirit; but to introduce the principle into the various relations of the actual world, involves a more extensive problem than its simple implantation; a problem whose solution and application require a severe and lengthened process of culture. In proof of this, we may note that slavery did not cease immediately on the reception of Christianity. Still less did liberty predominate in States; or Governments and Constitutions adopt a rational organization, or recognise freedom as their basis. That application of the principle to political relations; the thorough moulding and interpenetration of the constitution of society by it, is a process identical with history itself. I have already directed attention to the distinction here involved, between a principle as such, and its *application; i.e.* its introduction and carrying out in the actual phenomena of Spirit and Life.

This is a point of fundamental importance in our science, and one which must be constantly respected as essential. And in the same way as this distinction has attracted attention in view of the *Christian* principle of self-consciousness— Freedom; it also shews itself as an essential one, in view of the principle of Freedom *generally.* The History of the World is none other than the progress of the consciousness of Freedom; a progress whose development according to the necessity of its nature, it is our business to investigate.

The general statement given above, of the various grades in the consciousness of Freedom—and which we applied in the first instance to the fact that the Eastern nations knew only that *one* is free; the Greek and Roman world only that some are free; while *we* know that all men absolutely (man *as man*) are free,—supplies us with the natural division of Universal History, and suggests the mode of its discussion. This is remarked, however, only incidentally and anticipatively; some other ideas must be first explained.

The destiny of the spiritual World, and,—since this is the *substantial World*, while the physical remains subordinate to it, or, in the language of speculation, has no truth *as against* the spiritual,—the *final cause of the World at large*, we allege to be the *consciousness* of its own freedom on the part of Spirit, and *ipso facto*, the *reality* of that freedom. But that this term, "Freedom," without further qualification, is an indefinite, and incalculable ambiguous term; and that while that which it represents is the *ne plus ultra* of attainment, it is liable to an infinity of misunderstandings, confusions and errors, and to become the occasion for all imaginable excesses,—has never been more clearly known and felt than in modern times. Yet, for the present, we must content ourselves with the term itself without farther definition. Attention was also directed to the importance of the infinite difference between a principle in the abstract, and its realisation in the concrete. In the process before us, the essential nature of freedom—which involves in it absolute necessity,—is to be displayed as coming to a consciousness of itself (for it is in its very nature, self-consciousness) and thereby realising its existence. Itself is its own object of attainment, and the sole aim of Spirit. This result it is, at which the process of the World's History has been continually aiming; and to which the sacrifices that have ever and anon been laid on the vast altar of the earth, through the long lapse of ages, have been offered. This is the only aim that sees itself realised and fulfilled; the only pole of repose amid the ceaseless change of events and conditions, and the sole efficient principle that pervades them. This final aim is God's purpose with the world; but God is the absolutely perfect Being, and can, therefore, will nothing other than himself—his own Will. The Nature of His Will—that is, His Nature itself—is what we here call the Idea of Freedom; translating the language of Religion into that of Thought. The question, then, which we may next put, is: What means does this principle of Freedom use for its realisation? This is the second point we have to consider.

## (2) THE MEANS OF SPIRIT

The question of the *means* by which Freedom develops itself to a World, conducts us to the phenomenon of History itself. Although Freedom is, primarily, an undeveloped idea, the means it uses are external and phenomenal; presenting themselves in History to our sensuous vision. The first glance at History convinces us that the actions of men proceed from their needs, their passions, their characters and talents; and impresses us with the belief that such needs, passions and interests are the sole springs of action—the efficient agents in this scene of activity. Among these may, perhaps, be found aims of a liberal or universal kind—benevolence it may be, or noble patriotism; but such virtues and general views are but insignificant as compared with the World and its doings. We may perhaps see the Ideal of Reason actualized in those who adopt such aims, and within the sphere of their influence; but they bear only a trifling proportion to the mass of the human race; and the extent of that influence is limited accordingly. Passions, private aims, and the satisfaction of selfish desires, are on the other hand, most effective springs of action. Their power lies in the fact that they respect none of the limitations which justice and morality would impose on them; and that these natural impulses have a more direct influence over man than the artificial and tedious discipline that tends to order and self-restraint, law and morality. When we look at this display of passions, and the consequences of their violence; the Unreason which is associated not only with them, but even (rather we might say *especially*) with *good* designs and righteous aims; when we see the evil, the vice, the ruin that has befallen the most flourishing kingdoms which the mind of man ever created, we can scarce avoid being filled with sorrow at this universal taint of corruption: and, since this decay is not the work of mere Nature, but of the Human Will— a moral embitterment—a revolt of the Good Spirit (if it have a place within us) may well be the result of our reflections. Without rhetorical exaggeration, a simply truthful combination of the miseries that have overwhelmed the noblest of nations and politics, and the finest exemplars of private virtue,—forms a picture of most fearful aspect, and excites emotions of the profoundest and most hopeless sadness, counter-balanced by no consolatory result. We endure in beholding it a mental torture, allowing no defence or escape but the consideration that what has happened could not be otherwise; that it is a fatality which no intervention could alter. And at last we draw back from the intolerable disgust with which these sorrowful reflections threaten us, into the more agreeable environment of our individual life—the Present formed by our private aims and interests. In short we retreat into the selfishness that stands on the quiet shore, and thence enjoy in safety the distant spectacle of "wrecks confusedly hurled." But even regarding History as the slaughterbench at which the happiness of peoples, the wisdom of States, and the virtue of individuals have been victimised—the question involuntarily arises—to what principle, to what final aim these enormous sacrifices have been offered. From this point the investigation usually proceeds to that which we have made the general commencement of our enquiry. Starting from this we pointed out those phenomena which made up a picture so suggestive of gloomy emotions and thoughtful reflections—as *the very field* which we, for our part, regard as exhibiting only the means for realising what we assert to be the essential destiny—the absolute aim, or—which come to the same thing—the true *result* of the World's History. We have all along purposely eschewed "moral reflections" as a method of rising from the scene of historical specialties to the general principles which they embody. Besides, it is not the interest of such sentimentalities, really to rise above those depressing emotions; and to solve the enigmas of Providence which the considerations that occasioned them, present. It is essential to their character to find a gloomy satisfaction in the empty and fruitless sublimities of that negative result. We return then to the point of view which we have adopted; observing that the successive steps (*Momente*) of the analysis to which it will lead us, will also evolve the conditions requisite for answering the enquiries suggested by the panorama of sin and suffering that history unfolds.

The *first* remark we have to make, and which—though already presented more than once—cannot be too often repeated when the occasion seems to call for it,—is that what we call *principle, aim, destiny,* or the nature and idea of Spirit, is something merely general and abstract. Principle—Plan of Existence—Law—is a hidden, undeveloped essence, which *as such*—however true in itself—is not completely real. Aims, principles, &c., have a place in our thoughts, in our subjective design only; but not yet in the sphere of reality. That which exists for itself only, is a possibility, a potentiality; but has not yet emerged into Existence. A *second* element must be introduced in order to produce actuality—*viz.* actuation, realization; and whose motive power is the Will—the activity of man in the widest sense. It is only by this activity that that Idea as well as abstract characteristics generally, are realised, actualised; for of themselves they are powerless. The motive power that puts them in operation, and gives them determinate existence, is the need, instinct, inclination, and passion of man. That some conception of mine should be developed into act and existence, is my earnest desire: I wish to assert my personality in connection with it: I wish to be satisfied by its execution. If I am to exert myself for any object, it must in some way or other be *my* object. In the accomplishment of such or such designs I must at the same time find *my* satisfaction; although the purpose for which I exert myself includes a complication of results, many of which have no interest for me. This is the absolute right of personal existence—to find *itself* satisfied in its activity and labour. If men are to interest themselves for anything, they must (so to speak) have part of their existence involved in it; find their individuality gratified by its attainment. Here a mistake must be avoided. We intend blame, and justly impute it as a fault, when we say of an individual, that he is "interested" (in taking part in such or such transactions) that is, seeks only his private advantage. In reprehending this we find fault with him for furthering his personal aims without any regard to a more comprehensive design; of which he takes advantage to promote his own interest, or which he even sacrifices with this view. But he who is active in *promoting an object*, is not simply "interested," but interested in that object itself. Language faithfully expresses this distinction.—Nothing therefore happens, nothing is accomplished, unless the individuals concerned, seek their own satisfaction in the issue. They are particular units of society; *i.e.* they have special needs, instincts, and interests generally, peculiar to themselves. Among these needs are not only such as we usually call necessities—the stimuli of individual desire and volition—but also those connected with individual views and convictions; or—to use a term expressing less decision—leanings of opinion; supposing the impulses of reflection, understanding, and reason, to have been awakened. In these cases people demand, if they are to exert themselves in any direction, that the object should commend itself to them; that in point of opinion,—whether as to its goodness, justice, advantage, profit,—they should be able to "enter into it" (*dabei seyn*). This is a consideration of especial importance in our age, when people are less than formerly influenced by reliance on others, and by authority; when, on the contrary, they devote their activities to a cause on the ground of their own understanding, their independent conviction and opinion.

We assert then that nothing has been accomplished without interest on the part of the actors; and—if interest be called passion, inasmuch as the whole individuality, to the neglect of all other actual or possible interests and claims, is devoted to an object with every fibre of volition, concentrating all its desires and powers upon it—we may affirm absolutely that *nothing great* in *the World* has been accomplished without *passion*. Two elements, therefore, enter into the object of our investigation; the first the Idea, and second the complex of human passions; the one the warp, the other the woof of the vast arras-web of Universal History. The concrete mean and union of the two is Liberty, under the conditions of morality in a State. We have spoken of the Idea of Freedom as the nature of Spirit, and the absolute goal of History. Passion is regarded as a thing of sinister aspect, as more or less immoral. Man is required to have no passions. Passion, it is true, is not quite the suitable word for what I wish to express. I mean here nothing more than human activity as resulting from private interests—special, or if you will, self-seeking designs—with this qualification, that the whole energy of will and character is devoted to their attainment; that other interests (which would in themselves constitute attractive aims), or rather all things else, are sacrificed to them. The object in question is so bound up with the man's will, that it entirely and alone determines the "hue of resolution," and is inseparable from it. It has become the very essence of his volition. For a person is a specific existence; not man in general (a term to which no real existence corresponds), but a particular human being. The term "character" likewise expresses this idiosyncrasy of Will and Intelligence. But *Character* comprehends all peculiarities whatever; the way in which a person conducts himself in private relations, &c., and is not limited to his idiosyncrasy in its practical and active phase. I shall, therefore, use the term "passion;" understanding thereby the particular bent of character, as far as the peculiarities of volition are not limited to private interest, but supply the impelling and actuating force for accomplishing deeds shared in by the community at large. Passion is in the first instance the *subjective*, and therefore the *formal* side of energy, will, and activity—leaving the object or aim still undetermined. And there is a similar relation of formality to reality in merely individual conviction, individual views, individual *conscience*. It is always a question, of essential importance, what is the purport of my conviction, what the object of my passion, in deciding whether the one or the other is of a true and substantial nature. Conversely, if it is so, it will inevitably attain actual existence—be realised.

From this comment on the second essential element in the historical embodiment of an aim, we infer—glancing at the institution of the State in passing—that a State is then well constituted and internally powerful, when the private interest of its citizens is one with the common interest of the State; when the one finds its gratification and realization in the other,—a proposition in itself very important. But in a State many institutions must be adopted, much political machinery invented, accompanied by appropriate political arrangements,—necessitating long struggles of the understanding before what is really appropriate can be discovered,—involving moreover, contentions with private interest and passions, and a tedious discipline of these latter, in order to bring about the desired harmony. The epoch when a State attains this harmonious condition, marks the period of its bloom, its virtue, its vigour, and its prosperity. But the history of mankind does not begin with a *conscious* aim of any kind, as it is the case with the particular circles into which men form themselves of set purpose. The mere social instinct implies a conscious purpose of security for life and property; and when society has been constituted, this purpose becomes more comprehensive. The History of the World begins with its general aim—the realization of the Idea of Spirit—only in an *implicit* form (*an sich*) that is, as Nature; a hidden, most profoundly hidden, unconscious instinct; and the whole process of History (as already observed), is directed to rendering this unconscious impulse a conscious one. Thus appearing in the form of merely natural existence, natural will—that which has been called the subjective side,—physical craving, instinct, passion, private interest, as also opinion and subjective conception,—spontaneously present themselves at the very commencement. The vast congeries of volitions, interests and activities, constitute the instruments and means of the World-Spirit for attaining its object; bringing it to consciousness, and realising it. And this aim is none other than finding itself—coming to itself—and contemplating itself in concrete actuality. But that those manifestations of vitality on the part of individuals and peoples, in which they seek and satisfy their own purposes, are, at the same time, the means and instruments of a higher and broader purpose of which they know nothing,—which they realise unconsciously,—might be made a matter of question; rather has been questioned, and in every variety of form negatived, decried and contemned as mere dreaming and "Philosophy." But on this point I announced my view at the very outset, and asserted our hypotheses,—which, however, will appear in the sequel, in the form of a legitimate inference,—and our belief, that Reason governs the world, and has consequently governed its history. In relation to this independently universal and substantial existence—all else is subordinate, subservient to it, and the means for its development.—The Union of Universal Abstract Existence generally with the Individual,—the Subjective—that this alone is Truth, belongs to the department of speculation, and is treated in this general form in Logic.—But in the process of the World's History itself,—as still incomplete,—the abstract final aim of history is not yet made the distinct object of desire and interest. While these limited sentiments are still unconscious of the purpose they are fulfilling, the universal principle is implicit in them, and is realizing itself through them. The question also assumes the form of the union of *Freedom* and *Necessity;* the latent abstract process of Spirit being regarded as *Necessity*, while that which exhibits itself in the conscious will of men, as their interest, belongs to the domain of *Freedom.* As the metaphysical connection (*i.e.* the connection in the Idea) of these forms of thought, belongs to Logic, it would be out of place to analyse it here. The chief and cardinal points only shall be mentioned.

Philosophy shews that the Idea advances to an infinite antithesis; that, *viz.* between the Idea in its free, universal form—in which it exists for itself—and the contrasted form of abstract introversion, reflection on self, which is formal existence-for-self, personality, formal freedom, such as belongs to Spirit only. The universal Idea exists thus as the substantial totality of things on the one side, and as the abstract essence of free volition on the other side. This reflection of the mind on itself is individual self-consciousness—the polar opposite of the Idea in its general form, and therefore existing in absolute Limitation. This polar opposite is consequently limitation, particularization, for the universal absolute being; it is the side of its *definite existence;* the sphere of its formal reality, the sphere of the reverence paid to God.—To comprehend the absolute connection of this antithesis, is the profound task of metaphysics. This Limitation originates all forms of particularity of whatever kind. The formal volition [of which we have spoken] wills itself; desires to make its own personality valid in all that it purposes and does: even the pious individual wishes to be saved and happy. This pole of the antithesis, existing for itself, is—in contrast with the Absolute Universal Being—a special separate existence, taking cognizance of specialty only, and willing that alone. In short it plays its part in the region of mere phenomena. This is the sphere of particular purposes, in effecting which individuals exert themselves on behalf of their individuality—give it full play and objective realization. This is also the sphere of happiness and its opposite. He is happy who finds his condition suited to his special character, will, and fancy, and so enjoys himself in that condition. The History of the World is not the theatre of happiness. Periods of happiness are blank pages in it, for they are periods of harmony,—periods when the antithesis is in abeyance. Reflection on self,—the Freedom above described—is abstractly defined as the formal element of the activity of the absolute Idea. The realizing activity of which we have spoken is the middle term of the Syllogism, one of whose extremes is the Universal essence, the *Idea*, which reposes in the penetralia of the Spirit; and the other, the complex of external things, objective matter. That activity is the medium by which the universal latent principle is translated into the domain of objectivity.

I will endeavour to make what has been said more vivid and clear by examples.

The building of a house is, in the first instance, a subjective aim and design. On the other hand we have, as means, the several substances required for the work,—Iron, Wood, Stones. The elements are made use of in working up this material: fire to melt the iron, wind to blow the fire, water to set wheels in motion, in order to cut the wood, &c. The result is, that the wind, which has helped to build the house, is shut out by the house; so also are the violence of rains and floods, and the destructive powers of fire, so far as the house is made fire-proof. The stones and beams obey the law of gravity,—press downwards,—and so high walls are carried up. Thus the elements are made use of in accordance with their nature, and yet to co-operate for a product, by which their operation is limited. Thus the passions of men are gratified; they develop themselves and their aims in accordance with their natural tendencies, and build up the edifice of human society; thus fortifying a position of Right and Order *against themselves.*

The connection of events above indicated, involves also the fact, that in history an additional result is commonly produced by human actions beyond that which they aim at and obtain—that which they immediately recognise and desire. They gratify their own interest; but something farther is thereby accomplished, latent in the actions in question, though not present to their consciousness, and not included in their design. An analogous example is offered in the case of a man who, from a feeling of revenge,—perhaps not an unjust one, but produced by injury on the other's part,—burns that other man's house. A connection is immediately established between the deed itself and a train of circumstances not directly included in it, taken abstractedly. In itself it consisted in merely presenting a small flame to a small portion of a beam. Events not involved in that simple act follow of themselves. The part of the beam which was set fire to is connected with its remote portions; the beam itself is united with the woodwork of the house generally, and this with other houses; so that a wide conflagration ensues, which destroys the goods and chattels of many other persons besides his against whom the act of revenge was first directed; perhaps even costs not a few men their lives. This lay neither in the deed abstractedly, nor in the design of the man who committed it. But the action has a further general bearing. In the design of the doer it was only revenge executed against an individual in the destruction of his property, but it is moreover a crime, and that involves punishment also. This may not have been present to the mind of the perpetrator, still less in his intention; but his deed itself, the general principles it calls into play, its substantial content entails it. By this example I wish only to impress on you the consideration, that in a simple act, something farther may be implicated than lies in the intention and consciousness of the agent. The example before us involves, however, this additional consideration, that the substance of the act, consequently we may say the act itself, recoils upon the perpetrator,—reacts upon him with destructive tendency. This union of the two extremes—the embodiment of a general idea in the form of direct reality, and the elevation of a specialty into connection with universal truth—is brought to pass, at first sight, under the conditions of an utter diversity of nature between the two, and an indifference of the one extreme towards the other. The aims which the agent set before them are limited and special; but it must be remarked that the agents themselves are intelligent thinking beings. The purport of their desires is interwoven with *general, essential* considerations of justice, good, duty, &c.; for mere desire—volition in its rough and savage forms—falls not with the scene and sphere of Universal History. Those general considerations, which form at the same time a norm for directing aims and actions, have a determinate purport; for such an abstraction as "good for its own sake," has no place in living reality. If men are to act, they must not only intend the Good, but must have decided for themselves whether this or that particular thing is a Good. What special course of action, however, is good or not, is determined, as regards the ordinary contingencies of private life, by the laws and customs of a State; and here no great difficulty is presented. Each individual has his position; he knows on the whole what a just, honourable course of conduct is. As to ordinary, private relations, the assertion that it is difficult to choose the right and good,—the regarding it as the mark of an exalted morality to find difficulties and raise scruples on that score,—may be set down to an evil or perverse will, which seeks to evade duties not in themselves of a perplexing nature; or, at any rate, to an idly reflective habit of mind—where a feeble will affords no sufficient exercise to the faculties,—leaving them therefore to find occupation within themselves, and to expend themselves on moral self-adulation.

It is quite otherwise with the comprehensive relations that History has to do with. In this sphere are presented those momentous collisions between existing, acknowledged duties, laws, and rights, and those contingencies which are adverse to this fixed system; which assail and even destroy its foundations and existence; whose tenor may nevertheless seem good,—on the large scale advantageous,—yes, even indispensable and necessary. These contingencies realise themselves in History: they involve a general principle of a different order from that on which depends the *permanence* of a people or a State. This principle is an essential phase in the development of the *creating* Idea, of Truth striving and urging towards [consciousness of] itself. Historical men—*World-Historical Individuals*—are those in whose aims such a general principle lies.

Caesar, in danger of losing a position, not perhaps at that time of superiority, yet at least of equality with the others who were at the head of the State, and of succumbing to those who were just on the point of becoming his enemies,— belongs essentially to this category. These enemies—who were at the same time pursuing *their* personal aims—had the form of the constitution, and the power conferred by an appearance of justice, on their side. Caesar was contending for the maintenance of his position, honour, and safety; and, since the power of his opponents included the sovereignty over the provinces of the Roman Empire, his victory secured for him the conquest of that entire Empire; and he thus became— though leaving the form of the constitution—the Autocrat of the State. That which secured for him the execution of a design, which in the first instance was of negative import—the Autocracy of Rome,—was, however, at the same time an independently necessary feature in the History of Rome and of the World. It was not, then, his private gain merely, but an unconscious impulse that occasioned the accomplishment of that for which the time was ripe. Such are all great historical men,—whose own particular aims involve those large issues which are the will of the World-Spirit. They may be called Heroes, inasmuch as they have derived their purposes and their vocation, not from the calm, regular course of things, sanctioned by the existing order; but from a concealed fount—one which has not attained to phenomenal, present existence,—from that inner Spirit, still hidden beneath the surface, which, impinging on the outer world as on a shell, bursts it in pieces, because it is another kernel than that which belonged to the shell in question. They are men, therefore, who appear to draw the impulse of their life from themselves; and whose deeds have produced a condition of things and a complex of historical relations which appear to be only *their* interest, and *their* work.

Such individuals had no consciousness of the general Idea they were unfolding, while prosecuting those aims of theirs; on the contrary, they were practical, political men. But at the same time they were thinking men, who had an insight into the requirements of the time—*what was ripe for development.* This was the very Truth for their age, for their world; the species next in order, so to speak, and which was already formed in the womb of time. It was theirs to know this nascent principle; the necessary, directly sequent step in progress, which their world was to take; to make this their aim, and to expend their energy in promoting it. World-Historical men—the Heroes of an epoch—must, therefore, be recognised as its clear-sighted ones; *their* deeds, *their* words are the best of that time. Great men have formed purposes to satisfy themselves, not others. Whatever prudent designs and counsels they might have learned from others, would be the more limited and inconsistent features in their career; for it was they who best understood affairs; from whom *others* learned, and approved or at least acquiesced in—their policy. For that Spirit which had taken this fresh step in history is the inmost soul of all individuals; but in a state of unconsciousness which the great men in question aroused. Their fellows, therefore, follow these soul-leaders; for they feel the irresistible power of their own inner Spirit thus embodied. If we go on to cast a look at the fate of these World-Historical persons, whose vocation it was to be the agents of the World-Spirit,—we shall find it to have been no happy one. They attained no calm enjoyment; their whole life was labour and trouble; their whole nature was nought else but their master-passion. When their object is attained they fall off like empty hulls from the kernel. They die early, like Alexander; they are murdered, like Caesar; transported to St. Helena, like Napoleon....

But though we might tolerate the idea that individuals, their desires and the gratification of them, are thus sacrificed, and their happiness given up to the empire of chance, to which it belongs; and that as a general rule, individuals come under the category of means to an ulterior end,—there is one aspect of human individuality which we should hesitate to regard in that subordinate light, even in relation to the highest; since it is absolutely no subordinate element, but exists in those individuals as inherently eternal and divine. I mean *Morality, Ethics, Religion.* Even when speaking of the realization of the great idea aim by means of individuals, the *subjective* element in them—their interest and that of their cravings and impulses, their views and judgments, though exhibited as the merely formal side of their existence,—was spoken of as having an infinite right to be consulted. The first idea that presents itself in speaking of *means* is that of something external to the object, and having no share in the object itself. But merely natural things—even the commonest lifeless objects—used as means, must be of such a kind as adapts them to their purpose; they must possess something in common with it. Human beings least of all, sustain the bare external relation of mere means to the great ideal aim. Not only do they in the very act of realising it, make it the occasion of satisfying personal desires, whose purport is diverse from that aim—but they share in that ideal aim itself; and are for that very reason objects of their own existence; not *formally* merely, as the world of living beings generally is—whose individual life is essential subordinate to that of man, and is properly used *up* as an instrument. Men, on the contrary, are objects of existence to themselves, as regards the intrinsic import of the aim in question. To this order belongs that in them which we would exclude from the category of mere means,—Morality, Ethics, Religion. That is to say, man is an object of existence in himself only in virtue of the Divine that is in him,—that which was designated at the outset as *Reason;* which, in view of its activity and power of self-determination, was called *Freedom.* And we affirm—without entering at present on the proof of the assertion—that Religion, Morality, &c. have their foundation and source in that principle, and so are essentially elevated above all alien necessity and chance. And here we must remark that individuals, to the extent of their freedom, are responsible for the depravation and enfeeblement of morals and religion. This is the seal of the absolute and sublime destiny of man—that he knows what is good and what is evil; that his destiny *is* his very ability to will either good or evil,—in one word, that he is the subject of moral imputation, imputation not only of evil, but of good; and not only concerning this or that particular matter, and all that happens *ab extra,* but *also* the good and evil attaching to his individual freedom. The brute alone is simply innocent....

... In affirming ... that the Universal Reason *does* realise itself, we have indeed nothing to do with the individual empirically regarded. That admits of degrees of better and worse, since here chance and specialty have received authority from the Idea to exercise their monstrous power. Much, therefore, in particular aspects of the grand phenomenon might be found fault with. This subjective fault-finding,—which, however, only keeps in view the individual and its deficiency, without taking notice of Reason pervading the whole,—is easy; and inasmuch as it asserts an excellent intention with regard to the good of the whole, and seems to result from a kindly heart, it feels authorized to give itself airs and assume great consequence. It is easier to discover a deficiency in individuals, in states, and in Providence, than to see their real import and value. For in this merely negative fault-finding a proud position is taken,—one which overlooks the object, without having entered into it,—without having comprehended its positive aspect. Age generally makes men more tolerant; youth is always discontented. The tolerance of age is the result of the ripeness of a judgment which, not merely as the result of indifference, is satisfied even with what is inferior; but, more deeply taught by the grave experience of life, has been led to perceive the substantial, solid worth of the object in question. The insight then to which—in contradistinction from those ideals—philosophy is to lead us, is, that the real world is as it ought to be—that the truly good—the universal divine reason—is not a mere abstraction, but a vital principle capable of realising itself. This *Good*, this *Reason*, in its most concrete form, is God. God governs the world; the actual working of his government—the carrying out of his plan—is the History of the World. This plan philosophy strives to comprehend; for only that which has been developed as the result of it, possesses *bona fide* reality. That which does not accord with it, is negative, worthless existence. Before the pure light of this divine Idea—which is no mere Ideal—the phantom of a world whose events are an incoherent concourse of fortuitous circumstances, utterly vanishes. Philosophy wishes to discover the substantial purport, the real side of the divine idea, and to justify the so much despised Reality of things; for Reason is the comprehension of the Divine work. But as to what concerns the perversion, corruption, and ruin of religious, ethical and moral purposes, and states of society generally, it must be affirmed, that in their *essence* these are infinite and eternal; but that the forms they assume may be of a limited order, and consequently belong to the domain of mere nature, and be subject to the sway of chance. They are therefore perishable, and exposed to decay and corruption. Religion and morality—in the same way as inherently universal essences—have the peculiarity of being present in the individual soul, in the full extent of their Idea, and therefore truly and really; although they may not manifest themselves in it *in extenso*, and are not applied to fully developed relations. The religion, the morality of a limited sphere of life— that of a shepherd or a peasant, *e.g.*—in its intensive concentration and limitation to a few perfectly simply relations of life,—has infinite worth; the same worth as the religion and morality of extensive knowledge, and of an existence rich in the compass of relations and actions. This inner focus—this simple region of the claims of subjective freedom,—the home of volition, resolution, and action,—the abstract sphere of conscience,—that which comprises the responsibility and moral value of the individual, remain untouched; and is quite shut out from the noisy din of the World's History—including not merely external and temporal changes, but also those entailed by the absolute necessity inseparable from the realization of the Idea of Freedom itself. But as a general truth this must be regarded as settled, that whatever in the world possesses claims as noble and glorious, has nevertheless a higher existence above it. The claim of the World-Spirit rises above all special claims.

These observations may suffice in reference to the means which the World-Spirit uses for realising its Idea. Stated simply and abstractly, this mediation involves the activity of personal existences in whom Reason is present as their absolute, substantial being; but a basis, in the first instance, still obscure and unknown to them. But the subject becomes more complicated and difficult when we regard individuals not merely in their aspect of activity, but more concretely, in conjunction with a particular manifestation of that activity in their religion and morality,—forms of existence which are intimately connected with Reason, and share in its absolute claims. Here the relation of mere means of an end disappears, and the chief bearings of this seeming difficulty in reference to the absolute aim of Spirit, have been briefly considered.

### (3) THE EMBODIMENT OF SPIRIT

The third point to be analysed is, therefore—what is the object to be realised by these means; *i.e.* what is the form it assumes in the realm of reality. We have spoken of *means;* but in carrying out of a subjective, limited aim, we have also to take into consideration the element of a *material,* either already present or which has to be procured. Thus the question would arise: What is the material in which the Ideal of Reason is wrought out? The primary answer would be,—Personality itself—human desires—Subjectivity generally. In human knowledge and volition, as its material element, Reason attains positive existence. We have considered subjective volition where it has an object which is the truth and essence of a reality, *viz.* where it constitutes a great world-historical passion. As a subjective will, occupied with limited passions, it is dependent, and can gratify its desires only within the limits of this dependence. But the subjective will has also a substantial life—a reality,—in which it moves in the region of *essential* being and has the essential itself as the object of its existence. This essential being is the union of the *subjective* with the *rational* Will: it is the moral Whole, the State, which is that form of reality in which the individual has and enjoys his freedom; but on the condition of his recognition, believing in and willing that which is common to the Whole. And this must not be understood as if the subjective will of the social unit attained its gratification and enjoyment through that common Will; as if this were a means provided for its benefit; as if the individual, in his relations to other individuals, thus limited his freedom, in order that this universal limitation—the mutual constraint of all—might secure a small space of liberty for each. Rather, we affirm, are Law, Morality, Government, and they alone, the positive reality and completion of Freedom. Freedom of a low and limited order, is mere caprice; which finds its exercise in the sphere of particular and limited desires.

Subjective volition—Passion—is that which sets men in activity, that which effects "practical" realization. The Idea is the inner spring of action; the State is the actually existing, realised moral life. For it is the Unity of the universal, essential Will, with that of the individual; and this is "Morality." The Individual living in this unity has a moral life; possesses a value that consists in this substantially alone. Sophocles in his *Antigone* says, "The divine commands are not of yesterday, nor of today; no, they have an infinite existence, and no one could say whence they came." The laws of morality are not accidental, but are the essentially Rational. It is the very object of the State that what is essential in the practical activity of men, and in their dispositions, should be duly recognized; that it should have a manifest existence, and maintain its position. It is the absolute interest of Reason that this moral Whole should exist; and herein lies the justification and merit of heroes who have founded states,—however rude these may have been. In the History of the World, only those peoples can come under our notice which form a state. For it must be understood that this latter is the realization of Freedom, *i.e.* of the absolute final aim, and that it exists for its own sake. It must further be understood that all the worth which the human being possesses—all spiritual reality, he possesses only through the State. For his spiritual reality consists in this, that his own essence—Reason—is objectively present in him, that it possesses objective immediate existence for him. Thus only is he fully conscious; thus only is he a partaker of morality—of a just and moral social and political life. For Truth is the Unity of the universal and subjective Will; and the Universal is to be found in the State, in its laws, its universal and rational arrangements. The State is the

Divine Idea as it exists on Earth. We have in it, therefore, the object of History in a more definite shape than before; that in which Freedom obtains objectivity, and lives in the enjoyment of this objectivity. For Law is the objectivity of Spirit; volition in its true form. Only that will which obeys law, is free; for it obeys itself— it is independent and so free. When the State or our country constitutes a community of existence; when the subjective will of man submits to laws,—the contradiction between Liberty and Necessity vanishes. The Rational has necessary existence, as being the reality and substance of things, and we are free in recognising it as law, and following it as the substance of our own being. The objective and the subjective will are then reconciled, and present one identical homogeneous whole. For the morality (*Sittlichkeit*) of the State is not of that ethical (*moralische*) reflective kind, in which one's own conviction bears sway; this latter is rather the peculiarity of the modern time, while the true antique morality is based on the principle of abiding by one's duty [to the state at large]. An Athenian citizen did what was required of him, as it were from instinct; but if I reflect on the object of my activity, I must have the consciousness that my will has been called into exercise. But morality is Duty—substantial Right—a "*second nature*" as it has been justly called; for the *first* nature of man is his primary merely animal existence....

Summing up what has been said of the State, we find that we have been led to call its vital principle, as actuating the individuals who compose it,—Morality. The State, its laws, its arrangements, constitute the rights of its members; its natural features, its mountains, air, and waters, are *their* country, their fatherland, their outward material property; the history of this State, *their* deeds; what their ancestors have produced, belongs to them and lives in their memory. All is their possession, just as they are possessed by it; for it constitutes their existence, their being.

Their imagination is occupied with the ideas thus presented, while the adoption of these laws, and of a fatherland so conditioned is the expression of their will. It is this matured totality which thus constitutes *one* Being, the spirit of *one* People. To it the individual members belong; each unit is the Son of his Nation, and at the same time—in as far as the State to which he belongs is undergoing development—the Son of his Age. None remains behind it, still less advances beyond it. This spiritual Being (the Spirit of his Time) is his; he is a representative of it; it is that in which he originated, and in which he lives. Among the Athenians the word Athens had a double import; suggesting primarily, a complex of political institutions, but no less, in the second place, that Goddess who represented the Spirit of the People and its unity.

This Spirit of a People is a *determinate* and particular Spirit, and is, as just stated, further modified by the degree of its historical development. This Spirit, then, constitutes the basis and substance of those other forms of a nation's consciousness, which have been noticed. For Spirit in its self-consciousness must become an object of contemplation to itself, and objectivity involves, in the first instance, the rise of differences which make up a total of distinct spheres of objective spirit; in the same way as the Soul exists only as the complex of its faculties; which in their form of concentration in a simple unity produce that Soul. It is thus *One Individuality* which, presented in its essence as God, is honoured and enjoyed in *Religion;* which is exhibited as an object of sensuous contemplation in *Art;* and is apprehended as an intellectual conception, in *Philosophy.* In virtue of the original identity of their essence, purport, and object, these various forms are inseparably united with the Spirit of the State. Only in connection with this particular religion, can this particular political constitution exist; just as in such or such a State, such or such a Philosophy or order of Art.

The remark next in order is, that each particular National genius is to be treated as only One Individual in the process of Universal History. For that history is the exhibition of the divine, absolute development of Spirit in its highest forms,—that gradation by which it attains its truth and consciousness of itself. The forms which these grades of progress assume are the characteristic "National Spirits" of History; the peculiar tenor of their moral life, of their Government, their Art, Religion, and Science. To realise these grades is the boundless impulse of the World-Spirit—the goal of its irresistible urging; for this division into organic members, and the full development of each, is its Idea.—Universal History is exclusively occupied with shewing how Spirit comes to a recognition and adoption of the Truth: the dawn of knowledge appears; it begins to discover salient principles, and at last it arrives at full consciousness.

Having, therefore, learned the abstract characteristics of the nature of Spirit, the means which it uses to realise its Idea, and the shape assumed by it in its complete realisation in phenomenal existence—namely, the State—nothing further remains for this introductory section to contemplate but

### 3. *The Course of the World's History*

The mutations which history presents have been long characterised in the general, as an advance to something better, more perfect. The changes that take place in Nature—how infinitely manifold soever they may be—exhibit only a perpetually self-repeating cycle; in Nature there happens "nothing new under the sun," and the multiform play of its phenomena so far induces a feeling of *ennui;* only in those changes which take place in the region of Spirit does anything new arise. This peculiarity in the world of mind has indicated in the case of man an altogether different destiny from that of merely natural objects—in which we find always one and the same stable character, to which all change reverts;—namely, a *real* capacity for change, and that for the better,—an impulse of *perfectibility.* This principle, which reduces change itself under a law, has met with an unfavourable reception from religions—such as the Catholic— and from States claiming as their just right a stereotyped, or at least a stable position. If the mutability of worldly things in general—political constitutions, for instance—is conceded, either Religion (as the Religion of *Truth*) is absolutely excepted, or the difficulty escaped by ascribing changes, revolutions, and abrogations of immaculate theories and institutions, to accidents or imprudence,—but principally to the levity and evil passions of man. The principle of Perfectibility indeed is almost as indefinite a term as mutability in general; it is without scope or goal, and has no standard by which to estimate the changes in question: the improved, more perfect, state of things towards which it professedly tends is altogether determined.

The principle of *Development* involves also the existence of a latent germ of being—a capacity or potentiality striving to realise itself. This formal conception finds actual existence in Spirit; which has the History of the World for its theatre, its possession, and the sphere of its realisation. It is not of such a nature as to be tossed to and fro amid the superficial play of accidents, but is rather the absolute arbiter of things; entirely unmoved by contingencies, which, indeed, it applies and manages for its own purposes. Development, however, is also a property of organized natural objects. Their existence presents itself, not as an exclusively dependent one, subjected to external changes, but as one which expands itself in virtue of an external unchangeable principle; a simple essence,— whose existence, *i.e.,* as a germ, is primarily simple,—but which subsequently develops a variety of parts, that become involved with other objects, and consequently live through a continuous process of changes;—a process nevertheless, that results in the very contrary of change, and is even transformed into a *vis conservatrix* [preserving power] of the organic principle, and the form embodying it. Thus the organized *individuum* [association of individuals] produces itself; it expands itself *actually* to what it was always *potentially:* So Spirit is only that which it attains by its own efforts; it makes itself *actually* what it always was *potentially*. —That development (of *natural organisms*) takes place in a direct, unopposed, unhindered manner. Between the Idea and its realisation— the essential constitution of the original germ and the conformity to it of the existence derived from it—no disturbing influence can intrude. But in relation to Spirit it is quite otherwise. The realisation of *its* Idea is mediated by consciousness and will; these very faculties are, in the first instance, sunk in their primary *merely* natural life; the first object and goal of their striving is the realisation of their merely natural destiny,—but which, since it is Spirit that animates it, is possessed of vast attractions and displays great power and [moral] richness. Thus Spirit is at war with itself; it has to overcome itself as its most formidable obstacle. That development which in the sphere of Nature is a peaceful growth, is in that of Spirit, a severe, a mighty conflict with itself. What Spirit really strives for is the realisation of its Ideal being; but in doing so, it hides that goal from its own vision, and is proud and well satisfied in this alienation from it.

Its expansion, therefore, does not present the harmless tranquility of mere growth, as does that of organic life, but a stern reluctant working against itself. It exhibits, moreover, not the mere formal conception of development, but the attainment of a definite result. The goal of attainment we determined at the outset: it is Spirit in its *completeness*, in its essential nature, *i.e.*, Freedom. This is the fundamental object, and therefore also the leading principle of the development,—that whereby it receives meaning and importance (as in the Roman history, Rome is the object—consequently that which directs our consideration of the facts related); as, conversely, the phenomena of the process have resulted from this principle alone, and only as referred to it, possess a sense and value. There are many considerable periods in History in which this development seems to have been intermitted; in which, we might rather say, the whole enormous gain of previous culture appears to have been entirely lost; after which, unhappily, a new commencement has been necessary, made in the hope of recovering—by the assistance of some remains saved from the wreck of a former civilization, and by dint of a renewed incalculable expenditure of strength and time,—one of the regions which had been an ancient possession of that civilization. We behold also *continued* processes of growth; structures and systems of culture in particular spheres, rich in kind, and well developed in every direction. The merely formal and indeterminate view of development in general can neither assign to one form of expansion superiority over the other, nor render comprehensible the object of that decay of older periods of growth; but must regard such occurrence,—or, to speak more particularly, the retrocessions they exhibit,—as external contingencies; and can only judge of particular modes of development from indeterminate points of view; which—since the development as such, is all in all—are relative and not absolute goals of attainment.

Universal History exhibits the *gradation* in the development of that principle whose substantial *purport* is the consciousness of Freedom. The analysis of the successive grades, in their abstract form, belongs to Logic; in their concrete aspect to the Philosophy of Spirit. Here it is sufficient to state that the first step in the process presents that immersion of Spirit in Nature which has been already referred to; the second shows it as advancing to the consciousness of its freedom. But this initial separation from Nature is imperfect and partial, since it is derived immediately from the merely natural state, is consequently related to it, and is still encumbered with it as an essentially connected element. The third step is the elevation of the soul from this still limited and special form of freedom to its pure universal form; that state in which the spiritual essence attains the consciousness and feeling of itself. These grades are the ground-principles of the general process; but how each of them on the other hand involves within *itself* a process of formation,—constituting the links in a dialectic of transition,—to particularise this may be reserved for the sequel....

Universal History ... shews the development of the consciousness of Freedom on the part of Spirit, and of the consequent realization of that Freedom. This development implies a gradation—a series of increasingly adequate expressions or manifestations of Freedom, which result from its Idea. The logical, and—as still more prominent—the *dialectical* nature of the Idea in general, *viz.* that it is self-determined—that it assumes successive forms which it successively transcends; and by this very process of transcending its earlier stages, gains an affirmative, and, in fact, a richer and more concrete shape;—this necessity of its nature, and the necessary series of pure abstract forms which the Idea successively assumes—is exhibited in the department of *Logic*. Here we need adopt only one of its results, *viz.* that every step in the process, as differing from any other, has its determinate peculiar principle. In history this principle is idiosyncrasy of Spirit—peculiar National Genius. It is within the limitations of this idiosyncrasy that the spirit of the nation, concretely manifested, expresses every aspect of its consciousness and will—the whole cycle of its realization. Its religion, its polity, its ethics, its legislation, and even its science, art, and mechanical skill, all bear its stamp. These special peculiarities find their key in that common peculiarity,—the particular principle that characterises a people; as, on the other hand, in the facts which History presents in detail, that common characteristic principle may be detected. That such or such a specific quality constitutes the peculiar genius of a people, is the element of our inquiry which must be derived from experience, and historically proved....

# THE PHILOSOPHY OF RIGHT

## The State

### *Idea and Aim of the State*

The State is the realization of the ethical idea. It is the ethical spirit as revealed, self-conscious, substantial will. It is the will which thinks and knows itself, and carries out what it knows, and in so far as it knows. The unreflected existence of the State rests on custom, and its reflected existence on the self-consciousness of the individual, on his knowledge and activity. The individual, in return, has his substantial freedom in the State, as the essence, purpose, and product of his activity.

The true State is the ethical whole and the realization of freedom. It is the absolute purpose of reason that freedom should be realized. The State is the spirit, which lives in the world and there realizes itself consciously; while in nature it is actual only as its own other or as dormant spirit. Only as present in consciousness, knowing itself as an existing object, is it the State. The State is the march of God through the world, its ground is the power of reason realizing itself as will. The idea of the State should not denote any particular State, or particular institution; one must rather consider the Idea only, this actual God, by itself. Because it is more easy to find defects than to grasp the positive meaning, one readily falls into the mistake of emphasizing so much the particular nature of the State as to overlook its inner organic essence. The State is no work of art. It exists in the world, and thus is the realm of caprice, accident, and error. Evil behavior toward it may disfigure it on many sides. But the ugliest man, the criminal, the invalid, and the cripple, are still living human beings. The affirmative, life, persists in spite of defects, and it is this affirmative which alone is here in question.

In the State, everything depends upon the unity of the universal and the particular. In the ancient States the subjective purpose was absolutely one with the will of the State. In modern times, on the contrary, we demand an individual opinion, an individual will and conscience. The ancients had none of these in the modern

---

**N.B.** The topic headings inserted in the text have been added by J. Loewenberg.

sense; the final thing for them was the will of the State. While in Asiatic despotisms the individual had no inner self and no self-justification, in the modern world man demands to be honored for the sake of his subjective individuality.

The union of duty and right has the twofold aspect that what the State demands as duty should directly be the right of the individual, since the State is nothing but the organization of the concept of freedom. The determinations of the individual will are given by the State objectively, and it is through the State alone that they attain truth and realization. The State is the sole condition of the attainment of the particular end and good.

Political disposition, called patriotism—the assurance resting in truth and the will which has become a custom—is simply the result of the institutions subsisting in the State, institutions in which reason is actually present.

Under patriotism one frequently understands a mere willingness to perform extraordinary acts and sacrifices. But patriotism is essentially the sentiment of regarding, in the ordinary circumstances and ways of life, the weal of the community as the substantial basis and the final end. It is upon this consciousness, present in the ordinary course of life and under all circumstances, that the disposition to heroic effort is founded. But as people are often rather magnanimous than just, they easily persuade themselves that they possess the heroic kind of patriotism, in order to save themselves the trouble of having the truly patriotic sentiment, or to excuse the lack of it.

Political sentiment, as appearance, must be distinguished from what people truly will. What they at bottom will is the real cause, but they cling to particular interests and delight in the vain contemplation of improvements. The conviction of the necessary stability of the State in which alone the particular interests can be realized, people indeed possess, but custom makes invisible that upon which our whole existence rests; it does not occur to any one, when he safely passes through the streets at night, that it could be otherwise. The habit of safety has become a second nature, and we do not reflect that it is the result of the activity of special institutions. It is through force—this is frequently the superficial opinion—that the State coheres, but what alone holds it together is the fundamental sense of order, which is possessed by all.

The state is an organism or the development of the idea into its differences. These different sides are the different powers of the State with their functions and activities, by means of which the universal is constantly and necessarily producing itself, and, being presupposed in its own productive function, it is thus always actively present. This organism is the political constitution. It eternally springs from the State, just as the State in turn maintains itself through the constitution. If these two things fall asunder, if both different sides become independent of each other, then the unity which the constitution produces is no longer operative; the fable of the stomach and the other organs may be applied to it. It is the nature of an organism that all its parts must constitute a certain unity; if one part asserts its independence the other parts must go to destruction. No predicates, principles, and the like suffice to express the nature of the State; it must be comprehended as an organism.

The State is real, and its reality consists in the interest of the whole being realized in particular ends. Actuality is always the unity of universality and particularity, and the differentiation of the universal into particular ends. These particular ends seem independent, though they are borne and sustained by the whole only. In so far as this unity is absent, no thing is real, though it may exist. A bad State is one which merely exists. A sick body also exists, but it has no true reality. A hand, which is cut off, still looks like a hand and exists, but it has no reality. True reality is necessity. What is real is eternally necessary.

To the complete State belongs, essentially, consciousness and thought. The State knows thus what it wills, and it knows it under the form of thought.

The essential difference between the State and religion consists in that the commands of the State have the form of legal duty, irrespective of the feelings accompanying their performance; the sphere of religion, on the other hand, is in the inner life. Just as the State, were it to frame its commands as religion does, would endanger the right of the inner life, so the church, if it acts as a State and imposes punishment, degenerates into a tyrannical religion.

In the State one must want nothing which is not an expression of rationality. The State is the world which the spirit has made for itself; it has therefore a determinate and self-conscious course. One often speaks of the wisdom of God in nature, but one must not believe that the physical world of nature is higher than the world of spirit. Just as spirit is superior to nature, so is the State superior to the physical life. We must therefore worship the State as the manifestation of the divine on earth, and consider that, if it is difficult to comprehend nature, it is infinitely harder to grasp the essence of the State. It is an important fact that we, in modern times, have attained definite insight into the State in general and are much engaged in discussing and making constitutions; but that does not advance the problem much. It is necessary to treat a rational matter in the light of reason, in order to learn its essential nature and to know that the obvious does not always constitute the essential.

When we speak of the different functions of the powers of the State, we must not fall into the enormous error of supposing each power to have an abstract, independent existence, since the powers are rather to be differentiated as elements in the conception of the State. Were the powers to be in abstract independence, however, it is clear that two independent things could never constitute a unity, but must produce war, and the result would be destruction of the whole or restoration of unity by force. Thus, in the French Revolution, at one time the legislative power had swallowed up the executive, at another time the executive had usurped the legislative power.

## The Constitution

The constitution is rational, in so far as the State defines and differentiates its functions according to the nature of its concept.

Who shall make the constitution? This question seems intelligible, yet on closer examination reveals itself as meaningless, for it presupposes the existence of no constitution, but only a mere mass of atomic individuals. How a mass of individuals is to come by a constitution whether by its own efforts or by those of others, whether by goodness, thought, or force, it must decide for itself, for with a disorganized mob the concept of the State has nothing to do. But if the question does presuppose an already existing constitution, then to make a constitution means only to change it. The presupposition of a constitution implies, however, at once, that any modification in it must take place constitutionally. It is absolutely essential that the constitution, though having a temporal origin, should not be regarded as made. It (the principle of constitution) is rather to be conceived as absolutely perpetual and rational, and therefore as divine, substantial, and above and beyond the sphere of what is made.

Subjective freedom is the principle of the whole modern world—the principle that all essential aspects of the spiritual totality should develop and attain their right. From this point of view one can hardly raise the idle question as to which form is the better, monarchy or democracy. One can but say that the forms of all constitutions are one-sided that are not able to tolerate the principle of free subjectivity and that do not know how to conform to the fully developed reason.

Since spirit is real only in what it knows itself to be, and since the State, as the nation's spirit, is the law permeating all its affairs, its ethical code, and the consciousness of its individuals, the constitution of a people chiefly depends upon the kind and the character of its self-consciousness. In it lies both its subjective freedom and the reality of the constitution.

To think of giving people a constitution *a priori*, though according to its content a more or less rational one—such a whim would precisely overlook that element which renders a constitution more than a mere abstract object. Every nation, therefore, has the constitution which is appropriate to it and belongs to it.

The State must, in its constitution, permeate all situations. A constitution is not a thing just made; it is the work of centuries, the idea and the consciousness of what is rational, in so far as it is developed in a people. No constitution, therefore, is merely created by the subjects of the State. The nation must feel that its constitution embodies its right and its status, otherwise the constitution may exist externally, but has no meaning or value. The need and the longing for a better constitution may often indeed be present in individuals, but that is quite different from the whole multitude being permeated with such an idea—that comes much later. The principle of morality, the inwardness of Socrates originated necessarily in his day, but it took time before it could pass into general self-consciousness.

## *The Power of the Prince*

Because sovereignty contains in ideal all special privileges, the common misconception is quite natural, which takes it to be mere force, empty caprice, and synonymous with despotism. But despotism means a state of lawlessness, in which the particular will as such, whether that of monarch or people (*ochlocracy*), is the law, or rather instead of the law. Sovereignty, on the contrary, constitutes the element of ideality of particular spheres and functions under lawful and constitutional conditions.

The sovereignty of the people, conceived in opposition to the sovereignty residing in the monarch, stands for the common view of democracy, which has come to prevail in modern times. The idea of the sovereignty of the people, taken in this opposition, belongs to a confused idea of what is commonly and crudely understood by "the people." The people without its monarch and without that whole organization necessarily and directly connected with him is a formless mass, which is no longer a State. In a people, not conceived in a lawless and unorganized condition, but as a self-developed and truly organic totality—in such a people sovereignty is the personality of the whole, and this is represented in reality by the person of the monarch.

The State must be regarded as a great architectonic edifice, a hieroglyph of reason, manifesting itself in reality. Everything referring merely to utility, externality, and the like, must be excluded from its philosophic treatment. That the State is the self-determining and the completely sovereign will, the final decision being nec-essarily referred to it—that is easy to comprehend. The difficulty lies in grasping this "I will" as a person. By this it is not meant that the monarch can act arbitrarily. He is bound, in truth, by the concrete content of the deliberations of his council, and, when the constitution is stable, he has often nothing more to do than sign his name—but this name is important; it is the point than which there is nothing higher.

It may be said that an organic State has already existed in the beautiful democ-racy of Athens. The Greeks, however, derived the final decision from entirely ex-ternal phenomena, from oracles, entrails of sacrificed animals, and from the flight of birds. Nature they considered as a power which in this wise made known and gave expression to what was good for the people. Self-consciousness had at that time not yet attained to the abstraction of subjectivity; it had not yet come to the realization that an "I will" must be pronounced by man himself concerning the decisions of the State. This "I will" constitutes the great difference between the ancient and the modern world, and must therefore have its peculiar place in the great edifice of the State. Unfortunately this modern characteristic is regarded as merely external and arbitrary.

It is often maintained against the monarch that he may be ill-educated or un-worthy to stand at the helm chance. It is therefore absurd to assume the rationality of the institution of the monarch. The presupposition, however, that the fortunes of the State depend upon the particular character of the monarch is false. In the per-fect organization of the State the important thing is only the finality of formal de-cision and the stability against passion. One must not therefore demand objective qualification of the monarch; he has but to say "yes" and to put the dot upon the "i." The crown shall be of such a nature that the particular character of its bearer is of no significance. Beyond his function of administering the final decision, the monarch is a particular being who is of no concern. Situations may indeed arise in which his particularity alone asserts itself, but in that case the State is not yet fully developed, or else is ill constructed. In a well-ordered monarchy the law alone has objective power to which the monarch has but to affix the subjective "I will."

Monarchs do not excel in bodily strength or intellect and yet millions per-mit themselves to be ruled by them. To say that the people permit themselves to be governed contrary to their interests, aims, and intentions is preposterous, for people are not so stupid. It is their need, it is the inner power of the idea, which, in opposition to their apparent consciousness, urges them to this situation and retains them therein.

Out of the sovereignty of the monarch flows the prerogative of pardoning criminals. Only to the sovereignty belongs the spiritual power to undo what has been done and to cancel the crime by forgiving and forgetting.

Pardon is the remission of punishment, but does not abolish right. Right remains, and the pardoned is a criminal as he was before the pardon. The act of mercy does not mean that no crime has been committed. This remission of punishment may be effected in religion, for by and in spirit what has been done can be made undone. But in so far as remission occurs in the world, it has its place only in majesty and is due only to its arbitrary decision.

## The Executive

The main point upon which the function of the government depends is the division of labor. This division is concerned with the transition from the universal to the particular and the individual; and the business is to be divided according to the different branches. The difficulty lies in harmonizing the superior and the inferior functions. For some time past the main effort has been spent in organizing from above, the lower and bulky part of the whole being left more or less unorganized; yet it is highly important that it should become organic, for only thus is it a power and a force; otherwise it is but a heap or mass of scattered atoms. Authoritative power resides only in the organic state of the particular spheres.

The State cannot count on service which is capricious and voluntary (the administration of justice by knights-errant, for instance), precisely because it is capricious and voluntary. Such service presupposes acting according to subjective opinion, and also the possibility of neglect and of the realization of public ends. The opposite extreme to the knight-errant in reference to public service would be the State-servant who was attached to his task solely by want, without genuine duty and right.

The efficiency of the State depends upon individuals, who, however, are not entitled to carry on the business of the State through natural [or untutored] fitness, but according to their objective qualifications. Ability, skill, character, belong to the particular nature of the individual; for a particular office, however, he must be specially educated and trained. An office in the State can, therefore, be neither sold nor bequeathed.

Public service demands the sacrifice of independent self-satisfaction, and the giving up of the pursuit of private ends, but grants the right of finding these in dutiful service, and in it only. Herein lies the unity of the universal and the particular interests which constitutes the concept and the inner stability of the State.

The members of the executive and the officials of the State form the main part of the middle class which represents the educated intelligence and the consciousness of right of the mass of a people. This middle class is prevented by the institutions of sovereignty from above and the rights of corporation from below, from assuming the exclusive position of an aristocracy and making education and intelligence the means for caprice and despotism. Thus the administration of justice, whose object is the proper interest of all individuals, had at one time been perverted into an instrument of gain and despotism, owing to the fact that the knowledge of the law was hidden under a learned and foreign language, and the knowledge of legal procedure under an involved formalism.

In the middle class, to which the State officials belong, resides the consciousness of the State and the most conspicuous cultivation; the middle class constitutes therefore the ground pillar of the State in regard to uprightness and intelligence. The State in which there is no middle class stands as yet on no high level.

## The Legislature

The legislature is concerned with the interpretation of the laws and with the internal affairs of the State, in so far as they have a universal content. This function is itself a part of the constitution and thus presupposes it. Being presupposed, the constitution lies, to that degree, outside the direct province of the legislature, but in the forward development of the laws and the progressive character of the universal affairs of government, the constitution receives its development also.

The constitution must alone be the firm ground on which the legislature stands; hence it must not be created for purposes of legislation. But the constitution not only *is*, its essence is also to *become*—that is, it progresses with the advance of civilization. This progress is an alteration which is imperceptible, but has not the form of an alteration. Thus, for example, the emperor was formerly judge, and went about the empire administering justice. Through the merely apparent advance of civilization it has become practically necessary the emperor should gradually yield his judicial function to others, and thus came about the transition of the judicial function from the person of the prince to a body of judges; thus the progress of any condition is an apparently calm and imperceptible one. In this way and after a lapse of time a constitution attains a character quite different from what it had before.

In the legislative power as a whole are operative both the monarchical element and the executive. To the former belongs the final decision; the latter as advisory element possesses concrete knowledge, perspective over the whole in all its ramifications, and acquaintance with the objective principles and wants of the power of the State. Finally, in the legislature the different classes or estates are also active. These classes or estates represent in the legislature the element of subjective formal freedom, the public consciousness, the empirical totality of the views and thought of the many.

The expression "The Many" (οι πολλοι) characterizes the empirical totality more correctly than the customary word "All." Though one may reply that, from this "all," children, women, etc., are obviously meant to be excluded, yet it is more obvious that the definite expression "all" should not be used when something quite indefinite is in question.

There are, in general, current among the public so unspeakably many distorted and false notions and phrases about the people, the constitution, and the classes, that it would be a vain task to mention, explain, and correct them. The prevalent idea concerning the necessity and utility of an assembly of estates amounts to the assumption that the people's deputies, nay, the people itself, best understand what would promote the common weal, and that they have indubitably the good will to promote it. As for the first point, the case is just the reverse. The people, in so far as this term signifies a special part of the citizens, stands precisely for the part that does not know what it wills. To know what one wills, and, what is more difficult, to know what the absolute will, viz., reason, wills, is the fruit of deep knowledge and insight; and that is obviously not a possession of the people. As for the especially good will, which the classes are supposed to have for the common good, the usual point of view of the masses is the negative one of suspecting the government of a will which is evil or of little good.

The attitude of the government toward the classes must not be essentially a hostile one. Belief in the necessity of this hostile relation is a sad mistake. The government is not one part in opposition to another, so that both are engaged in wrestling something from each other. When the State is in such a situation it is a misfortune and not a mark of health. Furthermore, the taxes, for which the classes vote, are not to be looked upon as gifts, but are consented to for the best interests of those consenting. What constitutes the true meaning of the classes is this—that through them the State enters into the subjective consciousness of the people and thus the people begin to share in the State.

In despotic countries, where there are only princes and people, the people assert themselves, whenever they act, as a destructive force directed against the organization, but the masses, when they become organically related to the State, obtain their interests in a lawful and orderly way. When this organic relation is lacking, the self-expression of the masses is always violent; in despotic States the despot shows, therefore, indulgence for his people, and his rage is always felt by those surrounding him. Moreover, the people of a despotic State pay light taxes, which in a constitutional State are increased through the very consciousness of the people. In no other country are taxes so heavy as they are in England.

There exists a current notion to the effect that, since the private class is raised in the legislature to a participation in the universal cause, it must appear in the form of individuals—either that representatives are chosen for the function, or that every individual exercises a vote. This abstract atomic view prevails neither in the family nor in civic society, in both of which the individual appears only a member of a universal. The State, however, is in essence an organization of members, and these members are themselves spheres; in it no element shall show itself as an unorganized mass. The many, as individuals, whom one chooses to call the people, are indeed a collection, but only as a multitude, a formless mass, whose movement and action would be elemental, irrational, savage, and terrible.

The concrete State is the whole, organized into its particular spheres, and the member of the State is a member of such a particular class. Only in this objective determination can the individual find recognition in the State. Only in his cooperative capacity, as member of the community and the like, can the individual first find a real and vital place in the universal. It remains, of course, open to him to rise through his skill to any class for which he can qualify himself, including even the universal class.

It is a matter of great advantage to have among the delegates representatives of every special branch of society, such as trade, manufacture, etc.—individuals thoroughly familiar with their branch and belonging to it. In the notion of a loose and indefinite election this important matter is left to accident; every branch, however, has the same right to be represented as every other. To view the delegates as representatives has, then, an organic and rational meaning only if they are not representatives of mere individuals, of the mere multitude, but of one of the essential spheres of society and of its large interests. Representation thus no longer means substitution of one person by another, but it means, rather, that the interest itself is actually present in the representative.

Of the elections by many separate individuals it may be observed that there is necessarily an indifference, especially in large States, about using one's vote, since one vote is of such slight importance; and those who have the right to vote will not do so, no matter how much one may extol the privilege of voting. Hence this institution turns into the opposite of what it stands for. The election becomes the business of a few, of a single party, of a special interest, which should, in fact, be neutralized.

Through the publicity of the assembly of classes public opinion first acquires true thoughts and an insight into the condition and the notion of the State and its affairs, and thus develops the capacity of judging more rationally concerning them; it learns, furthermore, to know and respect the routine, talents, virtues, and skill of the authorities and officers of the State. While publicity stimulates these talents in their future development and incites their honorable display, it is also an antidote for the pride of individuals and of the multitude, and is one of the greatest opportunities for their education.

It is a widespread popular notion that everybody already knows what is good for the State, and that it is this common knowledge which finds expression in the assembly. Here, in the assembly, are developed virtues, talents, skill, which have to serve as examples. To be sure, the ministers may find these assemblies onerous, for ministers must possess large resources of wit and eloquence to resist the attacks which are hurled against them. Nevertheless, publicity is one of the best means of instruction in the interests of the State generally, for where publicity is found the people manifest an entirely different regard for the State than in those places where there are no assemblies or where they are not public. Only through the publication of every one of their proceedings are the chambers related to the larger public opinion; and it is shown that what one imagines at home with his wife and friends is one thing, and what happens in a great assembly, where one feat of eloquence wrecks another, is quite a different thing.

## Public Opinion

Public opinion is the unorganized way in which what a people wants and thinks is promulgated. That which is actually effective in the State must be so in an organic fashion. In the constitution this is the case. But at all times public opinion has been a great power, and it is particularly so in our time, when the principle of subjective freedom has such importance and significance. What shall now prevail, prevails no longer through force, little through use and custom, but rather through insight and reasons.

Public opinion contains, therefore, the eternal substantial principles of justice, the true content, and the result of the whole constitution, legislation, and the universal condition in general. The form underlying public opinion is sound common sense, which is a fundamental ethical principle winding its way through everything, in spite of prepossessions. But when this inner character is formulated in the shape of general propositions, partly for their own sake, partly for the purpose of actual reasoning about events, institutions, relations, and the recognized wants of the State, there appears also the whole character of accidental opinion, with its ignorance and perversity, its false knowledge and incorrect judgment.

It is therefore not to be regarded as merely a difference in subjective opinion when it is asserted on the one hand—

"*Vox populi, vox dei*";

and on the other (in Ariosto, for instance)—[1]

"*Che'l Volgare ignorante ogn' un riprenda
E parli più de quel che meno intenda.*"

[The ignorant vulgar reproves everyone
and talks most of what it understands least.]

Both sides co-exist in public opinion. Since truth and endless error are so directly united in it, neither one nor the other side is truly in earnest. Which one is in earnest, is difficult to decide—difficult, indeed, if one confines oneself to the direct expression of public opinion. But as the substantial principle is the inner character of public opinion, this alone is its truly earnest aspect; yet this insight cannot be obtained from public opinion itself, for a substantial principle can only be apprehended apart from public opinion and by a consideration of its own nature. No matter with what passion an opinion is invested, no matter with what earnestness a view is asserted, attacked, and defended, this is no criterion of its real essence. And least of all could public opinion be made to see that its seriousness is nothing serious at all.

---

[1] Or in Goethe:

"*Zuschlagen kann die Masse,
Da ist sie respektabel;
Urteilen gelingt ihr miserabel.*"

[The masses are respectable hands at fighting, but miserable hands at judging.— J.M.P.]

A great mind has publicly raised the question whether it is permissible to deceive a people. The answer is that a people will not permit itself to be deceived concerning its substantial basis, the essence, and the definite character of its spirit, but it deceives *itself* about the way in which it knows this, and according to which it judges of its acts, events, etc.

Public opinion deserves, therefore, to be esteemed as much as to be despised; to be despised for its concrete consciousness and expression, to be esteemed for its essential fundamental principle, which only shines, more or less dimly, through its concrete expression. Since public opinion possesses within itself no standard of discrimination, no capacity to rise to a recognition of the substantial, independence of it is the first formal condition of any great and rational enterprise (in actuality as well as in science). Anything great and rational is eventually sure to please public opinion, to be espoused by it, and to be made one of its prepossessions.

In public opinion all is false and true, but to discover the truth in it is the business of the great man. The great man of his time is he who expresses the will and the meaning of that time, and then brings it to completion; he acts according to the inner spirit and essence of his time, which he realizes. And he who does not understand how to despise public opinion, as it makes itself heard here and there, will never accomplish anything great.

## Freedom of the Press

The freedom of public utterance (of which the press is one means, having advantage over speech in its more extended reach, though inferior to it in vivacity), the gratification of that prickling impulse to express and to have expressed one's opinion, is directly controlled by the police and State laws and regulations, which partly hinder and partly punish its excesses. The indirect guarantee lies in its innocuousness, and this again is mainly based on the rationality of the constitution, the stability of the government, and also on the publicity given to the assemblies of the classes. Another security is offered by the indifference and contempt with which insipid and malicious words are, as a rule, quickly met.

The definition of the freedom of the press as freedom to say and write what one pleases, is parallel to the one of freedom in general, viz., as freedom to do what one pleases. Such view belongs to the uneducated crudity and superficiality of naïve thinking. The press, with its infinite variety of content and expression, represents what is most transient, particular, and accidental in human opinion. Beyond the direct incitation to theft, murder, revolt, etc., lies the art of cultivating the expression which in itself seems general and indefinite enough, but which, in a measure, conceals a perfectly definite meaning. Such expressions are partly responsible for consequences of which, since they are not actually expressed, one is never sure how far they are contained in the utterances and really follow from them. It is this indefiniteness of the content and form of the press which prevents the laws governing it from assuming that precision which one demands of laws. Thus the extreme subjectivity of the wrong, injury, and crime committed by the press, causes the decision and sentence to be equally subjective. The laws are not only indefinite, but the press can, by the skill and subtlety of its expressions, evade them, or criticise the judgment of the court as wholly arbitrary. Furthermore, if the utterance of the press is treated as an offensive deed, one may retort that it is not a deed at all, but only an opinion, a thought, a mere saying. Consequently, impunity is expected for opinions and words, because they are merely subjective, trivial, and insignificant, and, in the same breath, great respect and esteem is demanded for these opinions and words—for the opinions, because they are mine and my mental property, and for the words, because they are the free expression and use of that property. And yet the basic principle remains that injury to the honor of individuals generally, abuse, libel, contemptuous caricaturing of the government, its officers and officials, especially the person of the prince, defiance of the laws, incitement to revolt, etc., are all offenses and crimes of different grades.

However, the peculiar and dangerous effect of these acts for the individuals, the community, and the State depends upon the nature of the soil on which they are committed, just as a spark, if thrown upon a heap of gunpowder, has a much more dangerous result than if thrown on the mere ground, where it vanishes and leaves no trace. But, on the whole, a good many such acts, though punishable by law, may come under a certain kind of Nemesis which internal impotence is forced to bring about. In entering upon opposition to the superior talents and virtues, by which impotence feels oppressed, it comes to a realization of its inferiority and to a consciousness of its own nothingness, and the Nemesis, even when bad and odious, is, by treating it with contempt, rendered ineffectual. Like the public, which forms a circle for such activity, it is confined to a harmless malicious joy, and to a condemnation which reflects upon itself.

*Meaning of War*

There is an ethical element in war. It must not be regarded as an absolute ill, or as merely an external calamity which is accidentally based upon the passions of despotic individuals or nations, upon acts of injustice, and, in general, upon what ought not to be. The recognition of the finite, such as property and life, as accidental, is necessary. This necessity is at first wont to appear under the form of a force of nature, for all things finite are mortal and transient. In the ethical order, in the State, however, nature is robbed of its force, and the necessity is exalted to a work of freedom, to an ethical law. The transient and negative nature of all things is transformed in the State into an expression of the ethical will. War, often painted by edifying speech as a state in which the vanity of temporal things is demonstrated, now becomes an element whereby the ideal character of the particular receives its right and reality. War has the deep meaning that by it the ethical health of the nations is preserved and their finite aims uprooted. And as the winds which sweep over the ocean prevent the decay that would result from its perpetual calm, so war protects the people from the corruption which an everlasting peace would bring upon it. History shows phases which illustrate how successful wars have checked internal unrest and have strengthened the entire stability of the State.

In peace, civic life becomes more extended, every sphere is hedged in and grows immobile, and at last all men stagnate, their particular nature becoming more and more hardened and ossified. Only in the unity of a body is health, and, where the organs become still, there is death. Eternal peace is often demanded as an ideal toward which mankind should move. Thus Kant proposed an alliance of princes, which should settle the controversies of States, and the Holy Alliance probably aspired to be an institution of this kind. The State, however, is individual, and in individuality negation is essentially contained. A number of States may constitute themselves into a family, but this confederation, as an individuality, must create an opposition and so beget an enemy. Not only do nations issue forth invigorated from their wars, but those nations torn by internal strife win peace at home as a result of war abroad. War indeed causes insecurity in property, but this real insecurity is only a necessary commotion. From the pulpits much is preached concerning the insecurity, vanity, and instability of temporal things, and yet every one, though he may be touched by his own words, thinks that he, at least, will manage to hold on to his possessions. Let the insecurity finally come, in the form of Hussars with glistening sabres, and show its earnest activity, and that touching edification which foresaw all this now turns upon the enemy with curses. In spite of this, wars will break out whenever necessity demands them; but the seeds spring up anew, and speech is silenced before the grave repetitions of history.

The military class is the class of universality. The defense of the State is its privilege, and its duty is to realize the ideality contained in it, which consists in self-sacrifice. There are different kinds of bravery. The courage of the animal, or the robber, the bravery which arises from a sense of honor, the chivalrous bravery, are not yet the true forms of bravery. In civilized nations true bravery consists in the readiness to give oneself wholly to the service of the State, so that the individual counts but as one among many. Not personal valor alone is significant; the important aspect of it lies in self-subordination to the universal cause.

To risk one's life is indeed something more than mere fear of death, but this is only negative; only a positive character—an aim and content—gives meaning to bravery. Robbers and murderers in the pursuit of crime, adventurers in the search of their fanciful objects, etc., also possess courage, and do not fear death. The principle of the modern world—the power of thought and of the universal—has given to bravery a higher form; the higher form causes the expression of bravery to appear more mechanical. The brave deeds are not the deeds of any particular person, but those of the members of a whole. And, again, since hostility is directed, not against separate individuals, but against a hostile whole, personal valor appears as impersonal. This principle it is which has caused the invention of the gun; it is not a chance invention that has brought about the change of the mere personal form of bravery into the more abstract.

## International Relations

Just as the individual is not a real person unless related to other persons, so the State is no real individuality unless related to other States. The legitimate power of a State, and more especially its princely power, is, from the point of view of its foreign relations, a wholly internal affair. A State shall, therefore, not interfere with the internal affairs of another State. On the other hand, for a complete State, it is essential that it be recognized by others; but this recognition demands as a guarantee that it shall recognize those States which recognize it, and shall respect their independence. Hence its internal affairs cannot be a matter of indifference to them.

When Napoleon, before the peace of Campoformio, said, "The French Republic requires recognition as little as the sun needs to be recognized," his words suggest nothing but the strength of existence, which already carries with it the guarantee of recognition, without needing to be expressed.

When the particular wills of the State can come to no agreement their controversy can be decided only by war. What offense shall be regarded as a breach of treaty, or as a violation of respect and honor, must remain indefinite, since many and various injuries can easily accrue from the wide range of the interests of the States and from the complex relations of their citizens. The State may identify its infinitude and honor with every one of its single aspects. And if a State, as a strong individuality, has experienced an unduly protracted internal rest, it will naturally be more inclined to irritability, in order to find an occasion and field for intense activity.

The nations of Europe form a family according to the universal principle of their legislation, their ethical code, and their civilization. But the relation among States fluctuates, and no judge exists to adjust their differences. The higher judge is the universal and absolute Spirit alone—the World-Spirit.

The relation of one particular State to another presents, on the largest possible scale, the most shifting play of individual passions, interests, aims, talents, virtues, power, injustice, vice, and mere external chance. It is a play in which even the ethical whole, the independence of the State, is exposed to accident. The principles which control the many national spirits are limited. Each nation as an existing individuality is guided by its particular principles, and only as a particular individuality can each national spirit win objectivity and self-consciousness; but the fortunes and deeds of States in their relation to one another reveal the dialectic of the finite nature of these spirits. Out of this dialectic rises the universal Spirit, the unlimited World-Spirit, pronouncing its judgment—and its judgment is the highest—upon the finite nations of the world's history; for the history of the world is the world's court of justice.

# JOHN STUART MILL

*John Stuart Mill (1806–1873) was born in London to James Mill, a famous utilitarian philosopher. As a youngster Mill was fortunately extremely precocious, since he was educated almost from infancy according to the rigid principles of Jeremy Bentham, the father of modern utilitarianism. In his* Autobiography, *Mill explains that he began his education at the age of two; at three he was reading Greek; and by 12 he was versed in a wide array of classical literature, mathematics, and philosophy. Without attending university, he went to work for the East India Company at the age of 17 and remained for 35 years. The rigorous educational regimen of his youth did mould Mill, but at the age of 20 he suffered a serious breakdown. He laments in his* Autobiography: *"I never was a boy; never played cricket; it is better to let Nature have her way." When he was 24 he began a friendship with a beautiful, highly educated, married woman, named Harriet Taylor, wife of John Taylor, a merchant. This friendship, the source of much gossip, led to marriage in 1851, after the death of John Taylor. The couple withdrew, in Mill's words, from "insipid society" and lived happily until Harriet's death in 1858. Throughout his career Mill published on philosophy, politics, and economics as well as actively promoting a variety of social reforms. His writings were quite influential. His textbook in economics, as one example, was the standard work in the last half of the nineteenth century. For a short time, from 1865 to 1868, he was a member of Parliament. After his election defeat he moved with his stepdaughter, Helen Taylor, to Avignon, France, where he died suddenly in 1873.*

*The chief works for understanding Mill's political philosophy are:* A System of Logic *(1843);* Principles of Political Economy *(1848);* On Liberty *(1859);* Thoughts on Parliamentary Reform *(1859);* Considerations on Representative Government *(1861);* Utilitarianism *(1863); and* The Subjection of Women *(written in 1861 and published in 1869).*

— J.M.P.

# ON LIBERTY

## *Chapter I*

### *Introductory*

The subject of this essay is not the so-called liberty of the will, so unfortunately opposed to the misnamed doctrine of philosophical necessity; but civil, or social liberty: the nature and limits of power which can be legitimately exercised by society over the individual. A question seldom stated and hardly ever discussed in general terms, but which profoundly influences the practical controversies of the age by its latent presence, and is likely soon to make itself recognised as the vital question of the future. It is so far from being new, that, in a certain sense, it has divided mankind almost from the remotest ages; but in the stage of progress into which the more civilised portions of the species have now entered, it presents itself under new conditions, and requires a different and more fundamental treatment.

The struggle between liberty and authority is the most conspicuous feature in the portions of history with which we are earliest familiar, particularly in that of Greece, Rome, and England. But in old times this contest was between subjects, or some classes of subjects, and the government. By liberty, was meant protection against the tyranny of the political rulers. The rulers were conceived (except in some of the popular governments of Greece) as in a necessarily antagonistic position to the people whom they ruled. They consisted of a governing One, or a governing tribe or caste, who derived their authority from inheritance or conquest, who, at all events, did not hold it at the pleasure of the governed, and whose supremacy men did not venture, perhaps did not desire, to contest, whatever precautions might be taken against its oppressive exercise. Their power was regarded as necessary, but also as highly dangerous; as a weapon which they would attempt to use against their subjects, no less than against external enemies. To prevent the weaker members of the community from being preyed upon by innumerable vultures, it was needful that there should be an animal of prey stronger than the rest, commissioned to keep them down. But as the king of the vultures would be no less bent upon preying on the flock than any of the minor harpies, it was indispensable to be in a perpetual attitude of defence against his beak and claws. The aim, therefore, of patriots was to set limits to the power which the ruler should be suffered to exercise over the community; and this limitation was what they meant by liberty.

It was attempted in two ways. First, by obtaining a recognition of certain immunities, called political liberties or rights, which it was to be regarded as a breach of duty in the ruler to infringe, and which if he did infringe, specific resistance, or general rebellion, was held to be justifiable. A second, and generally a later expedient, was the establishment of constitutional checks, by which the consent of the community, or of a body of some sort, supposed to represent its interests, was made a necessary condition to some of the more important acts of the governing power. To the first of these modes of limitation, the ruling power, in most European countries, was compelled, more or less, to submit. It was not so with the second; and, to attain this, or when already in some degree possessed, to attain it more completely, became everywhere the principal object of the lovers of liberty. And so long as mankind were content to combat one enemy by another, and to be ruled by a master, on condition of being guaranteed more or less efficaciously against his tyranny, they did not carry their aspirations beyond this point.

A time, however, came, in the progress of human affairs, when men ceased to think it a necessity of nature that their governors should be an independent power, opposed in interest to themselves. It appeared to them much better that the various magistrates of the State should be their tenants or delegates, revocable at their pleasure. In that way alone, it seemed, could they have complete security that the powers of government would never be abused to their disadvantage. By degrees this new demand for elective and temporary rulers became the prominent object of the exertions of the popular party, wherever any such party existed; and superseded, to a considerable extent, the previous efforts to limit the power of rulers. As the struggle proceeded for making the ruling power emanate from the periodical choice of the ruled, some persons began to think that too much importance had been attached to the limitation of the power itself. *That* (it might seem) was a resource against rulers whose interests were habitually opposed to those of the people. What was now wanted was, that the rulers should be identified with the people; that their interest and will should be the interest and will of the nation. The nation did not need to be protected against its own will. There was no fear of its tyrannising over itself. Let the rulers be effectually responsible to it, promptly removable by it, and it could afford to trust them with power of which it could itself dictate the use to be made. Their power was but the nation's own power, concentrated, and in a form convenient for exercise. This mode of thought, or perhaps of feeling, was common among the last generation of European liberalism, in the Continental section of which it still apparently predominates. Those who admit any limit to what a government may do, except in the case of such governments as they think ought not to exist, stand out as brilliant exceptions among the political thinkers of the Continent. A similar tone of sentiment might by this time have been prevalent in our own country, if the circumstances which for a time encouraged it had continued unaltered.

But in political and philosophical theories, as well as in persons, success discloses faults and infirmities which failure might have concealed from observation. The notion that the people have no need to limit their power over themselves might seem axiomatic, when popular government was a thing only dreamed about, or read of as having existed at some distant period of the past. Neither was that notion necessarily disturbed by such temporary aberrations as those of the French Revolution, the worst of which were the work of a usurping few, and which, in any case, belonged, not to the permanent working of popular institutions, but to a sudden and convulsive outbreak against monarchical and aristocratic despotism. In time, however, a democratic republic came to occupy a large portion of the earth's surface and made itself felt as one of the most powerful members of the community of nations; and elective and responsible governments became subject to the observations and criticisms which wait upon a great existing fact. It was now perceived that such phrases as "self-government," and "the power of the people over themselves," do not express the true state of the case. The "people" who exercise the power are not always the same people with those over whom it is exercised; and the "self-government" spoken of is not the government of each by himself, but of each by all the rest. The will of the people, moreover, practically means the will of the most numerous or the most active *part* of the people—the majority, or those who succeed in making themselves accepted as the majority; the people, consequently, *may* desire to oppress a part of their number, and precautions are as much needed against this as against any other abuse of power. The limitation, therefore, of the power of government over individuals loses none of its importance when the holders of power are regularly accountable to the community, that is, to the strongest party therein. This view of things, recommending itself equally to the intelligence of thinkers and to the inclination of those important classes in European society to whose real or supposed interests democracy is adverse, has had no difficulty in establishing itself; and in political speculations "the tyranny of the majority" is now generally included among the evils against which society requires to be on its guard.

Like other tyrannies, the tyranny of the majority was at first, and is still vulgarly, held in dread, chiefly as operating through the acts of the public authorities. But reflecting persons perceived that when society is itself the tyrant—society collectively over the separate individuals who compose it—its means of tyrannising are not restricted to the acts which it may do by the hands of its political functionaries. Society can and does execute its own mandates; and if it issues wrong mandates instead of right, or any mandates at all in things with which it ought not to meddle, it practises a social tyranny more formidable than many kinds of political oppression, since, though not usually upheld by such extreme penalties, it leaves fewer means of escape, penetrating much more deeply into the details of life, and enslaving the soul itself. Protection, therefore, against the tyranny of the magistrate is not enough; there needs protection also against the tyranny of the prevailing opinion and feeling, against the tendency of society to impose, by other means than civil penalties, its own ideas and practices as rules of conduct on those who dissent from them; to fetter the development and, if possible, prevent the formation of any individuality not in harmony with its ways, and compels all characters to fashion themselves upon the model of its own. There is a limit to the legitimate interference of collective opinion with individual independence; and to find that limit, and maintain it against encroachment, is as indispensable to a good condition of human affairs as protection against political despotism.

But though this proposition is not likely to be contested in general terms, the practical question, where to place the limit—how to make the fitting adjustment between individual independence and social control—is a subject on which nearly everything remains to be done....

The object of this essay is to assert one very simple principle, as entitled to govern absolutely the dealings of society with the individual in the way of compulsion and control, whether the means used be physical force in the form of legal penalties or the moral coercion of public opinion. That principle is, that the sole end for which mankind are warranted, individually or collectively, in interfering with the liberty of action of any of their number, is self-protection. That the only purpose for which power can be rightfully exercised over any member of a civilised community, against his will, is to prevent harm to others. His own good, either physical or moral, is not a sufficient warrant. He cannot rightfully be compelled to do or forbear because it will be better for him to do so, because it will make him happier, because, in the opinions of others, to do so would be wise or even right. These are good reasons for remonstrating with him, or reasoning with him, or persuading him, or entreating him, but not for compelling him or visiting him with any evil in case he do otherwise. To justify that, the conduct from which it is desired to deter him must be calculated to produce evil to someone else. The only part of the conduct of anyone, for which he is amenable to society, is that which concerns others. In the part which merely concerns himself, his independence is, of right, absolute. Over himself, over his own body and mind, the individual is sovereign.

It is, perhaps, hardly necessary to say that this doctrine is meant to apply only to human beings in the maturity of their faculties. We are not speaking of children, or of young persons below the age which the law may fix as that of manhood or womanhood. Those who are still in a state to require being taken care of by others, must be protected against their own actions as well as against external injury. For the same reason, we may leave out of consideration those backward states of society in which the race itself may be considered as in its nonage. The early difficulties in the way of spontaneous progress are so great, and there is seldom any choice of means for overcoming them; and a ruler full of the spirit of improvement is warranted in the use of any expedients that will attain an end, perhaps otherwise unattainable. Despotism is a legitimate mode of government in dealing with barbarians, provided the end be their improvement, and the means justified by actually effecting that end. Liberty, as a principle, has no application to any state of things anterior to the time when mankind have become capable of being improved by free and equal discussion. Until then, there is nothing for them but implicit obedience to an Akbar or a Charlemagne, if they are so fortunate as to find one. But as soon as mankind have attained the capacity of being guided to their own improvement by conviction or persuasion (a period long since reached in all nations with whom we need here concern ourselves), compulsion, either in the direct form or in that of pains and penalties for noncompliance, is no longer admissible as a means to their own good, and justifiable only for the security of others.

It is proper to state that I forego any advantage which could be derived to my argument from the idea of abstract right, as a thing independent of utility. I regard utility as the ultimate appeal on all ethical questions; but it must be utility in the largest sense, grounded on the permanent interests of a man as a progressive being. These interests, I contend, authorized the subjection of individual spontaneity to external control, only in respect to those actions of each which concern the interest of other people. If anyone does an act hurtful to others, there is a *prima facie* case for punishing him, by law, or, where legal penalties are not safely applicable, by general disapprobation. There are also many positive acts for the benefit of others, which he may rightfully be compelled to perform: such as to give evidence in a court of justice; to bear his fair share in the common defence, or in any other joint work necessary to the interest of the society of which he enjoys the protection; and to perform certain acts of individual beneficence, such as saving a fellow-creature's life, or interposing to protect the defenceless against ill-usage, things which whenever it is obviously a man's duty to do, he may rightfully be made responsible to society for not doing. A person may cause evil to others not only by his actions but by his inaction, and in either case he is justly accountable to them for the injury. The latter case, it is true, requires a much more cautious exercise of compulsion than the former. To make anyone answerable for doing evil to others is the rule; to make him answerable for not preventing evil is, comparatively speaking, the exception. Yet there are many cases clear enough and grave enough to justify that exception. In all things which regard the external relations of the individual, he is *de jure* amenable to those whose interests are concerned, and, if need be, to society as their protector. There are often good reasons for not holding him to the responsibility; but these reasons must arise from the special expediencies of the case: either because it is a kind of case in which he is on the whole likely to act better, when left to his own discretion, than when controlled in any way in which society have it in their power to control him; or because the attempt to exercise control would produce other evils, greater than those which it would prevent. When such reasons as these preclude the enforcement of responsibility, the conscience of the agent himself should step into the vacant judgement seat, and protect those interests of others which have no external protection; judging himself all the more rigidly, because the case does not admit of his being made accountable to the judgement of his fellow-creatures.

But there is a sphere of action in which society, as distinguished from the individual, has, if any, only an indirect interest; comprehending all that portion of a person's life and conduct which affects only himself, or if it also affects others, only with their free, voluntary, and undeceived consent and participation. When I say only himself, I mean directly, and in the first instance; for whatever affects himself, may affect others through himself; and the objection which may be grounded on this contingency, will receive consideration in the sequel. This, then is the appropriate region of human liberty. It comprises, *first,* the inward domain of consciousness; demanding liberty of conscience in the most comprehensive sense; liberty of thought and feeling; absolute freedom of opinion and sentiment on all subjects, practical or speculative, scientific, moral or theological. The liberty of expressing and publishing opinions may seem to fall under a different principle, since it belongs to that part of the conduct of an individual which concerns other people; but, being almost of as much importance as the liberty of thought itself, and resting in great part on the same reasons, is practically inseparable from it. *Secondly*, the principle requires liberty of tastes and pursuits; of framing the plan of our life to suit our own character; of doing as we like, subject to such consequences as may follow: without impediment from our fellow-creatures, so long as what we do does not harm them, even though they should think our conduct foolish, perverse, or wrong. *Thirdly*, from this liberty of each individual, follows the liberty, within the same limits, of combinations among individuals; freedom to unite, for any purpose not involving harm to others: the persons combining being supposed to be of full age, and not forced or deceived.

No society in which these liberties are not, on the whole, respected, is free, whatever may be its form of government; and none is completely free in which they do not exist absolute and unqualified. The only freedom which deserves the name, is that of pursuing our own good in our own way, as long as we do not attempt to deprive others of theirs, or impede their efforts to obtain it. Each is the proper guardian of his own health, whether bodily, or mental and spiritual. Mankind are greater gainers by suffering each other to live as seems good to themselves, than by compelling each to live as seems good to the rest....

## Chapter II

### Of the Liberty of Thought and Discussion

The time, it is to be hoped, is gone by, when any defence would be necessary of the "liberty of the press" as one of the securities against corrupt or tyrannical government. No argument, we may suppose, can now be needed against permitting a legislature or an executive, not identified in interest with the people, to prescribe opinions to them, and determine what doctrines or what arguments they shall be allowed to hear. This aspect of the question, besides, has been so often and so triumphantly enforced by preceding writers, that it need not be specially insisted on in this place. Though the law of England, on the subject of the press, is as servile to this day as it was in the time of the Tudors, there is little danger of its being actually put in force against political discussion, except during some temporary panic, when fear of insurrection drives ministers and judges from their propriety; and, speaking generally, it is not, in constitutional countries, to be apprehended that the government, whether completely responsible to the people or not, will often attempt to control the expression of opinion, except when in doing so it makes itself the organ of the general intolerance of the public. Let us suppose, therefore, that the government is entirely at one with the people, and never thinks of exerting any power of coercion unless in agreement with what it conceives to be their voice. But I deny the right of the people to exercise such coercion, either by themselves or by the government. The power itself is illegitimate. The best government has no more title to it than the worst. It is as noxious, or more noxious, when exerted in accordance with public opinion, than when in opposition to it. If all mankind minus one were of one opinion, and only one person were of the contrary opinion, mankind would be no more justified in silencing that one person, than he, if he had the power, would be justified in silencing mankind. Were an opinion a personal possession of no value except to the owner; if to be obstructed in the enjoyment of it were simply a private injury, it would make some difference whether the injury was inflicted only on a few persons or on many. But the peculiar evil of silencing the expression of an opinion is, that it is robbing the human race: posterity as well as the existing generation; those who dissent from the opinion, still more than those who hold it. If the opinion is right, they are deprived of the opportunity of exchanging error for truth; if wrong, they lose, what is almost as great a benefit, the clearer proportion and livelier impression of truth, produced by its collision with error.

It is necessary to consider separately these two hypotheses, each of which has a distinct branch of the argument corresponding to it. We can never be sure that the opinion we are endeavouring to stifle is a false opinion; and if we were sure, stifling it would be an evil still.

First: the opinion which it is attempted to suppress by authority may possibly be true. Those who desire to suppress it, of course deny its truth; but they are not infallible. They have no authority to decide the question for all mankind, and exclude every other person from the means of judging. To refuse a hearing to an opinion, because they are sure that it is false, is to assume that *their* certainty is the same thing as *absolute* certainty. All silencing of discussion is an assumption of infallibility. Its condemnation may be allowed to rest on this common argument, not the worse for being common....

Let us now pass to the second division of the argument, and dismissing the supposition that any of the received opinions may be false, let us assume them to be true, and examine into the worth of the manner in which they are likely to be held, when their truth is not freely and openly canvassed. However unwillingly a person who has a strong opinion may admit the possibility that his opinion may be false, he ought to be moved by the consideration that, however true it may be, if it is not fully, frequently, and fearlessly discussed, it will be held as a dead dogma, not a living truth....

It is illustrated in the experience of almost all ethical doctrines and religious creeds. They are all full of meaning and vitality to those who originate them, and to the direct disciples of the originators. Their meaning continues to be felt in undiminished strength, and is perhaps brought out into even fuller consciousness, so long as the struggle lasts to give the doctrine or creed an ascendancy over other creeds. At last it either prevails, and becomes the general opinion, or its progress stops; it keeps possession of the ground it has gained, but ceases to spread further. When either of these results has become apparent, controversy on the subject flags, and gradually dies away. The doctrine has taken its place, if not as a received opinion, as one of the admitted sects or divisions of opinion: those who hold it have generally inherited, not adopted it; and conversion from one of these doctrines to another, being now an exceptional fact, occupies little place in the thoughts of their professors. Instead of being, as at first, constantly on the alert either to defend themselves against the world, or to bring the world over to them, they have subsided into acquiescence, and neither listen, when they can help it, to arguments against their creed, nor trouble dissentients (if there be such) with arguments in its favour. From this time may usually be dated the decline in the living power of the doctrine. We often hear the teachers of all creeds lamenting the difficulty of keeping up in the minds of believers a lively apprehension of the truth which they nominally recognize, so that it may penetrate the feelings, and acquire a real mastery over the conduct. No such difficulty is complained of while the creed is still fighting for its existence: even the weaker combatants then know and feel what they are fighting for, and the difference between it and other doctrines; and in that period of every creed's existence, not a few persons may be found, who have realized its fundamental principles in all the forms of thought, have weighed and considered them in all their important bearings and have experienced the full effect on the character which belief in that creed ought to produce in a mind thoroughly imbued with it. But when it has come to be an hereditary creed, and to be received passively, not actively; when the mind is no longer compelled, in the same degree as at first, to exercise its vital powers on the questions which its belief presents to it: there is a progressive tendency to forget all of the belief except the formularies, or to give it a dull and torpid assent, as if accepting it on trust dispensed with the necessity of realizing it in consciousness, or testing it by personal experience, until it almost ceases to connect itself at all with the inner life of the human being. Then are seen the cases, so frequent in this age of the world as almost to form the majority, in which the creed remains as it were outside the mind, incrusting and petrifying it against all other influences addressed to the higher parts of our nature; manifesting its power by not suffering any fresh and living conviction to get in, but itself doing nothing for the mind or heart, except standing sentinel over them to keep them vacant....

It still remains to speak of one of the principal causes which make diversity of opinion advantageous, and will continue to do so until mankind shall have entered a stage of intellectual advancement which at present seems at an incalculable distance. We have hitherto considered only two possibilities: that the received opinion may be false, and some other opinion consequently true; or that, the received opinion being true, a conflict with the opposite error is essential to a clear apprehension and deep feeling of its truth. But there is a commoner case than either of these: when the conflicting doctrines, instead of being one true and the other false, share the truth between them; and the nonconforming opinion is needed to supply the remainder of the truth, of which the received doctrine embodies only a part. Popular opinions, on subjects not palpable to sense, are often true, but seldom or never the whole truth. They are a part of the truth; sometimes a greater, sometimes a smaller part, but exaggerated, distorted, and disjointed from the truths by which they ought to be accompanied and limited. Heretical opinions, on the other hand, are generally some of these suppressed and neglected truths, bursting the bonds which kept them down, and either seeking reconciliation with the truth contained in the common opinion, or fronting it as enemies, and setting themselves up, with similar exclusiveness, as the whole truth. The latter case is hitherto the most frequent, as, in the human mind, one-sidedness has always been the rule, and many-sidedness the exception. Hence, even in revolutions of opinion, one part of the truth usually sets while another rises. Even progress, which ought to superadd, for the most part only substitutes, one partial and incomplete truth for another; improvement consisting chiefly in this, that the new fragment of truth is more wanted, more adapted to the needs of the time, than that which it displaces. Such being the partial character of prevailing opinions, even when resting on a true foundation, every opinion which embodies somewhat of the portion of truth which the common opinion omits, ought to be considered precious, with whatever amount of error and confusion that truth may be blended. No sober judge of human affairs will feel bound to be indignant because those who force on our notice truths which we should otherwise have overlooked, overlook some of those which we see. Rather, he will think that so long as popular truth is one-sided, it is more desirable than otherwise that unpopular truth should have one-sided assertors too; such being usually the most energetic, and the most likely to compel reluctant attention to the fragment of wisdom which they proclaim as if it were the whole....

We have now recognised the necessity to the mental well-being of mankind (on which all their other well-being depends) of freedom of opinion, and freedom of the expression of opinion, on four distinct grounds; which we will now briefly recapitulate.

First, if any opinion is compelled to silence, that opinion may, for aught we can certainly know, be true. To deny this is to assume our own infallibility.

Secondly, though the silenced opinion be an error, it may, and very commonly does, contain a portion of truth; and since the general or prevailing opinion on any subject is rarely or never the whole truth, it is only by the collision of adverse opinions that the remainder of the truth has any chance of being supplied.

Thirdly, even if the received opinion be not only true, but the whole truth; unless it is suffered to be, and actually is, vigorously and earnestly contested, it will, by most of those who receive it, be held in the manner of a prejudice, with little comprehension or feeling of its rational grounds. And not only this, but, fourthly, the meaning of the doctrine itself will be in danger of being lost, or enfeebled, and deprived of its vital effect on the character and conduct: the dogma becoming a mere formal profession, inefficacious for good, but cumbering the ground and preventing the growth of any real and heartfelt conviction, from reason or personal experience.

Before quitting the subject of freedom of opinion, it is fit to take some notice of those who say that the free expression of all opinions should be permitted, on condition that the manner be temperate, and do not pass the bounds of fair discussion. Much might be said on the impossibility of fixing where these supposed bounds are to be placed; for if the test be offence to those whose opinions are attacked, I think experience testifies that this offence is given whenever the attack is telling and powerful, and that every opponent who pushes them hard, and whom they find it difficult to answer, appears to them, if he shows any strong feeling on the subject, an intemperate opponent. But this, though an important consideration in a practical point of view, merges in a more fundamental objection. Undoubtedly the manner of asserting an opinion, even though it be a true one, may be very objectionable, and may justly incur severe censure. But the principal offences of the kind are such as it is mostly impossible, unless by accidental self-betrayal, to bring home to conviction. The gravest of them is, to argue sophistically, to suppress facts or arguments, to misstate the elements of the case, or misrepresent the opposite opinion. But all this, even to the most aggravated degree, is so continually done in perfect good faith, by persons who are not considered, and in many other respects may not deserve to be considered, ignorant or incompetent, that it is rarely possible, on adequate grounds, conscientiously to stamp the misrepresentation as morally culpable; and still less could law presume to interfere with this kind of controversial misconduct. With regard to what is commonly meant by intemperate discussion, namely invective, sarcasm, personality, and the like, the denunciation of these weapons would deserve more sympathy if it were ever proposed to interdict them equally to both sides; but it is only desired to restrain the employment of them against the prevailing opinion: against the unprevailing they may not only be used without general disapproval, but will be likely to obtain for him who uses them the praise of honest zeal and righteous indignation. Yet whatever mischief arises from their use is greatest when they are employed against the comparatively defenceless; and whatever unfair advantage can be derived by any opinion from this mode of asserting it, accrues almost exclusively to received opinions. The worst offence of this kind which can be committed by a polemic is to stigmatize those who hold the contrary opinion as bad and immoral men. To calumny of this sort, those who hold any unpopular opinion are peculiarly exposed, because they are in general few and uninfluential, and nobody but themselves feels much interested in seeing justice done them; but this weapon is, from the nature of the case, denied to those who attack a prevailing opinion: they can neither use it with safety to themselves, nor, if they could, would it do anything but recoil on their own cause. In general, opinions contrary to those commonly received can only obtain a hearing by studied moderation of language, and the most cautious avoidance of unnecessary offence, from which they hardly ever deviate even in a slight degree without losing ground; while unmeasured vituperation employed on the side of the prevailing opinion really does deter people from professing contrary opinions, and from listening to those who profess them. For the interest, therefore, of truth and justice, it is far more important to restrain this employment of vituperative language than the other; and, for example, if it were necessary to choose, there would be much more need to discourage offensive attacks on infidelity than on religion. It is, however, obvious that law and authority have no business restraining either, while opinion ought, in every instance, to determine its verdict by the circumstances of the individual case; condemning everyone, on whichever side of the argument he places himself, in whose mode of advocacy either want of candour, or malignity, bigotry, or intolerance of feeling manifest themselves; but not inferring these vices from the side which a person takes, though it be the contrary side of the question of our own; and giving merited honour to everyone, whatever opinion he may hold, who has calmness to see and honesty to state what his opponents and their opinions really are, exaggerating nothing to their discredit, keeping nothing back which tells or can be supposed to tell, in their favour. This is the real morality of public discussion; and if often violated, I am happy to think that there are many controversialists who to a great extent observe it, and a still greater number who conscientiously strive towards it.

## Chapter III

### Of Individuality, As One of the Elements of Well-Being

Such being the reasons which make it imperative that human beings should be free to form opinions, and to express their opinions without reserve; and such the baneful consequences to the intellectual, and through that to the moral nature of man, unless this liberty is either conceded, or asserted in spite of prohibition; let us next examine whether the same reasons do not require that men should be free to act upon their opinions—to carry these out in their lives, without hindrance, either physical or moral, from their fellow-men, so long as it is at their own risk and peril. This last provision is of course indispensable. No one pretends that actions should be as free as opinions. On the contrary, even opinions lose their immunity when the circumstances in which they are expressed are such as to constitute their expression a positive instigation to some mischievous act. An opinion that corn-dealers are starvers of the poor, or that private property is robbery, ought to be unmolested when simply circulated through the press, but may justly incur punishment when delivered orally to an excited mob assembled before the house of a corn-dealer, or when handed about among the same mob in the form of a placard. Acts, of whatever kind, which without justifiable cause do harm to others, may be, and in the more important cases absolutely require to be, controlled by the unfavourable sentiments, and, when needful, by the active interference of mankind. The liberty of the individual must be thus far limited; he must not make himself a nuisance to other people. But if he refrains from molesting others in what concerns them, and merely acts according to his own inclination and judgement in things which concern himself, the same reasons which show that opinion should be free, prove also that he should be allowed, without molestation, to carry his opinions into practice at his own cost. That mankind are not infallible; that their truths, for the most part, are only half-truths; that unity of opinion, unless resulting from the fullest and freest comparison of opposite opinions, is not desirable, and diversity not an evil, but a good, until mankind are much more capable than at present of recognizing all sides of the truth, are principles applicable to men's modes of action, not less than to their opinions. As it is useful that while mankind are imperfect there should be different opinions, so it is that there should be different experiments of living; that free scope should be given to varieties of character, short of injury to others; and that the worth of different modes of life should be proved practically, when anyone thinks fit to try them. It is desirable, in short, that in things which do not primarily concern others, individuality should assert itself. Where not the person's own character, but the traditions or customs of other people are the rule of conduct, there is wanting one of the principal ingredients of human happiness, and quite the chief ingredient of individual and social progress.

In maintaining this principle, the greatest difficulty to be encountered does not lie in the appreciation of means towards an acknowledged end, but in the indifference of persons in general to the end itself. If it were felt that the free development of individuality is one of the leading essentials of well-being; that it is not only a co-ordinate element with all that is designated by the terms civilization, instruction, education, culture, but is itself a necessary part and condition of all those things; there would be no danger that liberty should be undervalued, and the adjustment of the boundaries between it and social control would present no extraordinary difficulty. But the evil is, that individual spontaneity is hardly recognized by the common modes of thinking as having any intrinsic worth, or deserving any regard on its own account. The majority, being satisfied with the ways of mankind as they now are (for it is they who make them what they are), cannot comprehend why those ways should not be good enough for everybody; and what is more, spontaneity forms no part of the ideal of the majority of moral and social reformers, but is rather looked on with jealousy, as a troublesome and perhaps rebellious obstruction to the general acceptance of what these reformers, in their own judgement, think would be best for mankind. Few persons, out of Germany, even comprehend the meaning of the doctrine which Wilhelm von Humboldt, so eminent both as a savant and as a politician, made the text of a treatise—that "the end of man, or that which is prescribed by the eternal or immutable dictates of reason, and not suggested by vague and transient desires, is the highest and most harmonious development of his powers to a complete and consistent whole," that, therefore, the object "towards which every human being must ceaselessly direct his efforts, and on which especially those who design to influence their fellow-men must ever keep their eyes, is the individuality of power and development;" that for this there are two requisites, "freedom, and variety of situations;" and that from the union of these arise "individual vigour and manifold diversity," which combine themselves in "originality." ...

He who lets the world, or his own portion of it, choose his plan of life for him, has no need of any other faculty than the ape-like one of imitation. He who chooses his plan for himself, employs all his faculties. He must use observation to see, reasoning and judgements to foresee, activity to gather materials for decision, discrimination to decide, and when he has decided, firmness and self-control to hold to his deliberate decision. And these qualities he requires and exercises exactly in proportion as the part of his conduct which he determines according to his own judgement and feelings is a large one. It is possible that he might be guided in some good path, and kept out of harm's way, without any of these things. But what will be his comparative worth as a human being? It really is of importance, not only what men do, but also what manner of men they are that do it. Among the works of man which human life is rightly employed in perfecting and beautifying, the first in importance surely is man himself. Supposing it were possible to get houses built, corn grown, battles fought, causes tried, and even churches erected and prayers said, by machinery—by automatons in human form—it would be a considerable loss to exchange for these automatons even the men and women who at present inhabit the more civilised parts of the world, and who assuredly are but starved specimens of what nature can and will produce. Human nature is not a machine to be built after a model, and set to do exactly the work prescribed for it, but a tree, which requires to grow and develop itself on all sides, according to the tendency of the inward forces which make it a living thing....

... But society has now fairly got the better of individuality; and the danger which threatens human nature is not the excess, but the deficiency, of personal impulses and preferences. Things are vastly changed since the passions of those who were strong by station or by personal endowment were in a state of habitual rebellion against laws and ordinances, and required to be rigorously chained up to enable the persons within their reach to enjoy any particle of security. In our times, from the highest class of society down to the lowest, everyone lives as under the eye of a hostile and dreaded censorship. Not only in what concerns others, but in what concerns only themselves, the individual or the family do not ask themselves—what do I prefer? or, what would suit my character and disposition? or, what would allow the best and highest in me to have fair play, and enable it to grow and thrive? They ask themselves, what is suitable to my position? what is usually done by persons of my station and pecuniary circumstances? or (worse still) what is usually done by persons of a station and circumstances superior to mine? I do not mean that they choose what is customary in preference to what suits their own inclination. It does not occur to them to have any inclination, except for what is customary. Thus the mind itself is bowed to the yoke: even in what people do for pleasure, conformity is the first thing thought of; they like crowds; they exercise choice only among things commonly done: peculiarity of taste, eccentricity of conduct, are shunned equally with crimes: until by dint of not following their own nature they have no nature to follow: their human capacities are withered and starved: they become incapable of any strong wishes or native pleasures, and are generally without either opinions or feelings of home growth, or properly their own. Now is this, or is it not, the desirable condition of human nature? ...

## Chapter IV

### Of the Limits to the Authority of Society Over the Individual

What, then, is the rightful limit to the sovereignty of the individual over himself? Where does the authority of society begin? How much of human life should be assigned to individuality, and how much to society?

Each will receive its proper share, if each has that which more particularly concerns it. To individuality should belong the part of life in which it is chiefly the individual that is interested; to society, the part which chiefly interests society.

Though society is not founded on a contract, and though no good purpose is answered by inventing a contract in order to deduce social obligations from it, everyone who receives the protection of society owes a return for the benefit, and the fact of living in society renders it indispensable that each should be bound to observe a certain line of conduct towards the rest. This conduct consists, *first*, in not injuring the interests of one another; or rather certain interests, which, either by express legal provision or by tacit understanding, ought to be considered as rights; and *secondly*, in each person's bearing his share (to be fixed on some equitable principle) of the labours and sacrifices incurred for defending the society or its members from injury and molestation. These conditions society is justified in enforcing, at all costs to those who endeavour to withhold fulfilment. Nor is this all that society may do. The acts of an individual may be hurtful to others, or wanting in due consideration for their welfare, without going to the length of violating any of their constituted rights. The offender may then be justly punished by opinion, though not by law. As soon as any part of a person's conduct affects prejudicially the interests of others, society has jurisdiction over it, and the question whether the general welfare will or will not be promoted by interfering with it, becomes open to discussion. But there is no room for entertaining any such question when a person's conduct affects the interests of no persons besides himself, or need not affect them unless they like (all the persons concerned being of full age, and the ordinary amount of understanding). In all such cases, there should be perfect freedom, legal and social, to do the action and stand the consequences.

It would be a great misunderstanding of this doctrine to suppose that it is one of selfish indifference, which pretends that human beings have no business with each other's conduct in life, and that they should not concern themselves about the well-doing or well-being of one another, unless their own interest is involved. Instead of any diminution, there is need of a great increase of disinterested exertion to promote the good of others. But disinterested benevolence can find other instruments to persuade people to their good than whips and scourges, either of the literal or the metaphorical sort. I am the last person to undervalue the self-regarding virtues: they are only second in importance, if even second, to the social. It is equally the business of education to cultivate both. But even education works by conviction and persuasion as well as by compulsion, and it is by the former only that, when the period of education is passed, the self-regarding virtues should be inculcated. Human beings owe to each other help to distinguish the better from the worse, and encouragement to choose the former and avoid the latter. They should be forever stimulating each other to increased exercise of their higher faculties, and increased direction of their feelings and aims towards wise instead of foolish, elevating instead of degrading, objects and contemplations. But neither one person, nor any number of persons, is warranted in saying to another human creature of ripe years, that he shall not do with his life for his own benefit what he chooses to do with it. He is the person most interested in his own well-being: the interest which any other person, except in cases of strong personal attachment, can have in it, is trifling, compared with that which he himself has; the interest which society has in him individually (except as to his conduct to others) is fractional, and altogether indirect; while with respect to his own feelings and circumstances, the most ordinary man or woman has means of knowledge immeasurably surpassing those that can be possessed by anyone else. The interference of society to overrule his judgement and purposes in what only regards himself must be grounded on general presumptions; which may be altogether wrong, and even if right, are as likely as not to be misapplied to individual cases, by persons no better acquainted with the circumstances of such cases than those are who look at them merely from without. In this department, therefore, of human affairs, individuality has its proper field of action. In the conduct of human beings towards one another it is necessary that general rules should for the most part be observed, in order that people may know what they have to expect; but in each person's own concerns his individual spontaneity is entitled to free exercise. Considerations to aid his judgement, exhortations to strengthen his will, may be offered to him, even obtruded on him, by others: but he himself is the final judge. All errors which he is likely to commit against advice and warning are far outweighed by the evil of allowing others to constrain him to what they deem his good.

I do not mean that the feelings with which a person is regarded by others ought not to be in any way affected by his self-regarding qualities or deficiencies. This is neither possible nor desirable. If he is eminent in any of the qualities which conduce to his own good, he is, so far, a proper object of admiration. He is so much the nearer to the ideal perfection of human nature. If he is grossly deficient in those qualities, a sentiment the opposite of admiration will follow. There is a degree of folly, and a degree of what may be called (though the phrase is not unobjectionable) lowness or depravation of taste, which, though it cannot justify doing harm to the person who manifests it, renders him necessarily and properly a subject of distaste, or, in extreme cases, even of contempt: a person could not have the opposite qualities in due strength without entertaining these feelings. Though doing no wrong to anyone, a person may so act as to compel us to judge him, and feel to him, as a fool, or as a being of an inferior order; and since this judgement and feeling are a fact which he would prefer to avoid, it is doing him a service to warn him of it beforehand, as of any other disagreeable consequence to which he exposes himself. It would be well, indeed, if this good office were much more freely rendered than the common notions of politeness at present permit, and if one person could honestly point out to another that he thinks him in fault, without being considered unmannerly or presuming. We have a right, also, in various ways, to act upon our unfavourable opinion of anyone, not to the oppression of his individuality, but in the exercise of ours. We are not bound, for example, to seek his society; we have a right to avoid it (though not to parade the avoidance), for we have a right to choose the society most acceptable to us. We have a right, and it may be our duty, to caution others against him, if we think his example or conversation likely to have a pernicious effect on those with whom he associates. We may give others a preference over him in optional good offices, except those which tend to his improvement. In these various modes a person may suffer very severe penalties at the hands of others for faults which directly concern only himself; but he suffers these penalties only in so far as they are the natural and, as it were, the spontaneous consequences of the faults themselves, not because they are purposely inflicted on him for the sake of punishment. A person who shows rashness, obstinacy, self-conceit—who cannot live within moderate means—who cannot restrain himself from hurtful indulgences—who pursues animal pleasures at the expense of those of feeling and intellect—must expect to be lowered in the opinion of others, and to have a less share of their favourable sentiments; but of this he has no right to complain, unless he has merited their favour by special excellence in his social relations, and has thus established a title to their good offices, which is not affected by his demerits towards himself.

What I contend for is, that the inconveniences which are strictly inseparable from the unfavourable judgement of others, are the only ones to which a person should ever be subjected for that portion of his conduct and character which concerns his own good, but which does not affect the interest of others in their relations with him. Acts injurious to others require a totally different treatment. Encroachment on their rights; infliction on them of any loss or damage not justified by his own rights; falsehood or duplicity in dealing with them; unfair or ungenerous use of advantages over them; even selfish abstinence from defending them against injury—these are fit objects of moral reprobation, and, in grave cases, of moral retribution and punishment. And not only these acts, but the dispositions which lead to them, are properly immoral, and fit subjects of disapprobation which may rise to abhorrence. Cruelty of disposition; malice and ill-nature; that most antisocial and odious of all passions, envy; dissimulation and insincerity, irascibility on insufficient cause, and resentment disproportioned to the provocation; the love of domineering over other; the desire to engross more than one's share of advantages (the greediness of the Greeks); the pride which derives gratification from the abasement of others; the egotism which thinks self and its concerns more important than everything else, and decides all doubtful questions in its own favour;—these are moral vices, and constitute a bad and odious moral character; unlike the self-regarding faults previously mentioned, which are not properly immoralities, and to whatever pitch they may be carried, do not constitute wickedness. They may be proofs of any amount of folly, or want of personal dignity and self-respect; but they are only a subject of moral reprobation when they involve a breach of duty to others, for whose sake the individual is bound to have care for himself. What are called duties to ourselves are not socially obligatory, unless circumstances render them at the same time duties to others. The term "duty to oneself," when it means anything more than prudence, means self-respect or self-development, and for none of these is anyone accountable to his fellow-creatures, because for none of them is it for the good of mankind that he be held accountable to them....

The distinction here pointed out between the part of a person's life which concerns only himself, and that which concerns others, many persons will refuse to admit. How (it may be asked) can any part of the conduct of a member of society be a matter of indifference to the other members? No person is an entirely isolated being; it is impossible for a person to do anything seriously or permanently hurtful to himself, without mischief reaching at least to his near connections, and often far beyond them. If he injures his property, he does harm to those who directly or indirectly derived support from it, and usually diminishes, by a greater or less amount, the general resources of the community. If he deteriorates his bodily or mental faculties, he not only brings evil upon all who depended on him for any portion of their happiness, but disqualifies himself for rendering the services which he owes to his fellow-creatures generally; perhaps becomes a burden on their affection or benevolence; and if such conduct were very frequent, hardly an offence that is committed would detract more from the general sum of good. Finally, if by his vices or follies a person does no direct harm to others, he is nevertheless (it may be said) injurious by his example; and ought to be compelled to control himself, for the sake of those whom the sight or knowledge of his conduct might corrupt or mislead.

And even (it will be added) if the consequences of misconduct could be confined to the vicious or thoughtless individual, ought society to abandon to their own guidance those who are manifestly unfit for it? If protection against themselves is confessedly due to children and persons under age, is not society equally bound to afford it to persons of mature years who are equally incapable of self-government? If gambling, or drunkenness, or incontinence, or idleness, or uncleanliness, are as injurious to happiness, and as great a hindrance to improvement, as many or most of the acts prohibited by law, why (it may be asked) should not law, so far as is consistent with practicability and social convenience, endeavour to repress these also? And as a supplement to the unavoidable imperfections of law, ought not opinion at least to organize a powerful police against these vices, and visit rigidly with social penalties those who are known to practise them? There is no question here (it may be said) about restricting individuality, or impeding the trial of new and original experiments in living. The only things it is sought to prevent are things which have been tried and condemned from the beginning of the world until now; things which experience has shown not to be useful or suitable to any person's individuality. There must be some length of time and amount of experience after which a moral or prudential truth may be regarded as established: and it is merely desired to prevent generation after generation from falling over the same precipice which has been fatal to their predecessors.

I fully admit that the mischief which a person does to himself may seriously affect, both through their sympathies and their interests, those nearly connected with him and, in a minor degree, society at large. When, by conduct of this sort, a person is led to violate a distinct and assignable obligation to any other person or persons, the case is taken out of the self-regarding class and becomes amenable to moral disapprobation in the proper sense of the term. If, for example, a man, through intemperance or extravagance, becomes unable to pay his debts, or, having undertaken the moral responsibility of a family, becomes from the same cause incapable of supporting or educating them, he is deservedly reprobated, and might be justly punished; but it is for the breach of duty to his family or creditors, not for the extravagance. If the resources which ought to have been devoted to them, had been diverted from them for the most prudent investment, the moral culpability would have been the same. George Barnwell murdered his uncle to get money for his mistress, but if he had done it to set himself up in business he would equally have been hanged. Again, in the frequent case of a man who causes grief to his family by addiction to bad habits, he deserves reproach for his unkindness or ingratitude; but so he may for cultivating habits not in themselves vicious, if they are painful to those with whom he passes his life, or who from personal ties are dependent on him for their comfort. Whoever fails in the consideration generally due to the interests and feelings of others, not being compelled by some more imperative duty, or justified by allowable self-preference, is a subject of moral disapprobation for that failure, but not for the cause of it, nor for the errors, merely personal to himself, which may have remotely led to it. In like manner, when a person disables himself, by conduct purely self-regarding, from the performance of some definite duty incumbent on him to the public, he is guilty of a social offence. No person ought to be punished simply for being drunk; but a soldier or a policeman should be punished for being drunk on duty. Whenever, in short, there is a definite damage, or a definite risk of damage, either to an individual or to the public, the case is taken out of the province of liberty, and placed in that of morality or law.

But with regard to the merely contingent, or, as it may be called, constructive injury which a person causes to society, by conduct which neither violates any specific duty to the public, nor occasions perceptible hurt to any assignable individual except himself, the inconvenience is one which society can afford to bear, for the sake of the greater good of human freedom. If grown persons are to be punished for not taking proper care of themselves, I would rather it were for their own sake, than under pretence of preventing them from impairing their capacity of rendering to society benefits which society does not pretend it has a right to exact....

## Chapter V

## Applications

… It was pointed out in an early part of this essay, that the liberty of the individual, in things wherein the individual is alone concerned, implies a corresponding liberty in any number of individuals to regulate by mutual agreement such things as regard them jointly, and regard no persons but themselves. This question presents no difficulty, so long as the will of all the persons implicated remains unaltered; but since that will may change, it is often necessary, even in things in which they alone are concerned, that they should enter into engagements with one another; and when they do, it is fit, as a general rule, that those engagements should be kept. Yet, in the laws, probably, of every country, this general rule has some exceptions. Not only persons are not held to engagements which violate the rights of third parties, but it is sometimes considered a sufficient reason for releasing them from an engagement, that it is injurious to themselves. In this and most other civilized countries, for example, an engagement by which a person should sell himself, or allow himself to be sold, as a slave, would be null and void; neither enforced by law nor by opinion. The ground for thus limiting his power of voluntarily disposing of his own lot in life, is apparent, and is very clearly seen in this extreme case. The reason for not interfering unless for the sake of others, with a person's voluntary acts, is consideration for his liberty. His voluntary choice is evidence that what he so chooses is desirable, or at least endurable, to him, and his good is on the whole best provided for by allowing him to take his own means of pursuing it. But by selling himself for a slave, he abdicates his liberty; he foregoes any future use of it beyond that single act. He therefore defeats, in his own case, the very purpose which is the justification of allowing him to dispose of himself. He is no longer free; but is thenceforth in a position which has no longer the presumption in its favour, that would be afforded by his voluntarily remaining in it. The principle of freedom cannot require that he should be free not to be free. It is not freedom to be allowed to alienate his freedom. These reasons, the force of which is so conspicuous in this peculiar case, are evidently of far wider application; yet a limit is everywhere set to them by the necessities of life, which continually require, not indeed that we should resign our freedom, but that we should consent to this and the other limitation of it. The principle, however, which demands uncontrolled freedom of action in all that concerns only the agents themselves, requires that those who have become bound to one another, in things which concern no third party, should be able to release one another from the engagement: and even without such voluntary release there are perhaps no contracts or engagements, except those that relate to money or money's worth, of which one can venture to say that there ought to be no liberty whatever of retraction....

I have reserved for the last place a large class of questions respecting the limits of government interference, which, though closely connected with the subject of this essay, do not, in strictness, belong to it. These are cases in which the reasons against interference do not turn upon the principle of liberty: the question is not about restraining the actions of individuals, but about helping them; it is asked whether the government should do, or cause to be done, something for their benefit, instead of leaving it to be done by themselves, individually or in voluntary combination.

The objections to government interference, when it is not such as to involve infringement of liberty, may be of three kinds.

The first is, when the thing to be done is likely to be better done by individuals than by the government. Speaking generally, there is no one so fit to conduct any business, or to determine how or by whom it shall be conducted, as those who are personally interested in it. This principle condemns the interferences, once so common, of the legislature, or the officers of government, with the ordinary processes of industry. But this part of the subject has been sufficiently enlarged upon by political economists, and is not particularly related to the principles of this essay.

The second objection is more nearly allied to our subject. In many cases, though individuals may not do the particular thing so well, on the average, as the officers of government, it is nevertheless desirable that it should be done by them rather than by the government, as a means to their own mental education—a mode of strengthening their active faculties, exercising their judgement, and giving them a familiar knowledge of the subjects with which they are thus left to deal. This is a principal, though not the sole, recommendation of jury trial (in cases not political); of free and popular local and municipal institutions; of the conduct of industrial and philanthropic enterprises by voluntary associations. These are not questions of liberty, and are connected with that subject only by remote tendencies; but they are questions of development. It belongs to a different occasion from the present to dwell on these things as parts of national education; as being, in truth, the peculiar training of a citizen, the practical part of the political education of a free people, taking them out of the narrow circle of personal and family selfishness, and accustoming them to the comprehension of joint interests, the management of joint concerns—habituating them to act from public or semi-public motives, and guide their conduct by aims which unite instead of isolating them from one another. Without these habits and powers, a free constitution can neither be worked nor preserved; as is exemplified by the too often transitory nature of political freedom in countries where it does not rest upon a sufficient basis of local liberties. The management of purely local business by the localities, and of the great enterprises of industry by the union of those who voluntarily supply the pecuniary means, is further recommended by all the advantages which have been set forth in this essay as belonging to individuality of development, and diversity of modes of action. Government operations tend to be everywhere alike. With individuals and voluntary associations, on the contrary, there are varied experiments, and endless diversity of experience. What the State can usefully do is to make itself the central depository, and active circulator and diffuser, of the experience resulting from many trials. Its business is to enable each experimentalist to benefit by the experiments of others, instead of tolerating no experiments but its own.

The third and most cogent reason for restricting the interference of government is the great evil of adding unnecessarily to its power. Every function superadded to those already exercised by the government causes its influence over hopes and fears to be more widely diffused, and converts, more and more, the active and ambitious part of the public into hangers-on of the government, or of some party which aims at becoming the government. If the roads, the railways, the banks, the insurance offices, the great joint-stock companies, the universities, and the public charities, were all of them branches of the government; if, in addition, the municipal corporations and local boards, with all that now devolves on them, become departments of the central administration; if the employees of all these different enterprises were appointed and paid by the government, and looked to the government for every rise in life; not all the freedom of the press and popular constitution of the legislature would make this or any other country free otherwise than in name. And the evil would be greater, the more efficiently and scientifically the administrative machinery was constructed—the more skilful the arrangements for obtaining the best qualified hands and heads with which to work it....

# UTILITARIANISM

*Chapter II*

*What Utilitarianism Is*

… The creed which accepts as the foundation of morals *utility* or the *greatest happiness principle* holds that actions are right in proportion as they tend to promote happiness, wrong as they tend to produce the reverse of happiness. By "happiness" is intended pleasure, and the absence of pain; by "unhappiness," pain, and the privation of pleasure. To give a clear view of the moral standard set up by the theory, much more requires to be said; in particular, what things it includes in the ideas of pain and pleasure, and to what extent this is left an open question. But these supplementary explanations do not affect the theory of life on which this theory of morality is grounded—namely, that pleasure, and freedom from pain, are the only things desirable as ends; and that all desirable things (which are as numerous in the utilitarian as in any other scheme) are desirable either for the pleasure inherent in themselves, or as means to the promotion of pleasure and the prevention of pain.

Now such a theory of life excites in many minds, and among them in some of the most estimable in feeling and purpose, inveterate dislike. To suppose that life has (as they express it) no higher end than pleasure—no better and nobler object of desire and pursuit—they designate as utterly mean and grovelling; as a doctrine worthy only of swine, to whom the followers of Epicurus were, at a very early period, contemptuously likened; and modern holders of the doctrine are occasionally made the subject of equally polite comparisons by its German, French, and English assailants.

When thus attacked, the Epicureans have always answered that it is not they but their accusers who represent human nature in a degrading light; since the accusation supposes human beings to be capable of no pleasures except those of which swine are capable. If this supposition were true, the charge could not be gainsaid, but would then be no longer an imputation; for if the sources of pleasure were precisely the same to human beings and to swine, the rule of life which is good enough for the one would be good enough for the other. The comparison of the Epicurean life to that of beasts is felt as degrading, precisely because a beast's pleasures do not satisfy a human being's conceptions of happiness. Human beings have faculties more elevated than the animal appetites, and when once made conscious of them, do not regard anything as happiness which does not include their gratification. I do not, indeed, consider the Epicureans to have been by any means faultless in drawing out their scheme of consequences from the utilitarian principle. To do this in any sufficient manner, many Stoic, as well as Christian elements require to be included. But there is no known Epicurean theory of life which does not assign to the pleasures of the intellect, of the feelings and imagination, and of the moral sentiments, a much higher value as pleasures than to those of mere sensation. It must be admitted, however, that utilitarian writers in general have placed the superiority of mental over bodily pleasures chiefly in the greater permanency, safety, uncostliness, etc., of the former—that is, in their circumstantial advantages rather than in their intrinsic nature. And on all these points utilitarians have fully proved their case; but they might have taken the other, and, as it may be called, higher ground, with entire consistency. It is quite compatible with the principle of utility to recognise the fact, that some *kinds* of pleasure are more desirable and more valuable than others. It would be absurd that while, in estimating all other things, quality is considered as well as quantity, the estimation of pleasures should be supposed to depend on quantity alone.

If I am asked what I mean by difference of quality in pleasures, or what makes one pleasure more valuable than another merely as a pleasure, except its being greater in amount, there is but one possible answer. Of two pleasures, if there be one to which all or almost all who have experience of both give a decided preference, irrespective of any feeling of moral obligation to prefer it, that is the more desirable pleasure. If one of the two is, by those who are competently acquainted with both, placed so far above the other that they prefer it, even though knowing it to be attended with a greater amount of discontent, and would not resign it for any quantity of the other pleasure which their nature is capable of, we are justified in ascribing to the preferred enjoyment a superiority in quality, so far outweighing quantity as to render it, in comparison, of small account.

Now it is an unquestionable fact that those who are equally acquainted with, and equally capable of appreciating and enjoying, both, do give a most marked preference to the manner of existence which employs their higher faculties. Few human creatures would consent to be changed into any of the lower animals, for a promise of the fullest allowance of a beast's pleasures; no intelligent human being would consent to be a fool; no instructed person would be an ignoramus, no person of feeling and conscience would be selfish and base, even though they should be persuaded that the fool, the dunce, or the rascal is better satisfied with his lot than they are with theirs. They would not resign what they possess more than he for the most complete satisfaction of all the desires which they have in common with him. If they ever fancy they would, it is only in cases of unhappiness so extreme, that to escape from it they would exchange their lot for almost any other, however undesirable in their own eyes. A being of higher faculties requires more to make him happy, is capable probably of more acute suffering, and certainly accessible to it at more points, than one of an inferior type; but in spite of these liabilities, he can never really wish to sink into what he feels to be a lower grade of existence. We may give what explanation we please of this unwillingness: we may attribute it to pride, a name which is given indiscriminately to some of the most and to some of the least estimable feelings of which mankind are capable; we may refer it to the love of liberty and personal independence, an appeal to which was with the Stoics one of the most effective means for the inculcation of it; to the love of power, or to the love of excitement, both of which do really enter into and contribute to it: but its most appropriate appellation is a sense of dignity, which all human beings possess in one form or other, and in some, though by no means in exact, proportion to their higher faculties, and which is so essential a part of the happiness of those in whom it is strong, that nothing which conflicts with it could be, otherwise than momentarily, an object of desire to them. Whoever supposes that this preference takes place at a sacrifice of happiness—that the superior being, in anything like equal circumstances, is not happier than the inferior—confounds the two very different ideas, of *happiness* and *content*. It is indisputable that the being whose capacities of enjoyment are low, has the greatest chance of having them fully satisfied; and a highly endowed being will always feel that any happiness which he can look for, as the world is constituted, is imperfect. But he can learn to bear its imperfections, if they are at all bearable; and they will not make him envy the being who is indeed unconscious of the imperfections, but only because he feels not at all the good which those imperfections qualify. It is better to be a human being dissatisfied than a pig satisfied; better to be Socrates dissatisfied than a fool satisfied. And if the fool, or the pig, are of a different opinion, it is because they only know their own side of the question. The other party to the comparison knows both sides.

It may be objected that many who are capable of the higher pleasures, occasionally, under the influence of temptation, postpone them to the lower. But this is quite compatible with a full appreciation of the intrinsic superiority of the higher. Men often, from infirmity of character, make their election for the nearer good, though they know it to be the less valuable; and this no less when the choice is between two bodily pleasures, than when it is between bodily and mental. They pursue sensual indulgences to the injury of health, though perfectly aware that health is the greater good. It may be further objected that many who begin with youthful enthusiasm for everything noble, as they advance in years sink into indolence and selfishness. But I do not believe that those who undergo this very common change, voluntarily choose the lower description of pleasures in preference to the higher. I believe that before they devote themselves exclusively to the one, they have already become incapable of the other. Capacity for the nobler feelings is in most natures a very tender plant, easily killed, not only by hostile influences, but by mere want of sustenance; and in the majority of young persons it speedily dies away if the occupations to which their position in life has devoted them, and the society into which it has thrown them, are not favourable to keeping that higher capacity in exercise. Men lose their high aspirations as they lose their intellectual tastes, because they have not time or opportunity for indulging them; and they addict themselves to inferior pleasures not because they deliberately prefer them, but because they are either the only ones to which they have access or the only ones which they are any longer capable of enjoying. It may be questioned whether anyone who had remained equally susceptible to both classes of pleasures, ever knowingly and calmly preferred the lower; though many, in all ages, have broken down in an ineffectual attempt to combine both.

From this verdict of the only competent judges I apprehend there can be no appeal. On a question which is the best worth having of two pleasures, or which of two modes of existence is the most grateful to the feelings, apart from its moral attributes and from its consequences, the judgement of those who are qualified by knowledge of both, or, if they differ, that of the majority among them, must be admitted as final. And there need be the less hesitation to accept this judgement respecting the quality of pleasures, since there is no other tribunal to be referred to even on the question of quantity. What means are there of determining which is the acutest of two pains, or the intensest of two pleasurable sensations, except the general suffrage of those who are familiar with both? Neither pains nor pleasures are homogeneous, and pain is always heterogeneous with pleasure. What is there to decide whether a particular pleasure is worth purchasing at the cost of a particular pain, except the feelings and judgement of the experienced? When, therefore, those feelings and judgement declare the pleasures derived from the higher faculties to be preferable in kind, apart from the question of intensity, to those of which the animal nature, disjoined from the higher faculties, is susceptible, they are entitled on this subject to the same regard.

I have dwelt on this point, as being a necessary part of a perfectly just conception of utility, or happiness, considered as the directive role of human conduct. But it is by no means an indispensable condition to the acceptance of the utilitarian standard; for that standard is not the agent's own greatest happiness, but the greatest amount of happiness altogether; and if it may possibly be doubted whether a noble character is always the happier for its nobleness, there can be no doubt that it makes other people happier, and that the world in general is immensely a gainer by it. Utilitarianism, therefore, could only attain its end by the general cultivation of nobleness of character, even if each individual were only benefitted by the nobleness of others, and his own, so far as happiness is concerned, were a sheer deduction from the benefit. But the bare enunciation of such an absurdity as this last renders refutation superfluous.

According to the "greatest happiness principle," as above explained, the ultimate end, with reference to and for the sake of which all other things are desirable (whether we are considering our own good or that of other people), is an existence exempt as far as possible from pain, and as rich as possible in enjoyments, both in point of quantity and quality; the test of quality, and the rule for measuring it against quantity, being the preference felt by those who in their opportunities of experience, to which must be added their habits of self-consciousness and self-observation, are best furnished with the means of comparison. This, being, according to the utilitarian opinion, the end of human action, is necessarily also the standard of morality; which may accordingly be defined, the rules and precepts for human conduct, by the observance of which an existence such as has been described might be, to the greatest extent possible, secured to all mankind; and not to them only, but, so far as the nature of things admits, to the whole sentient creation....

Though it is only in a very imperfect state of the world's arrangements that anyone can best serve the happiness of others by the absolute sacrifice of his own, yet so long as the world is in that imperfect state, I fully acknowledge that the readiness to make such a sacrifice is the highest virtue which can be found in man. I will add that in this condition of the world, paradoxical as the assertion may be, the conscious ability to do without happiness gives the best prospect of realizing such happiness as is attainable. For nothing except that consciousness can raise a person above the chances of life, by making him feel that, let fate and fortune do their worst, they have not power to subdue him; which, once felt, frees him from excess of anxiety concerning the evils of life, and enables him, like many a Stoic in the worst times of the Roman Empire, to cultivate in tranquillity the sources of satisfaction accessible to him, without concerning himself about the uncertainty of their duration, any more than about their inevitable end.

Meanwhile, let utilitarians never cease to claim the morality of self-devotion as a possession which belongs by as good a right to them, as either to the Stoic or to the Transcendentalist. The utilitarian morality does recognize in human beings the power of sacrificing their own greatest good for the good of others. It only refuses to admit that the sacrifice is itself a good. A sacrifice which does not increase, or tend to increase, the sum total of happiness, it considers as wasted. The only self-renunciation which it applauds, is devotion to the happiness, or to some of the means of happiness, of others; either of mankind collectively, or of individuals within the limits imposed by the collective interests of mankind.

I must again repeat, what the assailants of utilitarianism seldom have the justice to acknowledge, that the happiness which forms the utilitarian standard of what is right in conduct, is not the agent's own happiness, but that of all concerned. As between his own happiness and that of others, utilitarianism requires him to be as strictly impartial as a disinterested and benevolent spectator....

## Chapter III

### Of the Ultimate Sanction of the Principle of Utility

The question is often asked, and properly so, in regard to any supposed moral standard—What is its sanction? what are the motives to obey it? or more specifically, what is the source of its obligation? whence does it derive its binding force? It is a necessary part of moral philosophy to provide the answer to this question; which, though frequently assuming the shape of an objection to the utilitarian morality, as if it had some special applicability to that above others, really arises in regard to all standards. It arises, in fact, whenever a person is called on to *adopt* a standard, or refer morality to any basis on which he has not been accustomed to rest in. For the customary morality, that which education and opinion have consecrated, is the only one which presents itself to the mind with the feeling of being *in itself* obligatory; and when a person is asked to believe that this morality *derives* its obligation from some general principle round which custom has not thrown the same halo, the assertion is to him a paradox; the supposed corollaries seem to have a more binding force than the original theorem; the superstructure seems to stand better without, than with, what is represented as its foundation. He says to himself, I feel that I am bound not to rob or murder, betray or deceive; but why am I bound to promote the general happiness? If my own happiness lies in something else, why may I not give that the preference?

If the view adopted by the utilitarian philosophy of the nature of the moral sense be correct, this difficulty will always present itself, until the influences which form moral character have taken the same hold of the principle which they have taken of some of the consequences—until, by the improvement of education, the feeling of unity with our fellow-creatures shall be (what it cannot be denied that Christ intended it to be) as deeply rooted in our character, and to our own consciousness as completely a part of our nature, as the horror of crime is in an ordinarily well brought up young person. In the meantime, however, the difficulty has no peculiar application to the doctrine of utility, but is inherent in every attempt to analyse morality and reduce it to principles; which, unless the principle is already in men's minds invested with as much sacredness as any of its applications, always seem to divest them of a part of their sanctity.

The principle of utility either has, or there is no reason why it might not have, all the sanctions which belong to any other system of morals. Those sanctions are either external or internal. Of the external sanctions it is not necessary to speak at any length. They are, the hope of favour and the fear of displeasure, from our fellow-creatures or from the Ruler of the Universe, along with whatever we may have of sympathy or affection for them, or of love and awe of Him, inclining us to do his will independently of selfish consequences. There is evidently no reason why all these motives for observance should not attach themselves to the utilitarian morality, as completely and as powerfully as to any other....

So far as to external sanctions. The internal sanction of duty, whatever our standard of duty may be, is one and the same—a feeling in our own mind: a pain, more or less intense, attendant on violation of duty, which in properly cultivated moral natures rises, in the more serious cases, into shrinking from it as an impossibility. This feeling, when disinterested, and connecting itself with the

545

pure idea of duty, and not with some particular form of it, or with any of the merely accessory circumstances, is the essence of conscience; though in that complex phenomenon as it actually exists, the simple fact is in general all encrusted over with collateral associations, derived from sympathy, from love, and still more from fear; from all the forms of religious feeling; from the recollections of childhood and of all our past life; from self-esteem, desire of the esteem of others, and occasionally even self-abasement....

The ultimate sanction, therefore, of all morality (external motives apart) being a subjective feeling in our own minds, I see nothing embarrassing to those whose standard is utility, in the question, what is the sanction of that particular standard? We may answer, the same as of all other moral standards—the conscientious feelings of mankind. Undoubtedly this sanction has no binding efficacy on those who do not possess the feelings it appeals to; but neither will these persons be more obedient to any other moral principle than to the utilitarian one. On them morality of any kind has no hold but through the external sanctions. Meanwhile the feelings exist, a fact in human nature, the reality of which, and the great power with which they are capable of acting on those in whom they have been duly cultivated, are proved by experience. No reason has ever been shown why they may not be cultivated to as great intensity in connection with the utilitarian, as with any other rule of morals.

There is, I am aware, a disposition to believe that a person who sees in moral obligation a transcendental fact, an objective reality belonging to the province of "things in themselves," is likely to be more obedient to it than one who believes it to be entirely subjective, having its seat in human consciousness only. But whatever a person's opinion may be on this point of ontology, the force he is really urged by is his own subjective feeling, and is exactly measured by its strength. No one's belief that duty is an objective reality, is stronger than the belief that God is so; yet the belief in God, apart from the expectation of actual reward and punishment, only operates on conduct through, and in proportion to, the subjective religious feeling....

But there *is* this basis of powerful natural sentiment; and this it is which, when once the general happiness is recognized as the ethical standard, will constitute the strength of the utilitarian morality. This firm foundation is that of the social feelings of mankind; the desire to be in unity with our fellow-creatures, which is already a powerful principle in human nature, and happily one of those which tend to become stronger, even without express inculcation, from the influences of advancing civilisation. The social state is at once so natural, so necessary, and so habitual to man, that, except in some unusual circumstances or by an effort of voluntary abstraction, he never conceives himself otherwise than as a member of a body; and this association is rivetted more and more as mankind are further removed from the state of savage independence. Any condition, therefore, which is essential to a state of society, becomes more and more an inseparable part of every person's conception of the state of things which he is born into, and which is the destiny of a human being....

## Chapter V

### On the Connection Between Justice and Utility

In all ages of speculation, one of the strongest obstacles to the reception of the doctrine that Utility or Happiness is the criterion of right and wrong, has been drawn from the idea of Justice. The powerful sentiment, and apparently clear perception, which that word recalls with a rapidity and certainty resembling an instinct, have seemed to the majority of thinkers to point to an inherent quality in things; to show that the Just must have an existence in nature as something absolute, generically distinct from every variety of the expedient, and, in idea, opposed to it, though (as is commonly acknowledged) never, in the long run, disjoined from it in fact....

To throw light upon this question, it is necessary to attempt to ascertain what is the distinguishing character of justice, or of injustice: what is the quality, or whether there is any quality, attributed in common to all modes of conduct designated as unjust (for justice, like many other moral attributes, is best defined by its opposite), and distinguishing them from such modes of conduct as are disapproved, but without having that particular epithet of disapprobation applied to them....

*In the first place*, it is mostly considered unjust to deprive anyone of his personal liberty, his property, or any other thing which belongs to him by law. Here, therefore, is one instance of the application of the terms just and unjust in a perfectly definite sense, namely, that it is just to respect, unjust to violate, the *legal rights* of any one. But this judgement admits of several exceptions, arising from the other forms in which the notions of justice and injustice present themselves. For example, the person who suffers the deprivation may (as the phrase is) have *forfeited* the rights which he is so deprived of: a case to which we shall return presently.

*Secondly,* the legal rights of which he is deprived, may be rights which *ought not* to have belonged to him; in other words, the law which confers on him these rights, may be a bad law. When it is so, or when (which is the same thing for our purpose) it is supposed to be so, opinions will differ as to the justice or injustice of infringing it…. When, however, a law is thought to be unjust, it seems always to be regarded as being so in the same way in which a breach of law is unjust, namely, by infringing somebody's right; which, as it cannot in this case be a legal right, receives a different appellation, and is called a moral right. We may say, therefore, that a second case of injustice consists in taking or withholding from any person that to which he has a *moral right*.

*Thirdly*, it is universally considered just that each person should obtain that (whether good or evil) which he *deserves*; and unjust that he should obtain a good, or be made to undergo an evil, which he does not deserve. This is, perhaps, the clearest and most emphatic form in which the idea of justice is conceived by the general mind. As it involves the notion of desert, the question arises, what constitutes desert? Speaking in a general way, a person is understood to deserve good if he does right, evil if he does wrong; and in a more particular sense, to deserve good from those to whom he does or has done good, and evil from those to whom he does or has done evil. The precept of returning good for evil has never been regarded as a case of the fulfilment of justice, but as one in which the claims of justice are waived, in obedience to other considerations.

*Fourthly*, it is confessedly unjust to *break faith* with any one: to violate an engagement, either express or implied, or disappoint expectations raised by our own conduct, at least if we have raised those expectations knowingly and voluntarily. Like the other obligations of justice already spoken of, this one is not regarded as absolute, but as capable of being overruled by a stronger obligation of justice on the other side; or by such conduct on the part of the person concerned as is deemed to absolve us from our obligation to him, and to constitute a *forfeiture* of the benefit which he has been led to expect.

*Fifthly*, it is, by universal admission, inconsistent with justice to be *partial*; to show favour or preference to one person over another, in matters to which favour and preference do not properly apply. Impartiality, however, does not seem to be regarded as a duty in itself, but rather as instrumental to some other duty; for it is admitted that favour and preference are not always censurable, and indeed the cases in which they are condemned are rather the exception than the rule…. Impartiality, in short, as an obligation of justice, may be said to mean, being exclusively influenced by the considerations which it is supposed ought to influence the particular case in hand; and resisting the solicitation of any motives which prompt to conduct different from what those considerations would dictate.

Nearly allied to the idea of impartiality is that of *equality;* which often enters as a component part both into the conception of justice and into the practice of it, and, in the eyes of many persons, constitutes its essence. But in this, still more than in any other case, the notion of justice varies in different persons, and always conforms in its variations to their notion of utility....

Among so many diverse applications of the term Justice, which yet is not regarded as ambiguous, it is a matter of some difficulty to seize the mental link which holds them together, and on which the moral sentiment adhering to the term essentially depends....

...We do not call anything wrong, unless we mean to imply that a person ought to be punished in some way or other for doing it; if not by law, by the opinion of his fellow-creatures; if not by opinion, by the reproaches of his own con-science. This seems the real turning point of the distinction between morality and simple expediency. It is a part of the notion of Duty in every one of its forms, that a person may rightfully be compelled to fulfil it. Duty is a thing which may be exacted from a person, as one exacts a debt. Unless we think that it may be *exacted* from him, we do not call it his duty. Reasons of prudence, or the interest of other people, may militate against actually exacting it; but the person him-self, it is clearly understood, would not be entitled to complain. There are other things, on the contrary, which we wish that people should do, which we like or admire them for doing, perhaps dislike or despise them for not doing, but yet admit that they are not bound to do; it is not a case or moral obligation; we do not blame them, that is, we do not think that they are proper objects of punish-ment. How we come by these ideas of deserving and not deserving punishment, will appear, perhaps, in the sequel; but I think there is no doubt that this dis-tinction lies at the bottom of the notions of right and wrong; that we call any conduct wrong, or employ, instead, some other term of dislike or disparagement, according as we think that the person ought, or ought not, to be punished for it; and we say, it would be right to do so and so, or merely that it would be desirable or laudable, according as we would wish to see the person whom it concerns, compelled, or only persuaded and exhorted, to act in that manner.[1]

---

[1] See this point enforced and illustrated by Professor Bain, in an admirable Chapter (entitled "The Ethical Emotions, or the Moral Sense"), of the second of the two treatises composing his elaborate and profound work on the Mind.

This, therefore, being the characteristic difference which marks off, not justice, but morality in general, from the remaining provinces of Expediency and Worthiness; the character is still to be sought which distinguishes justice from other branches of morality. Now it is known that ethical writers divide moral duties into two classes, denoted by the ill-chosen expressions, duties of perfect and of imperfect obligation; the latter being those in which, though the act is obligatory, the particular occasions of performing it are left to our choice; as in the case of charity or beneficence, which we are indeed bound to practise, but not towards any definite person, nor at any prescribed time. In the more precise language of philosophic purists, duties of perfect obligation are those duties in virtue of which a correlative *right* resides in some person or persons; duties of imperfect obligation are those moral obligations which do not give birth to any right. I think it will be found that this distinction exactly coincides with that which exists between justice and the other obligations of morality. In our survey of the various popular acceptations of justice, the term appeared generally to involve the idea of a personal right—a claim on the part of one or more individuals, like that which the law gives when it confers a proprietary or other legal right. Whether the injustice consists in depriving a person of a possession, or in breaking faith with him, or in treating him worse than he deserves, or worse than other people who have no greater claims, in each case the supposition implies two things—a wrong done, and some assignable person who is wronged. Injustice may also be done by treating a person better than others; but the wrong in this case is to his competitors, who are also assignable persons. It seems to me that this feature in the case—a right in some person, correlative to the moral obligation—constitutes the specific difference between justice, and generosity or beneficence. Justice implies something which is not only right to do, and wrong not to do, but which some individual person can claim from us as his moral right.... Having thus endeavoured to determine the distinctive elements which enter into the composition of the idea of justice, we are ready to enter on the inquiry, whether the feeling, which accompanies the idea, is attached to it by a special dispensation of nature, or whether it could have grown up, by any known laws, out of the idea itself; and in particular, whether it can have originated in considerations of general expediency.

I conceive that the sentiment itself does not arise from anything which would commonly, or correctly, be termed an idea of expediency; but that though the sentiment does not, whatever is moral in it does.

We have seen that the two essential ingredients in the sentiment of justice are, the desire to punish a person who has done harm, and the knowledge or belief that there is some definite individual or individuals to whom harm has been done.

Now it appears to me, that the desire to punish a person who has done harm to some individual is a spontaneous outgrowth from two sentiments, both in the highest degree natural, and which either are or resemble instincts; the impulse of self-defence, and the feeling of sympathy.

It is natural to resent, and to repel or retaliate, any harm done or attempted against ourselves, or against those with whom we sympathise. The origin of this sentiment it is not necessary here to discuss. Whether it be an instinct or a result of intelligence, it is, we know, common to all animal nature; for every animal tries to hurt those who have hurt, or who it thinks are about to hurt, itself or its young. Human beings, on this point, only differ from other animals in two particulars. First, in being capable of sympathising, not solely with their offspring, or, like some of the more noble animals, with some superior animal who is kind to them, but with all human, and even with all sentient beings. Secondly, in having a more developed intelligence, which gives a wider range to the whole of their sentiments, whether self-regarding or sympathetic. By virtue of his superior intelligence, even apart from his superior range of sympathy, a human being is capable of apprehending a community of interest between himself and the human society of which he forms a part, such that any conduct which threatens the security of the society generally, is threatening to his own, and calls forth his instinct (if instinct it be) of self-defence. The same superiority of intelligence, joined to the power of sympathising with human beings generally, enables him to attach himself to the collective idea of his tribe, his country, or mankind, in such a manner that any act hurtful to them, raises his instinct of sympathy, and urges him to resistance.

The sentiment of justice, in that one of its elements which consists of the desire to punish, is thus, I conceive, the natural feeling of retaliation or vengeance, rendered by intellect and sympathy applicable to those injuries, that is, to those hurts, which wound us through, or in common with, society at large. This sentiment, in itself, has nothing moral in it; what is moral is, the exclusive subordination of it to the social sympathies, so as to wait on and obey their call. For the natural feeling would make us resent indiscriminately whatever any one does that is disagreeable to us; but when moralised by the social feeling, it only acts in the directions conformable to the general good: just persons resenting a hurt to society, though not otherwise a hurt to themselves, and not resenting a hurt to themselves, however painful, unless it be of the kind which society has a common interest with them in the repression of....

To recapitulate: the idea of justice supposes two things; a rule of conduct, and a sentiment which sanctions the rule. The first must be supposed common to all mankind, and intended for their good. The other (the sentiment) is a desire that punishment may be suffered by those who infringe the rule. There is involved, in addition, the conception of some definite person who suffers by the infringement; whose rights (to use the expression appropriated to the case) are violated by it. And the sentiment of justice appears to me to be, the animal desire to repel or retaliate a hurt or damage to oneself, or to those with whom one sympathises, widened so as to include all persons, by the human capacity of enlarged sympathy, and the human conception of intelligent self-interest. From the latter elements, the feeling derives its morality; from the former, its peculiar impressiveness, and energy of self-assertion.

I have, throughout, treated the idea of a *right* residing in the injured person, and violated by the injury, not as a separate element in the composition of the idea and sentiment, but as one of the forms in which the other two elements clothe themselves. These elements are, a hurt to some assignable person or persons on the one hand, and a demand for punishment on the other. An examination of our own minds, I think, will show, that these two things include all that we mean when we speak of violation of a right. When we call anything a person's right, we mean that he has a valid claim on society to protect him in the possession of it, either by the force of law, or by that of education and opinion. If he has what we consider a sufficient claim, on whatever account, to have something guaranteed to him by society, we say that he has a right to it. If we desire to prove that anything does not belong to him by right, we think this done as soon as it is admitted that society ought not to take measures for securing it to him, but should leave him to chance, or to his own exertions. Thus, a person is said to have a right to what he can earn in fair professional competition; because society ought not to allow any other person to hinder him from endeavouring to earn in that manner as much as he can. But he has not a right to three hundred a year, though he may happen to be earning it; because society is not called on to provide that he shall earn that sum. On the contrary, if he owns ten thousand pounds three per cent, stock, he has a right to three hundred a year; because society has come under an obligation to provide him with an income of that amount.

To have a right, then, is, I conceive, to have something which society ought to defend me in the possession of. If the objector goes on to ask, why it ought? I can give him no other reason than general utility....

# KARL MARX

*Karl Marx (1818–1883) was born in Germany to Rhineland Jewish parents. His father was a prosperous middle-class lawyer and an admirer of the French enlightenment. When Marx was five his father had to convert to Protestantism in order to retain his legal position in the Prussian civil service. Marx was originally sent to the University of Bonn. He transferred one year later to the University of Berlin, where he principally studied, and he graduated with a doctorate in philosophy from the University of Jena in 1841. His first job was with a newspaper in Cologne, but the newspaper was suppressed in 1843. That same year, after a seven-year engagement, he married Jenny Westphalen, daughter of Baron von Westphalen, in June. In November they moved to Paris where Marx became co-editor of a new magazine,* The German-French Annals. *He met in Paris his lifelong collaborator and financial supporter, Friedrich Engels, son of a wealthy German textile manufacturer. The stay in Paris was cut short when in 1845 the Prussian government pressured the French authorities to expel Marx for the political views expressed in his magazine. He moved to Brussels where he became active in various worker organizations, including the Communist League, and, with Engels, wrote the* Communist Manifesto of the Communist Party *(1848). Belgium also expelled Marx for his political activity. He returned briefly to Paris and then to Germany. His work on a newspaper again led to trouble with the authorities; he was arrested for sedition. At his trial he made a dramatic speech in own his defence and was acquitted. In July 1849 he left for England where he spent the rest of his life. His meagre living came from working as a correspondent for the* New York Daily Tribune *and from the faithful Engels. Throughout this period he wrote, in the British Museum,* Das Kapital (Capital), *a three-volume work which he never completed. During his lifetime, his writings were known to only a small number of people.*

*Marx wrote an enormous amount, much of which was not published until long after his death. The following titles are some of the essential works. As well as the* Communist Manifesto, *Marx and Engels jointly wrote* The German Ideology *(from 1845 to 1846, and first published in Moscow in 1932). Marx wrote* The Poverty of Philosophy *(1847);* Wage, Labour, and Capital *(1849);* A Contribution to a Critique of Political Economy *(1859);* Capital, *volume I (1867; the English edition was edited by Engels in 1887 as well as the last two volumes in 1885 and 1894); and* The Civil War in France *(1871). Two other important works were published in the twentieth century:* Economic and Philosophic Manuscripts *(written in 1844, published in Moscow in 1932), and* Grundrisse (Foundations) *(written from 1857 to 1858 and published in Moscow in 1939–1941).*

— J.M.P.

# SPEECH AT THE GRAVESIDE
# OF KARL MARX
# (1883)

*by Friedrich Engels*

... Just as Darwin discovered the law of development of organic nature, so Marx discovered the law of development of human history: the simple fact, hitherto concealed by an overgrowth of ideology, that mankind must first of all eat, drink, have shelter and clothing, before it can pursue politics, science, art, religion, etc.; that therefore the production of the immediate material means of subsistence and consequently the degree of economic development attained by a given people or during a given epoch form the foundation upon which the state institutions, the legal conceptions, art, and even the ideas on religion, of the people concerned have been evolved, and in the light of which they must, therefore, be explained, instead of vice-versa, as had hitherto been the case.

But that is not all. Marx also discovered the special law of motion governing the present-day capitalist mode of production and the bourgeois society that this mode of production has created. The discovery of surplus value suddenly threw light on the problem, in trying to solve which all previous investigations, of both bourgeois economists and socialist critics, had been groping in the dark....

For Marx was before all else a revolutionist. His real mission in life was to contribute, in one way or another, to the overthrow of capitalist society and of the state institutions which it had brought into being, to contribute to the liberation of the modern proletariat, which he was the first to make conscious of its own position and its needs, conscious of the conditions of its emancipation. Fighting was his element. And he fought with a passion, a tenacity and a success such as few could rival....

# ECONOMIC AND PHILOSOPHIC MANUSCRIPTS

### ⇥ FIRST MANUSCRIPT ⇤

### Alienated Labour

### *by Karl Marx*

We have begun from the presuppositions of political economy. We have accepted its terminology and its laws. We presupposed private property; the separation of labour, capital and land, as also of wages, profit and rent; the division of labour; competition; the concept of exchange value, etc. From political economy itself, in its own words, we have shown that the worker sinks to the level of a commodity, and to a most miserable commodity; that the misery of the worker increases with the power and volume of his production; that the necessary result of competition is the accumulation of capital in a few hands, and thus a restoration of monopoly in a more terrible form; and finally that the distinction between capitalist and landlord, and between agricultural labourer and industrial worker, must disappear, and the whole of society divide into the two classes of property *owners* and *propertyless* workers.

Political economy begins with the fact of private property; it does not explain it. It conceives the *material* process of private property, as this occurs in reality, in general and abstract formulas which then serve it as laws. It does not *comprehend* these laws; that is, it does not show how they arise out of the nature of private property. Political economy provides no explanation of the basis for the distinction of labour from capital, of capital from land. When, for example, the relation of wages to profits is defined, this is explained in terms of the interests of capitalists; in other words, what should be explained is assumed. Similarly, competition is referred to at every point and is explained in terms of external conditions. Political economy tells us nothing about the extent to which these external and apparently accidental conditions are simply the expression of a necessary

---

*First Manuscript: Alienated Labour,* by Karl Marx, from *Karl Marx: Early Writings,* translated and edited by T. B. Bottomore, © T. B. Bottomore, 1963. Reprinted by permission of McGraw-Hill Book Company and C. A. Watts and Company Ltd.

development. We have seen how exchange itself seems an accidental fact. The only motive forces which political economy recognises are *avarice* and the *war between the avaricious, competition.*

Just because political economy fails to understand the interconnexions within this movement it was possible to oppose the doctrine of competition to that of monopoly, the doctrine of freedom of the crafts to that of the guilds, the doctrine of the division of landed property to that of the great estates; for competition, freedom of crafts, and the division of landed property were conceived only as accidental consequences brought about by will and force, rather than as necessary, inevitable and natural consequences of monopoly, the guild system and feudal property.

Thus we have now to grasp the real connexion between this whole system of alienation—private property, acquisitiveness, the separation of labour, capital and land, exchange and competition, value and the devaluation of man, monopoly and competition—and the system of *money.*

Let us not begin our explanation, as does the economist, from a legendary primordial condition. Such a primordial condition does not explain anything; it merely removes the question into a grey and nebulous distance. It asserts as a fact or event what it should deduce, namely, the necessary relation between two things; for example, between the division of labour and exchange. In the same way theology explains the origin of evil by the fall of man; that is, it asserts as a historical fact what it should explain.

We shall begin from a *contemporary* economic fact. The worker becomes poorer the more wealth he produces and the more his production increases in power and extent. The worker becomes an ever cheaper commodity the more goods he creates. The *devaluation* of the human world increases in direct relation with the *increase in value* of the world of things. Labour does not only create goods; it also produces itself and the worker as a *commodity,* and indeed in the same proportion as it produces goods.

This fact simply implies that the object produced by labour, its product, now stands opposed to it as an *alien being,* as a *power independent* of the producer. The product of labour is labour which has been embodied in an object and turned into a physical thing; this product is an *objectification* of labour. The performance of work is at the same time its objectification. The performance of work appears in the sphere of political economy as a *vitiation* of the worker, objectification as a *loss* and as *servitude to the object,* and appropriation as *alienation.*

So much does the performance of work appear as vitiation that the worker is vitiated to the point of starvation. So much does objectification appear as loss of the object that the worker is deprived of the most essential things not only of life but also of work. Labour itself becomes an object which he can acquire only by the greatest effort and with unpredictable interruptions. So much does the appropriation of the object appear as alienation that the more objects the worker produces the fewer he can possess and the more he falls under the domination of his product, of capital.

All these consequences follow from the fact that the worker is related to the *product of his labour* as to an *alien* object. For it is clear on this presupposition that the more the worker expends himself in work the more powerful becomes the world of objects which he creates in face of himself, the poorer he becomes in his inner life, and the less he belongs to himself. It is just the same as in religion. The more of himself man attributes to God the less he has left in himself. The worker puts his life into the object, and his life then belongs no longer to himself but to the object. The greater his activity, therefore, the less he possesses. What is embodied in the product of his labour is no longer his own. The greater this product is, therefore, the more he is diminished. The *alienation* of the worker in his product means not only that his labour becomes an object, assumes an *external* existence, but that it exists independently, *outside himself*, and alien to him, and that it stands opposed to him, and that it stands opposed to him as an autonomous power. The life which he has given to the objects sets itself against him as an alien and hostile force.

Let us now examine more closely the phenomenon of *objectification;* the worker's production and the *alienation* and *loss* of the object it produces, which is involved in it. The worker can create nothing without *nature*, without the *sensuous external world*. The latter is the material in which his labour is realised, in which it is active, out of which and through which it produces things.

But just as nature affords the *means of existence* of labour, in the sense that labour cannot live without objects upon which it can be exercised, so also it provides the *means of existence* in a narrower sense; namely the means of physical existence for the *worker* himself. Thus, the more the worker appropriates the external world of sensuous nature by his labour the more he deprives himself of *means of existence*, in two respects: first, that the sensuous external world becomes progressively less an object belonging to his labour or a means of existence of his labour, and secondly, that it becomes progressively less a means of existence in the direct sense, a means for the physical subsistence of the worker.

In both respects, therefore, the worker becomes a slave of the object; first, in that he receives an *object of work*, i.e. receives *work*, and secondly, in that he receives *means of subsistence*. Thus the object enables him to exist, first as a worker and secondly, as a *physical subject*. The culmination of this enslavement is that he can only maintain himself as a *physical subject* so far as he is a *worker*, and that it is only as a *physical subject* that he is a worker.

(The alienation of the worker in his object is expressed as follows in the laws of political economy: the more the worker produces the less he has to consume; the more value he creates the more worthless he becomes; the more refined his product the more crude and misshapen the worker; the more civilised the product the more barbarous the worker; the more powerful the work the more feeble the worker; the more the work manifests intelligence the more the worker declines in intelligence and becomes a slave of nature.)

*Political economy conceals the alienation in the nature of labour in so far as it does not examine the direct relationship between the worker (work) and production.* Labour certainly produces marvels for the rich but it produces privation for the worker. It produces palaces, but hovels for the worker. It produces beauty, but deformity for the worker. It replaces labour by machinery, but it casts some of the workers back into a barbarous kind of work and turns the others into machines. It produces intelligence, but also stupidity and cretinism for the workers.

*The direct relationship of labour to its products is the relationship of the worker to the objects of his production.* The relationship of property owners to the objects of production and to production itself is merely a *consequence* of this first relationship and confirms it. We shall consider this second aspect later.

Thus, when we ask what is the important relationship of labour, we are concerned with the relationship of the *worker* to production.

So far we have considered the alienation of the worker only from one aspect; namely, *his relationship with the products of his labour*. However, alienation appears not merely in the result but also in the *process of production*, within *productive activity* itself. How could the worker stand in an alien relationship to the product of his activity if he did not alienate himself in the act of production itself? The product is indeed only the *résumé* of activity, of production. Consequently, if the product of labour is alienation, production itself must be active alienation—the alienation of activity and the activity of alienation. The alienation of the object of labour merely summarises the alienation in the work activity itself.

What constitutes the alienation of labour? First, that the work is *external* to the worker, that it is not part of his nature; and that, consequently, he does not fulfil himself in his work but denies himself, has a feeling of misery rather than well-being, does not develop freely his mental and physical energies but is physically exhausted and mentally debased. The worker, therefore, feels himself at home only during his leisure time, whereas at work he feels homeless. His work is not voluntary but imposed, *forced labour*. It is not the satisfaction of a need, but only a *means* for satisfying other needs. Its alien character is clearly shown by the fact that as soon as there is no physical or other compulsion it is avoided like the plague. External labour, labour in which man alienates himself, is a labour of self-sacrifice, of mortification. Finally, the external character of work for the worker is shown by the fact that it is not his own work but work for someone else, that in work he does not belong to himself but to another person.

Just as in religion the spontaneous activity of human fantasy, of the human brain and heart, reacts independently as an alien activity of gods or devils upon the individual, so the activity of the worker is not his own spontaneous activity. It is another's activity and a loss of his own spontaneity.

We arrive at the result that man (the worker) feels himself to be freely active only in his animal functions—eating, drinking and procreating, or at most also in his dwelling and in personal adornment—while in his human functions he is reduced to an animal. The animal becomes human and the human becomes animal.

Eating, drinking and procreating are of course also genuine human functions. But abstractly considered, apart from the environment of human activities, and turned into final and sole ends, they are animal functions.

We have now considered the act of alienation of practical human activity, labour, from two aspects: (1) the relationship of the worker to the *product of labour* as an alien object which dominates him. This relationship is at the same time the relationship to the sensuous external world, to natural objects, as an alien and hostile world; (2) the relationship of labour to the *act of production* within *labour*. This is the relationship of the worker to his own activity as something alien and not belonging to him, activity as suffering (passivity), strength as powerlessness, creation as emasculation, the *personal* physical and mental energy of the worker, his personal life (for what is life but activity?), as an activity which is directed against himself, independent of him and not belonging to him. This is *self-alienation* as against the above-mentioned alienation of the *thing*.

We have now to infer a third characteristic of *alienated labour* from the two we have considered.

Man is a species-being not only in the sense that he makes the community (his own as well as those of other things) his object both practically and theoretically, but also (and this is simply another expression for the same thing) in the sense that he treats himself as the present, living species, as a *universal* and consequently free being.

Species-life, for man as for animals, has its physical basis in the fact that man (like animals) lives from inorganic nature, and since man is more universal than an animal so the range of inorganic nature from which he lives is more universal. Plants, animals, minerals, air, light, etc. constitute, from the theoretical aspect, a part of human consciousness as objects of natural science and art; they are man's spiritual inorganic nature, his intellectual means of life, which he must first prepare for enjoyment and perpetuation. So also, from the practical aspect, they form a part of human life and activity. In practice man lives only from these natural products, whether in the form of food, heating, clothing, housing, etc. The universality of man appears in practice in the universality which makes the whole of nature into his inorganic body: (1) as a direct means of life; and equally (2) as the material object and instrument of his life activity. Nature is the inorganic body of man; that is to say nature, excluding the human body itself. To say that man *lives* from nature means that nature is his *body* with which he must remain in a continuous interchange in order not to die. The statement that the physical and mental life of man, and nature, are interdependent means simply that nature is interdependent with itself, for man is a part of nature.

Since alienated labour: (1) alienates nature from man; and (2) alienates man from himself, from his own active function, his activity; so it alienates him from the species. It makes *species-life* into a means of individual life. In the first place it alienates species-life and individual life, and secondly, it turns the latter, as an abstraction, into the purpose of the former, also in its abstract and alienated form.

For labour, *life activity, productive life*, now appear to man only as *means* for the satisfaction of a need, the need to maintain his physical existence. Productive life is, however, species-life. It is life creating life. In the type of life activity resides the whole character of a species, its species-character; and free, conscious activity is the species-character of human beings. Life itself appears only as a *means of life*.

The animal is one with its life activity. It does not distinguish the activity from itself. It is *its activity*. But man makes his life activity itself an object of his will and consciousness. He has a conscious life activity. It is not a determination with which he is completely identified. Conscious life activity distinguishes man from the life activity of animals. Only for this reason is he a species-being. Or rather, he is only a self-conscious being, i.e. his own life is an object for him, because he is a species-being. Only for this reason is his activity free activity. Alienated labour reverses the relationship, in that man because he is a self-conscious being makes his life activity, his *being*, only a means for his *existence*.

The practical construction of an *objective world*, the *manipulation* of inorganic nature, is the confirmation of man as a conscious species-being, i.e. a being who treats the species as his own being or himself as a species-being. Of course, animals also produce. They construct nests, dwellings, as in the case of bees, beavers, ants, etc. But they only produce what is strictly necessary for themselves or their young. They produce only in a single direction, while man produces universally. They produce only under the compulsion of direct physical needs, while man produces when he is free from physical need and only truly produces in freedom from such need. Animals produce only themselves, while man reproduces the whole of nature. The products of animal production belong directly to their physical bodies, while man is free in fact of his product. Animals construct only in accordance with the standards and needs of the species to which they belong, while man knows how to produce in accordance with the standards of every species and knows how to apply the appropriate standard to the object. Thus man constructs also in accordance with the laws of beauty.

It is just in his work upon the objective world that man really proves himself as a *species-being*. This production is his active species-life. By means of it nature appears as his work and his reality. The object of labour is, therefore, the *objectification of man's species-life*; for he no longer reproduces himself merely intellectually, as in consciousness, but actively and in a real sense, and he sees his own reflection in a world which he has constructed. While, therefore, alienated labour takes away the object of production from man, it also takes away his *species-life*, his real objectivity as a species-being, and changes his advantage over animals into a disadvantage in so far as his inorganic body, nature, is taken from him.

Just as alienated labour transforms free and self-directed activity into a means, so it transforms the species-life of man into a means of physical existence.

Consciousness, which man has from his species, is transformed through alienation so that species-life becomes only a means for him. (3) Thus alienated labour turns the *species-life of man*, and also nature as his mental species-property, into an *alien* being and into a *means* for his *individual existence*. It alienates from man his own body, external nature, his mental life and his *human* life. (4) A direct consequence of the alienation of man from the product of his labour, from his life activity and from his species-life, is that *man is alienated* from other *men*. When man confronts himself he also confronts other men. What is true of man's relationship to his work, to the product of his work and to himself, is also true of his relationship to other men, to their labour and to the objects of their labour. In general, the statement that man is alienated from his species-life means that each man is alienated from others, and that each of the others is likewise alienated from human life.

Human alienation, and above all the relation of man to himself, is first realized and expressed in the relationship between each man and other men. Thus in the relationship of alienated labour every man regards other men according to the standards and relationships in which he finds himself placed as a worker.

We began with an economic fact, the alienation of the worker and his production. We have expressed this fact in conceptual terms as *alienated labour*, and in analysing the concept we have merely analysed an economic fact.

Let us now examine further how this concept of alienated labour must express and reveal itself in reality. If the product of labour is alien to me and confronts me as an alien power, to whom does it belong? If my own activity does not belong to me but is an alien, forced activity, to whom does it belong? To a being *other* than myself. And who is this being? The *gods?* It is apparent in the earliest stages of advanced production, e.g. temple building, etc. in Egypt, India, Mexico, and in the service rendered to gods, that the product belonged to the gods. But the gods alone were never the lords of labour. And no more was *nature*. What a contradiction it would be if the more man subjugates nature by his labour, and the more the marvels of the gods are rendered superfluous by the marvels of industry, the more he should abstain from his joy in producing and his enjoyment of the product for love of these powers.

The *alien* being to whom labour and the product of labour belong, to whose service labour is devoted, and to whose enjoyment the product of labour goes, can only be *man* himself. If the product of labour does not belong to the worker, but confronts him as an alien power, this can only be because it belongs to a *man other than the worker*. If his activity is a torment to him it must be a source of *enjoyment* and pleasure to another. Not the gods, nor nature, but only man himself can be this alien power over men.

Consider the earlier statement that the relation of man to himself is first realised, *objectified*, through his relation to other men. If he is related to the product of his labour, his objectified labour, as to an *alien*, hostile, powerful and independent object, he is related in such a way that another alien, hostile, powerful and independent man is the lord of this object. If he is related to his own activity as to unfree activity, then he is related to it as activity in the service, and under the domination, coercion and yoke, of another man.

Every self-alienation of man, from himself and from nature, appears in the relation which he postulates between other men and himself and nature. Thus religious self-alienation is necessarily exemplified in the relation between laity and priest, or, since it is here a question of the spiritual world, between the laity and a mediator. In the real world of practice this self-alienation can only be expressed in the real, practical relation of man to his fellow men. The medium through which alienation occurs is itself a *practical* one. Through alienated labour, therefore, man not only produces his relation to the object and to the process of production as to alien and hostile men; he also produces the relation of other men to his production and his product; and the relation between himself and other men. Just as he creates his own production as a vitiation, a punishment, and his own product as a loss, as a product which does not belong to him, so he creates the domination of the non-producer over production and its product. As he alienates his own activity, so he bestows upon the stranger an activity which is not his own....

# ECONOMIC AND PHILOSOPHIC MANUSCRIPTS

## → THIRD MANUSCRIPT ←

### Private Property and Communism

#### *by Karl Marx*

... *Communism* is the *positive* abolition of *private property*, of *human self-alienation*, and thus the real *appropriation* of *human* nature through and for man. It is, therefore, the return of man himself as a *social*, i.e. really human, being, a complete and conscious return which assimilates all the wealth of previous development. Communism as a fully developed naturalism is humanism and as a fully developed humanism is naturalism. It is the *definitive* resolution of the antagonism between man and nature, and between man and man. It is the true solution of the conflict between existence and essence, between objectification and self-affirmation, between freedom and necessity, between individual and species. It is the solution of the riddle of history and knows itself to be this solution....

A being does not regard himself as independent unless he is his own master, and he is only his own master when he owes his existence to himself. A man who lives by the favour of another considers himself a dependent being. But I live completely by another person's favour when I owe to him not only the continuance of my life but also *its creation*; when he is its *source*. My life has necessarily such a cause outside itself if it is not my own creation. The idea of *creation* is thus one which it is difficult to eliminate from popular consciousness. This consciousness is *unable to conceive* that nature and man exist on their own account, because such an existence contradicts all the tangible facts of practical life.

The idea of the creation of the *earth* has received a severe blow from the science of geogeny, i.e. from the science which portrays the formation and development of the earth as a process of spontaneous generation. *Generatio æquivoca* (spontaneous generation) is the only practical refutation of the theory of creation.

But it is easy indeed to say to the particular individual what Aristotle said: You are engendered by your father and mother, and consequently it is the coitus of two human beings, a human species-act, which has produced the human being. You see, therefore, that even in a physical sense man owes his existence to man. Consequently, it is not enough to keep in view only one of the two aspects, the *infinite* progression, and to ask further: who engendered my father and my grand-father? You must also keep in mind the circular movement which is perceptible in that progress, according to which man, in the act of generation reproduces himself; thus man always remains the subject. But you will reply: I grant you this *circular movement*, but you must in turn concede the progression, which leads ever further to the point where I ask; who created the first man and nature as a whole? I can only reply: your question is itself a product of abstraction. Ask yourself how you arrive at that question. Ask yourself whether your question does not arise from a point of view to which I cannot reply because it is a perverted one. Ask yourself whether that progression exists as such for rational thought. If you ask a question about the creation of nature and man you abstract from nature and man. You suppose them *non-existent* and you want me to demonstrate that they *exist*. I reply: give up your abstraction and at the same time you abandon your question. Or else, if you want to maintain your abstraction, be consistent, and if you think of man and nature as non-existent, think of yourself too as non-exis-tent, for you are also man and nature. Do not think, do not ask me any questions, for as soon as you think and ask questions your abstraction from the existence of nature and man becomes meaningless. Or are you such an egoist that you conceive everything as non-existent and yet want to exist yourself?

You may reply: I do not want to conceive the nothingness of nature, etc.; I only ask you about the act of its creation, just as I ask the anatomist about the for-mation of bones, etc.

Since, however, for socialist man, the *whole of what is called world history* is noth-ing but the creation of man by human labour, and the emergence of nature for man, he, therefore, has the evident and irrefutable proof of his *self-creation*, of his own *origins*. Once the essence of man and of nature, man as a natural being and nature as a human reality, has become evident in practical life, in sense ex-perience, the quest for an *alien* being, a being above man and nature (a quest which is an avowal of the unreality of man and nature) becomes impossible in prac-tice. *Atheism*, as a denial of this unreality, is no longer meaningful, for atheism is a *negation of God* and seeks to assert by this negation the *existence of man*. Socialism no longer requires such a roundabout method; it begins from the *theoretical* and *practical sense perception* of man and nature as essential beings. It is positive human *self-consciousness*, no longer a self-consciousness attained through the negation of religion; just as the *real life* of man is positive and no longer attained through the negation of private property, through *communism*. Communism is the phase of negation of the negation and is, consequently, for the next stage of historical development, a real and necessary factor in the emancipation and rehabilitation of man. Communism is the necessary form and the dynamic principle of the immediate future, but communism is not itself the goal of human development —the form of human society.

# THE GERMAN IDEOLOGY

## by Karl Max and Friedrich Engels

... Men can be distinguished from animals by consciousness, by religion or any-thing else you like. They themselves begin to distinguish themselves from ani-mals as soon as they begin to *produce* their means of subsistence, a step which is conditioned by their physical organisation. By producing their means of subsis-tence men are indirectly producing their actual material life.

The way in which men produce their means of subsistence depends first of all on the nature of the actual means of subsistence they find in existence and have to reproduce. This mode of production must not be considered simply as being the reproduction of the physical existence of the individuals. Rather it is a defi-nite form of activity of these individuals, a definite form of expressing their life, a definite *mode of life* on their part. As individuals express their life, so they are. What they are, therefore, coincides with their production, both with *what* they pro-duce and with *how* they produce. The nature of individuals thus depends on the material conditions determining their production.

This production only makes its appearance with the *increase of population*. In its turn this presupposes the intercourse [*Verkehr*] of individuals with one an-other. The form of this intercourse is again determined by production.

The relations of different nations among themselves depend upon the extent to which each has developed its productive forces, the division of labour and in-ternal intercourse. This statement is generally recognised. But not only the rela-tion of one nation to others, but also the whole internal structure of the nation itself depends on the stage of development reached by its production and its internal and external intercourse. How far the productive forces of a nation are devel-oped is shown most manifestly by the degree to which the division of labour has been carried. Each new productive force, insofar as it is not merely a quantitative extension of productive forces already known (for instance the bringing into cultivation of fresh land), causes a further development of the division of labour.

The division of labour inside a nation leads at first to the separation of in-dustrial and commercial from agricultural labour, and hence to the separation

*The German Ideology*, by Karl Marx and Friedrich Engels, from *The Marx-Engels Reader, Second Edition*, edited by Robert C. Tucker. New York: W.W. Norton (1972). Reprinted by permission.

of *town* and *country* and to the conflict of their interests. Its further development leads to the separation of commercial from industrial labour. At the same time through the division of labour inside these various branches there develop various divisions among the individuals co-operating in definite kinds of labour. The relative position of these individual groups is determined by the methods employed in agriculture, industry and commerce (patriarchalism, slavery, estates, classes). These same conditions are to be seen (given a more developed intercourse) in the relations of different nations to one another.

The various stages of development in the division of labour are just so many different forms of ownership, i.e., the existing stage in the division of labour determines also the relations of individuals to one another with reference to the material, instrument, and product of labour.

The first form of ownership is tribal [*Stammeigentum*] ownership. It corresponds to the undeveloped stage of production, at which a people lives by hunting and fishing, by the rearing of beasts or, in the highest stage, agriculture. In the latter case it presupposes a great mass of uncultivated stretches of land. The division of labour is at this stage still very elementary and is confined to a further extension of the natural division of labour existing in the family. The social structure is, therefore, limited to an extension of the family; patriarchal family chieftains, below them the members of the tribe, finally slaves. The slavery latent in the family only develops gradually with the increase of population, the growth of wants, and with the extension of external relations, both of war and of barter.

The second form is the ancient communal and State ownership which proceeds especially from the union of several tribes into a *city* by agreement or by conquest, and which is still accompanied by slavery. Beside communal ownership we already find movable, and later also immovable, private property developing, but as an abnormal form subordinate to communal ownership. The citizens hold power over their labouring slaves only in their community, and on this account alone, therefore, they are bound to the form of communal ownership. It is the communal private property which compels the active citizens to remain in this spontaneously derived form of association over against their slaves. For this reason the whole structure of society based on this communal ownership, and with it the power of the people, decays in the same measure as, in particular, immovable private property evolves. The division of labour is already more developed. We already find the antagonism of town and country; later the antagonism between those states which represent town interests and those which represent country interests, and inside the towns themselves the antagonism between industry and maritime commerce. The class relation between citizens and slaves is now completely developed.

This whole interpretation of history appears to be contradicted by the fact of conquest. Up till now violence, war, pillage, murder and robbery, etc., have been accepted as the driving force of history. Here we must limit ourselves to the chief points and take, therefore, only the most striking example—the destruction of an old civilisation by a barbarous people and the resulting formation of an entirely new organisation of society. (Rome and the barbarians; feudalism and Gaul; the Byzantine Empire and the Turks.) With the conquering barbarian people war itself is still, as indicated above, a regular form of intercourse, which is the more eagerly exploited as the increase in population together with the traditional and, for it, the only possible, crude mode of production gives rise to the need for new means of production. In Italy, on the other hand, the concentration of landed property (caused not only by buying-up and indebtedness but also by inheritance, since loose living being rife and marriage rare, the old families gradually died out and their possessions fell into the hands of a few) and its conversion into grazing-land (caused not only by the usual economic forces still operative today but by the importation of plundered and tribute corn and the resultant lack of demand for Italian corn) brought about the almost total disappearance of the free population. The very slaves died out again and again, and had constantly to be replaced by new ones. Slavery remained the basis of the whole productive system. The plebeians, midway between freemen and slaves, never succeeded in becoming more than a proletarian rabble. Rome indeed never became more than a city; its connection with the provinces was almost exclusively political and could, therefore, easily be broken again by political events.

With the development of private property, we find here for the first time the same conditions which we shall find again, only on a more extensive scale, with modern private property. On the one hand, the concentration of private property, which began very early in Rome (as the Licinian agrarian law proves) and proceeded very rapidly from the time of the civil wars and especially under the Emperors; on the other hand, coupled with this, the transformation of the plebeian small peasantry into a proletariat, which, however, owing to its intermediate position between propertied citizens and slaves, never achieved an independent development.

The third form of ownership is feudal or estate property. If antiquity started out from the town and its little territory, the Middle Ages started out from the *country*. This different starting-point was determined by the sparseness of the population at that time, which was scattered over a large area and which received no large increase from the conquerors. In contrast to Greece and Rome, feudal development at the outset, therefore, extends over a much wider territory, prepared by the Roman conquests and the spread of agriculture at first associated with them. The last centuries of the declining Roman Empire and its conquest by the barbarians destroyed a number of productive forces; agriculture had declined, industry had decayed for want of a market, trade had died out or been violently suspended, the rural and urban population had decreased. From these conditions and the mode of organisation of the conquest determined by them, feudal property developed under the influence of the Germanic military constitution. Like tribal and communal ownership, it is based again on a community; but the directly producing class standing over against it is not, as in the case of the ancient community, the slaves, but the enserfed small peasantry. As soon as feudalism is fully developed, there also arises antagonism to the towns. The hierarchical structure of landownership, and the armed bodies of retainers associated with it, gave the nobility power over the serfs. This feudal organisation was, just as much as the ancient communal ownership, an association against a subjected producing class; but the form of association and the relation to the direct producers were different because of the different conditions of production.

This feudal system of landownership had its counterpart in the *towns* in the shape of corporative property, the feudal organisation of trades. Here property consisted chiefly in the labour of each individual person. The necessity for association against the organised robber nobility, the need for communal covered markets in an age when the industrialist was at the same time a merchant, the growing competition of the escaped serfs swarming into the rising towns, the feudal structure of the whole country: these combined to bring about the *guilds*. The gradually accumulated small capital of individual craftsmen and their stable numbers, as against the growing population, evolved the relation of journeyman and apprentice, which brought into being in the towns a hierarchy similar to that in the country.

Thus the chief form of property during the feudal epoch consisted on the one hand of landed property with serf labour chained to it, and on the other of the labour of the individual with small capital commanding the labour of journeymen.

The organisation of both was determined by the restricted conditions of production—the small-scale and primitive cultivation of the land, and the craft type of industry. There was little division of labour in the heyday of feudalism. Each country bore in itself the antithesis of town and country; the division into estates was certainly strongly marked; but apart from the differentiation of princes, nobility, clergy and peasants in the country, and masters, journeymen, apprentices and soon also the rabble of casual labourers in the towns, no division of importance took place. In agriculture it was rendered difficult by the strip-system, beside which the cottage industry of the peasants themselves emerged. In industry there was no division of labour at all in the individual trades themselves, and very little between them. The separation of industry and commerce was found already in existence in older towns; in the newer it only developed later, when the towns entered into mutual relations.

The grouping of larger territories into feudal kingdoms was a necessity for the landed nobility as for the towns. The organisation of the ruling class, the nobility, had, therefore, everywhere a monarch at its head.

The fact is, therefore, that definite individuals who are productively active in a definite way enter into these definite social and political relations. Empirical observation must in each separate instance bring out empirically, and without any mystification and speculation, the connection of the social and political structure with production. The social structure and the State are continually evolving out of the life process of definite individuals, but of individuals, not as they may appear in their own or other people's imagination, but as they *really* are; i.e., as they operate, produce materially, and hence as they work under definite material limits, presuppositions and conditions independent of their will.

The production of ideas, of conceptions, of consciousness, is at first directly interwoven with the material activity and the material intercourse of men, the language of real life. Conceiving, thinking, the mental intercourse of men, appear at this stage as the direct efflux of their material behaviour. The same applies to mental production as expressed in the language of politics, laws, morality, religion, metaphysics, etc., of a people. Men are the producers of their conceptions, ideas, etc.—real, active men, as they are conditioned by a definite development of their productive forces and of the intercourse corresponding to these, up to its furthest forms. Consciousness can never be anything else than conscious existence, and the existence of men is their actual life-process. If in all ideology men and their circumstances appear upside-down as in a *camera obscura*, this phenomenon arises just as much from their historical life-process as the inversion of objects on the retina does from their physical life-process.

In direct contrast to German philosophy which descends from heaven to earth, here we ascend from earth to heaven. That is to say, we do not set out from what men say, imagine, conceive, nor from men as narrated, thought of, imagined, conceived, in order to arrive at men in the flesh. We set out from real, active men, and on the basis of their real life-process we demonstrate the development of the ideological reflexes and echoes of this life-process. The phantoms formed in the human brain are also, necessarily, sublimates of their material life-process, which is empirically verifiable and bound to material premises. Morality, religion, metaphysics, all the rest of ideology and their corresponding forms of consciousness, thus no longer retain the semblance of independence. They have no history, no development; but men, developing their material production and their material intercourse, alter, along with this their real existence, their thinking and the products of their thinking. Life is not determined by consciousness, but consciousness by life. In the first method of approach the starting-point is consciousness taken as the living individual; in the second method, which conforms to real life, it is the real living individuals themselves, and consciousness is considered solely as *their* consciousness.

This method of approach is not devoid of premises. It starts out from the real premises and does not abandon them for a moment. Its premises are men, not in any fantastic isolation and rigidity, but in their actual, empirically perceptible process of development under definite conditions. As soon as this active life-process is described, history ceases to be a collection of dead facts as it is with the empiricists (themselves still abstract), or an imagined activity of imagined subjects, as with the idealists.

Where speculation ends—in real life—there real, positive science begins: the representation of the practical activity, of the practical process of development of men. Empty talk about consciousness ceases, and real knowledge has to take its place. When reality is depicted, philosophy as an independent branch of knowledge loses its medium of existence. At the best its place can only be taken by a summing-up of the most general results, abstractions which arise from the observation of the historical development of men. Viewed apart from real history, these abstractions have in themselves no value whatsoever. They can only serve to facilitate the arrangement of historical material, to indicate the sequence of its separate strata. But they by no means afford a recipe or schema, as does philosophy, for neatly trimming the epochs of history. On the contrary, our difficulties begin only when we set about the observation and the arrangement—the real depiction—of our historical material, whether of a past epoch or of the present. The removal of these difficulties is governed by premises which it is quite impossible to state here, but which only the study of the actual life-process and the activity of the individuals of each epoch will make evident. We shall select here some of these abstractions, which we use in contradistinction to the ideologists, and shall illustrate them by historical examples.

Since we are dealing with the Germans, who are devoid of premises, we must begin by stating the first premise of all human existence and, therefore, of all history, the premise, namely, that men must be in a position to live in order to be able to "make history." But life involves before everything else eating and drinking, a habitation, clothing and many other things. The first historical act is thus the production of the means to satisfy these needs, the production of material life itself. And indeed this is an historical act, a fundamental condition of all history, which today, as thousands of years ago, must daily and hourly be fulfilled merely in order to sustain human life. Even when the sensuous world is reduced to a minimum, to a stick as with Saint Bruno, it presupposes the action of producing the stick. Therefore in any interpretation of history one has first of all to observe this fundamental fact in all its significance and all its implications and to accord it its due importance. It is well known that the Germans have never done this, and they have never, therefore, had an *earthly* basis for history and consequently never a historian. The French and the English, even if they have conceived the relation of this fact with so-called history only in an extremely one-sided fashion, particularly as long as they remained in the toils of political ideology, have nevertheless made the first attempts to give the writing of history a materialistic basis by being the first to write histories of civil society, of commerce and industry.

The second point is that the satisfaction of the first need (the action of satisfying, and the instrument of satisfaction which has been acquired) leads to new needs; and this production of new needs is the first historical act. Here we recognise immediately the spiritual ancestry of the great historical wisdom of the Germans who, when they run out of positive material and when they can serve up neither theological nor political nor literary rubbish, assert that this is not history at all, but the "prehistoric era." They do not, however, enlighten us as to how we proceed from this nonsensical "prehistory" to history proper; although, on the other hand, in their historical speculation they seize upon this "prehistory" with especial eagerness because they imagine themselves safe there from interference on the part of "crude facts," and, at the same time, because there they can give full rein to their speculative impulse and set up and knock down hypotheses by the thousand.

The third circumstance which, from the very outset, enters into historical development, is that men, who daily remake their own life, begin to make other men, to propagate their kind: the relation between man and woman, parents and children, the *family*. The family, which to begin with is the only social relationship, becomes later, when increased needs create new social relations and the increased population new needs, a subordinate one (except in Germany), and must then be treated and analysed according to the existing empirical data, not according to "the concept of the family," as is the custom in Germany.[1] These three aspects of social activity are not of course to be taken as three different stages, but just as three aspects or, to make it clear to the Germans, three "moments," which have existed simultaneously since the dawn of history and the first men, and which still assert themselves in history today.

The production of life, both of one's own in labour and of fresh life in procreation, now appears as a double relationship: on the one hand as a natural, on the other as a social relationship. By social we understand the co-operation of several individuals, no matter under what conditions, in what manner and to what end. It follows from this that a certain mode of production, or industrial stage, is always

---

[1] The building of houses. With savages each family has as a matter of course its own cave or hut like the separate family tent of the nomads. This separate domestic economy is made only the more necessary by the further development of private property. With the agricultural peoples a communal domestic economy is just as impossible as a communal cultivation of the soil. A great advance was the building of towns. In all previous periods, however, the abolition of individual economy, which is inseparable from the abolition of private property, was impossible for the simple reason that the material conditions governing it were not present. The setting-up of a communal domestic economy presupposes the development of machinery, of the use of natural forces and of many other productive forces—e.g., of water-supplies, of gas-lighting, steam-heating, etc., the removal [of the antagonism] of town and country. Without these conditions a communal economy would not in itself form a new productive force; lacking any material basis and resting on a purely theoretical foundation, it would be a mere freak and would end in nothing more than a monastic economy.—What was possible can be seen in the towns brought about by condensation and the erection of communal buildings for various definite purposes (prisons, barracks, etc.). That the abolition of individual economy is inseparable from the abolition of the family is self-evident. [*Marx*]

combined with a certain mode of co-operation, or social stage, and this mode of co-operation is itself a "productive force." Further that the multitude of productive forces accessible to men determines the nature of society, hence, that the "history of humanity" must always be studied and treated in relation to the history of industry and exchange. But it is also clear how in Germany it is impossible to write this sort of history, because the Germans lack not only the necessary power of comprehension and the material but also the "evidence of their senses," for across the Rhine you cannot have any experience of these things since history has stopped happening. Thus it is quite obvious from the start that there exists a materialistic connection of men with one another, which is determined by their needs and their mode of production, and which is as old as men themselves. This connection is ever taking on new forms, and thus presents a "history" independently of the existence of any political or religious nonsense which would especially hold men together.

Only now, after having considered four moments, four aspects of the primary historical relationships, do we find that man also possesses "consciousness";[2] but, even so, not inherent, not "pure" consciousness. From the start the "spirit" is afflicted with the curse of being "burdened" with matter, which here makes its appearance in the form of agitated layers of air, sounds, in short, of language. Language is as old as consciousness, language *is* practical consciousness that exists also for other men, and for that reason alone it really exists for me personally as well; language, like consciousness, only arises from the need, the necessity, of intercourse with other men. Where there exists a relationship, it exists for me: the animal does not enter into "*relations*" with anything, it does not enter into any relation at all. For the animal, its relation to others does not exist as a relation. Consciousness is, therefore, from the very beginning a social product, and remains so as long as men exist at all. Consciousness is at first, of course, merely consciousness concerning the *immediate* sensuous environment and consciousness of the limited connection with other persons and things outside the individual who is growing self-conscious. At the same time it is consciousness of nature, which first appears to men as a completely alien, all-powerful and unassailable force, with which men's relations are purely animal and by which they are overawed like beasts; it is thus a purely animal consciousness of nature (natural religion).

---

2 *Marginal note by Marx:* "Men have history because they must *produce* their life, and because they must produce it moreover in a *certain* way: this is determined by their physical organisation; their consciousness is determined in just the same way."

We see here immediately: this natural religion or this particular relation of men to nature is determined by the form of society and vice versa. Here, as everywhere, the identity of nature and man appears in such a way that the restricted relation of men to nature determines their restricted relation to one another, and their restricted relation to one another determines men's restricted relation to nature, just because nature is as yet hardly modified historically; and, on the other hand, man's consciousness of the necessity of associating with the individuals around him is the beginning of the consciousness that he is living in society at all. This beginning is as animal as social life itself at this stage. It is mere herd-consciousness, and at this point man is only distinguished from sheep by the fact that with him consciousness takes the place of instinct or that his instinct is a conscious one. This sheep-like or tribal consciousness receives its further development and extension through increased productivity, the increase of needs, and, what is fundamental to both of these, the increase of population. With these there develops the division of labour, which was originally nothing but the division of labour in the sexual act, then that division of labour which develops spontaneously or "naturally" by virtue of natural predisposition (e.g., physical strength), needs, accidents, etc., etc. Division of labour only becomes truly such from the moment when a division of material and mental labour appears. From this moment onwards consciousness *can* really flatter itself that it is something other than consciousness of existing practice, that it *really* represents something without representing something real; from now on consciousness is in a position to emancipate itself from the world and to proceed to the formation of "pure" theory, theology, philosophy, ethics, etc. But even if this theory, theology, philosophy, ethics, etc., comes into contradiction with the existing relations, this can only occur because existing social relations have come into contradiction with existing forces of production; this, moreover, can also occur in a particular national sphere of relations through the appearance of the contradiction, not within the national orbit, but between this national consciousness and the practice of other nations, i.e., between the national and the general consciousness of a nation (as we see it now in Germany).

Moreover, it is quite immaterial what consciousness starts to do on its own: out of all such muck we get only the one inference that these three moments, the forces of production, the state of society, and consciousness, can and must come into contradiction with one another, because the *division of labour* implies the possibility, nay the fact that intellectual and material activity—enjoyment and

# MANIFESTO OF THE COMMUNIST PARTY

*by Karl Marx and Friedrich Engels*

A specter is haunting Europe—the specter of communism. All the powers of old Europe have entered into a holy alliance to exorcise this specter: Pope and Czar, Metternich and Guizot, French radicals and German police spies.

Where is the party in opposition that has not been decried as communistic by its opponents in power? Where the opposition that has not hurled back the branding reproach of communism against the more advanced opposition parties, as well as against its reactionary adversaries?

Two things result from this fact:

    I. Communism is already acknowledged by all European powers to be itself a power.

    II. It is high time that communists should openly, in the face of the whole world, publish their views, their aims, their tendencies, and meet this nursery tale of the specter of communism with a Manifesto of the party itself.

To this end, communists of various nationalities have assembled in London and sketched the following Manifesto, to be published in the English, French, German, Italian, Flemish and Danish languages.

## I. Bourgeois and Proletarians

The history of all hitherto existing society is the history of class struggles.

Free man and slave, patrician and plebian, lord and serf, guild master and journeyman, in a word, oppressor and oppressed, stood in constant opposition to one another, carried on an uninterrupted, now hidden, now open fight, a fight that each time ended either in a revolutionary reconstitution of society at large or in the common ruin of the contending classes.

In the earlier epochs of history we find almost everywhere a complicated arrangement of society into various orders, a manifold gradation of social rank. In ancient Rome we have patricians, knights, plebians, slaves; in the Middle Ages, feudal lords, vassals, guild masters, journeymen, apprentices, serfs; in almost all of these classes, again, subordinate gradations.

The modern bourgeois society that has sprouted from the ruins of feudal society has not done away with class antagonisms. It has but established new classes, new conditions of oppression, new forms of struggle in place of the old ones.

Our epoch, the epoch of the bourgeoisie, possesses, however, this distinctive feature: it has simplified the class antagonisms. Society as a whole is more and more splitting up into two great hostile camps, into two great classes directly facing each other: bourgeoisie and proletariat.

From the serfs of the Middle Ages sprang the chartered burghers of the earliest towns. From these burgesses the first elements of the bourgeoisie were developed.

The discovery of America, the rounding of the Cape opened up fresh ground for the rising bourgeoisie. The East Indian and Chinese markets, the colonization of America, trade with the colonies, the increase in the means of exchange and in commodities generally, gave to commerce, to navigation, to industry an impulse never before known, and thereby, to the revolutionary element in the tottering feudal society, a rapid development.

The feudal system of industry, under which industrial production was monopolized by closed guilds, now no longer sufficed for the growing wants of the new markets. The manufacturing system took its place. The guild-masters were pushed on one side by the manufacturing middle class; division of labor between the different corporate guilds vanished in the face of division of labor in each single workshop.

Meantime the markets kept ever growing, the demand ever rising. Even manufacturers no longer sufficed. Thereupon steam and machinery revolutionized industrial production. The place of manufacture was taken by the giant, modern industry, the place of the industrial middle class by industrial millionaires, the leaders of whole industrial armies, the modern bourgeois.

Modern industry has established the world market, for which the discovery of America paved the way. This market has given an immense development to commerce, to navigation, to communication by land. This development has, in its turn, reacted on the extension of industry; and in proportion as industry, commerce, navigation, railways extended, in the same proportion the bourgeoisie developed, increased its capital, and pushed into the background every class handed down from the Middle Ages.

We see, therefore, how the modern bourgeoisie is itself the product of a long course of development, of a series of revolutions in the modes of production and of exchange.

Each step in the development of the bourgeoisie was accompanied by a corresponding political advance of that class. An oppressed class under the sway of the feudal nobility, an armed and self-governing association in the medieval commune; here independent urban republic (as in Italy and Germany), there taxable "third estate" of the monarchy (as in France), afterwards, in the period of manufacture proper, serving either the semifeudal or the absolute monarchy as a counterpoise against the nobility, and, in fact, cornerstone of the great monarchies in general, the bourgeoisie has at last, since the establishment of modern industry and of the world market, conquered for itself, in the modern representative state, exclusive political sway. The executive of the modern state is but a committee for managing the common affairs of the whole bourgeoisie.

The bourgeoisie, historically, has played a most revolutionary part.

The bourgeoisie, wherever it has got the upper hand, has put an end to all feudal, patriarchal, idyllic relations. It has pitilessly torn asunder the motley feudal ties that bound man to his "natural superiors," and has left remaining no other nexus between man and man than naked self-interest, than callous "cash payment." It has drowned the most heavenly ecstasies of religious fervor, of chivalrous enthusiasm, of Philistine sentimentalism in the icy water of egotistical calculation. It has resolved personal worth into exchange value and, in place of the numberless indefeasible chartered freedoms, has set up that single, unconscionable freedom—free trade. In one word, for exploitation, veiled by religious and political illusions, it has substituted naked, shameless, direct, brutal exploitation.

The bourgeoisie has stripped of its halo every occupation hitherto honored and looked up to with reverent awe. It has converted the physician, the lawyer, the priest, the poet, the man of science into its paid wage laborers.

The bourgeoisie has torn away from the family its sentimental veil, and has reduced the family relation to a mere money relation.

The bourgeoisie has disclosed how it came to pass that the brutal display of vigor in the Middle Ages, which reactionists so much admire, found its fitting complement in the most slothful indolence. It has been the first to show what man's activity can bring about. It has accomplished wonders far surpassing Egyptian pyramids, Roman aqueducts, and Gothic cathedrals; it has conducted expeditions that put in the shade all former exoduses of nations and crusades.

The bourgeoisie cannot exist without constantly revolutionizing the instruments of production, and thereby the relations of production, and with them the whole relations of society. Conservation of the old modes of production in unaltered form was, on the contrary, the first condition of existence for all earlier industrial classes. Constant revolutionizing of production, uninterrupted disturbance of all social conditions, everlasting uncertainty and agitation distinguish the bourgeois epoch from all earlier ones. All fixed, fast-frozen relations, with their train of ancient and venerable prejudices and opinions, are swept away, all new-formed ones become antiquated before they can ossify. All that is solid melts into air, all that is holy is profaned, and man is at last compelled to face with sober senses his real conditions of life and his relations with his kind.

The need of a constantly expanding market for its products chases the bourgeoisie over the whole surface of the globe. It must nestle everywhere, settle everywhere, establish connections everywhere.

The bourgeoisie has through its exploitation of the world market given a cosmopolitan character to production and consumption in every country. To the great chagrin of reactionists, it has drawn from under the feet of industry the national ground on which it stood. All old-established national industries have been destroyed or are daily being destroyed. They are dislodged by new industries, whose introduction becomes a life and death question for all civilized nations, by industries that no longer work up indigenous raw material, but raw material drawn from the remotest zones; industries whose products are consumed not only at home, but in every quarter of the globe. In place of the old wants, satisfied by the productions of the country, we find new wants, requiring for their satisfaction the products of distant lands and climes. In place of the old local and national seclusion and self-sufficiency we have intercourse in every direction, universal interdependence of nations. And as in material, so also in intellectual production. The intellectual creations of individual nations become common property. National one-sidedness and narrow-mindedness become more and more impossible, and from the numerous national and local literatures there arises a world literature.

The bourgeoisie, by the rapid improvement of all instruments of production, by the immensely facilitated means of communication, draws all, even the most barbarian, nations into civilization. The cheap prices of its commodities are the heavy artillery with which it batters down all Chinese walls, with which it forces the barbarians' intensely obstinate hatred of foreigners to capitulate. It compels all nations, on pain of extinction, to adopt the bourgeois mode of production; it compels them to introduce what it calls civilization into their midst, i.e., to become bourgeois themselves. In one word, it creates a world after its own image.

The bourgeoisie has subjected the country to the rule of the towns. It has created enormous cities, has greatly increased the urban population as compared with the rural, and has thus rescued a considerable part of the population from the idiocy of rural life. Just as it has made the country dependent on the towns, so it has made barbarian and semi-barbarian countries dependent on the civilized ones, nations of peasants on nations of bourgeois, the East on the West.

The bourgeoisie keeps more and more doing away with the scattered state of the population, of the means of production, and of property. It has agglomerated population, centralized means of production, and has concentrated property in a few hands. The necessary consequence of this was political centralization. Independent, or but loosely connected provinces, with separate interests, laws, governments and systems of taxation, became lumped together into one nation, with one government, one code of laws, one national class interest, one frontier, and one customs tariff.

The bourgeoisie, during its rule of scarce one hundred years, has created more massive and more colossal productive forces than have all preceding generations together. Subjection of nature's forces to man, machinery, application of chemistry to industry and agriculture, steam navigation, railways, electric telegraphs, clearing of whole continents for cultivation, canalization of rivers, whole populations conjured out of the ground—what earlier century had even a presentiment that such productive forces slumbered in the lap of social labor?

We see then: the means of production and of exchange, on whose foundation the bourgeoisie built itself up, were generated in feudal society. At a certain stage in the development of these means of production and of exchange, the conditions under which feudal society produced and exchanged, the feudal organization of agriculture and manufacturing industry, in one word, the feudal relations of property, became no longer compatible with the already developed productive forces; they became so many fetters. They had to be burst asunder; they were burst asunder.

Into their place stepped free competition, accompanied by a social and political constitution adapted to it, and by the economic and political sway of the bourgeois class.

A similar movement is going on before our own eyes. Modern bourgeois society with its relations of production, of exchange, and of property, a society that has conjured up such gigantic means of production and of exchange, is like the sorcerer who is no longer able to control the powers of the nether world whom he has called up by his spells. For many a decade past, the history of industry and commerce is but the history of the revolt of modern productive forces against modern conditions of production, against the property relations that are the conditions for the existence of the bourgeoisie and of its rule. It is enough to mention the commercial crises that by their periodic return put on its trial, each time more threateningly, the existence of the entire bourgeois society. In these crises a great part not only of the existing products but also of the previously created productive forces are periodically destroyed. In these crises there breaks out an epidemic that in all earlier epochs would have seemed an absurdity—the epidemic of over-production. Society suddenly finds itself put back into a state of momentary barbarism; it appears as if a famine, a universal war of devastation had cut off the supply of every means of subsistence; industry and commerce seem to be destroyed; and why? Because there is too much civilization, too much means of subsistence, too much industry, too much commerce. The productive forces at the disposal of society no longer tend to further the development of the conditions of bourgeois property; on the contrary, they have become too powerful for these conditions, by which they are fettered, and as soon as they overcome these fetters they bring disorder into the whole of bourgeois society, endanger the existence of bourgeois property. The conditions of bourgeois society are too narrow to comprise the wealth created by them. And how does the bourgeoisie get over these crises? On the one hand, by enforced destruction of a mass of productive forces; on the other, by the conquest of new markets, and by the more thorough exploitation of the old ones. That is to say, by paving the way for more extensive and more destructive crises, and by diminishing the means whereby crises are prevented.

The weapons with which the bourgeoisie felled feudalism to the ground are now turned against the bourgeoisie itself.

But not only has the bourgeoisie forged the weapons that bring death to itself; it has also called into existence the men who are to wield those weapons—the modern working class—the proletarians.

In proportion as the bourgeoisie, i.e., capital, is developed, in the same proportion is the proletariat, the modern working class, developed—a class of laborers, who live only so long as they find work, and who find work only so long as their labor increases capital. These laborers, who must sell themselves piecemeal, are a commodity, like every other article of commerce, and are consequently exposed to all the vicissitudes of competition, to all the fluctuations of the market.

Owing to the extensive use of machinery and to division of labor, the work of the proletarians has lost all individual character and, consequently, all charm for the workman. He becomes an appendage of the machine, and it is only the simplest, most monotonous, and most easily acquired knack that is required of him. Hence the cost of production of a workman is restricted, almost entirely, to the means of subsistence that he requires for his maintenance and for the propagation of his race. But the price of a commodity, and therefore also of labor, is equal to its cost of production. In proportion, therefore, as the repulsiveness of the work increases, the wage decreases. Nay, more, in proportion as the use of machinery and division of labor increases, in the same proportion the burden of toil also increases, whether by prolongation of the working hours, by increase of the work exacted in a given time, or by increased speed of the machinery, etc.

Modern industry has converted the little workshop of the patriarchal master into the great factory of the industrial capitalist. Masses of laborers, crowded into the factory, are organized like soldiers. As privates of the industrial army they are placed under a command of a perfect hierarchy of officers and sergeants. Not only are they slaves of the bourgeois class, and of the bourgeois state; they are daily and hourly enslaved by the machine, by the overlooker, and, above all, by the individual bourgeois manufacturer himself. The more openly this despotism proclaims gain to be its end and aim, the more petty, the more hateful, and the more embittering it is.

The less the skill and exertion of strength implied in manual labor, in other words, the more modern industry becomes developed, the more is the labor of men superseded by that of women. Differences of age and sex have no longer any distinctive social validity for the working class. All are instruments of labor, more or less expensive to use, according to their age and sex.

No sooner is the exploitation of the laborer by the manufacturer over, to the extent that he receives his wages in cash, than he is set upon by the other portions of the bourgeoisie, the landlord, the shopkeeper, the pawnbroker, etc.

The lower strata of the middle class—the small tradespeople, shopkeepers, and retired tradesmen generally, the handicraftsmen and peasants—all these sink gradually into the proletariat, partly because their diminutive capital does not suffice for the scale on which modern industry is carried on, and is swamped in the competition with the large capitalists, partly because their specialized skill is rendered worthless by new methods of production. Thus the proletariat is recruited from all classes of the population.

The proletariat goes through various stages of development. With its birth begins its struggle with the bourgeoisie. At first the contest is carried on by individual laborers, then by the workpeople of a factory, then by the operatives of one trade, in one locality, against the individual bourgeois who directly exploits them. They direct their attacks not against the bourgeois conditions of production, but against the instruments of production themselves; they destroy imported wares that compete with their labor, they smash to pieces machinery, they set factories ablaze, they seek to restore by force the vanished status of the workman of the Middle Ages.

At this stage the laborers still form an incoherent mass scattered over the whole country and broken up by their mutual competition. If anywhere they unite to form more compact bodies, this is not yet the consequence of their own active union, but of the union of the bourgeoisie, which class, in order to attain its own political ends, is compelled to set the whole proletariat in motion, and is moreover yet, for a time, able to do so. At this stage, therefore, the proletarians do not fight their enemies, but the enemies of their enemies, the remnants of absolute monarchy, the landowners, the non-industrial bourgeois, the petty bourgeoisie. Thus the whole historical movement is concentrated in the hands of the bourgeoisie; every victory so obtained is a victory for the bourgeoisie.

But with the development of industry the proletariat not only increases in number; it becomes concentrated in greater masses, its strength grows, and it feels that strength more. The various interests and conditions of life within the ranks of the proletariat are more and more equalized, in proportion as machinery obliterates all distinctions of labor and nearly everywhere reduces wages to the same low level. The growing competition among the bourgeois and the resulting commercial crises make the wages of the workers ever more fluctuating. The unceasing improvement of machinery, ever more rapidly developing, makes their livelihood more and more precarious; the collisions between individual workmen and individual bourgeois take more and more the character of collisions between two classes. Thereupon the workers begin to form combinations (trade unions) against the bourgeois; they club together in order to keep up the rate of wages; they found permanent associations in order to make provision beforehand for these occasional revolts. Here and there the contest breaks out into riots.

Now and then the workers are victorious, but only for a time. The real fruit of their battles lies not in the immediate result, but in the ever expanding union of the workers. This union is helped on by the improved means of communication that are created by modern industry and that place the workers of different localities in contact with one another. It was just this contact that was needed to centralize the numerous local struggles, all of the same character, into one national struggle between classes. But every class struggle is a political struggle. And that union, to attain which the burghers of the Middle Ages, with their miserable highways, required centuries, the modern proletarians, thanks to railways, achieve in a few years.

This organization of the proletarians into a class, and consequently into a political party, is continually being upset again by the competition between the workers themselves. But it ever rises up again, stronger, firmer, mightier. It compels legislative recognition of particular interests of the workers by taking advantage of the divisions among the bourgeoisie itself. Thus the ten-hour bill in England was carried.

Altogether collisions between the classes of the old society further, in many ways, the course of development of the proletariat. The bourgeoisie finds itself involved in a constant battle. At first with the aristocracy; later on, with those portions of the bourgeoisie itself whose interests have become antagonistic to the progress of industry; at all times, with the bourgeoisie of foreign countries. In all these battles it sees itself compelled to appeal to the proletariat, to ask for its help, and thus to drag it into the political arena. The bourgeoisie itself, therefore, supplies the proletariat with its own elements of political and general education: in other words, it furnishes the proletariat with weapons for fighting the bourgeoisie.

Further, as we have already seen, entire sections of the ruling classes are, by the advance of industry, precipitated into the proletariat, or are at least threatened in their conditions of existence. These also supply the proletariat with fresh elements of enlightenment and progress.

Finally, in times when the class struggle nears the decisive hour, the process of dissolution going on within the ruling class, in fact within the whole range of old society, assumes such a violent, glaring character that a small section of the ruling class cuts itself adrift and joins the revolutionary class, the class that holds the future in its hands. Just as, therefore, at an earlier period, a section of the nobility went over to the bourgeoisie, so now a portion of the bourgeoisie goes over to the proletariat, and in particular, a portion of the bourgeois ideologists, who have raised themselves to the level of comprehending theoretically the historical movement as a whole.

Of all the classes that stand face to face with the bourgeoisie today, the proletariat alone is a really revolutionary class. The other classes decay and finally disappear in the face of modern industry; the proletariat is its special and essential product.

The lower-middle class, the small manufacturer, the shopkeeper, the artisan, the peasant, all these fight against the bourgeoisie, to save from extinction their existence as fractions of the middle class. They are therefore not revolutionary, but conservative. Nay, more, they are reactionary, for they try to roll back the wheel of history. If by chance they are revolutionary they are so only in view of their impending transfer into the proletariat; they thus defend not their present but their future interests, they desert their own standpoint to place themselves at that of the proletariat.

The "dangerous class," the social scum, that passively rotting mass thrown off by the lowest layers of old society, may, here and there, be swept into the movement by a proletarian revolution; its conditions of life, however, prepare it far more for the part of a bribed tool of reactionary intrigue.

In the conditions of the proletariat those of old society at large are already virtually swamped. The proletarian is without property; his relation to his wife and children has no longer anything in common with the bourgeois family relations; modern industrial labor, modern subjection to capital, the same in England as in France, in America as in Germany, has stripped him of every trace of national character. Law, morality, religion are to him so many bourgeois prejudices, behind which lurk in ambush just as many bourgeois interests.

All the preceding classes that got the upper hand sought to fortify their already acquired status by subjecting society at large to their conditions of appropriation. The proletarians cannot become masters of the productive forces of society, except by abolishing their own previous mode of appropriation, and thereby also every other previous mode of appropriation. They have nothing of their own to secure and to fortify; their mission is to destroy all previous securities for, and insurance of, individual property.

All previous historical movements were movements of minorities, or in the interest of minorities. The proletarian movement is the self-conscious, independent movement of the immense majority, in the interests of the immense majority. The proletariat, the lowest stratum of our present society, cannot stir, cannot raise itself up, without the whole super-incumbent strata of official society being sprung into the air.

Though not in substance, yet in form, the struggle of the proletariat with the bourgeoisie is at first a national struggle. The proletariat of each country must, of course, first of all settle matters with its own bourgeoisie.

In depicting the most general phases of the development of the proletariat, we traced the more or less veiled civil war, raging within existing society, up to the point where that war breaks out into open revolution, and where the violent overthrow of the bourgeoisie lays the foundation for the sway of the proletariat.

Hitherto every form of society has been based, as we have already seen, on the antagonism of oppression and oppressed classes. But in order to oppress a class certain conditions must be assured to it under which it can, at least, continue its slavish existence. The serf, in the period of serfdom, raised himself to membership in the commune, just as the petty bourgeois, under the yoke of feudal absolutism, managed to develop into a bourgeois. The modern laborer, on the contrary, instead of rising with the progress of industry, sinks deeper and deeper below the conditions of existence of his own class. He becomes a pauper, and pauperism develops more rapidly than population and wealth. And here it becomes evident that the bourgeoisie is unfit any longer to be the ruling class in society, and to impose its conditions of existence upon society as an overriding law. It is unfit to rule because it is incompetent to assure an existence to its slave within his slavery, because it cannot help letting him sink into such a state that it has to feed him instead of being fed by him. Society can no longer live under this bourgeoisie: in other words, its existence is no longer compatible with society.

The essential condition for the existence, and for the sway of the bourgeois class, is the formation and augmentation of capital; the condition for capital is wage labor. Wage labor rests exclusively on competition between the laborers. The advance of industry, whose involuntary promoter is the bourgeoisie, replaces the isolation of the laborers, due to competition, by their revolutionary combination, due to association. The development of modern industry, therefore, cuts from under its feet the very foundation on which the bourgeoisie produces and appropriates products. What the bourgeoisie, therefore, produces, above all, is its own grave-diggers. Its fall and the victory of the proletariat are equally inevitable.

## II. Proletarians and Communists

In what relation do the communists stand to the proletarians as a whole?

The communists do not form a separate party opposed to other working-class parties.

They have no interests separate and apart from those of the proletariat as a whole.

They do not set up any sectarian principles of their own, by which to shape and mold the proletarian movement.

The communists are distinguished from the other working-class parties by this only: 1. In the national struggles of the proletarians of the different countries they point out and bring to the front the common interests of the entire proletariat, independent of all nationality. 2. In the various stages of development which the struggle of the working class against the bourgeoisie has to pass through, they always and everywhere represent the interests of the movement as a whole.

The communists, therefore, are on the one hand, practically, the most advanced and resolute section of the working-class parties of every country, that section which pushes forward all others; on the other hand, theoretically, they have over the great mass of the proletariat the advantage of clearly understanding the line of march, the conditions, and the ultimate general results of the proletarian movement.

The immediate aim of the communists is the same as that of all the other proletarian parties: formation of the proletariat into a class, overthrow of the bourgeois supremacy, conquest of political power by the proletariat.

The theoretical conclusions of the communists are in no way based on ideas or principles that have been invented, or discovered, by this or that would-be universal reformer.

They merely express, in general terms, actual relations springing from an existing class struggle, from a historical movement going on under our very eyes. The abolition of existing property relations is not at all a distinctive feature of communism.

All property relations in the past have continually been subject to historical change consequent upon the change in historical conditions.

The French Revolution, for example, abolished feudal property in favor of bourgeois property.

The distinguishing feature of communism is not the abolition of property generally, but the abolition of bourgeois property. But modern bourgeois private property is the final and most complete expression of the system of producing and appropriating products that is based on class antagonisms, on the exploitation of the many by the few.

In this sense the theory of the communists may be summed up in the single sentence: Abolition of private property.

We communists have been reproached with the desire of abolishing the right of personally acquiring property as the fruit of man's own labor, which property is alleged to be the groundwork of all personal freedom, activity, and independence.

Hard-won, self-acquired, self-earned property! Do you mean the property of the petty artisan and of the small peasant, a form of property that preceded the bourgeois form? There is no need to abolish that; the development of industry has to a great extent already destroyed it, and is still destroying it daily.

Or do you mean modern bourgeois private property?

But does wage labor create any property for the laborer? Not a bit. It creates capital, i.e., that kind of property which exploits wage labor, and which cannot increase except upon condition of begetting a new supply of wage labor for fresh exploitation. Property, in its present form, is based on the antagonism of capital and wage labor. Let us examine both sides of this antagonism.

To be a capitalist is to have not only a purely personal but a social status in production. Capital is a collective product, and only by the united action of many members, nay, in the last resort only by the united action of all members of society, can it be set in motion.

Capital is, therefore, not a personal, it is a social power.

When, therefore, capital is converted into common property, into the property of all members of society, personal property is not thereby transformed into social property. It is only the social character of the property that is changed. It loses its class character.

Let us now take wage labor.

The average price of wage labor is the minimum wage, i.e., that quantum of the means of subsistence which is absolutely requisite to keep the laborer in bare existence as a laborer. What, therefore, the wage laborer appropriates by means of his labor merely suffices to prolong and reproduce a bare existence. We by no means intend to abolish this personal appropriation of the products of labor, an appropriation that is made for the maintenance and reproduction of human life, and that leaves no surplus wherewith to command the labor of others. All that we want to do away with is the miserable character of this appropriation, under which the laborer lives merely to increase capital, and is allowed to live only in so far as the interest of the ruling class requires it.

In bourgeois society, living labor is but a means to increase accumulated labor. In communist society accumulated labor is but a means to widen, to enrich, to promote the existence of the laborer.

In bourgeois society, therefore, the past dominates the present; in communist society the present dominates the past. In bourgeois society capital is independent and has individuality, while the living person is dependent and has no individuality.

And the abolition of this state of things is called by the bourgeois, abolition of individuality and freedom! And rightly so. The abolition of bourgeois individuality, bourgeois independence, and bourgeois freedom is undoubtedly aimed at.

By freedom is meant, under the present bourgeois conditions of production, free trade, free selling and buying.

But if selling and buying disappear, free selling and buying disappear also. This talk about free selling and buying, and all the other "brave words" of our bourgeoisie about free in general, have a meaning, if any, only in contrast with restricted selling and buying, with the fettered traders of the Middle Ages, but have no meaning when opposed to the communistic abolition of buying and selling, of the bourgeois conditions of production, and of the bourgeoisie itself.

You are horrified at our intending to do away with private property. But in your existing society private property is already done away with for nine tenths of the population; its existence for the few is solely due to its non-existence in the hands of those nine tenths. You reproach us, therefore, with intending to do away with a form of property the necessary condition for whose existence is the non-existence of any property for the immense majority of society.

In one word, you reproach us with intending to do away with your property. Precisely so; that is just what we intend.

From the moment when labor can no longer be converted into capital, money, or rent, into a social power capable of being monopolized, i.e., from the moment when individual property can no longer be transformed into bourgeois property, into capital, from that moment, you say, individuality vanishes.

You must, therefore, confess that by "individual" you mean no other person than the bourgeois, than the middle-class owner of property. This person must, indeed, be swept out of the way and made impossible.

Communism deprives no man of the power to appropriate the products of society; all that it does is to deprive him of the power to subjugate the labor of others by means of such appropriation.

It has been objected that upon the abolition of private property all work will cease and universal laziness will overtake us.

According to this, bourgeois society ought long ago have gone to the dogs through sheer idleness, for those of its members who work acquire nothing and those who acquire anything do not work. The whole of this objection is but another expression of the tautology that there can no longer be any wage labor when there is no longer any capital.

All objections urged against the communistic mode of producing and appropriating material products have, in the same way, been urged against the communistic modes of producing and appropriating intellectual products. Just as, to the bourgeois, the disappearance of class property is the disappearance of production itself, so the disappearance of class culture is to him identical with the disappearance of all culture.

That culture, the loss of which he laments, is, for the enormous majority, a mere training to act as a machine.

But don't wrangle with us so long as you apply, to our intended abolition of bourgeois property, the standard of your bourgeois notions of freedom, culture, law, etc. Your very ideas are but the outgrowth of the conditions of your bourgeois production and bourgeois property, just as your jurisprudence is but the will of your class made into a law for all, a will whose essential character and direction are determined by the economic conditions of existence of your class.

The selfish misconception that induces you to transform into eternal laws of nature and of reason the social forms springing from your present mode of production and form of property—historical relations that rise and disappear in the progress of production—this misconception you share with every ruling class that has preceded you. What you see clearly in the case of ancient property, what you admit in the case of feudal property, you are of course forbidden to admit in the case of your own bourgeois form of property.

Abolition of the family! Even the most radical flare up at this infamous proposal of the communists.

On what foundation is the present family, the bourgeois family based? On capital, on private gain. In its completely developed form this family exists only among the bourgeoisie. But this state of things finds its complement in the practical absence of the family among the proletarians, and in public prostitution.

The bourgeois family will vanish as a matter of course when its complement vanishes, and both will vanish with the vanishing of capital.

Do you charge us with wanting to stop the exploitation of children by their parents? To this crime we plead guilty.

But you will say, we destroy the most hallowed of relations when we replace home education by social.

And your education! Is not that also social, and determined by the social conditions under which you educate, by the intervention, direct or indirect, of society, by means of schools, etc.? The communists have not invented the intervention of society in education; they do but seek to alter the character of that intervention, and to rescue education from the influence of the ruling class.

The bourgeois claptrap about the family and education, about the hallowed co-relation of parent and child, becomes all the more disgusting, the more, by the action of modern industry, all family ties among the proletarians are torn asunder and their children transformed into simple articles of commerce and instruments of labor.

"But you communists would introduce community of women," screams the whole bourgeoisie in chorus.

The bourgeois sees in his wife a mere instrument of production. He hears that the instruments of production are to be exploited in common and, naturally, can come to no other conclusion than that the lot of being common to all will likewise fall to the women.

He has not even a suspicion that the real point aimed at is to do away with the status of women as mere instruments of production.

For the rest, nothing is more ridiculous than the virtuous indignation of our bourgeois at the community of women which, they pretend, is to be openly and officially established by the communists. The communists have no need to introduce community of women; it has existed almost from time immemorial.

Our bourgeois, not content with having the wives and daughters of their proletarians at their disposal, not to speak of common prostitutes, take the greatest pleasure in seducing each other's wives.

Bourgeois marriage is in reality a system of wives in common and thus, at the most, what the communists might possibly be reproached with is that they desire to introduce, in substitution for a hypocritically concealed, an openly legalized community of women. For the rest, it is self-evident that the abolition of the present system of production must bring with it the abolition of the community of women springing from that system, i.e., of prostitution, both public and private.

The communists are further reproached with desiring to abolish countries and nationality.

The workingmen have no country. We cannot take from them what they have not got. Since the proletariat must first of all acquire political supremacy, must rise to be the leading class of the nation, must constitute itself *the* nation, it is, so far, itself national, though not in the bourgeois sense of the word.

National differences and antagonisms between peoples are daily more and more vanishing, owing to the development of the bourgeoisie, to freedom of commerce, to the world market, to uniformity in the mode of production and in the conditions of life corresponding thereto.

The supremacy of the proletariat will cause them to vanish still faster. United action, of the leading civilized countries at least, is one of the first conditions for the emancipation of the proletariat.

In proportion as the exploitation of one individual by another is put to an end, the exploitation of one nation by another will also be put to an end. In proportion as the antagonism between classes within the nation vanishes, the hostility of one nation to another will come to an end.

The charges against communism made from a religious, a philosophical, and, generally, from an ideological standpoint are not deserving of serious examination.

Does it require deep intuition to comprehend that man's ideas, views, and conceptions, in one word, man's consciousness, change with every change in the conditions of his material existence, in his social relations, and in his social life?

What else does the history of ideas prove than that intellectual production changes its character in proportion as material production is changed? The ruling ideas of each age have been the ideas of its ruling class.

When people speak of ideas that revolutionize society they do not express the fact that within the old society the elements of a new one have been created, and that the dissolution of the old ideas keeps even pace with the dissolution of the old conditions of existence.

When the ancient world was in its last throes, the ancient religions were overcome by Christianity. When Christian ideas succumbed in the eighteenth century to rationalist ideas, feudal society fought its death battle with the then revolutionary bourgeoisie. The ideas of religious liberty and freedom of conscience merely gave expression to the sway of free competition within the domain of knowledge.

"Undoubtedly," it will be said, "religious, moral, philosophical, and juridical ideas have been modified in the course of historical development. But religion, morality, philosophy, political science, and law constantly survived this change.

"There are, besides, eternal truths, such as freedom, justice, etc., that are common to all states of society. But communism abolishes eternal truths, it abolishes all religion, and all morality, instead of constituting them on a new basis; it therefore acts in contradiction to all past historical experience."

What does this accusation reduce itself to? The history of all past society has consisted in the development of class antagonisms, antagonisms that assumed different forms at different epochs.

But whatever form they may have taken, one fact is common to all past ages, viz., the exploitation of one part of society by the other. No wonder then that the social consciousness of past ages, despite all the multiplicity and variety it displays, moves within certain common forms, or general ideas, which cannot completely vanish except with the total disappearance of class antagonisms.

The communist revolution is the most radical rupture with traditional property relations; no wonder that its development involves the most radical rupture with traditional ideas.

But let us have done with the bourgeois objections to communism.

We have seen above that the first step in the revolution by the working class is to raise the proletariat to the position of ruling class, to win the battle of democracy.

The proletariat will use its political supremacy to wrest, by degrees, all capital from the bourgeoisie, to centralize all instruments of production in the hands of the state, i.e., of the proletariat organized as the ruling class, and to increase the total of productive forces as rapidly as possible.

Of course, in the beginning this cannot be effected except by means of despotic inroads on the rights of property and on the conditions of bourgeois production; by means of measures, therefore, which appear economically insufficient and untenable, but which, in the course of the movement, outstrip themselves, necessitate further inroads upon the old social order, and are unavoidable as a means of entirely revolutionizing the mode of production.

These measures will of course be different in different countries.

Nevertheless, in the most advanced countries the following will be pretty generally applicable:

1. Abolition of property in land and application of all rents of land to public purposes.

2. A heavy progressive or graduated income tax.
3. Abolition of all right of inheritance.
4. Confiscation of the property of all emigrants and rebels.
5. Centralization of credit in the hands of the state, by means of a national bank with state capital and an exclusive monopoly.
6. Centralization of the means of communication and transport in the hands of the state.
7. Extension of factories and instruments of production owned by the state; the bringing into cultivation of wastelands, and the improvement of the soil generally in accordance with a common plan.
8. Equal liability of all to labor. Establishment of industrial armies, especially for agriculture.
9. Combination of agriculture with manufacturing industries; gradual abolition of the distinction between town and country, by a more equable distribution of the population over the country.
10. Free education for all children in public schools. Abolition of children's factory labor in its present form. Combination of education with industrial production, etc.

When, in the course of development, class distinctions have disappeared and all production has been concentrated in the hands of a vast association of the whole nation, the public power will lose its political character. Political power, properly so called, is merely the organized power of one class for oppressing another. If the proletariat during its contest with the bourgeoisie is compelled, by the force of circumstances, to organize itself as a class, if, by means of a revolution, it makes itself the ruling class and, as such, sweeps away by force the old conditions of production, then it will, along with these conditions, have swept away the conditions for the existence of class antagonisms and of classes generally, and will thereby have abolished its own supremacy as a class.

In place of the old bourgeois society, with its classes and class antagonisms, we shall have an association in which the free development of each is the condition for the free development of all.

## *IV. Position of the Communists in Relation to the Various Existing Opposition Parties*

Section II has made clear the relations of the communists to the existing working-class parties, such as the Chartists in England and the agrarian reformers in America.

The communists fight for the attainment of the immediate aims, for the enforcement of the monetary interests of the working class, but in the movement of the present they also represent and take care of the future of that movement. In France the communists ally themselves with the social democrats, against the conservative and radical bourgeoisie, reserving, however, the right to take up a critical position in regard to phrases and illusions traditionally handed down from the Great Revolution.

In Switzerland they support the radicals, without losing sight of the fact that this party consists of antagonistic elements, partly of democratic socialists, in the French sense, partly of radical bourgeois.

In Poland they support the party that insists on an agrarian revolution as the prime condition for national emancipation, that party which fomented the insurrection of Cracow in 1846.

In Germany they fight with the bourgeoisie whenever it acts in a revolutionary way, against the absolute monarchy, the feudal squirearchy, and the petty bourgeoisie.

But they never cease, for a single instant, to instill into the working class the clearest possible recognition of the hostile antagonism between the bourgeoisie and proletariat, in order that the German workers may straightway use, as so many weapons against the bourgeoisie, the social and political conditions that the bourgeoisie must necessarily introduce along with its supremacy, and in order that, after the fall of the reactionary classes in Germany, the fight against the bourgeoisie itself may immediately begin.

The communists turn their attention chiefly to Germany, because that country is on the eve of a bourgeois revolution that is bound to be carried out under more advanced conditions of European civilization, and with a much more developed proletariat, than that of England was in the seventeenth and of France in the eighteenth century, and because the bourgeois revolution in Germany will be but the prelude to an immediately following proletarian revolution.

In short, the communists everywhere support every revolutionary movement against the existing social and political order of things.

In all these movements they bring to the front, as the leading question in each, the property question, no matter what its degree of development at the time.

Finally, they labor everywhere for the union and agreement of the democratic parties of all countries.

The communists disdain to conceal their views and aims. They openly declare that their ends can be attained only by the forcible overthrow of all existing social conditions. Let the ruling classes tremble at a communistic revolution. The proletarians have nothing to lose but their chains. They have a world to win.

---

# WORKINGMEN OF ALL COUNTRIES, UNITE!

# A CONTRIBUTION TO THE CRITIQUE OF POLITICAL ECONOMY

*by Karl Marx*

... The general conclusion at which I arrived and which, once reached, continued to serve as the leading thread in my studies may be briefly summed up as follows: In the social production which men carry on they enter into definite relations that are indispensable and independent of their will; these relations of production correspond to a definite stage of development of their material powers of production. The sum total of these relations of production constitutes the economic structure of society—the real foundation, on which rise legal and political superstructures and to which correspond definite forms of social consciousness. The mode of production in material life determines the general character of the social, political, and spiritual processes of life. It is not the consciousness of men that determines their existence, but, on the contrary, their social existence determines their consciousness. At a certain stage of their development the material forces of production in society come into conflict with the existing relations of production, or—what is but a legal expression for the same thing—with the property relations within which they had been at work before. From forms of development of the forces of production these relations turn into their fetters. Then comes the period of social revolution. With the change of the economic foundation the entire immense superstructure is more or less rapidly transformed. In considering such transformations the distinction should always be made between the material transformation of the economic conditions of production, which can be determined with the precision of natural science, and the legal, political, religious, aesthetic, or philosophic—in short, ideological—forms in which men become conscious of this conflict and fight it out. Just as our opinion of an individual is not based on what he thinks of himself, so can we not judge such a period of transformation by its own consciousness; on the contrary, this consciousness must rather be explained from the contradictions of material life, from the existing conflict between the social forces of production and the relations of production. No social order ever disappears before all the productive forces for which there is room in it have been developed, and new, higher relations of production never appear before the material conditions of their existence have matured in the womb of the old society. Therefore mankind always takes up only such problems as it can solve, since, looking at the matter more closely, we will always find that the problem itself arises only when the material conditions necessary for its solution already exist or are at least in the process of formation. In broad outlines we can designate the Asiatic, the ancient, the feudal, and the modern bourgeois methods of production as so many epochs in the progress of the economic formation of society. The bourgeois relations of production are the last antagonistic form of the social process of production—antagonistic not in the sense of individual antagonism, but of one arising from conditions surrounding the life of individuals in society; at the same time the productive forces developing in the womb of bourgeois society create the material conditions for the solution of that antagonism. This social formation constitutes, therefore, the closing chapter of the prehistoric stage of human society....

# CAPITAL

## *by Karl Marx*

### *Commodities: Use-Value and Exchange-Value*

The wealth of those societies in which the capitalist mode of production prevails presents itself as "an immense accumulation of commodities," its unit being a single commodity. Our investigation must therefore begin with the analysis of a commodity.

A commodity is, in the first place, an object outside us, a thing that by its properties satisfies human wants of some sort or another. The nature of such wants, whether, for instance, they spring from the stomach or from fancy, makes no difference. Neither are we here concerned to know how the object satisfies these wants, whether directly as means of subsistence, or indirectly as means of production.

Every useful thing, as iron, paper, etc., may be looked at from the two points of view: of quality and quantity. It is an assemblage of many properties, and may therefore be of use in various ways. To discover the various uses of things is the work of history. So also is the establishment of socially recognized standards of measure for the quantities of these useful objects. The diversity of these measures has its origin partly in the diverse nature of the objects to be measured, partly in convention.

The utility of a thing makes it a use-value. But this utility is not a thing of air. Being limited by the physical properties of the commodity, it has no existence apart from that commodity. A commodity, such as iron, corn, or a diamond, is therefore, so far as it is a material thing, a use-value, something useful. This property of a commodity is independent of the amount of labour required to appropriate its useful qualities. When treating of use-value, we always assume we are dealing with definite quantities, such as dozens of watches, yards of linen, or tons of iron. The use-values of commodities furnish the material for a special study, that of the commercial knowledge of commodities. Use-values become a reality only by use or consumption; they also constitute the substance of all wealth, whatever may be the social form of that wealth. In the form of society we are about to consider, they are, in addition, the material depositories of exchange-value.

Exchange-value, at first sight, presents itself as a quantitative relation, as the proportion in which values in use of one sort are exchanged for those of another sort, a relation constantly changing with time and place. Hence exchange-value appears to be something accidental and purely relative, and consequently an intrinsic value, i.e. an exchange-value that is inseparably connected with, inherent in, commodities, seems a contradiction in terms. Let us consider the matter a little more closely.

A given commodity, e.g., a quarter of wheat is exchanged for x blacking, y silk, or z gold, etc.—in short, for other commodities in the most different proportions. Instead of one exchange-value, the wheat has, therefore, a great many. But since x blacking, y silk, or z gold, etc., each represent the exchange-value of one quarter of wheat, x blacking, y silk, z gold, etc., must, as exchange-values, be replaceable by each other, or equal to each other. Therefore, first: the valid exchange-values of a given commodity express something equal; secondly, exchange-value, generally, is only the mode of expression, the phenomenal form, of something contained in it, yet distinguishable from it.

Let us take two commodities, e.g., corn and iron. The proportions in which they are exchangeable, whatever those proportions may be, can always be represented by an equation in which a given quantity of corn is equated to some quantity of iron: e.g., 1 quarter corn = x cwt. iron. What does this equation tell us? It tells us that in two different things—in 1 quarter of corn and x cwt. of iron, there exists in equal quantities something common to both. The two things must therefore be equal to a third, which in itself is neither the one nor the other. Each of them, so far as it is exchange-value, must therefore be reducible to this third.

A simple geometrical illustration will make this clear. In order to calculate and compare the areas of rectilinear figures, we decompose them into triangles. But the area of the triangle itself is expressed by something totally different from its visible figure, namely, by half the product of the base into the altitude. In the same way the exchange-values of commodities must be capable of being expressed in terms of something common to them all, of which thing they represent a greater or less quantity.

This common "something" cannot be either a geometrical, a chemical, or any other natural property of commodities. Such properties claim our attention only in so far as they affect the utility of those commodities, make them use-values. But the exchange of commodities is evidently an act characterized by a total abstraction from use-value. Then one use-value is just as good as another, provided only it be present in sufficient quantity. Or, as old Barbon says, "one sort of wares is as good as another, if the values be equal. There is no difference or distinction in things of equal value.... A hundred pounds' worth of lead or iron is of as great value as one hundred pounds' worth of silver or gold." As use-values, commodities are, above all, of different qualities, but as exchange-values they are merely different quantities, and consequently do not contain an atom of use-value.

If then we leave out of consideration the use-value of commodities, they have only one common property left, that of being products of labour. But even the product of labour itself has undergone a change in our hands. If we make abstraction from its use-value, we make abstraction at the same time from the material elements and shapes that make the product a use-value; we see in it no longer a table, a house, yarn, or any other useful thing. Its existence as a material thing is put out of sight. Neither can it any longer be regarded as the product of the labour of the joiner, the mason, the spinner, or of any other definite kind of productive labour. Along with the useful qualities of the products themselves, we put out of sight both the useful character of the various kinds of labour embodied in them, and the concrete forms of that labour; there is nothing left but what is common to them all; all are reduced to one and the same sort of labour, human labour in the abstract.

Let us now consider the residue of each of these products; it consists of the same unsubstantial reality in each, a mere congelation of homogeneous human labour, of labour power expended without regard to the mode of its expenditure. All that these things now tell us is that human labour power has been expended in their production, that human labour is embodied in them. When looked at as crystals of this social substance, common to them all, they are—Values.

We have seen that when commodities are exchanged, their exchange-value manifests itself as something totally independent of their use-value. But if we abstract from their use-value, there remains their Value as defined above. Therefore, the common substance that manifests itself in the exchange-value of commodities, whenever they are exchanged, is their value. The progress of our investigation will show that exchange-value is the only form in which the value of commodities can manifest itself or be expressed. For the present, however, we have to consider the nature of value independently of this, its form.

A use-value, or useful article, therefore, has value only because human labour in the abstract has been embodied or materialized in it. How, then, is the magnitude of this value to be measured? Plainly, by the quantity of the value-creating substance, the labour, contained in the article. The quantity of labour, however, is measured by its duration, and labour time in its turn finds its standard in weeks, days, and hours.

Some people might think that if the value of a commodity is determined by the quantity of labour spent on it, the more idle and unskilful the labourer, the more valuable would his commodity be, because more time would be required in its production. The labour, however, that forms the substance of value, is homogeneous human labour, expenditure of one uniform labour power. The total labour power of society, which is embodied in the sum total of the values of all commodities produced by that society, counts here as one homogeneous mass of human labour power, composed though it be of innumerable individual units. Each of these units is the same as any other, so far as it has the character of the average labour power of society, and takes effect as such; that is, so far as it requires for producing a commodity no more time than is needed on average, no more than is socially necessary. The labour time socially necessary is that required to produce an article under the normal conditions of production, and with the average degree of skill and intensity prevalent at the time. The introduction of power-looms into England probably reduced by one-half the labour required to weave a given quantity of yarn into cloth. The hand-loom weavers, as a matter of fact, continued to require the same time as before; but for all that, the product of one hour of their labour represented after the change only half an hour's social labour, and consequently fell to one-half its former value.

We see then that that which determines the magnitude of the value of any article is the amount of labour socially necessary, or the labour time socially necessary for its production. Each individual commodity, in this connection, is to be considered as an average sample of its class. Commodities, therefore, in which equal quantities of labour are embodied, or which can be produced in the same time, have the same value. The value of one commodity is to the value of any other, as the labour time necessary for the production of the one is to that necessary for the production of the other. "As values, all commodities are only definite masses of congealed labour time."

The value of a commodity would therefore remain constant, if the labour time required for its production also remained constant. But the latter changes with every variation in the productiveness of labour. This productiveness is determined by various circumstances, among others, by the average amount of skill of the workmen, the state of science, and the degree of its practical application, the social organization of production, the extent and capabilities of the means of production, and by physical conditions. For example, the same amount of labour in favourable seasons is embodied in eight bushels of corn, and in unfavourable, only in four. The same labour extracts from rich mines more metal than from poor mines. Diamonds are of very rare occurrence on the earth's surface, and hence their discovery costs, on an average, a great deal of labour time. Consequently much labour is represented in a small compass. Jacob doubts whether gold has ever been paid for at its full value. This applies still more to diamonds. According to Eschwege, the total produce of the Brazilian diamond mines for the eighty years ending in 1823, had not realized the price of one-and-a-half years' average produce of the sugar and coffee plantations of the same country, although the diamonds cost much more labour, and therefore represented more value. With richer mines, the same quantity of labour would embody itself in more diamonds, and their value would fall. If we could succeed, at a small expenditure of labour, in converting carbon into diamonds, their value might fall below that of bricks. In general, the greater the productiveness of labour, the less is the labour time required for the production of an article, the less is the amount of labour crystallized in that article, and the less is its value; and vice versa, the less the productiveness of labour, the greater is the labour time required for the production of an article, and the greater is its value. The value of a commodity, therefore, varies directly as the quantity, and inversely as the productiveness, of the labour incorporated in it.

A thing can be a use-value, without having value. This is the case whenever its utility to man is not due to labour. Such are air, virgin soil, natural meadows, etc. A thing can be useful, and the product of human labour, without being a commodity. Whoever directly satisfies his wants with the produce of his own labour creates, indeed, use-values, but not commodities. In order to produce the latter, he must not only produce use-values, but use-values for others, social use-values. (And not only for others. The medieval peasant produced quit-rent-corn for his feudal lord and tithe-corn for his parson. But neither the quit-rent-corn nor the tithe-corn became commodities by reason of the fact that they had been produced for others. To become a commodity a product must be transferred to another, whom it will serve as a use-value, by means of an exchange.) Lastly, nothing can have value without being an object of utility. If the thing is useless, so is the labour contained in it; the labour does not count as labour, and therefore creates no value....

## The Rate of Surplus Value

... If we look at the means of production, in their relation to the creation of value, and to the variation in the quantity of value, apart from anything else, they appear simply as the material in which labour power, the value-creator, incorporates itself. Neither the nature, nor the value of this material is of any importance. The only requisite is that there be a sufficient supply to absorb the labour expended in the process of production. That supply once given, the material may rise or fall in value, or even be, as land and the sea, without any value in itself; but this will have no influence on the creation of value or on the variation in the quantity of value.

In the first place then we equate the constant capital to zero. The capital advanced is consequently reduced from c + v to v, and instead of the value of the product (c + v) + s we have now the value produced (v + s). Given the new value produced = £180, which sum consequently represents the whole labour expended during the process, then subtracting from it £90, the value of the variable capital, we have remaining £90, the amount of the surplus value. This sum of £90 or s expresses the absolute quantity of surplus value produced. The relative quantity produced, or the increase per cent of the variable capital, is determined, it is plain, by the ratio of the surplus value to the variable capital, or is expressed by s/v. In our example this ratio is 90/90, which gives an increase of 140 per cent. This relative increase in the value of the variable capital, or the relative magnitude of the surplus value, I call, "The rate of surplus value."

We have seen that the labourer, during one portion of the labour process, produces only the value of his labour power, that is, the value of his means of subsistence. Now since his work forms part of a system, based on the social division of labour, he does not directly produce the actual necessaries which he himself consumes; he produces instead a particular commodity, yarn for example, whose value is equal to the value of those necessaries or of the money with which they can be bought. The portion of his day's labour devoted to this purpose will be greater or less, in proportion to the value of the necessaries that he daily requires on an average, or, what amounts to the same thing, in proportion to the labour time required on an average to produce them. If the value of those necessaries represent on an average the expenditure of six hours' labour, the workman must on an average work for six hours to produce that value. If instead of working for the capitalist, he worked independently on his own account, he would, other things being equal, still be obliged to labour for the same number of hours, in order to produce the value of his labour power, and thereby to gain the means of subsistence necessary for his conservation or continued reproduction. But as we have seen, during that portion of his day's labour in which he produces the value of his labour power, say three shillings, he produces only an equivalent for the value of his labour power already advanced by the capitalist; the new value created only replaces the variable capital advanced. It is owing to this fact, that the production of the new value of three shillings takes the semblance of a mere reproduction. That portion of the working-day, then, during which this reproduction takes place, I call "necessary" labour time, and the labour expended during that time I call "necessary" labour. Necessary, as regards the labourer, because independent of the particular social form of his labour; necessary, as regards capital, and the world of capitalists, because on the continued existence of the labourer depends their existence also.

During the second period of the labour process, that in which his labour is no longer necessary labour, the workman, it is true, labours, expends labour power; but his labour, being no longer necessary labour, he creates no value for himself. He creates surplus value which, for the capitalist, has all the charms of a creation out of nothing. This portion of the working-day, I name surplus labour time, and to the labour expended during that time, I give the name of surplus labour. It is every bit as important, for a correct understanding of surplus value, to conceive it as a mere congelation of surplus labour time, as nothing but materialized surplus labour, as it is, for a proper comprehension of value, to conceive it as a mere congelation of so many hours of labour, as nothing but materialized labour. The essential difference between the various economic forms of society, between, for instance, a society based on slave-labour, and one based on wage-labour, lies only in the mode in which this surplus labour is in each case extracted from the actual producer, the labourer.

# FRIEDRICH NIETZSCHE

~

*Friedrich Nietzsche (1804–1900) was born into a long line of German Lutheran pastors, yet he has become most famous for his announcement that "God is dead." His father died when Friedrich was five, but he had a happy childhood in general and grew up in a comfortable household with his mother, sister, grandmother, and two maiden aunts. He went to an excellent, private boarding school and from there to the University of Bonn, where he studied theology. After a year, he switched to the study of philology and to the University of Leipzig. He had an outstanding academic career and even received an appointment in philology at the University of Basel in Switzerland before receiving his Ph.D. After ten years (1869–1879) he resigned his position, abandoned philology for philosophy, and spent the rest of his life living in various small rooms in Switzerland and Italy. Although often in poor health, he worked extremely hard writing and publishing his philosophic works. He suddenly collapsed in January 1889, apparently due to syphilis that he may have contracted during his year in Bonn. After this episode, he was incurably insane and died 11 years later.*

*While Nietzsche never wrote a work strictly in political philosophy, his views of history and philosophy are directly pertinent to political philosophy and to the study of politics in the twentieth century. His early writings are in conventional essay form, but his later philosophic works are often full of aphorisms, songs, poems, stories, and myths. Nietzsche used dramatic, literary forms in order to persuade the reader to embrace his highly original philosophy. The following works are particularly useful for students of political philosophy:* On Truth and Lie in an Extra-Moral Sense *(written in 1873 and published posthumously),* Untimely Meditations *(1873–76),* Human, All-Too-Human *(1878–79),* The Gay Science *(1882, the fifth book published in 1887),* Thus Spoke Zarathustra *(1883–85),* Beyond Good and Evil *(1886),* A Genealogy of Morals *(1887), and the* Will to Power *(1883–88 and left unfinished).*

—J.M.P.

# ON TRUTH AND LIE
# IN AN EXTRA-MORAL SENSE[1]

In some remote corner of the universe, poured out and glittering in innumerable solar systems, there once was a star on which clever animals invented knowledge. That was the haughtiest and most mendacious minute of "world history"—yet only a minute. After nature had drawn a few breaths the star grew cold, and the clever animals had to die.

One might invent such a fable and still not have illustrated sufficiently how wretched, how shadowy and flighty, how aimless and arbitrary, the human intellect appears in nature. There have been eternities when it did not exist; and when it is done for again, nothing will have happened. For this intellect has no further mission that would lead beyond human life. It is human, rather, and only its owner and producer gives it such importance, as if the world pivoted around it. But if we could communicate with the mosquito, then we would learn that it floats through the air with the same self-importance, feeling within itself the flying center of the world. There is nothing in nature so despicable or insignificant that it cannot immediately be blown up like a bag by a slight breath of this power of knowledge; and just as every porter wants an admirer, the proudest human being, the philosopher, thinks that he sees the eyes of the universe telescopically focused from all sides on his actions and thoughts.

It is strange that this should be the effect of the intellect, for after all it was given only as an aid to the most unfortunate, most delicate, most evanescent beings in order to hold them for a minute in existence, from which otherwise, without this gift, they would have every reason to flee as quickly as Lessing's son. That haughtiness which goes with knowledge and feeling, which shrouds the eyes and senses of man in a blinding fog, therefore deceives him about the value of existence by carrying in itself the most flattering evaluation of knowledge itself. Its most universal effect is deception; but even its most particular effects have something of the same character.

*On Truth and Lie in an Extra-Moral Sense,* by Friedrich Nietzsche, from *The Portable Nietzsche,* edited and translated by Walter Kaufmann. New York: The Viking Press (1954). Reprinted by permission.

[1]  [A fragment published posthumously.]

The intellect, as a means for the preservation of the individual, unfolds its chief powers in simulation; for this is the means by which the weaker, less robust individuals preserve themselves, since they are denied the chance of waging the struggle for existence with horns or the fangs of beasts of prey. In man this art of simulation reaches its peak: here deception, flattery, lying and cheating, talking behind the back, posing, living in borrowed splendor, being masked, the disguise of convention, acting a role before others and before oneself—in short, the constant fluttering around the single flame of vanity is so much the rule and the law that almost nothing is more incomprehensible than how an honest and pure urge for truth could make its appearance among men. They are deeply immersed in illusions and dream images; their eye glides only over the surface of things and sees "forms"; their feeling nowhere leads into truth, but contents itself with the reception of stimuli, playing, as it were, a game of blindman's buff on the backs of things. Moreover, man permits himself to be lied to at night, his life long, when he dreams, and his moral sense never even tries to prevent this—although men have been said to have overcome snoring by sheer will power.

What, indeed, does man know of himself! Can he even once perceive himself completely, laid out as if in an illuminated glass case? Does not nature keep much the most from him, even about his body, to spellbind and confine him in a proud, deceptive consciousness, far from the coils of the intestines, the quick current of the blood stream, and the involved tremors of the fibers? She threw away the key; and woe to the calamitous curiosity which might peer just once through a crack in the chamber of consciousness and look down, and sense that man rests upon the merciless, the greedy, the insatiable, the murderous, in the indifference of his ignorance—hanging in dreams, as it were, upon the back of a tiger. In view of this, whence in all the world comes the urge for truth?

Insofar as the individual wants to preserve himself against other individuals, in a natural state of affairs he employs the intellect mostly for simulation alone. But because man, out of need and boredom, wants to exist socially, herd-fashion, he requires a peace pact and he endeavors to banish at least the very crudest *bellum omnium contra omnes*[2] from his world. This peace pact brings with it something that looks like the first step toward the attainment of this enigmatic urge for truth. For now that is fixed which henceforth shall be "truth"; that is, a regularly valid and

---

2 ["War of all against all."]

obligatory designation of things is invented, and this linguistic legislation also furnishes the first laws of truth: for it is here that the contrast between truth and lie first originates. The liar uses the valid designations, the words, to make the unreal appear as real; he says, for example, "I am rich," when the word "poor" would be the correct designation of his situation. He abuses the fixed conventions by arbitrary changes or even by reversals of the names. When he does this in a self-serving way damaging to others, then society will no longer trust him but exclude him. Thereby men do not flee from being deceived as much as from being damaged by deception: what they hate at this stage is basically not the deception but the bad, hostile consequences of certain kinds of deceptions. In a similarly limited way man wants the truth: he desires the agreeable life-preserving consequences of truth, but he is indifferent to pure knowledge, which has no consequences; he is even hostile to possibly damaging and destructive truths. And, moreover, what about these conventions of language? Are they really the products of knowledge, of the sense of truth? Do the designations and the things coincide? Is language the adequate expression of all realities?

Only through forgetfulness can man ever achieve the illusion of possessing a "truth" in the sense just designated. If he does not wish to be satisfied with truth in the form of a tautology—that is, with empty shells—then he will forever buy illusions for truths. What is a word? The image of a nerve stimulus in sounds. But to infer from the nerve stimulus, a cause outside us, that is already the result of a false and unjustified application of the principle of reason.... The different languages, set side by side, show that what matters with words is never the truth, never an adequate expression; else there would not be so many languages. The "thing in itself" (for that is what pure truth, without consequences, would be) is quite incomprehensible to the creators of language and not at all worth aiming for. One designates only the relations of things to man, and to express them one calls on the boldest metaphors. A nerve stimulus, first transposed into an image—first metaphor. The image, in turn, imitated by a sound—second metaphor....

Let us still give special consideration to the formation of concepts. Every word immediately becomes a concept, inasmuch as it is not intended to serve as a reminder of the unique and wholly individualized original experience to which it owes its birth, but must at the same time fit innumerable, more or less similar cases—which means, strictly speaking, never equal—in other words, a lot of unequal cases. Every concept originates through our equating what is unequal. No leaf ever wholly equals another, and the concept "leaf" is formed through an arbitrary abstraction from these individual differences, through forgetting the distinctions; and now it gives rise to the idea that in nature there might be something besides the leaves which would be "leaf"—some kind of original form after which all leaves have been woven, marked, copied, colored, curled, and painted, but by unskilled hands, so that no copy turned out to be a correct, reliable, and faithful image of the original form. We call a person "honest." Why did he act so honestly today? we ask. Our answer usually sounds like this: because of his honesty. Honesty! That is to say again: the leaf is the cause of the leaves. After all, we know nothing of an essence-like quality named "honesty"; we know only numerous individualized, and thus unequal actions, which we equate by omitting the unequal and by then calling them honest actions. In the end, we distill from them a *qualitas occulta* [hidden quality] with the name of "honesty"....

What, then, is truth? A mobile army of metaphors, metonyms, and anthropomorphisms—in short, a sum of human relations, which have been enhanced, transposed, and embellished poetically and rhetorically, and which after long use seem firm, canonical, and obligatory to a people: truths are illusions about which one has forgotten that this is what they are; metaphors which are worn out and without sensuous power; coins which have lost their pictures and now matter only as metal, no longer as coins.

We still do not know where the urge for truth comes from; for as yet we have heard only of the obligation imposed by society that it should exist: to be truthful means using the customary metaphors—in moral terms: the obligation to lie according to a fixed convention, to lie herd-like in a style obligatory for all....

# THE GAY SCIENCE

## 4

**What preserves the species.** The strongest and most evil spirits have so far advanced humanity the most: they have always rekindled the drowsing passions—all ordered society puts the passions to sleep; they have always reawakened the sense of comparison, of contradiction, of joy in the new, the daring, and the untried; they force men to meet opinion with opinion, model with model. For the most part by arms, by the overthrow of boundary stones, and by offense to the pieties, but also by new religions and moralities. The same "malice" is to be found in every teacher and preacher of the new…. The new is always the *evil*, as that which wants to conquer, to overthrow the old boundary stones and the old pieties; and only the old is the good. The good men of every age are those who dig the old ideas deep down and bear fruit with them, the husbandmen of the spirit. But all land is finally exhausted, and the plow of evil must always return.

There is a fundamentally erroneous doctrine in contemporary morality, celebrated particularly in England: according to this, the judgments "good" and "evil" are condensations of the experiences concerning "expedient" and "inexpedient"; what is called good preserves the species, while what is called evil is harmful to the species. In truth, however, the evil urges are expedient and indispensable and preserve the species to as high a degree as the good ones—only their function is different.

## 7

**Something for the industrious.** … So far, everything that has given color to existence still lacks a history: or, where could one find a history of love, of avarice, of envy, of conscience, of piety, or of cruelty? Even a comparative history of law, or merely of punishment, is completely lacking so far. Has anyone yet conducted research into the different ways of dividing the day and the consequences of a regular arrangement of work, holiday, and rest? Does one know the moral effects of food? Is there a philosophy of nourishment? (The ever-renewed clamor for

---

*The Gay Science*, by Friederich Nietzsche, from *The Portable Nietzsche*, edited and translated by Walter Kaufmann. New York: The Viking Press (1954). Reprinted by permission.

and against vegetarianism is sufficient proof that there is no such philosophy as yet.) Have the experiences of living together been assembled; for example, the experiences in the monasteries? Has the dialectic of marriage and friendship been presented as yet? …

## 34

**Historia abscondita [Concealed History].** Every great human being has a retroactive force: all history is again placed in the scales for his sake, and a thousand secrets of the past crawl out of their hideouts—into *his* sun. There is no way of telling what may yet become history some day. Perhaps the past is still essentially undiscovered! So many retroactive forces are still required!

## 125

**The Madman.** Have you not heard of that madman who lit a lantern in the bright morning hours, ran to the marketplace, and cried incessantly, "I seek God! I seek God!" As many of those who do not believe in God were standing around just then, he provoked much laughter. Why, did he get lost? said one. Did he lose his way like a child? said another. Or is he hiding? Is he afraid of us? Has he gone on a voyage? or emigrated? Thus they yelled and laughed. The madman jumped into their midst and pierced them with his glances.

"Whither is God" he cried. "I shall tell you. *We have killed him*—you and I. All of us are his murderers. But how have we done this? How were we able to drink up the sea? Who gave us the sponge to wipe away the entire horizon? What did we do when we unchained this earth from its sun? Whither is it moving now? Whither are we moving now? Away from all suns? Are we not plunging continually? Backward, sideward, forward, in all directions? Is there any up or down left? Are we not straying as through an infinite nothing? Do we not feel the breath of empty space? Has it not become colder? Is not night and more night coming on all the while? Must not lanterns be lit in the morning? Do we not hear anything yet of the noise of the gravediggers who are burying God? Do we not smell anything yet of God's decomposition? Gods too decompose. God is dead. God remains dead. And we have killed him. How shall we, the murderers of all murderers, comfort ourselves? What was holiest and most powerful of all that the world has yet owned has bled to death under our knives. Who will wipe this blood off us?

What water is there for us to clean ourselves? What festivals of atonement, what sacred games shall we have to invent? Is not the greatness of this deed too great for us? Must not we ourselves become gods simply to seem worthy of it? There has never been a greater deed; and whoever will be born after us—for the sake of this deed he will be part of a higher history than all history hitherto."

Here the madman fell silent and looked again at his listeners; and they too were silent and stared at him in astonishment. At last he threw his lantern on the ground, and it broke and went out. "I come too early," he said then; "my time has not come yet. This tremendous event is still on its way, still wandering—it has not yet reached the ears of man. Lightning and thunder require time, the light of the stars requires time, deeds require time even after they are done, before they can be seen and heard. This deed is still more distant from them than the most distant stars—*and yet they have done it themselves.*"

It has been related further that on that same day the madman entered divers churches and there sang his *requiem aeternam deo* [rest eternally, Lord]. Led out and called to account, he is said to have replied each time, "What are these churches now if they are not the tombs and sepulchers of God?"

## *193*

**Kant's joke.** Kant wanted to prove in a way that would dumfound the common man that the common man was right: that was the secret joke of this soul. He wrote against the scholars in favor of the popular prejudice, but for scholars and not popularly.

## *250*

**Guilt.** Although the most acute judges of the witches, and even the witches themselves, were convinced of the guilt of witchery, the guilt nevertheless was non-existent. It is thus with all guilt.

## *283*

**Preparatory men.** I welcome all signs that a more manly, a warlike, age is about to begin, an age which, above all, will give honor to valor once again. For this age shall prepare the way for one yet higher, and it shall gather the strength which this higher age will need one day—this age which is to carry heroism into the pursuit of knowledge and *wage wars* for the sake of thoughts and their consequences. To this end we now need many preparatory valorous men who cannot leap into being out of nothing—any more than out of the sand and slime of our present civilization and metropolitanism: men who are bent on seeking for that aspect in all things which must be *overcome;* men characterized by cheerfulness, patience, unpretentiousness, and contempt for all great vanities, as well as by magnanimity in victory and forbearance regarding the small vanities of the vanquished; men possessed of keen and free judgment concerning all victors and the share of chance in every victory and every fame; men who have their own festivals, their own weekdays, their own periods of mourning, who are accustomed to command with assurance and are no less ready to obey when necessary, in both cases equally proud and serving their own cause; men who are in greater danger, more fruitful, and happier! For, believe me, the secret of the greatest fruitfulness and the greatest enjoyment of existence is: to *live dangerously!* Build your cities under Vesuvius! Send your ships into uncharted seas! Live at war with your peers and yourselves! Be robbers and conquerors, as long as you cannot be rulers and owners, you lovers of knowledge! Soon the age will be past when you could be satisfied to live like shy deer, hidden in the woods! At long last the pursuit of knowledge will reach out for its due: it will want to *rule* and *own*, and you with it!

## 285

**Excelsior!** "You will never pray again, never adore again, never again rest in endless trust; you deny yourself any stopping before ultimate wisdom, ultimate goodness, ultimate power, while unharnessing your thoughts; you have no perpetual guardian and friend for your seven solitudes; you live without a view of mountains with snow on their peaks and fire in their hearts; there is no avenger for you, no eventual improver; there is no reason anymore in what happens, no love in what will happen to you; no resting place is any longer open to your heart, where it has only to find and no longer to seek; you resist any ultimate peace, you want the eternal recurrence of war and peace. Man of renunciation, do you want to renounce all this? Who will give you the necessary strength? Nobody yet has had this strength." There is a lake which one day refused to flow off and erected a dam where it had hitherto flowed off: ever since, this lake has been rising higher and higher. Perhaps that very renunciation will also lend us the strength to bear the renunciation itself; perhaps man will rise ever higher when he once ceases to *flow out* into a god.

## *290*

**One thing is needful.** "Giving style" to one's character—a great and rare art! It is exercised by those who see all the strengths and weaknesses of their own natures and then comprehend them in an artistic plan until everything appears as art and reason and even weakness delights the eye. Here a large mass of second nature has been added; there a piece of original nature has been removed: both by long practice and daily labor. Here the ugly which could not be removed is hidden; there it has been reinterpreted and made sublime.... It will be the strong and domineering natures who enjoy their finest gaiety in such compulsion, in such constraint and perfection under a law of their own; the passion of their tremendous will relents when confronted with stylized, conquered, and serving nature; even when they have to build palaces and lay out gardens, they demur at giving nature a free hand. Conversely, it is the weak characters without power over themselves who hate the constraint of style.... They become slaves as soon as they serve; they hate to serve. Such spirits—and they may be of the first rank—are always out to interpret themselves and their environment as *free* nature—wild, arbitrary, fantastic, disorderly, astonishing; and they do well because only in this way do they please themselves. For one thing is needful: that a human being attain his satisfaction with himself—whether it be by this or by that poetry and art; only then is a human being at all tolerable to behold. Whoever is dissatisfied with himself is always ready to revenge himself therefor; we others will be his victims, if only by always having to stand his ugly sight. For the sight of the ugly makes men bad and gloomy.

## *310*

**Will and wave.** How greedily this wave approaches, as if there were some objective to be reached! How, with awe-inspiring haste, it crawls into the inmost nooks of the rocky cliff! It seems that it wants to anticipate somebody; it seems that something is hidden there, something of value, high value.

And now it comes back, a little more slowly, still quite white with excitement—is it disappointed? But already another wave is approaching, still greedier and wilder than the first, and its soul too seems to be full of secrets and the lust to dig up treasures. Thus live the waves—thus live we who will—more I shall not say.

So? You mistrust me? You are angry with me, you beautiful monsters? Are you afraid that I might betray your secret entirely? Well, then be angry with me! Raise your dangerous green bodies as high as you can! Make a wall between me and the sun—as you do now! Verily, even now nothing is left of the world but green dusk and green lightning flashes. Carry on as you please, you pranksters; roar with delight and malice—or dive again, pouring your emeralds into the deepest depths, and cast your endless white manes of foam and spray over them—everything suits me, for everything suits you so well, and I am so well disposed toward you for everything: how could I think of betraying *you!* For—heed it well!—I know you and your secret, I know your kind! You and I—are we not of one kind? You and I—do we not have *one* secret?

## 319

**As interpreters of our experiences.** A kind of honesty has been alien to all founders of religions and others like them: they have never made their experiences a matter of conscience for knowledge. "What did I really experience? What happened in me then, and around me? Was my reason bright enough? Was my will turned against all deceptions of the senses and was it courageous in its resistance to the fantastic?"—none of them has raised such questions; all the dear religious people still do not raise such questions even now: rather, they have a thirst for things that are *against reason*, and they do not want to make it too hard for themselves to satisfy it. And so they experience "miracles" and "rebirths" and hear the voices of the little angels! We, however, we others, who thirst for reason, want to look our experiences as straight in the eye as if they represented a scientific experiment, hour after hour, day after day. We ourselves want to be our experiments and guinea pigs.

## 340

**The dying Socrates.** I admire the courage and wisdom of Socrates in everything he did, said—and did not say. This mocking and enamored monster and pied piper of Athens, who made the most arrogant youths tremble and sob, was not only the wisest talker who ever lived; he was just as great in his silence....

## *341*

**The greatest stress.** How, if some day or night a demon were to sneak after you into your loneliest loneliness and say to you, "This life as you now live it and have lived it, you will have to live once more and innumerable times more; and there will be nothing new in it, but every pain and every joy and every thought and sigh and everything immeasurably small or great in your life must return to you—all in the same succession and sequence—even this spider and this moonlight between the trees, and even this moment and I myself. The eternal hourglass of existence is turned over and over, and you with it, a dust grain of dust." Would you not throw yourself down and gnash your teeth and curse the demon who spoke thus? Or did you once experience a tremendous moment when you would have answered him, "You are a god, and never have I heard anything more godly." If this thought were to gain possession of you, it would change you, as you are, or perhaps crush you. The question in each and every thing, "Do you want this once more and innumerable times more?" would weigh upon your actions as the greatest stress. Or how well disposed would you have to become to yourself and to life to *crave nothing more fervently* than this ultimate eternal confirmation and seal?

# THE GAY SCIENCE: BOOK V (1887)

## *343*

**The background of our cheerfulness.** The greatest recent event—that "God is dead," that the belief in the Christian God has ceased to be believable—is even now beginning to cast its first shadows over Europe. For the few, at least, whose eyes, whose *suspicion* in their eyes, is strong and sensitive enough for this spectacle, some sun seems to have set just now.... In the main, however, this may be said: the event itself is much too great, too distant, too far from the comprehension of the many even for the tidings of it to be thought of as having *arrived* yet, not to speak of the notion that many people might know what has really happened here, and what must collapse now that this belief has been undermined—all that was built upon it, leaned on it, grew into it; for example, our whole European morality....

Even we born guessers of riddles who are, as it were, waiting on the mountains, put there between today and tomorrow and stretched in the contradiction between today and tomorrow, we firstlings and premature births of the coming century, to whom the shadows that must soon envelop Europe really *should* have appeared by now—why is it that even we look forward to it without any real compassion for this darkening, and above all without any worry and fear for *ourselves?* Is it perhaps that we are still too deeply impressed by the first consequences of this event—and these first consequences, the consequences for *us*, are perhaps the reverse of what one might expect: not at all sad and dark, but rather like a new, scarcely describable kind of light, happiness, relief, exhilaration, encouragement, dawn? Indeed, we philosophers and "free spirits" feel as if a new dawn were shining on us when we receive the tidings that "the old god is dead"; our heart overflows with gratitude, amazement, anticipation, expectation. At last the horizon appears free again to us, even granted that it is not bright; at last our ships may venture out again, venture out to face any danger; all the daring of the lover of knowledge is permitted again; the sea, our sea, lies open again; perhaps there has never yet been such an "open sea."

## 344

**How far we too are still pious.** In science, convictions have no rights of citizenship, as is said with good reason. Only when they decide to descend to the modesty of a hypothesis, of a provisional experimental point of view, of a regulative fiction, may they be granted admission and even a certain value within the realm of knowledge—though always with the restriction that they remain under police supervision, under the police of mistrust. But does this not mean, more precisely considered, that a conviction may obtain admission to science only when it ceases to be a conviction? Would not the discipline of the scientific spirit begin with this, no longer to permit oneself any convictions? Probably that is how it is. But one must still ask whether it is not the case that, *in order that this discipline could begin*, a conviction must have been there already, and even such a commanding and unconditional one that it sacrificed all other convictions for its own sake. It is clear that science too rests on a faith; there is no science "without presuppositions." The question whether truth is needed must not only have been affirmed in advance, but affirmed to the extent that the principle, the faith, the conviction is expressed: "*nothing* is needed *more* than truth, and in relation to it everything else has only second-rate value."

This unconditional will to truth: what is it? ... What do you know in advance of the character of existence, to be able to decide whether the greater advantage is on the side of the unconditionally mistrustful or of the unconditionally trusting?

Yet if both are required, much trust *and* much mistrust: whence might science then take its unconditional faith, its conviction, on which it rests, that truth is more important than anything else, even than any other conviction? Just this conviction could not have come into being if both truth and untruth showed themselves to be continually useful, as is the case. Thus, though there undeniably exists a faith in science, it cannot owe its origin to such a utilitarian calculus but it must rather have originated *in spite* of the fact that the inutility and dangerousness of the "will to truth," of "truth at any price," are proved to it continually....

Consequently, "will to truth" does not mean "I will not let myself be deceived" but—there is no choice—"I will not deceive, not even myself": *and with this we are on the ground of morality.* For one should ask oneself carefully: "Why don't you want to deceive?" especially if it should appear—and it certainly does appear—that life depends on appearance; I mean, on error, simulation, deception, self-deception; and when life has as a matter of fact, always shown itself to be on the side of the most unscrupulous *polytropoi.* Such an intent charitably interpreted, could perhaps be a quixotism, a little enthusiastic impudence; but it could also be something worse, namely, a destructive principle, hostile to life. "Will to truth"—that might be a concealed will to death.

Thus the question "Why science?" leads back to the moral problem, "For what end any morality at all" if life, nature, and history are "not moral"? ... But one will have gathered what I am driving at, namely, that it always remains a *metaphysical faith* upon which our faith in science rests—that even we devotees of knowledge today, we godless ones and anti-metaphysicians, still take *our* fire too from the flame which a faith thousands of years old has kindled: that Christian faith, which was also Plato's faith, that God is truth, that truth is divine....

# Thus Spoke Zarathustra

## Zarathustra's Prologue

### *1*

When Zarathustra was thirty years old he left his home and the lake of his home and went into the mountains. Here he enjoyed his spirit and his solitude, and for ten years did not tire of it. But at last a change came over his heart, and one morning he rose with the dawn, stepped before the sun, and spoke to it thus:

"You great star, what would your happiness be had you not those for whom you shine?

"For ten years you have climbed to my cave: you would have tired of your light and of the journey had it not been for me and my eagle and my serpent.

"But we waited for you every morning, took your overflow from you, and blessed you for it.

"Behold, I am weary of my wisdom, like a bee that has gathered too much honey; I need hands outstretched to receive it.

"I would give away and distribute, until the wise among men find joy once again in their folly, and the poor in their riches.

"For that I must descend to the depths, as you do in the evening when you go behind the sea and still bring light to the underworld, you overrich star.

"Like you, I must *go under*—go down, as is said by man, to whom I want to descend.

"So bless me then, you quiet eye that can look even upon an all-too-great happiness without envy!

"Bless the cup that wants to overflow, that the water may flow from it golden and carry everywhere the reflection of your delight.

"Behold, this cup wants to become empty again, and Zarathustra wants to become man again."

Thus Zarathustra began to go under.

*Thus Spoke Zarathustra,* by Friedrich Nietzsche, from *The Portable Nietzsche,* edited and translated by Walter Kaufmann. New York: The Viking Press (1954). Reprinted by permission.

## 2

Zarathustra descended alone from the mountains, encountering no one. But when he came into the forest, all at once there stood before him an old man who had left his holy cottage to look for roots in the woods. And thus spoke the old man to Zarathustra:

"No stranger to me is this wanderer: many years ago he passed this way. Zarathustra he was called, but he has changed. At that time you carried your ashes to the mountains; would you now carry your fire into the valleys? Do you not fear to be punished as an arsonist?

"Yes, I recognize Zarathustra. His eyes are pure, and around his mouth there hides no disgust. Does he not walk like a dancer?

"Zarathustra has changed, Zarathustra has become a child, Zarathustra is an awakened one; what do you now want among the sleepers? You lived in your solitude as in the sea, and the sea carried you. Alas, would you now climb ashore? Alas, would you again drag your own body?"

Zarathustra answered: "I love man."

"Why," asked the saint, "did I go into the forest and the desert? Was it not because I loved man all-too-much? Now I love God; man I love not. Man is for me too imperfect a thing. Love of man would kill me."

Zarathustra answered: "Did I speak of love? I bring men a gift."

"Give them nothing!" said the saint. "Rather, take part of their load and help them to bear it—that will be best for them, if only it does you good! And if you want to give them something, give no more than alms, and let them beg for that!"

"No," answered Zarathustra. "I give no alms. For that I am not poor enough."

The saint laughed at Zarathustra and spoke thus: "Then see to it that they accept your treasures. They are suspicious of hermits and do not believe that we come with gifts. Our steps sound too lonely through the streets. And what if at night, in their beds, they hear a man walk by long before the sun has risen— they probably ask themselves, Where is the thief going?

"Do not go to man. Stay in the forest! Go rather even to the animals! Why do you not want to be as I am—a bear among bears, a bird among birds?"

"And what is the saint doing in the forest?" asked Zarathustra.

The saint answered: "I make songs and sing them; and when I make songs, I laugh, cry, and hum: thus I praise God. With singing, crying, laughing, and humming, I praise the god who is my god. But what do you bring us as a gift?"

When Zarathustra had heard these words he bade the saint farewell and said: "What could I have to give you? But let me go quickly lest I take something from you!" And thus they separated, the old one and the man, laughing as two boys laugh.

But when Zarathustra was alone he spoke thus to his heart: "Could it be possible? This old saint in the forest has not yet heard anything of this, that *God is dead!*"

## 3

When Zarathustra came into the next town, which lies on the edge of the forest, he found many people gathered together in the market place; for it had been promised that there would be a tightrope walker. And Zarathustra spoke thus to the people:

"*I teach you the overman.* Man is something that shall be overcome. What have you done to overcome him?

"All beings so far have created something beyond themselves; and do you want to be the ebb of this great flood and even go back to the beasts rather than overcome man? What is the ape to man? A laughingstock or a painful embarrassment. And man shall be just that for the overman: a laughingstock or a painful embarrassment. You have made your way from worm to man, and much in you is still worm. Once you were apes, and even now, too, man is more ape than any ape.

"Whoever is the wisest among you is also a mere conflict and cross between plant and ghost. But do I bid you become ghosts or plants?

"Behold, I teach you the overman. The overman is the meaning of the earth. Let your will say: the overman *shall be* the meaning of the earth! I beseech you, my brothers, remain *faithful to the earth,* and do not believe those who speak to you of otherworldly hopes! Poison-mixers are they, whether they know it or not. Despisers of life are they, decaying and poisoned themselves, of whom the earth is weary: so let them go.

"Once the sin against God was the greatest sin; but God died, and these sinners died with him. To sin against the earth is now the most dreadful thing, and to esteem the entrails of the unknowable higher than the meaning of the earth.

"Once the soul looked contemptuously upon the body, and then this contempt was the highest: she wanted the body meager, ghastly, and starved. Thus she hoped to escape it and the earth. Oh, this soul herself was still meager, ghastly, and starved: and cruelty was the lust of this soul. But you, too, my brothers, tell me: what does your body proclaim of your soul? Is not your soul poverty and filth and wretched contentment?

"Verily, a polluted stream is man. One must be a sea to be able to receive a polluted stream without becoming unclean. Behold, I teach you the overman: he is this sea; in him your great contempt can go under.

"What is the greatest experience you can have? It is the hour of the great contempt. The hour in which your happiness, too, arouses your disgust, and even your reason and your virtue.

"The hour when you say, 'What matters my happiness? It is poverty and filth and wretched contentment. But my happiness ought to justify existence itself.'

"The hour when you say, 'What matters my reason? Does it crave knowledge as the lion his food? It is poverty and filth and wretched contentment.'

"The hour when you say, 'What matters my virtue? As yet it has not made me rage. How weary I am of my good and my evil! All that is poverty and filth and wretched contentment.'

"The hour when you say, 'What matters my justice? I do not see that I am flames and fuel. But the just are flames and fuel.'

"The hour when you say, 'What matters my pity? Is not pity the cross on which he is nailed who loves man? But my pity is no crucifixion.'

"Have you yet spoken thus? Have you yet cried thus? Oh, that I might have heard you cry thus!

"Not your sin but your thrift cries to heaven; your meanness even in your sin cries to heaven.

"Where is the lightning to lick you with its tongue? Where is the frenzy with which you should be inoculated?

"Behold, I teach you the overman: he is this lightning, he is this frenzy."

When Zarathustra had spoken thus, one of the people cried: "Now we have heard enough about the tightrope walker; now let us see him too!" And all the people laughed at Zarathustra. But the tightrope walker, believing that the word concerned him, began his performance.

## 4

Zarathustra, however, beheld the people and was amazed. Then he spoke thus:

"Man is a rope, tied between beast and overman—a rope over an abyss. A dangerous across, a dangerous on-the-way, a dangerous looking-back, a dangerous shuddering and stopping.

"What is great in man is that he is a bridge and not an end: what can be loved in man is that he is an *overture* and a *going under*.

"I love those who do not know how to live, except by going under, for they are those who cross over.

"I love the great despisers because they are the great reverers and arrows of longing for the other shore.

"I love those who do not first seek behind the stars for a reason to go under and be a sacrifice, but who sacrifice themselves for the earth, that the earth may some day become the overman's.

"I love him who lives to know, and who wants to know so that the overman may live some day. And thus he wants to go under.

"I love him who works and invents to build a house for the overman and to prepare earth, animal, and plant for him: for thus he wants to go under.

"I love him who loves his virtue, for virtue is the will to go under and an arrow of longing.

"I love him who does not hold back one drop of spirit for himself, but wants to be entirely the spirit of his virtue: thus he strides over the bridge as spirit.

"I love him who makes his virtue his addiction and his catastrophe: for his virtue's sake he wants to live on and to live no longer.

"I love him who does not want to have too many virtues. One virtue is more virtue than two, because it is more of a noose on which his catastrophe may hang.

"I love him whose soul squanders itself, who wants no thanks and returns none: for he always gives away and does not want to preserve himself.

"I love him who is abashed when the dice fall to make his fortune, and asks, 'Am I then a crooked gambler?' For he wants to perish.

"I love him who casts golden words before his deeds and always does even more than he promises: for he wants to go under.

"I love him who justifies future and redeems past generations: for he wants to perish of the present.

"I love him who chastens his god because he loves his god: for he must perish of the wrath of his god.

"I love him whose soul is deep, even in being wounded, and who can perish of a small experience: thus he goes gladly over the bridge.

"I love him whose soul is overfull so that he forgets himself, and all things are in him: thus all things spell his going under.

"I love him who has a free spirit and a free heart: thus his head is only the entrails of his heart, but his heart drives him to go under.

"I love all those who are as heavy drops, falling one by one out of the dark cloud that hangs over men: they herald the advent of lightning, and, as heralds, they perish.

"Behold, I am a herald of the lightning and a heavy drop from the cloud; but this lightning is called *overman*."

## 5

When Zarathustra had spoken these words he beheld the people again and was silent. "There they stand," he said to his heart; "there they laugh. They do not understand me; I am not the mouth for these ears. Must one smash their ears before they learn to listen with their eyes? Must one clatter like kettledrums and preachers of repentance? Or do they believe only the stammerer?

"They have something of which they are proud. What do they call that which makes them proud? Education they call it; it distinguishes them from goatherds. That is why they do not like to hear the word 'contempt' applied to them. Let me then address their pride. Let me speak to them of what is most contemptible: but that is the *last man*."

And thus spoke Zarathustra to the people: "The time has come for man to set himself a goal. The time has come for man to plant the seed of his highest hope. His soil is still rich enough. But one day this soil will be poor and domesticated, and no tall tree will be able to grow in it. Alas, the time is coming when man will no longer shoot the arrow of his longing beyond man, and the string of his bow will have forgotten how to whir!

"I say unto you: one must still have chaos in oneself to be able to give birth to a dancing star. I say unto you: you still have chaos in yourselves.

"Alas, the time is coming when man will no longer give birth to a star. Alas, the time of the most despicable man is coming, he that is no longer able to despise himself. Behold, I show you the *last man*.

"What is love? What is creation? What is longing? What is a star?' thus asks the last man, and he blinks.

"The earth has become small, and on it hops the last man, who makes everything small. His race is as ineradicable as the flea-beetle; the last man lives longest.

"'We have invented happiness,' say the last men, and they blink. They have left the regions where it was hard to live, for one needs warmth. One still loves one's neighbor and rubs against him, for one needs warmth.

"Becoming sick and harboring suspicion are sinful to them: one proceeds carefully. A fool, whoever still stumbles over stones or human beings! A little poison now and then: that makes for agreeable dreams. And much poison in the end, for an agreeable death.

"One still works, for work is a form of entertainment. But one is careful lest the entertainment be too harrowing. One no longer becomes poor or rich: both require too much exertion. Who still wants to rule? Who obey? Both require too much exertion.

"No shepherd and one herd! Everybody wants the same, everybody is the same: whoever feels different goes voluntarily into a madhouse.

"'Formerly, all the world was mad,' say the most refined, and they blink.

"One is clever and knows everything that has ever happened: so there is no end of derision. One still quarrels, but one is soon reconciled—else it might spoil the digestion.

"One has one's little pleasure for the day and one's little pleasure for the night: but one has a regard for health.

"'We have invented happiness,' say the last men, and they blink."

And here ended Zarathustra's first speech, which is also called "the Prologue"; for at this point he was interrupted by the clamor and delight of the crowd. "Give us this last man, O Zarathustra," they shouted. "Turn us into these last men! Then we shall make you a gift of the overman!" And all the people jubilated and clucked with their tongues.

But Zarathustra became sad and said to his heart: "They do not understand me: I am not the mouth for these ears. I seem to have lived too long in the mountains; I listened too much to brooks and trees: now I talk to them as to goatherds. My soul is unmoved and bright as the mountains in the morning. But they think I am cold and I jeer and make dreadful jests. And now they look at me and laugh: and as they laugh they even hate me. There is ice in their laughter."

## 6

Then something happened that made every mouth dumb and every eye rigid. For meanwhile the tight rope walker had begun his performance: he had stepped out of a small door and was walking over the rope, stretched between two towers and suspended over the marketplace and the people. When he had reached the exact middle of his course the small door opened once more and a fellow in motley clothes, looking like a jester, jumped out and followed the first one with quick steps.

"Forward, lamefoot!" he shouted in an awe-inspiring voice. "Forward, lazybones, smuggler, pale-face, or I shall tickle you with my heel! What are you doing here between towers? The tower is where you belong. You ought to be locked up; you block the way for one better than yourself." And with every word he came closer and closer; but when he was but one step behind, the dreadful thing happened which made every mouth dumb and every eye rigid: he uttered a devilish cry and jumped over the man who stood in his way. This man, however, seeing his rival win, lost his head and the rope, tossed away his pole, and plunged into the depth even faster, a whirlpool of arms and legs. The marketplace became as the sea when a tempest pierces it: the people rushed apart and over one another, especially at the place where the body must hit the ground.

Zarathustra, however, did not move; and it was right next to him that the body fell, badly maimed and disfigured, but not yet dead. After a while the shattered man recovered consciousness and saw Zarathustra kneeling beside him. "What are you doing here?" he asked at last. "I have long known that the devil would trip me. Now he will drag me to hell. Would you prevent him?"

"By my honor, friend," answered Zarathustra, "all that of which you speak does not exist: there is no devil and no hell. Your soul will be dead even before your body: fear nothing further."

The man looked up suspiciously. "If you speak the truth," he said, "I lose nothing when I lose my life. I am not much more than a beast that has been taught to dance by blows and a few meager morsels."

"By no means," said Zarathustra. "You have made danger your vocation; there is nothing contemptible in that. Now you perish of your vocation: for that I will bury you with my own hands."

When Zarathustra had said this, the dying man answered no more; but he moved his hand as if he sought Zarathustra's hand in thanks.

## 7

Meanwhile the evening came, and the marketplace hid in darkness. Then the people scattered, for even curiosity and terror grow weary. But Zarathustra sat on the ground near the dead man, and he was lost in thought, forgetting the time. At last night came, and a cold wind blew over the lonely one.

Then Zarathustra rose and said to his heart: "Verily, it is a beautiful catch of fish that Zarathustra has brought in today! Not a man has he caught but a corpse.

Human existence is uncanny and still without meaning: a jester can become man's fatality. I will teach men the meaning of their existence—the overman, the lightning out of the dark cloud of man. But I am still far from them, and my sense does not speak to their senses. To men I am still the mean between a fool and a corpse.

"Dark is the night, dark are Zarathustra's ways. Come, cold, stiff companion! I shall carry you where I may bury you with my own hands."

## 8

When Zarathustra had said this to his heart he hoisted the corpse on his back and started on his way. And he had not taken a hundred steps when a man sneaked up to him and whispered in his ear—and behold, it was the jester from the tower. "Go away from this town, Zarathustra," said he; "there are too many here who hate you. You are hated by the good and the just, and they call you their enemy and despiser; you are hated by the believers in the true faith, and they call you the danger of the multitude. It was your good fortune that you were laughed at; and verily, you talked like a jester. It was your good fortune that you stooped to the dead dog; when you lowered yourself so far, you saved your own life for today. But go away from this town, or tomorrow I shall leap over you, one living over one dead." And when he had said this the man vanished; but Zarathustra went on through the dark lanes.

At the gate of the town he met the gravediggers; they shone their torches in his face, recognized Zarathustra, and mocked him. "Zarathustra carries off the dead dog: how nice that Zarathustra has become a gravedigger! For our hands are too clean for this roast. Would Zarathustra steal this bite from the devil? Well then, we wish you a good meal. If only the devil were not a better thief than Zarathustra: he will steal them both, he will gobble up both." And they laughed and put their heads together.

Zarathustra never said a word and went his way. When he had walked two hours, past forests and swamps, he heard so much of the hungry howling of the wolves that he himself felt hungry. So he stopped at a lonely house in which a light was burning.

"Like a robber, hunger overtakes me," said Zarathustra. "In forests and swamps my hunger overtakes me, and in the deep of night. My hunger is certainly capricious: often it comes to me only after a meal, and today it did not come all day; where could it have been?"

And at that Zarathustra knocked at the door of the house. An old man appeared, carrying the light, and asked: "Who is it that comes to me and to my bad sleep?"

"A living and a dead man," said Zarathustra. "Give me something to eat and to drink; I forgot about it during the day. He who feeds the hungry refreshes his own soul: thus speaks wisdom."

The old man went away, but returned shortly and offered Zarathustra bread and wine. "This is an evil region for the hungry," he said; "that is why I live here. Beast and man come to me, the hermit. But bid your companion, too, eat and drink; he is wearier than you are."

Zarathustra replied: "My companion is dead; I should hardly be able to persuade him."

"I don't care," said the old man peevishly. "Whoever knocks at my door must also take what I offer. Eat and be off!"

Thereupon Zarathustra walked another two hours, trusting the path and the light of the stars; for he was used to walking at night and he liked to look in the face of all that slept. But when the dawn came Zarathustra found himself in a deep forest, and he did not see a path anywhere. So he laid the dead man into a hollow tree—for he wanted to protect him from the wolves—and he himself lay down on the ground and the moss, his head under the tree. And soon he fell asleep, his body weary but his soul unmoved.

# 9

For a long time Zarathustra slept, and not only dawn passed over his face but the morning too. At last, however, his eyes opened: amazed, Zarathustra looked into the woods and the silence; amazed, he looked into himself. Then he rose quickly, like a seafarer who suddenly sees land, and jubilated, for he saw a new truth. And thus he spoke to his heart:

"An insight has come to me: companions I need, living ones—not dead companions and corpses whom I carry with myself wherever I want to. Living companions I need, who follow me because they want to follow themselves—wherever I want.

"An insight has come to me: let Zarathustra speak not to the people but to companions. Zarathustra shall not become the shepherd and dog of a herd.

"To lure many away from the herd, for that I have come. The people and the herd shall be angry with me: Zarathustra wants to be called a robber by the shepherds.

"Shepherds, I say; but they call themselves the good and the just. Shepherds, I say; but they call themselves believers in the true faith.

"Behold the good and the just! Whom do they hate most? The man who breaks their tables of values, the breaker, the lawbreaker; yet he is the creator.

"Behold the believers of all faiths! Whom do they hate most? The man who breaks their tables of values, the breaker, the lawbreaker; yet he is the creator.

"Companions, the creator seeks, not corpses, not herds and believers. Fellow creators, the creator seeks—those who write new values on new tablets. Companions, the creator seeks, and fellow harvesters; for everything about him is ripe for the harvest. But he lacks a hundred sickles: so he plucks ears and is annoyed. Companions, the creator seeks, and such as know how to whet their sickles. Destroyers they will be called, and despisers of good and evil. But they are the harvesters and those who celebrate. Fellow creators, Zarathustra seeks, fellow harvesters and fellow celebrants: what are herds and shepherds and corpses to him?

"And you, my first companion, farewell! I buried you well in your hollow tree; I have hidden you well from the wolves. But I part from you; the time is up. Between dawn and dawn a new truth has come to me. No shepherd shall I be, nor gravedigger. Never again shall I speak to the people: for the last time have I spoken to the dead.

"I shall join the creators, the harvesters, the celebrants: I shall show them the rainbow and all the steps to the overman. To the hermits I shall sing my song, to the lonesome and the twosome; and whoever still has ears for the unheard-of—his heart shall become heavy with my happiness.

"To my goal I will go—on my own way; over those who hesitate and lag behind I shall leap. Thus let my going be their going under."

## 10

This is what Zarathustra had told his heart when the sun stood high at noon; then he looked into the air, questioning, for overhead he heard the sharp call of a bird. And behold! An eagle soared through the sky in wide circles, and on him there hung a serpent, not like prey but like a friend: for she kept herself wound around his neck.

"These are my animals," said Zarathustra and was happy in his heart. "The proudest animal under the sun and the wisest animal under the sun—they have gone out on a search. They want to determine whether Zarathustra is still alive. Verily, do I still live? I found life more dangerous among men than among animals; on dangerous paths walks Zarathustra. May my animals lead me!"

When Zarathustra had said this he recalled the words of the saint in the forest, sighed, and spoke thus to his heart: "That I might be wiser! That I might be wise through and through like my serpent! But there I ask the impossible: so I ask my pride that it always go along with my wisdom. And when my wisdom leaves me one day—alas, it loves to fly away—let my pride then fly with my folly."

Thus Zarathustra began to go under.

# THE GENEALOGY OF MORALS

## ⇥ FIRST ESSAY ⇤

## "Good and Evil," "Good and Bad"

### 2

… Now the first argument that comes ready to my hand is that the real homestead of the concept "good" is sought and located in the wrong place: the judgment "good" did *not* originate among those to whom goodness was shown. Much rather has it been the good themselves, that is, the aristocratic, the powerful, the high-stationed, the high-minded, who have felt that they themselves were good, and that their actions were good, that is to say of the first order, in contra-distinction to all the low, the low-minded, the vulgar, and the plebeian. It was out of this pathos of distance that they first arrogated the right to create values for their own profit, and to coin the names of such values: what had they to do with utility? The standpoint of utility is as alien and as inapplicable as it could possibly be, when we have to deal with so volcanic an effervescence of supreme values, creating and demarcating as they do a hierarchy within themselves: it is at this junc-ture that one arrives at an appreciation of the contrast to that tepid temperature, which is the presupposition on which every combination of worldly wisdom and every calculation of practical expediency is always based—and not for one occa-sional, not for one exceptional instance, but chronically. The pathos of nobility and distance, as I have said, the chronic and despotic *esprit de corps* and fundamental instinct of a higher dominant race coming into association with a meaner race, an "under race," this is the origin of the antithesis of good and bad.

(The masters' right of giving names goes so far that it is permissible to look upon language itself as the expression of the power of the masters: they say "this *is* that, and that," they seal finally every object and every event with a sound, and thereby at the same time take possession of it.) It is because of this origin that the word "good" is far from having any necessary connection with altruistic acts, in accordance with the superstitious belief of these moral philosophers. On

*The Genealogy of Morals*, by Friedrich Nietzsche, translated by Horace B. Samuel. From *The Philosophy of Nietzsche*, New York: The Modern Library © copyright 1927, 1954. Reprinted by permission.

the contrary, it is on the occasion of the *decay* of aristocratic values, that the antitheses between "egoistic" and "altruistic" press more and more heavily on the human conscience—it is, to use my own language, the *herd instinct* which finds in this antithesis an expression in many ways. And even then it takes a considerable time for this instinct to become sufficiently dominant, for the valuation to be inextricably dependent on this antithesis (as is the case in contemporary Europe); for today the prejudice is predominant, which, acting even now with all the intensity of an obsession and brain disease, holds that "moral," "altruistic," and "*désintéressé*" are concepts of equal value.

## 4

The guide-post which first put me on the *right* track was this question—what is the true etymological significance of the various symbols for the idea "good" which have been coined in the various languages? I then found that they all led back to *the same evolution of the same idea*—that everywhere "aristocrat," "noble" (in the social sense), is the root idea, out of which have necessarily developed "good" in the sense of "with aristocratic soul," "noble," in the sense of "with a soul of high calibre," "with a privileged soul"—a development which invariably runs parallel with that other evolution by which "vulgar," "plebeian," "low," are made to change finally into "bad."…

## 7

The reader will have already surmised with what ease the priestly mode of valuation can branch off from the knightly aristocratic mode, and then develop into the very antithesis of the latter: special impetus is given to this opposition, by every occasion when the castes of the priests and warriors confront each other with mutual jealousy and cannot agree over the prize. The knightly-aristocratic "values" are based on a careful cult of the physical, on a flowering, rich, and even effervescing healthiness, that goes considerably beyond what is necessary for maintaining life, on war, adventure, the chase, the dance, the tourney—on everything, in fact, which is contained in strong, free, and joyous action. The priestly-aristocratic mode of valuation is—we have seen—based on other hypotheses: it is bad enough for this class when it is question of war! Yet the priests are, as is notorious, *the worst enemies*—why? Because they are the weakest. Their weakness causes their hate to expand into a monstrous and sinister shape, a shape which is most crafty and most poisonous. The really great haters in the history of the world have always been priests, who are also the cleverest haters—in comparison with the cleverness of priestly revenge, every other piece of cleverness is practically negligible. Human history would be too fatuous for anything were it not for the cleverness imported into it by the weak—take at once the most important instance. All the world's efforts against the "aristocrats," the "mighty," the "masters," the "holders of power," are negligible by comparison with what has been accomplished against those classes by *the Jews*—the Jews, that priestly nation which eventually realised that the one method of effecting satisfaction on its enemies and tyrants was by means of a radical transvaluation of values, which was at the same time an act of the *cleverest revenge*. Yet the method was only appropriate to a nation of priests, to a nation of the most jealously nursed priestly revengefulness. It was the Jews who, in opposition to the aristocratic equation (good = aristocratic = beautiful = happy = loved by the gods), dared with a terrifying logic to suggest the contrary equation, and indeed to maintain with the teeth of the most profound hatred (the hatred of weakness) this contrary equation, namely, "the wretched are alone the good; the poor, the weak, the lowly, are alone the good; the suffering, the needy, the sick, the loathsome, are the only ones who are pious, the only ones who are blessed, for them alone is salvation—but you, on the other hand, you aristocrats, you men of power, you are to all eternity the evil, the horrible, the covetous, the insatiate, the godless; eternally also shall you be the unblessed, the cursed, the damned!" We know who it was who reaped the heritage of this Jewish transvaluation. In the context of the monstrous and inordinately fateful initiative which the Jews have exhibited in connection with this most fundamental of all declarations of war, I remember the passage which came to my pen on another occasion [*Beyond Good and Evil*, Aph. 195]—that it was, in fact, with the Jews that the *revolt of the slaves* begins in the sphere of morals; that revolt which has behind it a history of two millennia, and which at the present day has only moved out of our sight, because it—has achieved victory.

## 10

The revolt of the slaves in morals begins in the very principle of *resentment* becoming creative and giving birth to values—a resentment experienced by creatures who, deprived as they are of the proper outlet of action, are forced to find their compensation in an imaginary revenge. While every aristocratic morality springs from a triumphant affirmation of its own demands, the slave morality says "no" from the very outset to what is "outside itself," "different from itself," and "not itself": and this "no" is its creative deed. This volte-face of the valuing standpoint—this *inevitable* gravitation to the objective instead of back to the subjective—is typical of "resentment": the slave-morality requires as the condition of its existence an external and objective world, to employ physiological terminology, it requires objective stimuli to be capable of action at all—its action is fundamentally a reaction. The contrary is the case when we come to the aristocrat's system of values: it acts and grows spontaneously, it merely seeks its antithesis in order to pronounce a more grateful and exultant "yes" to its own self;—its negative conception, "low," "vulgar," "bad," is merely a pale late-born foil in comparison with its positive and fundamental conception (saturated as it is with life and passion), of "we aristocrats, we good ones, we beautiful ones, we happy ones."…

While the aristocratic man lived in confidence and openness with himself…, the resentful man, on the other hand, is neither sincere nor naïf, nor honest and candid with himself. His soul *squints;* his mind loves hidden crannies, tortuous paths and backdoors, everything secret appeals to him as *his* word, *his* safety, *his* balm; he is past master in silence, in not forgetting, in waiting, in provisional self-depreciation and self-abasement. A race of such *resentful* men will of necessity eventually prove more *prudent* than any aristocratic race, it will honour prudence on quite a distinct scale, as, in fact, a paramount condition of existence, while prudence among aristocratic men is apt to be tinged with a delicate flavour of luxury and refinement; so among them it plays nothing like so integral a part as that complete certainty of function of the governing *unconscious* instincts, or as indeed a certain lack of prudence, such as a vehement and valiant charge, whether against danger or the enemy, or as those ecstatic bursts of rage, love, reverence, gratitude, by which at all times noble souls have recognised each other. When the resentment of the aristocratic man manifests itself, it fulfils and exhausts itself in an immediate reaction, and consequently instills no *venom:* on the other hand, it never manifests itself at all in countless instances, when in the case of the feeble and weak it would be inevitable. An inability to take seriously for any length of time their enemies, their disasters, their *misdeeds*—that is the sign of the full strong natures who possess a superfluity of moulding plastic force, that heals completely and produces forgetfulness: a good example of this in the modern world is Mirabeau[1], who had no memory for any insults and meannesses which were practised on him, and who was only incapable of forgiving because he forgot. Such a man indeed shakes off with a shrug many a worm which would have buried itself in another; it is only in characters like these that we see the possibility (supposing, of course, that there is such a possibility in the world) of the real "*love* of one's enemies." What respect for his enemies is found, forsooth, in an aristocratic man—and such a reverence is already a bridge to love! He insists on having his enemy to himself as his distinction. He tolerates no other enemy but a man in whose character there is nothing to despise and *much* to honour! On the other hand, imagine the "enemy" as the resentful man conceives him—and it is here exactly that we see his work, his creativeness; he has conceived "the evil enemy," the "evil one," and indeed that is the root idea from which he now evolves as a contrasting and corresponding figure a "good one," himself—his very self!

## 13

… What wonder, if the suppressed and stealthily simmering passions of revenge and hatred exploit for their own advantage their belief, and indeed hold no belief with a more steadfast enthusiasm than this—"that the strong has the *option* of being weak, and the bird of prey of being a lamb." Thereby do they win for themselves the right of attributing to the birds of prey the *responsibility* for being birds of prey: when the oppressed, downtrodden, and overpowered say to themselves with the vindictive guile of weakness, "Let us be otherwise than the evil, namely, good! and good is every one who does not oppress, who hurts no one, who does not attack, who does not pay back, who hands over revenge to God, who holds himself, as we do, in hiding; who goes out of the way of evil, and demands, in short, little from life; like ourselves the patient, the meek, the just,"—yet all this, in its cold and unprejudiced interpretation, means nothing more than "once for all, the weak are weak; it is good to do *nothing for which we are not strong enough*"; but this dismal state of affairs, this prudence of the lowest order, which even insects possess (which in a great danger are fain to sham death so as to avoid doing "too much"), has, thanks to the counterfeiting and self-deception of weakness, come to masquerade in the pomp of an ascetic, mute, and expectant virtue, just as

---

[1]  [A French revolutionary and orator, who lived from 1749 to 1791. — J.M.P.]

though the *very* weakness of the weak—that is, forsooth, its *being*, its working, its whole unique inevitable inseparable reality—were a voluntary result, something wished, chosen, a deed, an act of *merit*. This kind of man finds the belief in a neutral, free-choosing "subject" *necessary* from an instinct of self-preservation, of self-assertion, in which every lie is fain to sanctify itself. The subject (or, to use popular language, the *soul*) has perhaps proved itself the best dogma in the world simply because it rendered possible to the horde of mortal, weak, and oppressed individuals of every kind, that most sublime specimen of self-deception, the interpretation of weakness as freedom, of being this, or being that, as *merit*.

## ⤍ SECOND ESSAY ⤌

## "Guilt," "Bad Conscience," and the Like

### *3*

His conscience?—One apprehends at once that the idea "conscience," which is here seen in its supreme manifestation, supreme in fact to almost the point of strangeness, should already have behind it a long history and evolution. The ability to guarantee one's self with all due pride, and also at the same time to *say yes* to one's self—that is, as has been said, a ripe fruit, but also a *late* fruit:—How long must needs this fruit hang sour and bitter on the tree! And for an even longer period there was not a glimpse of such a fruit to be had—no one had taken it on himself to promise it, although everything on the tree was quite ready for it, and everything was maturing for that very consummation. "How is a memory to be made for the man-animal? How is an impression to be so deeply fixed upon this ephemeral understanding, half dense, and half silly, upon this incarnate forgetfulness, that it will be permanently present?" As one may imagine, this primeval problem was not solved by exactly gentle answers and gentle means; perhaps there is nothing more awful and more sinister in the early history of man than his *system of mnemonics*. "Something is burnt in so as to remain in his memory: only that which never stops *hurting* remains in his memory." This is an axiom of the oldest (unfortunately also the longest) psychology in the world. It might even be said that wherever solemnity, seriousness, mystery, and gloomy colours are now found in the life of the men and of nations of the world, there is some *survival* of that horror which was once the universal concomitant of all promises, pledges, and obligations. The past, the past with all its length, depth, and hardness, wafts to us its breath, and bubbles up in us again, when we become "serious." When man thinks it necessary to make for himself a memory, he never accomplishes it without blood, tortures and sacrifice; the most dreadful sacrifices and forfeitures (among them the sacrifice of the first-born), the most loathsome mutilation (for instance, castration), the most cruel rituals of all the religious cults (for all religions are really at bottom systems of cruelty)—all these things originate from that instinct which found in pain its most potent mnemonic. In a certain sense the whole of asceticism is to be ascribed to this: certain ideas have got to be made inextinguishable, omnipresent, "fixed," with the object of hypnotising the whole nervous and intellectual system through these "fixed ideas"—and the ascetic methods and modes of life are the means of freeing those ideas from the competition of all other ideas so as to make them "unforgettable."...

...These Germans employed terrible means to make for themselves a memory, to enable them to master their rooted plebeian instincts and the brutal crudity of those instincts: think of the old German punishments, for instance, stoning (as far back as the legend, the millstone falls on the head of the guilty man), breaking on the wheel (the most original invention and speciality of the German genius in the sphere of punishment), dart-throwing, tearing, or trampling by horses ("quartering"), boiling the criminal in oil or wine (still prevalent in the fourteenth and fifteenth centuries), the highly popular flaying ("slicing into strips"), cutting the flesh out of the breast; think also of the evil-doer being besmeared with honey, and then exposed to the flies in a blazing sun. It was by the help of such images and precedents that man eventually kept in his memory five or six "I will nots" with regard to which he had already given his *promise*, so as to be able to enjoy the advantages of society—and verily with the help of this kind of memory man eventually attained "reason"! Alas! reason, seriousness, mastery over the emotions, all these gloomy, dismal things which are called reflection, all these privileges and pageantries of humanity: how dear is the price that they have exacted! How much blood and cruelty is the foundation of all "good things"!

## 4

But how is it that that other melancholy object, the consciousness of sin, the whole "bad conscience," came into the world? And it is here that we turn back to our genealogists of morals. For the second time I say—or have I not said it yet?

—that they are worth nothing. Just their own five-spans-long limited modern experience; no knowledge of the past, and no wish to know it; still less a historic instinct, a power of "second sight" (which is what is really required in this case)—and despite this to go in for the history of morals. It stands to reason that this must needs produce results which are removed from the truth by something more than a respectful distance.

Have these current genealogists of morals ever allowed themselves to have even the vaguest notion, for instance, that the cardinal moral idea of "ought"[2] originates from the very material idea of "owe"? Or that punishment developed as a *retaliation* absolutely independently of any preliminary hypothesis of the freedom or determination of the will?—And this to such an extent, that a *high* degree of civilisation was always first necessary for the animal man to begin to make those much more primitive distinctions of "intentional," "negligent," "accidental," "responsible," and their contraries, and apply them in the assessing of punishment…. Throughout the longest period of human history punishment was *never* based on the responsibility of the evil-doer for his action, and was consequently *not* based on the hypothesis that only the guilty should be punished;—on the contrary, punishment was inflicted in those days for the same reason that parents punish their children even nowadays, out of anger at an injury that they have suffered, an anger which vents itself mechanically on the author of the injury—but this anger is kept in bounds and modified through the idea that every injury has somewhere or other its *equivalent* price, and can really be paid off, even though it be by means of pain to the author. Whence is it that this ancient deep-rooted and now perhaps ineradicable idea has drawn its strength, this idea of an equivalency between injury and pain? I have already revealed its origin, in the contractual relationship between *creditor* and *ower*, that is as old as the existence of legal rights at all, and in its turn points back to the primary forms of purchase, sale, barter, and trade.

*6*

It is then in *this* sphere of the law of contract that we find the cradle of the whole moral world of the ideas of "guilt," "conscience," "duty," the "sacredness of duty,"—their commencement, like the commencement of all great things in the world, is

---

2 [The German word *schuld* means both debt and guilt. *Cp.* the English "owe" and "ought," by which I occasionally render the double meaning.— H.B.S.]

thoroughly and continuously saturated with blood. And should we not add that this world has never really lost a certain savour of blood and torture (not even in old Kant: the categorical imperative reeks of cruelty). It was in this sphere likewise that there first became formed that sinister and perhaps now indissoluble association of the ideas of "guilt" and "suffering." To put the question yet again, why can suffering be a compensation for "owing"?—Because the *infliction* of suffering produces the highest degree of happiness, because the injured party will get in exchange for his loss (including his vexation at his loss) an extraordinary counter-pleasure: the *infliction* of suffering—a *real* feast, something that, as I have said, was all the more appreciated the greater the paradox created by the rank and social status of the creditor. These observations are purely conjectural; for, apart from the painful nature of the task, it is hard to plumb such profound depths: the clumsy introduction of the idea of "revenge" as a connecting-link simply hides and obscures the view instead of rendering it clearer (revenge itself simply leads back again to the identical problem—"How can the infliction of suffering be a satisfaction?"). In my opinion it is repugnant to the delicacy, and still more to the hypocrisy of tame domestic animals (that is, modern men; that is, ourselves) to realise with all their energy the extent to which *cruelty* constituted the great joy and delight of ancient man, was an ingredient which seasoned nearly all his pleasures, and conversely the extent of the naïveté and innocence with which he manifested his need for cruelty, when he actually made as a matter of principle "disinterested malice" (or, to use Spinoza's expression, the *sympathia malevolens*) into a *normal* characteristic of man—as consequently something to which the conscience says a hearty *yes....*

## 12

A word more on the origin and end of punishment—two problems which are or ought to be kept distinct, but which unfortunately are usually lumped into one. And what tactics have our moral genealogists employed up to the present in these cases? Their inveterate naïveté. They find out some "end" in the punishment, for instance, revenge and deterrence, and then in all their innocence set this end at the beginning, as the *causa fiendi* [fiendish cause] of the punishment, and—they have done the trick. But the patching up of a history of the origin of law is the last use to which the "End in Law"[3] ought to be put. Perhaps there is

---

3  [An allusion to *Der Zweck im Recht*, by the great German jurist, Professor Ihering.]

no more pregnant principle for any kind of history than the following, which, difficult though it is to master, *should* none the less be *mastered* in every detail. —The origin of the existence of a thing and its final utility, its practical application and incorporation in a system of ends, are *toto cælo* opposed to each other—everything, anything, which exists and which prevails anywhere, will always be put to new purposes by a force superior to itself, will be commandeered afresh, will be turned and transformed to new uses; all "happening" in the organic world consists of *overpowering* and dominating, and again all overpowering and domination is a new interpretation and adjustment, which must necessarily obscure or absolutely extinguish the subsisting "meaning" and "end." The most perfect comprehension of the utility of any physiological organ (or also of a legal institution, social custom, political habit, form in art or in religious worship) does not for a minute imply any simultaneous comprehension of its origin: this may seem uncomfortable and unpalatable to the older men,—for it has been the immemorial belief that understanding the final cause or the utility of a thing, a form, an institution, means also understanding the reason for its origin: to give an example of this logic, the eye was made to see, the hand was made to grasp. So even punishment was conceived as invented with a view to punishing. But all ends and all utilities are only *signs* that a Will to Power has mastered a less powerful force, has impressed thereon out of its own self the meaning of a function....

## 13

To return to our subject, namely *punishment*, we must make consequently a double distinction: first, the relatively permanent *element*, the custom, the act, the "drama," a certain rigid sequence of methods of procedure; on the other hand, the fluid element, the meaning, the end, the expectation which is attached to the operation of such procedure.... With regard to the other element in *punishment*, its fluid element, its meaning, the idea of punishment in a very late stage of civilisation (for instance, contemporary Europe) is not content with manifesting merely one meaning, but manifests a whole synthesis "of meanings." The past general history of punishment, the history of its employment for the most diverse ends, crystallises eventually into a kind of unity, which is difficult to analyse into its parts, and which, it is necessary to emphasise, absolutely defies definition. (It is nowadays impossible to say definitely *the precise reason* for punishment: all ideas, in which a whole process is promiscuously comprehended, elude definition; it is only that which has no history, which can be defined.)...

## *16*

At this juncture I cannot avoid trying to give a tentative and provisional expression to my own hypothesis concerning the origin of the bad conscience: it is difficult to make it fully appreciated, and it requires continuous meditation, attention, and digestion. I regard the bad conscience as the serious illness which man was bound to contract under the stress of the most radical change which he has ever experienced—that change, when he found himself finally imprisoned within the pale of society and of peace.

Just like the plight of the water-animals, when they were compelled either to become land-animals or to perish, so was the plight of these half-animals, perfectly adapted as they were to the savage life of war, prowling, and adventure—suddenly all their instincts were rendered worthless and "switched off." Henceforward they had to walk on their feet—"carry themselves," whereas heretofore they had been carried by the water: a terrible heaviness oppressed them. They found themselves clumsy in obeying the simplest directions, confronted with this new and unknown world they had no longer their old guides—the regulative instincts that had led them unconsciously to safety—they were reduced, were those unhappy creatures, to thinking, inferring, calculating, putting together causes and results, reduced to that poorest and most erratic organ of theirs, their "consciousness." I do not believe there was ever in the world such a feeling of misery, such a leaden discomfort—further, those old instincts had not immediately ceased their demands! Only it was difficult and rarely possible to gratify them: speaking broadly, they were compelled to satisfy themselves by new and, as it were, hole-and-corner methods. All instincts which do not find a vent without, *turn inwards*—this is what I mean by the growing "internalisation" of man: consequently we have the first growth in man, of what subsequently was called his soul. The whole inner world, originally as thin as if it had been stretched between two layers of skin, burst apart and expanded proportionately, and obtained depth, breadth, and height, when man's external outlet became *obstructed.* These terrible bulwarks, with which the social organisation protected itself against the old instincts of freedom (punishments belong preeminently to these bulwarks), brought it about that all those instincts of wild, free, prowling man became turned backwards *against man himself.* Enmity, cruelty, the delight in persecution, in surprises, change, destruction—the turning all these instincts against their own possessors: this is the origin of the "bad conscience." It was man, who, lacking external enemies and obstacles, and imprisoned as he was in the oppressive narrowness and monotony of custom, in his own impatience lacerated, persecuted, gnawed, frightened, and ill-treated himself; it was this animal in the hands of the tamer, which beat itself against the bars of its cage; it was this being who, pining and yearning for that desert home of which it had been deprived, was compelled to create out of its own self, an adventure, a torture-chamber, a hazardous and perilous desert—it was this fool, this homesick and desperate prisoner—who invented the "bad conscience." But thereby he introduced that most grave and sinister illness, from which mankind has not yet recovered, the suffering of man from the disease called man, as the result of a violent breaking from his animal past, the result, as it were, of a spasmodic plunge into a new environment and new conditions of existence, the result of a declaration of war against the old instincts, which up to that time had been the staple of his power, his joy, his formidableness. Let us immediately add that this fact of an animal ego turning against itself, taking part against itself, produced in the world so novel, profound, unheard-of, problematic, inconsistent, and *pregnant* a phenomenon, that the aspect of the world was radically altered thereby. In sooth, only divine spectators could have appreciated the drama that then began, and whose end baffles conjecture as yet—a drama too subtle, too wonderful, too paradoxical to warrant its undergoing a nonsensical and unheeded performance on some random grotesque planet! Henceforth man is to be counted as one of the most unexpected and sensational lucky shots in the game of the "big baby" of Heracleitus, whether he be called Zeus or Chance—he awakens on his behalf the interest, excitement, hope, almost the confidence, of his being the harbinger and forerunner of something, of man being no end, but only a stage, an interlude, a bridge, a great promise.

## 17

It is primarily involved in this hypothesis of the origin of the bad conscience, that that alteration was no gradual and no voluntary alteration, and that it did not manifest itself as an organic adaptation to new conditions, but as a break, a jump, a necessity, an inevitable fate, against which there was no resistance and never a spark of resentment. And secondly, that the fitting of a hitherto unchecked and amorphous population into a fixed form, starting as it had done in an act of violence, could only be accomplished by acts of violence and nothing else—that the oldest

"State" appeared consequently as a ghastly tyranny, a grinding ruthless piece of machinery, which went on working, till this raw material of a semi-animal populace was not only thoroughly kneaded and elastic, but also *moulded.* I used the word "State"; my meaning is self-evident, namely, a herd of blonde beasts of prey, a race of conquerors and masters, which with all its war-like organisation and all its organising power pounces with its terrible claws on a population, in numbers possibly tremendously superior, but as yet formless, as yet nomad. Such is the origin of the "State." That fantastic theory that makes it begin with a contract is, I think, disposed of. He who can command, he who is a master by "nature," he who comes on the scene forceful in deed and gesture—what has he to do with contracts? Such beings defy calculation, they come like fate, without cause, reason, notice, excuse, they are there as the lightning is there, too terrible, too sudden, too convincing, too "different," to be personally even hated. Their work is an instinctive creating and impressing of forms, they are the most involuntary, unconscious artists that there are:—their appearance produces instantaneously a scheme of sovereignty which is *live,* in which the functions are partitioned and apportioned, in which above all no part is received or finds a place, until pregnant with a "meaning" in regard to the whole. They are ignorant of the meaning of guilt, responsibility, consideration, are these born organisers; in them predominates that terrible artist-egoism, that gleams like brass, and that knows itself justified to all eternity, in its work, even as a mother in her child. It is not in *them* that there grew the bad conscience, that is elementary—but it would not have grown *without them,* repulsive growth as it was, it would be missing, had not a tremendous quantity of freedom been expelled from the world by the stress of their hammer-strokes, their artist violence, or been at any rate made invisible and, as it were, *latent.* This *instinct of freedom* forced into being latent—it is already clear—this instinct of freedom forced back, trodden back, imprisoned within itself, and finally only able to find vent and relief in itself; this, only this, is the beginning of the "bad conscience."

## 24

… Man has for too long regarded his natural proclivities with an "evil eye," so that eventually they have become in his system affiliated with a bad conscience. A converse endeavour would be intrinsically feasible—but who is strong enough to attempt it?—namely, to affiliate to the "bad conscience" all those *unnatural* proclivities, all those transcendental aspirations, contrary to sense, instinct, nature, and

## → THIRD ESSAY ←

### What Is the Meaning of Ascetic Ideals?

"Careless, mocking, forceful—so does wisdom wish us: she is a woman, and never loves any one but a warrior."

*Thus Spake Zarathustra*

## 8

... We know what are the three great catch-words of the ascetic ideal: poverty, humility, chastity; and now just look closely at the life of all the great fruitful inventive spirits—you will always find again and again these three qualities up to a certain extent. *Not* for a minute, as is self-evident, as though, perchance, they were part of their virtues—what has this type of man to do with virtues—but as the most essential and natural conditions of their *best* existence, their *finest* fruitfulness. In this connection it is quite possible that their predominant intellectualism had first to curb an unruly and irritable pride, or an insolent sensualism, or that it had all its work cut out to maintain its wish for the "desert" against perhaps an inclination to luxury and dilettantism, or similarly against an extravagant liberality of heart and hand. But their intellect did effect all this, simply because it was the *dominant* instinct, which carried through its orders in the case of all the other instincts. It effects it still; if it ceased to do so, it would simply not be dominant. But there is not one iota of "virtue" in all this....

## 28

If you except the ascetic ideal, man, the *animal* man had no meaning. His existence on earth contained no end; "What is the purpose of man at all?" was a question without an answer; the *will* for man and the world was lacking; behind every great human destiny rang as a refrain a still greater "Vanity!" The ascetic ideal simply means this: that something *was lacking*, that a tremendous void encircled man —he did not know how to justify himself, to explain himself, to affirm himself, he *suffered* from the problem of his own meaning. He suffered also in other ways, he was in the main a *diseased* animal; but his problem was not suffering itself, but the lack of an answer to that crying question, "*To what purpose* do we suffer?"

Man, the bravest animal and the one most inured to suffering, does *not* repudiate suffering in itself: he *wills* it, he even seeks it out, provided that he is shown a meaning for it, a *purpose* of suffering. Not suffering, but the senselessness of suffering was the curse which till then lay spread over humanity—*and the ascetic ideal gave it a meaning!* It was up till then the only meaning; but any meaning is better than no meaning; the ascetic ideal was in that connection the *"faute de mieux" par excellence* that existed at that time. In that ideal suffering *found an explanation;* the tremendous gap seemed filled; the door to all suicidal Nihilism was closed. The explanation—there is no doubt about it—brought in its train new suffering, deeper, more penetrating, more venomous, gnawing more brutally into life: it brought all suffering under the perspective of *guilt;* but in spite of all that—man was *saved* thereby, he had a *meaning,* and from henceforth was no more like a leaf in the wind, a shuttlecock of chance, of nonsense, he could now "will" something—absolutely immaterial to what end, to what purpose, with what means he wished: *the will itself was saved*. It is absolutely impossible to disguise *what* in point of fact is made clear by every complete will that has taken its direction from the ascetic ideal: this hate of the human, and even more of the animal, and more still of the material, this horror of the senses, of reason itself, this fear of happiness and beauty, this desire to get right away from all illusion, change, growth, death, wishing and even desiring—all this means—let us have the courage to grasp it—a will for Nothingness, a will opposed to life, a repudiation of the most fundamental conditions of life, but it is and remains *a will!*—and to say at the end that which I said at the beginning—man will wish *Nothingness* rather than not wish *at all.*

# BIBLIOGRAPHY

## GENERAL READINGS

Arnhart, Larry. *Political Questions,* 2nd edition. Prospect Heights, Ill.: Waveland Press, 1993.

Ball, Terrence. *Reappraising Political Theory.* Oxford: Clarendon, 1995.

Copleston, Frederick. *A History of Philosophy,* 9 vols. New York: Doubleday, 1985.

Hallowell, John H. and Jene M. Porter. *Political Philosophy: The Search for Humanity and Order.* Scarborough: Prentice-Hall, 1997.

Hampshire-Monk. *A History of Modern Political Thought: Major Political Thinkers from Hobbes to Marx.* Oxford: Blackwell, 1992.

McDonald, Lee. *Western Political Theory: From Its Origins to the Present.* New York: Harcourt, Brace and World, 1968.

Plamenatz, John. *Man and Society,* 2 vols. New York: McGraw-Hill, 1963.

Skinner, Quentin. *The Foundation of Modern Political Thought,* 2 vols. New York: Cambridge University Press: 1978.

Strauss, Leo and Joseph Cropsey. *History of Political Philosophy,* 3rd edition. Chicago: University of Chicago Press, 1987.

Voegelin, Eric. *Order and History,* 5 vols. Baton Rouge: Louisiana State University Press, 1956-87.

Wiser, James L. *Political Philosophy: A History of the Search for Order.* Englewood Cliffs: Prentice-Hall, 1983.

Wolin, Sheldon. *Politics and Vision: Continuity and Innovation in Western Political Thought.* Boston: Little, Brown, 1960.

## PLATO

### *Translations*

Bloom, Allan, trans. With notes and an Interpretative Essay. *The Republic of Plato.* New York: Basic Books, 1968.

Grube, G.M.A., trans. *The Republic.* Indianapolis: Hackett, 1973.

————. trans. *Trial and Death of Socrates*. Indianapolis: Hackett, 1975.

Hamilton, Edith and Huntington Cairns, eds. *The Collected Dialogues of Plato*. New York: Pantheon, 1961.

Pangle, Thomas, trans. With notes and an Interpretative Essay. *The Laws of Plato*. New York: Basic Books, 1980.

### *Commentaries*

Annas, Julia. *An Introduction to Plato's Republic*. Oxford: Oxford University Press, 1981.

Barker, Ernest. *Greek Political Theory: Plato and His Predecessors*. London: Methuen & Co., 1918.

Crombie, I. M. *An Examination of Plato's Doctrines*, 2 vols. London: Methuen, 1962-3.

Craig, Leon Harold. *The War Lover: A Study of Plato's Republic*. Toronto: University of Toronto Press, 1994.

Cushman, Robert E. *Therapiea: Plato's Conception of Philosophy*. Chapel Hill: University of North Carolina Press, 1958.

Euben, Peter J. *The Tragedy of Political Theory: The Road Not Taken*. Princeton: Princeton University Press, 1990.

Friedlander, Paul. *Plato*, 3 vols. Trans. Hans Meyerhoff. Princeton: Princeton University Press, 1969.

Griswold, Jr., Charles L., ed. *Platonic Writings: Platonic Readings*. New York: Routledge, 1988.

Grube, G.M.A. *Plato's Thought*, 2nd edition. Indianapolis: Hackett, 1980.

Hall, Robert W. *Plato*. London: George Allen & Unwin, 1981.

Hare, R.M. *Plato*. New York: Oxford University Press, 1982.

Havelock, Eric A. *Preface to Plato*. Cambridge: Harvard University Press, 1963.

Irwin, Terence. *Plato's Moral Theory: The Early and Middle Dialogues*. Oxford: Clarendon, 1977.

Klosko, George. *The Development of Plato's Political Theory*. New York: Methuen, 1986.

Kraut, Richard, ed. *The Cambridge Companion to Plato*. Cambridge: Cambridge University Press, 1992.

Levinson, R. *In Defense of Plato*. Cambridge: Harvard University Press, 1953.

Melling, David J. *Understanding Plato*. Oxford: Oxford University Press, 1987.

Murdoch, Iris. *The Fire and the Sun: Why Plato Banished the Artist*. Oxford: Oxford University Press, 1977.

Nettleship, Richard Lewis. *Lectures on the Republic of Plato*. London: Macmillan, 1922.

Nussbaum, Martha C. *The Fragility of Goodness: Luck and Ethics in Greek Tragedy and Philosophy*. Cambridge: Cambridge University Press, 1986.

Ophir, Adi. *Plato's Invisible Cities: Discourse and Power in the Republic*. London: Routledge, 1991.

Popper, Karl. *The Open Society and Its Enemies*, 2 vols. London: Routledge and Kegan Paul, 1945.

Ryle, Gilbert. *Plato's Progress.* Cambridge: Cambridge University Press, 1966.

Sallis, John. *Being and Logos: The Way of Platonic Dialogue,* 2nd ed. Atlantic Highlands: Humanities Press International, 1986.

Stokes, Michael C. *Plato's Socratic Conversations: Drama and Dialectic in Three Dialogues.* Baltimore: Johns Hopkins University Press, 1986.

Strauss, Leo. *The City and Man.* Chicago: Rand McNally, 1964.

Taylor, A.E. *Plato: The Man and His Works,* 7th ed. London: Methuen, 1960.

Thorson, Thomas L., ed. *Plato: Totalitarian or Democrat?* Englewood Cliffs: Prentice-Hall, 1963.

Vlastos, Gregory, ed. *Plato: A Collection of Critical Essays,* 2 vols. Notre Dame: University of Notre Dame Press, 1978.

Voegelin, Eric. *Order and History: Plato and Aristotle,* vol. III. Baton Rouge: Louisiana State University Press, 1957.

White, Nicholas P. *A Companion to Plato's Republic.* Indianapolis: Hackett, 1979.

## Social and Political Background

Cornford, Francis M. *Before and After Socrates.* Cambridge: Cambridge University Press, 1932.

Finley, M.I. *Politics in the Ancient World.* Cambridge: Cambridge University Press, 1983.

Grene, David. *Greek Political Theory: The Image of Man in Thucydides and Plato.* Chicago: University of Chicago Press, 1965.

Guthrie, W.K.C. *Socrates.* New York: Cambridge University Press, 1971.

Hansen, Mogens H. *The Athentian Democracy in the Age of Demosthenes: Structure, Principles and Ideology.* Oxford: Blackwell, 1991.

Jaeger, Werner. *Paideia: The Ideals of Greek Culture,* 3 vols. Translated by Gilbert Highet. New York: Oxford University Press, 1939–44.

Kagan, Donald. *Pericles of Athens and the Birth of Democracy.* London: Secken and Warburg, 1990.

Kitto, H.D.F. *The Greeks.* London: Penguin Books, 1951.

Meier, Christian. *The Greek Discovery of Politics,* trans. David McLintock. Cambridge: Harvard University Press, 1990.

Ober, Josiah. *Mass and Elite in Democrataic Athens: Rhetoric, Ideology and the Power of the People.* Princeton: Princeton University Press, 1989.

Roberts, Jennifer Tolbert. *Athens on Trial: The Antidemocratic Tradition in Western Thought..* Princeton: Princeton University Press, 1994.

Sinclair, R.K. *Democracy and Participation in Athens.* Cambridge: Cambridge University Press, 1988.

Snell, Bruno. *The Discovery of the Mind: The Greek Origins of European Thought,* trans. T.G. Rosenmeyer. Oxford: Basil Blackwell, 1953.

Voegelin, Eric. *Order and History: The World of the Polis,* vol. II. Baton Rouge: Louisiana State University Press, 1957.

# ARISTOTLE

## Translations

Barker, Ernest, trans. *The Politics of Aristotle*. Oxford: Oxford University Press, 1946.

Everson, Stephen, ed. *Aristotle: The Politics*, trans. Benjamin Jowett and revised by Jonathan Barnes. Cambridge: Cambridge University Press, 1988.

Irwin, Terence, trans. *Nicomachean Ethics*. Indianapolis: Hackett, 1985.

Lord, Carnes, trans. *Aristotle: The Politics*. Chicago: University of Chicago Press, 1984.

Ross, David and revised by J.L. Ackrill and J.O. Urmson, trans. *Aristotle: The Nicomachean Ethics*. Oxford: Oxford University Press, 1980.

Thomson, J.A.K., trans. *The Ethics of Aristotle*. London: Penguin Books, 1955.

## Commentaries

Ackrill, J.L. *Aristotle the Philosopher*. Oxford: Oxford University Press, 1981.

Arnhart, Larry. *Aristotle on Political Reasoning*. DeKalb: Northern Illinois University Press, 1981.

Bambrough, Renford, ed. *New Essays on Plato and Aristotle*. London: Routledge & Kegan Paul, 1965.

Barker, Ernest. *The Political Thought of Plato and Aristotle*. New York: Dover Publications, 1959.

Barnes, Jonathan. *Aristotle*. New York: Oxford University Press, 1982.

Barnes, Jonathan, Malcolm Schofield, Richard Sorabji, eds. *Articles on Aristotle*, 4 vols. London: Duckworth, 1975–79.

Chroust, Anton-Hermann. *Aristotle*, vol. I. Notre Dame: University of Notre Dame Press, 1973.

Clark, Stephen R.L. *Aristotle's Man*. Oxford: Clarendon Press, 1975.

Cooper, John M. *Reason and Human Good in Aristotle*. Cambridge: Harvard University Press, 1975.

Grene, Marjorie. *A Portrait of Aristotle*. Chicago: University of Chicago Press, 1963.

Guthrie, W.K.C. *A History of Greek Philosophy*, vol. VI, *Aristotle: An Encounter*. Cambridge: Cambridge University Press, 1981.

Hardie, W.F.R. *Aristotle's Ethical Theory*. New York: Oxford University Press 1968.

Jaeger, Werner. *Aristotle: Fundamentals of the History of His Development*. Translated by Richard Robinson. New York: Oxford University Press, 1962.

Keyt, David and Fred D. Miller, Jr., eds. *A Companion to Aristotle's Politics*. Oxford: Blackwell, 1991.

Lloyd, G.E.R. *Aristotle: The Growth and Structure of His Thought*. Cambridge: Cambridge University Press, 1968.

Lord, Carnes. *Education and Culture in the Political Thought of Aristotle*. Ithaca: Cornell University Press, 1982.

Lord, Carnes and David K. O'Connor, eds., *Essays on the Foundations of Aristotelian Political Science*. Berkeley: University of California Press, 1991

MacIntyre, Alasdair. *After Virtue: A Study in Moral Theory*. Notre Dame: University of Notre Dame Press, 1981.

Morrall, John B. *Aristotle*. London: George Allen & Unwin, 1977.

Mulgan, R.G. *Aristotle's Political Theory*. New York: Oxford University Press, 1977.

Nichols, Mary P. *Citizens and Statesmen: A Study of Aristotle's Politics*. Lanham: Rowman and Littlefield, 1992.

Nussbaum, Martha. *The Fragility of Goodness: Luck and Ethics in Greek Tragedy and Philosophy*. Cambridge: Cambridge University Press, 1986.

Rorty, Amelie Oksenberg, ed. *Essays on Aristotle's Ethics*. Berkeley: University of California Press, 1980.

Ross, W.D. *Aristotle*, 3rd edition. London: Methuen, 1973.

Sherman, Nancy. *The Fabric of Character: Aristotle's Theory of Virtue*. Oxford: Clarendon Press, 1989.

Strauss, Leo. *The City and Man*. Chicago: Rand McNally & Co., 1964.

Veatch, Henry B. *Aristotle: A Contemporary Appreciation*. Bloomington: Indiana University Press, 1974.

Voegelin, *Order and History*, vol. III, *Plato and Aristotle*. Baton Rouge: Louisiana State University Press, 1957.

Yack, Bernard. *The Problems of a Political Animal*. Berkeley: University of California Press, 1993.

### Social and Political Background

Barker, Ernest, trans. *The Politics of Aristotle*. Oxford: Oxford University Press, 1946.

Bowra, C.M. *The Greek Experience*. New York: Mentor, 1957.

Finley, M.I. *Democracy in the Ancient World*, revised edition. New Brunswick, New Jersey: Rutgers University Press, 1985.

Hamilton, Edith. *The Greek Way*. New York: Norton, 1958.

Vernant, Jean-Pierre. *The Origins of Greek Thought*. Ithaca: Cornell University Press, 1982.

## ST. AUGUSTINE

### Translations

Bettenson, Henry, trans. *City of God*. Harmondsworth: Penguin, 1972.

Bourke, Vernon, J. ed. *The Essential Augustine*. Indianapolis: Hackett, 1974.

Oates, Whitney J., ed. *Basic Writings of Saint Augustine*, 2 vols. New York: Random House, 1948.

Paolucci, Henry, trans. *The Political Writings of St. Augustine*. Chicago: Gateway, 1962.

## *Commentaries*

Battenhouse, Roy, ed. *A Companion to St. Augustine*. New York: Oxford University Press, 1955.

Brooks, Edgar H. *The City of God and the Politics of Crisis*. New York: Oxford University Press, 1955.

Brown, Peter. *Augustine of Hippo*. New York: Dorset Press, 1987.

_____. *The Body and Society: Men, Women, and Sexual Renunciation in Early Christianity*. New York: Columbia University Press, 1988.

Chadwick, Henry. *Augustine*. Oxford: Oxford University Press, 1986.

Deane, Herbert A. *The Political and Social Ideas of St. Augustine*. New York: Columbia University Press, 1963.

Evans, G.R. *Augustine on Evil*. Cambridge: Cambridge University Press, 1983.

Gilson, Étienne. *The Christian Philosophy of St. Augustine*. New York: Random House, 1960.

Kirwan, Christopher. *Augustine*. London: Routledge, 1989.

Markus, R.A. *Augustine: A Collection of Critical Essays*. New York: Doubleday, 1972.

_____. *"Saeculum": History and Society in the Theology of Saint Augustine*. Cambridge: Cambridge University Press, 1970.

Miles, Margaret R. *Fullness of Life: Historical Foundations for a New Asceticism*. Philadelphia: Westminster Press, 1981.

Meagher, Robert. *Augustine: An Introduction*. New York: Harper & Row, 1979.

O'Donovan, Oliver. *The Problem of Self-Love in St. Augustine*. New Haven: Yale University Press, 1980.

Pelikan, Jaroslav. *The Mystery of Continuity: Time and History, Memory and Eternity in the Thought of Saint Augustine*. Charlottesville: University of Virginia, 1986.

Wetzel, James. *Augustine and the Limits of Virtue*. Cambridge: Cambridge University Press, 1992.

## *Social and Political Background*

Armstrong, A.H. *The Cambridge History of Later Greek and Early Mediaeval Philosophy*. Cambridge: Cambridge University Press, 1967.

Burns, J.H., ed. *The Cambridge History of Mediaeval Political Thought: c.350–c. 1450*. Cambridge: Cambridge University Press, 1988.

Cochrane, Charles Norris. *Christianity and Classical Culture*. New York: Oxford University Press, 1957.

Hexter, J.H. *The Judaeo-Christian Tradition*. New York: Harper & Row, 1966.

Jaeger, Werner. *Early Christianity and Greek Paideia*. New York: Oxford University Press, 1969.

MacMullen, Ramsay. *Christianizing the Roman Empire*. New Haven: Yale University Press, 1982.

Markus, R.A. *From Augustine to Gregory the Great*. London: Varkiorum Reprints, 1983.

McIlwain, Charles H. *The Growth of Political Thought in the West*. New York: Macmillan, 1932.

Randall, John Herman. *Hellenistic Ways of Deliverance and the Making of the Christian Synthesis.* New York: Columbia University Press, 1970.

Segal, Alan F. *Rebecca's Children: Judaism and Christianity in the Roman World.* Cambridge: Harvard University Press, 1986.

Voegelin, Eric. *Order and History: Israel and Revelation,* vol. 1. Baton Rouge: Louisiana State University Press, 1956.

_____. *Order and History: The Ecumenic Age,* vol. 4. Baton Rouge: Louisiana State University Press, 1974.

# ST. THOMAS AQUINAS

## Translations

Baumgarth, William B. and Richard J. Reagan, S. J., eds. *Aquinas: On Law, Morality and Politics.* Indianapolis: Hackett, 1988.

D'Entreves, A. P., ed. *Thomas Aquinas: Selected Political Writings.* New York: Barnes & Noble, 1981.

Pegis, Anton C., ed. *Basic Writings of Thomas Aquina,* 2 vols. New York: Random House, 1945.

_____, ed. *Introduction to St. Thomas Aquinas: The Summa Theologica and The Summa Contra Gentiles.* New York: Modern Library, 1948.

Phelan, Gerald B. and I. Th. Eschmann, *On Kingship, to the King of Cyprus.* Toronto: Pontifical Institute of Medieval Studies, 1949.

*The Summa Theologica of St. Thomas Aquinas,* 2nd ed. rev., 3 vols. New York: Benziger, 1947.

## Commentaries

Armstrong, R. A. *Primary and Secondary Precepts in Thomistic Natural Law Teaching.* The Hague: Martinus Nijhoff, 1966.

Chenu, Marie Dominique. *Toward Understanding Saint Thomas.* Chicago: Regnery, 1964.

Copleston, Frederick. *Aquinas.* Baltimore: Penguin, 1955.

Gilby, Thomas. *The Political Thought of Thomas Aquinas.* Chicago: University of Chicago Press, 1958.

Gilson, Étienne. *The Christian Philosophy of St. Thomas Aquinas.* New York: Hippocrene Books, 1983.

Jaffa, Harry V. *Thomism and Aristotelianism.* Chicago: University of Chicago Press, 1952.

Kenny, Anthony. *Aquinas.* New York: Hill and Wang, 1980.

Kenny, Anthony, ed. *Aquinas: A Collection of Critical Essays.* London: Macmillan, 1969.

Lonergan, Bernard. *Verbum: Word and Idea in Aquinas,* ed. David B. Burrell. Notre Dame: University of Notre Dame Press, 1967.

Maritain, Jacques. *St. Thomas Aquinas.* New York: Sheed and Ward, 1946.

McInerny, Ralph. *Ethica Thomistica: The Moral Philosophy of Thomas Aquinas.* Washington: The Catholic University of America Press, 1982.

McInerny, Ralph. *A First Glance at St. Thomas Aquinas: A Handbook for Peeping Thomists.* Notre Dame: University of Notre Dame Press, 1990.

Miles, Margaret R. *Fullness of Life: Historical Foundations for a New Asceticism.* Philadelphia: Westminster Press, 1981.

O'Connor, Daniel J. *Aquinas and Natural Law.* New York: Crowell-Collier-Macmillan, 1968.

Parel, Anthony, ed. *Calgary Aquinas Studies.* Toronto: Pontifical Institute of Medieval Studies, 1978.

Pieper, Josef. *Guide to Thomas Aquinas.* New York: Pantheon, 1962.

Regan, Richard J. *The Moral Dimension of Politics.* Oxford: Oxford University Press, 1986.

Sigmund, Paul E., ed. *St. Thomas Aquinas on Politics and Ethics.* New York: Norton, 1988.

### *Social and Political Background*

Berman, Harold J. *Law and Revolution: The Formation of the Western Legal Traditon.* Cambridge: Harvard University Press, 1983.

Black, Antony. *Political Thought in Europe, 1250-1450.* Cambridge: Cambridge University Press, 1992.

Burns, J. H. ed. *The Cambridge History of Mediaeval Political Thought, c. 350-c.1450.* Cambridge: Cambridge University Press, 1988.

Copleston, Frederick. *A History of Philosophy: Mediaeval Philosophy,* vol. II, part II; *Late Mediaeval and Renaissance Philosophy,* vol. III, part I. Garden City: Doubleday, 1962.

Geach, Peter. *The Virtues.* Cambridge: Cambridge University Press, 1977.

Haren, Michael. *Medieval Thought: The Western Intellectual Tradition from Antiquity to the Thirteenth Century.* New York: St. Martin's 1985.

Hearnshaw, F. J. C., ed. *The Social and Political Ideas of Some Great Medieval Thinkers.* New York: Barnes & Noble, 1967.

Huizinga, J. *The Waning of the Middle Ages.* New York: Anchor Books, 1954.

Knowles, David. *The Evolution of Medieval Thought.* 2nd edition, ed. D. E. Luscombe and C. N. L. Brooke. London: Longman, 1988.

Lovejoy, Arthur O. *The Great Chain of Being.* Cambridge: Harvard University Press, 1936.

MacIntyre, Alasdair. *Three Rival Versions of Moral Enquiry* . Notre Dame: University of Notre Dame Press, 1990.

Morrall, John B. *Political Thought in Medieval Times.* New York: Harper, 1958.

Murray, Alexander. *Reason and Society in the Middle Ages.* Oxford: Clarendon Press, 1985.

Pelikan, Jaroslav. *The Christian Tradition,* vol. 3, *The Growth of Medieval Theology (600-1300).* Chicago: University of Chicago Press, 1978.

Skinner, Quentin and Eckhard Kessler, Jill Kraze, eds. *The Cambridge History of Renaissance Philosophy.* Cambridge: Cambridge University Press, 1988.

Strayer, Joseph R. *On the Medieval Origins of the Modern State.* Princeton: Princeton University Press, 1979.

Tierney, Brian. *Religion, Law, and, the Growth of Constitutional Thought (1150-1650)*. Cambridge: Cambridge University Press, 1982.

Ullmann, Walter. *A History of Political Thought: The Middle Ages*. Baltimore: Penguin, 1965.

## MACHIAVELLI

### Translations

Adams, Robert M., trans. and ed. *The Prince: A New Translation, Backgrounds, Interpretations*. New York: Norton, 1992.

Bondavella, Peter and Mark Musa. *The Portable Machiavelli*. New York: Penguin, 1979.

Gilbert, Allan, trans. and ed. *Machiavelli: The Chief Works and Others*, 3 vols., Durham: Duke University Press, 1965.

Musa, Mark, trans. *The Prince*, a bilingual edition. New York: St. Martin's Press, 1964.

Ricci, Luigi, trans. and revised by E.R.P. Vincent. *The Prince and the Discourses. The Discourses,* trans. by Christian E. Detmold. New York: Modern Library, 1950.

Skinner, Quentin and Russell Price, eds. *The Prince*. Cambridge: Cambridge University Press, 1988.

Walker, Leslie J., trans. *The Discourses of Niccolò Machiavelli*, 2 vols., introduction by Cecil H. Clough, revised edition. New Haven: Yale University Press, 1975.

### Commentaries

Bock, Gisela, Quentin Skinner, Maurizio Viroli, eds. *Machiavelli and Republicanism*. Cambridge: Cambridge University Press, 1990.

Butterfield, Herbert. *The Statecraft of Machiavelli*. New York: Collier, 1962.

Chabod, Federico. *Machiavelli and the Renaissance*. New York: Harpers, 1958.

De Grazia, Sebastian. *Machiavelli in Hell*. Princeton: Princeton University Press, 1989.

Fleisher, Martin, ed. *Machiavelli and the Nature of Political Thought*. New York: Atheneum, 1972.

Garver, Eugene. *Machiavelli and the History of Prudence*. Madison: University of Wisconsin Press, 1987.

Gilbert, Allan H. *Machiavelli's Prince and Its Forerunners*. Durham: Duke University Press, 1938.

Gilbert, Felix. *Machiavelli and Guicciardini: Politics and History in Sixteenth-Century Florence*. Princeton: Princeton University Press, 1965.

Hale, J. R. *Machiavelli and Renaissance Italy*. New York: Macmillan, 1961.

Hulliung, Mark. *Citizen Machiavelli*. Princeton: Princeton University Press, 1983.

Mansfield, Harvey C., Jr. *Machiavelli's New Modes and Orders: A Study of the 'Discourses on Livy'*. Ithaca: Cornell University Press, 1979.

Parel, Anthony, ed. *The Political Calculus: Essays on Machiavelli's Philosophy*. Toronto: University of Toronto Press, 1972.

Parel, Anthony. *The Machiavellian Cosmos*. New Haven: Yale University Press, 1992.

Pitkin, Hanna Fenichel. *Fortune Is a Woman: Gender and Politics in the Thought of Niccolo Machiavelli*. Berkeley: University of California Press, 1984.

Pocock, J. G. A. *The Machiavellian Moment: Florentine Political Thought and the Atlantic Republican Tradition*. Princeton: Princeton University Press, 1975.

Rebhorn, Wayne A. *Foxes and Lions: Machiavelli's Confidence Men*. Ithaca: Cornell University Press, 1988.

Ridolfi, Roberto. *The Life of Niccolò Machiavelli*. Chicago: University of Chicago Press, 1963.

Skinner, Quentin. *Machiavelli*. Oxford: Oxford University Press, 1981.

Smith, Bruce James. *Politics and Remembrance: Republican Themes in Machiavelli, Burke, and Tocqueville*. Princeton: Princeton University Press, 1985.

Strauss, Leo. *Thoughts on Machiavelli*. Glencoe, Ill.: Free Press, 1958.

### Social and Political Background

Baron, Hans. *In Search of Florentine Civic Humanism* , vol. 2. Princeton: Princeton University Press, 1988.

Burckhardt, Jacob. *The Civilization of the Renaissance in Italy*. New York: Random House, 1954.

Kerrigan, William and Gordon Braden. *The Idea of the Renaissance*. Baltimore: The Johns Hopkins University Press, 1989.

McKnight, Stephen A. *Sacralizing the Secular: The Renaissance Origins of Morality* . Baton Rouge: Louisiana State University Press, 1989.

Meinecke, Friedrich. *Machiavellism*. Translated by Douglas Scott. London: Routledge and Kegan Paul, 1957.

Rabil, Jr., Albert. *Renaissance Humanism: Foundations, Forms, and Legacy* . Philadelphia: University of Pennsylvania Press, 1988.

Skinner, Quentin and Eckhard Kessler, eds. *The Cambridge History of Renaissance Philosophy*. Cambridge: Cambridge University Press, 1988.

Skinner, Quentin. *The Foundations of Modern Political Thought: The Renaissance,* vol. I. Cambridge: Cambridge University Press, 1978.

Viroli, Maurizo. *From Politics to Reason of State: The Acquisition and Transformation of the Language of Politics, 1250-1600*. Cambridge: Cambridge University Press, 1992.

---

# HOBBES

---

### Works

*Behemoth or The Long Parliament* , ed. Ferdinand Tönnies and introduction by Stephen Holmes. Chicago: University of Chicago Press, 1990.

*De Cive, The English Version* , ed. Howard Warrender. Oxford: Clarendon Press, 1983.

*The Elements of Law, Natural and Politic* , ed. Ferdinand Tönnies and introduction by M. Goldsmith. London: Cass, 1969.

*The English Works of Thomas Hobbes* , 11 vols. London: Bohn, 1839-1845.

*Leviathan* , ed. C. B. MacPherson. London: Penguin, 1968.

*Leviathan* , ed. Michael Oakeshott. New York: Collier, 1962.

*Leviathan* , ed. Richard Tuck. Cambridge: Cambridge University Press, 1991.

"The Life of Thomas Hobbes of Malmesbury," J. E. Parasons, Jr. and Whitney Blair, *Interpretation*, 10, 1 (January, 1982), 1-7.

*Man and Citizen* (*De Homine* and *De Cive* ), ed. Bernard Gert. Indianapolis: Hackett, 1991.

*Three Discourses of Thomas Hobbes*, ed. Noel B. Reynolds and Arlene Saxonhouse. Chicago: University of Chicago Press, 1995.

### Commentaries

Baumgold, Deborah. *Hobbes's Political Theory* . Cambridge: Cambridge University Press, 1988.

Baumrin, Bernard, ed. *Hobbes's Leviathan: Interpretation and Criticism.* Belmont: Wadsworth, 1969.

Boonin-Vail, David. *Thomas Hobbes and the Science of Moral Virtue.* Cambridge: Cambridge University Press, 1994.

Brown, Keith, ed. *Hobbes Studies.* Oxford: Blackwell, 1965.

Cranston, Maurice and Richard Peters, eds. *Hobbes and Rousseau: A Collection of Critical Essays* . Garden City: Doubleday, 1972.

Dick, Oliver Lawson, ed. *Aubrey's Brief Lives.* London: Secker and Warburg, 1949.

Dietz, Mary G., ed. *Thomas Hobbes and Political Theory* . Lawrence: University of Kansas Press, 1990.

Ewin, R. E. *Virtues and Rights: The Moral Philosophy of Thomas Hobbes* . Boulder: Westview Press, 1991.

Flathman, Richard. *Thomas Hobbes: Skepticism, Individuality, and Chastened Politics.* Newbury, Ca.: Sage, 1993.

Gauthier, David. *The Logic of Leviathan: The Moral and Political Theory of Thomas Hobbes.* Oxford: Clarendon Press, 1969.

Hampton, Jean. *Hobbes and the Social Contract Tradition.* Cambridge: Cambridge University Press, 1986.

Herbert, Gary B. *Thomas Hobbes: The Unity of Scientific and Moral Wisdom* . Vancouver: University of British Columbia Press, 1989.

Hood, F. C. *The Divine Politics of Thomas Hobbes.* Oxford: Oxford University Press, 1964.

Johnston, David. *The Rhetoric of the Leviathan: Thomas Hobbes and the Politics of Cultural Transformation* . Princeton: Princeton University Press, 1986.

Kavka, Gregory S. *Hobbesian Moral and Political Theory* . Princeton: Princeton University Press, 1986.

King, Preston, ed. *Hobbes: Critical Assessments*, 4 vols. London: Routledge, 1992.

Kraynak, Robert P. *History and Modernity in the Thought of Thomas Hobbes*. Ithaca: Cornell University Press, 1990.

Lloyd, S. A. *Ideals as Interests in Hobbes's Leviathan*. Cambridge: Cambridge University Press, 1992.

MacPherson, C. B. *The Political Theory of Possessive Individualism: Hobbes to Locke*. Oxford: Oxford University Press, 1962.

Martinich, A. P. *The Two Gods of Leviathan: Thomas Hobbes on Religion and Politics*. New York: Cambridge University Press, 1992.

McNeilly, F. S. *The Anatomy of Leviathan*. New York: St. Martin's Press, 1968.

Oakeshott, Michael. *Hobbes on Civil Association*. Oxford: Basil Blackwell, 1975.

Peters, Richard. *Hobbes*. London: Penguin, 1967.

Rapaczynski, Andrzej. *Nature and Politics: Liberalism in the Philosophies of Hobbes, Locke and Rousseau*. Ithaca: Cornell University Press, 1987.

Raphael, D. D. *Hobbes: Morals and Politics*. London: Allen & Unwin, 1977.

Rogers, G. A. J. and Alan Ryan, eds. *Perspectives on Thomas Hobbes*. Oxford: Clarendon, 1988.

Rogow, Arnold A. *Thomas Hobbes: Radical in the Service of Reaction*. New York: W. W. Norton, 1986.

Sommerville, Johann P. *Thomas Hobbes: Political Ideas in Historical Context*. New York: St. Martin's Press, 1992.

Sorell, Tom. *Hobbes*. London: Routledge & Kegan Paul, 1986.

_____, ed. *The Cambridge Companion to Hobbes*. Cambridge: Cambridge University Press, 1996.

Spragens, Jr., Thomas A. *The Politics of Motion: The World of Thomas Hobbes*. London: Croom Helm, 1973.

Strauss, Leo. *The Political Philosophy of Hobbes: Its Basis and Its Genesis*. Chicago: University of Chicago Press, 1952.

Tuck, Richard. *Hobbes*. Oxford: Oxford University Press, 1989.

Warrender, Howard. *The Political Philosophy of Hobbes: His Theory of Obligation*. Oxford: Oxford University Press, 1957.

Watkins, J. W. N. *Hobbes' System of Ideas*. London: Hutchinson, 1965.

### *Intellectual Background*

Allen, J. W. *English Political Thought, 1603-1660*. London: Methuen, 1938.

Burns, J. H., ed. *The Cambridge History of Political Thought: 1450-1700*. Cambridge: Cambridge University Press, 1991.

Butterfield, Herbert. *The Origins of Modern Science, 1300-1800*. Toronto: Clarke, Irwin & Co., 1968.

Greenleaf, W. H. *Order, Empiricism, and Politics: Two Traditions of English Political Thought, 1500-1700*. London: Oxford University Press, 1964.

Hall, A. Rupert. *The Scientific Revolution: 1500-1800.* London: Longmans, 1962.

Hill, Christopher. *Puritanism and Revolution: Studies in Interpretation of the English Revolution of the 17th Century*. London: Secker & Warburg, 1958.

Oakley, Francis. *Omnipotence, Covenant, and Order: An Excursion in the History of Ideas from Abelaard to Leibniz*. Ithaca: Cornell University Press, 1984.

Popkin, Richard. *The History of Scepticism from Erasmus to Descartes.* New York: Humanities Press, 1964.

Skinner, Quentin. *The Foundations of Modern Political Thought: The Age of Reformation,* vol. II. Cambridge: Cambridge University Press, 1978.

Tuck, Richard. *Philosophy and Government 1525-1651.* Cambridge: Cambridge University Press, 1993.

Willey, Basil. *The Seventeenth-Century Background.* New York: Columbia University Press, 1934.

---

# LOCKE

---

## Works

*An Essay Concerning Human Understanding,* ed. Peter H. Nidditch. Oxford: Clarendon Press, 1975.

*Essays on the Law of Nature,* ed. W. von Leyden. Oxford: Clarendon Press, 1954.

*A Letter Concerning Toleration,* ed. James H. Tully. Indianapolis: Hackett, 1983.

*John Locke: Political Writings,* ed. David Wootton. London: Penguin, 1993.

*Some Thoughts Concerning Education,* eds. John W. Yolton and Jean S. Yolton. Oxford: Clarendon Press, 1989.

*Two Tracts on Government,* ed. Philip Abrams. Cambridge: Cambridge University Press, 1967.

*Two Treatises of Government,* ed. Peter Laslett, 2nd edition. Cambridge: Cambridge University Press, 1967.

*The Works of John Locke,* 12th edition, 9 vols, 1824.

## Commentaries

Aaron, R. I. *John Locke,* 2nd edition. Oxford: Oxford University Press, 1955.

Andrew, Edward. *Shylock's Rights: A Grammar of Lockian Claims.* Toronto: University of Toronto Press, 1988.

Ashcraft, Richard. *Revolutionary Politics and Locke's Two Treatises of Government.* Princeton: Princeton University Press, 1986.

———. *Locke's Two Treatises of Government.* London: Allen & Unwin, 1987.

Ayers, Michael. *Locke,* 2 vols. London: Routledge, 1991.

Cox, Richard H. *Locke on Peace and War.* New York: Oxford University Press, 1960.

Cranston, Maurice. *John Locke: A Biography.* London: Longmans, 1966.

Dunn, John. *The Political Thought of John Locke: An Historical Account of the Arguments of the 'Two Treatises of Government.'* Cambridge: Cambridge University Press, 1969.

———. *Locke.* New York: Oxford University Press, 1984.

Fox-Bourne, H. R. *The Life of John Locke,* 2 vols. London: King, 1876.

Franklin, Julian H. *John Locke and the Theory of Sovereignty: Mixed Monarchy and the Right of Resistance in the Political Thought of the English Revolution.* Cambridge: Cambridge University Press, 1978.

Gough, J. W. *John Locke's Political Philosophy: Eight Studies.* Oxford: Oxford University Press, 1950.

Grant, Ruth W. *John Locke's Liberalism.* Chicago: University of Chicago Press, 1987.

Harpham, Edward J., ed. *John Locke's 'Two Treatises of Government': New Interpretations.* Lawrence: University Press of Kansas, 1992.

Lloyd Thomas, D. A. *Locke on Government.* London: Routledge, 1995.

Lowe, F. J. *Locke on Human Understanding.* New York: Routledge, 1995.

MacPherson, C. B. *The Political Theory of Possessive Individualism.* Oxford: Oxford University Press, 1962.

Marshall, John. *John Locke: Resistance, Religion and Responsibility.* Cambridge: Cambridge University Press, 1994.

Minogue, Kenneth. *The Liberal Mind.* New York: Random House, 1968.

Mitchell, Joshua. *Not by Reason Alone.* Chicago: University of Chicago Press, 1993.

Parry, Geraint. *John Locke.* London: Allen & Unwin, 1978.

Rapaczynski, Andrzej. *Nature and Politics: Liberalism in the Philosphies of Hobbes, Locke, and Rousseau.* Ithaca: Cornell University Press, 1987.

Ryan, Alan. *Property and Political Theory.* Oxford: Basil Blackwell, 1984.

Schouls, Peter A. *Reasoned Freedom: John Locke and Enlightenment.* Ithaca: Cornell University Press, 1992.

Simmons, A. John. *The Lockean Theory of Rights.* Princeton: Princeton University Press, 1992.

Strauss, Leo. *Natural Rights and History.* Chicago: University of Chicago Press, 1953.

Tarcov, Nathan. *Locke's Education for Liberty.* Chicago: University of Chicago Press, 1984.

Tully, James. *A Discourse on Property.* Cambridge: Cambridge University Press, 1980.

Vaughan, Karen I. *John Locke: Economist and Social Scientist.* Chicago: University of Chicago Press, 1980.

Wood, Neal. *John Locke and Agrarian Capitalism.* Berkelely: University of California Press, 1984.

Yolton, John M. *John Locke: An Introduction.* New York: Basil Blackwell, 1985.

———. ed. *John Locke: Problems and Perspectives.* New York: Cambridge University Press, 1968.

### Intellectual Background

Bailyn, Bernard. *The Ideological Origins of the American Revolution.* Cambridge: Belknap Press, 1967.

Burns, J. H., ed. *The Cambridge History of Political Thought: 1450-1700*. Cambridge: Cambridge University Press, 1991.

Daly, James. *Sir Robert Filmer and English Political Thought*. Toronto: University of Toronto Press, 1979.

Greenleaf, W. H. *Order, Empiricism and Politics: Two Traditions of English Political Thought*. Oxford: Oxford University Press, 1964.

Hill, Christopher. *The World Turned Upside Town: Radical Ideas During the English Revolution*. London: Temple Smith, 1972.

Laslett, Peter, ed. *Patriarcha and Other Political Works of Sir Robert Filmer*. Oxford: Blackwell, 1949.

Pangle, Thomas. *The Spirit of Modern Republicanism: The Moral Vision of the American Founders and the Philosophy of Locke*. Chicago: University of Chicago Press, 1988.

Pocock, *The Ancient Constitution and the Feudal Law*. Cambridge: Cambridge University Press, 1967.

Schochet, Gordon J. *Patriarchalism in Political Thought*. Oxford: Blackwell, 1975.

Skinner, Quentin. *The Foundations of Modern Political Thought*, vol. 2: *The Age of Reformation*. Cambridge: Cambridge University Press, 1978.

Trevelyan, G. M. *England Under the Stuarts*. London: Methuen, 1965.

Tuck, Richard. *Natural Rights Theories: Their Origins and Devlelopment*. New York: Cambridge University Press, 1979.

Zuckert, Michael P. *Natural Rights and the New Republicanism*. Princeton: Princeton University Press, 1994.

# ROUSSEAU

## *Translations*

Bloom, Allan, trans. *Politics and the Arts: Letter to M. d'Alembert on the Theater*. Ithaca: Cornell University Press, 1968.

Butterworth, Charles, trans. *The Reveries of the Solitary Walker*. New York: Harper & Row, 1979.

Cohen, J. M., trans. *The Confessions*. New York Penguin Books, 1953.

Cole, G. D. H. *Social Contract and the Discourses*, revised by J. H. Bumfitt and John C. Hall. New York: E. P. Dutton, 1973.

Cranston, Maurice. *Rousseau: The Social Contract*. Middlesex: Penguin, 1968.

Cress, Donald A., trans. *Rousseau: Basic Political Writings*. Indianapolis: Hackett, 1987.

Gourevitch, Victor. *The First and Second Discourses, Together with the Replies to Critics, and Essay on the Origin of Languages*. New York: Harper & Row, 1986.

Masters, Roger D., ed., and translated by Roger D. Masters and Judith R. Masters. *The First and Second Discourses by Jean-Jacques Rousseau*. New York: St. Martin's, 1969.

Masters, Roger D., ed., and translated by Judith R. Masters. *On the Social Contract with Geneva Manuscript and Political Economy*. New York: St. Martin's, 1978.

Masters, Roger and Christopher Kelly, eds. *Rousseau's Collected Writings*. Hanover, N.H.: University Press of New England, 1990.

Vaughn, C. E., ed. *The Political Writings of Jean Jacques Rousseau*, 2 vols. New York: John Wiley, 1962.

### *Commentaries*

Althusser, Louis. *Politics and History: Montesquieu, Rousseau, and Marx.*, trans., Ben Brester. London: Routledge, 1982.

Barnard, F. M. *Self-Direction and Political Legitimacy: Rousseau and Herder*. Oxford: Oxford University Press, 1988.

Berman, Marshall. *The Politics of Authenticity*. New York: Athenaeum, 1970.

Bloom, Allan. *Love and Friendship*. New York: Simon and Schuster, 1993.

Blum, Carol. *Rousseau and the Republic of Virtue: The Language of Politics in the French Revolution*. New York: Cornell University Press, 1986.

Cassirer, Ernst. *The Question of Jean-Jacques Rousseau*. Translated by Peter Gay. Bloomington: Indiana University Press, 1963.

Chapman, John H. *Rousseau—Totalitarian or Liberal?* New York: Columbia University Press, 1956.

Charvet, John. *The Social Problem in the Philosophy of Rousseau*. Cambridge: Cambridge University Press, 1974.

Cranston, Maurice. *Jean-Jacques: The Early Life and Work of Jean-Jacques Rousseau, 1712-1754*, vol I. New York: Norton, 1982.

_____. *The Noble Savage: Jean-Jacques Rousseau, 1754-1762*, vol. II. Chicago: University of Chicago Press, 1991.

Cranston, Maurice and Richard Peters, eds. *Hobbes and Rousseau: A Collection of Critical Essays*. Garden City: Doubleday, 1972.

Einaudi, Mario. *The Early Rousseau*. Ithaca: Cornell University Press, 1967.

Ellenburg, Stephen. *Rousseeau's Political Philosophy: An Interpretation from Within*. Ithaca: Cornell University Press, 1976.

Fralin, Richard. *Rousseau and Representation*. New York: Columbia University Press, 1978.

Gildin, Hilail. *Rousseau's Social Contract: The Design of the Argument*. Chicago: University of Chicago Press, 1983.

Grimsley, Ronald. *The Philosophy of Rousseau*. Oxford: Oxford University Press, 1969.

Guéhenno, Jean. *Jean-Jacques Rousseau, vol. I: 1712-1758; Jean-Jacques Rousseau, vol. II: 1758-1778*. Trans. John and Doreen Weightmann. London: Routledge and Kegan Paul, 1967.

Hartle, Ann. *The Modern Self in Rousseau's Confession: A Reply to St. Augustine*. Notre Dame: Notre Dame University Press, 1984.

Horowitz, Asher. *Rousseau, Nature, and History*. Toronto: University of Toronto Press, 1987.

Hulliung, Mark. *The Autocritique of Enlightenment: Rousseau and the Philosophes*. Cambridge: Harvard University Press, 1994.

Kelly, Christopher. *Rousseau's Exemplary Life: The 'Confessions' as Political Philosophy*. Ithaca: Cornell University Press, 1987.

Leigh, R. A., ed. *Rousseau after Two Hundred Years*. Cambridge: Cambridge University Press, 1982.

Levine, Andrew. *The Politics of Autonomy*. Amherst: University of Massachusetts Press, 1976.

_____. *The General Will: Rousseau, Marx, Communism*. Cambridge: Cambridge University Press, 1993.

Masters, Roger D. *The Political Philosophy of Rousseau*. Princeton: Princeton University Press, 1968.

Melzer, Arthur M. *The Natural Goodness of Man: On the System of Rousseau's Thought*. Chicago: University of Chicago Press, 1990.

Miller, James. *Rousseau: Dreamer of Democracy*. New Haven: Yale University Press, 1986.

Mitchell, Joshua. *Not by Reason Alone*. Chicago: University of Chicago Press, 1993.

Noble, Richard. *Language, Subjectivity, and Freedom in Rousseau's Moral Philosophy*. New York: Garland Publilshing, 1991.

Ragaczynski, Andrzej. *Nature and Politics: Libealism and the Philosophies of Hobbes, Locke, and Rousseau*. Ithaca: Cornell University Press, 1987.

Riley, Patrick. *The General Will Before Rousseau: The Transformation of the Divine into the Civic*. Princeton: Princeton University Press, 1986.

_____. *Will and Political Legitimacy*. Cambridge: Harvard University Press, 1982.

Schwartz, Joel. *The Sexual Politics of Jean-Jacques Rousseau*. Chicago: University of Chicago Press, 1984.

Shklar, Judith N. *Men and Citizens: A Study of Rousseau's Social Theory*. London: Cambridge University Press, 1969.

Starobinski, Jean. *Jean-Jacques Rousseau: Transparency and Obstruction*. Translated by Arthur Goldhammer. Chicago: University of Chicago Press, 1988.

Strong, Tracy B. *Jean Jacques Rousseau: The Politics of the Ordinary*. Thousand Oaks: Sage, 1994.

Trachtenberg, Zev M. *Making Citizens: Rousseau's Political Theory of Culture*. London: Routledge, 1993.

Wokler, Robert. *Rousseau*. Oxford: Oxford University Press, 1995.

### Intellectual Background

Becker, Carl L. *The Heavenly City of the Eighteenth-Century Philosophers*. New Haven: Yale University Press, 1932.

Berlin, Isaiah., ed. *The Age of Enlightenment: The Eighteenth Century Philosophers*. New York: New American Library, 1956.

_____. *Four Essays on Liberty*. New York: Oxford University Press, 1969.

Cassirer, Ernst. *The Philosophy of the Enlightenment*, trans. F. C. A. Koelin and J. P. Pettegrove. Boston: Beacon Press, 1955.

Cobban, Alfred. *In Search of Humanity: The Role of the Enlightenment in Modern History.* New York: Braziller, 1960.

Crocker, Lester, ed. *The Age of Enlightenment.* New York: Walker and Co., 1969.

Gay, Peter. *The Enlightenment: An Interpretation.* (New York: Knopf, 1966).

Havens, George. *The Age of Ideas: From Reaction to Revolution in Eighteenth Century France.* New York: Holt, 1965.

Keohane, Nannerl O. *Philosophy and the State in France.* Princeton: Princeton University Press, 1980.

Manuel, Frank E. *The Eighteenth Century Confronts the Gods.* Cambridge: Harvard University Press, 1959.

Talmon, J. L. *The Origins of Totalitarian Democracy.* New York: Praeger, 1960.

Voegelin, Eric. *From Enlightenment to Revolution,* ed. John Hallowell. Durham: Duke University Press, 1975.

Walzer, Michael. *The Revolution of the Saints.* New York: Atheneum, 1969.

Yack, Bernard. *The Longing for Total Revolution: Philosophic Sources of Social Discontent from Rousseau to Marx and Nietzsche.* Berkeley: Univesity of California Press, 1992.

# JOHN STUART MILL

## Works

*The Collected Works of John Stuart Mill,* 35 vols., ed. John M. Robson. Toronto: University of Toronto Press, 1963-91.

*John Stuart Mill: On Liberty and Other Essays,* ed. John Gray. Oxford: Oxford University Press, 1991.

*John Stuart Mill: A Selection of His Works,* ed. John M. Robson. Toronto: Macmillan, 1966.

*J. S. Mill: On Liberty and Other Writings,* ed. Stefan Collini. Cambridge: Cambridge University Press, 1989.

## Commentaries

Anschutz, R. P. *The Philosophy of J. S. Mill.* New York: Oxford University Press, 1953.

Britton, Karl. *John Stuart Mill.* London: Penguin, 1953.

Collini, Stefan and Donald Winch, John Burrow. *That Noble Science of Politics: A Study in Nineteenth-Century History.* Cambridge: Cambridge University Press, 1983.

Cowling, Maurice. *Mill and Liberalism.* New York: Cambridge University Press, 1963.

Duncan, Graham. *Marx and Mill: Two Views of Social Conflict and Social Harmony.* Cambridge: Cambridge University Press, 1973.

Halliday, R. J. *John Stuart Mill.* London: Allen & Unwin, 1976.

Hayek, F. A. *John Stuart Mill and Harriet Taylor.* London: Routledge & Kegan Paul, 1951.

Himmelfarb, Gertrude. *On Liberty and Liberalism: The Case of John Stuart Mill.* New York: Knopf, 1974.

Laine, Michael, ed. *Essays on J. S. Mill: Presented to John M. Robson.* Toronto: University of Toronto Press, 1991.

Mazlish, Bruce. *James and John Stuart Mill.* New York: Basic Books, 1975.

McCloskey, Henry J. *John Stuart Mill: A Critical Study.* London: Macmillan, 1971.

Plamenatz, John. *The English Utilitarians.* Oxford: Blackwell, 1949.

Radcliff, Peter, ed. *Limits of Liberty: Studies of Mill's 'On Liberty'.* Belmont, California: Wadsworth, 1966.

Rees, John C. *John Stuart Mill's 'On Liberty'.* Oxford: Oxford University Press, 1985.

Robson, John M. *The Improvement of Mankind: The Social and Political Thought of John Stuart Mill.* Toronto: University of Toronto Press, 1968.

Ryan, Alan. *J. S. Mill.* New York: Pantheon Books, 1970.

_____, ed. *The Idea of Freedom: Essay in Honour of Isaiah Berlin.* Oxford: Oxford University, 1979.

Schneewind, J. B., ed. *Mill: A Collection of Critical Essays.* Garden City: Anchor, 1968.

Semmel, Bernard. *John Stuart Mill and the Pursuit of Virtue.* New Haven: Yale University Press, 1984.

Stevens, James Flitzjames. *Liberty, Equality and Fraternity.* Chicago: University of Chicago Press, 1991.

Ten, C. T. *Mill on Liberty.* Oxford: Clarendon Press, 1980.

Thomas, William. *Mill.* Oxford: Oxford University Press, 1985.

Thompson, Dennis F. *John Stuart Mill and Representative Government.* Princeton: Princeton University Press, 1976.

### Intellectual Background

Berlin, Isaiah. *Four Essays on Liberty.* Oxford: Oxford University Press, 1969.

Halévy, Elie. *The Growth of Philosophic Radicalism*, trans. Mary Morris. London: Faber & Faber, 1928.

Roberts, David. *Victorian Origins of the Welfare State.* New Haven: Yale University Press, 1960.

Willey, Basil. *Nineteenth Century Studies.* London: Chaltto & Windsor, 1949.

# HEGEL

### Translations

Friedrich, C. J., ed. *The Philosophy of Hegel.* New York: Modern Library, 1953.

Loewenberg, Jacob, ed. *Hegel Selections.* New York: Scribner's, 1929.

Pelczynski, Z. A., ed. *Hegel's Political Writings.* Oxford: Oxford University Press, 1961.

Rauch, Leo, trans. *G. W. F. Hegel: Introduction to the Philosophy of History and selections from the Philosophy of Right.* Indianapolis: Hackett, 1988.

Wood, Allen W. *Elements of the Philosophy of Right*, trans. H. B. Nisbet. Cambridge: Cambridge University Press, 1991.

### Commentaries

Avineri, Shlomo. *Hegel's Theory of the Modern State.* Cambridge: Cambridge University Press, 1972.

Findlay, John N. *Hegel: A Reexamination.* London: George Allen, 1958.

Hook, Sidney. *From Hegel to Marx.* New York: Humanities Press, 1950.

Kaufmann, Walter, ed. *Hegel's Political Philosophy.* New York: Atherton, 1970.

Kelly, George A. *Idealism, Politics and History.* Cambridge: Cambridge University Press, 1969.

Löwith, Karl. *From Hegel to Nietzsche.* New York: Holt, Rinehart and Winston, 1964.

MacIntyre, Alasdair, ed. *Hegel: A Collection of Critical Essays.* Notre Dame: University of Notre Dame Press, 1976.

Pelczynski, Z., ed. *The State and Civil Society: Studies in Hegel's Political Philosophy.* Cambridge: Cambridge University Press, 1984.

Plant, Raymond. *Hegel.* New York: Basil Blackwell, 1984.

Riedel, Manfred. *Between Tradition and Revolution: The Hegelian Transformation of Political Philosophy.* Cambridge: Cambridge University Press, 1984.

Singer, Peter. *Hegel.* Oxford: Oxford University Press, 1983.

Taylor, Charles. *Hegel.* Cambridge: Cambridge University Press, 1975.

_____. *Hegel and Modern Society.* Cambridge: Cambridge University Press, 1979.

# MARX

### Works

*Grundrisse,* trans. Martin Nicolaus. New York: Vintage, 1973.

*Karl Marx: A Reader,* ed. John Elster. Cambridge: Cambridge University Press, 1986.

*Karl Marx: Early Texts,* ed. John Elster. Oxford: Oxford University Press, 1971.

*Karl Marx: Early Writings,* trans. and ed. T.B./Bottomore. New York: McGraw-Hill, 1963.

*The Marx-Engels Reader,* Tucker, Robert C., ed. New York: Norton, 1972.

*Selected Writings,* ed. David McLellan. Oxford: Oxford University Press, 1977.

### Commentaries

Althusser, Louis. *For Marx,* translated by Ben Brewster. New York: Random House, 1970.

Avineri, Shlomo. *The Social and Political Thought of Karl Marx.* New York: Cambridge University Press, 1968.

Berlin, Isaiah. *Karl Marx: His Life and Environment,* 4th edition. New York: Oxford University Press, 1963.

Bober, M. M. *Karl Marx's Interpretation of History,* 2nd edition. New York: Norton, 1948.

Carver, Terrell, ed. *The Cambridge Companion to Marx.* Cambridge: Cambridge University Press, 1991.

Cohen, G. A. *Karl Marx's Theory of History: A Defense.* Princeton: Princeton University Press, 1980.

_____. *History, Labour, and Freedom: Themes From Marx.* Oxford: Clarendon Press, 1988.

Cohen, Marshall, Thomas Nagel, and Thomas Scanlon, eds. *Marx, Justice, and History.* Princeton: Princeton University Press, 1980.

Duncan, Graeme. *Marx and Mill: Two Views of Social Conflict and Social Harmony.* Cambridge: Cambridge University Press, 1973.

Dupré, Louis. *The Philosophical Foundations of Marxism.* New York: Harcourt, 1966.

Elster, Jon. *Making Sense of Marx.* Cambridge: Cambridge University Press, 1985.

Evans, Michael. *Karl Marx.* London: Allen & Unwin, 1975.

Freedman, Robert. *The Marxist System: Economic, Political, and Social Perspectives.* Chatham: Chatham House, 1990.

Fromm, Erich. *Marx's Concept of Man.* New York: Ungar, 1961.

Giddens, Anthony. *Capitalism and Modern Social Theory: An Analysis of the Writings of Marx, Durkheim, and Max Weber.* Cambridge: Cambridge University Press, 1971.

Gould, Carol C. *Marx's Social Ontology: Individuality and Community in Marx's Theory of Social Reality.* Cambridge: MIT Press, 1980.

Heilbroner, Robert. *Marxism: For and Against.* New York: Norton, 1980.

Hook, Sidney. *From Hegel to Marx: Studies in the Intellectual Development of Karl Marx.* Ann Arbor: University of Michigan Press, 1962.

Kamenka, E. *Marxism and Ethics.* London: Macmillan, 1969.

Kolakowski, Leszek. *Main Currents of Marxism.* 3 vols. Translated by P. S. Falla. Oxford: Oxford University Press, 1978.

Lichtheim, George. *Marxism: An Historical and Critical Study.* New York: Praeger, 1965.

Lobkowicz, Nicholas, ed. *Marx and the Western World.* Notre Dame: University of Notre Dame Press, 1967.

MacIntyre, Alasdair. *Marxism and Christianity.* London: 1968.

Mandel, Ernest. *Marxist Economic Theory.* 2 vols. Translated by Brian Pearce. New York: Monthly Review Press, 1970.

Mazlish, Bruce. *The Meaning of Karl Marx.* Oxford: Oxford University Press, 1987.

McLellan, David. *Karl Marx: His Life and Thought.* New York: Harper & Row, 1973.

_____. *The Young Hegelians and Karl Marx.* London: Macmillan, 1969.

_____. *Marx before Marxism.* New York: Harper & Row, 1970.

McMurtry, John. *The Structure of Marx's World-View.* Princeton: Princeton University Press, 1978.

Meszaros, Istvan. *Marx's Theory of Alienation.* New York: Harper & Row, 1972.

Miliband, Ralph. *Marxism and Politics.* Oxford: Oxford University Press, 1977.

Ollman, Bertell. *Alienation: Marx's Conception of Man in Capitalist Society.* New York: Cambridge University Press, 1971.

Rader, Melvin. *Marx's Interpretation of History.* Oxford: Oxford University Press, 1979.

Roemer, John., ed. *Analytical Marxism.* Cambridge: Cambridge University Press, 1986.

Singer, Peter. *Karl Marx.* Oxford: Oxford University Press, 1980.

Sowell, Thomas. *Marxism, Philosophy and Economics.* London: 1986.

Tucker, Robert C. *Philosophy and Myth in Karl Marx.* 2nd ed. Cambridge: Cambridge University Press, 1972.

# NIETZSCHE

## Translations

Hollingdale., R.J., trans. *Human, All Too Human.* London: Cambridge University Press, 1986.

_____. *Thus Spake Zarathustra.* Harmondsworths: Penguin, 1975.

_____. *Twlight of the Idols.* Harmondworth: Penguin, 1972.

_____. *Untimely Meditations.* Cambridge: Cambridge University Press, 1983.

Kaufmann, Walter, trans. *Beyond Good and Evil.* New York: Vintage, 1966.

_____, trans. *The Birth of Tragedy* and *The Case of Wagner.* New York: Vintage, 1967.

_____, trans. *The Gay Science.* New York: Vintage, 1974.

_____, ed. *The Portable Nietzsche.* New York: Viking Press, 1963.

Kaufmann, Walter and R.J. Hollingdale, trans. *On the Genealogy of Morals* and *Ecce Homo.* New York: Vintage: 1966.

_____, trans. *The Will to Power.* New York: Vintage, 1968.

*The Philosophy of Nietzsche: Thus Spake Zarathustra, Beyond Good and Evil, The Genealogy of Morals, Ecce Homo, The Birth of Tragedy.* New York: Modern Library, 1954.

## Commentaries

Ahern, Daniel R. *Nietzsche as Cultural Physician.* University Park: Pennsylvania State University Press, 1995.

Ansell-Pearson, Keith. *Nietzsche Contra Rousseau: A Study of Nietzsche's Moral and Political Philosophy.* Cambridge: Cambridge University Press, 1991.

Allison, David, ed. *The New Nietzsche.* Cambridge: MIT Press, 1985.

Berkowitz, Peter. *Nietzsche: The Ethics of an Immoralist.* Cambridge: Harvard University Press, 1995.

Blondel, Eric. *Nietzsche: The Body and Culture.* Trans., Séan Hand. Stanford: Stanford University Press, 1991.

Dannhauser, Werner. *Nietzsche's View of Socrates.* Ithaca: Cornell University Press, 1974.

Danto, Arthur C. *Nietzsche as Philosopher: An Original Study.* New York: Columbia Press, 1965.

Deleuze, Gilles. *Nietzsche and Philosophy.* Trans., Hugh Tomlinson. New York: Columbia University Press, 1983.

Detwiler, B. *Nietzsche and the Politics of Aristocratic Radicalism*. Chicago: University of Chicago Press, 1990.

Eden, Robert. *Political Leadership and Nihilism: A Study of Weber and Nietzsche*. Gainesville: University Press of Florida, 1983.

Gillespie, M. A. and Tracy B. Strong, eds. *Nietzsche's New Seas*. Chicago: University of Chicago Press, 1988.

Hayman, Ronald. *Nietzsche: A Critical Life*. New York: Penguin, 1984.

Heidegger, Martin. *Nietzsche*. vol. 4. New York: Harper and Row, 1979-1982.

Heller, Erich. *The Importance of Nietzsche: Ten Essays*. Chicago: University of Chicago Press, 1988.

Hollingdale, R. J. *Nietzsche: The Man and His Philosophy*. Baton Rouge: Louisiana State University Press, 1965.

Kaufmann, Walter. *Nietzsche: Philosopher, Psychologist, Antichrist*. 3rd edition. New York: Vintage, 1968.

Lampert, Laurence. *Nietzsche's Teaching: An Interpretation of 'Thus Spoke Zarathustra'*. New Haven: Yale University Press, 1986.

Löwith, Karl. *From Hegel to Nietzsche: The Revolution in Nineteenth-Century Thought*. Trans., David E. Green. New York: Holt, Rinehart and Winston, 1994.

Magnus, Bernd and Kathleen M. Higgins, eds. *The Cambridge Companion to Nietzsche*. Cambridge: Cambridge University Press, 1996.

Megil, Allan. *Prophets of Extremity: Nietzsche, Heidegger, Foucault, Derrida*. Berkeley: University of California Press, 1985.

Nehamas, Alexander. *Nietzsche: Life as Literature*. Cambridge: Harvard University Press, 1985.

Pletsch, Carl. *Young Nietzsche: Becoming a Genius*. New York: Free Press, 1991.

Rosen, Stanley. *Nihilism: A Philosophical Essay*. New Haven: Yale University Press, 1969.

Schacht, Richard. *Nietzsche*. London: Routledge and Kegan Paul, 1983.

Solomon, Robert C., ed. *Nietzsche: A Collection of Critical Essays*. New York: Anchor, 1973.

Solomon, Robert C. and Kathleen M. Higgins. *Reading Nietzsche*. New York: Oxford University Press, 1988.

Stern, J. P. *Nietzsche*. Hassocks, Sussex: Harvester Press, 1978.

Strong, Tracy B. *Friedrich Nietzsche and the Politics of Transfiguration*. Berkeley: University of California Press, 1975.

Warren, Mark. *Nietzsche and Political Thought*. Cambridge: MIT Press, 1987.

Yack, Bernard. *The Longing for Total Revolution*. Berkeley: University of California Press, 1992.

# SUBJECT INDEX